ACHIEVER
Exam Prep Guide for
AP® EUROPEAN HISTORY

Christopher Freiler

Mc
Graw
Hill
Education

mheducation.com/prek-12

Send all inquiries to:
McGraw-Hill Education
8787 Orion Place
Columbus, OH 43240

ISBN: 978-0-07-897642-1
MHID: 0-07-897642-1

Printed in the United States of America.

4 5 6 7 8 9 LOV 25 24 23 22 21

Acknowledgments

Writing a book is mostly solo work, but the writer stands in front of an unheralded network of support, without which his labors would be for naught. With that in mind, I lovingly thank my family—my wife Michele, for her emotional support and copy-editing expertise; my daughter Megan, for her help in tracking down permissions; and my son Kyle, for handling important editorial and logistical issues. In addition, I wouldn't have been able to undertake this project without the expertise and professionalism of the editorial and production staff at McGraw-Hill Education, namely Mickey Cox, Amy Smallwood-Ringenberg, and Brieanna Hammond. Special thanks go to Victoria Thompson for her help with French translations, and Drew Vande Creek of Northern Illinois University Libraries for tracking down permissions information. Finally, the following students at Hinsdale Central were kind enough to share their writing as samples: Zaina Ahmed, Sophie Brown, Katie Cernugel, Andrea Collins, Alice Ding, Tara Entezar, Jayne Gelman, Amy Guo, Minna Hassballa, Sophia Horowicz, Riya Jain, JoonSoo Kim, Nikolai J. Kowalchuk, Milen Spegar, Sherman Thompson, Nick Tienken, and Scott Watson.

About the Author

Christopher Freiler has taught Advanced Placement European History at Hinsdale Central High School in Hinsdale, IL, since 1993. Additionally, he has taught Philosophy Honors since 2003, a course he proposed and developed. He has been involved with the national AP program since 1997, serving as a workshop consultant and in leadership positions for the annual exam scoring, the re-design of the AP European History course curriculum, and for the development of the test. Chris earned his B.A. in History at Northwestern University, M.A. in History at University of Virginia, and M.A. in Philosophy at Northern Illinois University.

Preface

You, the AP student, will find several products on the market designed to help prepare you for the Advanced Placement European History exam. The author, a former co-chair of the committee that designed the current curriculum and exam, as well as a leader at the annual exam scoring, designed the volume you now hold to be the most representative and comprehensive test preparation manual available. The following features make it stand apart:

- This book mirrors the curriculum framework and exam format that define the course, providing an inside look at how to approach European History as an apprentice historian.

- This review guide addresses the required content of the course briefly but substantively, ensuring that you will not be left in the dark for any possible item on the AP exam.

- Theme Music, Skill Set, and Example Base features throughout the guide are designed to help students link content meaningfully to course themes, reinforce historical thinking skills (HTS), and connect illustrative examples to broader developments.

- Practice exam questions were developed to follow closely both the content and types of questions you will encounter on the exam.

- Document-based (DBQ), short-answer (SAQ), and long essay (LEQ) questions follow the format and approach of those on the AP exam.

You have a choice in selecting a review guide, and we are confident the Achiever will provide the guidance you need for success in the course and on the exam.

A Note from the Author

Welcome to your study of Advanced Placement European History. You should find the course material challenging yet rewarding, as the curriculum covers significant developments and events that affect our lives still today. Though the sheer amount of material—the people, places, events, art works, and literature—may seem overwhelming, you will not be expected to remember everything. Rather than approaching the course as a retainer of facts, think of yourself as an apprentice historian—engaging historical interpretations and employing a set of important historical thinking skills (HTS) in making and evaluating arguments with the evidence of primary sources and content knowledge.

My experience as a teacher has shown me that virtually any motivated student can succeed in the course and on the AP exam. Two keys to success are 1) a commitment to develop your historical thinking skills and 2) a toolkit of proven strategies to prepare for the exam. You will supply the first key; this guide will provide you with the second.

This book is organized into three sections. In the first section you'll learn how the exam is structured and scored. This section also surveys important strategies for increasing comprehension of your daily reading, meeting the tasks required by the various items on the exam, particularly those that involve writing. The second section comprises the crux of this review guide, with chapters surveying important content of different topics, divided into the 4 chronological periods of the course. Each chapter provides helpful study tips, a brief discussion of interpretive issues, and review questions. You will also find a concise list of suggested resources. At the end of each time period, a diagnostic test is offered online, so that you can apply your content knowledge and practice your HTS on the various test item types.

This review guide can be used on its own or in conjunction with any textbook. It is recommended that you consult outside resources—such as historical interpretations, primary sources, works of art—whenever useful to your engagement with content or to practice the HTS.

The final section provides two full practice examinations, complete with 55-question multiple-choice sections, four SAQS, a DBQ, and an LEQ. In all, you will find over 350 multiple-choice questions with substantial answer explanations, as well as sample DBQ, SAQ, and LEQ responses. Sample essays have been included in the belief that seeing writing that succeeds, and also that which is lacking, serves as the best way to hone your own writing skills. Finally, with the premise that chronology is important for understanding the skills of historical thinking, I have included three different timelines in the appendices to this volume.

Good luck in your review of the course!

Christopher Freiler

Table of Contents

SECTION II   CONTENT REVIEW

Section I
Studying for the Exam

1 The Structure of the AP Exam

Overview of the Test Structure

Each year's exam is designed by the AP European History Test Development Committee and covers the period from 1450 to the recent past. Because the exam is created several years before actual testing, it is unlikely that any recent events (i.e., within the past 5–10 years) will appear on the exam. However, material from the post-1945 will appear on the exam, likely a multiple-choice (MC) set or two, perhaps a Short-Answer Question (SAQ) or Long-Essay Question (LEQ), or maybe the Document-Based Question (DBQ). The test writers will aim to provide *roughly* equal treatment to the four time periods: 1) 1450-1648, 2) 1648-1815, 3) 1815-1914, 4) 1914-"present."

The exam consists of four parts. In Section I there are 55 stimulus-based multiple-choice (MC) questions (see below). Students are provided 55 minutes to complete this multiple choice section, or about 1 minute per question (for pacing purposes). Once you complete Section I, you will not be able to return to it; the proctors will collect your test and scan sheet and start you immediately on the next section. Section II comprises 4 Short-Answer Questions (SAQs), 2 or 3 of which will involve stimulus material. Once completed with this section (50 minutes), the proctors will provide a 5- to 10-minute break, during which they will prepare the room for the next sections. Upon resuming, you will have 90 minutes to complete the Document-Based Question (DBQ) and Long-Essay Question (LEQ). This portion of the exam includes a 15-minute "reading period," intended for reading through the DBQ documents and planning out your response; however, you may divide your time any way you wish. Because the DBQ is the more complex task, you are strongly encouraged to begin with this question.

For many of you, AP European history will be your first AP exam. If so, you will find it to be not only an intellectual test, but a physical and psychological one. It is important, therefore, to pace yourself and come to the exam well-prepared and well-rested.

Section	Number of Questions	Time	% of Score
I	55 Multiple-Choice	55 minutes	40%
II	4 Short-Answer	50 minutes	20%
Scheduled break of 5–10 minutes			
III	1 Document-Based	55 minutes	25%
IV	1 Long-Essay (choice of 2)	35 minutes	15%
	Total	3 hours, 15 minutes	

Part I: Multiple Choice (MC)

The multiple-choice (MC) questions on the AP exam are designed to test the following: 1) required content knowledge (see the Concept Outline of the College Board Course Exam and Description for European History, 2) the 9 historical thinking skills (HTS), 3) the 5 course themes, and 4) any of the relevant 19 key concepts (KCs). As such, it is vital that you not approach this portion of the test as simply a regurgitation of what you've encountered throughout your course. To put it simply—you *will* be reading, processing, and thinking throughout the MC section. Because these stimulus-based questions—i.e., employing different types of source materials—involve more "moving parts," it is critical to your overall success that you have practice with them.

Even with 55 questions, there will be some gaps of material covered, and thus, one of the topics you studied may not appear on the exam. However, if you've focused strongly on the essential narratives and overarching questions presented through the themes and KCs, you will be prepared to apply your understanding to this portion of the exam. All of the questions will come in sets, oriented around a specific source. Sets will consist of at least 2 and no more than 5 questions, generally testing several of the HTS. Even with a set being centered on one source, your inability to answer one question of the set correctly should not affect your ability to answer others. Each correct answer stands on its own and is not dependent on previous questions. The last question of the set may include a question that tests "skills only," meaning that it does not require content knowledge but simply your ability to think historically. In addition, this last question of a set may be "content only" or "stimulus not required," which means you can merely draw from what you know. The former type of question will likely only appear 2-4 times, and the latter about 6-10 times on an exam format.

Each question will have four possible choices, consisting of the key (correct answer) and 3 distractors (wrong answers). As you practice the MC questions in this guide, you will notice that the distractors often seem appealing. This is by design. Compared to previous test formats, you will encounter less "made-up history," or developments that never happened. Instead, you will probably be faced with 3-4 accurate statements; your job is to consider which one is most applicable to the source and the "stem" (what the question asks). At first, this may strike you as difficult and more time-consuming, but you will improve your ability on these items the more you practice them—especially in recognizing the HTS involved with the question, reading the sources efficiently, and familiarizing yourself with the Concept Outline.

Part II: Short-Answer Questions (SAQs)

The four short-answer questions (SAQs) measure your understanding of important content topics and 1 or 2 historical thinking skills. Of the four prompts you'll be given, 2 or 3 of them will include stimulus material, similar to what you'll see on the MC section. Though you must answer all four questions, the tasks are open enough to allow a wide range of student choices. Once again, this point should remind you of the importance of getting a high-level picture of the themes and key concepts of the course. Simply recalling facts is unlikely to help you on the SAQs.

It is likely that you will encounter a range of time periods, themes, and historical thinking skills (HTS) on the SAQs. Bring your attention especially to the HTS. If you know how to handle, say, a Causation question, this will assist in your recall and application of relevant content. Your facility with different types of questions will also assist in your transition from one question type to another and spare you time and stress.

Each question will require a little more than 10 minutes to answer, and given the purpose of the SAQs, this should be plenty. In fact, you will write each response on a designated template on one side of paper, with a box that must contain your entire answer. If you go beyond the box, that portion of your writing will not be scored. Unlike the other written portions of the exam, the SAQs do not have a formal rubric. Since each question comprises three parts, you can earn only three points for each SAQ. Going beyond what earns you the point, will not add any bonus or qualitative points to your overall score. With appropriate preparation and practice, the SAQs may be the least taxing and stressful portion of the exam.

Part III: Document-Based Question (DBQ)

If this is your first Advanced Placement history class, you may be unfamiliar with the concept of a document-based question. The task involves interpreting sources and applying your content knowledge to the development of an argument. Since the question requires content knowledge, the prompt will address a mainstream topic, i.e., one found explicitly in the Concept Outline, often ranging over several KCs or periods. All DBQs will require you to apply the HTS of 1) argumentation, 2) use of evidence in support of an argument, 3) analyzing evidence—content and sourcing, 4) contextualization, and 5) synthesis. In fact, you will notice sections on the DBQ rubric (below) where these skills are directly assessed.

Each DBQ will include 7 documents, and you are strongly urged to use all of them in support of your argument. The rubric calls for use of at least 6 documents to earn Point 2 above, but if you should make a major error of interpretation, you will be left with no margin for error. Total time for the DBQ is 55 minutes, made up of 10–15 minutes for reading through the documents and planning your response, and 40–45 minutes to write your response.

Your practice with the DBQ is vital to your effective time management and ability to juggle the various tasks on the rubric in writing a focused and coherent argument. To that effect, you will find DBQs in this guide, including sample essays. Just as with any skill—like playing an instrument or a sport—the DBQ is best approached as a craft that is mastered through deliberate practice and reflection on one's areas of weakness.

Part IV: Long-Essay Question (LEQ)

The long essay (LEQ) measures your ability to use your content knowledge to make an argument on a major theme or topic in the course. You will choose from two prompts, likely from the same theme (e.g., Interaction of Europe and the World) and with a parallel structure. That is, each prompt will involve the same number of tasks, so there should be no advantage for students in choosing one over the other.

You are allotted approximately 35 minutes to write your LEQ, but you can take a few extra minutes if you like, as long as you realize that you'll be sacrificing time on the DBQ to do so. The directions recommend taking 5 minutes to organize your response, and you are strongly encouraged to take this suggestion. Many students on the national exam demonstrate knowledge of the topic but score weakly on their essays, for these reasons: 1) lack of a clear argument or direction, 2) lack of focus and going on tangents, and 3) making errors in defining the parameters of the question (e.g., geographic, chronological, or topical scope). Most of these errors can be attributed to panicked rather than measured writing. Remember: a briefer, focused essay that addresses the question will earn higher marks than a lengthy, rambling one.

How the Exam Is Scored

All AP exams employ the same overall scoring system:

- 5 Extremely well qualified
- 4 Well qualified
- 3 Qualified
- 2 Possibly qualified
- 1 No recommendation

To calculate your overall total, a complex formula converts the raw score of each section of the exam toward a possible of 130 points total. However, one should not think in terms of the standard 90-80-70-60% scale. "Break points" between each of the above overall scores are determined after the test is administered based on historical standards and how well students performed that particular year on the exam. It is best not to think of the exam by an unreasonable standard of perfection based on points, but with each item as an opportunity to demonstrate your understanding of what you've learned and its application to the course.

Scoring of the Multiple Choice Section

There is no penalty for guessing on this section, so you should make sure you answer each question. Even if you can narrow the choices down to 2, it is in your interest to guess. After all, if you do that 10 times (of 55 questions), you are likely by averages to get 5 of them correct.

Scoring of the Essays

Both the DBQ and LEQ are scored with a rubric that awards points based on a measure of student proficiency with the historical thinking skills. Both essays will always measure: 1) Argumentation, 2) Use of Evidence, and 3) Synthesis. In addition, the DBQ will measure student ability to provide content and sourcing analysis for the DBQ documents *as documents*, in addition to *their use as support for an argument*. Both the DBQ and LEQ will be geared toward ONE targeted historical thinking skill, though this will not constitute a separate point on the DBQ rubric, as the skill is measured under the portions of the rubric dealing with argumentation. However, the LEQ rubric calls out two specific points for the targeted skill, with a qualitative distinction between 0, 1, and 2 points, depending on how well students address the targeted skill with their argument. The targeted HTS for the LEQ are: 1) Comparison, 2) Causation, 3) Change and Continuity Over Time (CCOT), and 4) Periodization. The generic rubrics below will provide a clearer sense of how your essays will be scored. It is vital that you know these rubrics and practice the skills well enough so that you can demonstrate your mastery as you write your essays.

DBQ RUBRIC

A. Thesis and Argument Development	2 points
Presents a thesis that makes a historically defensible claim and responds to all parts of the question. The thesis must consist of one or more sentences located in one place, either in the introduction or the conclusion.	1 point
Develops and supports a cohesive argument that recognizes and accounts for historical complexity by explicitly illustrating relationships among historical evidence such as contradiction, corroboration, and/or qualification.	1 point
B. Document Analysis	**2 points**
Utilizes the content of at least SIX of the documents to support the stated thesis or a relevant argument.	1 point
Explains the significance of the author's point of view, author's purpose, historical context, and/or audience for at least FOUR documents.	1 point
C. Using Evidence Beyond the Documents	**2 points**
Contextualization Situates the argument by explaining the broader historical events, developments, or processes immediately relevant to the question. *Scoring Note: Contextualization requires using knowledge not found in the documents to situate the argument within broader historical events, developments, or processes immediately relevant to the question. The contextualization point is not awarded for merely a phrase or reference, but instead requires an explanation, typically consisting of multiple sentences or a full paragraph.*	1 point
Evidence Beyond the Documents Provides an example or additional piece of specific evidence beyond those found in the documents to support or qualify the argument. *Scoring Notes: This example must be different from the evidence used to earn other points on this rubric. This point is not awarded for merely a phrase or reference. Responses need to reference an additional piece of specific evidence and explain how that evidence supports or qualifies the argument.*	1 point

D. Synthesis	1 point
Extends the argument by explaining the connections between the argument and ONE of the following: a) A development in a different historical period, situation, era, or geographical area. b) A course theme and/or approach to history that is not the focus of the essay (such as political, economic, social, cultural, or intellectual history). c) A different discipline or field of inquiry (such as economics, government and politics, art history, or anthropology) ***Scoring Note:*** *The synthesis point requires an explanation of the connections to a different historical period, situation, era, or geographical area, and is not awarded for merely a phrase or reference.*	1 point
Total	7 points

On Accuracy: The components of this rubric each require that students demonstrate historically defensible content knowledge. Given the timed nature of the exam, the essay may contain errors that do not detract from the overall quality, as long as the historical content used to advance the argument is accurate.

On Clarity: These essays should be considered first drafts and thus may contain grammatical errors. Those errors will not be counted against a student unless they obscure the successful demonstration of the content knowledge and skills described above.

LEQ RUBRIC

A. Thesis	1 point
Presents a thesis that makes a historically defensible claim and responds to all parts of the question. The thesis must consist of one or more sentences located in one place, either in the introduction or the conclusion.	1 point

B. Argument Development: Using the Targeted Historical Thinking Skill	2 points
Comparison: Describes similarities AND differences among historical individuals, events, developments, or processes.	1 point
Explains the reasons for similarities AND differences among historical individuals, events, developments, or processes.	1 point
Causation: Describes causes AND/OR effects of a historical event, development, or process.	1 point
Explains the reasons for the causes AND/OR effects of a historical event, development, or process. ***Scoring Note:*** *If the prompt requires discussion of both causes and effects, responses must address both causes and effects in order to earn both points.*	1 point
CCOT: Describes historical continuity AND change over time.	1 point
Explains the reasons for historical continuity AND change over time.	1 point
Periodization: Describes the ways in which the historical development specified in the prompt was different from and similar to developments that preceded AND/OR followed.	1 point
Explains the extent to which the historical development specified in the prompt was different from and similar to developments that preceded AND/OR followed. ***Scoring Note:*** *For both points, if the prompt requires evaluation of a turning point, then responses must discuss developments that preceded AND followed. For both points, if the prompt requires evaluation of the characteristics of an era, then responses can discuss developments that EITHER preceded OR followed.*	1 point

C. Argument Development: Using Evidence	2 points
Addresses the topic of the question with specific examples of relevant evidence.	1 point
Utilizes specific examples of evidence to fully and effectively substantiate the stated thesis or a relevant argument.	1 point
Scoring Note: *To fully and effectively substantiate the stated thesis or a relevant argument, responses must include a broad range of evidence that, through analysis and explanation, justifies the stated thesis or a relevant argument.*	

D. Synthesis	1 point
Extends the argument by explaining the connections between the argument and ONE of the following: a) A development in a different historical period, situation, era, or geographical area. b) A course theme and/or approach to history that is not the focus of the essay (such as political, economic, social, cultural, or intellectual history). c) A different discipline or field of inquiry (such as economics, government and politics, art history, or anthropology) (Note: For European and World History only).	1 point
Scoring Note: *The synthesis point requires an explanation of the connections to a different historical period, situation, era, or geographical area, and is not awarded for merely a phrase or reference.*	

Total	6 points

On Accuracy: The components of this rubric each require that students demonstrate historically defensible content knowledge. Given the timed nature of the exam, the essay may contain errors that do not detract from the overall quality, as long as the historical content used to advance the argument is accurate.

On Clarity: These essays should be considered first drafts and thus may contain grammatical errors. Those errors will not be counted against a student unless they obscure the successful demonstration of the content knowledge and skills described above.

Registration and Fees

For most students, registering for the exam is fairly easy. It is generally handled by your school's AP coordinator, often someone in your guidance department. If you are unsure how to register and have not received any information by late winter, you may wish to ask your teacher or an administrator at your school. Should your school not administer the exam, contact AP Services at the College Board for a list of schools in your area that do. The current fee for taking the exam is $92.

Fee reductions

Visit https://professionals.collegeboard.org/testing/waivers/guidelines/ap for information about eligibility criteria and the procedure for claiming College Board fee reductions for AP Exams. Go to http://professionals.collegeboard.com/testing/ap/coordinate/fee-assistance for information about additional federal and state fee reductions that may be available for students in your state.

For more information about financial aid, contact your AP coordinator.

Source: Rubrics for AP Histories + Historical Thinking Skills, Fall 2015. Copyright © 2015 The College Board. Reproduced with permission. http://apcentral.collegeboard.com.

For more information on anything related to the AP program, visit www.apcentral.collegeboard. com or contact AP Services:

AP Services
P.O. Box 6671
Princeton, New Jersey 08541-6671
Phone: 877-274-6474 (toll-free in the United States and Canada) or 212-632-1781
Email: apexams@info.collegeboard.org

What to Bring to the Exam

To reduce any anxiety, it is important that you come prepared on the day of the exam. Here is a list of items you will need:

- **Several sharpened No. 2 pencils** (with erasers) for all responses on their multiple-choice answer sheet.
- **Pens with black or dark-blue ink** for completing areas on the exam booklet covers and for free-response questions in most exams.
- **Your school's code** if testing at a school different from the one you regularly attend. Home-schooled students will be provided with their state's or country's home-school code at the time of the exam.
- **A watch** that does not beep or have an alarm (in case the exam room does not have a clock that can be easily seen).
- **AP Student Pack.** If you do not attend the school where you are taking the exam, also bring a government-issued or school-issued photo ID.
- If applicable, **SSD Student Accommodation Letter** which verifies that they have been approved for a testing accommodation such as Braille or large-type exams.

Prohibited items on AP Exam day

- **Electronic equipment:** Phone, smartphone, smartwatch, laptop, tablet computer, etc., portable listening or recording devices (MP3 player, iPod, etc.), cameras or other photographic equipment, devices that can access the Internet, and any other electronic or communication devices.
- **Unapproved aids:** Books, compasses, protractors, mechanical pencils, correction fluid, dictionaries, highlighters*, notes, or colored pencils.*
- **Scratch paper;** notes can be made on portions of the exam booklets.
- **Watches that beep** or have an alarm, or smartwatches.
- **Computers***
- **Reference guides, keyboard maps** or other typing instructions.
- **Clothing with subject-related information**
- **Food or drink***

* Unless this has been preapproved as an accommodation by the College Board Services for Students with Disabilities office prior to the exam date.

Additional Resources to Help You Prepare
Using Your Textbook Effectively

For almost all students, the primary source of information is their textbook. Textbooks convey material in a standard manner, though they often differ in their areas of emphasis as well as the features they offer. Many texts now come standard with access to a Web site where you can get chapter summaries, take quizzes, find links to other useful resources, and even obtain feedback on practice essays that you write. In addition, your teacher may have had you purchase or provided a study guide that accompanies the text. These can often vary in quality, but you may find it useful to follow along with the text reading by consulting your study guide.

Just because a textbook is your main resource shouldn't prevent you from employing other useful resources, such as reference works, additional readings, periodicals, online materials, or even literature. Certainly, it is possible for you to succeed on the exam simply by making the most effective use of your textbook, but if you find other sources enlightening, convenient, or interesting, your teacher will probably not discourage and is likely to positively encourage them as a way to get a better feel for what you are learning. **NOTE:** It is NOT your textbook that defines the parameters of the course but the College Board Course Exam and Description (see below). Any material in the Concept Outline (except for the illustrative examples in gray boxes) is fair game for a test item. However, this works in your favor too: if the specific term is not in the concept outline, it cannot be the answer for an MC question.

AP Central

Your contact point for the latest information regarding the AP program is the official site of the College Board: apcentral.collegeboard.com. Any basic questions you have related to the administration of the exam, its scoring, policies, and others can be found at this Web site. In addition, you can purchase products that may help you in your review, such as free-response questions and sample essays. If you are a senior or would simply like to know policies of particular universities related to AP credit, the site features links to hundreds of colleges that can guide your decision making.

In addition, you can access subject specific materials through the course home pages (easily found from the general home page). Some of the materials and sites are unique to teachers, but you will find materials of benefit to students as well.

Internet Resources

Many students find that they are savvier Internet users than their teachers. Certainly, the Internet has opened new sources of information, particularly related to history, unknown to historians and students of history in years past. However, the Internet is a tool like any other and should be used judiciously to meet the appropriate need. Before you rely too heavily on any specific site—say one that you found using one of the major search engines like Google or Bing—you should ensure that the site is reliable and authoritative. Those sites affiliated with a known college or university, or perhaps sponsored by a teacher of the course, may prove useful to your studying. With that in mind, I have listed below some Web sites that have been helpful to me and my students in the past.

https://secure-media.collegeboard.org/digitalServices/pdf/ap/ap-european-history-course-and-exam-description.pdf—From the College Board site, this Course and Exam Description is the official statement of the curriculum of the course. It is your go-to source for required knowledge and skills.

http://www.historyteacher.net/APEuroCourse/APEuroCourseMainPage.htm—This site is one of the best by a teacher of the course—Susan Pojer, from Horace Greeley High School in Chappaqua, NY—and contains extensive review materials, practice DBQs, and links to other sources.

http://eudocs.lib.byu.edu/index.php/Main_Page—This site offers a thorough collection of primary sources organized by nation, and also includes a section titled "Europe as a Supranational Region."

http://legacy.fordham.edu/halsall/mod/modsbook.asp—Perhaps the best resource for primary sources related to European history. You will find the site more user-friendly than the one above and the chronological organization easier to follow. The site carries classics, like Luther's Ninety-Five Theses, but also interesting nuggets you're unlikely to find elsewhere.

http://www.phschool.com/curriculum_support/map_bank/—This site provides blank maps from a variety of historical eras that can be used to chart the shifting political balance of power in Europe.

http://www.worldology.com/Europe/europe_history_lg.htm—A collection of interactive maps with a scrolling timeline, this site provides a useful review of the shifting geography of Europe, especially related to warfare.

http://spartacus-educational.com/—An encyclopedic database for modern history, this site is easy to navigate and effective for research projects.

http://www.johndclare.net/—This site provides interpretations and sources on major topics in 20th-century diplomatic and political history.

www.wga.hu/index.html—You will find this easily searchable site a treasure of visual images. Search chronologically or alphabetically by artist for paintings, sculpture, or architecture. In addition, you can use a special feature to place images side-by-side for comparison. The site, however, is limited to the period before 1900.

http://www.artchive.com/—Excellent searchable site for art that covers the ground thoroughly, if you can stand the prevalence of ads and pop-ups.

Of course, the above list is only a small sampling of sites available. As you read through the content review in Section 2, you will find additional suggestions for resources. With modern search engines at your fingertips, many more sites are waiting to be discovered for the motivated. Though these sites can be fun and useful, keep in mind that the rules of citation and rendering proper credit still apply. If you use one of these sites for research, make sure that you supply a bibliography and give proper credit, advice that applies to all of your studies and academic work. Help in formatting bibliographies can be found at www.easybib.com.

CHAPTER 2 Strategies for Success

How to Use This Review Guide

The review book you now hold is intended to supplement, not replace, your textbook. Yet, you will find that any major topic covered within the course or on the exam will be addressed here. As you read and study, make sure that you connect content (e.g., key persons, events, artworks, books, etc.) to the course themes, historical thinking skills (HTS), and key concepts (KCs). The study strategies covered here should improve your comprehension as you move through your daily reading and prepare for quizzes and exams.

Another way you can employ this guide is to use Section II to review material prior to any assessment, particularly the AP exam. To test your knowledge and apply HTS, try the sets of MC questions and the SAQ or LEQ at the end of each chapter. In addition, available online following each historical period, there is a diagnostic exam, including 30 MC questions, 2 SAQs, a DBQ, and an LEQ. To help you develop your all-important writing skills, you will also find sample essays that provide insight into how the exam is scored, as well as indicators of effective strategies and common errors. As you read these essays, your skill in determining the score for each sample should improve, an indication that you are understanding the features of a powerful essay.

As you approach the exam, perhaps starting with your Spring break or around late March, you should get more serious about breaking down what you have learned into more manageable chunks for review. Go back to those chapters that you have already covered and refresh your memory with some practice questions. As you near the test date, you should attempt one or both of the full practice tests, using the timing guidelines indicated in Chapter 1. This practice will help you get a feel for the emotional and psychological stresses of the test. Finally, one of the last items you should review is the full chronological scope of the course, including the timelines in the Appendix. Make sure you can place art movements, social developments, intellectual changes, wars, etc. in the appropriate chronological period, as well as examine the rationale for such periodization schemes. As with any resource, this review guide should prove as helpful as you are willing to make it.

The Historical Thinking Skills

All three AP history subjects (US, European, World) now share the same language of historical thinking skills (HTS). These skills are used both to shape test construction and to guide your approach to the subject. **Warning**: it is not sufficient simply to know content without the ability to apply that content knowledge in demonstration of deeper thinking about the discipline of history. In short, you should consider yourself an apprentice historian rather than a mere reciter of information. On one hand, the focus on HTS creates challenges, but on the other, it makes the course more engaging, especially in that you are expected to approach history as a contested argument over interpretations and evidence. There are 9 HTS, divided as follows:

Analyzing Historical Sources and Evidence

Just as science takes as its raw material the natural world, history similarly engages with a "raw material" to drive its investigation. For historians, these materials are both the primary sources of the past (letters, government documents, art, speeches, objects, etc.) and also other historians' interpretations on a topic of study. If you were to study, say, the reform of cities around the turn of the 20th century, it would make sense to begin with relevant sources—maps, architectural treatises, grievances from urbanites, data on infectious diseases. Before focusing your research, you'd want to situate your investigation and subsequent writing in the ongoing literature produced by other historians on that topic, known as *historiography*. Then you would attempt to answer a question in that field or even pose a new question. Though you won't likely complete this process in the AP European History course, you will simulate that methodology in your studies and on the AP exam. (Please note for future reference the abbreviations below.)

Analyzing Evidence: Content and Sourcing (EVCS) Very few documents speak for themselves; they require interpretation and context. Ahead of using a source as evidence, historians first consider the document's source and type. For example, if investigating the origins of the French Revolution and examining letters from the monarch as evidence, you would not consider the source as a fact in itself. After all, monarchs may provide only a perspective from above, without knowledge of how their policies affect various groups or individuals. And of course, they will view government policy from the perspective of dynastic rule and what's best for their or the state's interests. Documents from monarchs are useful to the historian, but more so to reveal the attitudes and perceptions of decision-makers, maybe even to reveal the discrepancy between their perspectives and those of their subjects, rather than a straightforward identification of cause. More will be written below on specific strategies for analyzing sources in the DBQ section.

Interpretation (INTR) The main resource for this course is probably your textbook (a secondary source), but the primary job of historians is to generate interpretations, not simply chronicle the past. Take the Cold War, for example. A highly charged event, it was first interpreted in the 1940s and 1950s by American historians as attributable to traditional Russian expansionism, a Marxist inclination toward world revolution, and perhaps the paranoia of Stalin. However, as classified documents from the early Cold War were released and American foreign policy in Vietnam came under increasing criticism, historians developed a revisionist perspective emphasizing American economic dominance (exercised through the Marshall Plan), its nuclear monopoly, and the weakness of the Soviet Union. By the end of the Cold War (1989–1991), historians moved beyond the question of mere responsibility (U.S. vs. Soviet) to focus on the process of competition between two rival ideologies and politico-economic systems and the cycle of misperception and overreaction. On the exam, you will not be required to know any one particular viewpoint or school of interpretation, but you need to be prepared to recognize and evaluate various historical interpretations on major events and developments.

Making Historical Connections

Whenever you encounter a person, event, or document in a history course, you should consider: Why is it important? With what developments in this or other eras does it relate? How does this fact reveal an ongoing issue or conflict in my course? When you address these types of questions, you are making connections, the heart and soul of historical thinking. For purposes of test items, you establish your connections through making comparisons, drawing on context, and synthesizing your understanding into a coherent, broader picture.

Comparison (COMP) In comparing two items, we learn more about both of them, as many of the features we had taken for granted when viewed in isolation now become more prominent by being placed side-by-side with another relevant item. Historical thinking means drawing comparisons between nations or regions, between different periods or eras, and between contemporaneous developments or trends. If you are charged with comparing two or more items, make certain that you address both similarities and differences, though you may emphasize one or the other. Also, appropriate comparisons should be between "apples and apples," i.e., explaining economic causes of the French and Russian Revolutions, rather than, say, economic causes for one and intellectual causes for the other. Though basic, you will find it helpful to use a standard Venn diagram to organize your thoughts before setting out with your analysis. Consider the following example:

Renaissance   ## Enlightenment

* revival of classics
* focus on the arts
* Church patronage

* elite focus
* state patronage
* printing press

* methods of New Science
* critical reform movement
* religious skepticism

With these similarities and differences briefly and quickly established, you are now prepared to respond to a possible DBQ or LEQ comparing these two key cultural movements.

Contextualization (CTX) Contextualization is both the most basic and subtle of historical thinking skills. Whenever an historian encounters a source or novel fact, she will survey (probably without even being aware of the process) what she knows on the topic, attempting to place it within an already existing structure of knowledge. For examples, let's suppose you come across a source from a Spanish official (known as a *corregidor*) to the Spanish monarch, around 1550, regarding local grievances directed against high taxes and inflation. In interpreting this source, you may consider developments at the local, national, regional, and global levels. The chart below provides a shorthand version of this process.

Global:
exploration

Europe:
New Monarchs and mercantilism

Spain:
centralization

Castile:
center of Spain with high taxes

As you progress through the course and attend to its themes and key concepts, this subtle inferential process will become more ingrained and apparent to you. Can you see how the chart above may help with interpreting and understanding the hypothetical document above?

Synthesis (SYN) The deepest connections in historical thinking involve synthesis. Whenever you connect a recurring issue (e.g., conceptions of gender) from one period to another, or consider how a topic (e.g., industrialization) affected two nations or regions in varying ways, or maybe even use knowledge from a discipline outside history (science, art, statistics, anthropology, et al.), you are employing the skill of synthesis. Simply put, synthesis entails creating a coherent and persuasive view of the past drawing on all the other historical thinking skills. For purposes of the AP exam, the only formats that can realistically gauge synthesis are the DBQ and LEQ, both of which include a specific point in the rubric for this skill. However, you will want to practice your ability to synthesize in your studies or class activities provided by your teacher. As you read or participate in class discussion, always ask: 1) When and where else have we studied this problem or topic? 2) What is similar or different about the topic compared to the other instances I've encountered? 3) In what other classes has a similar topic or issue arisen, and can I use a skill or method from that class to help me understand this one? You may find it helpful to set aside a space in a notebook or the like to keep track of any insights from one period or unit and see in future units how you might establish connections across geography, space, and disciplines.

Chronological Reasoning

All historical events take place in time and place; the skills of chronological reasoning relate directly to the fundamental tasks of explaining the how and why of such events, developments, or processes. As you'll see, chronological reasoning is fundamental to practicing history.

Causation (CAUS) We live in a world of causation (excluding quantum physics), and it is the job of the historian to examine the often complex processes of what brings about important events or processes. Given its nature, the skill of causation can be applied to almost any historical inquiry. Historians often divide causation into long- and short-term causes. It is not enough simply to identify a range of causes; rather, it is important to provide a persuasive account of how such causes interacted to produce an event. Let's look at one of the most important and debated debates over historical causation—the French Revolution. The chart below provides a high-level overview of what the historian might consider in analyzing this issue.

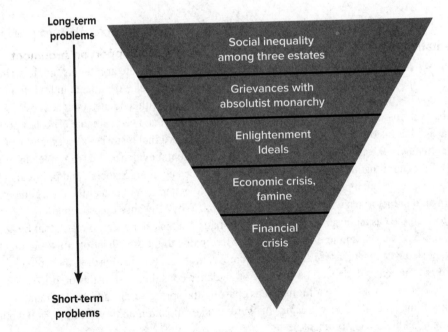

So if the financial crisis sparked the French Revolution, then it is up to the historian to explain the manner in which events unfolded and how the nature and course of events were influenced by the combination and interaction of other causes that underlay the immediate problems the monarchy attempted to address in 1788–1789.

Patterns of Continuity and Change Over Time (CCOT) We tend to emphasize change in considering the past; after all, we are eager to explain how we arrived at our current state from what seem like differing circumstances centuries ago. However, as the course themes will remind us, many issues echo throughout the centuries, just in differing contexts. For example, let's consider the issue of industrialization. If you traveled Europe around 1840, you would find pockets of widespread transformation (Britain, Belgium, parts of Germany, cities in France) in the means of manufacturing and transporting goods. These new patterns of production marked a seismic shift for some in the nature of work—not simply conditions, but also control over the pace and manner of work. However, for many areas of Europe (Russia, southern Italy, central Spain), these new trends seemed remote because agricultural practices continued much as they had for centuries. Even within moments of change, much can remain guided by traditional practices and ideas. Though women participated in the Renaissance, Reformation, and Scientific Revolution, these movements of intellectual and cultural change left attitudes toward gender relatively unaffected, despite sparking debates over women's nature and proper role in society. When you encounter a question of CCOT, remember to note both what changes, what remains the same, and, most importantly, provide an explanation for the diverse outcomes.

Periodization (PER) Most likely you've used terms of periodization in everyday conversation—"Dark Ages," "the Age of Reason," "modern." Historians create narratives—by emphasizing some processes over others, by prioritizing some evidence over others (e.g., pamphlets of Enlightenment philosophes vs. sermons by Pietist ministers), a process that leads to characterizations involving the labels noted above. Questions regarding periodization may revolve around the notion of a "turning point." Some consider the Protestant Reformation a turning point; of course, for religion, but also for the relation of the church to the state, diplomacy, education, and even the growth of capitalism. You will also be asked to consider whether a label (Age of Absolutism) accurately captures an era. As you might expect, what makes such questions appropriate for testing purposes is that the evidence cuts both ways. As you study eras and key events throughout the course, avoid simply absorbing these designations and consider how appropriate they are as you engage the content of that topic or unit of study.

Creating and Supporting an Argument (one skill divided into two parts)

Argumentation (ARG) and **Argumentation: Using Evidence to Support an Argument (EVARG)** The primary task of historians is to engage with and generate arguments, not to write textbooks. We can compare historical arguments to scientific theories. Arguments in both fields take a position (as in testing a hypothesis), defend the argument with evidence (science uses natural observations while history uses documents and artifacts), and be falsifiable. This last point means that another historian could theoretically challenge the original historian's argument, just like a scientific hypothesis might be disproven with experimental evidence. For example, an historian might claim that the Industrial Revolution produced economic, social, and political problems; however, though patently true, this claim would generally not constitute an argument, at least not among historians who study industrialization. Why? Because this statement is manifest to even the casual observer. If, on the other hand, an historian were to claim that by 1850, Britain experienced an increased standard of living due to industrialization, this statement would establish an argument, as it is an area of contest among historians. Further, the truth or falsity of this argument will depend on the type of evidence consulted—statistics on prices of products, accounts of working conditions, maps charting the spread of disease, census data, reform legislation, et al. In other words, if you were to take a position on this question, you would be engaging in an historical argument.

For both the DBQ and LEQ, you will be expected to establish a position (or argument) that you can defend, with evidence, throughout your essay. Once again, it should be a position with which another writer could disagree. To cite one more instance: take the question of war guilt and the First World War. Article 231 from the Versailles Treaty established Germany's sole guilt for the war—the first "official" historical interpretation on the war's causes and one with profound political implications (e.g., rise of the Nazi Party and World War II). If you were acting as an amateur historian, you could clearly take issue with the "war guilt" clause and establish a rival interpretation. Perhaps you might emphasize the buildup of tensions over decades, consider diplomatic correspondence of other powers, or better yet, go beyond "responsibility" and emphasize the dysfunctional structure of diplomacy, the arms race, or growing tensions in the Balkans. Whatever position you take, your choice will dictate the type of evidence you consider or stress. Final point: whenever you write a thesis, take a second look and ask yourself—could someone disagree with this statement and set up a rival argument? If not, then consider another tack. If yes, then your ability to consider and answer counterarguments to your thesis will demonstrate complexity and sophistication, a marker of strong essays.

Reading Strategies

Your content source for this course is likely to be your textbook. Chances are, you will find yourself spending about 30–60 minutes per day reading about 7–10 pages in it. It is important that you get the most out of the time you spend reading. My experience as a teacher has shown me that many students do not read as effectively as possible because they lack strategies that can increase their comprehension. Such strategies need not add significantly to your homework, but the extra 5 minutes or so that you spend with them will pay dividends in the long run, both in your performance and in saving time later.

First, you will need to find a time and place that is conducive to your studying. For many students, this is a quiet place with few distractions, but not necessarily the most comfortable, such as your bed, where you are liable to become drowsy or lose concentration. Many studies confirm that multitasking is a myth, so I strongly recommend that when reading, you shut off/down your TV, phone, social media, and other electronic devices. Several years ago, one of my students raised his grade in my class from a B to an A and reduced his homework time in all of his classes by 50% simply by focusing with all of his attention on the task directly in front of him. Beyond the improvements in performance, you may find that bringing focus and intensity to what you're doing will produce the side benefit of enhancing your enjoyment of it as well.

One way to make reading and studying more engaging is to avoid reading passively, as if history were a story that "speaks for itself." Certainly there is element of story and drama in history, particularly at its best, but this is usually not the format of most textbooks. Most are written in a fairly standard manner with a set of analytical cues, which with some practice, you can pick up on and become adept at deciphering.

A textbook chapter often begins with a hook—a story, personality, event, work of art—that is designed to grab the reader's attention. Beneath the flowery language, the authors are trying to convey the themes, or main ideas, of the chapter. Challenge yourself to identify what the big picture is before you continue with your reading. Other texts begin with a more standard introduction to the chapter content and themes. Perhaps it would be helpful to write out 1–2 sentences based on this introduction that summarize the key points covered in the chapter. This could be done immediately after reading the introduction or after completing the entire chapter. It is vital in your reading that you focus on the Big Picture—defining key terms, identifying cause and effect, linking to previous topics, and especially connecting specific content to course themes, period key concepts, and practicing your HTS.

Though there are numerous strategies, not all work as well for each student. Feel free to experiment with strategies until you find those that work well for you. Whatever you do, make sure that you are *actively* reading your text, much as a builder constructs a scaffolding or framework of a house, before moving on to the siding, roof, interior. The difference is that your scaffolding acts as an analytical structure for your understanding of the entire chapter. To assist you in this process, I have included several specific strategies below to get you started. Keep in mind that there is nothing magical about these strategies; their positive effect depends on your perseverance in developing skills of historical analysis and working at connecting the specific content of the course to the Big Picture.

Scaffolding and Annotating

How do you get started with a scaffold? History revolves more around asking productive questions than having the right answers. Again, you are encouraged to focus on the interpretive issues prompted by historical moments and, further, to anticipate possible essay prompts (including DBQs) by thinking of possible arguments that you could make with the evidence that you encounter. Begin your reading each night with an overarching question that you will attempt to answer when you've finished with the reading. This question will generally lead to further sub-questions. Remember, you will invariably find the answers to your questions within the text itself.

Suppose that you are reading about the Italian Renaissance[1]. In the passage below, from a major course textbook, the authors introduce a key interpretive issue, provide an explanation of cause and effect, and identify important conceptual terms. I've marked up the passage to provide an idea of how to engage a text. Keep in mind that what follows is *one* way to approach a text and should not be considered a foolproof formula.

The basic institutions of Europe...all originated in the Middle Ages. But the Renaissance marked a new era in thought and feeling[2], by which Europe and its institutions were in the long run to be transformed. The Renaissance pertained to high culture, and hence to a *limited number of persons*, but extended over the whole area represented by literature and the arts[3]—literature meaning all kinds of writing and the arts including all products of human skill. The effects of the Italian Renaissance, though much modified with the passage of time, were evident in the books and art galleries of Europe and America, and in the architecture of their cities, even after the revolution of modern art in the early twentieth century. They involved the whole area of culture which was neither theological nor scientific but concerned with moral and civic questions about what human beings ought to be or ought to do, with the answers reflected in matters of taste, style, propriety, decorum, personal character, and education. In particular, it was in Renaissance Italy that an almost purely **secular attitude**[4] first appeared, in which life was no longer seen by leading thinkers as a brief preparation for the hereafter.

The towns of Italy, so long as trade converged in the Mediterranean, were the biggest and most bustling of all the towns that rose in Europe during the Middle Ages.... [They] were independent city-states. There was no king to build up a government for Italy as a whole, and for several generations the popes were either absent at Avignon or engaged in disputes arising from the Great Schism, so that the influence of Rome was unimportant. The merchant oligarchies, each in its own city, enjoyed an unhampered stage on which to pursue interests other than those of business. They had the experience of contending for public office, of suppressing popular revolt or winning popular favor, of producing works of public munificence, of making alliances, hiring armies, outwitting rivals, and conducting affairs of state. In short, Italy offered an environment in which many facets of human personality could be developed[5].

Formerly, the ideal behavior had been seen in renunciation, in a certain disdain for the concerns of this world. **Now a life of involvement was also prized.** Formerly, poverty had been greatly respected, at least in Christian doctrine. **Now there was more praise for a proper enjoyment of wealth.** Medieval Europeans had admired a life of contemplation, or meditative withdrawal. **Now** the humanist Leonardo Bruni could write, in 1433, **"The whole glory of man lies in activity**[6]...."

The new esteem for human activity took both a social and an **individualistic** turn. In cities maintaining their republican forms, a new **civic consciousness** or sense of **public duty** was expressed. For this purpose the writings of Cicero and other ancients were found to be highly relevant, since they provided an ethics independent of the Christian and medieval tradition. There was also a kind of cult of the great individual, hardly known to the ancients, which gave little attention to collective responsibility. Renaissance individualism emphasized the outstanding attainments of extraordinary men (*women, by contrast, were usually expected to pursue the ordinary tasks of domestic life*). The great man shaped his own destiny in a world governed by fortune. He had ***virtù***, the quality of being a man (*vir*, "man"), the successful demonstration of human powers. A man of *virtù* in the arts, in war, or in statecraft, was a man who knew what he was doing, who, from resources within himself, made the best use of his opportunities, hewing his way through the world and **excelling in all that he did**[7].

The growing preoccupation with human actions can be traced in new forms of painting, sculpture, and architecture that arose in Italy at this time. These arts likewise reflected an increasing this-worldliness—a new sense of reality and a new sense of space,—that was different from that of the Middle Ages and *would underlie much European thought until the early twentieth century*[8]. Space was no longer indeterminate, unknowable, or divine; it was a zone occupied by physical human beings, or one in which human beings might at least imagine themselves moving about. Reality meant visible and tangible persons or objects in this space, "objective" in the sense that they looked or felt the same to all normal persons who perceived them. It was a function of the arts to convey this reality, however idealized or suffused by the artist's individual feeling, in such a way that observers could recognize in the image the identity of the subject portrayed[9].

In the above chapter introduction, I have underlined important terms and analytical statements that help home in on the main points of the chapter. At first, these may be more difficult for you to locate, particularly if you are accustomed to thinking of history as fact-driven rather than analysis- and interpretation-driven as historians do. Though many students rely on highlighting texts, I urge you to annotate instead. The highlighting above was meant to draw your attention to the relevant portions of the text, but if reading for myself, I would selectively underline and then make margin notes, in an effort to keep a running outline that demands my continuous engagement with the text. Though the annotations beside the introduction above are fairly detailed, try your hand at using basic phrases, such as "civic consciousness" or "individualism" that will serve to remind you of these concepts when later you return to study this material. Think of yourself as *creating* meaning rather than *absorbing* it. Comprehension relies on asking productive questions and then seeking the answers to those questions.

Let's anticipate some possible essay prompts by creating some questions based on the passage:

- To what extent and in what ways did the Renaissance differ culturally from the Middle Ages?

- Why did the Renaissance begin first and take strongest root in Italy?

- To what extent did the Renaissance change the arts, politics, and culture?

- What social factors, such as class or gender, limited the reach of the Renaissance?

- In what ways did the Renaissance anticipate or lay the foundations for the modern world?

These questions represent a high level of analysis and thinking for a student just beginning this course. Think of them as a goal at which to aim. Keep in mind that you need not specifically write out the answers to each question, though as you can see from the annotation above, questions of this nature were in mind as I marked up the text. As a general rule, you should spend 2–3 minutes prior to reading constructing such questions and about 5 minutes when you've completed the reading creating a brief outline to review what you have read. Rushing through the reading and flipping your book closed is of little use in the long run. Reviewing immediately after reading will reinforce what you have learned and help you more easily erect future scaffolding for the next reading assignment. Studies show that unless you both focus on and reinforce studying or reading, your comprehension and retention will not likely transfer from your working memory (the tasks at hand for your cognition) to your long-term memory. To assist you in your efforts at creating useful yet easily managed outlines, I have included a sample here.

Middle Ages to Renaissance (HTS: PER)

- basic institutions from Middle Ages
- new attitudes and approaches with the Renaissance
- high culture and limitations of class
- secular attitude—moral and civic questions

R.R. Palmer, Joel Colton, and Lloyd Kramer, *A History of Europe in the Modern World*, 11th ed., pp. 56–60. Copyright © 2014 by McGraw-Hill Education. Reprinted with permission.

8 NOTE

The Renaissance transformed the arts and literature, as this section reminds us. In addition, the italics underscore the chronological reach of these changes in the arts.

9 NOTE

In this final, more technical, selection, we see a strong connection of the OS theme as the arts moved toward a more objective depiction of reality. Considering course themes, we can also establish connections in the entire selection to: PP, in the discussion of wealth in prompting secular attitudes; SP, in the political character and role of the city-states; and IS, in the growth of individualism and the class and gender limitations of humanism.

Why Italy? (HTS: CAUS)

- independent city-states (SP)
- center of trade and access to wealth/ideas (PP)
- lack of centralized authority (SP)
- merchant oligarchies interested in individual accomplishment (PP & IS)

Old and New Ideals (HTS: CCOT)

- medieval renunciation vs. humanist involvement
- medieval ideal of poverty vs. humanist embrace of wealth

Renaissance Humanism

- individualism (IS)
- civic consciousness/public duty (SP)
- classics (like Cicero) provide pre-Christian ethical framework (OS)
- virtù—excellence in all areas (limitations for women, IS)

Impact

- human-centered
- painting, sculpture, architecture defined until 20th century
- new sense of space and objectivity (OS)

An outline of this type can be completed briefly as you read, though you should avoid making it too extensive, as this will render it less effective as a subsequent study tool, and, at some point, adding to it defeats its purpose as a distillation of what you have read. Please take note the multiple times I've called out and connected the content to the HTS and Themes: not only will this help build your mastery of the course, it will also render your reading and studying more interesting by orienting yourself toward connections and analysis, rather than a painful and fruitless exercise in factual memorization and recall.

Before we move on to other strategies, we need to address another often-neglected feature of most textbooks—visuals, such as maps, charts, cartoons, and primary sources. Many students tend to view these items as pleasant breaks from the monotony of a full page of double-column text. Though they do offer a break, they also serve an important purpose in reinforcing the major themes of the unit. It is a truism that we learn best by what we hear and see, rather than either by itself. Think of these non-text items as visual cues for the historical era under study. Again, you can ask useful questions and jot down answers next to the sources themselves.

- How does this map represent the political situation of Europe in _____?
- What about this painting reflects the concerns of the era?
- How does this political cartoon show conflicts or issues important to this period?
- What data in this chart helps me understand the developments of this chapter?
- Why was this primary source chosen as a representation of chapter themes?

Primary sources, such as those noted above, drive test items on the AP exam, which makes it imperative for you to practice interpreting them. In fact, if you engage with the sources and visuals in your text substantively, you are very likely to encounter these or similar sources on exam items, either in your class or on the AP exam.

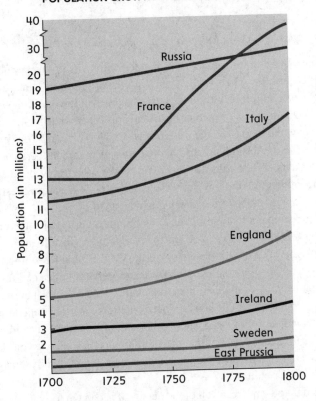

POPULATION GROWTH IN EUROPE, 1700–1800

Dennis Sherman and Joyce Salisbury, *The West in the World: A History of Western Civilization* (New York: McGraw-Hill Education, 2014), p. 474.

Consider what use you might make of the chart above. This simple population chart provides you with some essential information regarding demographic changes over a century. Population movements coincide with economic, political, and social developments. Try to identify and explain the factors that caused the patterns on the chart, both over time and also by geography. By linking visuals to content in this way, you both hone your skills of visual analysis and reinforce your thematic understanding of a particular period in history. Finally, you can anticipate questions that might arise from this chart based on the HTS:

- What factors caused the population patterns in the 18th century (CAUS)?

- Compare and contrast population trends based on nation or region (COMP).

- Explain how these patterns changed over time, e.g., stronger increase after about 1720 (CCOT).

- What other developments during the 18th century do these trends reflect (CTX)?

- What historical eras might be defined, in part, by these trends, e.g., the Enlightenment (PER)?

Timelines and the Importance of Chronology

Perhaps like my students, one of the first questions you asked in your AP European history class was, "Do we have to know dates?" There are two parts to the answer. First, the course and the exam do *not* test your knowledge of trivia. Dates are generally not important in and of themselves. That's the easy answer. The second part is more nuanced. Chronology *is* essential to the understanding of history; in fact, without it, the fundamental historical tasks of analyzing cause-effect relationships, making connections across topic areas, and dealing with historical periods would be impossible. So yes, you must have a strong grasp of chronology to perform well in the course and on the exam. This will involve knowledge of historical eras, as well as some dates.

To see why chronology plays this key role in your understanding, let's look at a long-essay question:

Analyze the impact of global trade on European diplomacy and society in the period 1650–1763.

Clearly, if you have little or no knowledge of the developments in this period, you will be unable to address this question. There are few cues in the prompt itself, other than an assumption that global trade influenced diplomacy and society. The dates in the question were chosen with a purpose, probably to encompass a particular historical era. What is the significance of 1650? This is approximately when the last of the religious wars (Thirty Years' War) ended, and it marks the beginning of the Age of Absolutism, also named after its dominant personality—the Age of Louis XIV. The latter date (1763) ends the Seven Years' War, the last of the major colonial conflicts prior to the French Revolution. Note also that this is a Causation question, since it asks you to explain how and why global trade *affected* two areas of life.

If you happened to remember that the 17th and 18th centuries corresponded with the Commercial Revolution, then you would be off to a good start in being able to handle this prompt. This question, then, wants you to deal with the effects of the Commercial Revolution on diplomacy and society in the Age of Absolutism. With the competition for colonies and resources, along with the economic philosophy of mercantilism that emphasized scarcity, nations engaged in near-constant warfare to advance their power. These conflicts are often called the Commercial Wars. You needn't remember all of them, simply their nature and general results, e.g., on the balance of power. For the second part of the question (effects on society), you should think in terms of demographics (the study of populations); changes in class, family, and gender; and the development of a consumer culture.

Don't be concerned if you can't recall all of the details. It is enough for you to begin your essay with some specific historical context. This context serves as a useful way to begin your introductory paragraph and establish your control of the question; in fact, on the DBQ, your effective integration of contextualization can easily earn you the point on the rubric for that specific HTS. A good portion of your studying, then, should involve reviewing the events and developments that define historical eras. For example, if you were asked, "What significant intellectual development occurred in the 18th century?", you should be able to answer: "the Enlightenment." This knowledge will act as your key to entering any given DBQ or LEQ.

To assist you in your mastery of historical chronology, the Appendix includes three different timelines, one of which is divided into topic areas, so that you can see not only the important developments but also how these topics are connected. As you review the timelines, you will find it helpful to define the characteristics of an historical era (e.g., explain how Baroque art reflected the religious and political climate of 17th-century Europe). Remember that dates are markers—important primarily for how they delineate and define historical eras. Also keep in mind that questions may refer to centuries rather than dates. A century refers to the hundred years numerically prior to the number of the century; e.g., the 16th century covers the 1500s. This may seem basic, but many students blunder on their essays owing to chronological lapses.

On the following page is a slice of chronology, about 70 years in length, which highlights developments for the five course themes. As you peruse the data, look across the chart to establish connections, or threads, that tie together developments. For this example, I have already cross-referenced the themes with the KCs (see Chapter 3 for further description) for Period 1 at the bottom of the timeline.

This timeline, which could be filled with more or less detail, provides cues that help you place the major events and developments in time and that characterize this particular slice of chronology. As is clear, the events and developments here mark those important movements that begin your course—the Renaissance and Protestant Reformation. Just as you use landmarks and maps to guide your movement around geographical space, dates and timelines will assist you in marking historical eras, cause-and-effect patterns, and the themes of a historical period. You will find it helpful to

THEME Timeline (1450–1525)

Theme	Events
Interaction of Europe & World (INT)	Navigational and mapmaking advances; Portuguese exploration of African coast; 1492 Columbus' discovery of Americas; 1498 Vasco da Gama reaches India; 1519–21 Cortez conquers Aztecs
Poverty & Prosperity	Decline of manorialism; Rise of commercial agriculture; Global trade begins with exploration; Price Revolution
Objective Knowledge & Subjective Visions (OS)	1450s Development of printing press; da Vinci born (1452); 1473 Sistine Chapel built; Erasmus' & More's Christian humanism; High Renaissance—centered in Rome; Michelangelo's masterpieces; 1513 Machiavelli's *The Prince*; Spread of Renaissance to northern Europe; 1517 Luther's 95 Theses
States & Other Institutions of Power (SP)	1417–1540s RENAISSANCE PAPACY; 1453 Fall of Constantinople; 1453 End of the Hundred Years' War; 1454 Peace of Lodi; 1478 Spanish Inquisition established; 1479 Ferdinand and Isabella unite Spain; 1492 *Reconquista* completed; RISE OF NEW MONARCHS; MILITARY REVOLUTION; 1519–56 Charles V as HRE
Individual & Society (IS)	Decline of feudalism; POPULATION INCREASE (to ca. 1600); 1492 Jews expelled from Spain; Rise of nobility of the robe

Year scale: 1450, 1455, 1460, 1465, 1470, 1475, 1480, 1485, 1490, 1495, 1500, 1505, 1510, 1515, 1520, 1525

KC 1.1	KC 1.2	KC 1.3	KC 1.4	KC 1.5
Humanist revival of classics introduced new artistic values and methods of knowledge.	States attempted to centralize power within competitive diplomatic structure.	A weakened Church faced growing criticism and calls for reform.	Driven by profits and technology, Europeans expanded overseas and established colonies.	Medieval social and economic structures persisted despite the growth of global trade and a money economy.

make your own timelines, varying from general (perhaps for broad social developments) to more specific (the religious wars and French Revolution). Just keep in mind that the goal is always for you to see the big picture and how the trees make up the forest.

Strategies for the Multiple-Choice Questions

Though Section I takes only 55 minutes of the exam's total time, the multiple choice questions count for 40% of your overall score. For some, this is a source of comfort, for others, fear. If you struggle with objective assessments, the goal of this review guide is not to persuade you to prefer them to writing, only that you can gain confidence and achieve improved scores with the right approaches.

All of the MC questions (for all three history subjects) are now based on stimulus material, meaning a source (either primary or secondary) that forms the basis for a set of questions (between 2 and 5). The source might be a text (pamphlet, speech, diary entry, treatise, etc.), chart or graph, photograph, artwork, map, political cartoon, drawing/etching, or an interpretation by an historian. Occasionally one of the set may not require the stimulus or assess skills only; however, these are exceptions. Given this structure, it is in your interest to practice reading and interpreting sources and work with stimulus questions before you take the AP exam, not to mention any unit tests in your course. Here is a Top 10 list of tips before we try a set:

1. Read the source carefully and entirely before you determine its perspective. Look for nuances and subtleties, as these often make appealing sources for question sets.

2. Consider glancing briefly at the stem of each item, so that you'll know the topics of the questions *before* you engage the source.

3. Before even looking at the choices, quickly survey what you know about the topic or theme. This will become more intuitive as you practice.

4. Each question tests a specific HTS, so try to identify that skill and bring any strategies you've learned to the process of settling on the key.

5. Pick the BEST answer. All of the choices may appeal, since they are likely based on actual history, but go with the one that reflects BOTH the perspective of the source AND your content knowledge.

6. Don't worry about getting 100%; that's highly unlikely, and if you're a perfectionist, this expectation will only create anxiety and derail your intuitive thinking process for the test as a whole.

7. How many times have you changed an answer based on doubt, only to find later that you had the right answer the first time? Trust your gut!

8. Before you take MC exams, study from the Concept Outline of the Course Description. It's the Roman numeral portion after the Key Concept narratives. Every right answer must arise from this section—either directly, by paraphrase, or through inference.

9. Practice the many questions in this guide. Peruse the answer explanations (see Chapter 18) to help you sharpen your powers of deduction.

10. Outside-the-box suggestion: find a source, and try to write your own set of questions, using the Concept Outline and HTS. This will help you gain insight into how the tests are constructed and provide you with insider strategic thinking.

Now let's try a set based on the visual on the following page. Consider what you see in and can infer from this image—content, style of presentation, purpose, symbolism, historical context, etc. When you're ready, read the set of 5 questions based on the image. Note: each question has been correlated with the relevant HTS, course themes, and period key concepts.

An execution of alleged witches in 16th-century Germany

1. The event depicted above best reflects which of the following intellectual features of early modern Europe?

   A. Belief in social hierarchy based on a Great Chain of Being

   B. Persistence of folk beliefs in supernatural causation

   C. Spread of Bible reading due to the printing press

   D. Revival of classical texts that emphasized civic humanism

HTS—Contextualization (CTX). Theme: OS. KC: 1.1. This is a standard contextualization question, since it asks you to draw on what you know about the period to determine the ways in which the image reflects, in this case, the intellectual atmosphere of early modern Europe, an OS course theme. If you consult the Concept Outline, you'll see that the correct answer (B) is drawn from KC 1.1, specifically IV.D. You may notice that choices A, C, and D are all true of the period, but they don't explain directly why witches were persecuted. For example, it is true that increased Bible reading reasserted belief in demons, but D is not as directly related to the image as is B.

2. All of the following social and economic developments contributed to the phenomenon portrayed above EXCEPT:

   A. the price revolution, which disrupted traditional patterns of economic activity.

   B. a significant increase in poverty and the associated problem of begging.

   C. leisure activities oriented around the agricultural cycle and church calendar.

   D. migration to cities that strained resources and challenged traditional elites.

HTS—Causation (CAUS). Theme: PP. KC: 1.5. Here you have an EXCEPT question, of which there will likely be no more than 5-6 on any given test form. For this item type, you are looking for the one explanation that does not fit, which in this case is C. Again, all of the choices represent features of early modern economic and social life, but C does not relate directly to causing witchcraft accusations. Can you see why this is a Causation question? All of these factors helped, mostly indirectly, to create social dislocation and deepen the sense of crisis that found expression in witchcraft accusations.

3. An historian would most likely use the source above to make conclusions regarding:

   A. early modern attitudes toward women and magic.

   B. the impact of the religious wars on social stability.

   C. how artistic styles developed among the lower classes.

   D. the effect of centralized monarchies on the legal system.

HTS—Analyzing Evidence: Content & Sourcing (EVCS) and Using Evidence to Support an Argument (EVARG). Themes: OS, IS. KC: 1.1, 1.5. This question involves your judgment, a faculty that will become more sharply honed with your practice in the course. You are asked to think like an historian and consider what type of evidence works best to answer particular historical questions. All of the choices might be related to the image; however, since the image addresses belief in magic and perceptions of women–the most common victims of witchcraft accusations— those constitute the most likely use of this piece of evidence (A). The other choices would require further historical context and corroboration from other sources to be of much use to an historian. Based on the choices, the question addresses both culture (OS) and gender (IS) attitudes.

4. The situation of the main subjects in the image is most similar to:

    A. artistic geniuses, such as Michelangelo.

    B. religious minorities, such as the Anabaptists.

    C. humanist scholars, such as Machiavelli.

    D. new economic elites, such as the gentry.

HTS—Comparison (COMP). Theme: IS. KC: 1.3. We deal with a historical comparison in this question: what other group might have faced a similar situation and perception as women did during the witchcraft phenomenon? One of the elements of the IS course theme addresses the notion of "the Other," i.e., how groups can be alienated from the larger society through depictions, symbols, and forms of expression. Women were often targeted as witches because of gender beliefs emphasizing their lack of reason, credulity, and power over the human body. All but B represent individuals or groups of power and prestige. Anabaptists experienced persecutions by both Protestants and Catholics because their religious beliefs were considered outside the mainstream and a threat to the integrity of the state, similar to witches.

5. Which of the following most directly helped to end the phenomenon depicted?

    A. The end of the religious wars

    B. The Columbian Exchange

    C. The Scientific Revolution

    D. The French Revolution

HTS—Change and Continuity Over Time (CCOT) and Periodization (PER). Theme: OS. KC: 1.1. This question asks how and why the witchcraft accusations ended, simply by listing several important developments or events. It counts on your implicit thinking process regarding change and continuity over time and also turning points, i.e., an event that changed the way in which the world was viewed. Though all four choices can be argued as turning points, it was the Scientific Revolution (C) that most altered the explanation of causation, replacing supernatural explanations with materialism and mathematics. Once again, the question relates to the OS theme and KC 1.1, the variation of that theme in Period 1.

In retrospect, you'll notice that this set of MC questions covers almost all of the HTS; however, most sets you encounter on the AP exam will likely involve 3–4 questions and cover a more limited range of HTS as in the example above. Here are the most common types:

- **Causation**–The content of the document will either be the result of a previous cause or itself the cause of a subsequent effect. Notice how Questions 2 and 5 in the set above function in this fashion.

- **Contextualization**–You are asked about how a source "reflects" or "demonstrates" features of an event, period, or development.

- **Comparison**–Comparisons involve similarities and/or differences between two geographic areas, periods, or groups. Focuses on your ability to make connections.

- **Change/Continuity Over Time**–Less common than the above types, these items ask you to consider how features of a topic might have remained the same or been altered chronologically.

- **Argumentation, Evidence, and Source Analysis**–Question 3 above represents this type, in which you are asked to think like an historian and also draw on your content knowledge to test the link between evidence and conclusion.

- **Interpretation**–On any given exam format, you are likely to encounter 2 or 3 of these sets. Here you are generally given an excerpt from a secondary source and asked to consider evidence that might support or counter the claims of the historian.

- **Periodization**–Difficult type to write, so expect only a handful on the AP exam. In these questions, you consider turning points or events that ended or began a specific era.

- **Synthesis**–Tested primarily on the DBQ and LEQ, and given the nature of the HTS, very difficult to write for the multiple choice.

Strategies for the Written Section of the Exam

Short-Answer Questions (SAQs)

With Short-Answer Questions (SAQs), you have an opportunity to demonstrate your facility with 1–2 targeted HTS and to draw on your content knowledge to address a prompt *briefly*. For these items, do *not* write an essay–avoid introductions, thesis statements, and conclusions. Don't elaborate your response beyond what is necessary to establish your grasp of the HTS and the content involved in the prompt. In fact, your response must be limited to one side of a sheet of paper defined by a lined box. Spare your energy and time for the set of 4 questions (not to mention the later DBQ and LEQ) by maintaining your focus on *what the item format expects*–brevity and concision.

SAQs may or may not involve stimulus. At least 2 of the set of 4 will be stimulus-based; since these tend to be more complicated, let's examine such an example below. Read the following prompt, consider how you might respond, and then read the sample provided. Remember that each SAQ involves 3 scoring points, with no qualitative dimension, meaning you get the point or you don't. No extra points, no half-points, just 0 or 1.

"The Versailles Treaty," June 28, 1919: Part VIII, Article 231. The Avalon Project, Yale Law School, http://avalon.lawyale.edu/subject_menus/versailles_menu.asp

---

Article 231

"The Allied and Associated Governments affirm and Germany accepts the responsibility of Germany and her allies for causing all the loss and damage to which the Allied and Associated Governments and their nationals have been subjected as a consequence of the war imposed upon them by the aggression of Germany and her allies."

–Treaty of Versailles, between Allied Powers and Germany, June 1919

A. Using your understanding of European diplomacy and politics, 1871–1914, explain ONE example that supports the interpretation above.

B. Using your understanding of European diplomacy and politics, 1871–1914, explain ONE example that contradicts the interpretation above.

C. Explain ONE specific effect of the treaty provision above on European politics and diplomacy, 1919–1939.

As you consider this question, notice that it involves mainstream topics from your course: World War I, the Treaty of Versailles, and pre- and post-war diplomacy. You are presented with the "war guilt" clause from the Treaty of Versailles and asked to assess the validity of Article 231 by considering the origins of WWI *and* the effect of the treaty on postwar diplomacy. Notice that the question comprises 3 parts, and it is strongly suggested that you letter your response accordingly, as a clear indication to the AP reader and yourself that you are addressing all parts of the question. Now consider the following sample response and commentary:

A. Germany was mostly to blame for WWI, as Article 231 states. After Bismarck was dismissed, Germany was led by Kaiser William II, who tried to match England's traditional naval supremacy and aggressively pursued colonies. Because of the Kaiser's reckless diplomacy, Germany was feared by the other powers, except the stumbling Austria. The war was caused when Germany gave Austria a "blank check" in 1914 to deal with the Serbian threat.

B. Though Article 231 blamed Germany for WWI, this was based on the Allies' desire to punish Germany and make it pay for reparations. However, all nations had responsibility for the war. France wanted to retake Alsace-Lorraine and thus backed Russia's full mobilization when Austria declared war on Serbia, Russia's ally.

C. Versailles was a disaster for diplomacy after 1919. German anger over the unfair treaty led to the rise of Hitler and the Nazis, who were determined to overturn its weakening of Germany. This led directly to WWII, despite the failed efforts of the League of Nations.

There is no formal rubric for the SAQ; points are awarded based on whether or not the student adequately answers the three parts of the prompt. This questions tests the HTS of 1) Use of Evidence in Argumentation and 2) Causation. Notice how briefly this response addresses the question, and in so doing, earning all three points. She takes a position in Parts A and B, providing at least one specific example to support her claim. Then the student in Part C connects Versailles to the diplomatic failures of the interwar period that led to World War II. However, she resists the urge to turn the exercise into an essay question—there are no intros, conclusions, or body paragraphs. Just an immediate jump into what the prompt asks.

Certainly this response might have been longer (or briefer), but once you've earned the point by responding adequately to that part of the prompt, it will not serve your interests in extending your argument or attempting to be thorough. You will find many more SAQs throughout this review guide, and it is recommended that you build your facility through practice. With such practice, you will find the SAQs one of the easier parts of the course and exam to master.

Strategies for the Essay Questions

Dissecting the Prompt: Answer the Question Asked! Having read thousands of essays as an AP exam scorer and leader, I can attest that the main reason for student underachievement in writing is the inability to address effectively the question that was asked. As your quivering hands grasp the newly opened booklet of essay prompts (DBQ and LEQ), there is a tendency to fly right into the writing process. Resist this impulse. If planning a road trip, you would consult a map and only then decide on a route. Writing is no different.

Before writing, spend 5 minutes for the LEQ and 15 minutes for the DBQ planning out your approach. First, make sure you understand what the question is asking you to *know* and *do*, especially in relation to 1) chronological scope, 2) geographic scope, and 3) topical scope (e.g., economics, politics, culture, etc.). Both the LEQ and DBQ will always measure the HTS of 1) Argumentation, 2) Use of Evidence, and 3) Synthesis. Each question, either DBQ or LEQ, will also test a targeted HTS. The prompts below represent examples of questions based on these targeted skills:

Causation–Analyze the political and economic reasons for the onset and continuation of the Cold War, 1943–1961.

Comparison–Compare and contrast the political and economic development of France and England from 1640 to 1763.

Change and Continuity Over Time–To what extent did Napoleon continue the principles of the French Revolution in politics and religion?

Periodization–In what ways and to what extent can the Protestant Reformation be viewed as a turning point in European politics and culture?

Each of these prompts might form the basis for either a DBQ or an LEQ, but let's imagine that you were confronted on an exam with the CCOT question as an LEQ.

To what extent did <u>Napoleon continue</u> the <u>principles</u> of the <u>French Revolution</u> in <u>politics</u> and <u>religion</u>?

To ensure that you understand the tasks involved in the question, underline the relevant tasks and terms as I have done above. This should lead to the identification of a thesis and any appropriate examples as you take 5 minutes to organize your approach. The question asks you to make an assessment regarding the *extent* to which Napoleon continued (or changed) the ideals of the French Revolution. For your argument, avoid statements of degree, such as "to a great extent." Instead, be more specific regarding the ways in which and *why* Napoleon may have altered these ideals. Though the chronological scope is not specified, it is implied—i.e., the reign of Napoleon I (1799–1815). In addition, you will need to make reference to the French Revolution, if only broadly, to pick up the *principles* part of the question.

Organize Your Ideas Once clear on what the question is asking, you can begin organizing the essay. Keep in mind that this is a brainstorming process of limited time, not a research paper. Think of all the examples and specifics related to the topic. If you end up with an unmanageable amount of information, select those most relevant to the prompt and consider how you can use them to support a thesis. Here is an example of what your notes might look like:

<u>Principles of French Revolution</u>
"Liberty, equality, fraternity"—the last can be construed as "nationalism"

<u>Napoleon's policies</u>
Liberty—secret police, censorship, manipulation of public opinion, allowed freedom of worship, conquest of foreign lands, ending of feudalism and serfdom in conquered lands
Assessment: on balance, Napoleon did not promote liberty, ruled dictatorially posing as a "man of the people"

Equality—Napoleonic Code, restricted rights for women, abolition of feudalism and serfdom, establishment of schools, creation of uniform bureaucracy, "careers open to talent," nepotism, reestablished slavery in colonies
Assessment: in general, Napoleon's life and policies represent commitment to equality, but excluded women and compromised when it suited his power

Fraternity—Promoted nationalism in army, used revolutionary warfare, rewarded service with Legion of Honor, indirectly fed nationalism in conquered foreign lands
Assessment: Napoleon used nationalism effectively to gain and maintain power, but his indirect promotion of nationalism in foreign lands led to his downfall

This outline may be more detailed than time or your immediately recalled knowledge will allow. Don't worry. A student could easily write a top-notch essay with less detail than is given here. More important than simply facts is that you demonstrate an understanding of the question and provide a clear and direct thesis in response to the prompt.

Start Strong: Introduction and Thesis You've probably heard it from your teachers before: "Make sure your essay has a thesis." "Where's your thesis?" "Your thesis needs to be clearer." An explicit thesis statement gives your essay direction and provides something on which to hang the evidence. A thesis is a (usually) one-sentence statement of the main arguments or points you will develop in your essay. Further, to earn the rubric points, it must be in either your introduction (preferred) or conclusion. Unfortunately, many essays lack such specificity and direction. As you practice your writing, work to develop your skills in articulating a thesis for your essays. What, then, makes for a powerful thesis?

First, a strong thesis does more than simply restate the question. Let's say you are responding to this essay prompt: "Analyze the economic, geographic, and social factors that caused the Industrial Revolution to occur first in Great Britain, 1750–1850." In their rush to get into the question with examples, many students may produce a generic statement, like: "There were many economic, geographic, and social factors that led to the Industrial Revolution in Great Britain." This is merely a restatement of the prompt, and it adds little to your essay. Your thesis must be *informative*, which means the reader should know something more about the topic in question than they did before reading your introduction. Consider incorporating defining terms and essential concepts into your thesis to demonstrate your *specific* grasp of the topic under consideration.

A strong thesis is specific in relation to the question. In the above prompt, you are asked (implicitly) to identify the economic, geographic, and social factors that promoted British industrialism, so your introduction should call out or at least characterize these factors. Since you are asked to "analyze," make sure you begin your discussion of the *how* and *why* of causation. It is not enough simply to line up events in chronological order and leave the work of explanation to the reader. For the introduction, numerous examples are not necessary; save them for your body paragraphs. Stop and allow yourself time to recollect what you know about the topic. Consider the following for the level of detail and explanation at which to aim:

> Economic: Britain boasted important institutions that helped raise capital and promoted industry—Bank of England, strong navy, commercial empire, productive agriculture
>
> Geographic: abundant natural resources, easy access to the sea, security from invasion
>
> Social: mobile and surplus labor force, elites open to money-making, strong inventive tradition from Scientific Revolution and Enlightenment

Make sure to allow time for this brainstorming process. Again, do not be concerned if you generate less in the way of examples. Try to identify for each area in one sentence *how* developments there contributed to Great Britain's advantage. Once this is done, you are ready to formulate your thesis. But first, let's look at how to structure an effective introduction.

No one strategy works like magic, yet there is a formula that can serve you well. Begin your introduction with one or two sentences of relevant historical context. Avoid philosophizing or taking your question too far outside the time period. For the question above, you might begin:

> Prior to 1750, Great Britain was a major commercial power, passing rivals like the Dutch and Spanish. While most of Europe, 1750–1850, was involved in revolutions, Great Britain used its advantages to become the major industrial nation.

This context serves as a trajectory into the question and establishes with solid chronological foundations that you have control of the question. Now you are ready to take the brainstorming above and formulate a thesis—in this case, one that has three parts (economic, geographic, and social):

> The British used capitalistic economic institutions, such as the Bank of England, a secure geographic position with many resources, and a society that focused on invention and profit to become the world economic leader by 1850.

For added punch, finish off your introduction with a clincher that pulls the thesis together with an interpretation and perhaps signals the synthesis strategy you will use in the conclusion (such as connecting the topic to previous or subsequent similar issues). In this case, Britain influenced other nations to adopt similar production strategies, leading eventually to Europe's economic dominance and imperial control of world trade:

> Over the next century, other European nations followed the British example and developed their own economies to compete for trade and power all across the world.

Remember that this model is a process that you will need to hone in your class and as you use the practice questions in this book. The most important lesson you should take from our discussion is not that your thesis need be beautifully articulate (though that's an added bonus), rather that you are specific in addressing the question that is being asked. Avoid simply restating the question, which adds little to your essay and gives you no direction when you compose your body paragraphs.

The Body Paragraphs: Fleshing Out Your Thesis Though an introduction provides direction and focus to your essay, you serve the meat of your argument in the body paragraphs. As you write the body of your essay, always have one eye on your thesis. Often, students get caught up in telling a story or "data dumping," which has no relation to the ultimate point of the essay. All AP prompts are designed to gauge your *understanding* of the targeted HTS *and* the relevant content, not your factual recall. Keep focused on connecting your evidence to the thesis, avoiding tangential issues and commentary.

An effective body paragraph always begins with a strong topic sentence that goes beyond restating the question. If we take the essay above on Britain and industrialization, our first body paragraph might be on economic factors. Keep in mind that you need to show *how* and *why* these factors assisted Britain in industrializing. Statements of this nature are insufficient: "Now I will talk about economics" OR "Economic factors also helped Great Britain to industrialize." Aim to capture the primary role that factor played: "Great Britain's supportive economic institutions provided the capital it needed to industrialize." This conclusion now gives the remainder of the paragraph and your examples the direction you need. After all, you are making an *argument*, not merely describing or summarizing. An argument is a claim with which another historian could theoretically disagree, e.g., if you were to claim that social, rather than geographic or economic, factors served as the most important factor in promoting British industry.

When it comes to support for your argument, you must select evidence purposefully. More is not necessarily better. Several well-chosen examples that are clearly and explicitly connected to the topic sentence, and ultimately the thesis, are preferable to an unorganized or unexplained catalogue. As you write, try to think of yourself as establishing connections between the examples and the concept. Schematically, the body paragraph will appear as below, with explanations running along each line that connects the example to the topic sentence. For example, along the line from "strong navy" to the central idea of the paragraph, we might have: "England's strong navy allowed it to establish new colonies and defeat rival powers. The trade that resulted from England's colonial empire allowed entrepreneurs to finance industry back in the home country."

These four examples provide ample support for this paragraph. In fact, for each body paragraph, aim for approximately 2–4 examples as support. Fully explained examples show your control of the question and ability to develop a central idea–the thesis–as well as demonstrate your application of the targeted HTS (in this case, Causation). Finally, to conclude your body paragraph, write a transitional sentence that sets up your next paragraph, such as: "While these institutions were important, perhaps they would not even have existed without Britain's favored geographic location." Sentences like this help take a reader systematically through an argument and show how each component part fits with the others. If you made it this far, sometimes, as with speaking, the most important task is knowing when and how to stop.

The Conclusion: How to End on a High Note Think of the conclusion of your essay as a dismount in a gymnastic routine—a last chance to influence the scorer positively. It is important here that you *add* to what you've already written. Therefore, avoid merely repeating the introductory paragraph or reiterating a point already made. For both the DBQ and LEQ, the conclusion is an ideal spot to earn your Synthesis point. The most complex of all the HTS, Synthesis involves the ability to make deep historical connections—from your argument to other periods, geographic areas, and issues—OR to extend your argument with an additional category of analysis. Both the DBQ and LEQ rubrics specify three strategies for earning the synthesis point:

1. Extend your argument to a development in a different historical period, situation, era, or geographical area.

2. Extend your argument by connecting to a course theme or a topic not addressed by the prompt (e.g., political or cultural history).

3. Using a different field of inquiry as a tool for analysis, such as art history, economics, psychology, et al.).

Unless you've taken courses or read widely in one of the fields listed in 3), you should rely on the first two strategies. These strategies offer a variety of approaches, but whichever you use, make sure you explain your reasoning adequately. Name-dropping an example, without explanation, will not earn you the point.

Let's make this advice more concrete by looking at a specific example from another question:

Analyze the economic and political factors that account for the failure of the German Weimar Republic, 1918–1933.

First, the dates in the question cue you into setting up both the introduction and conclusion. The year 1918 marks the end of the First World War, and 1933, the appointment of Adolf Hitler as Chancellor of Germany. This chronological context will form the structure of our response: this topic is bracketed by the two world wars of the 20th century. In fact, the question would have been written by the Test Development Committee to test the SP and PP themes, which, if you notice, will help you strategize your concluding paragraph for the Synthesis point.

Your recognition of the question's link to related issues across chronology should make its way into your conclusion. Let's take our starting point as 1933 and consider how that date represents the failure of the Weimar Republic and context of the two world wars. Here is one way we might approach the conclusion of this essay (using the Synthesis 1 strategy above).

> The Weimar Republic was born amid chaos and revolution after the First World War. Economic problems, along with Germany's lack of a democratic history and anger over the Versailles Treaty, proved unsolvable. Weimar's failure was significant. Because Germany was unable to establish democracy, Hitler came to power in 1933 and quickly overthrew Versailles. These policies led to a larger and more violent conflict—the Second World War. However, after WWII, the western Allies realized that they needed to rebuild Germany and reintegrate it into an alliance, rather than punishing it for causing yet another war. Thus Germany was reintegrated into European diplomacy and politics, unlike in the period after 1918.

At this point in the exam, you may feel pressed for time, so practice being economical with your synthesis strategy, as demonstrated above. Notice how the conclusion connects the topic of the question to a similar diplomatic situation–the way in which the Allies treated Germany differently after World War II. Though brief, this paragraph effectively establishes and explains a meaningful connection to a related issue in a subsequent chronological period (Strategy 1 above). As you read through the sample essays in this volume, you will encounter additional strategies for the Synthesis—both those that work and those that fall short.

How long should your essay be? As already mentioned, longer essays do not necessarily equate with higher scores. With that in mind, most LEQs responses end up about 2 handwritten pages. Of course, this suggestion should serve as a guideline not a hard-and-fast rule. After all, the time limit of 35 minutes (for the LEQ) will ultimately shape the length of your response.

Mastering the Long-Essay Questions (LEQs)

What Should I Expect? For the long essays, you will be presented with two question choices. These questions will test your knowledge of the same targeted HTS (e.g., Causation), often the same course theme (e.g., Poverty and Prosperity), involve parallel tasks, and will often be drawn from two different chronological eras. Since the content addressed by the long-essay prompts must be addressed within the Concept Outline of the Course Description, the questions should be mainstream. Of course, you may encounter creative applications of this notion. For example, a question may ask you to pull together content from a broad chronological span focusing on a recurring issue, such as attitudes toward gender or artistic representations.

Look at the set below and try to identify the targeted HTS and course themes.

1. Analyze in what ways and to what extent the French Revolution represents a turning point in European politics and society.

2. Analyze in what ways and to what extent the First World War represents a turning point in European politics and society.

The questions target the HTS of Periodization, since they ask you to deal with the idea of a turning point. To write an effective essay, you must explain the characteristics (with examples) of politics and society either before and during each event, or during and after each event. Also, you'll notice that each question addresses the course themes of States and Other Institutions of Power (SP) and Individual and Society (IS).

Managing Your Time Keep in mind that the second phase of the AP exam (following the 10-minute break) requires you to write the DBQ and LEQ in a total of 90 minutes. Of this time, you should spend approximately 35 minutes on the LEQ. Although there is a designated 15-minute reading period for this phase of the exam, you are not required to divide up your time on the two essays in any particular way. Given the tasks you have to juggle, you may find it helpful to spend the first 5 minutes of the reading period organizing your LEQ (settling on a thesis, surveying content, determining paragraph structure, identifying synthesis strategy) and then turning to the DBQ.

After you finish the DBQ (in roughly 55 minutes), you can return to the LEQ. Having already planned out your response, you can go right into the writing process. This will make up for the 5-minute lag with the proctor's instructions (since you likely started the DBQ 5 minutes "late" because you outlined your LEQ). By using this strategy, you can create a plan of action for both essays and reduce your anxiety. Also, by this time of the exam, you may be experiencing mental and physical fatigue, which tend to produce mistakes. By organizing your ideas at the beginning of the 90 minutes—when your mind is still fresh—you're less likely to experience the pitfalls of chronological errors and misinterpreting the required tasks of a question. To manage your time, it is suggested that you bring a watch (no alarms or data allowed) and consult it throughout this and the previous sections of the exam.

Final Tips for Writing an Effective Essay Before moving on to the unique features of the Document-Based Question, let's pull together the suggestions for effective writing, some of which apply to both the LEQs and DBQ. AP readers will think of your essays as a first draft, so spelling errors, grammar, and less-than-elegant penmanship generally do not detract from your score. With that said, there is no doubt that a clear, cogent writing style can only assist in conveying your understanding. It is in your interest, then, to work at making your writing as tight as possible—that is, making every word count with no wasted motion. AP readers want to see your performance, not your warm-up routine. To assist in improving your writing style, a brief yet essential resource is William Strunk and E.B. White, *The Elements of Style* (Boston: Allyn & Bacon, 2000). This short primer on usage and style will give your writing power and clarity. So should the following suggestions:

- Allow yourself about 5 minutes (LEQ) to organize your ideas and establish a clear direction for your essay.

- Get to your points as quickly as possible; avoid flowery prose, rhetorical questions, dramatic scene-setting.

- Be specific in identifying your thesis; do not simply restate the question—make an argument.

- Make sure you engage both the HTS and course theme(s) on which the question is based. Draw on the strategies you've developed and address the HTS explicitly.

- Provide topic sentences to your body paragraphs that relate directly to your thesis.

- *Apply* examples to the thesis, rather than simply mentioning or listing them.

- Steer clear of value judgments or opinions. Your role is as an impartial historian.

- Write directly and clearly. Try to avoid too many or needlessly complex prepositional phrases. Employ action verbs, such as "advanced," "opposed," and "established," whenever possible.

- Manage your time effectively. Don't get bogged down in side issues; focus on your argument.

- Finish strong. Use the conclusion to establish strong historical connections and earn your Synthesis point.

Even if you lose track of time or are rushed, don't panic. Some years ago, I had a student who found himself with only 12 minutes at the end of our final exam (a full AP exam) to complete his long essay. He approached me and asked, "What should I do?" My response was, "Go back and write as much as you can in those 12 minutes." He complied and earned a solid score on his response. Not that I would recommend putting yourself under this time pressure, but it might boost your confidence to know that you don't have to be perfect on all components of the exam to score highly. However, you should try to make the most of your opportunities.

An Example Before we move on to the DBQ, let's look at a sample essay from an actual student of the course. As you read the response below, you'll notice that I've added commentary as to how the student earned her points on the rubric (see p. 5 from Chapter 1 to follow along with the scoring requirements). The essay below is in response to the Periodization question above on the French Revolution.

(see p. 5 from Chapter 1 to follow along with the scoring requirements)

From 1789 to 1799 in France, there was massive upheaval in an attempt for the French citizens to replace the Old Regime[10] with a new political and social system where equality and legal rights were exercised. The French Revolution was a significant turning point in European history because it got rid of the inequalities of the social classes and it established natural law that granted more equality to the citizens[11].

One reason that the French Revolution was a major turning point was because it attempted to abolish the inequalities between social classes[12]. Before the French Revolution, the three estates were not granted equal rights, as the nobles and clergy had many privileges and tax exemptions. However, since a great portion of the revolution was led by the overlooked Third Estate, it led to efforts to establish equal social rights. This was especially important during the Liberal phase of the Revolution, where all privileges were abolished,

10 NOTE

Brief but relevant reference to the Old Regime.

11 NOTE

This is a brief introduction; however, the student offers a specific thesis, earning the first point in the rubric.

12 NOTE

This topic sentence refers back to the relevant HTS and establishes the student's focus on Periodization.

Thomas S. Greenspon, *Moving Past Perfect: How Perfectionism May Be Holding Back Your Kids (and You!) and What You Can Do About It* (Minneapolis: Free Spirit Publishing, 2012), p. 24.

as were any remnants of serfdom and feudalism. These changes were made by the National Assembly in the Declaration of Rights of Man and Citizen. The Revolution also attempted to abolish class distinctions by making positions available by merit rather than birth, something that was continued during the rule of Napoleon. During the Revolution, other social classes needed the right to seek military ranks and high offices, especially the sans-culottes in the Reign of Terror[13].

The Revolution was also a major turning point in history because it attempted to legally grant equality to its citizens through democratic reform[14]. Prior to the Revolution, France was a monarchy where the king had a significant amount of say over its citizens. Although it wasn't entirely an absolute monarchy, it did have some remnants of that type of rule. However, this changed dramatically because of the input of ordinary citizens during the revolution. The revolution was mostly led by the Third Estate, the common citizens. They created a new constitution and documents such as Declaration of Rights of Man and Citizen. Later on during the Reign of Terror, the sans-culottes influenced the Committee of Public Safety, which promoted equality through many reforms. This shows that the balance of power changed from one in which only the highest classes had the most rights to one in which the lower classes had a chance to rule[15]. However, this was only true to some extent. Women were still left out of governments and, during the radicalization and Reign of Terror, even forbidden to join women's groups and associations. Although women's roles in the revolution were decreased, their participation during the Liberal phase, especially during the October Days and the storming of Bastille, played a significant role in creating feminist attitudes[16].

Overall, the French Revolution was a significant turning point in European history because it changed the balance of power and showed the power the lower classes could have when given equality. The topic of the French Revolution also was both impacted and had an impact on the rest of the world. In the United States, the American Revolution had just taken place, increasing the revolutionary spirit and admiration of Enlightenment policies, such as equality and liberty, both of which had an impact on France and inspired the trend of revolution. On the other hand, France impacted other states to reform their governments. This was especially evident during the Haitian slave revolt, the first successful slave revolt in history. Here the Haitian slaves overthrew the slave-keepers, fighting for equality and liberty as well. This goes to show how a revolutionary spirit can make lasting changes[17].

This essay overall earned a 6, the highest possible on the LEQ. It earned the point for Thesis (see intro), the point for Synthesis (see conclusion), 2 points for addressing the HTS of Periodization through substantive analysis of the French Revolution as a turning point, and 2 points for Use of Evidence in supporting the thesis. Is this a perfect response? By no means. It might be enhanced by a more developed introduction and several more specific examples. However, it should remind you that with a strong grounding in the chronology of European history, attention to the course themes, practice with the HTS, and a focused approach, you too can write essays that earn top scores. A professional historian of the French Revolution would certainly write a much more impressive essay, yet it would still only earn a 6, as did this one. "Excellence is risk. Perfection is fear. Excellence is confidence. Perfection is doubt." –Author unknown

How to Approach the Document-Based Question (DBQ)

Purpose of the DBQ The document-based question is designed to test your skill in using historical sources and content evidence to make an argument. With the 7 documents provided, you will detect patterns from the sources; evaluate evidence for bias; note multiple perspectives on an issue; detect nuance, irony, and purpose in documents; and apply varying techniques of analysis depending on the type of source. In the current Information Age, we are bombarded by images, many connected to product sales, lofty advertising promises, high political rhetoric, and unsubstantiated claims by bloggers. As a citizen, you need to be able to sort fact from fiction, recognize the agendas behind the words, and appreciate that there can be many ways of looking at an issue. By practicing such skills with historical sources, it is hoped that you not only

13 NOTE
This paragraph offers several examples. Though 1–2 more specific examples might provide further depth, the evidence relates directly back to the student's argument regarding a turning point.

14 NOTE
Again, this topic sentence, while somewhat general, effectively returns to the HTS and the argument.

15 NOTE
In this section, the student introduces several examples and suggests a grasp of the chronological scope of the revolution. Also, she notes how a specific social group–the sans-culottes– were affected by the Revolution's policies.

16 NOTE
This is one of the more impressive features of this essay: the student notes a limitation on the Revolution as a turning point by analyzing its (lack of) impact on women. But she also notes its future effects.

17 NOTE
With references to the Enlightenment, American Revolution, and Haitian slave revolt, the student demonstrates amply her ability to make historical connections by introducing a new theme, Interaction of Europe and the World (INT), which was not part of the prompt.

appreciate how historians arrive at interpretations and explanations, but translate these skills into whatever field you choose.

Before delving into DBQ strategies, let's consider an actual question. After you note the general directions below, I recommend reading through the DBQ question that follows. If this is your first foray into DBQs, don't worry if you find the task confusing. We'll go through it step-by-step, and then you can try the question as an exercise.

General Directions

1. You have 55 minutes to complete the DBQ, of which 15 minutes is allotted for reading the documents and planning your response.

2. Read the question precisely, underlining key words and tasks you are charged to complete.

3. Read the documents completely and carefully; oftentimes, you will encounter a document that shifts tone or that outlines an argument with which the author *disagrees*, and then lays out his own perspective.

4. As you read the sources, consider how the evidence from the documents AND your content knowledge can be used to develop an argument.

5. Pay careful attention to each source—its type, information about the author, historical context, etc. Brainstorm approaches on how to use this information for source analysis.

6. When you are finished reading the documents, make a brief outline that includes: paragraph topics, organization of documents, content examples, and strategies for source analysis.

7. As you begin writing, keep referring back to the question to ensure that you are addressing it explicitly, with the documents and content examples.

Practice DBQ Exercise

Document-Based Question
Maximum reading and writing time: 55 minutes
It is suggested that you spend about 15 minutes reading the documents and 40 minutes writing your response.

Directions: Question 1 is based on the accompanying documents. The documents have been edited for the purpose of this exercise.

In your response you should do the following:

- **Thesis:** Present a thesis that makes a historically defensible claim and responds to all parts of the question. The thesis must consist of one or more sentences located in one place, either in the introduction or the conclusion.

- **Argument Development:** Develop and support a cohesive argument that recognizes and accounts for historical complexity by explicitly illustrating relationships among historical evidence such as contradiction, corroboration, and/or qualification.

- **Use of the Documents:** Utilize the content of at least six of the documents to support the stated thesis or a relevant argument.

- **Sourcing the Documents:** Explain the significance of the author's point of view, author's purpose, historical context, and/or audience for at least four documents.

- **Contextualization:** Situate the argument by explaining the broader historical events, developments, or processes immediately relevant to the question.

- **Outside Evidence:** Provide an example or additional piece of specific evidence beyond those found in the documents to support or qualify the argument.

Samuel Wilberforce, "Darwin's 'Origin of Species,'" in *The Quarterly Review*, Vol. 108 (London: John Murray, 1860): pp. 257–58.; Clémence Royer, preface to French translation of *On the Origin of Species* in *Charles Darwin Evolutionary Writings*, ed. James A. Secord, (Oxford: Oxford University Press, 2008).; Charles Darwin, *The Autobiography of Charles Darwin*, orig. pub. 1887 (New York: Barnes & Noble Books, 2005), pp. 67, 70.

- **Synthesis:** Extend the argument by explaining the connections between the argument and one of the following.
  - A development in a different historical period, situation, era, or geographical area.
  - A course theme and/or approach to history that is not the focus of the essay (such as political, economic, social, cultural, or intellectual history).
  - A different discipline or field of inquiry (such as economics, government and politics, art history, or anthropology).

1. Assess the impact of Charles Darwin's theory of natural selection on European culture and politics in the period 1859-1914 (HTS: Causation).

Document 1

Source: Samuel Wilberforce, English bishop and writer, *Darwin's* Origin of Species, 1860

First, then, [Darwin] not obscurely declares that he applies his scheme of the action of the principle of natural selection to MAN himself, as well as to the animals around him. Now, we must say at once, and openly, that such a notion is absolutely incompatible not only with single expressions in the word of God on that subject of natural science with which it is not immediately concerned, but, which in our judgment is of far more importance, with the whole representation of that moral and spiritual condition of man which is its proper subject-matter. Man's derived supremacy over the earth; man's power of articulate speech; man's gift of reason; man's free-will and responsibility; man's fall and man's redemption; the incarnation of the Eternal Son; the indwelling of the Eternal Spirit,—all are equally and utterly irreconcilable with the degrading notion of the brute origin of him who was created in the image of God, and redeemed by the Eternal Son assuming to himself his nature.

Document 2

Source: Clémence Royer, French translator of Darwin, anthropologist, and feminist, Preface to *On the Origin of Species*, 1866

The doctrine of Mr. Darwin is the rational revelation of progress, pitting itself in logical antagonism with the irrational revelation of the fall*. These are two principles, two religions in struggle, a thesis and an antithesis of which I defy any German to synthesize. It is a categorical yes and no between which it is necessary to choose, and whoever declares for the one is against the other. For myself, the choice is made.

I believe in progress.

*A reference to the account of Adam and Eve from the Old Testament.

Document 3

Source: Charles Darwin, biologist and developer of doctrine of natural selection in evolution, *Autobiography*, 1887

Thus disbelief [in God] crept over me at very slow rate, but was at last complete. The rate was so slow that I felt no distress.

The old argument from design in nature, as given by [William] Paley*, which formerly seemed to me so conclusive, fails, now that the law of natural selection has been discovered. We can no longer argue that, for instance, the beautiful hinge of a bivalve shell must have been made by an intelligent being, like the hinge of a door by man. There seems to be no more design in the variability of organic beings, and in the action of natural selection, than in the course the wind blows. Everything in nature is the result of fixed laws.

The mystery of the beginning of all things is insoluble to us; and I for one must be content to remain an Agnostic.

*William Paley was an early 19th-century natural theologian who devised a famous argument for intelligent design.

Source: Man is But a Worm," *Punch's Almanack for 1882*, satirical magazine addressing social and political issues

MAN·IS·BVT·A·WORM.

Document 5

Source: Herbert Spencer, British philosopher and sociologist, *Social Statics*, 1873

Pervading all nature we see at work a stern discipline, which is a little cruel that it may be very kind.... Meanwhile the well-being of existing humanity, and its unfolding into this ultimate perfection, are both secured by the same beneficent, though severe discipline, to which animate creation [animals] at large is subject.

It seems hard that a laborer incapacitated by sickness from competing with his stronger fellows, should have to bear the resulting privations. It seems hard that widows and orphans should be left to struggle for life or death. Nevertheless, when regarded not separately but in connection with the interests of universal humanity, these harsh fatalities are seen to be full of beneficence—the same beneficence which brings to early graves the children of diseased parents, and singles out the low-spirited, the intemperate, and the debilitated as the victims of an epidemic.

Document 6

Source: Karl Pearson, British mathematician and scientist, professor of eugenics*, *National Life: From the Standpoint of Science*, 1901

History shows me one way, and one way only, in which a high state of civilization has been produced, namely, the struggle of race with race, and the survival of the physically and mentally fitter race....

The struggle means suffering, intense suffering, while it is in progress; but that struggle and that suffering have been the stages by which the white man has reached his present stage of development, and they account for the fact that he no longer lives in caves and feeds on roots and nuts. This dependence of progress on the survival of the fitter race, terribly dark as it may seem to some of you, gives the struggle for existence its redeeming features; it is the fiery crucible out of which comes the finer metal.

*Eugenics is the supposed science of studying and classifying racial characteristics.

PHOTO: Linda Steward/E+/Getty Images; TEXT: Herbert Spencer, *Social Statics; or, The Conditions Essential to Human Happiness* (New York: D. Appleton and Company, 1873), pp. 352–354.; Karl Pearson, *National Life: From the Standpoint of Science* (London: Adam and Charles Black, 1901), pp. 19, 24.

Source: Friedrich von Bernhardi, German general and writer on military affairs, *Germany and the Next War*, 1912

This aspiration [for universal peace] is directly antagonistic to the great universal laws which rule all life. War is a biological necessity of the first importance, a regulative element in the life of mankind which cannot be dispensed with, since without it an unhealthy development will follow, which excludes every advancement of the race, and therefore all real civilization. "War is the father of all things."* The sages of antiquity long before Darwin recognized this.

*Heraclitus of Ephesus, ancient Greek philosopher

Interpreting the Question Once you look at the DBQ, make sure you understand what the prompt is asking you to **know** and to **do.** In fact, not only should you re-read it and underline key terms, you should also look back at the question *after* you write your introduction, to make sure you've addressed all parts of the question. In this case, the markup of the question might look like this:

Assess the impact of Charles Darwin's theory of natural selection on European culture and politics in the period 1859–1914.

The above process will reinforce the topical (culture, politics), geographical (Europe as a whole), and chronological (1859–1914) scope of the question. In this case, you can likely construe culture broadly to include issues such as religion, ideas, arts, gender, and attitudes toward class and race. Politics may include government policies, ideologies, political parties and movements, foreign affairs, and military issues. Also, try to use the dates as a cue for organizing your essay and considering content examples. Darwin published *On the Origin of Species* in 1859, and the end date marks the onset of World War I. Knowledge of that span should help you survey relevant content and employ helpful historical context.

The next objective is to identify the targeted HTS, which I called out for you above. Though the targeted HTS does not show up on the rubric as a separate category, you should address Causation in A) the development of your argument, B) the use of documents to support your thesis, and C) the use of context and content evidence in support of your argument.

As you read the documents, make connections to what you know about the period. Remember, you only need 1–2 specific content examples (*not* related to source analysis) to earn the Evidence Beyond Documents (EBD) point. To remind yourself about the EBD point, brainstorm content ideas as you read the documents and make note of them. Don't worry about being comprehensive. There will be a range of choices; the more important task is linking the content explicitly to your argument. Here are some content examples suggested by the documents:

- Social and Racial Darwinism

- "White Man's Burden" (Kipling poem)

- Marx's use in history of Darwin's notion of evolution

- Theories challenging traditional ideas, such as Freud, Nietzsche, Einstein, quantum physics

- Scramble for Africa

- Nationalism and national unification campaigns (esp. Germany), including wars

- Arms race

- Increased nationalist tensions on eve of World War I

As you develop your outline and consider use of documents, strategize where you can integrate 1–2 examples like those above.

General Friedrich von Bernhardi, *Germany and the Next War*, trans. Allen H. Powles (New York: Longmans, Green, and Co., 1914), p. 18.

Interpreting the Documents All DBQs will include different types of documents: letters, speeches, books, articles, pamphlets, diaries, cartoons, charts, and illustrations. In one way your task is the same for each document: explain how it relates to your thesis. In another way, each document offers a different opportunity to engage in substantive source analysis. These strategies can vary based on the type of document. In which situation—making a speech before a political gathering or writing a personal letter—would a politician be more forthright in explaining his true motives and intent? Political cartoonists boast a rich history of poking fun at the high and mighty. Illustrators and even photographers (in the manner of how they choose and compose their subjects) act as effective propagandists for and against political movements.

Each of the above scenarios highlights an essential theme of your AP European history course: history is not simply facts but a contested story seen from multiple perspectives. Your job in the DBQ is to demonstrate that you can see through the smokescreen of bias and hidden motives, as well as consider the purpose and intended audience of the document. When addressing point of view, you may speculate as to authors' motives and reliability. Just make sure that you *explain* the reasons for your assertions. Simply stating that "the author of Document 3 is biased" is insufficient and will not earn you credit for point of view. As revealed in the DBQ rubric, there are four specific source analysis strategies identified. We will look at them in general terms before examining specific uses in this particular DBQ.

- **Author's Point of View:** Here you take a known fact about the author's identity and use it to consider (or speculate as to) how that factor may have influenced the content or manner in which she presents her ideas. Such factors of identity can include: 1) class/status, 2) gender, 3) age, 4) occupation, 5) ethnicity/race, 6) political affiliation, 7) religion, and 8) economic role.

- **Author's Purpose:** Even if it's not evident, every document was originally created for some purpose, even if it was merely for a chronicler to record his thoughts in a personal diary. With this strategy, you should infer the purpose of the document based on the type of document. For example, a speech by a political leader before an assembly aims at persuasion, so as you read such a document, pay attention to the rhetoric of the speaker.

- **Historical Context:** Any document reflects the time period in which it was created, either obviously or subtly. Look at the source attribution and note the date or era of the document's provenance. Most likely the source reveals concerns or issues from the period in which it was recorded. For example, imagine a pamphlet on crime and punishment written in 1762. Since this was during the Enlightenment, the source may show the influence of ideals of reason, reform, progress, or humanitarianism—all features of enlightened thought.

- **Intended Audience:** The intended audience may be called out specifically by the author, or you may infer it based on the type of document. In either case, try to use your determination as to the intended audience to analyze the tone and reliability of the source. Two documents can address the same topic and make similar points, yet they may differ markedly in tone, and thus reliability. Imagine an autobiography recounting events that occurred decades before its writing. The more removed in time we are from our memories, the more unreliable they become. Also, autobiographies are often written to "set the record straight" or "tell my side of the story." All these considerations should factor into your evaluation of the source.

Before we look at each document individually, let me add two cautions. First, every document included is relevant to the exercise; there are no trick documents. Though the relevance of some documents may be harder for you to see than others, each can be related to your argument and other documents, which leads to the next point. In any DBQ, two or three more subtle and nuanced documents will be included. Their purpose is to separate the average or above-average response from those that offer sharp and detailed insight into how the documents support a thesis. Now let's look at the content of each document, its possible relation to an argument, and possible strategies for source analysis.

Document 1—Samuel Wilberforce, English bishop and writer, *On Darwin's* Origin of Species, 1860: The first document provides a clearly negative perspective on Darwin's theory. The author, an English bishop, sets up a repeated contrast between the qualities of humans (as created in the image of God) and the "degrading" implications of humans' origins from lower forms of life. Wilberforce finds natural selection scandalous not simply because it seems to contradict the Bible, but also for what it implies about the moral status of humans. This document appears to be a treatise or pamphlet, written the year after the *On the Origin of Species*. One may wonder whether Wilberforce even read Darwin's book, and certainly his standing as a bishop indicates his point of view as an advocate for a predominantly moral and religious view of the world.

Document 2—Clémence Royer, French translator of Darwin, anthropologist, and feminist, Preface to *On the Origin of Species*, 1866: Royer's perspective contrasts sharply with that of Wilberforce above. Though she accepts Wilberforce's dichotomy between religion and science, she opts for the opposing side, or "progress" as she sees it. Considering that this is the preface to Royer's translation of Darwin, her intended audience will be those either interested in or supportive of natural selection. Royer aims to convince her readers of Darwin's accomplishment and to accept the theory as a valid scientific law. Finally, it makes sense that a woman (and feminist), having been subjected to inferior treatment, may convey antagonism toward the traditional political and social order, as well as sympathize with the underdog.

Document 3—Charles Darwin, biologist and developer of doctrine of natural selection in evolution, *Autobiography, 1887*: Darwin explains the course of his theological beliefs due to his involvement in biology. The document addresses many of the same religious issues as Documents 1 and 2, though Darwin's adopts a more subtle tone. For him, the acceptance of the randomness inherent in natural selection leads to agnosticism, i.e., the removal of the explanatory power of a Supreme Being to account for nature or humans. As an autobiography, written almost 20 years after *On the Origin of Species* (but not published till much later), we may wonder whether Darwin's account of his intellectual journey overlooks the inner and outer conflict that his theory produced.

Document 4—"Man Is But a Worm," *Punch's Almanack for 1882*, satirical magazine addressing social and political issues: A complex image, this source offers multiple possibilities for interpretation. You may note first that the source comes from a magazine with a satirical approach, though it may not be obvious what is being mocked in the cartoon—the validity of natural selection and the idea of man's lowly roots OR those who may be unwilling to accept that humans do not hold the lofty place in Creation they once believed (as expressed in Document 1). If unsure, you can make explicit those multiple ways of interpreting the source into your argument. In the bottom left, you'll notice what look like letters. These spell out "CHAOS," and then following the time arc, this process leads to present-day humans, all with Darwin watching over, sitting on what seems to be a classical throne. Whatever the interpretation, it is clear that Document 4 demonstrates the new perception of the human position in the living world.

Document 5—Herbert Spencer, British philosopher and sociologist, *Social Statics*, 1873: Spencer helped found the field of sociology and advocated for the position we now call Social Darwinism. Spencer's use of "survival of the fittest" is starkly evident in this passage, as Spencer discusses the situation of the working classes and poor, issues that would have gained increased attention during the Second Industrial Revolution. As an academic and a respected member of society, Spencer probably lacked first-hand knowledge of the situation of poverty. Also, the sources seems to be a scholarly volume designed for fellow intellectuals, hence his tone of academic distance. Spencer's application of Darwin influenced government policy and political debates, as evidenced in the following two documents.

Document 6—Karl Pearson, British mathematician and scientist, professor of eugenics, *National Life From the Standpoint of Science*, 1901: Though less scholarly in tone, Pearson's treatise echoes that of Spencer above. Again, we see the emphasis on struggle, except in this instance, with a decidedly racial tone. The phrase "white race" may have jumped out to you and reminded you that this was an age of imperialism and competition among the great powers in the Scramble for Africa. Pearson justifies this conquest as the natural outcome of competition among civilization, a process that results in the advance of the human race. Please note the gloss on eugenics: though the field claimed the mantle of scientific credibility, it has since been discredited (after the Nazis) as a pseudo-science motivated more by racism than disinterested inquiry into human characteristics. We may conclude that Pearson wished to justify intellectually the expansion and height of the British Empire under Queen Victoria.

Document 7—Friedrich von Bernhardi, German general and writer on military affairs, *Germany and the Next War*, 1912: In this brief source, a German military theorist justifies war as a "biological necessity," certainly a phrase taken from Darwin, not to mention that von Bernhardi invokes him later in the paragraph. Since war is the business of a general, von Bernhardi deems military affairs as vital to a nation's survival and natural advance. If you consider the historical context, von Bernhardi writes 2 years prior to the outbreak of the First World War, as tensions grew among the great powers and amidst the arms race and mad pursuit of colonies.

The Scoring Rubric It is unlikely a student could score well on the DBQ without knowing the scoring rubric. The rubric is not difficult to learn, and your continued practice with DBQs will build mastery and fluency. In fact, if there is one area of the AP exam where practice can do the most to improve your score, it is on the DBQ. Since the DBQ comprises many moving parts, it is vital that you practice, review areas of difficulty, and then use strategies to develop mastery. As you practice the DBQs in this review book, make sure you keep referring back to the rubric on pp. 4-5 (Chapter 1) and assess the samples essays. In fact, you might try rewriting parts of deficient samples to raise their scores to a 7. Before we take a first look at several such samples for the Darwin question, let's go more in-depth on two areas that are likely to present the strongest challenge to students in earning top scores on this exercise.

General Strategies for Source Analysis You will have noticed some strategies in addressing point of view in the previous examples. Here are some general questions to ask about the documents you encounter:

1. How might the author's identity (race, ethnic background, occupation, social class, age, nationality, religion) have influenced her position?

2. Does this source have first-hand knowledge about what it is reporting? In other words, how reliable is the source?

3. What seems to be the purpose of the source or its intended audience? Is this a public or private document? Does the document have a clear purpose, perhaps as propaganda (especially useful for visual sources)?

4. How close in time to the events being reported was this document written or published? Could the author's memory be faulty or idealized by nostalgic reflection?

5. What is the tone of the document? Are there strong words that suggest an explicit bias?

6. What historical events or processes might have influenced the content or manner of presentation in the document?

One way to demonstrate your mastery of point of view is to employ adjectives or verbs, other than "says" or "states," to capture the tone of the document. Try some of the following words to characterize the tone of the document:

condemned	attacked	typified	observed
encouraged	questioned	implied	criticized
praised	doubted	postulated	showed
sarcastic	excoriated	exhorted	berated
extolled	embraced	idealized	modified
satirized	rejected	stereotyped	adapted
ridiculed	challenged	generalized	issued
informed	depicted	ignored	decreed
patronizing	exalted	overlooked	suggested
dismissive	claimed	glorified	categorized
speculated	rationalized	contrasted	classified
condoned	compared	recorded	defended
mocked	exemplified	noted	represented

Remember, to receive credit on the rubric for source analysis, you must provide FOUR explicit examples. Your source analysis must provide adequate explanation of its rationale to earn points. Many students simply make assertions, like "Since he's a noble, he would think that way." This statement represents only a first step, i.e., noting that the author's status as a noble likely affected his stance on the issue in question. However, the statement lacks sufficient explanation; in contrast, the following assertion *would* earn credit: "Since nobles controlled positions in government and the army, Duke Charles fears the entrance of the middle-class into political power and thus denounces the proposed law."

Writing the Introduction and Thesis The introduction to your DBQ sets you up for success; in fact, you can easily earn 2 points on the rubric even before embarking on the body of your essay. To set up the specific topic, be sure to provide background on any developments or processes that set the historical context. For example, in the Darwin question above, you might mention the general advance of scientific theories and prestige of science and technology, including positivism. Or you might explain the role of imperialism, nationalism, or secularism to help set the stage for your later discussion of how natural selection affected or was affected by these ideas. With 2–3 sentences of substantive linkage to the DBQ prompt, you can earn your Contextualization point.

After establishing the chronological and/or geographic setting, you turn to your thesis. Under no circumstances should you merely restate the question or provide vague references to whatever HTS is being assessed, such as "changed politics a lot," "made culture way different," or "had a big impact on Europe." With the Darwin question, you are dealing with Causation, so you must address the *how* and *why* of the cause bringing about the effect. Be specific, clear, and precise: "Darwin's theory of natural selection challenged religious authority and the exalted place of humans in European culture. At the same time, Darwinism inadvertently hardened politics by emphasizing the struggle among classes, nations, and even races." Notice, first, that this thesis employs two sentences (which is acceptable), and second, that it provides specific explanation of the manner of cause and effect. More importantly, this thesis will provide direction to your analysis of the sources and the development of your argument.

Don't get bogged down in the introductory paragraph; it should be no more than 5–7 sentences. Resist the temptation to provide extensive background or commentary on the topic. The focus of your essay will be the body paragraphs and treatment of the documents.

Effective Body Paragraphs Using the Documents It is in the body paragraphs where you make your argument. In my view, the second Argumentation point on the DBQ rubric will be the most difficult to earn, since you are charged to demonstrate "historical complexity" through showing how documents "contradict, corroborate, or qualify one another." Many students fall into a pattern of summarizing or quoting a document, adding analysis that is merely a paraphrase, and then unceremoniously moving on to the next source. If you adopt this approach, you will not earn the Argumentation point. To help you internalize these requirements, we will use some basic formulas, which you can practice and adapt as you develop your skills on the DBQ.

First, begin your body paragraphs with a powerful topic sentence that indicates how the paragraph supports your thesis. Avoid simply stating the topic: "Darwin's ideas affected culture." Give the reader more direction: "The theory of natural selection opened further rifts between religious and scientific views of the world and ethics." Next, move into your documents. When you use a document, cite the author and the title or type of source. This is the first step toward addressing source analysis. It is also a good practice to put the document number in parentheses after using it, e.g. (Doc. 4), to make it easy for the reader to count the documents should she be in doubt whether you used the required number. When you use a document, you should 1) explain how it supports the topic sentence of the paragraph, 2) consider opportunities for source analysis with it, and 3) discuss how it juxtaposes with other documents.

Think of the documents as being part of a conversation on the issue. If you can get the evidence to interact, you will be be moving toward the charge of the second Argumentation point (see above). Before looking at specific techniques, let's define the requirements for this point:

Contradiction—As you read the sources, look for how documents contradict one another on a similar point. For example, Documents 1 and 2 on the Darwin question offer two opposing perspectives on the theological implications of natural selection. Try to capture this antithesis by using an appropriate transition, e.g., "In Document 2, Royer contradicts Wilberforce's denunciation of Darwin, instead arguing that…." If you are taking a position (e.g., that Darwin's ideas harmed culture), then you will need to address evidence that runs counter to your claim (e.g., that Darwin's ideas enhanced culture). Don't ignore such evidence; your engagement of it demonstrates your recognition of complexity.

Corroboration—If you think of a trial, one type of evidence (e.g., DNA) can confirm or support another type of evidence (e.g., eyewitness testimony). This is corroboration. Though sources may provide differing viewpoints, they can arrive at a similar conclusion. In Document 5, Spencer applies Darwin's notion of "survival of the fittest" to government policy as it relates to internal issues of poverty and inequality. Pearson (Document 6) agrees with Spencer's conclusion, except that he applies the struggle inherent in nature to foreign policy, justifying imperial domination.

Qualification—We often make generalizations that need to be modified in recognition of complexity, and in the same way, sources can be in general agreement but provide differing justifications for their conclusions. Moreover, when we consider certain types of sources, we pick up on nuances or shades of meaning not noticed in other types of evidence. Darwin explains his path from belief to unbelief (Document 3) as a slow process of replacing one set of explanations (religious) with another (scientific). The Punch cartoon (Document 4) seems also to realize this implication of natural selection; however, as a cartoon, it employs exaggeration (in the depiction of the figures and the compression of time) and humor (from CHAOS to worms to reptilian creatures to monkeys to the "missing link" to humans). All this while Darwin, like God, watches over the process. There is similar recognition of the issues involved, but divergence on what this means for humanity.

To capture the above features of documents, employ transition words as you move from one document to the next. Think of the phrases below as a template for engaging your evidence in a conversation. They will give your writing power and indicate your awareness of the complexity involved in argumentation.

- "This document is supported by…"

- "On the other hand,…"

- "His view is directly contradicted by…"

- "The author agrees, but with different reasoning…"

- "This perspective is echoed by…"

- "This viewpoint receives confirmation from…"

As you develop your argument in this way, pay attention to possibilities for source analysis—the rubric requires 4 explicit examples—and attend to this task as well. Like those above, the following phrases will serve as indicators of your analysis of the sources:

- It is not surprising that X should take this view, given that Y...

- Considering his/her position/status as X, this source is a reliable account of Y because of Z.

- Since the document was created during X, the perspective was likely influenced by Y.

- X probably created this document for the explicit purpose of Y, which implies that Z.

- This speech/writing/visual/etc. was aimed at X to convince them that Y.

- Taking into account his/her X, the source is (un)biased because Y.

- Because of the gap between the writing of this source and X, it cannot be considered reliable.

Phrases and transitions like these are not specifically required by the rubric, nor should they be considered to have magical properties. They act as reminders to you and your reader that the DBQ is about making an argument, using and recognizing the complexities of evidence. For further examples and insight into these strategies, please see Gerald Graff's and Cathy Birkenstein's *They Say, I Say*, 3rd ed. (New York: Norton, 2014).

The Conclusion Your conclusion offers an ideal chance to earn your Synthesis point. Of course, remind the reader of your argument, but then connect the topic to related historical issues (from a different period or nation/region). You can also add another category of analysis (e.g., economic) or, if you have relevant background, employ techniques from another discipline, such as art history, biology, sociology, all of which could apply to the Darwin question. Attending to the Synthesis point can provide a strong focus to your conclusion, yet you can earn your Synthesis point at any time during the essay. As you read through the DBQ samples throughout this guide, please take note of the varying synthesis strategies.

The "Ten Commandments" of DBQ Writing

1. Avoid long quotations from the documents. They add nothing to source analysis and waste time you might spend on higher-level tasks. Paraphrase specific information in the documents or use brief quotes and/or phrases.

2. The question is designed to gauge your skills of historical analysis, not as a platform for your own position on the issue. Avoid indicating your own opinion and using "I" words.

3. Make sure you address *all* parts (if it has parts) of the question throughout your essay.

4. Cite the documents appropriately. Identify the author, source (this can be abbreviated if it's lengthy), and place the document number in parentheses.

5. Make the structure of your argument clear by employing a direct thesis, strong topic sentences, and transitional phrases.

6. Use the documents *explicitly* to advance your argument. Avoid simply summarizing or paraphrasing without connecting to a thesis.

7. Be explicit in explaining your rationales for source analysis. Simply stating, "The author is biased," is insufficient. Aim for at least 4–5 examples of source analysis and try to vary your strategies.

8. Try to use all of the documents to support your response (in case you make a major error with one). It is acceptable to spend more time on a document that offers rich opportunities for analysis, but avoid getting bogged down with any particular document. Try to be efficient in using the documents to support your answer.

9. Refer to appropriate evidence beyond the documents: as background to introduce your thesis, as historical context to analyze sources, and as additional content evidence that advances your argument.

10. If the question asks you to take a position, then make sure you do so AND provide reason(s) for your position. Address evidence contradicting your argument (to show complexity) and work toward engaging the documents in an ongoing conversation/debate on the topic.

Practice Writing Now you should be ready to begin writing the sample DBQ. Take about 15 minutes to read through the documents and plan your response. Once you begin writing (you have 40 minutes), stay focused on the question. When you are finished, compare your response to the samples below, which also have commentary included. Use the scoring rubric (on p. 4) to evaluate your essay. Remember that this is a first effort, so you may feel a time crunch. Don't worry, that's common and you will improve your efficiency with each effort.

Sample Essay The essay below demonstrates how to approach the writing of the DBQ. You can follow along with the commentary to see how the student earned *all* points in the rubric.

Charles Darwin's theory of natural selection and evolution developed during a time period of great changes in scientific ideas. Natural selection changed European cultural ideas, challenging the traditional Christian view of intelligent design. Darwin's ideas also caused the development of eugenics, a pseudo-science that provided "scientific" support for nationalism and caused that doctrine to gain more political influence[18].

Christians in Europe traditionally believed in a God who, being perfect in every way, created the world to be perfect, like Himself. As evidenced by Document 1, Darwin's ideas presented a contradiction to this theory of intelligent design by a perfect God. Wilberforce, who was a bishop, and therefore wished to preserve his traditional beliefs about religion in writing this document[19], wrote that mankind's power over all other species on Earth could not have been an accident, and that man's creation must have been done by some perfect Master Being. This document shows that Darwinism indeed did not agree with traditional Christian doctrine. Although Bishop Wilberforce was not convinced that evolution should replace intelligent design as the theory of choice, Clémence Royer, the author of Document 2, was. She wrote that anyone who used logic should most definitely recognize that Darwin's theory was superior to the "irrational" happenings of the Bible. Royer wrote this document to preface "The Origins of Species," Darwin's definitive work on evolution, and that is probably why she spoke with so much praise about Darwin's ideas; she wanted to sell more books[20]. Corroborating Document 2[21], Document 3, written by Darwin himself, continues the idea that natural selection and religion came into direct conflict. Darwin wrote that he became an agnostic because of his ideas of natural selection. Since nature came about entirely by accident, according to him, there must be no God to perfectly design everything. Darwin, of course, as the original developer of the theory of evolution, would wish to believe in its truth, and would defend his theory against detractors, which is probably why he spoke about natural selection in such a positive light[22].

Natural selection also influenced European political ideas of the time. The period 1859–1914 was the great age of European imperialism. Not only did Darwinism cause the development of eugenics and a further increase in nationalistic fervor, but it also provided evidence for the superiority of Europe and the need to colonize. Eugenics was a pseudo-science that studied races and classified their characteristics, claiming it could prove certain races were superior or inferior to others[23]. In Document 6, Pearson, a professor of eugenics, wrote that history reveals that the survival of the fitter and stronger race is why Europe was so advanced at the time. Since Pearson was, after all a professor of

18 NOTE
These two sentences earn the Thesis point, as the student notes the cultural impact of Darwinism on religious belief and in politics with nationalism and eugenics.

19 NOTE
Brief but adequate source analysis for Doc. 1.

20 NOTE
Source analysis for Doc. 2.

21 NOTE
This transition effectively connects Docs. 2 and 3.

22 NOTE
Source analysis for Doc. 3.

23 NOTE
Not only a topic sentence, this preface to the body paragraph also earns the Contextualization point by noting imperialism and connecting it to theories of racial superiority.

eugenics, it makes sense that he firmly believed in its truth, and wished to prove it and influence others to believe in it as well by writing this document[24]. Eugenics, which taught such ideas as this, provided evidence for the superiority of Europeans, thus justifying colonization and imperialism. Rudyard Kipling, a British poet, wrote the famous poem, "White Man's Burden," which demonstrated, satirically, many popular European political attitudes of the time. The poem discusses the superiority of the titular "white man" and said that it would forever be the burden and responsibility of the white men, or Europeans, to civilize inferior races, who were compared to devils or children[25]. Darwinism, which morphed into social Darwinism, provided fodder for nationalism[26]. In Document 7, Friedrich von Bernhardi argued that war is beneficial to civilization, as presumably it impedes the development of weaker races and allows the stronger to come out on top. Bernhardi's ideas were written during the height of nationalism, right before World War I, which demonstrates the effects of natural selection on politics and explains his war-mongering. As he was German, he was probably extremely nationalistic, as that country had only recently been unified, and in writing about superior races, he wished probably to justify the warlike tendencies of his Kaiser, Wilhelm II[27]. Nationalism in conjunction with natural selection is also seen in Document 5[28], in which a British philosopher, Spencer, argues that the hardships of life, including war, disease, and hard work, are ultimately beneficial to humanity, as these trials help weed out the weaker members of society and leave only the strong to survive. These documents may be explained in the context of industrialization. With the poor working and living conditions that came along with industrialization during this time period, many workers lived short, miserable, sickly lives[29]. This document may have been trying to justify some of these conditions by calling them ultimately good. The rise in nationalism and imperialism that was also justified by natural selection was additionally part of this movement of industrialization. Since Europeans possessed more advanced weaponry and technology, such as ships, guns, and cures for diseases like malaria, they were easily able to conquer and subdue native inhabitants of their colonies, thus leading them to point to natural selection as the cause of their victory[30].

Europe during 1859–1914 was greatly influenced by Darwin's ideas, both culturally and politically. Natural selection also affected European attitudes and policies toward the non-European world. Europeans took evolution and used it to justify the brutal colonization of areas in Africa, Asia, and the Middle East. Imperialism forever changed the way Europe interacted with the world. Instead of being equals or the inferior party in negotiations, as Europeans were during the time of the Silk Road, Europe was most definitely the master of the world because of its superior attitudes and technology. During this period, Europe surpassed China and the Middle East to become to undisputed, most powerful, advanced area on the map. Europeans created a most global economy and brought European goods, ideas, and culture ever to corner of the earth[31].

As you read the essay and comments, you may have noticed the student's mastery of the scoring rubric and deliberate effort to earn all of the points. Her response earned the Argumentation point by consistently noting complexity through document interaction, noting contradiction, corroboration, and qualification. Score: 7. Let's look at one more sample.

The theory of natural selection created by Charles Darwin created great uproar in the European aspects of culture and politics. As a result of his theory, the reliability of the church came into question and who was to trust between the two—the church or natural selection and evolution? The argument for the church being that the moral and spiritual aspects of man cannot be developed, while those who supported Darwin argued natural selection and evolution created humans today[32].

The spread of Darwin's theory had great impact on Europe, and promoted aggressive beliefs in life for "survival of the fittest."[33] It ranged from day-to-day life actions to business operations. Document 5, written by a social Darwinist Herbert Spencer explains how natural selection is positive for Europe. He explicitly states how natural selection is able to remove the weak and promote a stronger species. The possible purpose of the statements by Herbert Spencer might be him attempting to promote his own belief, social

24 NOTE
Source analysis for Doc. 6, identifying its purpose.

25 NOTE
With this example and full explanation, the student earns the Evidence Beyond Document point.

26 NOTE
An effective transition to the next document.

27 NOTE
With this use of Historical Context, the student establishes her 4th source analysis for a document, earning that point in the rubric.

28 NOTE
The student's 6th document, earning that point for Using Documents as Evidence.

29 NOTE
Another effective link to Contextualization.

30 NOTE
To conclude the paragraph, the student once again draws on her extensive knowledge of historical context.

31 NOTE
The concluding paragraph provides a strong Synthesis example, effectively linking the topic to the INT theme (Strategy 2) and suggests a sense of CCOT.

32 NOTE
There is an attempt at the Thesis point, but the student does not address politics. Also, no Contextualization is provided in the intro or elsewhere.

33 NOTE
An effort at a topic sentence, but it could be more specific in what it means by "aggressive."

34 NOTE

Minimal but adequate source analysis for Document 5.

35 NOTE

Effective transition to next document.

36 NOTE

An effort at Evidence Beyond Document (slavery) but requires further explanation.

37 NOTE

Again, a minimal yet adequate source analysis for Document 3.

38 NOTE

This attempt at source analysis (through historical context) does not provide adequate explanation.

39 NOTE

Source analysis for Document 1 also falls short, as there is no explanation as to why a bishop would be biased on the issue.

40 NOTE

This is the student's 6th document used, earning Content Use point.

41 NOTE

Here the student earns source analysis for the purpose of the magazine and the cartoon.

42 NOTE

Solid connection of the issue to a related one in a different period. Enough to earn Synthesis point.

Darwinism, in an attempt to gain popularity[34]. Many agreed with Herbert Spencer's beliefs[35], such as Karl Pearson from document 6. Throughout document 6, Karl Pearson, a professor of eugenics, points to the fact that class and racial struggle exists. His reasoning for white supremacy is simply stated by the fact that Europeans developed sooner than others, and how any nation that experienced horrors and poor living conditions is because they are inferior and it is only a matter of time before natural selection removes them. A very similar situation also took place, when North American slavery grew in numbers. It is very likely that Karl Pearson would also support that[36]. Document 3 also promoted Darwinism, as it was written by Darwin himself. Darwin argues that his belief in god disappeared slowly, but he felt no distress. He then argues on the fact that natural selection is good for mankind. His belief is that everything in nature has resulted from something else, and has formed in a positive way from its previous generation. Darwin might have included his statement about god because he wanted to promote his own theory instead of Christianity[37]. Friedrich von Bernhardi also agreed with Darwin, on the premise that war promoted natural selection. Bernhardi believed that war is a necessity to mankind. It promotes regulation and if it does not take place, unhealthy developments may occur. Friedrich von Bernhardi might've said this as a preface to the looming First World War[38].

However not everyone agreed with Darwin. As an attempt to promote the church, Samuel Wilberforce explicitly states how it's impossible for Darwinism to exist, as physical developments have nothing to do with the spiritual and moral aspects of a man. Samuel Wilberforce beliefs in document 1 are likely biased, as he was a bishop of the church[39]. Though document 4[40] does appear to have promoted evolution, it is actually sarcastic. The political cartoon represents man's evolution from a worm into modern day man but the cartoon takes place in a satirical magazine. Though the magazine does address social and political issues, it is likely throwing a jab at all the arguing that has occurred as a result of Darwin's theories. Also, the fact that the final "evolve" that takes place is from man to god, also points to the fact that is should not be taken seriously[41].

It is very clear that the opposing beliefs of the church and Darwin did cause great uproar and resulted in many new beliefs and aspects on life. A similar development that took place earlier in history is between the Catholic Church and Lutheranism. The spread of Luther's ideas caused controversy in politics (like religious war) and culture (the decline of the Church's power over education), just like Darwin's ideas. In both cases, many people were forced to choose sides, and this led to conflict within society[42].

This student provides some effective analysis but also seemed shakier than the first sample on the application of the rubric. He earned the Argumentation point (barely) through consistent transitions and recognition that Darwin's ideas provoked opposing views. However, nowhere did the student answer both parts (culture and politics) of the question explicitly, costing the Thesis point. In addition, the essay offered no explicit Contextualization, and its attempt at Evidence Beyond Documents fell short of adequate explanation. Though the student earned Document Content (for 6 accurate uses), he fell just short of the Source Analysis point, with 3 examples and several near-misses. Finally, the response offered an appropriate albeit brief connection to another period to earn Synthesis. Score: 3 (Argumentation, Document Use, Synthesis).

Conclusion

As you read through the content review section, keep practicing both your writing and application of the historical thinking skills. It is especially important that you refer back to the rubrics (for the DBQ and LEQ) whenever you attempt questions, as well as evaluate the various samples provided, which like those above, highlight excellent responses and those that might have been easily improved with clearer direction and an explicit application of skills. Good luck!

3 The Rise of Europe

Introduction

The following chapters review the content of the AP European History course. The material may correspond in content and organization to your textbook. When warranted, I have reorganized the material to provide a stronger focus on the format of the official curriculum framework for the course. As of the 2016 exam administration, AP European History will be organized around four time periods of roughly equal distribution for test items: 1) 1450–1648, 2) 1648–1815, 3) 1815–1914, and 4) 1914–present. This guide will employ the same chronological scheme, but you'll notice that each period will be subdivided into more focused topics, such as the Enlightenment or Industrial Revolution, each of which will offer test items to check your understanding. Within each period, you'll find connections called out to link the content review to features of the curriculum framework (**Theme Music, Skill Set,** and **Example Base**). Further, at the end of each Period, you will have the opportunity to take an online Diagnostic Test comprising a full DBQ, 30 multiple-choice questions, 2 SAQs, and choice of 2 LEQs.

Five course themes provide a narrative of the recurring issues across this time span. As you look over the themes, you may notice that they roughly correspond to the type of categories that are often used to drive test items, like social, economic, cultural, or diplomatic history. You are strongly advised to draw on the themes to create a narrative framework for the course and to employ them in your writing. Moreover, the themes serve to remind you that this course is NOT primarily oriented toward memorizing content, but instead for you to demonstrate an understanding of the overarching issues and interpretive questions that have marked European history. With the themes below, I have included the 19 Key Concepts that provide the narrative structure for each of the 4 Periods above. Each Key Concept can be connected either primarily or secondarily to the course themes. As you study the content review, thematic and key concept connections will be called out to ensure that you are keeping your attention focused on the big picture.

Themes and Key Concepts (KCs)

1. Interaction of Europe and the World (INT)

Summary If you've taken World History before this course, then you have a leg up for this theme. If not, you needn't fret, as this theme is the most straightforward of the 5. As of 1450, Europe had already begun its outward reach toward Africa and Asia in pursuit of gold and silver, luxury products, and spices. These motives coincided with the goal of spreading Christianity and states seeking political advantage over rivals. Since the Crusades, Europeans gradually accumulated knowledge of new navigational and ship-building techniques from Arab traders and the Chinese. The establishment of European colonies—first as trading outposts, then as territorial empires—helped create a global trading network by the end of the 17th century. These endeavors resulted in a two-way causal stream: Europe gained access to new commodities as part of the Columbian Exchange, while American Indians experienced demographic disaster through disease and mistreatment and Africans were subjected to the transatlantic slave trade.

Interaction with the non-European world also generated cultural and intellectual reassessment, as Europeans responded in a variety of ways to contact with the outside world—by articulating theories of racial superiority and cultural relativism, writing travel literature, and developing new commercial and financial practices. The slave trade, in particular, had by the 18th century raised questions of natural rights and citizenship that coincided with the Enlightenment and the age of revolutions. With the Industrial Revolution of the 19th century, European states sought global resources with a renewed vigor and established more expansive empires, the pursuit of which only heightened national rivalries while prompting internal debates and anti-colonial movements.

By 1914, a new player, the United States, had emerged on the world scene and as a European power. The world wars and Cold War reoriented Europe's position in the world and affirmed the importance of the United States to the European balance of power as the superpowers erected an Iron Curtain that divided East from West. The destructive wars and economic upheaval of the 20th century engendered, first, movements for indigenous autonomy, and then, outright independence for former colonies. Decolonization also contributed to new patterns of immigration and conflict, raising further issues regarding European identities and the continent's position in the world.

Overarching Questions:

- Why have Europeans sought contact and interaction with other parts of the world?

- What political, technological, and intellectual developments enabled European contact and interaction with other parts of the world?

- How have encounters between Europe and the world shaped European culture, politics, and society?

- What impact has contact with Europe had on non-European societies?

Key Concepts

- **KC 1.4** Europeans explored and settled overseas territories, encountering and interacting with indigenous populations.

- **KC 2.2** The expansion of European commerce accelerated the growth of a world-wide economic network.

- **KC 3.5** A variety of motives and methods led to the intensification of European global control and increased tensions among the Great Powers.

- **KC 4.1** Total war and political instability in the first half of the 20th century gave way to a polarized state order during the Cold War, and eventually to efforts at transnational union.

Major Topics and Developments

- Motives, means, and consequences of European exploration (15th–16th centuries)

- Establishment of gunpowder and colonial empires (15th–18th centuries)

- Global trading network → Commercial Revolution (16th–18th centuries)

- Slave trade, slavery, and race (15th–19th centuries)

- Travel literature and the Enlightenment (17th–18th centuries)

- Revolutionary ideas and anti-colonialism (18th–19th centuries)

- Imperialism in Asia and Africa (19th–20th centuries)

- Impact of interaction on the arts, culture, and ideas (18th–20th centuries)

- World wars and decolonization (20th century)

- Guest workers and issues of dependency and immigration (20th–21st centuries)

Source: AP European History Course and Exam Description, Fall 2015. Copyright © 2015 The College Board. Reproduced with permission. http://apcentral.collegeboard.com.

2. Poverty and Prosperity (PP)

Summary   After 1450, Europe gradually, and with wide regional variations, moved away from subsistence and preindustrial toward commercial and money-oriented economic activities. The Price Revolution—caused primarily by rising population bidding up the price of land and goods—privileged the development of cash crops for sale on the market. Rising prices paralleled the enclosure movement and the breakdown of communal agriculture practices, all of which encouraged the growth of larger landholdings and a new rural elite (the "gentry" in England). Preindustrial economic operations had been subject to the control of traditional institutions such as guilds and villages (communal agriculture). The transformation toward a money and commercial economy corresponded with 1) trade in goods from the Americas and other colonies, 2) a rising standard of living in new products, and 3) efforts by governments to promote commerce, in an effort to promote national wealth. Government policies to shepherd national wealth (thought of as hard money or specie) followed the theory of mercantilism.

Despite the increase in wealth during the period 1500–1750, Europe continued to confront the limits of resources and population strains (Malthusian Trap) on available resources. Enlightenment thinker Adam Smith formulated a systematic critique of mercantilism with his free-market theories known as capitalism. Capitalist principles and practices supported the growth of industry in the 18th century, first in Britain and spreading to the continent in the 19th century. Industrialization revolutionized production through the factory system and application of machinery, but at the same time produced new class inequalities (bourgeoisie and proletariat) and a range of social problems, such as overcrowded cities and child labor. Stimulated by these problems and the legacy of the French Revolution, socialism (and then Marxism) developed throughout the 19th century, reaching political power with the experiment of the Russian Revolution.

Two world wars and a Great Depression ended the pre-1914 European-dominated world economic system, allowing new centers of production and economic power to arise, particularly the United States. The economic crisis of the 20th century led to experimentation with new theories and policies in western Europe, such as Keynesianism and then the growth of a more extensive welfare state. During the Cold War, the Soviet Union and Eastern Europe offered a rival system of centralized control and collective ownership of property. The imperatives of the Cold War actually facilitated Europe's recovery from the Cold War, in the form of American aid and new policies of political and economic integration. The latter were highlighted by the formation of the European Union and euro currency around the turn of the 21st century, which were joined by the former Eastern bloc satellites following the collapse of communism. These policies of unity and the growing costs of the welfare state have not been without critics from both the left and right of the political spectrum, reminding Europeans of the perennial issue of organizing production efficiently while addressing issues of inequality and status of labor.

Overarching Questions:

- How has capitalism developed as an economic system?

- How has the organization of society changed as a result of or in response to the development and spread of capitalism?

- What were the causes and consequences of economic and social inequality?

- How did individuals, groups, and the state respond to economic and social inequality?

Key Concepts

- **KC 1.4** Europeans explored and settled overseas territories, encountering and interacting with indigenous populations.

- **KC 1.5** European society and the experiences of everyday life were increasingly shaped by commercial and agricultural capitalism, notwithstanding the persistence of medieval social and economic structures.

- **KC 2.2** The expansion of European commerce accelerated the growth of a worldwide economic network.

- **KC 2.4** The experiences of everyday life were shaped by demographic, environmental, medical, and technological changes.

- **KC 3.1** The Industrial Revolution spread from Great Britain to the continent, where the state played a greater role in promoting industry.

- **KC 3.2** The experiences of everyday life were shaped by industrialization, depending on the level of industrial development in a particular location.

- **KC 4.2** The stresses of economic collapse and total war engendered internal conflicts within European states and created conflicting conceptions of the relationship between the individual and the state, as demonstrated in the ideological battle among liberal democracy, communism, and fascism.

- **KC 4.4** Demographic changes, economic growth, total war, disruptions of traditional social patterns, and competing definitions of freedom and justice altered the experiences of everyday life.

Major Topics and Developments

- Traditional economy and subsistence agriculture (15th–17th centuries)

- Renaissance recovery (15th century)

- Price Revolution and money economy (16th–17th centuries)

- New financial and trading institutions (15th–18th centuries)

- Mercantilism → Capitalism (17th–18th centuries)

- 1st and 2nd Industrial Revolutions overcoming Malthusian Trap (18th–19th centuries)

- Inequality—reform and socialism (19th–20th centuries)

- Effects of world wars—Great Depression (20th century)

- Economic miracle and unity (20th–21st centuries)

3. Objective Knowledge and Subjective Visions (OS)

Summary Classical and medieval learning began with authoritative texts and institutions, like Aristotle's writings, the Bible, or the Catholic Church. After 1450, this approach was increasingly challenged by a new methodology of inquiry that involved more systematic investigation of the natural world and a quantitative rather than the classical qualitative perspective. During the Renaissance and Reformation, classical texts and standards of value continued to hold sway; however, these movements' attitude of questioning set the stage for the Scientific Revolution. The new science not only produced new conceptions of the cosmos and human body, it also adopted a radical new method of investigation involving empirical evidence, a reliance on mathematics, and the enunciation of natural laws.

The Scientific Revolution reached its culmination with Newton's mechanical view of the universe and set the stage of the application of "natural" laws to human affairs, the 18th-century movement known as the Enlightenment. The philosophes of the Enlightenment, such as Voltaire and Diderot, expressed skepticism toward religious authority with new ideas ranging from deism to outright atheism. All human endeavors, from education to politics to economics, fell under the aegis of reason and science, producing a widespread impulse toward reform and belief in progress. The new attitude of progress and confidence in reason reached fruition with the French and Industrial Revolutions, aimed at applying Enlightenment principles to political systems and its technologies to production. Along with impressive accomplishments in technology and the social sciences, the revolutionary era also sparked new ideologies aimed at providing systematic accounts of the human condition.

Despite the powerful appeal of the new science, many continued to adhere to a religious worldview and subjective interpretations of reality and knowledge. Romanticism reacted to the Enlightenment's perceived overemphasis on rationalism by countering with emotion, intuition, and a more subjective attitude toward the natural world. Just as science and technology seemed to reach their apogee during the 19th century—particularly with the development of positivism, which asserted that only observable objects and forces could exist—new theories in science and social science called objective truths into question. Freudian psychology, relativity theory, and quantum physics reinforced the subjective nature of reality and laid the foundations for movements in philosophy and the arts that questioned the possibility of absolute paradigms. After two world wars and the threat of nuclear destruction during the Cold War, intellectuals and artists greeted claims of objectivity with skepticism, instead embracing a plurality of intellectual perspectives and an eclectic blending of styles.

Overarching Questions:

- What roles have traditional sources of authority (church and classical antiquity) played in the creation and transmission of knowledge?

- How and why did Europeans come to rely on the scientific method and reason in place of traditional authorities?

- How and why did Europeans come to value subjective interpretations of reality?

Key Concepts

- **KC 1.1** The worldview of European intellectuals shifted from one based on ecclesiastical and classical authority to one based primarily on inquiry and observation of the natural world.

- **KC 1.3** Religious pluralism challenged the concept of a unified Europe.

- **KC 2.3** The popularization and dissemination of the Scientific Revolution and the application of its methods to political, social, and ethical issues led to an increased, although not unchallenged, emphasis on reason in European culture.

- **KC 3.6** European ideas and culture expressed a tension between objectivity and scientific realism on one hand, and subjectivity and individual expression on the other.

- **KC 4.3** During the 20th century, diverse intellectual and cultural movements questioned the existence of objective knowledge, the ability of reason to arrive at truth, and the role of religion in determining moral standards.

Major Topics and Developments

- Authoritative knowledge (classical and ecclesiastical sources) to objective knowledge (15th–17th centuries)

- Renaissance and Scientific Revolution—from qualitative to quantitative (15th–17th centuries)

- Enlightenment—"science of man" (18th century)

- Romanticism and subjectivity (18th–19th centuries)

- Positivism and modernism (19th–20th centuries)

- Questioning of rationality—Freud, Darwin, Einstein, quantum physics (19th–20th centuries)

- Age of Anxiety—effects of world wars (20th century)

- Post-modernism and plurality of intellectual frameworks (20th–21st centuries)

4. States and Other Institutions of Power (SP)

Summary By 1450, Europe was just beginning to develop the modern conception of nation-states. Prior political thinking focused on the ideal of reviving the ancient Roman Empire around Christianity. Spurred by new secular political theories, like Machiavelli's, and the imperative of warfare—now dominated by gunpowder and the foot-soldier—states began to develop new institutions and policies to centralize power around the monarch and curb the prerogatives of traditional groups like nobles, estates, and local assemblies. The Renaissance, exploration, and the Protestant Reformation inadvertently facilitated the centralizing trend—by providing a cadre of literate office-holders drawn from the middle class, opening a range of new wealth and resources, and strengthening control over religious institutions (even in nations that remained Catholic). The Peace of Westphalia of 1648, which followed over a century of religious warfare, confirmed the sovereignty of the nation-state over internal religious policy and created the secular order of competing states seeking to maintain the balance of power.

By the 17th century, a variety of differing types of states existed—from city-states to multiethnic empires—but the dominant trend was toward absolutism, as exemplified by France under Louis XIV (1643–1715). Some states, such as the Netherlands and Britain, developed into constitutional regimes, running counter to the centralizing trend. Nations also patronized the arts, sciences, and commerce in an effort to lend tangible and emotional props to their power. Commercial expansion supported the growth of the middle class and the creation of a civil society, i.e., public space outside the control of the government, such as coffeehouses, salons, and libraries. With the New Science and preference for secular progress, the Enlightenment stoked discussion over new political theories, culminating with the French Revolution's fundamental attack on the Old Regime in favor of natural rights. Though incomplete, the French Revolution engendered a new ideal of popular legitimacy, mass politics, and a touchstone for critics of existing governments. Furthermore, the Revolution and subsequent wars of Napoleon threatened the state system created at Westphalia.

Despite the efforts of diplomats to close the Pandora's box of revolution in 1814–1815 at Vienna, new ideologies arose to articulate blueprints for change and motivate political action. In combination with the issues raised by the industrialization, revolutionary politics sparked development of a political spectrum ranging from anarchism to socialism to Liberalism to Conservatism. Perhaps the most powerful ideology in the 19th and 20th centuries proved to be nationalism, particularly since it was stymied by the Vienna settlement. After the breakdown of Metternich's Concert of Europe with the revolutions of 1848 and Crimean War, the door opened to the unification of Italy and Germany, the creation of which disrupted the balance of power in Europe. With pursuit of colonies added to the mix, the system of alliances failed to integrate Germany into a stable diplomacy, leading to the two world wars of the 20th century. Diplomats in Versailles attempted to reconstruct a new order of collective security with the League of Nations; however, economic crisis and diplomatic instability—complicated by the existence of the first Marxist state in the Soviet Union—led to extremist political ideologies. The Second World War ended even more destructively than the First, with Europe now divided between the superpowers of the United States and Soviet Union. However, western Europe recovered quickly with the help of American aid and new policies of economic and political integration. The new ideal of a unified Europe has been stimulated, on one hand, by the collapse of communism after 1989, but also challenged, on the other, by a revival of nationalism in the Balkans and elsewhere and tensions over the euro currency.

Overarching Questions:

- What forms have European governments taken, and how have these changed over time?

- In what ways and why have European governments moved toward or reacted against representative and democratic principles and practices?

- How did civil institutions develop apart from governments, and what impact have they had upon European states?

- How and why did changes in warfare affect diplomacy, the European state system, and the balance of power?

- How did the concept of a balance of power emerge, develop, and eventually become institutionalized?

Key Concepts

- **KC 1.2** The struggle for sovereignty within and among states resulted in varying degrees of political centralization.

- **KC 1.3** Religious pluralism challenged the concept of a unified Europe.

- **KC 2.1** Different models of political sovereignty affected the relationship among states and between states and individuals.

- **KC 3.3** The problems of industrialization provoked a range of ideological, governmental, and collective responses.

- **KC 3.4** European states struggled to maintain international stability in an age of nationalism and revolutions.

- **KC 4.1** Total war and political instability in the first half of the 20th century gave way to a polarized state order during the Cold War, and eventually to efforts at transnational union.

- **KC 4.2** The stresses of economic collapse and total war engendered internal conflicts within European states and created conflicting conceptions of the relationship between the individual and the state, as demonstrated in the ideological battle among liberal democracy, communism, and fascism.

Major Topics and Developments

- Rise of centralized states and decline of empires (15th–17th centuries)

- Military revolution (15th–17th centuries)

- Theories of absolutism and resistance (16th–18th centuries)

- Great power system and balance of power (17th–18th centuries)

- Civil society and public opinion (17th–18th centuries)

- Enlightenment—social contract, natural rights, limited government (18th century)

- Revolutionary movements and ideologies (18th–19th centuries)

- Nationalism and unification (19th century)

- World wars and totalitarianism (20th century)

- Cold War and transnational unity (20th–21st centuries)

- Decolonization (20th–21st centuries)

5. Individual and Society (IS)

Summary This will be a challenging course theme for many, but with the appropriate approach, it can become a strength. Though the IS theme may seem primarily descriptive and to cover many different groups or issues, it is best to consider the content under the guidance of prevailing issues: (in)equality, role of social institutions (marriage, family, village, guild), gender norms and behavior, and effects of economic changes on social life. In addition, you may find it instructive to use the chronological division of medieval (15th–16th centuries), early modern (16th–18th centuries), and modern (19th–21st centuries).

Individuals in European society were traditionally defined by status, e.g., the three estates used in feudal France of the clergy, nobles, and commoners. Between and within these ranks, inequality, hierarchy, and privilege were assumed to rule attitudes and behaviors, such as with the Body Politic metaphor. Religious authority provided support for class and gender expectations. However, the revival of the classics during the Renaissance and new religious ideals of the Reformation prompted an ongoing debate over the extent to which intellectual and cultural movements should alter society, particularly in relation to women (*Querelle Des Femmes,* or the "woman question"). The preindustrial economy of limited resources reinforced the importance of household and village production. Women and men worked in complementary tasks to raise crops or manufacture products; though gender norms guided productive and reproductive activities, the idea of strictly separate spheres would not arise until mechanization. Despite instigating reform in some areas, intellectual movements often reaffirmed negative stereotypes of women, which, in addition to social and economic instability, promoted the witchcraft phenomenon of the 16th and 17th centuries.

With the Enlightenment and revolution in politics and industry in the 18th and 19th centuries, traditional social norms were fundamentally called into question. Supported by a rising standard of living and the notion of progress, the upper classes embraced new attitudes and practices toward children. The French Revolution abolished serfdom and feudalism (in many states) and introduced new conceptions of government stressing individualism and equality. With the First and Second Industrial Revolutions of the 19th and early 20th centuries, women both gained the means of economic independence, stimulating the modern feminist movement, and also created the notion of domesticity, or separate spheres for women (private) and men (public). A rising standard of living and increasing leisure time helped to create a new consumer culture and, in urban areas, a mass society involving access to newspapers, education, and redesigned city landscapes.

The two world wars of the 20th century called for the mass mobilization of society, altering the relationship between the state and the individual. In some cases—as with women gaining the vote—warfare promoted equality, but in others—as with the forced industrialization of the Soviet Union under Stalin or the racial policies of fascist governments—the organized violence of the state meant repression or, worse, mass murder. Totalitarian regimes generally overlooked the rights of individuals—women, kulaks, ethnic minorities—in pursuit of a "higher" ideal of complete equality or racial purity. The postwar economic recovery and Cold War fears produced a Second Wave feminism and new movements for equality, especially among immigrants. Though Europe has become more pluralistic since 1945, issues of equality and identity—whether over the extent of the welfare state or the status of immigrants—continue to generate conflict and change.

Overarching Questions:

- What forms have family, class, and social groups taken in European history, and how have they changed over time?

- How and why have tensions arisen between the individual and society over the course of European history?

- How and why has the status of specific groups within society changed over time?

Key Concepts

- **KC 1.5** European society and the experiences of everyday life were increasingly shaped by commercial and agricultural capitalism, notwithstanding the persistence of medieval social and economic structures.

- **KC 2.1** Different models of political sovereignty affected the relationship among states and between states and individuals.

- **KC 2.4** The experiences of everyday life were shaped by demographic, environmental, medical, and technological changes.

- **KC 3.2** The experiences of everyday life were shaped by industrialization, depending on the level of industrial development in a particular location.

- **KC 3.3** The problems of industrialization provoked a range of ideological, governmental, and collective responses.

- **KC 4.4** Demographic changes, economic growth, total war, disruptions of traditional social patterns, and competing definitions of freedom and justice altered the experiences of everyday life.

Major Topics and Developments

- Preindustrial economy and traditional social structure (15th–17th centuries)

- Family, village, guild, and the individual (15th–17th centuries)

- Intellectual and cultural movements—impact on society (15th–17th centuries)

- Concerns over marginal social groups—poverty and witchcraft (16th–17th centuries)

- Effects of commercial agriculture and expanding commerce (17th–18th centuries)

- Movements of equality—Enlightenment and French Revolution (18th–19th centuries)

- First and Second Industrial Revolutions—effect on gender and class (19th–20th centuries)

- Feminism and movements of liberation (19th–20th centuries)

- Effects of world wars and Great Depression on state power and individual (20th century)

- Changing identities in post-1945 Europe (20th–21st centuries)

- Second Wave Feminism (20th–21st centuries)

Learning Objectives (LOs)

The AP European History course employs 69 Learning Objectives (LOs) as statements of what students should know and be able to do. For studying and review, the LOs can serve as a self-check before a unit test or review for the AP exam. Further, each exam item will be keyed to one or more LOs. It is suggested that you revisit the LOs to familiarize yourself with the major developments and the conceptual language of the course. Here's an example of a LO from the States and Other Institutions of Power (SP) theme:

SP-10: Trace the ways in which new technologies from the printing press to the Internet have shaped the development of civil society and enhanced the role of public opinion.

Note that the LO is phrased broadly enough to encompass all 4 periods of the course, so that students can consider issues of causation, changes and continuities over time, comparisons across time and geography, and how specific examples illustrate the statement. For this particular LO, a number of technologies may come to mind that affected political theory and power: the printing press, expansion of literacy, new venues for a civil society, transportation (canals and railroads, e.g.), mass communications, total war, and finally, computers and the Internet. If you engage with these LOs in preparation for the AP exam, you will find them an effective way to cover the chronological and geographic expanse of the course, as well as help you make all-important connections between periods and between developments during the same period. Because of their sheer number, this review book will not address the LOs in detail, but you can access them at the College Board website for the course and exam description noted earlier.

A Note on Geography

Before we depart, it is important to know where we are and where we are going. Some claim that "geography is destiny." Though there is truth in this assertion, it is overstated. As with any geographic region, Europe has been tremendously influenced by its environmental context; economic activities, cultural practices, political forms, and even fashion have all been shaped by geographic and climatic circumstances.

Take note of the map below. Several observations come to mind. First, Europe is an oddly shaped peninsula gouged with numerous inland seas, bays, and gulfs; punctuated by islands small and large; and narrowing toward the Atlantic and widening into the great plain leading to the vast Eurasian landmass. Second, Europe's location from north to south places it in the temperate climate zone—with wide variations between summer and winter temperatures, though this moderates in proximity to large bodies of water, such as the Atlantic Ocean and

R.R. Palmer, Joel Colton, and Floyd Kramer, *A History of Europe in the Modern World* (New York: McGraw-Hill Education, 2014), pp. 4–5.

Mediterranean Sea. Third, a large variety of navigable rivers, mountain ranges, and plateaus indicate the tremendous diversity of landforms in such a small area (Europe is the second smallest of the seven continents).

What has been the impact of this geographic inheritance? For purposes of your course, two observations are offered. First, a wide variety of economic activities has marked the forward advance of European history. Europe's diverse climate and geography allow it to cultivate almost every important agricultural product—essential cereal grains, livestock, wine—and deploy important natural resources for a wide range of manufacturing and industrial activities—mining, metallurgy, textile production. This geographic inheritance accounts for Europe's economic vitality and its outward reach to control markets and resources abroad, linking geography to the historical developments of exploration and imperialism, the Commercial Revolution, and industrialization.

Second, the European landmass has proved incredibly difficult for one political entity to control. Even the Romans were unable to subjugate all of it, and subsequent conquerors have repeated this failure. As a result, Europe's political and diplomatic history has been defined by a variety of political forms—nation-states, city-states, republics, empires, contested border regions—and multiple centers of power. Because of the inability of one entity—be it the Holy Roman Empire or Napoleonic France—to control the entire region, frequent warfare and shifts in the balance of power define European political and diplomatic history. Though common ground exists among the nations of Europe, until recently, sufficient differences in language, culture, and history have prevented a strong enough shared identity to overcome conflicts that too often descended into warfare. Thus, we have a major theme of this course linked to the geographic context—the tension between the identities of the individual nations and the common heritage of Europe.

As you study the content to follow, it is in your interest to keep a vigilant eye on the geographic context for these events and developments. You are advised to refer to the maps within this guide and in your textbook to connect the ever-changing political map of Europe to events that caused these shifts. Moreover, knowing the major regions and nations of Europe will provide a visual cue for grounding you in the historical content to follow. The time spent internalizing the map of Europe will pay off in your understanding and performance on the AP exam.

The Ancient and Medieval Inheritance

Though the Advanced Placement European history exam covers the period from 1450, some general knowledge of the ancient and medieval world will prove useful in your study of the material. For example, it is difficult to understand the fascination of Renaissance humanists with classical values if one has little familiarity with ancient Greece and Rome. With that caveat in mind, this brief chapter offers background on the pre-1450 period.

Heritage of the Ancient World

Greek Civilization The Greeks are often called the founders of Western civilization, with justification. Greek civilization flourished from around 1000 B.C.E. until its conquest by Rome in 146 B.C.E, and its contributions in philosophy, science, architecture, drama, history, as well as other fields, became the standard and reference point for European civilization for years to come. The Greek heritage of human accomplishment echoed through the ages and defined excellence in the following areas:

- *Philosophy*—Greek thinkers used reason in asking the most basic questions of nature and humanity, such as "What is the most real?," "What is the good?," "What is a just society?" Philosophers such as Plato and Aristotle established important principles and knowledge that dominated almost all academic fields until the 16th century.

- *Politics*—Though the political arena was restricted to free property-owning males, democracy and the active civic environment of the Greek city-states inspired imitation among Renaissance humanists and created a model for future revolutionaries.

- *History*—Historians such as Herodotus and Thucydides emphasized the importance of social and political forces in historical causation. Moving away from mythology and divine providence, Greek historians wrote history to edify and warn against human pride and folly.

- *Drama and Poetry*—Literary works in ancient Greece served as mirrors held up to society's faults and the vanities of human nature. The tragedies of Aeschylus, Euripides, and Sophocles and the comedies of Aristophanes influenced later literature in their complex plots, rich characters, and thematic emphasis. Europe's great tradition of lyric poetry got its start with Pindar and Sappho.

- *Science and Mathematics*—Once again, Aristotle's ideas—wrong as they often were— defined the fields of physics, astronomy, zoology, and anatomy for centuries, later becoming the target of criticism during the Scientific Revolution. Borrowing much from surrounding civilizations, the Greeks contributed immensely to mathematics, particularly geometry with the theorems of Pythagoras and Euclid.

- *Classical Aesthetics*—Perhaps the most lasting impact of Greek culture remains its emphasis in art and architecture on the virtues of balance, symmetry, and order. Whether the sculptural attention to the human form or the harmony of great civic buildings, how Europeans ordered space and perceived human potential owes much to ancient Greek accomplishments.

Alexander the Great and the Hellenistic Age Like all good things, ancient Greek civilization came to an end. The devastating Peloponnesian War between the Athenians and Spartans weakened the city-states, opening the way for conquest by the Macedonians from the north. Alexander the Great's armies swept through southeastern Europe, into the Middle East, and eventually halting near India. Alexander died in 323 B.C.E., but not before spreading Greek civilization to the areas he conquered. The subsequent two centuries witnessed the gradual synthesis of Greek ideas with those of surrounding regions. This period is known as the Hellenistic Age.

Roman Civilization As a city, Rome was founded in 753 B.C.E. and graduated into a far-flung empire ruling the entire Mediterranean basin by the 2nd century C.E. This outcome was not predetermined, but was aided by luck, circumstance, and sheer determination. Certainly, the Romans deserve recognition for their contributions to many fields and the length of their rule, yet their initial importance lay in spreading Greek ideas to the remainder of Europe following the Roman conquest of the Balkan Peninsula in 146 B.C.E. With each conquest, Rome successfully integrated new ethnic groups and peoples into its realm, often by extending citizenship and conferring the benefits of Roman civilization upon those lands. Though Rome built on Greek learning in many areas, its greatness tends to rest upon its practical accomplishments and enduring legacy.

- *Administration and Law*—As a republic, Rome survived by constant adaptation to shifting circumstances and use of patriotism inspired in its citizens, whether fighting tenaciously in battle or drawing new citizens into its active political life. Internal social and political conflict, along with the rise of military despots, ultimately undid the republic and led to the creation of the empire. The empire's ability to centralize power and establish a uniform legal code across a vast expanse of territory became the touchstone and goal of many European rulers after the empire's fall in 476 C.E. (in the west; the eastern or Byzantine Empire continued until 1453).

- *Architecture and Infrastructure*—Rome thrived as a distinctly urban culture. Wherever Romans conquered, they brought roads, aqueducts, impressive public buildings, and other amenities previously unknown to their new subjects. Though much of this infrastructure eventually decayed owing to disrepair, even the ruins served as a legacy to be imitated. For example, Renaissance humanists scoured their Italian backyard searching for examples of Roman architecture, baths, and piazzas, not to mention sculptures and literary works, for artistic imitation.

- *The* Pax Romana—During its almost half-millennium rule, the Roman Empire generally succeeded in providing a political order that allowed both an active public life and a thriving intellectual and cultural setting. Certainly the empire experienced turmoil—especially in the 3rd century—due to barbarian invasions, military interference, and demographic decline, but it resiliently rode further on the fumes of its nearly exhausted glory. Even after it fell, many looked to recover the peace and stability of the *Pax Romana*, or Roman peace.

Christianity Though Christianity did not originate there, Europe has traditionally been the heartland of the Christian religion. After the 4th century, when it became the official religion of the Roman Empire, Christianity spread outward from the Mediterranean basin, reaching its final missionary outpost in the Eastern Baltic in the 14th century. Christianity's influence extends beyond the religious realm, into politics, ideas, culture, and the arts. Oftentimes, Christian dogma was reconciled and absorbed into pagan customs and beliefs, as can be seen with holiday practices during Halloween and Christmas. Nonetheless, the implications of Christian theology and practice held profound consequences for European society.

- *The Soul*—Belief in individual immortality and a moral structure that transcended the temporal (material or earthly) world radically altered the perception of the human person. Christianity holds that there is a spiritual reality, the soul, that exists beyond the material world accessible only to the senses.

- *Individual Dignity*—The notion that each individual is "created in the image of God" has often acted as a check on absolutist tendencies in politics and provided a moral basis for law and society.

- *Monotheism*—Drawing from their Jewish roots, the Christian fathers of the early Church maintained a strong belief in one God, while at the same time articulating the doctrine of the Holy Trinity, or the three persons of God (Father, Son, Holy Spirit) who share the same substance.

- *St. Augustine (354–430 c.e.)*—Perhaps the most influential of the early Christian saints, his writings emphasized the predominance of spiritual over temporal authority, the importance of the next world (the City of God vs. the City of Man), and the sovereignty and majesty of God.

- *Caesaropapism*—According to the traditions of the Roman Empire, political and spiritual authority were fused in the same person. While this tradition continued in the Eastern or Byzantine Empire, the two authorities developed separately in Latin Christianity. This split caused repeated controversies between the Roman Catholic Papacy and the Holy Roman Emperor during the Middle Ages, but its positive effect was to carve out a zone between both authorities for political diversity and corporate (meaning "in groups") liberties where neither political nor spiritual power could reach, each being checked by the other.

Heritage of the Medieval World

The Early Middle Ages, 476–1050 The period following the fall of the Roman Empire is often termed "the Dark Ages." To some extent, this designation is accurate, as Roman cities became depopulated, roads fell into disrepair, trade dried up, and various barbarian tribes replaced the universal empire with a variety of Germanic kingdoms. In addition, the learning of ancient Greece and Rome was kept alive dimly by the candlelight of monastic scriptoria.

- *Barbarian Invasions*—Due to a traffic jam on the plains of central Asia, barbarian tribes poured into Europe in the waning days of the Roman Empire. Most of these tribes gradually assimilated into the empire, often being deployed for their military skills or to guard distant outposts. What had originally been a strength of the empire—the ability to assimilate various ethnicities—gradually diluted the culture and greatness of Rome. Thus, in 476, a barbarian leader deposed the last emperor in the West.

- *Latin vs. Greek Christianity*—Once the Roman Empire was divided in the 4th century between east and west for administrative purposes, the two parts drifted further apart culturally and religiously. After the fall of Rome, the Byzantine Empire, centered in Constantinople (today Istanbul), continued the legacy of the empire, but with a distinctly Greek cultural accent. Disputes throughout the medieval period over the authority of the pope, the use of religious icons in church, and other theological controversies led to a formal break between the Latin (Catholic) and Orthodox branches of Christianity that was formalized in 1054, and remains to this day.

- *The Islamic World*—Islam came out of the desert in the 620s as the fastest growing religion in world history, quickly establishing political and cultural dominance of vast swaths of Asia, North Africa, and southern Europe. Arabs easily assimilated the intellectual legacy of the Greeks and Romans—keeping alive the learning of Aristotle and others more effectively than Europeans—at the same time making important contributions to mathematics (Arabic numerals, algebra), science (especially in astronomy and medicine), and literature. Since the early 8th century, Muslims have been a continuous presence in Europe, claiming a common religious heritage with Jews and Christians as "people of the Book," though believing Mohammad and the Koran to be the ultimate fulfillment of God's promise to His people.

- *Germanic Customs*—Unlike the Roman Empire, barbarian culture focused on loyalty to persons rather than institutions. Rather than adhering to abstract legal concepts or ideals, Germanic society revolved around tribal identities, which allowed in many ways for a greater amount of freedom than had existed in the Roman Empire. However, this freedom came at the cost of political unity, economic vitality, and an active civic culture.

- *Monasteries*—Monasteries served as more than houses for religious orders. Beginning in the 5th century, when they adopted the discipline of St. Benedict (ca. 480–543), monasteries retreated from the chaos of political life to concentrate on the life of the spirit and the mind. This meant that monks kept alive ancient Greek and Roman texts, at the same time inventing everything from champagne to pretzels.

- *Charlemagne*—A Frankish king (from the tribe of the Franks, later France), Charlemagne, provided a short-lived period of unity and intellectual revival in central Europe. Crowned emperor by the pope in 800, Charlemagne drove out rival barbarian chieftains and established a seat of government in Aix-la-Chapelle (Aachen) in imitation of the Roman ideal. Though he could not himself read, Charlemagne led a mini-Renaissance of learning, which faded when his successors fought among themselves over the political spoils after his death in 814.

- *Second Wave of Invasions (9th century)*—Following the rule of Charlemagne, Europe once again was beset by a period of instability and foreign invasion. During the 9th century, tribes from the north, east, and Muslim pirates from the south threatened to overrun the weak kingdoms of the European heartland. As before, the Norse from the Scandinavia and the Magyars from Asia were gradually incorporated into European political culture and converted to Christianity. By 1000, Europe had settled into relative political stability, with the map now filled in with virtually all of the major ethnic groups, though borders would continue to shift and evolve according to war, conquest, and migration.

The High Middle Ages, 1050–1300 As an historical era, the Middle Ages gets a bad rap, whether being spoofed by Monty Python or being associated with terms like "Dark Ages" or "gothic." A more appropriate way to view this millennium is as a gradual synthesis of the major strands of European culture, politics, and society—ancient Greek and Roman, Christianity, and barbarian. In fact, the High Middle Ages was a period of dynamic developments in ideas, economics, technology, politics, and society. Simply because medieval life looks different to our contemporary eyes doesn't mean it was backward or uncivilized. Perhaps the brief review below will convince the skeptic of this notion.

- *Agriculture*—Improvements in agriculture, such as three-crop field rotation, the iron plow, horse collar, and use of windmills, supported an increasing population. More land was brought under cultivation, in places producing a surplus, which helped to stimulate an increase in trade. By 1300, Europe had reached a population peak of 75 million, which represented a doubling from the level of 1000.

- *Feudalism*—Based on the decentralized nature of Germanic political culture and the insecurity of the Early Middle Ages, the system of feudalism emerged during the High Middle Ages. Relationships between lord and vassal were based on specific contractual obligations of loyalty and protection. In return for protection, peasants provided labor and gave loyalty to feudal elites, who controlled peasants and serfs through an intricate set of obligations, fees, rituals, and taxes. As warfare required continuous training and expensive equipment (a result of the invention of the stirrup allowing heavy mounted warriors), only an elite few could engage in the practice. Society became divided, at least in theory, into those who fought (nobles and knights), those who prayed (the clergy), and those who worked (peasants and artisans).

- *Towns and Commerce*—As the economy improved throughout the High Middle Ages, its effects were felt most strongly in the growth of towns. Medieval towns were not the teeming urban centers of the industrial era, but did attract skilled labor, ideas, and goods. Towns lay outside the feudal structure and jealously guarded their liberties, which were generally confirmed by charters. Towns often banded together in leagues to protect their independence or promote their commerce, as with the Hanse, the German trading centers in the Baltic. A central institution of most towns was the guild, which controlled the production of goods in a particular craft. Not only did the guild ensure a minimum quality of goods and license its members' skills, it also acted as a civic institution, reflecting the corporate (small, organized groups) nature of medieval society. With the continued growth and attraction of cities in western Europe, feudalism and serfdom declined in importance, to be replaced by a more commercial and money-oriented economy.

- *National Monarchies*—The states of the Middle Ages lacked the complexity and administrative tools of modern forms of government. Nonetheless, kings and queens of this era worked to establish hereditary claims to their thrones. In fact, the beginnings of bureaucracy (government agencies) and representative government can be seen in several nations. First, monarchies established some power to tax their subjects to support the state, though this often required the approval of other bodies. A well-known example demonstrating this trend is English nobles limiting the power of the king in 1215 with the Magna Carta, which eventually led to the formation of the Parliament. Royal councils and representative bodies confirmed limits on the power of monarchs and that traditional liberties must be respected.

- *The Church*—During this period, the Catholic Church reached the height of its political, spiritual, and cultural influence. Throughout the High Middle Ages, the pope and the Holy Roman Emperor continuously vied for power in central Europe, generally over the issue of clerical control, with the result that each checked the power of the other. For a time, popes were successful in establishing their claims to make and unmake kings. The climax of these grand ideals came with the papacy of Innocent III (1198–1216), who attempted to unify the entire Christian world under his authority. At the same time, there was growing criticism of the behavior of the clergy and the lack of regularity in church doctrine and practice. The result was a revival of the monastic ideal (termed the Cluniac movement) and the calling of an exceptional Church council in 1215—the Fourth Lateran—that established new regulations for the clergy and formalized many church doctrines related to the sacraments, which stand to this day.

- *Gender Roles*—As with many periods in history, women's roles in the Middle Ages were bound by legal and economic prescription. However, medieval women of different classes often found ways to express autonomy, initiative, and talent within these parameters. The nature of medieval warfare often left noblewomen to manage large manors, engage in politics, and organize the defense of castles. Younger noblewomen often joined convents, where they could pursue intellectual and spiritual interests outside the control of men. Women also played major roles in movements of religious change or in so-called heresies. Further, the ideal of courtly love and chivalry placed women at the center of an important cultural tradition. Cities and towns relied on the labor of women in artisan families, often as guild members in food preparation, brewing, and cloth production. Peasant and serf women labored alongside their husbands in mowing hay, tending to vegetable gardens, or in harvesting. Since peasant homes were simple, domestic chores actually played a minor role for women.

- *Universities and Scholasticism*—With the rise of towns came a quickening of intellectual life. Informal meetings of students and teachers evolved into the formal founding of the first universities in the early 13th century. Universities taught a variety of subjects in their various faculties, but our current separation of spiritual and material subjects did not exist in the medieval world view. In fact, theology stood as the "queen of the sciences," and liberally borrowed from other disciplines to elaborate its truths. The best example of this practice was the creation of Scholasticism. During the 13th century, a mini-Renaissance of Aristotle's philosophy took place. Pagan ideas governing logic and the natural world were synthesized into Christian dogma, especially by scholars such as St. Thomas Aquinas, to explain divine truths. This intellectual system dominated universities until well into the 18th century, though with growing criticism after 1500.

- *The Crusades*—A sign of the increasing power of Europe were the Crusades. Due to the expansion of commerce, population, and political organization, Christian Europe was able to go on the offensive against Islamic rule of the Holy Land. The First Crusade was launched in 1095, and subsequent efforts succeeded in establishing kingdoms in Palestine and surrounding areas. However, many of these efforts were driven by prejudice (against Jews, for example) and sheer bloodlust, often producing atrocities and tragic consequences, like the needless sack of Constantinople in 1204 (during the Fourth Crusade). Despite some of the baser motives, the Crusades demonstrated Europe's newfound assertiveness and interest in the outside world, stimulating exploration.

Expanding Europe As of 1300, Europe had become one of several important civilizations on the Eurasian landmass and Africa that came into increasing contact with one another. By this time, Europe stood in a much more advantageous position than it had only a century earlier, able to withstand the onslaught of the Mongols and Ottoman Turks in upcoming centuries. Despite its successes, Europe's technological and cultural accomplishments still paled in comparison to China's, yet in the next 600 years it was Europe that successfully projected its power abroad, not China. Why? Though it invented printing and gunpowder, China did not exploit these technologies in pursuit of global commerce and power. Ironically, Europe's lack of central political power, separation of secular and religious authority, and disorderly conflict among various nations (none of which existed in China) drove technological and scientific innovation, yielding a strange mix of conflict and war along with freedom and dynamism.

Additional Resources

Renate Bridenthal et al., *Becoming Visible* (1998)—Valuable collection of essays on women's history from ancient times to the present.

Norman Cantor, *The Civilization of the Middle Ages* (rev. 1993)—Straightforward and helpful review of all things medieval.

Jared Diamond, *Guns, Germs, and Steel* (1997)—An impressive work arguing for the importance of environmental factors in explaining the rise of Europe.

Michael Grant, *The Founders of the Western World: A History of Greece and Rome* (1990)—A popular writer surveys the topic in an accessible manner for students.

Michael Hart, *The 100: A Ranking of the Most Influential Persons in History,* 2nd ed. (1992)—The title gives the book's premise, and this volume is always good for sparking interesting debates. Many figures covered in the course can be found here.

Jonathan Riley Smith, *The Crusades: A Short History* (1987)—A good place to start for an understanding of this fascinating and tragic era.

Times Atlas of European History (1994)—Clean maps and brief text take the reader through a tour of European history.

Section II
Content Review

PERIOD 1

The chapters in Period 1 will address the following major developments and events:

- Italian and northern Renaissances
- New Monarchs and centralization of power
- Protestant and Catholic Reformations
- Early modern society
- Exploration and colonization
- Religious wars
- Growth of commerce and money economy
- Scientific Revolution

Each chapter will provide a content review and practice questions to test your understanding of the material. At the conclusion of the content chapters, you will be able both to gauge your grasp of the content and practice historical thinking skills in an online diagnostic test that will include:

- 30 MC questions
- 2 SAQs
- 1 DBQ
- 1 LEQ (choice of 2)

Each chapter will begin with a brief correlation to the Key Concepts from the Course Description. Good luck with your review!

1 NOTE

The bolded terms in this and subsequent chapters indicate required content knowledge from the Course Description Concept Outline. Underlined terms denote illustrative content–not required, but examples that can prove useful in explaining and elaborating on KCs.

 ## The Renaissance and Reformation[1]

If the High Middle Ages exhibited dynamic growth, then the 14th century represented the stick in the spokes of this runaway medieval cart that brought it crashing to the ground. Sometimes, however, tragedy can pave the way for the emergence of new cultural trends. In the wake of social, religious, cultural, and economic crisis, there emerged two defining movements of early modern European history—the Renaissance and the Protestant Reformation.

Key In Chapter 4 addresses the following KCs from the Course Description:

- **KC 1.1** Italian and northern Renaissances and impact of the printing press
- **KC 1.2** New monarchies and secular political theories
- **KC 1.3** Protestant and Catholic Reformations
- **KC 1.5** Role of women/gender/family and social effects of Renaissance and Reformation

The Upheavals of the 14th Century[2]

Europe's peak population in 1300 of 75 million was already pushing up against its natural boundaries, when the continent was hit by the Great Famine of 1315–1317 and the cataclysmic Black Death of 1348–1351. The latter represents one of the great natural disasters in world history, costing Europe upwards of 40% of its people. More important than sheer numbers were the psychological and social costs of the disease. Caused by fleas traveling on rats, the bubonic plague spread quickly along trade routes and especially devastated urban areas. No one could explain the cause of the pestilence. Flagellants took the calamity to be God's wrath upon man and whipped themselves in atonement. Many blamed Jews for poisoning wells, which led to a notorious persecution of that minority in Nuremberg. Art reflected the obsession with death; paintings featured skeletons performing the *danse macabre*. The Catholic Church could offer little solace, especially since the disease killed off well over 60% of the top clergy. Perhaps most significantly, the Black Death caused a labor shortage that undermined the feudal structure, as peasants bargained for improved labor conditions, winning lifetime tenures and converting other obligations to cash payments.

Improved peasant conditions did not last long. Governments and nobles reasserted their power throughout the century, which led to the *jacquerie* rebellion in 1358 in France and Wat Tyler's revolt in 1381 in England. Urban revolts also occurred in Florence; each of these revolts was eventually overturned, often with great violence. Of more lasting import was the blow delivered to the feudal system in the west.

National monarchies were young creations, and therefore fragile. Dynastic instability (e.g., the inability to produce male heirs) plagued many states throughout the 14th century and led most seriously to the Hundred Years' War (1337–1453). Actually a series of wars, this conflict between France and England over the French throne (and the cloth trade in the Low Countries) dealt a fatal blow to the medieval idea of warfare. Time and again, English longbowmen demonstrated the power of massed infantry against France's heavily mounted feudal knights. French fortunes revived upon the back of a divinely inspired peasant girl. In 1429, Joan of Arc believed the voice of God called her to break the siege of Orleans. Despite her military success, Joan was tried for witchcraft and burned at the stake (later made a saint in 1920). Yet the tide had turned, and by 1453, England held only the city of Calais on the continent. Each nation then turned inward to resolve pressing political conflicts.

The Catholic Church also stood in the midst of crisis. Since 1307, the papacy had lived in exile in France during the so-called Babylonian Captivity, where its prestige declined in proportion to the increase in its administrative apparatus and material wealth. When an Italian crowd forced the mostly French cardinals to elect one of their own, the church plunged into the Great Schism (1378–1417), with rival French and Italian popes forcing the nations of Europe to choose sides. Advocates of conciliarism attempted to use church councils (unsuccessfully) to solve the crisis *and* to check the power of the papacy. Reformers such as John Wyclif in England and John Hus in Bohemia (part of the Holy Roman Empire) attacked the institutional power and wealth of the church and called for a simpler Christianity. Though Hus was burned at the stake in 1415, his ideas set the stage for the Protestant Reformation of the 16th century.

The Setting of the Renaissance

Italy was the first area of Europe to experience the Renaissance. Several reasons account for this early lead[3].

- *Geographic*—Italy was not only the center of the Mediterranean, which made it a crossroads of trade, it also boasted centers of ancient culture. If artists wished to imitate classical motifs, they need look no further than their Roman backyard. Ideas followed in the wake of trade, particularly as humanists escaped the declining Byzantine Empire, being besieged by the Turks (and falling in 1453).

2 SKILL SET
Though the official course begins in 1450, some basic knowledge of the late Middle Ages will aid in your understanding of the Renaissance and set up a vital and intriguing interpretive issue (INTR): To what extent does the Renaissance represent a break from the Middle Ages and a new period in European history?

3 SKILL SET
The question of Italy's head start represents an important early causation question focused around a nation (CAUS). It parallels other issues, such as Britain and industrialization, France and its revolution, and Germany and the Nazis. You may wish to begin your practice by writing a focused paragraph in response to "why Italy?" based on the material below.

- *Urbanization*—While in most of Europe only 10% of the population lived in cities, up to 25% of Italians partook directly of the civic culture so essential to Renaissance humanism. Cities attracted trade, ideas, and culture—the lifeblood of the Renaissance.

- *Social Factors*—Nobles played a vital role in Italy, just as they did in every European nation, though their attitudes tended to be more oriented to money-making and cultural accomplishments than elsewhere. A common family blending in Italy involved a cash-strapped aristocrat and an up-and-coming wealthy merchant, thus creating a new elite, where wealth and worldly achievement mattered more than merely lineage.

- *Political Variety*—In the 14th century, Italy was a collection of small and large city-states. No centralized authority existed to stamp out potentially threatening ideas. If artists or intellectuals found difficulty in one place, they could simply move to another and continue their work. This disunity later became a liability, but at that time, Italy benefited from competing political centers.

With its thriving city-states, Italy imitated the ancient *poleis* of Greece and the Roman Republic. Citizenship and freedom in the ancient world sparked intellectual and cultural life, and the same held true of Renaissance Italy. A major concern of Renaissance thinkers was a life of active civic engagement. The life of the mind (*otium*) must eventually contribute to the bettering of one's city-state (*negotium*). Reflection *and* action promoted *virtù*, or excellence, in the Renaissance man or woman.

4 THEME MUSIC

The Individual and Society theme can pose challenges to students (IS). To get a head start, use this and the section below on the social impact of the Reformation to establish the "baseline" for issues like class, gender, family, child-rearing, and education.

As with today, family served as the central social institution of the Italian Renaissance.[4] Renaissance families were patriarchal, placing a great deal of power in the male head of the family, or *patria potesta*. Before a man could achieve legal autonomy, his father must officially liberate him before the appropriate authorities. Oftentimes, men were not able to establish an independent existence until their late 20s or early 30s. At the same time, families commonly married off their daughters as early as their mid-teens. Marriages were frequently arranged to the benefit of both families. Economic concerns predominated; compatibility of the couple came second, and often not at all, given the significant age difference between man and woman. As a result of this marriage-age gap, Italy experienced predictable side effects. First, prostitution was rampant, and since almost impossible to eliminate, generally tolerated and even regulated by governments. Second, the incidence of rape and sexual violence was high, though lower-class men were punished more severely if their victim was from the upper classes. Finally, spouses often predeceased their partners, who remarried quickly due to the difficulties involved in living an independent existence. This led to remarriage, numerous blended families, and an abundance of stepparents. Though the nuclear family (mother, father, and children) was the norm, Renaissance Italy also depended on African slavery, a result of the labor shortage created by the Black Death. Slaves lived with families and often performed domestic work. Though as much as 10% of Italy's population in 1400 was made up of slaves, the practice *in* Europe declined with the recovery of the population in the 15th century.

Renaissance Humanism and Art

The term "Renaissance" is the creation of the modern Swiss historian Jacob Burckhardt (writing in 1860). Though the average layperson will tend to view the Renaissance, or rebirth of classical culture, as a distinct break from the Middle Ages, historians often disagree over how useful this term is in describing a specific time period. One of the difficulties is, when do we date the beginning of the Renaissance? **Petrarch** (1304–1374), the father of humanism, already argued for a new age as early as the 1340s. However, this was before the Black Death, so does that mean the Black Death defines the Renaissance? In addition, one of the great painters of the late medieval period, Giotto, influenced later Renaissance painters. So where do we put Giotto? Even if there is much wisdom in viewing the Renaissance as a continuation of medieval trends, there is little doubt that a new self-consciousness regarding human beings and a new self-assertion is evident in Italy by 1350.

As the name suggests, humanists were fascinated by humans and their potential. The fabric of humanism is woven of several important strands[5].

- *Secularism*—Humanists focused their attention on the here-and-now, and less on the afterworld, as had been the tendency during the Middle Ages. Education, self-help manuals, and treatises on civility all reinforced the notion that humans stood to gain rewards—wealth, status, prestige, fame—in the temporal world. Even in religious paintings, humans take on increased significance, while painting itself becomes more an exercise to glorify the artist than to glorify God.

- *Classics*—Ancient Greece and Rome formed the moral center of many humanists' outlook. Collectors of manuscripts, such as Poggio Bracciolini, scoured monasteries, ruins—anywhere—to find evidence of the ancient way of life. For example, the ancient Roman Vitruvius's *On Architecture* provided a guide to the creation of buildings that imitated a coherent system of columns, arches, and pillars. Also, the recovery of the long-lost Hellenistic sculpture *Laocoön* in the early 16th century inspired Michelangelo to create his masterpiece, *David*. Ancient values and aesthetics, as pre-Christian, told a captivating story with humans at the center, from which humanists took inspiration.

- *Individualism*—By "individualism," humanists meant not a narrow, selfish conception of human actions, but rather that learning and human affairs should concern the individual. It was as if humanists had just discovered mankind and could not tear themselves away. This attitude can be seen in the self-consciousness of Petrarch's verse as well as Castiglione's suggestions for achieving fame, wealth, and position.

- *Power*—Amid the inspiring philosophy and mesmerizing art, it is easy to forget that the Renaissance was at its heart about human control of the environment. A central humanist aim was to provide society with intellectual tools that could be used to master everything from the globe (cartography), to sound (musical notation), to abstract space (three-dimensional perspective in painting), to business (double-entry bookkeeping), and finally politics. It's no coincidence that along with the great works of art came exploration and colonization, the centralization of New Monarchs, and urban planning.

Humanism found many expressions—literature, philosophy, education, politics, and, of course, art. As you review the list of representative figures below, keep in the mind the principles to which they connect above.

The Writers and Philosophers[6]

Leonardo Bruni (1369–1444): Bruni studied under Chrysoloras, a Greek scholar who had escaped from the faltering Byzantine Empire, and translated ancient Greek texts into Latin. In addition, Bruni served Florence in various political capacities and later wrote a Latin history of the city. He is most famous for his admiration of Cicero, the Roman statesman and model of civic virtue.

Lorenzo Valla (1406–1457): Valla excelled in philology, the study of ancient languages. Even though a member of the clergy, Valla demonstrated through textual analysis that the "Donation of Constantine," which supposedly granted the pope authority over political bodies, was a forgery.

Pico della Mirandola (1463–1494): Plato's philosophy (neo-Platonism) revived during the Renaissance, and there is no better example of the trend than Mirandola's "Oration on the Dignity of Man." Many consider it the classic statement of human potential. Neo-Platonism held that humans had once shared a divine nature and though they had freely chosen to enter the material world, they retained a spark of divinity, which could be recaptured through intellectual and spiritual regeneration.

Lorenzo de' Medici (1449–1492): Known as "the Magnificent," Lorenzo ruled Florence during its Golden Age. A strong advocate of **civic humanism** and a man of diverse interests, Lorenzo is most famous for this patronage of intellectuals and the arts. His untimely death in 1492 led to the invasion of Italy by foreign powers, as well as the decline of Renaissance culture in Florence.

5 THEME MUSIC

Since the OS theme deals with the most abstract topics in the course, it is vital that you focus on defining your terms. For this section, it is recommended that you write an historical definition of humanism in a paragraph.

6 EXAMPLE BASE

Here you'll find brief explanations of key figures in humanism. However, don't place your focus on rote learning; instead, use 4-5 of these intellectuals or artists to develop your explanation of humanism—in literature, philosophy, history, political theory, and the arts.

Niccolo Machiavelli (1469–1527): One of the most famous figures of the Renaissance, Machiavelli's claim to fame is ***The Prince***. Dedicated to the Medici family, the book serves as a manual for the pragmatic ruler who must appear virtuous, wise, and courageous (like a "lion"), at the same time ready to be ruthless and cunning (like a "fox"). Machiavelli denies the traditional notion that the political realm must uphold the laws of God. Politics follows its own logic in the hard-headed rules of power, or *raison d'etat* (reason of state), which is why *The Prince* is often considered the first modern work of political science. It is important to remember the context for Machiavelli's writing—the invasion of Italy and its subsequent domination by foreign powers. *The Prince*, as well as Machiavelli's other writings endorsing citizen militias and republican government, can be seen collectively as patriotic appeals for a free and united Italy. After being tortured and losing his position in government, Machiavelli tried desperately to win back his influence, with little success. Fairly or unfairly, Machiavelli's name is associated with a brand of amoral politics both condemned and practiced since the 16th century.

Petrarch (1304–1374): Often called the Father of Humanism, Petrarch helped popularize the notion that Italy was entering a new age of learning and individualism, distinct from the "ignorance" characteristic of the Middle Ages. Petrarch revived a more pure form of Latin and, as such, spent his literary energies composing verse in the language, much of it related to a psychological portrait of humans and the theme of love, wherein he wrote of his beloved Laura.

Baldassare Castiglione (1478–1529): Castiglione first gained fame as a diplomat, but is most known for his *Book of the Courtier*, a how-to manual on winning fame and influence among the rich and powerful. To gain position and fortune, Castiglione counsels the Renaissance Man to be widely read in the classics, including history, poetry, music, and philosophy, as well as to know how to conduct himself in public. The courtier will be skilled in the military arts *and* cultured and polished. In addition, Castiglione advocated education for women, but of a particular kind: a musical instrument, poetry, and literacy. Abstract subjects such as math and science were reserved for men.

7 SKILL SET

Whenever you encounter art in this course, think Contextualization (CTX). You may wish to consult one of the websites mentioned in Chapter 1 to view well-known works of architecture, painting, and sculpture. As you consider these images, explain how they reflect the concerns, values, and developments of the period in which they were created.

Works in Oil, Marble, and Stone[7]

The Renaissance achieved fame for its production of renowned works of art. Several developments mark the upward trend of Renaissance art:

- *Oil-based Paints*—Historically, artists had used tempera paints with an egg base, yet with oil-based paints (from the Low Countries), artists could achieve more startling effects with light and shadow by applying layer after thin layer of paint.

- *Perspective*—For centuries, artists had attempted to achieve a realistic effect of three-dimensional space, but their methods tended to be haphazard and approximate. With the rediscovery of theories of optics and perspective geometry, Renaissance painters were able to achieve a strikingly realistic view of a visual plane.

- *Naturalism*—The Renaissance preoccupation with the human body was reflected in its portrayals on canvas and in stone. Painters and sculptors gave increased attention to musculature and movement of the human body. This emphasis is clearly seen in Michelangelo's *Sistine Chapel*, where the master achieves a heroic view of humans, and also in da Vinci's sketches based on anatomical dissections.

- *Subject Matter*—While artists continued to focus on religious paintings, human beings, nature, and ancient architecture played a more central role in these works. In addition, artists began to experiment with classical scenes, landscapes, and portraits.

- *Order and Symmetry*—In all three media, Renaissance artists placed great importance on orderly composition. Architects employed proportion in their use of classical motifs such as the column, dome, and arch.

- *Status of the Artist*—Because they were considered craftsmen, most artists of the Middle Ages were anonymous. As patronage by wealthy merchants and the church increased during the Renaissance, the reputation of artists as creative geniuses—people set apart—became the standard.

<u>Donatello</u> (1386–1466): Donatello revived the free-standing sculpture. His depiction of *David* represents the first full-size statue cast in bronze since ancient times. The sculptor imbued his forms with psychological detail and expression, representing Renaissance naturalism.

<u>Masaccio</u> (1401–1428): Masaccio employed perspective geometry for the first time in his *Holy Trinity*, and also realized a depth of realism and three-dimensional space in a series of frescoes in the Brancacci Chapel, of which the *Expulsion of Adam and Eve from the Garden* is a highlight for depicting the agony and shame of the couple. Unfortunately, this master died young.

<u>Filippo Brunelleschi</u> (1377–1446): Though an architect, Brunelleschi expressed interest in all the arts, including cast bronze and painting—it was he who helped develop the use of perspective geometry in painting. By far, Brunelleschi's primary achievement is the massive dome (*Il Duomo*) he created for the Cathedral of Florence, a feat of artistic vision and engineering.

<u>Leonardo da Vinci</u> (1452–1519): Perhaps the foremost Renaissance Man, da Vinci gained fame for just a few paintings—*Mona Lisa*, *The Last Supper*, *Madonna of the Rocks*. His diverse interests led him into science, engineering, and anatomy. Da Vinci introduced the notion of systematic observation, which he tracked in his notebooks, written backwards to make it difficult for imitators to steal his ideas.

<u>Michelangelo Buonarroti</u> (1475–1564): Bearing a name synonymous with genius, Michelangelo excelled in all the artistic media—sculpture (*David*, *Pieta*), painting (*Sistine Chapel*, *Last Judgment*), and architecture (*St. Peter's Basilica Dome*, *Laurentian Library*). The master's nudes offer a heroic vision of the human form influenced by neo-Platonic philosophy, though his later works express a darker vision. In addition, Michelangelo composed poetry and was working on another Pieta at the age of 89 when he died.

<u>Raphael</u> (1483–1520): The youngest of the great masters, and considered a rival of Michelangelo's, Raphael often sought artistic patronage in Rome, where the Renaissance refocused after about 1490. Raphael's *School of Athens* honors ancient learning and his fellow artists, as the Greek philosophers take on the physical appearance of his contemporaries. In addition, Raphael painted numerous portraits of the Madonna, the Mother of Jesus.

Education and the Printing Press

Renaissance humanism spurred education. Humanists founded schools for both boys and girls, though the latter tended to focus more on keeping appearances rather than mastery of abstract subject matter. Latin and Greek were prized by scholars of the 15th and 16th centuries, yet a truly well-rounded person needed to be conversant in all the liberal arts—grammar, music, arithmetic, geometry, astronomy, rhetoric, and logic—not to mention poetry, horsemanship, and military arts. Renaissance schools provided structure and regular promotion of pupils from one level to the next, and in that sense, have influenced the values and curricula of schools today.

Though the Chinese invented printing, they did not capitalize on their success. Johann Gutenberg and his colleagues perfected the skill of movable type in the 1450s, publishing their famous Gutenberg Bible, of which several dozen still exist. Books continued to be expensive luxury items for the upper classes, but the die had been cast. No longer could church or state exercise a monopoly on education or intellectual life. The **printing press** assisted in spreading the Renaissance and helped to establish standardized texts, as well as promote **vernacular literature** ("in the language of the people," i.e., not Latin). Perhaps printing's most important impact was to secure the success of the Protestant Reformation. Few would deny that the invention of the printing press stands as one of the most, if not *the* most, significant technological developments of the past millennium.

8 THEME MUSIC
Starting now, you should trace the issue of women's participation in various movements of change and the extent to which such involvement altered women's position in society. This question relates both to the IS theme and the HTS of CCOT.

Was There a Renaissance For Women?[8]

Though there were several well-regarded female humanists, women faced significant barriers to their intellectual pursuits. The prevailing notion held that women's focus should be directed toward the domestic sphere. More enlightened humanists favored education for women, but it never equaled the type of learning available to men. Nonetheless, women often played key political roles, especially when their statesmen-husbands were off at war, and several gained fame for sponsoring the forerunners to the salons of the Enlightenment. In some ways, the status of women declined from the Middle Ages, as they came to be viewed as objects of art or pawns in marriage alliances, a fact accentuated by the gap in average ages between husband and wife. Some famous humanists and early feminists did leave a mark:

Christine de Pisan (1364–1431): A French noblewoman, de Pisan published one of the first modern statements of feminism, *The City of Ladies*, which defends women's intellectual capabilities against anti-female bias. After her husband's death, de Pisan fought to retain her property and turned to writing to support her family; she may have been the first woman in European history to make a living through her writings.

Isabella d'Este (1474–1539): Often called the First Lady of the World, d'Este married into the famous Gonzaga family of Mantua. After her husband departed for war, d'Este conducted diplomacy on his behalf (and sometimes behind his back). She also found time to establish schools for girls, attract humanists to her court, and write hundreds of letters of literary merit.

Laura Cereta (1469–1499): Cereta's life again illustrates the importance of marriage and early mortality. Her husband died after 18 months of marriage, and rather than enter a convent or remarry, Cereta wrote works advocating equality of opportunity for women. She, too, died young, however.

9 THEME MUSIC
The following section addresses the SP theme, focusing on the overarching issue of the centralization of power and resistance to it. Take note of the strategies and institutions used by monarchs to overcome provincialism as well as how corporate groups and institutions (nobles, towns, church, e.g.) resisted monarchical forays.

Renaissance Politics and the New Monarchs[9]

Politics was central to Renaissance views regarding power, status, and values such as civic humanism. As noted previously, Machiavelli's ideas played a major role in introducing a secular conception of politics, and historians such as Francesco Guicciardini emphasized social and political causes, rather than divine providence, in recounting the diplomacy and great events of the day. Given the divided nature of the Italian peninsula, regular diplomacy emerged to secure the balance of power. Ambassadors no longer served Christendom generally, but instead patriotically—and often deviously—represented their city- or nation-state. To ensure that no one power gained dominance, the five major city-states continually jockeyed for position, thus the concept of **balance-of-power** politics emerged, which would come to play a central role in European diplomatic thinking. Perhaps the best example of this attitude is the Peace of Lodi, signed in 1454, which created a fairly stable arrangement that ensured 40 years of peace. Furthermore, the so-called **New Monarchies** aimed to reassert strong dynastic claims with centralizing techniques in response to the disasters of the 14th century.

Though it is not necessary to have a detailed knowledge of each city-state, you may find it helpful to link the basics below to KCs 1.2 and 1.3.

City-State	Government	Key Figures	Assessment
Florence	A republic led by members of the many guilds, but in reality dominated behind the scenes by the Medici family, which made a fortune in banking.	*Cosimo de' Medici (1389–1464)—Patriarch of the family. Wealthy patron of humanism who helped found the Florentine Platonic Academy. (See Lorenzo, his grandson, above.) *Savanarola (1452–1498)—Preached against the secular focus on art and pagan philosophy, eventually taking over the city, before being burned at the stake.	Florence was the center of banking and textiles on the peninsula, and one of the richest of the city-states. This wealth helped make it the Queen City of the Renaissance before the French invasion in 1494. Many of the greats associated with Renaissance culture made their name in Florence.
Milan	A military dictatorship ruled by the Visconti family for centuries.	*Francesco Sforza (1401–1466)—Seized control of the city in the 1450s and a good example of how reliance on mercenary soldiers—*condottiere*— undermined Italy's independence.	Of the city-states, Milan was most closely tied to trading interests in central Europe. Strategically located, disputes over its control led to the invasion of foreign armies, and the ultimate end of the Renaissance.
Papal States	Technically ruled as a despotism by the papacy, it was really an elective monarchy that had difficulty managing the noble factions in its diverse territories.	*Alexander VI (1492–1503)—He represents the height of corruption in the Renaissance Papacy. Used his children to cement marriage alliances and regain power on the peninsula. *Julius II (1503–1513)—Known as the Warrior Pope, he led armies into battle and also sponsored grand art projects, like the Sistine Chapel.	The period from 1417 to the 1540s is known as the Renaissance Papacy, and it is not a proud moment in the history of the Catholic Church. Popes were deeply involved in politics and seemed to the faithful more focused on luxury, art, and rebuilding Rome, which became the center of the High Renaissance after 1490. Because a line of popes ignored pleas for reform, the problems that would lead to the Protestant Reformation festered.
Venice	An oligarchic republic ruled by wealthy merchant families. Nicknamed the "Serene Republic" for its stability throughout the era.	*Doge—Leader of the Venetian government chosen by wealthy merchants. *Book of Gold—Registry of the leading families in Venice; membership implied full citizenship rights.	The major trading power of the Italian city-states due to its contact with the Byzantine and later the Ottoman Empires. Its arsenal represents one of the first factories in history. Finally, Venetian artists, such as Titian and Bellini, stressed light and color over line and composition.
Naples	Relatively backward feudal monarchy claimed and eventually won by Ferdinand of Aragon.		Though the city of Naples was Europe's largest in 1500, the kingdom participated minimally in the intellectual and artistic Renaissance.

The state as we know it today did not exist in 1500, yet the New Monarchies of this era were laying its foundations. To rebuild after the devastation of the 14th and early 15th centuries, monarchs engaged in similar policies, while at the same time addressing problems unique to their geographic location with more focused policies. General strategies of centralization comprised the following:

economic

1. *Taxation*—Securing access to revenue, preferably without legislative approval.

Political

2. *Taming the aristocracy*—Monarchs established that they outranked other aristocrats by forming alliances with the middle class in towns and creating new nobles as officials, called the "nobles of the robe" (because their status came from their official capacities).

Political

3. *Codifying laws and creating courts*—Most nations were still a patchwork of customs, dialects, and legal traditions in 1500, so monarchs attempted to establish royal courts that applied more uniform laws.

4. *Controlling warfare*—Medieval armies were private entities and less than reliable. The New Monarchies worked to make armies and war the prerogative of the state, which made sense given the increasingly complex nature of war.

5. *Early bureaucracy and officials*—Emerging states lacked the mechanisms to enforce their will, let alone keep track of the affairs of government. To remedy this, monarchs began to use agencies, committees, representative bodies, and councils to assist in implementing royal authority.

6. *Religious control*—The medieval tension between religious and secular authority began to tilt in favor of the latter, even before the Protestant Reformation, as monarchs asserted increased authority over the clergy and the functions of religion within their national boundaries.

Now let's look briefly through the chart below at how these general strategies were applied in specific instances. Throughout this review guide, we will use a straightforward conceptual device to assist you in keeping track of nations, rulers, and policies: Challenges (the issues and problems rulers/nations faced) → Responses (policies the rulers/nations enacted to address these issues) → Results (the impact these policies had on the nation's strategic position).

Nation	Challenges	Responses	Results
England	Following the Hundred Years' War, England was plunged into the Wars of the Roses, between two factions of nobles. When the war ended in 1485, the Tudors set about rebuilding the power of the state.	*Henry VII (1485–1509) and **Henry VIII** (1509–1547) tamed the nobles, reducing the number of dukes from 9 to 2, and created a new aristocracy. *Star Chamber—royal system of courts, outside of parliamentary control, established. *Ended livery and maintenance, the private armies of the nobles. *Built England's first state navy. *Henry VIII took control of the Catholic Church in England and confiscated its lands.	The Tudors established the basis of English political and commercial power. However, Henry VIII's obsession with producing a male heir demonstrated the continuing fragility of royal rule and created a religious issue that would not be easily resolved.

Nation	Challenges	Responses	Results
France	France had experienced warfare on its soil for over 100 years, while its eastern neighbor Burgundy aimed to replace French leadership on the continent.	* Louis XI, the "Spider" (1461–1483) added new territory to the royal domain through strategic marriages and by conquering part of Burgundy. * Francis I (1515–1547), a Renaissance king, gained control of the French clergy through agreement with the pope (Concordat of Bologna). *Established taxation with *taille* (direct tax) and *gabelle* (government salt monopoly). *Claimed lands in Italy.	France extended its territory, laid a secure foundation for taxes, and created the largest army in Europe. This represents a strong recovery from the Hundred Years' War, but the kingdom continued to face encirclement by the Habsburgs.
Russia	The truncated duchy of Muscovy barely resembled the Russia of today, as it was threatened by powerful neighbors such as the Mongols and Poland.	*Ivan III, the "Great" (1462–1505), drove out the Mongols, claimed Moscow as the "Third Rome" by marrying niece of last Byzantine Emperor, and created the *streltsy*, a military service class. *Ivan IV, the "Terrible" (1547–1584), so nicknamed because of his hatred of the *boyars* (nobles), also continued Russian expansion.	Russia emerged as a great power, yet continued to face issues of cultural and technological backwardness. When Ivan IV killed his heir in a fit of rage, Russia fell into civil chaos and foreign invasion for 30 years.
Spain	Spain did not even exist until the marriage of Ferdinand and Isabella in 1469, and even then, Spain needed to complete the *reconquista* of the Moors and establish a national identity among its diverse kingdoms.	*Isabella of Castile's (1479–1504) and Ferdinand of Aragon's (1479–1516) marriage did not create a fully unified nation. *Made alliances with towns (*hermandades*) to establish law and order. * Completed *reconquista*. *Established strict religious orthodoxy with Spanish Inquisition (from 1478) and expelled Jews in 1492. *Sponsored voyages of exploration. ***Charles I** (aka Charles V in the Holy Roman Empire, 1516–1555) inherited diverse lands and became the most powerful monarch in Europe.	Spain emerged as the strongest nation in Europe. Access to the wealth of the New World and Charles's inheritance of numerous lands established Spain's Golden Age. However, its crusading mindset, onerous taxes, and persecution of talented minorities set the stage for its subsequent decline.

Northern Renaissance and Christian Humanism[10]

Renaissance culture began in Italy but quickly spread via the new printing press and along trade routes to the rest of Europe. It was particularly strong in the Low Countries (today's Netherlands and Belgium), France, England, and Germany, though almost every nation experienced some manifestation of humanist learning and classical revival.

Though northern humanists employed the same tactics of textual analysis and criticism as their Italian neighbors, their emphasis tended to be on Christian readings, such as the

10 SKILL SET

When you compare two objects, the process results in an improved grasp of both (COMP). For northern and Italian humanism, create a Venn diagram, making sure to note similarities and differences for the same topics (e.g., religion and art).

Bible, but also included the writings of the early church fathers (St. Augustine, for example). For this reason, northern humanism is often called **Christian humanism**. In general, Christian humanists criticized many of the Catholic Church's abuses, but wished to maintain the unity of Christianity by reforming from within. Many intelligent observers recognized that the ark of the church was listing badly and desperately needed repairs. The split that occurred in the 16th century revolved around this issue—whether the ship could be saved or should simply be abandoned in favor of a more stable vessel. Years before Luther, Christian humanists urged a reform, primarily through education, which would rescue the church from its worldliness and corruption. Though numerous Christian humanists labored to save the church, two clearly stand out for their literary accomplishments and clear teachings.

Before we address Erasmus and Thomas More, we need to paint a picture of late medieval spirituality. Maybe the best word to describe the mood of the 14th and 15th centuries is "anxiety." Amidst the death and upheaval of the plague, Great Schism, and political breakdown, European Christians became obsessed with securing eternal life. On one hand, this fear fed the mechanical exercises of indulgences, relic veneration, and pilgrimages. Desiring a positive relationship with God, some Christians turned to mysticism—the belief that the believer can bridge the gap between himself and the Almighty through meditation, prayer, and other acts of devotion. A popular book in this regard was Thomas à Kempis's *Imitation of Christ*, which provided daily readings to commune with God. In the Low Countries and Germany, an organization of laypersons (not members of the clergy) called the Brothers and Sisters of the Common Life ministered to the poor, founded schools for the education of character, and supported each other in living a Christian life. Religion remained dear to many; if it had not, the influence of the Catholic Church might have faded slowly without any disruptive spread of a new and vibrant Protestant theology.

Desiderius Erasmus (1466–1536) became the most famous intellectual of his day, and his name remains a symbol of tolerance and scholarship. Raised in a monastic environment, he never took vows, claiming he had "a Catholic soul but a Lutheran stomach" (and thus not able to withstand the church's demand for ritual fasting). With humor and style, Erasmus mocked the clergy and its abuses in works such as the *Praise of Folly*, which was eventually placed on the Index of Prohibited Books. Erasmus's primary message, as seen in *Handbook of the Christian Knight* and *On Civility in Children*, lay in the power of education to promote true reverence for God and in living out the Gospel message. Protected by powerful patrons, Erasmus condemned fanaticism of all kinds, and while his reputation remained undiminished by his death, his voice of moderation had been drowned out by extremists on all sides. He might have opposed the sentiment, but it is often said that "Erasmus laid the egg that Luther hatched."

Perhaps no intellectual better represents the bridging of the medieval and modern worlds than Thomas More (1478–1535). A man of deep piety (More wore a hairshirt—a rough and painful undergarment made of goat's wool–to mortify his flesh throughout much of his life), More well understood the game of worldly success, but always kept a careful eye on the next world. More's talents brought him to the attention of the monarchy, where he served in Parliament and as the first nonclerical Lord Chancellor (the highest judicial position in England). More's literary fame rests primarily on *Utopia*, a satire of 16th-century European society, and vision of a better life based on communal living. A friend of Erasmus, More possessed less of his comrade's moderate tendencies. More *was* willing to die for his beliefs, which occurred when he opposed Henry VIII's takeover of the Catholic Church. More was also willing to kill for them, as he oversaw the burning of accused heretics as Lord Chancellor. The scholar's last days were spent in the Tower of London, before his beheading in 1535, another victim of the growing rift between religious and political authority.

In art, northern humanism eventually adopted the techniques of Italian painters, including perspective and an emphasis on naturalism. However, northern artists tended to focus more on the theological and emotional content of Christian depictions, instead of classical architecture and wealthy patrons, as among Italian artists. In addition, northern painters, such as Pieter Bruegel the Elder (1525–1569), portrayed scenes of **everyday life**, including peasants, agriculture, or the simple customs that tied together small communities.

Causes of the Protestant Reformation

We have already hinted at several causes of the Protestant Reformation—Christian humanism, late medieval spirituality, and the state of the Catholic Church—but now it is time to focus on the last of these. Simply put, the Catholic Church in 1500 confronted a crisis. Desperate to recapture its former glory and influence, the papacy focused more on artistic patronage and Machiavellian politics than the spiritual state of its flock. Abuses that began during the Babylonian Captivity festered and produced a general cry for reform, a cry ignored by corrupt popes fearful of limits on their power by church councils. These abuses were:

- *Simony*—The buying and selling of high church offices, which often produced a revenue (annates) for the holder.
- *Nepotism*—The granting of offices to relatives (e.g., Pope Alexander VI conferred a cardinal's hat upon his 16-year-old son).
- *Pluralism*—The holding of multiple church offices.
- *Absenteeism*—Not residing in one's spiritual domain because one held multiple positions.
- *Indulgences*—The most controversial, the belief that a believer could draw on Jesus' and the saints' previous stock of grace to reduce the sinner's or a relative's time in purgatory (that region between heaven and hell reserved for the final "purging" of sinful souls).

It was this last abuse that sparked the Reformation, but prior to this spark, recall that a goodly pile of tinder had been accumulating for generations.

The Protestant Reform Movements

Luther and Lutheranism

The Protestant Reformation began with one man's spiritual crisis. This crisis revolved around a nagging but central question in Christianity: "How can I be saved?" It is common to think of Luther as attacking the abuses of the church, but his critique went well beyond that. Luther questioned not only the practices of the church, but condemned it for *teaching* wrongly, calling into question the entire sacramental system of Catholicism as it related to salvation.

In a complex transaction, Pope Leo X (1513–1521) in 1517 allowed the sale of indulgences by the monk Johan Tetzel (a sort of medieval used car salesman) to finance the building of St. Peter's Basilica in Rome. Luther responded almost immediately with the Ninety-Five Theses, wherein he condemned indulgences as twisting the central mystery of Christianity—Jesus' crucifixion as a once-and-for-all sacrifice wiping the human slate clean of sin and death. Previous to the indulgence controversy, Luther had been working out in his reading and lecturing a different conception of salvation. The decisive break became clear to him over the next few years, as Luther published pamphlets elaborating his ideas and denouncing what he considered false teachings. Luther's new theology can be summarized in three Latin phrases:

- *Sola scriptura*—The only authority in Christianity is the Bible. While the Catholic Church had based authority on Scripture *and* the teaching function of the church (the magisterium) in the persons of the bishops, cardinals, and popes, Luther argued that doctrine or practice needed to be supported by the revealed word of God *alone*.
- *Sola fide*—Salvation comes from faith alone. As Luther put it, "Good works do not make a good man, but a good man does good works." Faith is a free gift of God and cannot be earned through human activity, such as pilgrimages, relic veneration, or indulgences.
- *Sola gratia*—Salvation comes by the free gift of God's grace. Grace is the spiritual quality that gives the sinner merit in the eyes of God. Since humans are incapable of acquiring this merit through their own sinful efforts, it must be God's free gift. In contrast, the Catholic Church held that the primary instruments of grace were the sacraments; in short, that grace was mediated through the clergy.

Luther's attack echoed many of the critiques made by Hus and even Erasmus. What made Lutheranism successful was the urgency and passion with which Luther conveyed his message and, more importantly, the printing press. It is hard to imagine the Protestant Reformation's success without the tremendous propaganda instrument of the cheaply printed word. To illustrate, in the first 10 years of the Reformation, one-quarter of the books published in Germany were by Luther. In addition, many of the publications were not designed to appeal to theologians. Songs, sermons, and woodcuts mocking the Pope all appealed to a mass audience. Several of Luther's publications that reveal his new interpretation of Christianity include:

- "On the Freedom of the Christian" (1520)—A short pamphlet in which Luther rejected the notion of free will over salvation. Why, Luther asked, would I want to be in charge of my salvation when God can effect it so much better? The work prompted Erasmus uncharacteristically to reply to Luther by defending free will.

- *On the Babylonian Captivity of the Church* (1520)—This is a longer work, in Latin, for theologians. Here Luther condemned the Catholic conception of the sacraments as holding the faithful "in bondage" to the earthly power of the clergy. In addition, Luther retained only two sacraments—baptism and the Lord's Supper—because these had scriptural justification.

- *An Address to the Nobility of the German Nation* (1520)—Recognizing he needed political support in the Empire, Luther patriotically appealed to the German princes to support his cause and resist Roman taxation and power.

- German translation of the Bible (1530s)—Traditionally, Bible reading had been reserved for theologians or clergymen. By rendering the Bible into his native tongue, Luther made clear that the Bible was to be read by all, including women, and placed it front and center as an act of Christian worship.

It is often said that Luther demonstrated the fire of a theological revolutionary but the caution of a social and political conservative. No doubt, Luther was a complex figure who recognized that his attack on the Catholic Church held the potential to rip the whole of society apart. For Luther, the real church was the spiritual one of the next world; because perfection could not be reached on earth due to the sinful nature of humans, social and political revolution was self-defeating.

Luther's message inspired a host of other reformers, many of whom interpreted it in more radical ways. German firebrands, such as Andreas Carlstadt and Thomas Müntzer, applied Luther's idea of the "priesthood of all believers" more literally, to indicate a move toward social equality. These leaders supported the Peasants' Revolt of 1524–1525, the product of long-standing economic grievances and the new religious ideals. Luther was incensed, denouncing the firebrands and the peasants in "Against the Murdering and Robbing Horde of Peasants," in which he called for the death of all who challenged legitimate authority and who twisted the true Christian message, which was spiritual not political. Ultimately, the peasants were crushed at the cost of 100,000 lives, and Luther gained a reputation for intolerance that might have spent some steam from his movement in the 1530s. Another reason for Luther's attitude toward social upheaval lay in his need for support among the German princes, the only force standing between him and Charles V, the Holy Roman Emperor, before whom Luther in 1521 stood in defiance at the Diet of Worms. As a result of Luther's attitudes, wherever Lutheranism became the dominant religion (much of Germany and Scandinavia), the church was placed under the control of the state[11].

Through a series of timely marriages and untimely deaths, **Charles V** (1516–1556) stood in 1519 as the most powerful ruler in Europe, controlling Spain, the Low Countries, the Holy Roman Empire, significant parts of Italy, and the Spanish Empire in the New World. Charles recognized the need for reform in the church and continually pressured the pope to call a general council (unsuccessfully until 1545). At the same time, Charles believed it his duty to maintain

[11] SKILL SET

Consider this classic interpretive question: Was Luther a revolutionary or a conservative? Answering this question requires you to engage an historical interpretation and make an argument using evidence (INTR & EVARG). Even if you decide not to write out your answer, reflect on what evidence from the preceding discussion might go on each side of the balance sheet.

the political unity of Catholicism. Unfortunately for him, Charles's entire reign was spent on horseback attempting to keep his far-flung possessions together in the face of his many enemies:

- *Ottoman Turks*—The Ottomans killed Charles' brother-in-law Louis in battle in 1526, taking Hungary, and moved to besiege Vienna (capital of the Habsburg empire) in 1529.

- *France (Valois)*—Francis I represented Charles' most consistent rival. The perennial goal of France aimed to avoid encirclement by the Habsburgs and prevent the centralization of power in Germany. The Habsburg-Valois Wars (1494–1559) began in Italy but eventually intruded into the outcome of the Reformation in Germany, as Francis, though a Catholic, took the side of the German Protestants.

- *Algerian pirates*—Spain's interests in the Mediterranean were continuously threatened by piracy based in North Africa. Charles launched an expedition in 1541 that temporarily helped the problem.

- *The papacy*—Though both Charles and the Pope shared an interest in salvaging Catholicism, they differed over tactics and political goals, especially when Charles's troops sacked Rome in 1527, effectively bringing the Renaissance to an end.

- *German Lutherans*—Due to other preoccupations, Charles was forced to compromise with Lutherans early in his reign. An imperial diet in 1529 at Speyer attempted to impose a religious settlement but failed when Lutherans protested (which accounts for the term "Protestant"). By 1546, Charles was prepared to solve the issue through force. The Lutheran princes formed the Schmalkaldic League and were prepared to resist with the aid of outside powers. After an initial victory in 1547 at Muhlberg, Charles was unable to follow up on his success.

To settle the religious conflict in Germany (sometimes termed the "First Thirty Years War"), Charles agreed in 1555 to the <u>Peace of Augsburg</u>, which employed the compromise formula *cuius region, eius religion* ("his the region, his the religion") to divide the Empire between Lutheran and Catholic areas, as determined by the rulers of those states. It is important to note that this settlement did *not* endorse religious toleration, but recognized the relatively even balance of religious power in Germany. In addition, Charles V abdicated in 1556, splitting his realm between his brother Ferdinand (as HRE) and his son Philip II, who took everything else.

Calvin's Second Wave

By 1540, the Protestant Reformation already required a boost; **John Calvin** (1509–1564) provided just that. A second-generation reformer, Calvin was born in France and received a strong humanist education. Unlike Luther, Calvin studied to be a priest but switched to the legal profession, which may account for the strong images in Calvinism of God as the omnipotent sovereign and law-giver. Calvin set up his reform movement in Switzerland, and after some initial turmoil was recognized as the unquestioned leader of <u>Geneva</u>.

Calvin accepted much of Luther's reformed theology (justification by faith alone, two sacraments) but placed more emphasis on predestination, the notion that God foreknows and forejudges salvation for each person before birth. Those who had been saved ("the elect") did not suffer from spiritual complacency, as one might expect, but exhibited a zealous determination to create the "Most Holy City on Earth." In *Institutes of the Christian Religion*, published in numerous editions, Calvin synthesized reformed theology and provided a practical program for founding a reformed religion. Genevan politics were guided by the Ecclesiastical Ordinances, which divided the church into doctors (who studied scripture), pastors (who preached the word of God), deacons (who administered charity), and elders (who ensured discipline). Elders employed the Consistory to practice "Christian watchfulness" and monitor public morality, such as public drunkenness or gambling. Compared with Luther, Calvin believed the political system must uphold the moral law of a Christian community. Though not a theocracy, church leaders played a major role in ensuring public affairs were governed by church teachings.

Calvinism spread quickly among the nobility and the middle class, many of whom likely believed themselves to be the elect and who resented the privileges of the clergy. To promote the spread of the Reformation, Calvin founded the Genevan Academy in 1559 to train leaders who would sow the seeds of Calvinism in other locales. Its most famous graduate was John Knox (1505–1572), who established Calvinism in Scotland. Taking their cue from their leader and their minority status in most nations, Calvinists represented the forefront of a militant Protestant movement dedicated to battling the still-strong power of Catholicism.

Evangelical Reformers

Some historians divide the Reformation into evangelical (or radical) and magisterial branches. The former refers to the grassroots movement of individual persons, towns, and communities spreading the new reform gospel through preaching, conversion, and town disputations. Some religious reforms, however, were imposed from the top down, by magistrates, princes, and monarchs. We'll discuss the most famous example of this magisterial reform in the next section, but for now, let's examine some of the radical reformers.

Ulrich Zwingli (1484–1531) served as a chaplain to the many Swiss mercenaries who were often forced by poor economics to sell their services to a variety of nations. It was in his native Zurich where Zwingli established a reformed movement more radical in style than Luther's. Like Luther, Zwingli accepted two sacraments but disagreed with him over the meaning of the Lord's Supper. While Luther argued that a real presence of Jesus coexisted with the bread and wine (called consubstantiation—"two substances together"), Zwingli held Luther's position to be illogical. Jesus was in heaven at the right hand of the Father and could not be present in body and blood during services; the sacrament was symbolic only. In the context of the mounting power of the emperor, Luther and Zwingli met to attempt to settle their disagreement. The subsequent Marburg Colloquy failed miserably. With no German allies, Zwingli was killed in 1531 in the Swiss Civil War. Before he died, however, Zwingli had laid the basis for a different style of worship. Followers of Zwingli broke organs, smashed statues, and painted churches white, all in an effort to focus the believer's attention on the Word of God by eliminating "distractions."

The first 20 years of the Reformation saw great ferment and experimentation. In many areas, women first accepted the reform message, spreading the gospel and converting their husbands, father, and brothers. A famous example was Catherine Zell (1498–1562), who along with her husband Matthias, preached, wrote, and ministered to the poor. One movement most associated with this trend toward equality was Anabaptism. **Anabaptists** believed membership in a Christian community issued from an adult choice, and therefore practiced adult baptism. More importantly, they tended to take the Bible literally when it came to living a life apart from worldly temptations. Because they practiced adult baptism—thereby putting the souls of unbaptized babies in peril—and advocated the total separation of church and state, Anabaptists were hated by Catholics and Protestants alike. However, with a few exceptions, Anabaptists lived in small, peaceful communities and posed little real threat to the state.

Magisterial Reform in England

The most famous example of **magisterial reform** occurred in England. Though Lutheran ideas had gained a few adherents in the kingdom, **Henry VIII** (1509–1547) tolerated no opposition to the Catholic faith, having earned the title Defender of the Faith for penning a response to Luther's attack on the sacraments. However, matters of state intervened. Henry had no male heir, which he blamed on his "barren" wife, Catherine of Aragon. Normally, Henry's appeal for a divorce would have been granted by Pope Clement VII (1523–1534), but he was under the control of Charles V, who happened to be the nephew of Catherine.

After years and numerous appeals, Henry decided in 1533–1534 to act with the support of the Parliament. First, the Parliament declared Henry the head of the new Anglican Church with the Act of Supremacy. Further, the Act of Succession legitimated the offspring (the future Elizabeth

I) of Henry and Anne Boleyn, his new wife. With the aid of his primary advisor, Thomas Cromwell, Henry also moved to confiscate the lands of the church. However, Henry held no interest in *religious* reform, getting parliament to confirm distinctive Catholic practices such as clerical celibacy in the Six Articles. Many English reformers, such as the new Archbishop of Canterbury Thomas Cranmer, wished to take the reform further. They would have to wait until Henry died and his sickly teenage son, Edward VI (1547–1553), succeeded him in 1547.

Under Edward, the reform moved in a Zwinglian direction, with a new Book of Common Prayer and Act of Uniformity providing a simpler interpretation of worship. Edward's early death in 1553 turned England back once again into the Catholic camp, under Mary I (1553–1558), the daughter of the scorned Catherine of Aragon and wife of the Most Holy Catholic Philip II (1556–1598), king of Spain. Mary's persecution of Protestants, memorialized in the famous *Foxe's Book of Martyrs*, and pro-Spanish foreign policy earned her the nickname Bloody Mary and did little in the long run to reestablish Catholicism in England.

It was **Elizabeth I** (1558–1603) who met with the most success in establishing a compromise, the Elizabethan Settlement. Under house arrest for much of her youth, Elizabeth learned the dangers of religious dogmatism. In fact, Elizabeth represented a new type of leader, termed a *politique*, or one who places political unity above conformity to religious dogma. During her reign, Elizabeth entertained many suitors but ultimately adopted the role of national matriarch, never marrying. She refrained from persecuting religious minorities—with the exception of Catholics—and sponsored a new Book of Common Prayer, vague enough in its language to satisfy all interpretations. These compromises were cemented in the Thirty-Nine Articles. At the same time, Elizabeth could play the "lion," as she demonstrated by executing her cousin, Mary of Scotland, for plotting against her, and defending England in 1588 against the impending Spanish Armada. By the end of her reign, often called the Golden Age, Elizabeth had established England as the leading Protestant power in Europe[12].

Social Impact of the Protestant Reformation

The Protestant Reformation was primarily a religious movement, but it also altered social life. Movements of intellectual or cultural change often attract those—women, peasants, workers, minorities—who wish to change other features of society. Invariably, these reform movements eventually come to institutionalize new beliefs and practices to avoid more wrenching changes. In that sense, the Protestant Reformation can be viewed as a significant shift but also a lost opportunity for many groups. We now look briefly at several affected areas:

- *Family and gender*—As a result of the Protestant Reformation, family was placed at the center of social life. Celibacy was abolished, and many former clergy, like Luther, took spouses and glorified the marital bond as the most natural and God-like. For women, the results were mixed. Though women preached early on and earned limited rights of divorce, as well as education, Luther, Calvin, and other reformers preached that women's natural sphere was the domestic. Finally, religious vocations and female religious images were removed from Protestant churches.

- *Education*—There is no doubt that the Protestant Reformation spurred education. With the emphasis on Bible-reading, it was important to ensure literacy for boys *and* girls. Luther's colleague and defender, Philip Melancthon (1497–1560), earned the nickname *Praeceptor Germanie* (Teacher of Germany) for advocating a system of basic schooling called the *Gymnasia*. After the establishment of the Jesuits, Catholic nations also began to place increasing importance on education.

- *Social classes*—Other than the firebrands, few reformers explicitly argued for social equality. However, some historians have argued that a "Protestant work ethic" spurred the development of capitalism, and thus strengthened the middle class. In theory, the emphasis on deferred gratification and building a godly city on earth led to an ethic of hard work

12 EXAMPLE BASE
Many of the examples in this section on the range of Protestant reformers are required knowledge; however, you should take a moment to place them on a continuum of radical to conservative. As you look across the diagram, take note of the diversity of interpretations of religious reform.

and capital accumulation. (This interpretation is problematic, but you probably will earn points in an essay for mentioning it.)

- *Religious practices*—For centuries, European religious life had centered around the church calendar, with its saints' feast days, <u>Carnival</u> and Lent, sacraments, and rituals. In many lands, these practices were either abolished or modified. Protestant nations placed more emphasis on Bible-reading and sought to eliminate externals, such as relics, pilgrimages, and festivals. Also, the Reformation led to an increased concern with regulation of public morality, and even many Catholic nations attempted more rigorously to monitor excessive practices and curb long-accepted sins like prostitution.

Catholic Revival and Reform

Even before 1517, many Catholics recognized the need for reform. In fact, reform was already under way if we consider the lay piety movement and the writings of Christian humanists. Under Cardinal Ximenes de Cisneros (1436–1517), Spain had already addressed many clerical abuses and had tightened regulations for the training of priests. However, the institutional church, led by the papacy throughout the early 16th century, "fiddled while Rome burned." Finally, under the pontificate of Paul III (1534–1549), the hierarchical church responded to the challenge of the Protestant Reformation. The Catholic response to the reformation was multi-pronged and complex. Those actions designed to revive Catholic spirituality are often termed the **Catholic Reformation**, while those designed to halt the spread of the Protestant Reformation are called the Counter-Reformation. Below is a list of the actions, positive and negative, taken by the Catholic Church in response to the Protestant Reformation[13].

13 SKILL SET

Another classic question to consider: compare and contrast the Protestant and Catholic Reformations on religious doctrines and practices (COMP). If you encounter such a question, remember to capture complexity in your interpretation and avoid a one-sided portrayal that may reflect your own sympathies.

- *New religious orders*—For most Catholics, their connection to the church was their parish priest. Thus, a major element of reform involved the revival of religious orders and the establishment of new ones. The most important of these was the Society of Jesus or **Jesuits**, founded by Ignatius Loyola (1491–1556) in the 1540s. Like Luther, Loyola underwent a spiritual conversion. After being injured in battle, Loyola practiced rigorous acts of self-discipline and recommitted himself to the mysteries of the church. His important book, *Spiritual Exercises*, contains the famous phrase, "If I see a thing to be white but the institutional church commands it to be black, I will see it as black." Jesuits had no national base, seeing themselves as the "troops of the Pope" and missionaries to those who did not know Christ. Jesuits worked primarily through education and argument, and their efforts paid off by re-Catholicizing large parts of Eastern Europe, including Poland and Hungary after 1560. Other religious orders focused on charitable works and education. Angela Merici (1474–1540) founded the <u>Ursulines</u> to bring education to girls. The Spanish mystic, <u>Teresa of Avila</u> (1515–1582), experienced visions of Jesus and founded the Carmelites, dedicated to a life of contemplation and service. Also, a group of clergy and laypeople formed the Oratory of Divine Love to push for reform in the church and assist one another in leading lives of simply piety. Finally, a new breed of austere and hard-working bishops emerged, such as Gian Matteo Giberti (1495–1543) of Verona and Cardinal Charles Borromeo (1538–1584) of Milan.

- *Council of Trent (1545–1563)*—Though rather tardy and poorly attended, this council finally put the church's house in order. First, the Cardinals (most from Italy and Spain) eliminated many church abuses and provided for better education and regulation of priests. Second, the church refused to compromise on religious doctrines, reaffirming distinctive Catholic practices like clerical celibacy, the importance of good works, the authority of the papacy, and transubstantiation. According to the last, the bread and wine, though retaining the incidents of bread and wine such as taste and texture, are truly transformed into another substance (the body and blood of Jesus) during the Mass.

- *Strengthening the papacy and Inquisition (1542)*—To better meet the challenge of unorthodox belief, the papal bureaucracy was centralized and strengthened. A major feature of this revamping was the creation of the Roman Inquisition (not to be confused with the Spanish Inquisition), designed to root out perceived heresies. In the long run, the Inquisition had a chilling effect on intellectual life in Italy, as can be seen by the Galileo incident in 1633 (see Chapter 6).

- *Index of Prohibited Books*—Under the conservative pontificate of Pope Paul IV (1555–1559), the church decided to clamp down on any printed materials that threatened to mislead the faithful away from the orthodox interpretations of the magisterium. Though of limited impact in stopping Protestantism, the Index continued until the 20th century.

- ***Baroque art***—In an effort to revive Catholic spirituality, the church patronized an artistic movement that emphasized grandeur, illusion, and dramatic religiosity. In music, Palestrina composed numerous masses and sacred pieces geared toward arousing strong religious emotion. Multi-talented artists such as Giovanni Lorenzo Bernini (1598–1680) rebuilt Rome as a showplace of Catholic piety (see Chapter 7 for more on Baroque).

How successful was the Catholic response? By 1560, the religious divide in Europe was an accomplished fact; in that sense, the Catholic response came too little and too late. However, some parts of Europe had been re-Catholicized, and the church emerged from its reforms stronger and more militant than in 1500, before the Reformation had begun. One fact is clear: after the completion of the Council of Trent's work in 1564, no religious compromise was possible. With a militant Calvinism and revived and rearmed Catholic Church, an extended period of religious conflict lay on the horizon.

Additional Resources

Roland Bainton, *Here I Stand: A Life of Martin Luther* (1994)—Considered the classic account of an important figure.

Peter Burke, *The Renaissance: Culture and Society in Italy* (1999)—Explains the concept of the Renaissance and offers a complex account of how applicable the term is.

Alfred W. Crosby, *The Measure of Reality: Quantification and Western Society, 1250–1600* (1997)—Explores the development of quantitative thinking in the Later Middle Ages and Renaissance. A challenging but fairly brief and interesting read. Highly recommended.

Diarmaid MacCulloch, *The Reformation: A History* (2003)—Magisterial history with coverage of often-neglected areas. Some biases but useful as a reference source.

Theodore K. Rabb, *Renaissance Lives: Portraits of an Age* (1993)—Brief and vivid biographies of representative and leading figures.

Eugene F. Rice and Anthony Grafton, *The Foundations of Early Modern Europe, 1460–1559* (1993)—The first volume in the accessible Norton History of Modern Europe provides a solid and well-written overview of the period.

Eric Till, *Luther* (2003)—This film, produced by the Lutheran Church, provides dramatization of important moments of the Reformation but omits more controversial features of Luther's life.

William H. McNeill, *Plagues and Peoples* (1976)—Examines the impact of disease in world history.

Practice MC Questions

Each chapter will end with 2–3 sets of MC questions and either an SAQ or LEQ for your practice with content and application of skills. For MC answer explanations, see Chapter 18. The SAQ or LEQ will conclude with a sample essay and scoring commentary. You may wish to write the essay first and then compare your answer to the sample. For LEQs, see the rubric on pp. 5-6 in Chapter 1.

Questions 1–4 are based on the passage below.

> "In the Middle Ages...human consciousness...lay dreaming or half awake beneath a common veil. The veil was woven of faith, illusion, and childish prepossession, through which the world and history were seen clad in strange hues. Man was conscious of himself only as a member of a race, people, party, family, or corporation—only through some general category. In Italy this veil first melted into air; an objective treatment and consideration of the state and of all the things of this world became possible....
>
> [During the Renaissance] Italy began to swarm with individuality; the charm [ban] laid upon human personality was dissolved; and a thousand figures meet us each in its own special shape and dress....The Italians of [this time] knew little of false modesty or of hypocrisy in any shape; not one of them was afraid of singularity, of being and seeming unlike his neighbours."
>
> Jacob Burckhardt, Swiss historian, *The Civilisation of the Renaissance in Italy*, 1860

1. Which of the following features of the Italian Renaissance does Burckhardt endorse most explicitly?

   A. Secularism

   B. Civic humanism

   C. Individualism

   D. Classical revival

2. The Renaissance mindset Burckhardt identifies led most directly in the arts to:

   A. a human-centered naturalism and portrayal of everyday life.

   B. use of distortion, drama, and illusion for state spectacle.

   C. challenging of Church doctrines and ecclesiastical authority.

   D. depictions of scientific inquiry and commercial activities.

3. Writing in 1860, Burckhardt seems most influenced by which of the following ideologies?

   A. Marxism

   B. Positivism

   C. Nationalism

   D. Conservatism

4. Burckhardt seems most concerned with addressing which of the following historical issues?

   A. That the Renaissance compares favorably with other intellectual movements

   B. That the Renaissance was caused by a variety of different factors and began in Italy

   C. That the humanists of the Renaissance were products of their historical context

   D. That the Renaissance represents a turning point and beginning of the modern world

Jacob Burckhardt, *The Civilisation of the Renaissance in Italy*, trans. S.G.C. Middlemore (London: S. Sonnenschein, 1904), pp. 129, 130.

> "At least twice a year, once in spring and again on the approach of winter, each pastor shall make in his sermons serious admonition to his parishioners that they must be diligent in sending their children to school. And let him stress the great benefit bound to come from this, schools being necessary not only for learning the liberal arts, but also the fear of God, virtue, and discipline. Where the young are neglected and kept out of school, permanent harm, both eternal and temporal, must result, as children grow up without fear and knowledge of God, without discipline, like the dumb beasts of the field, learning nothing about what is needed for their salvation, nor what is useful to them and their neighbors in worldly life."
>
> Wurttemberg (Germany) City Council ordinance, 1559

Gerald Strauss, *Luther's House of Learning: Indoctrination of the Young in the German Reformation* (Baltimore, MD: The Johns Hopkins University Press, 1978), pp. 45-46.

5. All of the following 16th-century developments contributed to the formation of the ordinance above EXCEPT:

   A. the invention of the printing press and advance of literacy.

   B. the emphasis in Protestant Christianity on reading the Bible.

   C. the ability of the Holy Roman Emperor to centralize power.

   D. the movement toward public regulation of morality.

6. Which of the following figures would most likely have agreed with the tone and purpose of the ordinance?

   A. Charles V

   B. John Calvin

   C. Henry VIII

   D. An Anabaptist

7. The purpose of education expressed above differs most strongly from that of the Italian Renaissance in:

   A. focusing primarily on learning for religious purposes.

   B. stressing the application of learning to a public role.

   C. overlooking the role of the liberal arts in forming character.

   D. believing that education should inspire and teach virtue.

8. How would the application of the principles behind education expressed above change most significantly after 1850?

   A. It would no longer address moral concerns.

   B. It would extend to citizens of all classes.

   C. It would promote revolutionary principles.

   D. It would no longer be supported by the state.

See Chapter 18 for answers and explanations.

Long Essay (LEQ) with Sample and Commentary

To what extent did the lives of women change as a result of the Renaissance and Reformation? (HTS: CCOT)

Throughout history, women have often been treated less than men. Women were made to be in charge of the domestic sphere and given few chances for education or political power. All of this changed with the Renaissance and Reformation. These were movements that tried to change the way people looked at ideas and religion. Many famous women, like Isabella d'Este and Elizabeth of England, played a major role in these movements. Not all changed for the better, because women were still inferior to men, but they were definitely better off.

The Renaissance was all about humanism, and a big part of that was education. Many intellectuals of this period thought that even women should receive an education. One of these was Castiglione in his *Book of Courtier*. Though this education was not the same as men's, it still was important because before this, women were usually illiterate. Also, there were even some famous women humanists. One of these was Isabella d'Este, a ruler of a city-state on the Italian peninsula. She gathered other thinkers at her court, a bit like a salon, and also wrote treatises about women having more rights. However, women had drawbacks as well. Since men were often much older than women when they were married, they were not always treated well. To escape the control of their husbands, women had affairs and exercised some power "behind the scenes." All in all, women gained an important role in the Renaissance, but this did not always apply to poor women, many of which turned to prostitution just to survive.

Women also gained some from the Reformation. In fact, many important rulers of this period were women, like Elizabeth and Mary Tudor. These rulers showed that politics was not just for men. Elizabeth may have been the best ruler in England's history. Why? She helped solve the religious conflict left over from her father, Henry VIII, and got the Protestants and Catholics back together again. In addition, she was able to fight off the Spanish and their armada in 1588, a great victory that made England the new sea power. Some women even played a role in religious issues, like Catherine Zell. Catherine was an Anabaptist—people who were radical and practiced adult baptism—and preached in churches with her husband. Catholic women even played a role, like Teresa of Avila. She had visions of Jesus and created a new group of nuns who helped the poor. So, as you can see, women did not just let men control politics and religion. They got involved and proved that they were up to the task.

Women's rights really came later in the twentieth century, when they got the vote, but the Renaissance and Reformation got the ball rolling. Some famous women played major roles in spreading both movements. Of course, not all women gained, especially lower classes, but that doesn't take away from the strides women made. Perhaps if women stand up for their rights, they will continue to gain equality with men.

This is a solid essay and one that, with improvements, could earn a top score. First, the student is in control of the question—she addresses it directly, offers a thesis (if simplified), and provides relevant support. Second, the essay is balanced, in providing roughly equal treatment of both the Renaissance and Reformation. Third, the response is clearly organized and contains no glaring errors of fact, though some misinterpretations (Elizabeth "got the Protestants and Catholics back together again"). What kept the essay from a top score? Though the thesis is evident, it is simplified. In fact, the student often relies on clichés ("get the ball rolling," "up to the task," "got involved") rather than a more specific analysis of how women's status changed or stayed the same (the targeted HTS–Change and Continuity over Time). Finally, though the student addresses synthesis–by carrying the topic forward to a later period–there is not sufficient explanation to earn that point. Score: 4 (Thesis, 1 for targeted HTS, 2 for Use of Evidence)

CHAPTER 5 Economic Expansion, Social Change, and Religious Wars, 1550–1650

The European encounter with the Americas, as a result of exploration and colonization, changed the world. Not only were Europeans forced to rethink cultural and intellectual assumptions, they gained access to riches, which shifted the balance of power politically in Europe and caused untold destruction to the colonized cultures. The resulting global economy, often termed the Commercial Revolution, altered economic and social structures in Europe. Moreover, this era also saw the effects of the Protestant and Catholic Reformations played out in a century of religious wars, never free from political and economic considerations. A major result of these developments was to shift the locus of European power from the Mediterranean to those nations on the Atlantic.

Key In Chapter 5 addresses the following KCs from the Course Description:

- **KC 1.2** The role of religion, warfare, and political theory in relation to states.

- **KC 1.3** Effects of religious reform and warfare on the state.

- **KC 1.4** Motives and means of exploration; establishment of empires; effects of colonization.

- **KC 1.5** Economic and social structures that reflect both growth of a money economy and persistence of medieval institutions and practices.

The Opening of the Atlantic[1]

Motives and Means

Europe's outward expansion began in 1095 with the Crusades and continued throughout the Middle Ages, with the *reconquista* in Spain, Marco Polo's journey to China, and the first tentative Portuguese steps to explore the coastline of Africa. What accounts for the burst of exploration in the 15th and 16th centuries? The usual explanation is "God, gold, and glory," a mantra that captures the missionary impulse, economic incentives, and personal motives of the conquistadores. However, we should not overlook the role that technological developments played, as well as the sponsorship provided by competitive states eager to reap the political advantages of this exploration.

For centuries, Europe's access to the coveted goods of the East was provided by Arab and Ottoman middlemen. Direct control of spices, silks, sugar, porcelain, precious metals, gems, and strategic minerals would reduce costs and ensure a ready supply of profit-making goods. With the growth of towns and commerce in the Middle Ages, merchants and governments were keen on exploiting opportunities to fill their private and state coffers with newfound wealth. And missionaries considered the lands of the East rich ground for spreading the Gospel message. Though many viewed religion as a pretext rather than a motive for exploration, others were genuinely driven by piety, even if it was misplaced. In fact, once the Reformation was under way, religious groups like the Jesuits viewed the new colonies as a proving ground of religious commitment. Motives, then, for exploration were clearly in place; now all that was needed were the means.

The 15th century climaxed a long chain of navigational and intellectual advances that supported overseas exploration. The Chinese had already made contact with Africa and the Indian Ocean basin in the early 15th century but did not follow up their successes. China considered itself culturally and economically superior and thus not desirous of the goods or ideas of other cultures. However, China's ingenuity served Europe well, as its compass and axial rudder allowed Columbus and others the ability to conduct voyages far from their homelands. In addition, the quadrant (and related astrolabe) allowed explorers to measure the angle of the Pole Star to

1 THEME MUSIC

Here we begin our investigation of the Interaction of Europe and the World theme (INT). As you study, focus on the motives, means, methods of control, and results of exploration. These issues will recur throughout the course.

2 EXAMPLE BASE
These examples of technology and learning may not be vital per se, but try to link them to broader intellectual and cultural developments, such as the Renaissance and subsequent Scientific Revolution.

determine latitude. New maps, called *portolani*, provided detailed information about headlands and direction, though limited information regarding the open ocean. New ship designs, such as the caravel (a light maneuverable craft) and <u>lateen</u> (or triangular) <u>sail</u>, which allowed a crew to tack against the direction of the wind, made blue-water voyages possible. Finally, perspective geometry and the rediscovery of Ptolemy's *Geographica* (a 2nd-century Greek astronomer) provided for the gridlike structure found on most modern maps, even if Ptolemy had overestimated the size of Asia (a fact that Columbus would use to his advantage)[2].

Not all states were positioned to exploit these technologies. Because Portugal and Spain were the first to establish monarchical control over their diverse realms, they became the first nations to sponsor long-distance sea voyages. Setting up and administering colonies on far-flung lands required resources, bureaucracy, and sustained political energy. Though many early explorers hailed from Italy (Columbus, Vespucci, Verrazano, the Cabots), that country sponsored no overseas voyages; it couldn't, because it was divided and preoccupied with foreign invasion. Also, centralized governments had gained a monopoly on violence and were thus able to employ new techniques and technologies in warfare, such as cannons, steel weapons, and plate armor, which simply overwhelmed colonial opponents.

The Development of Colonial Empires

One nation that experienced a substantial economic boost from exploration was Portugal. In retrospect, Portugal's rise is amazing. A nation lacking natural resources with only about 1 million inhabitants, tucked in the southwestern corner of Europe, Portugal by 1510 had established a worldwide trading empire. Prince Henry (1394–1460), nicknamed The Navigator, founded a school for seafarers at Sagres, which trained the first generation of sailors who settled the Azores Island chain (a basing area for transatlantic voyages) and explored along the west coast of Africa. Though the Portuguese plucked the gold, pepper, and slaves of Africa, they still had not found the coveted sea route to the East. Then Vasco da Gama (c. 1469–1524) in 1498 made it around the Cape of Good Hope and to the riches of India. The single returning boat earned a 1,000% profit for its investors!

Da Gama followed up his success by returning with cannons, which overwhelmed the advanced civilizations of the Indian Ocean basin. By 1510, the Portuguese had established control of several strategic choke points in the East, which allowed them to extract trade concessions and radically reduce the cost of luxury products. Though Portugal lacked the population and resources to maintain extensive settlements, their maritime empire fed Europe's appetite for trade with the East until it was taken over by the Dutch at the end of the 16th century.

Not far behind the Portuguese were the Spanish. Though Christopher Columbus (1451–1506) completed four voyages to the Americas, he never recognized his miscalculation of the earth's circumference. Subsequent explorers welcomed the prospect of exploiting two previously unknown continents, and in the decades that followed, the Spanish monarchy sponsored expeditions that would lead to the subjugation of an entirely "New World."

Before describing the Spanish empire, let's review the accomplishments of several major figures in the history of exploration, keeping in mind that with this topic, the AP exam will focus less on personalities and more on motives and effects:

- *Hernando Cortez* (1485–1547)—*Conquistador* who overwhelmed the advanced Aztec civilization through use of horses, cannons, and diplomacy. Cortez helped establish the Spanish presence in North America.

- *Ferdinand Magellan* (1480–1521)—Skilled Portuguese seaman who sailed under the flag of Spain. He led his men through the treacherous straits at the tip of South America, now named for him, before perishing in the Philippines. Magellan is credited with the first successful circumnavigation of the earth.

- *St. Francis Xavier* (1506–1552)—Jesuit missionary who used wit and zeal to establish Christianity in India, Indonesia, and Japan.

- *Francisco Pizarro* (c. 1475–1541)—Brutal conqueror of the Incas in the Andes. He was aided by disease, as he and less than 300 men laid claim to South America.

Following Columbus's discovery, the Portuguese and Spanish negotiated the Treaty of Tordesillas (1494), which divided the world in half for purposes of colonization. Eventually Portugal laid claim to Brazil in South America, but the primary force in the Americas proved to be Spain, a presence that had profound consequences for both the colonizer and the colonized.

Soon after the Spanish conquest of the Americas, the exploitation of native peoples began. To provide for the orderly development of the new continents, the Spanish introduced the *encomienda* system. According to this system, settlers were given grants of land and native labor, in return providing for the Christian instruction and protection of their workers. In reality, the indigenous people were brutally exploited in mining and other operations, prompting the rapid decline in their populations. The Potosi mine in present-day Bolivia stands as a fearful example of how the system quickly went awry. Though the mine became the primary supplier of Spanish silver, this wealth came at the expense of the native civilizations.

The indigenous population found a defender in the Dominican monk Bartolome de Las Casas (1484–1566), whose *Brief Account of the Devastation of the Indies* (1542) highlighted the issues of abuse and devastation. Las Casas's account eventually led to the New Laws, which reformed the *encomienda* system. Unfortunately, it was too late; most of the native population had been decimated by neglect and disease. The resulting labor shortage led to another negative legacy from exploration: African slavery. Though the slave trade dated back to the early 15th century, it didn't take off until exploitation of the Americas increased demand for menial labor. In all, approximately 12 million Africans suffered the horrors of the so-called Middle Passage across the Atlantic in Portuguese, Spanish, and ultimately Dutch and English ships. Though Africans were able to create new cultures in a new land, the issue of African slavery has left a deep imprint on the history of four continents.

Of all the colonial empires, Spain's operated in the most centralized fashion. Policies were administered directly, if sometimes slowly, by the Council of the Indies, under the control of the Spanish monarchy. Imperial administrators tended to be loyal to Spain rather than to the Spanish Americans they governed. The New World was divided into two viceroyalties—New Mexico and Peru—which were subdivided into captaincies-general for more direct control. To assist and oversee royal governors, *audiencias* served as advisory bodies and courts. To settle in Spanish America, one was required to adhere to the Catholic faith. Over time, remaining native peoples were converted to Catholicism, and the hierarchical structure of the Church was transferred to Spanish America, resulting even today in the largest concentration of Catholics in the world.

The Meeting of Two Worlds: Effects[3]

Intellectual and Cultural Impact

A key impact of exploration was the **Columbian Exchange**, the cultural and economic diffusion of practices and goods across the Atlantic. Exploration efforts were richly rewarded with a bounty of new crops and goods from the Americas, such as potatoes, tobacco, tomatoes, cocoa, gold and silver, beans, corn, peanuts, and possibly syphilis. Many of the crops and animals now considered natural to the Americas, in fact, originated in the Old World: horses, cattle, sheep, pigs, honey bees, rice, wheat, sugar cane, and, most notoriously, diseases. These last, including measles, smallpox, typhus, and malaria, decimated native peoples, who lacked immunity to such infectious pestilences. Along with abusive treatment, by the end of the 16th century the thriving populations of the Americas had been reduced by 90%, though historians disagree on the pre-1492 population levels (between 20–70 million).

Colonization also reoriented Europe's intellectual world. Contact between two previously unknown civilizations was bound to prompt all parties to rethink some of their cultural assumptions. First, Europeans set about creating new maps that more accurately depicted the world in precise, scientific, and abstract space (e.g., with grids and keys). The pioneer in this field was

3 SKILL SET
The Columbian Exchange offers a rich opportunity for applying HTS. First, you may wish to create a Venn diagram to compare and contrast its effects on both Europe and the Americas (COMP). Also, the Exchange sparked changes in the economy, which leads to a CCOT analysis. Finally, to help you develop your Argumentation (ARG) ability, try writing a brief statement of how 1492 represents a turning point in world economic and political history (PER).

Gerardus Mercator (1512–1594), a Flemish mapmaker who succeeded in mass-producing the first globes and also rendering a three-dimensional space (the earth) on a two-dimensional surface—the still-standard map that continues to bears his name. Also, even though Europeans approached indigenous peoples with little regard for their cultures, some used the encounter to reevaluate and even critique European society. Probably influenced by Las Casas, Michel de Montaigne (1533–1592), a French lawyer and inventor of the essay, introduced a new skeptical attitude toward European customs, even suggesting that native cannibalism was no worse than many of the atrocities of Europe's religious wars. A final legacy of 1492 was the creation of entirely new cultures in the New World from the mixing of the old. From the racial blending of the *mestizos* to the religious practices of voodoo to the Gullah and Creole dialects and finally to the music of jazz, the Americas continue to bear the legacy of exploration and colonization.

4 THEME MUSIC

This section provides a brief conceptual synopsis of the PP theme, particularly how Europe moved from a subsistence agriculture system to one based on money and capital. Be careful not to overstate the changes, as much of traditional economy persisted in regions and localities well into the 19th century.

The Commercial Revolution, Phase I[4]

Europe's colonization of the Americas and its creation of maritime empires led to significant changes within Europe. We examine some of the economic and social changes here; in a later chapter, we'll take a turn at the diplomatic and political results.

The economic result of exploration and colonization is termed the **Commercial Revolution**—an acceleration in global trade involving new goods and techniques. Often underestimated as a topic, the Commercial Revolution fed the growth of modern society. Two of these changes were an increase in Europe's population (to about 90 million in 1600, finally surpassing the pre-plague level) and a steady rise in prices. This latter development promoted a money-oriented economy, which further undermined the feudal system in western Europe. Though traditionally the **Price Revolution** was attributed to the importation of precious metals from New World, more recent interpretations have stressed population growth as the source. With rising demand chasing a limited supply of goods, prices for scarce products were bid up. Landowners benefited from the inflation, unless they had leased their land via long-term rents, and many turned to the production of cash crops (those for sale, not consumption). A new class of independent farmers, outside the feudal structure and focused on producing for the market, began to arise. In England, they were called the **gentry** (gentlemen), and they attempted to imitate the lifestyles of the lords and nobles. Like the bourgeoisie, they were resented by those below and scorned by those above.

Traditionally the **guilds** dominated the production of goods in towns and cities; workers owned the capital *and* performed the labor. With the increase in profit from trade, merchants began to invest their earnings in long-distance business ventures, often ending up in banking like the Medici in Italy or the Fuggers in Germany. Families such as the Fuggers formed close relationships with monarchs, as with Charles V, loaning money for state enterprises such as mining. Eventually larger banks were formed from the resources of numerous investors. One of the more prominent, the Bank of Amsterdam (founded in 1609), fueled the commercial dominance of the Netherlands. By this time, bankers ignored the traditional Christian prohibition against usury (the charging of interest on loans); the profits were just too great to ignore.

The separation of capital and labor is a major feature of **capitalism**, and the divergence became more pronounced beginning in the 16th and 17th centuries. Entrepreneurs began investing in their own manufacturing enterprises. To sidestep the guild structure, they provided (or "put out") the raw materials to rural families eager to supplement their marginal incomes by finishing goods. This was especially pronounced in the textile industries, where the various steps of manufacture—spinning, carding, weaving—were mechanized at different times. The **putting-out system (cottage industry)** signaled the decline of the guild structure and served as an intermerdiate step toward factory production in the late 18th century. Other industries did not fit neatly into the guild structure and also received stimulus from the new capital—printing, bookmaking, mining, shipbuilding, and weapons manufacture.

During the late 16th and into the 17th centuries, Europeans gained a strong appetite for luxury and staple items from overseas. As the goods became more common, such as tea and coffee, they gradually exercised a cultural influence on European styles and diet, often beginning with the aristocracy and seeping down through the bourgeoisie into the lower classes. The New World tomato and potato took a strong hold on European diets, though the latter had to overcome resistance to its appearance and taste. Eventually, however, the potato became the salvation of many nations, especially Russia, Germany, and Ireland, because of its versatility and ease of cultivation. Coffee- and tea-drinking provided opportunities for socializing outside more traditional networks (in <u>coffeehouses</u>) and also gave workers a jolt of midday energy, particularly when combined with the largest profit-maker of the era—<u>sugar</u>.

A status-conscious aristocracy and its middle-class imitators craved symbols of style and status. This meant silks and <u>porcelain</u> from China, calicoes (light, brightly colored cotton cloth) from India, and **spices** from the East Indies. Hunger for luxury goods fed the Commercial Revolution; competition among nations encouraged new trading techniques and the search for new goods, carried in the merchant marines of trading powers[5].

To pool financial resources and share risk, investors created joint-stock companies. Of these, the <u>Dutch</u> and <u>British East India Companies</u> (both founded in the first decade of the 17th century) were the most famous and profitable. Such companies gained monopoly status from government charters and were expected to provide an increase in trade as well as imports of gold and silver. Gradually the Dutch pushed the Portuguese out of the East Indies and, along with England, began to challenge the dominance of the Iberian empires. Colonial competition among the Netherlands, England, France, and Spain accelerated throughout the 17th and 18th centuries, culminating with a series of decisive commercial wars.

Global trade on a large scale fed the rise of commercial capitalism in Europe. The credit, financial, and mercantile systems described above defined the nature of capitalism until the rise of mechanized mass production in textiles in the late 18th century. In an effort to exploit the potential for wealth, European nations adopted the economic theory of **mercantilism**. This theory—which generally guided the policies of most nations until the *laissez-faire* ideas of Adam Smith—was based on three essential tenets:

- *Scarcity*—The total amount of global resources and wealth are limited. Therefore, any advances by one nation come at the expense of another; trade is a "zero-sum game."

- *Wealth = specie (hard money)*—Mercantilists held that real wealth equaled the amount of gold and silver flowing into a nation. Given this assumption, governments attempted to promote exports through trade monopolies, acquisition of colonies, and subsidies at the same time that they limited imports, via tariffs, trade restrictions, and war aimed at an enemy's mercantile potential.

- *Government intervention*—Though governments did not generally own the means of production, they did actively intervene to promote national objectives. States provided incentives to key industries, sought new colonies, and worked to establish national markets by building roads and canals and abolishing localism. The ultimate goal of these efforts proved to be a favorable balance of trade, i.e., more specie flowing into the nation than flowing out. In the next chapter, we'll examine the mercantilist policies of specific nations.

Changing Social Structures, 1500–1700

Early modern society experienced significant change alongside entrenched stability. Many of the social structures of the period 1500–1700 will seem alien to contemporary students. As you read through this section, try to step outside your assumptions and judgments. Capturing the mentalities of early modern Europeans requires sensitivity to historical context, aided by a vivid imagination. This period serves as a rich area for questions on the AP exam, though it is often overlooked by students. As you study the period, try to establish strong grounding in *specific* developments that influenced the lives of Europeans. When addressing any period, locate it clearly in time and place. Avoid expressions like "throughout history" or "women have always cooked and cleaned," as they reveal an anachronistic ("misplaced") understanding of the past.

5 EXAMPLE BASE

These products became key consumer goods, but in some instances, they also changed cultures. For example. the European desire for sugar stimulated the slave trade and plantation economies in the Americas. Coffee and tea led to new venues for public discussion of ideas and culture, which relates to the SP theme ("other institutions of power").

Demographic Changes and Social Structures

As noted previously, an increasing population caused a structural change in early modern European society. Until about 1550, this increase helped bring fertile land under cultivation as Europe recovered from the Black Death. After 1550, however, Europe's population began to strain existing resources, resulting in the Price Revolution described earlier. Population continued to increase throughout the rest of the century, but poor weather, war, lack of resources, and periodic famine caused a decline in population throughout the 17th century. The discrepancy between population and the resources to sustain it is termed the "**Malthusian trap6**," after the 18th-century British political economist. In fact, some nations, such as Spain, experienced a steep drop in population, which seriously hampered its economy and threatened its great-power status. Though governments did not keep accurate census data until the late 18th century, local studies have revealed the serious negative impact of poor economic conditions on daily life, as revealed by a serious drop in marriages and births during hard times. For the big picture—Europe's population maxed out at 100 million about 1550, dropped to around 80 million by 1650, and had recovered to 100 million again by 1700.

Economic developments altered the class structure. Though the traditional system was not overturned, some changes were evident by 1700. The aristocracy maintained its primary position despite the addition of new blood, that is, members of the middle class who were able to acquire noble status through the purchase of an office, which often became hereditary with a payment of a tax (called the *paulette* in France). Sometimes resented by the older nobles ("nobles of the sword"), these new nobles were termed the "nobles of the robe" and played a more important role as governments expanded their bureaucratic functions.

Below the nobles were the ***bourgeoisie***, or burghers, meaning those who lived in towns. Technically outside the feudal structure, the middle class made their livings in a variety of economic activities. The middle class was by no means a monolithic group. Some owned large tracts of land and lived off of rents, others traded goods as merchants, and still others filled out the growing professions, such as physicians, clergy, and attorneys. In addition, towns also thrived on the labor of the lower middle class or *petit bourgeoisie*, who labored as shopkeepers, artisans, grocers, and store owners. As the money economy and world trade expanded in the 16th and 17th centuries, the middle class increased, though they were not as yet able to translate these numbers into political power.

Agriculture and the Countryside

The lives of the vast majority of Europeans were dictated by the seasons and the paces of agricultural life. Agriculture was generally practiced in a village setting, with decisions made communally. This **subsistence agricultural system**—growing enough to feed the village with little left over for export—was defined by the **three-field crop rotation** system in the north and the **two-field** system in the south. In these systems, one section of land was left fallow (uncultivated) to allow for replenishment of the soil, limiting full use of resources. Each village included a commons area, used for livestock grazing, wood-gathering, hunting, or eking out a marginal existence for the landless. Throughout the 16th century, England began selling off common land for purchase by wealthy landowners. The practice had the double effect of creating a new non-aristocratic class of wealthy landowners, the **gentry**, as well as increasing the numbers of landless poor, who either had to contract out their labor or move to the cities. Between these two groups stood the yeomanry, small freeholders who owned their land. As often occurs with economic changes, some took advantage and improved their status while others found their already marginal existence threatened further.

The paths of western and eastern Europe began to diverge further during the 17th century. As most of the peasants of western Europe were freed from serfdom and other feudal obligations, those of eastern Europe were drawn more tightly into a highly codified system of laws governing an individual's life. While western peasants continued to owe their lords manorial

6 SKILL SET

Students often overlook the issue of demographics (study of population) throughout the course. A key figure on the topic is Thomas Malthus, who introduced a theory that explained why populations cannot expand progressively in the long term. You are strongly encouraged to trace European population developments throughout the course, especially in explaining the changes and continuities (CCOT) in Europe's interaction with its environment.

obligations, such as the payment of taxes, fees for the use of ovens and mills, and the hated labor service (called *corvee* in France, *robot* in the east), they were generally free to leave the land and could call on a set of traditional prerogatives to protect themselves against excessive landlords. Such was not the case in eastern Europe as, for example, **serfdom** became state law in the mid-17th century in Russia. Large manors, often exploiting the labor of up to 100,000 serfs, dominated nations such as Poland and Hungary, where nobles made up 10% of the population, compared to 2%–3% in France or England.

The Life of the Towns

Though only 10%–20% of Europeans lived in towns or cities, urban centers played an economic and a cultural role out of proportion to their numbers. Compared with our contemporary individualistic spirit, early modern Europeans were embedded in a web of social relationships—guild, village, neighborhood, church, city, class, family. In fact, popular metaphors for society construed it as a complex organism, with each group playing the appropriate role assigned it—the Great Chain of Being or the Body Politic. Institutions tended to be **hierarchical** in theory, though traditions and the desire to avoid social conflict often prevented social superiors from becoming arbitrary. In this period, cities attracted from the countryside both landless laborers and those seeking opportunity. By the end of the 16th century, most cities could no longer adequately handle the influx of new residents. The working poor comprised the majority of city dwellers and survived by finding odd jobs (e.g., unloading ships, hard manual labor, or domestic service) or by begging.

By 1550, when the economy was stressed, poverty reached crisis proportions in many European nations. Many of the poor resorted to begging; some even maimed themselves to garner sympathy. Traditional religious and charitable institutions were overwhelmed, so governments began to enact strict regulations that distinguished between the "**deserving**" (disabled, elderly, children) and "undeserving" (able-bodied males) **poor**. England's Poor Law of 1601, for example, provided charitable relief but also seriously punished those who violated its regulations.

Crime often accompanied poverty. Both property and violent crime increased in the period 1500–1700. Because governments lacked modern police forces and prisons, they tended to inflict cruel and often hideous punishments on captured criminals as an example to others. Public executions were common, even for property crimes such as theft. Not until the 18th century did reformers call for the changes in the legal and penal system.

Family and Communal Life[7]

As today, the most basic institution in European life was the family. In western Europe, the **nuclear family** (parents, children, and perhaps an elderly grandparent) predominated. Because taxes in nations like Russia and Hungary were assessed on households, extended families proved more common. Unlike Renaissance Italy, the average age of marriage for men was mid- to late 20s and early to mid-20s for women, though these averages increased in hard economic times. Women of the aristocracy tended to marry somewhat earlier and, on average, experienced eight to nine live births, whereas women of the middle and lower classes experienced on average six to seven live births. Part of this disparity can be explained by the use of wet nurses among the upper classes (breast-feeding tends to dampen fertility). Old age was rare because of high infant mortality and low life expectancy. As a result, remarriage and blended families were common. Despite the stereotype of female labor as primarily domestic, women were, in fact, integral to the family economy. A wife's death often drove a widower to remarry as soon as possible. In artisan households, for example, women supervised the workers, kept the books, and marketed the products.

By standard interpretation, the concept of childhood did not exist until its invention during the Enlightenment. In fact, evidence indicates that in the early modern period, parents did love their children and considered the loss of a child a tragedy. Nonetheless, children were expected to contribute labor to the family unit—often overseen by the father—and were subjected to corporal punishments for disobedience. Also, keep in mind that neither society nor parents

7 THEME MUSIC

Be careful of turning the Individual and Society (IS) theme into a collection of descriptions. Beginning with this period, try to establish a baseline of practices, customs, and attitudes for issues of gender, family, child-rearing, and village life. Also, be careful not to project modern stereotypes onto the past.

provided compulsory schooling or age-appropriate toys, reading materials, or clothing for children. In most nations, children did not earn full legal rights at a specific age, but only when they established their own residences. Female children were expected to bring a dowry into a marriage (land, furniture, personal property, cash), though in Germany, for example, tradition protected a father from arbitrarily depriving a daughter of her inheritance.

Early modern leisure differs significantly from our modern diversions. Whereas our forms of amusement tend to be consumptive (shopping, amusement parks, dining, etc.) and in small groups, Europeans of the 16th and 17th centuries engaged in **communal leisure**. Early-modern rhythms of life were governed by the seasons; periods of extended labor were followed by those of extended celebration. In Catholic nations, the **church calendar**, with its cycle of saints' feast days and rituals, dictated the pace of work and leisure. Carnival, the period right before Lenten fasting and penance, served as the largest of these festivals. For over a week, villagers and townspeople consumed large amounts of food and alcohol, while playing traditional games and engaging in a higher-than-normal amount of sexual activity. In addition, classes and genders switched roles for the "world turned upside down," which played the important role of letting off discontent in a ritualized way before returning to the normal hierarchy. With the Reformation, many Protestant and even some Catholic areas tried to restrain what they considered the excesses of the practice. Finally, to ensure social conformity, many localities imposed rituals of public humiliation on those who stepped outside of community standards, such as a husband who could not control his wife or a woman who committed adultery. In France, this practice was called *charivari* and in England skimmington.

Witchcraft Persecution

A striking phenomenon of early modern Europe was the **persecution of witches**. The height of the scare occurred from 1580 to 1700, during which approximately 100,000 people, mostly women, were executed for being in league with the devil. The practice strikes our modern sensibilities as backward and barbaric. However, we should try to understand what beliefs and socioeconomic conditions gave rise to the phenomenon. First, almost all Europeans, even the educated, believed in witches and demons. Increased Bible-reading because of the Protestant Reformation emphasized both the reality of the devil and the supposedly weak and credulous nature of women. Second, the early modern period experienced rapid social and economic change—enclosure, religious wars, poverty, crime, and overpopulation—that tended to undermine or challenge traditional practices. Third, religious passions were inflamed by the Protestant and Catholic Reformations and resulting religious wars, creating suspicion among communities, especially in regions divided by religious belief. Finally, those targeted for accusation tended to exist on the margins of the community—the poor, older women, those living alone—and thus beyond the reach of social norms. Women, in particular, were believed to have special knowledge of and powers over the body (because of their role in childbirth) and often supplemented family incomes by preparing traditional cures or potions. In fact, some may have even considered themselves to practice white magic. With the general acceptance of scientific explanations by elites, the witch trials declined markedly after 1720 and were almost gone by 1750[8].

8 SKILL SET
You may find the topic of witchcraft fascinating. It is, but make sure to avoid presentism, i.e., judging the past by present standards. Turn the topic into a Causation (CAUS) question and create a visual to show how and why the phenomenon accelerated (after 1550) and then faded (after 1680). Work toward capturing complexity in your portrayal.

The Religious Wars

One of the more complex and challenging topics you will study this year is the religious wars. Amidst the numerous personalities and rapidly changing motives, try to keep your eye on the key issues: the causes, nature, and end results of the wars. Though historians term these "religious" wars, each conflict was also influenced by political and territorial ambitions.

Philip II: Catholic Protector

At the center of the religious conflicts of the second half of the 16th century stood Philip II (1556–1598), ruler of Spain and the Low Countries, parts of Italy, and the New World. Like his

Habsburg father, Charles I (V as Holy Roman Emperor), Philip saw himself as the political protector of Catholicism in Europe, though Philip lacked Charles's more cosmopolitan background. Philip was a Spaniard and was influenced by that nation's strong Catholic tradition and crusading mentality. El Escorial, Philip's palace on the arid plains outside Madrid, reflected the ruler's personality. Part residence, part monastery and religious retreat, the Escorial formed the central governing point of a huge empire stretching across oceans. Philip insisted on overseeing even the minutest details of government, earning him the nickname the "King of Paper," after his habit of reviewing each document from his diverse realm. Philip's first area of concern was France, even though he did not directly rule that nation.

The French Wars of Religion

France's long series of religious conflicts (1560–1598) grew from religious *and* political roots. Despite Francis I's (1516–1547) attempts to stamp out the spread of Protestant faiths, Calvinism continued to grow in his kingdom, often indirectly aided by the patronage of his sister, Marguerite of Navarre (1492–1529), a deeply religious woman and author of several controversial stories and religious works. Calvinism found fertile ground among the French aristocracy in particular, perhaps because they already believed themselves "the elect." By 1560, 40% of French nobles advocated the Huguenot faith (as French Calvinists were called), which, because nobles held important positions in the government and military, posed a threat to the Catholic Valois monarchy. These religious causes were exacerbated when the strong French king Henry II (1547–1559) died tragically in a jousting accident. His death plunged France into a civil conflict over control of the throne *and* over France's religion.

The conflict in France is best viewed as a three-sided struggle. In the middle stood the Catholic Valois family, now led by Henry's widow, the moderate yet cunning Catherine de Medicis (1519–1589). Like the future Henry IV and Elizabeth I of England, Catherine advocated political stability over religious orthodoxy, being known as a *politique*. In addition, Catherine attempted to maintain the throne for her three weak sons—Francis II (1559–1560), Charles IX (1560–1574), and Henry III (1574–1589). Against the Catholic Valois, on one side, stood a faction of Protestant nobles who laid claim to the throne through Henry Bourbon (of Navarre) and wished free worship for those of the Huguenot faith. Also opposed to the Valois and with the backing of the Jesuits, the papacy, and Philip II were the Guise family, or ultra-Catholics. The ultra-Catholics viewed the Valois monarchy as weak in the face of the Protestant threat and wished to restore a more strongly Catholic king.

Religious conflict in France was played out in a series of 13 short wars, with numerous attempts at compromise by Catherine and her sons. One of these attempts at compromise led to one of the worst atrocities during this violent period. In 1572, Henry Bourbon agreed to marry Catherine de Medicis's daughter as a sign of reconciliation. However, during the wedding celebration in Paris, rumors flared that Protestants were plotting to take over the government. What followed was a slaughter of the Protestant nobles, in Paris and throughout France, known as the St. Bartholomew's Day Massacre. In all, approximately 10,000 French Protestants were killed, though Henry Bourbon escaped by converting to Catholicism (a conversion he quickly renounced). The event seemed to show the corruption of the Valois monarchy and deepened resistance to it.

The final stage of France's civil war is called the War of the Three Henries. In 1588, Henry Guise (leader of the ultra-Catholics) took the city of Paris, threatening the Valois hold on the nation. Henry III, of Valois, felt he had no alternative but to form an alliance against the ultra-Catholics with Henry Bourbon, whom he promised to make next in line to the throne. On the pretext of compromise, both Henries invited Guise to the palace and had him assassinated. In reprisal, a fanatical monk killed Henry III in 1589, making Henry Bourbon (IV) ruler of France. However, Henry IV's (1589–1610) way to Paris was barred by Spanish troops, and he would spend the next decade winning control of the nation. To bring peace to France, Henry converted back to Catholicism (the majority religion of France), supposedly saying "Paris is worth a mass," and then issued the **Edict of Nantes**, which allowed Huguenots to practice their religion outside Paris and to fortify towns to protect their hard-won liberties. Over the next several years, Henry IV became one of the most beloved monarchs in French history and established a strong Bourbon dynasty, laying the foundations for absolutism.

9 SKILL SET

You will notice the complexity of motives, changing courses, and groups/individuals involved in the religious wars. To prevent yourself from bogging down in minutia, focus on a major interpretative question–the relationship between religious and political or economic motives for the wars. Take a position and defend it, using examples from any of the conflicts in this section (INTR & EVARG).

The Wars of Spain[9]

An important part of Philip's inheritance was Burgundy, the 17 provinces known as the Low Countries, where his father Charles had been raised. Philip was an outsider to those in the Low Countries, who wished to maintain their traditional decentralized political structure and religious freedoms. Philip's policies eventually sparked a revolt, which had at its base religious, political, and economic causes. First, Philip attempted to increase taxes to fund the cost of the Spanish empire, thus alienating many in the middle classes. Next, Philip determined to stamp out heresy by tightening the church structure in the Netherlands (another name for Burgundy) and by employing the Inquisition. Because the 17 provinces stood astride important trade routes and had a tradition of religious tolerance, they attracted many adherents of Calvinism.

In response to Philip's tax policy, discontented Burgundians in 1566 directed their ire against the symbols of Catholicism, smashing statues and church decorations, in what was known as the iconoclast revolt. Philip sent the Duke of Alba to the Netherlands to crush the revolt. Alba established the so-called Council of Blood and executed a number of leading Protestant nobles, which only further inflamed the provinces. Soon a leader of the revolt emerged—William "the Silent" (1533–1584–from the House of Orange in Holland), so-called because of his reluctance to discuss his strategies with others. William was aided by the "sea beggars," ships that engaged in acts of piracy against the Spanish. When Spanish troops pillaged the city of Antwerp in 1576 (they had not been paid because Spain lacked funds), all 17 provinces called for the end of Spanish rule in the Netherlands, an event known as the Pacification of Ghent. This action caused Philip to change tactics, and it overshadowed the great Spanish naval victory over Ottoman forces in 1571 at Lepanto, which cleared the western Mediterranean of the Muslim threat.

Philip appointed his nephew Alexander Farnese (1545–1592), the Duke of Parma and a brilliant military leader, to subdue the Netherlands through reward and punishment. Farnese succeeded by 1578 in prying away the southern 10 provinces from the revolt and winning their allegiance to Spain with the Union of Arras. These provinces were populated primarily by the French-speaking Walloons. In response, the northern, mostly Dutch-speaking Flemish 7 provinces in 1581 formed the Union of Utrecht with the intent of separating from Spain. Throughout the conflict, Elizabeth I of England quietly provided the Dutch with financial and naval aid, including attacks on Spanish shipping by the "sea dogs" such as Sir Francis Drake (c. 1540–1596). By 1588, Philip was determined to end English meddling and teach Elizabeth, his one-time sister-in-law who had spurned his offer of marriage, a lesson. Philip's Spanish Armada did not have a chance against the more maneuverable English ships and because his plan for an invasion was too complex. Spain's "confident hope of a miracle" turned into a rout in the "Protestant wind," which signaled the rise of England and the relative decline of Spain as maritime powers, though Philip would raise other armadas and continue to fight on.

Though Philip never admitted defeat in the Netherlands, his successor Philip III in 1609 signed a Twelve Years' truce with the Union of Utrecht, which all but granted the Dutch independence. The southern 10 provinces remained loyal and became known as the Spanish Netherlands. Once the strongest nation in Europe, Spain slowly declined throughout the 17th century. There were several reasons for this loss of power. First, the Spanish had overextended themselves politically and militarily, taxing their subjects excessively and allowing the nation to fall behind economically. Second, the Iberian crusading mentality led the Spanish to persecute talented minorities, like the *moriscos* (Muslim converts to Catholicism), who were driven out in the early 17th century. Finally, internal revolts over high taxes and government centralization, combined with population decline, sapped Spain's internal energy. By the end of the Thirty Years' War, to which we now turn, Spain's *siglo de oro* (Golden Age) was over, an important lesson for nations that believe that power entails invincibility.

The Thirty Years' War, 1618–1648

Prior to the world wars of the 20th century, the most devastating conflict in European history was the Thirty Years' War. The conflict began as a civil war over religion in Germany but escalated into a continental conflagration involving territorial and political ambitions. Years before war started, German Catholics and Protestants geared up for battle by forming alliances with outside powers. These alliances—the Protestant Union and Catholic League—ensured that when war did come, it would involve the great powers of Europe.

Following the Peace of Augsburg (1555), Germany divided between Lutheran and Catholic states. However, the treaty did not take into account the fastest growing denomination after 1560—Calvinism. When the ruler of the Palatinate, Frederick V (1610–1623), converted to Calvinism, the delicate religious balance in Germany seemed threatened. It became apparent that neither Protestant nor Catholic leaders had any intention of treating Augsburg as a permanent settlement to Germany's religious division. What complicated matters was the elective nature of the Holy Roman Emperor, nominally the political leader of Catholicism and still a position of importance. According to the Golden Bull of 1356, the emperor was elected by seven states, three of which were controlled by Catholic rulers and three by Protestants. To gain control of the last electoral state (Bohemia), the next Habsburg in line (the traditional imperial ruling house)—Ferdinand II (1620–1637)—promised the Bohemian nobles he would respect their religious liberties if they would elect him the king of Bohemia (whereby he could in turn vote for himself as emperor). After Ferdinand was elected king in 1618, he betrayed his promise to the Bohemian nobles, thus initiating the conflict.

The event that set off the conflict was the so-called Defenestration of Prague (1618), in which Bohemian nobles tossed two imperial officials out of the Prague castle. Following this act of rebellion, the nobles elected Frederick V of Palatine as their new king. Subsequent fighting is often divided by historians into four distinct phases, which are outlined below. You are encouraged to take note of the shifting motivations and alliances of states.

Phase	Events	Groups/Leaders	Results
Bohemian, 1618–1625	The Protestant forces under Frederick V were defeated soundly at White Mountain. Once Ferdinand II (Habsburg) was elected emperor, he confiscated the lands of the rebellious Bohemian nobles, redistributed them, and then brought the Counter-Reformation to Bohemia.	*Frederick V of Palatine *Ferdinand II (Habsburg), Holy Roman Emperor	Catholic forces emerged victorious as Bavaria, leader of the Catholic League, took over much of the Electorate Palatine.

Phase	Events	Groups/Leaders	Results
Danish, 1625–1629	Christian IV, the Lutheran king of Denmark, entered the conflict both to support the Protestant cause and to gain territory in the Baltic. Wallenstein defeated Christian, thus giving imperial forces the upper hand.	*Christian IV (1588–1648) of Denmark *Albrecht von Wallenstein (1583–1634)—unpredictable leader of imperial forces who funded his own war machine.	Ferdinand confidently issued the Edict of Restitution (1629), which returned all confiscated Church lands since 1517, angering Protestant and Catholic nobles alike who had gained from this confiscation. The Habsburgs appeared on the verge of completing a centuries-old dream of centralizing power in central Europe.
Swedish, 1629–1635	Sweden's great military leader, Gustavus Adolphus, entered the conflict to revive the Protestant cause and to secure trade in the Baltic. At Breitenfield and Lützen, Gustavus succeeded in defeating the imperial forces and brought the war to the Catholic south. In an example of the war's horrifying effect, the city of Magdeburg was sacked and burned by imperial forces, killing thousands of civilians.	*Gustavus Adolphus (1611–1632) *Cardinal Richelieu (1585–1642)—advisor under Louis XIII (1610–1643) who brought France into the conflict to reduce the power of the Habsburgs. *Wallenstein was assassinated with the approval of the emperor for negotiating independently with the Swedes.	To end the war, the emperor (now Ferdinand III—1637–1657) revoked the Edict of Restitution and signed in 1635 the Peace of Prague with the other German states. However, the fighting continued and devolved into a continental struggle between the Spanish Habsburgs vs. the Swedes and French (also supported by the Dutch).
Franco-Swedish, 1635–1648	In the most violent phase of the war, Germany became the battleground for the territorial and political ambitions of its neighbors. At the battle of Rocroi (in the Spanish Netherlands) in 1643, the French soundly defeated the Spanish, signaling the rise of the former as the major military power in Europe.	*Philip IV (1621–1665) of Spain—continued to use Spain's dwindling resources to fight against France, despite facing internal rebellions by Portugal (which regained its independence in 1640) and the province of Catalonia.	By the end of the conflict, all sides were exhausted. However, peace negotiations dragged on for years before the war was finally ended in 1648.

The **Peace of Westphalia** (1648), which ended the Thirty Years' War, marks an important turning point in European politics and diplomacy. After this point, the **Holy Roman Empire no longer played a major role** in the affairs of central Europe, though the Austrian Habsburgs turned to the east in subsequent years to revive their imperial fortunes. The treaty formally recognized the independence of Switzerland and the Dutch Republic, as well as reflected a shift in the balance of power. Emerging stronger were France, Sweden, Prussia (in Germany), and the Dutch. Losing energy were the Holy Roman Empire and Spain, which now fell into the rank of the second-tier powers, beset by a declining population and economy[10].

Historians often view the Westphalia settlement as the "final nail in the coffin of the Middle Ages" because it recognized the sovereignty of each nation over its own religious affairs and ended any hopes of religious unity of Europe. Indeed, the papacy was virtually ignored in the peace negotiations and would play a sharply reduced role in future diplomacy. Though Europe as a whole moved toward a grudging religious tolerance, Germany was decimated. Estimates vary, but Germany's population may have declined by 20%–33%. In areas of heavy fighting, entire towns ceased to exist, and economic life was severely curtailed. Central Europe was left a power vacuum that would soon be filled by the emergence of two competing German powers—Prussia and Austria—whose fortunes will be traced in the next chapter.

As a result of the Thirty Years' War, Europe underwent a **military revolution**. Gunpowder and the foot-soldier (pikemen and musketeers) played a major role, with the **infantry** square formation employing massed volleys (firing at the same time). Tactics became more flexible, with the use of lighter and more mobile cavalry, pioneered by Gustavus Adolphus. In addition, to fund the increasing costs of war and oversee it complexity, governments grew larger and more centralized. Warfare had become the primary function of European states, who often spent up to 80% of their budgets on fielding, training, supplying, and of course, using armies (to meet their political objectives). As we'll see in Chapter 7, this trend caused a further expansion of the state's power in the age of absolutism.

10 THEME MUSIC

The Thirty Years' War and its settlement reveal key issues in the SP theme—the relationship between church and state, the role of warfare in expansion of state power, and the shifting balance of power among the nations of Europe. Be prepared to explain briefly each of these relationships.

Additional Resources

Felipe Fernandez-Armesto, *Columbus* (1991)—Interesting study of a complex figure, includes provocative interpretations.

Peter Burke, *Popular Culture in Early Modern Europe* (1994)—A vivid and engaging study of the topic.

Carlo Cipolla, *Before the Industrial Revolution: European Society and Economy, 1000–1700* (rev. 1994)—A wealth of information and data on every major feature of economic activity prior to the 18th century.

Alfred Crosby, *The Columbian Exchange: Biological and Cultural Consequences of 1492* (1972)—For those of a scientific bent, this book explains how colonization affected the world exchange of plants, animals, and diseases.

Richard S. Dunn, *The Age of Religious Wars, 1559–1715* (1979)—Another fine survey from the Norton History of the Modern World.

J.H. Elliott, *Europe Divided, 1559–98* (rev. 2000)—Fast-paced and informative introduction to European politics during the period.

Peter Laslett, *The World We Have Lost: England Before the Industrial Revolution* (1983)—A study of family life in England.

Brian Levack, *The Witch-Hunt in Early Modern Europe* (1987)—Surveys the many explanations for the phenomenon.

Steven Ozment, *The Burgermeister's Daughter: Scandal in a Sixteenth-Century German Town* (1997)—Told like a novel, this book shows how the historian works to recreate the features of everyday life.

Geoffrey Parker, *Europe in Crisis, 1598–1648* (1979)—Comprehensive overview of the many complex developments in European politics in this period.

J.H. Parry, *The Age of Reconnaissance: Discovery, Exploration, and Settlement, 1450–1650* (rev. 1981)—Brief introduction to the voyages of exploration and their effects.

Peter N. Stearns, ed., *Encyclopedia of European Social History, 1350–2000* (2000)—If you can find it at a nearby library, these volumes are a wonderful resource on all areas of social history.

http://www.encyclopedia.com/topic/Thirty_Years_War.aspx—Provides an overview of the Thirty Years' War.

http://yaleglobal.yale.edu/about/food.jsp—From Yale University, this site examines changes in food regimes as a result of the Columbian Exchange.

PERIOD 1

Practice MC Questions

Questions 1–4 are based on the image below.

Theodore de Bry, French engraver, silver mines of Potosi (Bolivia), 1602

1. The scene above directly resulted from all of the following factors EXCEPT:

   A. the desire of European states to gain direct access to goods and wealth.

   B. European military superiority in the form of steel weapons and cannons.

   C. the spread of classical ideas depicting mythical ancient civilizations.

   D. advances in navigational and cartographic techniques and technologies.

2. In what way did the process depicted above most change the European economy in the 16th and 17th centuries?

   A. It stimulated the growth of a new landed elite, such as the gentry in England.

   B. It led to the development of a money-oriented and commercial economy.

   C. It motivated the nobles and states of Eastern Europe to codify serfdom.

   D. It reinforced the importance of hierarchy in determining economic standing.

3. In contrast to the scene above, the impact of exploration on Africa:

   A. led to the establishment of large territorial empires in Africa.

   B. did not involve competition in Africa among states for resources.

   C. had minimal effect on Africa's role in the world economy.

   D. led to the slave trade and plantation economies in the Americas.

4. An historian studying the topic of exploration would most likely use this source as evidence to make conclusions in which of the following areas?

   A. The motivations of Europeans in seeking colonies

   B. The impact of exploration on artistic styles

   C. The effect of colonization on indigenous peoples

   D. The effects of colonization on European rivalries

Questions 5–8 are based on the map below.

EUROPE, 1648

KEY
- Ottoman Empire
- Brandenburg-Prussia
- Austrian Habsburgs
- Swedish Dominions
- Spanish Monarchy
- Boundary of Holy Roman Empire

Dennis Sherman and Joyce Salisbury, *The West in the World: A History of Western Civilization* (New York: McGraw-Hill Education, 2014), p. 352.

5. All of the following caused the situation above EXCEPT:

   A. competition among nation-states for territory and power.

   B. rivalry between England and France over colonies.

   C. efforts by the Habsburgs to restore Catholic unity.

   D. pursuit of commercial dominance in the Baltic.

6. The settlement above confirmed which of the following?

   A. Spanish control of the Mediterranean

   B. State control over internal religious policy

   C. The dominance of the Holy Roman Empire

   D. Noble control of state and military institutions

7. Which of the following best expresses how the situation above represented a turning point in European politics and diplomacy?

   A. Commercial and professional groups solidified their control of the state.

   B. Atlantic states were able to focus on the expansion of American empires.

   C. With aid of the Jesuits, the papacy reestablished its diplomatic influence.

   D. Religion ceased to be a major source of conflict among European states.

8. The state that experienced the most significant loss of power from the treaty above was:

   A. England.

   B. France.

   C. Spain.

   D. Sweden.

See Chapter 18 for answers and explanations.

Short-Answer Question with Sample and Commentary

"Every political action was publicly cloaked in religious terms, but religion seemed to be used more and more to rationalize actions motivated by secular interests."

Hajo Holborn, historian, *A History of Modern Germany: The Reformation*, 1959

A. Choose TWO examples from the religious wars and explain how they <u>support</u> the interpretation above.

B. Choose ONE example from the religious wars and explain how it <u>contradicts</u> the interpretation above.

(HTS: Interpretation and Use of Evidence)

A. The historian thinks that religion was really just a cover for secular motives, like power. This seems to be the case during warfare of this era. During the Thirty Years' War, France supported the Protestant side when they were fighting in Germany. This was done to promote the power of the French state, since France was a mainly Catholic nation helping the opposite religious side.

   Also, the Dutch revolted against the Spanish because they wanted to follow their own political rule. Philip II tried to impose Spanish rule, and the Netherlands resented this, since the people there thought of him as a foreign power. They just wanted to do their own thing.

B. France had its own internal religious conflict. Political factors mattered, like the competition for the throne between the Valois and Bourbon branches. But the war was really about control of religion. That's why outside Catholic groups, like the Jesuits, got involved. They wanted to promote the cause of Catholic unity. So in that sense, the historian was wrong.

This student takes the right approach in getting to her point quickly and also indicating which parts of the question she is addressing. Though brief, each example provides adequate explanation to earn the point. First, the response correctly if in simplified fashion notes French actions during the Thirty Years' War in support of Protestant forces. The second part on the Dutch argues the primacy of political factors; even if the example could relate more explicitly back to the religious dimension, the explanation is apropos and earns the point. In Part B, the student correctly points out a religious element to the French civil conflict, a seeming contradiction to Holborn's argument regarding the secular priority of the so-called religious wars. 3 points

Hajo Holborn, *A History of Modern Germany: The Reformation* (Princeton, NJ: Princeton University Press, 1959), p. 306.

CHAPTER 6 The Scientific View of the World

It would be difficult to overestimate the importance of the Scientific Revolution to the history of humanity. To many historians, the advent of a mathematical, scientific view of the world marks the beginnings of our modern age. For centuries, the achievements of ancient Greece and Rome had established the standard of excellence and reference point for all knowledge. However, during Europe's Age of Genius in the 17th century, scientists and philosophers demonstrated that this classical heritage could be surpassed through the application of the scientific method. Scientific thinking has come to infect almost all intellectual disciplines; the result has been not only improvements in technology but the challenging of traditional religious, political, and intellectual perspectives. Modern science represents an intellectual tool of great power, though a power that can also be used to destroy[1].

1 THEME MUSIC

The bulk of this chapter addresses the OS theme; in fact, the Scientific Revolution establishes its central narrative, in that it provides the "objective knowledge" framework and demonstrates the power of scientific thinking to surpass ancient knowledge.

Key In Chapter 6 addresses the following KCs from the Course Description:

- **KC 1.1** The theories and methods of the Scientific Revolution and persistence of beliefs in alchemy and astrology.
- **KC 1.5** Debate over women's involvement in science; folk beliefs of causation.
- **KC 2.1** State patronage of science to promote its interests.
- **KC 2.3** Development of political theories based on natural law.

The Old Science

Prior to the 16th century, scientific thinking about motion, the cosmos, and the human body was dominated by Aristotle (4th-century B.C.E. philosopher), Ptolemy (2nd-century Greek astronomer), and **Galen** (2nd-century Greek physician). In essence, the worldview of these ancient Greeks was *qualitative*—humans could employ their logical and rational capacities to determine the nature of objects, and from there, describe their behavior. Greek thinking was absorbed into Christianity in the 13th century with Scholasticism, which thereafter dominated the investigations of natural philosophy, as science was usually called. Scholastics dealt first with definitions and general propositions and went on to deduce further structures of knowledge from these, including properties of the natural world.

Systematic observation, experimentation, and **mathematics** played a limited role in the Scholastic system. Therefore, the Aristotelian-Ptolemaic view of the cosmos relied on the "logical" view that the earth lay at the center of the universe with the moon, sun, other planets, and stars revolving around it along crystalline spheres in perfect circles. The heavens were made of a separate substance (the quintessence, or fifth substance, to distinguish it from earth, air, fire, and water) and moved in circles, because the sphere represented the perfect geometric shape, reflecting the perfection of the heavens. Earthly objects moved along straight lines and fell toward earth, not because of a mysterious force called gravity, but to be at one with the substance from which they were made. Each object demonstrated properties unique to its nature; thus, heavy objects were believed to fall faster because they contained more matter and thus moved more quickly to their natural resting place. Though the ancient Greek philosophers Pythagoras and Plato did believe mathematical harmonies underlie all of nature, ancient and medieval scientific thought did not contemplate the notion of universal laws that could be expressed through mathematical *equations*.

Ancient cosmology was reflected in views of human anatomy. Galen postulated that the human body contained **four humors**: blood, phlegm, yellow bile, and black bile. Each of these humors was associated with a particular temperament, so individuals dominated by blood, for example, tended to be sanguine, or optimistic and cheerful. Bodily disorders arose from an imbalance of humors. Treatment involved correcting this imbalance through purging (inducing vomiting) and bleeding. Regardless of these treatments' failures, such ideas held sway among physicians for centuries, whose studies revolved more around reading ancient texts than anatomical study or clinical work with patients. Church prohibitions on dissection probably hindered anatomical knowledge in this regard; though Leonardo da Vinci violated this taboo, his detailed sketches of the human body, as well as other amazing diagrams of flying machines, led to few practical consequences, as they were not pursued systematically or taken up by future scientists.

Several factors stimulated the development of new scientific approaches in the 16th century: the Renaissance interest in nature, the need for celestial navigation to support exploration, and the Catholic Church's interest in an accurate calendar. Though the old model had worked well for centuries, the discrepancy between its theories and actual observations grew, and could not be explained satisfactorily by continued reference to its assumptions.

Advances in Astronomy and Physics

There are moments when ideas can change the world—literally. Such was the case with **Nicolaus Copernicus's** (1473–1543) *On the Revolutions of the Heavenly Spheres*, published just before the author's death in 1543. A Polish Catholic priest, Copernicus was called on by the church to develop a more accurate calendar. He presented the notion of a heliocentric, or sun-centered, universe as a mathematical supposition. Though Copernicus retained many features of the Ptolemaic cosmology ("model of the universe"), this radical notion that God's special creation—humans and their terrestrial home—were no longer the center of the universe served to spark criticism and further astronomical inquiry[2]. The developments that follow in astronomy and physics represent the primary field of advance during the Scientific Revolution; as you review, consider the relationship between new *ideas* and new *methods*.

The work of Copernicus demonstrates how a mathematics-driven astronomy could lead to and support new theories of planetary motion. Copernicanism temporarily stood as a theory without support from observations. Danish astronomer Tycho Brahe (1546–1601) provided these observations, as he spent over 20 years staring at the night sky on the isolated island of Hven off the coast of Denmark—all without the aid of a telescope! In 1577 Brahe charted the path of a comet that seemed to be traveling in an irregular (not circular) path as it passed through the supposed crystalline spheres, something that wasn't supposed to happen under the Ptolemaic system. While Brahe never fully accepted the heliocentric theory, his massive collection of data aided future scientists.

One of history's greatest scientists, Johannes Kepler (1571–1630), put Brahe's data to good use. Formerly Brahe's assistant, Kepler became court astronomer to the Holy Roman Emperor, despite being Lutheran. He used his mathematical genius to make a conceptual leap regarding planetary motion: many of the anomalies in the Copernican system were eliminated if the planets traveled in elliptical paths. Further, Kepler articulated three laws of planetary motion, all of which could be expressed precisely using equations. For example, Kepler demonstrated that the closer a planet orbited to the sun, the faster it moved, which fit with observations. Nonetheless, not all Kepler's view would be regarded as scientific today. Something of a religious mystic, Kepler believed that the orbits of the planets expressed a cosmic harmony, which could be heard in the "music of the spheres."

Galileo Galilei[3] (1564–1642) combined interests of wide scope with an ability to attract patronage and attention, not all of which was positive. First, the Italian scientist's correspondence with Kepler demonstrates the emergence of an international scientific community. Second, based on repeated experiments, Galileo devised one of the first mathematical formulas to explain and predict a natural phenomenon, the law of accelerating bodies: 32 ft/sec/sec. Providing **empirical** ("based on the senses") support for the heliocentric theory represents Galileo's most famous contribution to science. In 1609 Galileo created one of the first telescopes and trained it on the

2 SKILL SET

Intellectual frameworks involve an approach or method toward knowledge (epistemology) and a model of the universe (cosmology) to be investigated, which explains the objects and forces that inhabit it and how causation occurs. To reinforce your understanding of the transformation wrought by the new science, consider diagramming the ancient/medieval and modern epistemologies and cosmologies. Use the content in this section to make sure you understand how they compare (COMP) and how they changed during this period (CCOT).

3 EXAMPLE BASE

Whenever you encounter a series of examples, like the scientists here, it is important that you go beyond rote learning. To sharpen your focus, consider these interpretive questions: How revolutionary was the new science? To what extent did thinkers retain traditional approaches or ideas?

heavens. The resulting *Starry Messenger* (1610) depicted the moon with an imperfect and rough surface, sunspots, millions of stars, and moons orbiting Jupiter—all of which contradicted the notion of perfect heavenly bodies, the limited and static size of the universe, and that all bodies rotated around the earth. Despite an agreement with the papacy to teach **heliocentrism** as only a theory, Galileo later published a clear endorsement of it with *Dialogue Concerning the Two Chief World Systems: Ptolemaic and Copernican* (1632), which landed him before the Roman Inquisition in 1633. Galileo remained a Catholic who believed in the unity of truth—scientific and spiritual—and that any conflict between them required a reappraisal of biblical passages in light of new discoveries. In the midst of the Thirty Years' War, the Catholic Church silenced Galileo (placing him under house arrest for the next 9 years) and thereby stifled intellectual life in Italy for the foreseeable future.

Galileo's ideas could not be silenced, and his death in 1642 also marks the birth of the last great thinker of the Scientific Revolution—**Isaac Newton** (1642–1727). One of the true geniuses in history, Newton combined profound conceptual insights, precise mathematical expression, and systematic observation. Newton synthesized the work of over a century into a coherent view of the world, based on universal laws, as expressed in his *Principia Mathematica* (1687); as he later said, "If I have been able to see so far, it is only because I stood on the shoulders of giants." All objects behave similarly, according to Newton, because they all obey three laws of motion. What previous astronomers had observed piecemeal and with speculation, Newton synthesized into a cosmic machine, held together with the universal law of gravitation. In addition, to explain infinitesimal changes in motion, Newton invented a new form of mathematics—calculus. With these tools, the universe could now be viewed as a finely calibrated watch that obeyed natural laws with mathematical precision, which allowed it to be explained and controlled by human reason. Though Newton was a deeply religious man who retained the image of God's will behind all, his cosmology helped separate the world of matter from that of spirit, setting the stage for deism in the future (see Chapter 9).

Advances in Anatomy and Medicine

In the same year that Copernicus introduced his heliocentric theory (1543), Flemish anatomist Andreas Vesalius (1514–1564) published the landmark book in his field—*On the Fabric of the Human Body*. Based on dissections and precise drawings, Vesalius contradicted many of Galen's ideas regarding the human body, again by employing direct empirical evidence. Building on this success and working for years in a laboratory, the English physician **William Harvey** (1578–1657) developed the modern theory of blood flow, with arteries and veins circulating oxygen through human tissue.

Further discoveries in anatomy were greatly assisted by the development of the **microscope**, which became the basis for the investigations of a Dutch nobleman, Anton von Leeuwenhoek (1632–1723). For his discoveries of blood corpuscles, sperm, and bacteria (it was not linked to disease until later), Leeuwenhoek is often given the title, Father of Microbiology. Leeuwenhoek also corresponded with a secretary of the Royal Society of London (see below), Robert Hooke, who published his own book on the subject, *Micrographia* (1665) and worked with the chemist Robert Boyle (1627–1692). Boyle's book, *The Sceptical Chemist* (1661), criticized the blending of alchemy (the art of attempting to turn metals into gold) with chemistry, which should involve the scientific investigation of nature's most basic substances—the elements. In addition, Boyle articulated his famous law whereby the temperature, pressure, and volume of a gas can be related according to a mathematical formula.

Though these developments provided a more modern understanding of the human body and its functions, they did not translate into improved medical care for some time. In fact, many physicians continued to receive their training in the traditional classical style—reading Galen and Hippocrates, rather than through experimentation and clinical practice. Hospitals in the 17th and 18th centuries were as likely to house vagrants as the sick. Given the lack of understanding regarding bacteria and germs, hospitals generally served as places for the ill to die, not to be cured. Faith healers, midwives, and barber-surgeons, who engaged in the traditional bleeding and purging regimen, continued to provide medical care for the vast majority of Europeans[4].

The Scientific Method: Bacon and Descartes

Modern scientific thinking was the product of two differing intellectual temperaments—the Englishman **Francis Bacon** (1561–1626) and the Frenchman **René Descartes** (1596–1650). Both shared a disdain for the Scholastic tradition and a skepticism toward knowledge claims that had not been demonstrated through a rigorous system of thought. Bacon, from a noble family and occupying important positions in government, advocated a scientific approach based on **inductive reasoning**. As opposed to the Scholastic tradition of working first with definitions and propositions, Bacon called for systematic investigation and observation of nature, as well as experimentation, leading to generalizations about the physical world. In his uncompleted three-volume work, *Instauratio Magna* (the Great Renewal), Bacon called for a new start to human knowledge, for humanity to put aside ancient preconceptions and prejudices and look at nature with fresh eyes. For Bacon, science should be useful to human beings; it should make their lives longer, more secure, and more comfortable. To demonstrate the great potential of science, Bacon published his *New Atlantis* (1627), which portrayed a scientific utopia and prefigured many modern technological developments. Though his ideas proved influential, Bacon himself did not fully appreciate the importance of theory and mathematics in scientific investigation.

A brilliant mathematician, René Descartes initiated the modern turn in philosophy. Descartes deliberately rejected Scholastic notions; his intellectual project subjected every assertion of knowledge to systematic doubt. The goal of his skepticism was not to reject knowledge *per se*, but to build a surer foundation for it. Descartes even doubted that he existed. However, though he could doubt the existence of his body (because his senses often deceived him), Descartes could not doubt the existence of his mind, for in the very process of doubting, he affirmed that he had a mind—"I think; therefore, I am" (*cogito ergo sum*). From this thought experiment, Descartes argued for dualism, the idea that nature is made of two basic substances—an intangible, thinking substance known as mind and a tangible, extended (taking up space) substance known as matter. Descartes also demonstrated the power of mathematics in scientific thinking. With *Discourse on Method* (1637), he argued for a **deductive approach** to knowledge, much like a geometric proof, moving from general principles to more particular cases by steps of reason. With his Cartesian coordinate system (x, y, and z axes), Descartes provided a precise abstract depiction of space useful for engineering, architecture, and the military arts. Some of Descartes' ideas were later proved wrong—he speculated that animals were like machines and felt no pain—and his unorthodoxy almost landed him in hot water with the Catholic Church. Nonetheless, Descartes stands as one of the great philosophers in history and initiated the separation of matter and spirit that marks the path of secularism in subsequent centuries[5].

Women and Science

Women contributed to science and, in turn, were affected by scientific thinking. Given social constraints, it is a wonder that any women were able to contribute to science. Women were excluded from universities, scientific societies, and generally received an inferior education. Opportunities were available, however. In Germany, for example, the craft tradition allowed women to work alongside fathers and husbands; as a result, 15% of German astronomers in the 17th and 18th centuries were women. One such was Maria Winkelmann (1670–1720), who discovered a comet before her husband and helped to prepare the astronomical calendar for the Berlin Academy of Sciences. Despite these contributions, she was denied admission into the academy. Maria Sybilla Merian (1647–1717) traveled to South America to study insects, and her

4 THEME MUSIC

An often overlooked but essential issue of the PP and IS themes is demographics, the study of populations. Modern societies have generally supported a higher standard of living and longer life expectancy. These accomplishments begin with improved understanding of human anatomy and disease. Trace relevant content throughout the course; this topic represents an appropriate starting point.

5 SKILL SET

All of the natural philosophers (the term "scientist" came into general use during the 19th century) of this era expressed religious beliefs and saw their work as partly spiritual, i.e., understanding the "mind of God." However, by establishing a mechanistic view of the universe guided by materialism and mathematics, they set the stage for new religious attitudes, such as deism, agnosticism, and atheism. Take note of how explanations of nature can have an impact on religious belief and the role of religion over time (CCOT).

subsequent text and illustrations, *Metamorphosis of the Insects of Surinam*, became a standard in the field of entomology. Emilie du Chatelet (1706–1749) translated Newton to make his abstract works accessible to a mass audience, while Dorothea Erxleben (1715–1762) became one of the first women to earn a medical degree from a university.

Unfortunately, these women proved exceptions. Institutional barriers remained strong, though attitudes served as an even more effective roadblock. Throughout the 17th century, philosophers and scientists debated the *querelle de femmes*—the "women question." Ironically, some of science's greatest doubters—Spinoza, for example (see below)—could not extricate themselves from long-held prejudices when it came to women. Studies of anatomy seemed proof that women's smaller skulls and wider hips demonstrated their intellectual inferiority and fitness only for domestic roles. Investigation into human reproduction affirmed the greater importance of males in providing the "life force," with women providing only the matter or location of conception. It was not until 1823 that the ovum was discovered, proving otherwise. Did women, then, experience a Scientific Revolution? On one hand, women did participate in scientific discoveries despite the obstacles, but on the other, "science" was used to corset women even more tightly in limited social and intellectual roles. When it came to women, science in the 17th century proved most unrevolutionary[6].

6 THEME MUSIC
Once again, we see how a movement of cultural and intellectual change affected attitudes toward women and their position within society (IS). Continue to build on this theme as you study.

Religion and Skepticism

Though most scientists of the 17th and 18th centuries perceived no conflict between scientific inquiry and spirituality, the Scientific Revolution resulted in an increased skeptical and secular attitude among European elites. At first, many scientists blended (what would today be considered) superstitious beliefs in **alchemy and astrology** with materialist and mathematical perspectives. As time wore on, educated Europeans demanded empirical evidence or conformity with natural laws for claims of knowledge. This new standard is reflected in the decline of **witchcraft persecutions** after 1650, which no longer received the support of those in positions of power. New standards of evidence eliminating torture and hearsay testimony, especially in England, provided a more scientific basis for legal proceedings. Furthermore, European colonization stimulated travel literature, which in revealing the diversity of human societies and customs suggested the possibility of cultural relativism. Following in the path of the French humanist and skeptic Montaigne (see Chapter 5), Pierre Bayle (1647–1706) examined beliefs from a wide range of human endeavors in his *Historical and Critical Dictionary*, only to conclude that most owed more to human credulity than to rigorous and rational thought. Bayle's work forms a bridge from the Scientific Revolution to the 18th-century Enlightenment (see Chapter 9).

Two thinkers stand out in their attempts to create a synthesis of the scientific and the spiritual. Baruch Spinoza (1632–1677) came from a family of Portuguese Jews forced to emigrate to the Netherlands as a result of the Inquisition. Beginning in the Cartesian tradition of dualism regarding substances, Spinoza came to reject Descartes' understanding of God and substance. For Spinoza, all of nature was ultimately one substance: all that we experience is simply a modification of that substance, which is God. We can conceive of this substance with the attribute of extension (taking up space) or of thought (mind), but these attributes are ultimately manifestations of the same substance. Spinoza's substance monism made little sense to the Jewish community from which he was excommunicated, or to orthodox Christians who thought it no better than atheism. Spinoza's rejection of an anthropomorphic God (in the form of humans) led him to a naturalistic view of human affairs and ethics. Even the title of his most famous work, *Ethics, as Determined in a Geometric Manner* (1677), illustrates his rigorous rationalist style. In rejecting miracles, holy books, rituals, dogma, and even free will, Spinoza left human beings primarily with their minds to offer consolation, guidance, and whatever freedom comes from putting oneself in accord with the laws of nature.

Blaise Pascal (1623–1662) was a child prodigy of true mathematical genius. It is said that he independently discovered several theorems of Euclid's geometry at the age of 9. In addition, he later invented the first successful adding machine, developed Pascal's Triangle to show the pattern of ascending exponential functions of algebraic equations, and developed the geometry of solids as well as modern probability theory. After experiencing a profound religious conversion in 1654, Pascal gave up his work in science and mathematics for religion and philosophy. Pascal fell under the influence of the Jansenist movement in France, which rejected the Jesuits strong view of human freedom. In his famous work the *Pensées* ("Thoughts"), Pascal set out to show the proper relationship between reason and faith. Though scientific discoveries had demonstrated the insignificance of humans in the cosmos, Pascal nonetheless looked at human reason as a distinct capacity in the universe, or as he wrote, "Man is a reed, but he is a thinking reed." When it comes to religious faith, we will always want for evidence and arguments, said Pascal. Therefore, humans can weigh the alternatives—e.g., the promise of eternal reward vs. sacrifice of earthly pleasures—according to Pascal's Wager and gamble on belief, for we have much to gain and little to lose with faith.

A Scientific View of Human Affairs: Law and Political Theory

Scientific thinking inevitably crept into human affairs. If matter followed natural laws, why could human behavior not also be explained according to the same laws? The birth of natural law philosophy and the concept of **natural rights** have grounded much of modern political development toward democracy and equality. Natural law holds that humans can discover what is fair, just, and natural in the political and social realms by consulting reason. Custom, tradition, or the edicts of kings cannot override natural rights, which inhere in human beings because of their unique capacities. For example, the ability of humans to speak, write, and create symbols suggests that they have a natural right to freedoms in these areas. In diplomacy, several 17th-century jurists, such as Hugo Grotius in *Law of War and Peace* (1625) and Samuel Pufendorf in *Law of Nature and of Nations* (1672), attempted to define rules for commerce and war based on the common good of nations rather than simply the might of the strongest. Even with international organizations like the United Nations today, the world continues to struggle with winning adherence by all nations to a code of international law.

Thomas Hobbes

Natural law can also be used to justify absolutism. A sophisticated and secular justification (compare with Bossuet's divine-right account in Chapter 7) of absolutism comes from **Thomas Hobbes** (1588–1679). Hobbes wrote his *Leviathan* (1651) amidst the Scientific Revolution and the English Civil War, both of which left their mark on his political philosophy. According to Hobbes, humans are born into a state of nature, in which life is a continual war of "every man against every other man" for gain, glory, and security. If humans are equal, it is only in their ability to destroy one another. Hobbes viewed human society as akin to a closed system of energy, which tends to dissipate (into anarchy) over time. The only solution to this insecurity and chaos is for each individual to leave the state of nature by agreeing to a **social contract** with one another and with the sovereign, who will absorb the wills and power of each member of society into an all-powerful ruler. In the resulting commonwealth, the will of the sovereign (which could be a group of rulers) stands as law. Rebellion is prohibited, as it would only return society to the chaotic state of nature. Hobbes's justification is secular and scientific, and though it would be rejected by many in his native England, his notions of the state of nature and the social contract influenced subsequent thinkers.

John Locke

The most important defense of limited government based on natural law was written by the Englishman **John Locke** (1632–1704) to justify the Glorious Revolution (see Chapter 7).

Locke's *Second Treatise on Government* (1689) takes Hobbes and stands him on his head. In Locke's state of nature, man freely enjoys his natural rights of life, liberty, equality, and property. These inalienable rights come *before* the development of human society. Though humans are basically rational, they still conflict in the state of nature over property. Such disputes create insecurity and reduce the enjoyment of one's liberties. Thus, individuals enter into a social contract and leave the state of nature to secure those rights. Governments are limited by their original purpose—arbitrating disputes and providing order and public goods. Should governments become abusive toward these ends, society can invoke the right of rebellion to secure those rights anew. In all, governments are made by people and must display features of the limiting social contract—representation, guarantees of rights, respect of property. Locke's ideas helped promote the unique development of England in this era, though it should *not* be viewed as an endorsement of modern mass democracy.

Like Pierre Bayle, John Locke forms a bridge between the Scientific Revolution of the 17th century and the Enlightenment of the 18th century. Locke looked at the world from an empirical perspective, yet he believed that Christianity was a reasonable religion. At the same time, he supported religious toleration (except for the Catholics and atheists, whom he viewed as a threat to the state) as part of the settlement surrounding the Glorious Revolution. The ideas of Francis Bacon and John Locke form bookends to the 17th century regarding the importance of an empirical approach to the world. Locke became the foremost advocate of an empirical approach to knowledge in his philosophical writings. In *Essay Concerning Human Understanding* (1690), Locke rejected Descartes' notion of innate ideas, in favor of the mind as a *tabula rasa*, or "blank slate." Humans learn primarily from experience, which writes upon their minds and character their personality and knowledge. These ideas held radical implications when it came to education, as Locke argued in *Some Thoughts Concerning Education* (1689); children learn best not from rote memorization but from experience and from "praise and esteem." Locke's wide-ranging interests and writings sparked new thinking in several fields, including child-rearing, education, politics, and philosophy.

7 THEME MUSIC
Given the competitive environment of the European continent, states will seek advantages in many areas, science being one of them. For the SP theme, consider the factors that might affect a nation's political position related to science—commerce, navigation, and military weaponry.

Science Applied: Societies and Technology[7]

Governments saw great promise in science. Prestige accrued to nations who sponsored great scientific discoveries, but more importantly, states hoped to exploit theoretical advances for navigational and military purposes. To this end, the first great scientific societies were formed in the 1660s. In England, the privately run Royal Society of London received a government charter in 1662; eventually, Sir Isaac Newton served as its president. Not to be outdone, Louis XIV chartered, under stricter government supervision, the French Academy of Sciences in 1666. Smaller or more regional societies, academies, and universities for the study and perpetuation of science were also founded in the century. These organizations held meetings, published journals, established research projects, and shared their results with scientists across the continent. Even if governments wished to monopolize science for their narrow national interest, it would not have been possible given the modern printing press. An international scientific community seemed necessary to the very nature of modern science; to ensure reliability, experiments had to be repeated, data shared, and theories confirmed.

Science can be of the most abstract nature; at the same time, all humanity shares an interest in its practical results. New scientific equipment and machines—telescopes, microscopes, barometers, globes, marine chronometers, pendulum clocks, improved cannons, early steam engines—promised greater human control of the environment. In subsequent centuries, Europeans would exploit these advances to the fullest. The results have been both the greatest period of human technological creativity and the most destructive conflicts in history.

Additional Resources

Wilbur Applebaum, *The Scientific Revolution and the Foundations of Modern Science* (2005)—Accessible to high school students, this work comes from the Greenwood Guides to Historic Events.

John Henry, *The Scientific Revolution and the Origins of Modern Science* (2002)—From the Studies in European History series, this brief account provides the political, religious, and cultural background to the Scientific Revolution.

Steven Shapin, *The Scientific Revolution* (1996)—An excellent and brief, but challenging, overview of the topic.

Dava Sobel, *Galileo's Daughter: A Historical Memoir of Science, Faith, and Love* (2000)—A popular history that shows the trial of Galileo against the backdrop of his relationship with his daughter, a nun.

Dava Sobel, *Longitude: The True Story of a Lone Genius Who Solved the Greatest Scientific Problem of His Time* (1996)—Tells the story of how John Harrison created the first successful marine chronometer.

http://galileo.rice.edu/—Outstanding resource at Rice University related to Galileo's life, investigations, and accomplishments.

http://users.clas.ufl.edu/ufhatch/pages/03-Sci-Rev/SCI-REV-Home/index.htm#—By a university professor, this site provides brief essays on key topics, primary sources, and links to other sites.

Practice MC Questions

Questions 1–2 are based on the following passage.

> "But Nature, on the other hand, is inexorable and immutable; she never transgresses the laws imposed upon her, or cares a whit whether her abstruse reasons and methods of operation are understandable to men. For that reason it appears that nothing physical which sense-experience sets before our eyes, or which necessary demonstrations prove to us, ought to be called in question (much less condemned) upon the testimony of biblical passages which may have some different meaning beneath their words. For the Bible is not chained in every expression to conditions as strict as those which govern all physical effects; nor is God any less excellently revealed in Nature's actions than in the sacred statements of the Bible."
>
> Galileo Galilei, Italian mathematician and natural philosopher, "Letter to the Grand Duchess Christina of Tuscany," 1615

1. Based on the passage and your knowledge of the period, Galileo most directly challenged religious authority by:

   A. publishing his findings using the new print technology.

   B. appealing to elites for political support against the Church.

   C. cooperating with scientists from Protestant states.

   D. emphasizing physical observation over biblical authority.

2. In subsequent years, which of the following principles articulated by Galileo would come to dominate elite intellectual life?

   A. That there are no inherent conflicts between faith and science

   B. Classical learning is necessary to support new discoveries

   C. Nature is guided by universal and mathematical laws

   D. Appeals to political authority support new ideas

Questions 3–5 are based on the image below.

Illustration from a medical text, 1628

3. The illustration above reflects all of the following features of the new science EXCEPT:

   A. the importance of observation of the natural world.

   B. the use of experimentation to support explanations.

   C. the persistence of folk traditions about the universe.

   D. the challenge to Galen's humoral theory of the body.

4. Which of the following scientists is most responsible for the ideas represented in the image?

   A. Paracelsus

   B. Andreas Vesalius

   C. Francis Bacon

   D. William Harvey

5. According to 19th-century positivism, which of the following attitudes of natural philosophers from the 16th and 17th centuries would be considered nonscientific?

   A. Belief in a mathematical and mechanical model of the cosmos

   B. Support of alchemy and astrology as predictive systems

   C. Questioning the authority of ancient learning and methods

   D. Patronage of scientific inquiry by state authorities

Questions 6–8 are based on the image below.

Rembrandt van Rijn, Dutch artist, *The Anatomy Lesson of Dr. Nicolaes Tulp*, 1631

6. Which of the following principles of the new science is depicted in the painting?

   A. Empiricism

   B. Mathematics

   C. Deductive reasoning

   D. Cosmology

7. All of the following features of Dutch society would have contributed to the development portrayed in the painting EXCEPT:

   A. tolerance toward religious and intellectual dissent.

   B. commercial focus and dominance of merchant elites.

   C. strong central monarchy to patronize science.

   D. trade routes that allowed access to new ideas.

8. An art historian might use the image to support which of the following generalizations about art in the 17th century?

   A. "Baroque artists used painting to promote religiosity and state power."

   B. "Art came to reflect a secular outlook of progress and the public good."

   C. "New art movements rejected Renaissance ideas of naturalism and perspective."

   D. "Paintings emphasized Enlightenment ideals of political power and citizenship."

See Chapter 18 for answers and explanations.

Long Essay Question with Sample and Commentary

To what extent and in what ways did the Scientific Revolution represent a turning point in European ideas and culture?
(HTS: Periodization)

The Scientific Revolution represented a major change in European ideas and culture. Before it occurred, people used the classics and the Bible to understand nature. After scientists like Galileo and Newton, Europeans began to think about natural laws and observations as the focus of understanding. This new approach set the stage for the Enlightenment and other revolutions because it taught people to question authority and change the world through scientific thinking.

Before Copernicus published his heliocentric theory, the understanding of the universe was based on Aristotle and other Greek scholars. Intellectuals at the university would just study ancient texts to understand astronomy or the human body. With heliocentrism, people began to think differently about how the universe was structured. Like with no crystal spheres, as Brahe showed by observing a comet. This new thinking challenged authorities like the Church, who put Galileo on trial for teaching the heliocentric theory, which resulted in his execution. But it was impossible to stop the new thinking about science. Other scientists picked up the slack and continued their research. Bacon and Descartes created a new scientific method, with inductive and deductive reasoning, which allowed for proposing and testing hypotheses. All of this new thinking reached a high point with Newton, who broke down everything into natural laws using math (like calculus, which he invented). This accomplishment ("on the shoulders of giants") set the stage for the Enlightenment, which would use science to argue for progress in society.

New scientific ideas also affected culture greatly, as learning became more focused on observation of the world and less on classics and religion. This provided for a new secular focus. New universities and scientific societies were founded that tried to go beyond just lecturing on Ptolemy and Galen and repeating the same old debates. Instead, there was more experimentation and hands-on learning, as you can see in some of the art of this period. One example is the dissection lesson in the Dutch republic painted by Rembrandt; it shows a group of doctors learning about the human body through direct knowledge. Many states saw the importance of science and began to patronize it, like France under Louis XIV and in Britain with the Royal Society. Nations wanted to be more powerful and saw that science could do it. Also with politics, new theories came about from Hobbes and Locke that used the idea of natural laws to understand how governments were formed and should operate. These new theories would affect revolutions later.

The Scientific Revolution is definitely a turning point and a major event in European history. This development of an objective approach to knowledge, with a reliable method of testing of hypotheses with evidence, undermined the ancient worldview of taking Aristotle and the Church at their word. Enlightenment philosophes publicized this new scientific method and employed it arguing for new ideas in politics, like natural rights and the social contract. Without the new science, it is hard to see how Locke, Rousseau, and others might have developed a new philosophy of politics that eventually led to the French Revolution.

For LEQs addressing turning points, a student must describe the ways in which an event or era was similar to or different from the eras that both preceded and followed it, as well as explain the extent to which the era in question was similar to or different from the eras that preceded and/or followed it. In this sample, the student briefly outlines the methods of the pre-scientific era, identifies characteristics of the new science, and suggests how these new approaches helped create the Enlightenment. In the body of the essay, the student makes multiple references to the authorities of the classics and religion (Aristotle, Ptolemy, and Galileo's trial before the Inquisition). In addition, we read about the discoveries of various scientists with some implication about their methods and ideas. For the subsequent era, there are brief yet sufficient references to the Enlightenment, political theory, and revolutions. This student earned both points for the targeted HTS, even if the analysis tends to stay at a basic level. Despite the multiple examples, this essay does not provide a full enough analysis of the evidence nor apply it directly enough to the thesis to earn the second point for using evidence to support an argument. Finally, the conclusion provides adequate connection to subsequent developments (Enlightenment and French Revolution), as well as providing a brief analysis of politics (a new category of analysis). Score: 5 (Thesis. 2 for targeted HTS, 1 for Use of Evidence, Synthesis)

PERIOD 2

The chapters in Period 2 address the following major developments and events:

- Development of absolute monarchies
- Challenges to absolutism, such as republics and constitutional states
- Art movements that reflected absolutism, commerce, and civic ideals
- Commercial Revolution
- Commercial Wars and other conflicts affecting the balance of power
- Enlightened absolutism
- Social and cultural changes, such as the Agricultural Revolution, consumerism, and rise of the middle class
- Enlightenment
- French Revolution and Napoleonic era

Each chapter will provide a content review and practice questions to test your understanding of the material. At the conclusion of the content chapters, you will be able to both gauge your grasp of the content and practice historical thinking skills in an online diagnostic test that will include:

- 30 MC questions
- 2 SAQs
- 1 DBQ
- 1 LEQ (choice of 2)

Each chapter will begin with a brief correlation to the Key Concepts from the Course Description. Good luck with your review.

CHAPTER 7 Absolutism and the Balance of Power in West and East, 1640–1740

1 SKILL SET

To ensure your focus on the KCs and course theme (SP), think of this unit as an evaluation of how each state in its drive for power addressed: use of resources, religious divisions, alliances with other states, economic developments, administrative control, and military affairs. In other words, try to use the evidence of this chapter (EVARG) to develop an interpretation on the nature of political power and varying paths to success or failure (INTR and ARG).

This chapter covers a wide array of nations and rulers. To assist your comprehension, try employing the framework discussed earlier for each nation: Challenge → Response → Result[1]. In response to the devastation of the religious wars and the general upheaval in the period 1550–1650, rulers increasingly justified their power based on absolutist or divine-right theories of monarchy. As we'll see in this chapter, not all accepted such theoretically expansive powers and worked to limit monarchical authority. Rulers also exploited developments in commerce to enhance their nations' power. The resulting competition led to nearly continuous warfare in this period over colonies, trade, and territory. To prevent the predominance of any one power (usually France), European diplomacy relied on the **balance of power**. Both of these trends—development of strong centralized monarchies and balance-of-power diplomacy—played out in eastern and western Europe against the backdrop of various political forms and the differing geographic and social imperatives of east and west.

Key In Chapter 7 addresses the following KCs from the Course Description:

- **KC 2.1** Absolute monarchies in western, central, and eastern Europe
- **KC 2.1** Challenges to absolutism in England and the Dutch Republic
- **KC 2.1 and 2.2** Warfare among the great powers over territory and commerce
- **KC 2.2** The theory and practice of mercantilism
- **KC 2.3** Artistic movements that glorified the state and that reflected commercial society

Political Theories and the Age of Crisis

To understand the drive for centralized power in European states, it is useful to recall the context of the period 1550–1650. This period is often referred to as the Age of Crisis, owing to the cumulative effect of the following forces:

- Religious warfare
- Climate change involving poor weather
- Resulting shorter growing seasons, crop failures, and famines
- High taxes
- Internal rebellion
- Witchcraft accusations
- Intellectual changes in explaining natural phenomena (the Scientific Revolution)
- Economic changes: Price Revolution, enclosure, increase in poverty/begging
- Increase in violent and property crime

Though we prize our liberties today, this attitude may be a function of our relative political and social stability. In times of chaos and crisis, people often sacrifice rights in the interests of security and order. Such was the case for advocates of absolutism in the early 17th century. To provide for stability, some political theorists developed justifications for the enhanced power of rulers. Not all agreed with absolutist pretensions, and such opponents provided counter theories justifying limits on monarchical power (also see Chapter 6 for Hobbes and Locke).

Given the strong religious beliefs of the period, arguments based on the authority of God carried a natural resonance. Divine-right arguments were new only in the expansive powers with which theorists attempted to imbue them. The most famous advocate of divine-right rule was the French clergyman Bishop Bossuet (1627–1704). Quite simply, kings derive their power from God directly and rule on earth in his behalf. Once this view is understood, the resulting magnificent displays of power by Louis XIV and his imitators become clearer as a ruling strategy, as well as the abhorrence with which rebellion and treason were viewed in this era. Some defied the general trend toward absolutism, such as the Huguenots who endorsed resistance by local officials against what was perceived as a repressive monarchy.

The Age of Louis XIV in France

Foundations of French Absolutism: Henry IV and Louis XIII

Absolutism reached its highest expression in France during the reign of **Louis XIV** (r. 1643–1715). The previous two Bourbon monarchs laid the foundation for the sparkling but flawed edifice that was the Age of Louis XIV. Henry IV (r. 1589–1610), the first in the Bourbon line, after bringing the religious conflict to an end with the Edict of Nantes (1598), turned his attention to putting

France's financial and economic house in order. Under Henry and his primary advisor, the Duc de Sully, the French state balanced its budget and established a firmer basis for taxation. In addition, Henry promoted economic development through the building of roads and canals, draining swamps, and promoting colonization. His strong rule allowed France to survive his assassination in 1610 and the regency of his wife, Marie de Medicis, on behalf of their son, Louis XIII.

Louis XIII (r. 1610–1643) relied on the advice of his talented and shrewd advisor, Cardinal Richelieu (1585–1642), who increased direct (*taille*) and indirect (*gabelle*—government salt monopoly) taxes. Louis and Richelieu concerned themselves with curbing the power of the nobility. To this effect, Richelieu banned dueling (which suggested violence independent of the state), employed spies to monitor the provincial nobility, and appointed *intendants*, or local officials, whose job it was to be the "eyes and ears of the monarchy." In addition, while allowing Huguenots to maintain their religious practices, Richelieu forced them to relinquish their fortified towns. Though Richelieu was a prince of the Catholic Church, under his guidance France supported the *Protestant* forces during the Thirty Years' War. Like Machiavelli before him, politics was for Richelieu about *raison d'etat*, or "reason of state," as he expressed it in his *Political Testament*. According to Richelieu, it was in France's interests to limit the growing power of the surrounding Habsburgs (the political leaders of the Catholic cause), regardless of the religious allegiances of Richelieu, or France more generally.

2 THEME MUSIC

The SP theme in this period revolves around the theory and practice of absolute monarchy, including those in opposition, such as corporate groups, provinces, and religious minorities. As you consider the material here on the French experience, keep an eye forward to explaining the long-term causes of the French Revolution.

Louis XIV and French Absolutism[2]

When Louis XIV inherited the throne in 1643, France was once again faced with the prospect of a boy king (Louis was 5). Discontent over high taxes and foreign influence in government led to a series of rebellions in Paris and the countryside known as the Fronde (1648–1652). In fact, the young Louis's first memory involved fleeing from his capital in a carriage surrounded by an angry mob. The event convinced him to build his seat of government in the nearby suburb of Versailles and to establish an iron-fisted rule that could overwhelm any potential future opposition.

Early in Louis's reign, the real ruler of France was Cardinal Mazarin (1602–1661), who continued many of the policies of his predecessor, Richelieu. Upon Mazarin's death in 1661, Louis at the age of 23 took personal control of government and did not relinquish it until his death in 1715. A major concern for Louis was to overcome the provincialism and feudal remnants of the French state. Seventeenth-century France was divided by linguistic dialects, provincial customs and estates, and a variety of political bodies that potentially limited monarchical power. One such was the 15 regional *parlements*, or courts, controlled by the nobles, and who by tradition had to register the king's decrees to give them effect. To control these bodies, Louis wielded threats of exile and confiscation of property, or involved nobles in court patronage and intrigue at the glittering palace of Versailles.

The Palace at Versailles

No greater symbol of royal absolutism exists than Louis's palace at Versailles. Originally a hunting lodge, Versailles became under Louis a seat of government as well as a teeming city of patronage-seekers and the backdrop for the drama of Louis's kingship. Looking over the palace itself, the man-made canal, lush gardens, and grandiose outbuildings, one begins to understand the importance of Louis's expression "I am the state." The palace was constructed over several decades, and though the records were deliberately destroyed, it is estimated that the palace absorbed as much as 60%–80% of the state's revenues during the years of its construction. Versailles was more than a royal residence. Nobles were encouraged to live on the grounds and participate in the pageantry of Louis's rule. Court etiquette and seeking royal favor deliberately occupied the energies of thousands of the French aristocracy, safely under Louis's gaze and unable to make trouble in the provinces. All of Louis's activities were infused with religious solemnity; nobles competed to participate in the ceremonies of the king's waking, dining, and retiring to bed (*lever, dîner,* and *coucher*). French culture and the grandeur of Louis's Versailles became the envy of Europe, as elites across Europe sharpened their French language skills and rulers built their own mini-Versailles.

Economic Policies

Reflecting a continental trend, France under Louis practiced mercantilism to enhance its economic position. Under **Jean-Baptiste Colbert** (1619–1683), the minister of finance and Louis's primary advisor, France developed a unified internal market and also expanded its commercial presence around the world. Like many nations, France's economy was limited by internal tariffs; though Colbert did not eliminate these, he did create a free-trade zone, known as the Five Great Farms, to facilitate commerce. In addition, Colbert continued to enhance France's infrastructure with roads, a postal system, and the establishment of manufacturing codes. Industries were organized into corporations, which fell under the guidance of the state, a process that helped the nation earn a reputation for high-quality luxury goods. To promote commerce, Colbert established the French East India Company (to rival Britain's and the Netherlands') and built a royal navy. High tariffs (taxes on imports) limited foreign goods and, along with the high taxes imposed to finance Louis's many wars, had the effect of increasing the burden on the lower classes (especially peasants) by raising prices and taking much of their hard-earned subsistence. Members of the nobility had negotiated exemptions from many direct taxes over the years, creating a regressive and inefficient system that increased discontent as time wore on.

Religious and Cultural Policies

Louis's commitment to the principle of "one king, one faith, and one law" persuaded him that the Calvinist Huguenots constituted a threat to these theoretical powers. In 1685 Louis revoked the Edict of Nantes by issuing the Edict of Fontainebleau, attempting forcibly to convert French Protestants back to Catholicism. Rather than convert, most simply took refuge, along with their property and skills, in those lands that welcomed them, such as the Dutch Republic and Brandenburg-Prussia.

The grandeur of Louis's France was often associated with its artistic and intellectual achievements. In the 1660s, Louis established the French Academy of Arts and the **French Academy of Sciences**. The former created paintings, sculpture, architecture, music, and drama under clear aesthetic guidelines—artists should glorify Louis, France, and link its greatness with classical subjects and style. Much of this patronage revolved around Versailles, which featured an opera house/theater for playwrights to express their comic or tragic commentaries on classical themes. Under Louis, France achieved a continental reputation for combining the scale of the Baroque (see below) with the restraint of the neoclassical. In the area of science, Louis hoped to exploit advances in astronomy, medicine, and navigation to enhance France's prestige as well as its economic and military potential.

The Army

During the 17th century, France replaced Spain as the leading military power on the continent and the nation most often threatening the balance of power. Louis XIV tied his and France's greatness to the army. Under the Marquis de Louvois (1641–1691), Louis's minister of war, France's army became the largest in Europe at 400,000 men. Despite Louvois's skill and the addition of territory on France's eastern border, the wars of Louis XIV (see below) drained the treasury and severely taxed the country's manpower and resources[3].

A Commercial Republic: the Dutch

For all of France's greatness, its small neighbor to the northeast posed a challenge by being different in almost every possible way. The seven northern provinces of the Netherlands (or

3 THEME MUSIC
The most significant driver for the centralization of power (SP) was the military imperative. By 1650, most states had brought warfare under central control; however, the expense of war in the form of troops, munitions, and fortresses came to absorb the bulk of the state's budget, often prompting tax revolts and causing shifts in the fortunes of states.

United Provinces, officially the Dutch Republic after 1648) became Europe's leading commercial power in the first half of the 17th century. How did this nation of about 1 million people with few natural endowments threaten powerful France? First, the Dutch made efficient use of their resources. Land was recovered from the sea by use of dams and dikes and was then organized into *polders* for purposes of diverting water. After 1580, the Dutch moved into Portuguese markets in the East Indies and South America, establishing colonial outposts and reaping huge profits with their joint-stock companies. Second, the Dutch set themselves up as the "middlemen of Europe" by ignoring the prevailing mercantilist philosophy and using their fleet of maneuverable flyboats (or *fluyts*) to trade with all nations and their colonies. It didn't hurt that the Netherlands lay astride important trade routes in the Baltic and Atlantic. Amsterdam served as an *entrepot* city, where ships were efficiently uploaded and offloaded with goods (much like a modern computer file server), as well as the financial center of Europe, what with its Bank of Amsterdam and the Stock Exchange. Merchants played a key role in the Netherlands, and their activities drew investment and trade from all over Europe. Finally, the Netherlands practiced religious toleration, attracting Huguenot refugees from France, Jews, small Protestant denominations, and those fleeing the Inquisition in Spain. These talented minorities lent their business acumen and craftsmanship to the flourishing Dutch economy.

The period 1550–1650 marked the Dutch Golden Age. Its "embarrassment of riches" fueled an outpouring of cultural activity, which, unlike in France, focused on themes of middle-class domestic life, nature, and science. Talented painters, such as Jan Vermeer (1632–1675), Judith Leyster (1609–1660), Frans Hals (1588–1666), and Rembrandt von Rijn (1606–1669), reflected the Dutch preoccupation with light and shadow, natural landscapes, still lifes, domestic scenes, and group portraits. **René Descartes** (1596–1650) and Baruch Spinoza (1632–1677) found a home for their unorthodox philosophies in the Netherlands when they couldn't elsewhere. Such economic and cultural achievements attracted the envy of the Netherlands' larger neighbors.

Internal strife and external threat posed a problem for the Dutch. Constitutionally, the Netherlands were a loosely connected federation of seven provinces that often jealously guarded their liberties, but in times of war relied on leadership from the House of Orange in Holland. Because of continual threats to their security, the other six provinces elected William of Orange (later king of England) in 1673 the hereditary *stadholder* of the Netherlands, though the House of Orange never succeeded in creating a strong centralized monarchy. Given their inherent limitations, it was probably only a matter of time before the Netherlands was surpassed by its rivals. A major turning point proved to be the Anglo-Dutch Naval Wars, fought in three phases between 1652 and 1674 over the English Navigation Acts (1651, 1660), which attempted to restrict Dutch trade with England's colonies. Though the Dutch survived the onslaught, it seriously undercut their commercial power and set the stage for their later conflict with Louis XIV**4**.

Britain: Civil War and Limited Monarchy
Causes of the Conflict

Like the so-called religious wars, the **English Civil War** was both religious and political in nature. The political component involved conflict over sovereignty (ultimate authority) between the new Stuart line of monarchs and the **English Parliament**. Religiously, Puritans wished to purify the state Anglican Church of what they perceived as the residue of Catholic doctrine and worship, which the Stuarts seemed to endorse. Lasting almost a century (from 1603 to 1689), the conflict ultimately laid the foundations for England's unique system of government, which combined elements of monarchy, oligarchy ("rule by a few"), and democracy.

Elizabeth I died without an heir, leaving the throne (in 1603) to the son of Mary, Queen of Scots, James I. As a Scottish outsider, James failed to appreciate the important legislative role played by the English Parliament, whom he continually lectured about his divine-right powers and foolishly laid out in a book, *The True Law of Free Monarchies* (1598). In addition, James antagonized Puritans with the hierarchical structure he retained for the Anglican Church. To control the clergy and religion in general, James believed such an episcopal ("of bishops") structure was necessary; hence, his saying, "No bishop, no king." The growing number of Puritans in Parliament preferred a loose church configuration that allowed individual congregations to control local affairs but cooperate through regional governing boards. James's policies fueled anti-Catholic sentiment, which was only heightened in 1605 when radical Catholics failed to blow up the Parliament, an event known as the Gunpowder Plot.

The English Civil War

These issues came to head during the reign of James's son, Charles I (1625–1649). When Charles demanded revenue, Parliament instead issued the Petition of Right (1628), an assertion of its prerogatives regarding taxation and liberties from arbitrary arrest and imprisonment. This latter issue had arisen due to the Stuarts use of the Star Chamber, a royal court in which standard judicial procedures were ignored in favor of secrecy and arbitrary judgments. Frustrated with Parliament, Charles decided to rule alone from 1629 to 1639, relying on revenues from the royal domain and the use of ship money—in which coastal towns were required to contribute either ships or money for defense. This latter policy had the effect of alienating the growing mercantile elite. Further, Charles's religious policies, guided by Archbishop of Canterbury William Laud (1573–1645), seemed to Puritans little different than Catholicism. Laud attempted to impose uniformity on the realm in 1640 with a new Book of Common Prayer, causing the Scots, who favored a decentralized church structure, to rise in rebellion.

Now Charles had to call the Parliament back into session in order defend against a Scottish invasion. Rather than grant Charles his requested taxes, the Parliament once again asserted its liberties and placed two of his top officials on trial for treason. When Charles attempted in 1642 to arrest the parliamentary leaders of the Puritan cause, his action misfired and plunged England into civil war. The war between the forces of the king (Cavaliers) and those of Parliament (Roundheads) resulted in the capture of Charles in 1645. This conflict brought the brilliant and zealous leader of Parliament's New Model Army to the fore—Oliver Cromwell (1599–1658). Not only an outstanding military leader who employed many of the new more flexible tactics, Cromwell was a devout Puritan who believed, along with his men, in religious toleration for all Protestant denominations and a democratic church structure.

Oliver Cromwell and the Protectorate

When Parliament refused to take action against the captured king, Cromwell surrounded the Parliament and drove out its more moderate members. This new Rump Parliament placed the king under arrest and executed him for treason in 1649. Soon Cromwell had disposed of even the Rump Parliament and named himself Lord Protector under the only written constitution in England's history, the Instrument of Government (1653). Eventually Cromwell imposed military rule and pursued vigorous policies aimed at reforming English morals (by banning plays, gambling, and the celebration of Christmas, which smacked of Catholic "idolatry"), promoting English commerce via mercantilism, and violently subduing rebellion in Ireland and Scotland. After Cromwell's death in 1658, the English aristocracy, weary of military rule and Cromwell's Puritanism, agreed to restore the Stuart monarchy.

The Stuart Restoration and Glorious Revolution

With the Restoration of Charles II (1660–1685) as monarch, the same issues of religion and political control quickly reasserted themselves. Though Charles privately inclined toward Catholicism, he hid his sympathies behind a façade of religious tolerance, while appointing Catholics as justices of the peace (local officials). In 1673, Parliament responded with the Test Act, which required all officeholders to take communion in the Church of England. Further, Charles's pro-French policy ran counter to years of English diplomacy. In fact, Charles had signed in 1670 the secret Treaty of Dover with Louis XIV, in which he gained an annual subsidy from the French king while agreeing to reintroduce Catholicism in England at the first opportunity. With these funds, Charles was able to rule without Parliament in the last years of his reign.

What caused the end of the Stuart monarchy was the prospect of a Catholic dynasty for the foreseeable future. Charles's brother, James II (1685–88), ascended to the throne in 1685, despite the division in Parliament between those who supported his legitimate succession (Tories) and those who opposed him (Whigs). James was an avowed Catholic, which might have been tolerable, until his wife gave birth to a male heir in 1688. Faced with the prospect of a Catholic dynasty, Whig members of Parliament invited James's daughter Mary, a Protestant, and her husband, William of Orange, stadholder of the Netherlands, to invade the nation and claim the throne as corulers. The resulting **Glorious Revolution** proved a success, and William III (1689–1702) and Mary II (1688–1694) agreed to parliamentary sovereignty and recognition of English liberties with the Bill of Rights (1689). In addition, Parliament passed a Toleration Act (1689), which allowed Protestant dissenters to worship but excluded them from public service, and the Act of Succession (1701), which prohibited the English monarchy from ever being held by a Catholic. Finally, to cement ties formally with Scotland, the English Parliament agreed in 1707 to create the United Kingdom of Great Britain. The Glorious Revolution and this series of acts laid the foundation for Britain's unique but stable government and commercial dominance in the 18th century[5].

Art: From Mannerism to Baroque

Due to foreign invasion and economic decline, the Italian Renaissance style of symmetry, order, and classical themes gave way to one based on complex composition, distortion, and elongated human figures. This late 16th-century genre was known as **Mannerism**, meaning those who painted in the manner of the later Michelangelo, such as his *Last Judgment* (completed in 1542). The most famous Mannerist painter, who accomplished his greatest work during the Spanish Golden Age, was El Greco (1541–1614). Known for introducing yellows and grays into the painter's palette, El Greco expressed in works like *Burial of Count Orgaz* and *Landscapes of Toledo* a complex psychology toward a Spain on the verge of decline. To get an impression of the Mannerist style, you might also view Tintoretto's (1518–1594) version of *The Last Supper* and compare it with da Vinci's. Clearly, Catholic Counter-Reformation mysticism had replaced the classical style and one-point perspective of Leonardo's version[6].

Mannerism gradually evolved into the **Baroque** style, which dominated art and music from 1600 to about 1730. A major theme of the Baroque was power—reflecting rising absolute monarchs and a reviving Catholic Church, both of whom were the major patrons of Baroque artists. The figure most associated with the rebuilding of Rome in the age of the Counter-Reformation was Gian Lorenzo Bernini (1598–1680), an accomplished painter, sculptor, and architect. Bernini designed the magnificent altar in St. Peter's Basilica, the papal throne, and the welcoming arms of St. Peter's Square outside. In addition, Bernini's version of the *David* demonstrates the Baroque style eloquently: unlike Michelangelo's static psychological portrait, Bernini provides the viewer with the action of David flinging his slingshot. Bernini's most famous work—*The Ecstasy of St. Teresa*—combines sculpture and architecture to create a rapturous religious vision.

Absolute monarchs like Louis XIV needed artists to assist in conveying their grandeur. Court painters, such as Velazquez (1599–1660) of Spain, managed to win patronage by not only glorifying monarchy but also creating rich and complex commentaries on their subjects, as with *The Maids of Honor*. Another outstanding painter of the Baroque style who attracted many patrons was Peter Paul Rubens (1577–1640). Rubens was one of the first studio painters, employing a team of assistants to help him complete his many muscular and energetic compositions of scenes both religious, like *The Raising of the Cross*, and political, such as his *Portraits of Marie de Medicis* (wife of Henry IV of France). In music, the compositions of J.S. Bach, Antonio Vivaldi, G.F. Handel, and the operas of Monteverdi expressed the Baroque fascination with ornate, complex structure as well as religious and secular themes of power.

5 SKILL SET

England often seems a genteel and peaceful nation; however, its history involves ongoing conflicts over politics, religion, and ethnicity. Consider this periodization question: Which of the following dates represents the most significant turning point in English politics: 1534, 1603, 1649, 1689? Be prepared to justify your response.

6 THEME MUSIC

You may wish to find images of these artworks using an Internet search or by consulting one of art sites mentioned previously. As always, be prepared to place the art in context (CTX) by explaining the artist's technique and linking its subject matter to the concerns of the period. Baroque is the art of princes and popes, patronage and power. Can you make this conceptual link with a few examples of art?

The Wars of Louis XIV[7]

To understand European diplomacy, you must grasp the importance of the **balance of power**. Balance-of-power politics developed during the Italian Renaissance but reached its most explicit form during the Age of Louis XIV. Louis's desire to extend France to its "natural frontiers" (the Rhine River) and also accrue glory to himself led him into nearly constant warfare during his reign. As Spain continued its decline under the Habsburgs, France rushed in to exploit the vacuum of power in western Europe. In each of these wars, Louis animated a coalition of powers against him to prevent his threat to the balance of power, or the dominance of one nation over the rest. As you read over the wars below, focus on how the balance of power operates and shifts with each phase of conflict.

The first targets of Louis's ambitions were the Spanish Netherlands and Dutch Republic, the latter whose commercial success he envied. This Dutch War earned Louis the strategic province of Franche-Comté (formerly Burgundy), which outflanked Alsace-Lorraine, his next target. Taking advantage of the growing weakness of the Holy Roman Empire, Louis in 1689 then invaded Alsace-Lorraine. The subsequent Nine Years' War resulted in an anti-French alliance, also known as the League of Augsburg. Now both the stadholder of the Netherlands and king of England, William III (of Orange) pieced together this coalition to prevent Louis's bid for continental domination. Famines, sieges, and high taxes marked this desultory conflict, which ended in 1697 practically where it started, with Louis gaining only a few towns along his border. Bigger game awaited, as the Spanish monarch, Charles II, continued to decline in health, with no heir to the throne.

European royal houses had waited decades for the death of poor Charles II (1665–1700), the last Habsburg ruler of Spain and sad result of generations of interbreeding between the Spanish and Austrian Habsburg lines. Complicating matters, Louis XIV and the Holy Roman Emperor claimed the throne through family marriages to Charles's sisters. Both contenders signed a treaty in 1700 to partition the Spanish Empire and thus maintain the balance of power. These plans fell to naught when Charles left a will in 1700 after his death granting all possessions to his nephew, Philip V, the Bourbon grandson of Louis XIV. Louis decided to press his claim to the Spanish throne via his grandson. The resulting War of Spanish Succession (1702–1713) proved to be the most costly, important, and last of Louis's wars for continental domination. France and Spain faced off against England, the Netherlands, the Holy Roman Emperor, and a few smaller states. Warfare in the 18th century involved deliberate movements designed to outmaneuver opponents or capture strategic fortresses. The war dragged expensively on, as each nation—large and small—exploited the conflict to meet long-held territorial and political goals.

With the Peace of Utrecht in 1714 the conflict finally came to a close. Louis's grandson Philip V (1700–1749) did become the Bourbon ruler of Spain, but it was a truncated empire that could never be united with its northern Bourbon neighbor of France. To recognize the weaker position of Spain, the 10 southern provinces of the Netherlands were given to Austria (now the Austrian Netherlands), as were former Spanish territories in Italy. The big winner of the conflict proved to be England, which gained Gibraltar, a fortress at the opening of the Mediterranean, new territory in North America, and the privilege of trading with the Spanish Empire, known as the *asiento*. Britain's Protestant succession was also confirmed, and it was poised, with a stable government and enhanced commercial position, to become the leading maritime power in Europe. As we'll see below, other nations either emerged from the conflict with new found or curtailed power. However, the major consequences of the war and the treaty were to block Louis XIV's last effort to impose French domination on the continent and to confirm the European state system of sovereign nations constantly shifting positions to maintain or create a balance of power. On his deathbed in 1715, Louis told his heir and great-grandson (the future Louis XV) that he feared he "had loved war too much."

7 EXAMPLE BASE
You may be confused by the wars covered in this section. Focus your attention on the nature of war, the rivalries, the changing role of the state, and their effects on the balance of power. Military history on the AP exam tends to revolve around these issues and lesson on battles and strategy.

Aging Empires in the East

Three aging states dominated central Europe in the 17th century—the Holy Roman Empire, Poland, and the Ottoman Empire. The weakness of these "soft states"—so-called because of their loose organization—allowed for the emergence of a new constellation of powers.

Following the Thirty Years' War (1648), the Holy Roman Empire's status as a loose confederation of over 300 German states was confirmed. The traditional rulers of the empire, the Austrian Habsburgs, turned east over the next century to enhance their power, particularly at the expense of the declining Ottoman Empire. Though Austria was able to gain significant swaths of land in east-central Europe, these conquests continued to bring more non-German minorities (Slavs, Poles, Italians, Romanians, and Ukrainians) into the empire, which later proved a centrifugal force, as nationalism took hold in the 19th century[8].

8 SKILL SET

As you may have noticed, some states experienced success and others failure in their attempts to enhance their power and overcome internal divisions and external threats. Be able to place sets of nations side by side (e.g., France and Poland) and explain the reasons for the outcomes (COMP).

Poland was the weakest of the European kingdoms. Ironically, Poland had been in 1500 the largest nation in Europe. Throughout the 16th century, the powerful nobles of Poland—the *szlachta*, who made up almost 10% of the population—succeeded in limiting the power of the Polish kings. Eventually, the Polish monarchy evolved into an elective position, and one that was fought over by rival European powers, who bribed the noble-electors with promises of religious toleration and respect for their "liberties." After 1587, the nation was ruled by only two native-born monarchs. Further, a single noble could block the actions of the Sejm, Poland's representative body, by using the *liberum veto*. Poland's experience ran counter to the larger trend toward absolutism, and unable to establish permanent taxes or a standing army, Poland fell prey to larger rivals. The tragic result of this failure to centralize for the formerly great kingdom was **Poland's Partition** in 1795.

After the Turks captured Constantinople in 1453, the Ottoman Empire periodically sent shock waves of fear throughout central Europe with an ebb and flow of expansion. In 1529, the Turks had nearly captured Vienna, but eventually fell back into internal turmoil for over a century. Once again, in 1683 the Turks besieged the Habsburg capital, which was rescued triumphantly by a multinational Holy League (led by the last great native Polish king, Jan Sobieski) at the **Battle of Vienna**. Never again would the Turks pose a major threat to central Europe. What had once been Ottoman strengths, now decayed; the empire simply did not keep up with rest of Europe. First, the Turkish rulers, the Sultans, grew corrupt from court intrigue, assassination plots, and sensuous living. Second, the once-great Janissaries, the elite fighters comprised of former Christians, became a static force opposed to technological and strategic change. Finally, though the Ottoman rulers tolerated religious minorities (more so than most European nations), the resulting tradition of local rule made it difficult to draw effectively on the resources of the empire's far-flung provinces. Many states, such as France, desired the continued existence of the Ottoman Empire as a counterweight to the Austrian Habsburgs, but only if the Islamic state could be influenced and indirectly controlled from the outside.

Austria Turns East

Once the Austrian Habsburgs held off the Turkish invasion in 1683, they were able to turn the battle back toward their long-time enemies. Employing the talents of a castoff from the court of Louis XIV, Eugene of Savoy (1663–1736), the Austrians defeated the Turks, gaining back Hungary and adding Transylvania, as well as territory in the Balkan Peninsula, by treaty (1699). Austria needed to end the Turkish conflict so as to turn their attention to the impending War of Spanish Succession (see above). Though the Austrians were unable to reunite the two Habsburg branches (Spanish and Austrian) during the conflict, the Peace of Utrecht (1713–1714) granted them territory in the Netherlands and Italy.

The reign of Emperor Charles VI (1711–1740) was dominated by one issue: ensuring the succession of his daughter and heir, Maria Theresa (1740–1780), to the many Habsburg lands. To this effect, Charles negotiated the Pragmatic Sanction with Europe's rulers, whereby they agreed to respect the Habsburg inheritance to a female ruler. Given the circumstances, Austria adjusted effectively after its losses in the Thirty Years' War, but as we'll see in the next chapter, the succession issue would ultimately cost the Habsburgs their dominant position in central Europe.

The Rise of Prussia and Its Army

The rise of Brandenburg-Prussia (later simply Prussia) in the 17th century was a surprise. A scattered nation with a small population (2 million in 1650) and few natural resources, Prussia relied heavily on three factors for its amazing rise to power: 1) skillful and resolute leadership from the Hohenzollern dynasty, 2) efficient use of resources, and, most importantly, 3) an outstanding military tradition. As was often joked, "Prussia is not a state with an army, but an army with a state." For no other nation was the military so closely associated with its power and prestige.

Brandenburg stood in the middle of north-central Germany, of importance only as an Elector of the Holy Roman Emperor. However, in 1618 the Hohenzollerns inherited the Duchy of Prussia, so far east that it was surrounded by Poland. During the Thirty Years' War, Brandenburg experienced widespread devastation, its capital city of Berlin reduced to a village of rubble. Nonetheless, Brandenburg-Prussia gained territory in the west along the Rhine and in Pomerania as a result of the Peace of Westphalia (1648). Frederick William, the Great Elector (1640–1688), resolved that his nation would never again be overrun by invading armies.

Frederick William was the first in a line of great Prussian rulers. To gain the support of the Prussian nobility (the Junkers) Frederick William granted them important positions in the army and allowed them almost complete power over their serfs. In exchange, the aristocracy agreed to accept Hohenzollern leadership and an excise tax to fund the activities of the state. With these funds, Frederick William erected the skeleton of the Prussian state. To collect the taxes, Frederick William created the General War Commissariat, which at first provisioned the army but evolved into a state bureaucracy, famous for its punctuality and efficiency. The Hohenzollern rulers generally lived a Spartan existence, allowing most of the state's revenues to flow into the army. Though Frederick William enhanced the army to 40,000 men, his goal was not to use it for conquest, but for security and as the glue that held scattered Prussia together. In addition, Frederick William practiced mercantilism by establishing monopolies, raising tariffs on imported goods, and promoting economic development. When Louis XIV revoked the Edict of Nantes, the Prussian state welcomed the persecuted Huguenots, eager to cash in on their economic skills.

During the War of Spanish Succession, the Habsburg emperor called on the support of Brandenburg-Prussia to drive out the French from Germany. As a reward for his support, the duke of Brandenburg-Prussia earned himself a new title—king in Prussia. The first great king of Prussia proved to be Frederick William I (1713–1740), not to be confused with Frederick William, the Great Elector. Frederick William's personality and approach to governing were strict, paternalistic, and austere. The ruler could be seen patrolling the streets of his realm with a walking stick, admonishing government officials or wayward citizens. Efficiency and duty took precedence over all else. State funds were used judiciously to augment the size of the army (up to 83,000) and often at the expense of the royal household budget. Frederick William introduced merit to government service, often promoting the middle class, though this by no means challenged the primary position of the Junkers or the army. However, Frederick William fought no wars in his reign. This feat he left for the son with whom he never got along, Frederick II.

Peter and the Westernization of Russia[9]

Russia's Unique Position

Much of Russia is *in* Europe, but Russia has not always been *of* Europe. Many of the trends we have addressed thus far—Renaissance, Reformation, Scientific Revolution (see Chapter 6)—did not touch the Russian state or its people. For many in the west, Russia was a mystery, more

9 SKILL SET
The skill of CCOT applies especially well to Russian history. Though many rulers have attempted the modernization of Russia, a continual theme has been the difficulty of Russia to establish a functioning democracy able to harness the energies of its people, despite the changes in policies and regimes. The vast expanse and ethnic/linguistic diversity of Russia has often meant a top-down government. How does Peter I connect with this issue?

closely tied to the political and religious traditions of Asia. It is not as difficult, however, to identify the thrust of Russia's experience, as the themes of (1) expansion and (2) relative back-wardness define its role in European history.

As we've seen, Russia made strides in establishing a larger and more modern state under both Ivan III and Ivan IV in the 16th century. These rulers succeeded in driving the Mongols from much of central Asia, establishing some semblance of an administrative structure and creating a military class (*streltsy*). Unfortunately, Ivan IV killed his heir to the throne in a fit of rage, causing Russia to enter a difficult period of internal instability and foreign invasion known as the Time of Troubles (1604–1613). The situation was not resolved until the feudal estates (Zemsky Sobor) elected Michael Romanov (1613–1645) as the tsar of Russia. Romanov rule would last in Russia until the Russian Revolution in 1917 led to the end of the family line.

Russia now gained stability but continued to lag behind Europe. First, it was during the 17th century that Russia's oppressive system of **serfdom** was put into legal form. Though other nations in eastern and central Europe practiced serfdom, only in Russia could serfs be bought and sold like chattel. This slave-like existence often provoked massive rebellions, in which discontented serfs often allied with Cossacks (a warrior tribe) in proclaiming the overthrow of landlords and those in authority. Furthermore, Russia's dominant religion was the tradition-bound Orthodox Church, which tended to oppose social and religious changes. When the Russian patriarch Nikon (head of the Russian Orthodox Church) undertook reforms in the Bible and worship, a group called the Old Believers opposed the reforms and threatened to break away from the church. These represent only two issues facing Russia during this period, but they demonstrate well the divide between Russia's people and its government, as well as the conflict between tradition and modernization.

The Reforms of Peter the Great

Peter I, the Great (1682–1725) stands as one of the greatest and most fascinating figures in Russian history. On one hand, Peter was attracted by all that was modern—technology, science, industry; on the other, he could be brutal and ruthless in the pursuit of his goals. By the sheer force of his personality and vision, Peter within a generation brought Russia into the European state system and made his nation a great power. Though Peter did succeed in making the rest of Europe take note of Russia's might, his reforms did not seep down to the common person and often created divisions within Russian society.

As a boy in Moscow, Peter enjoyed the company of westerners who lived in the so-called German suburb of the city. Here he learned about engineering and manufacturing. When Peter took the throne, he decided to embark on a Great Embassy (1697–1698) to the west with hundreds of technical advisors. Peter attempted to travel incognito, but it was hard to miss the nearly 7-foot-tall Russian leader as he visited shipyards, manufactories, and colleges. The trip was cut short as Peter faced a rebellion at home by the *streltsy*, who perceived Peter's reforms as a threat to their power. Upon his return, Peter personally interrogated and executed many of the leaders of the rebellion, hanging their bodies on the city gates as a warning to others. With this storehouse of new technical skill, however, Peter helped build Russia's first navy and a more modern army. During his reign, Peter was nearly continuously at war, generally with the Ottoman Turks and Swedes.

Internally, Peter set out to strengthen the nation as well as reform the habits of his people. Taxes were imposed on a variety of items, including "heads," known as the poll tax. With these funds, Peter pursued mercantilist policies aimed at making Russia a commercial nation, with its own joint-stock companies, merchant fleet, and monopolies. Peter even employed serf labor in mining, metallurgy, and textile manufacture. Russians also needed to look modern, so Peter banned the wearing of long coats, beards, and the veiling of women. To promote loyalty to the state, Peter required all members of the landowning class to engage in state service. This later evolved into a system of merit, known as the Table of Ranks, whereby subjects could rise in status based on contributions to the state. To make governing the vast Russian expanse more effective, Peter eliminated the feudal organs of self-government and divided the nation into 10 governing units, with a senate of advisers to assist him in day-to-day administration. Finally, to resolve the conflict within the Russian Orthodox Church, Peter simply eliminated the position of patriarch and instead placed the church under the control of the state, a power that was exercised through a Holy Synod of bishops.

The Great Northern War

The primary goal of these changes was to gain territory at the expense of Russia's neighbors. At first, Peter directed his attention toward the Black Sea, hoping to gain a port city there. His campaigns failed to achieve much, except to demonstrate the backwardness of the Russian military. However, Peter's main rival was Sweden, whose territory and dominant position in the Baltic he wished to replace. After initial defeat in the Great Northern War (1700–1721) with Sweden, Peter learned from his mistakes and changed tactics and technology. Using the traditional Russian tactic of drawing the enemy into the Russian interior to face its brutal winter, Peter eventually gained a victory. By the Treaty of Nystadt (1721), Russia gained significant territory in the Baltic, which allowed Peter to build a new capital city, St. Petersburg, which represented his "window to the west." Never before had Russian influence extended so far into Europe.

No doubt, Peter accomplished much in his forced modernization of Russia. Prior to his reign, Russia was a large but backward entity relatively unknown to the rest of Europe. When Peter died in 1725, he left a Russia a great power of Europe, feared for its sheer size and military potential. Many elites in Russia eagerly adopted Peter's reforms, as they saw in them the potential for individual gain and national power. Nonetheless, most of Peter's reforms came at the expense of the masses—serfs, The Orthodox Church, lower classes. While Russia had adopted a veneer of technological and industrial might, its autocratic (rule by one person) system of government was fastened more tightly on the nation than ever before. In the short run, Russia was now a major power and always a threat to expand; in the long run, these perennial issues of backwardness and autocratic rule contributed to the Russian Revolution in the 20th century.

Additional Resources

Peter Burke, *The Fabrication of Louis XIV* (1992)—Studies the man and myth who was the Sun King.

Euan Cameron, *Early Modern Europe: An Oxford History* (1999)—Provides interpretations by leading historians on a variety of relevant topics.

Christopher Clark, *Iron Kingdom: The Rise and Downfall of Prussia, 1600–1947* (2009)–Provides a strong analysis of how the small kingdom rose to great power.

Cromwell (1970)—Fast-paced film portrayal of the English Civil War.

Norman Davies, *Europe: A History* (1998)—This massive history places Poland at the center of Europe. The appendices and anecdotal boxes are alone worth the price of the book.

Robert K. Massie, *Peter the Great: His Life and World* (1980)—Fascinating character study. A lengthy book that could be used in sections. Also recommended is the outstanding miniseries based on the book.

Derek McKay and H.M. Scott, *The Rise of the Great Powers, 1648–1815* (1983)—Detailed account of how and why the balance of power shifted during this period; useful in sections for research on specific nations.

http://www.classical.net/—For those interested in classical music, this site offers biographical sketches of important composers.

http://www.biography.com/people/louis-xiv–9386885/videos/louis-xiv-full-episode-2073406805 Helpful film biography of Louis XIV.

Practice MC Questions

Questions 1–4 are based on the passages below.

<u>Source 1</u>

"[W]ith all humble and due respect to your Majesty our Sovereign Lord and Head...we most truly avouch, First, That our privileges and liberties are our right and due inheritance, no less than our very lands and goods.

Secondly, That they cannot be withheld from us, denied, or impaired, but with apparent wrong to the whole state of the realm....

Fourthly, We avouch also, That our House is a Court of Record, and so ever esteemed."

Form of Apology and Satisfaction, statement of Parliament to James I, 1604

<u>Source 2</u>

"The state of Monarchy is the supremest thing upon earth; for kings are not only God's lieutenants upon earth and sit upon God's throne, but even by God himself they are called gods. There be three principal similitudes that illustrate the state of Monarchy: one taken out of the word of God and the two other out of the grounds of policy and philosophy. In the Scriptures kings are called gods, and so their power after a certain relation compared to the Divine power."

James I, king of England and Scotland, speech to Parliament, 1610

1. Which of the following trends of the 17th century do the passages reflect?

   A. The effort by monarchs to centralize administration and the opposition this created.

   B. The use of scientific principles to justify the sovereignty and power of governments.

   C. The continuation of traditional beliefs regarding knowledge and the cosmos.

   D. The growth of commerce and establishment of mercantilist policies by states.

2. Which of the following states represents the strongest exception to the political ideal articulated in Source 2?

   A. Russia

   B. France

   C. Poland

   D. Spain

3. The principles stated in Source 1 would be fulfilled with:

   A. The Commercial Revolution

   B. The Glorious Revolution

   C. The Scientific Revolution

   D. The Protestant Reformation

4. Which of the following would have most likely agreed with the sentiments expressed in Source 1 and disagreed with those in Source 2?

   A. John Calvin

   B. Thomas Hobbes

   C. John Locke

   D. Louis XIV

J. R. Tanner, Constitutional Documents of the Reign of James I 1603-1625 (London: Cambridge University Press, 1952), p. 221.; J. R. Tanner, "Speech to Parliament, 1610," Constitutional Documents of the Reign of James I 1603-1625 (London: Cambridge University Press, 1952), p. 15.

> "[The year 1648] looks like a sensible starting point because it was in that year that the Peace of Westphalia was concluded, bringing to an end a war that had lasted thirty years and had inflicted more devastation on Europe than any previous conflict. Moreover, it has settled two major issues, for the independence of the Dutch Republic from Spain was recognized, and the structure of German-speaking Europe was settled for a century and a half. More important still was what lay behind those two settlements: the recognition that [religious] pluralism had come to stay."
>
> Tim Blanning, historian, *The Pursuit of Glory*, 2007

5. Which of the following was a political or diplomatic result of the "religious pluralism" cited in Blanning's analysis?

   A. The Ottoman Empire ceased its westward expansion into the heart of Europe.

   B. Dynastic and state interest replaced faith as the main motive for warfare.

   C. Louis XIV of France felt empowered to revoke the Edict of Nantes.

   D. Britain and France engaged in a European and colonial conflict for dominance.

6. Which of the following developments fits most closely the periodization scheme offered by Blanning?

   A. The dominance of centralized nation-states engaged in competition for territory and resources

   B. The movement of the arts from the Baroque style to commercial and Enlightenment themes

   C. The rise of an economy based on commercial agriculture and new methods of finance and trade

   D. The movement toward empirical and rational explanations for natural phenomena

See Chapter 18 for answers and explanations.

7. Which of the following most directly affected the German-speaking settlement that Blanning mentions?

   A. The economic and demographic devastation caused by the Thirty Years' War

   B. The incursion of France under Louis XIV into the policies and structure of the Holy Roman Empire

   C. The rise of enlightened absolutism in several central and eastern European states

   D. The emergence of two German powers (Austria and Prussia), each checking the advances of the other

8. Which of the following led to the most serious challenge to the political and diplomatic structure described by Blanning?

   A. The Industrial Revolution and growth of technology

   B. The decline of Spain as a major European power

   C. The rise of the United States as a world power

   D. The French Revolution and Napoleonic wars

Tim Blanning, *The Pursuit of Glory: The Five Revolutions that Made Modern Europe: 1648-1815* (New York: Penguin Books, 2007), p. xxiii.

Short-Answer Question with Sample and Commentary

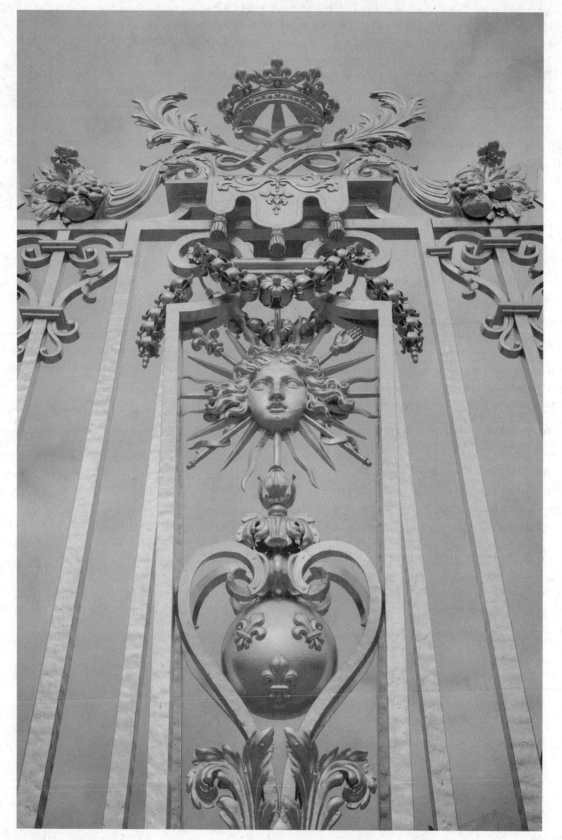

Detail of gate to Royal Courtyard, with image of Louis XIV, Chateau of Versailles, France, Europe, 17th century

Ferdinand Bol, Dutch painter. *Governors of the Wine Merchant's Guild.* ca. 1659

A. Explain TWO ways in which the works of art above reflect the economic, social, OR political differences between France and the Netherlands in the 17th century.

B. Explain ONE way in which art (as depicted above) changed OR remained the same from the time of the Renaissance.

(HTS: Contextualization, Comparison, CCOT)

> **A.** France and the Dutch could not have been more different in the 17th century. France was ruled by the Sun King, Louis XIV, who is portrayed in almost god-like fashion on the gate. In fact, this gate led into his extensive palace at Versailles, where he forced his nobles to participate in seeking his patronage. On the other hand, the Netherlands was a commercial republic focused on trade and gaining wealth through trade. It was decentralized and controlled by merchants; this helped spread ideas and promote tolerance, but it also made it hard for the Dutch to fight off their more powerful neighbors, like the French.
>
> **B.** Renaissance painters glorified the classics in their works and used perspective to provide a realistic view of their subjects. Louis the Sun King is shown in a classical style, like the ancient Greek sun-god Apollo. One change in art during this period is shown by the Dutch painting. Rather than grandiose scenes of Jesus (by Michelangelo or Raphael), the Dutch art reflected their prosperous middle-class society, as shown by the figures conducting business at the table.

Though well-written and with a strong sense of historical context, this response does not earn all points. The student accurately conveys the absolutism of France, contrasting it with the decentralized nature of the Netherlands. Though the student goes on to explain the economic values of commerce for the Dutch, she omits a second comparative feature for France (which could be drawn from either economic, social, or political life). Thus, Part A earns only 1 point. For Part B, the student accurately explains features of Renaissance art and established an appropriate similarity with the French painting and a difference with the Dutch painting, earning the point. 2 points

8 The Struggle for Wealth and Empire

The 18th century marks a turning point in the history of Europe. Many of the developments of previous centuries—the Scientific Revolution, centralized states, commercial advance—reached their full flower during this period. Hope for change and optimism regarding the future took hold, particularly among the upper classes. At the same time, this period was one of immense contradictions: tradition vs. progress, privilege vs. equality, wealth vs. poverty, elite vs. popular culture. In this chapter, we review the social structure of the Old Regime (on the eve of the French Revolution), recount the continuing advance of commerce, and show how competition over wealth and trade led to a major conflict in two phases that altered the European balance of power.

Key In Chapter 8 involves the following KCs from the Course Description:

- **KC 2.1** Competition among states for commerce and territory
- **KC 2.2** Further development of a market and global economy
- **KC 2.2** Higher standard of living from Agricultural Revolution and consumerism
- **KC 2.4** Developments in demographics, family, and society stimulated by the changing economy

---

Social Structure of the Old Regime

Demographic Changes[1]

1 THEME MUSIC

An oft-forgotten feature of the IS and PP themes is the so-called "vital revolution," the demographic shift to a society with a stable balance of births and deaths, based on improvements in medicine and hygiene that extend life expectancy and limit infant/child mortality. As you consult this section, consider how the 18th century laid the foundations for this trend.

Prior to the 18th century, Europe experienced periods of healthy population growth; inevitably, however, this had been followed by decline. Such declines usually resulted from scarcity of resources, warfare, and disease, known as a **Malthusian Trap**. The 18th century represented a shift in this trend–though not apparent at the time–in that Europe's population continued a steady and even significant growth in following centuries. From 1720, when the growth became evident, until the French Revolution (1789), Europe's population increased from about 120 to 180 million. What factors account for this growth?

- *Diet*—As a result of the Agricultural and Commercial Revolutions (see below), Europeans secured access to increased amounts and a <u>wider variety of food supplies</u>. Malnutrition and famine became rarer.

- ***Transportation improvements***—The building of roads and canals made it easier for national governments to address local shortages of grain and make good on crop failures.

- ***Decline of the plague***—Despite a few minor outbreaks, the dreaded bubonic plague, which every generation wiped out 10%–15% of the population in certain regions, mysteriously disappeared from the continent.

- *Weather*—Europe's **Little Ice Age** was coming to an end, especially after 1750, which meant a longer growing season and more reliable crops.

- *Medical improvements*—Though Edward Jenner introduced the **smallpox vaccine** in the 18th century, medical improvements actually played only a minor role in the population increase. Hospitals, medical training, and the understanding of disease remained woeful.

All of Europe took part in the population growth, but the increase tended to be more gradual in eastern than western Europe, except for Russia, which surpassed France as the most populous European nation around 1780. Urban areas grew the fastest, often straining their still-primitive infrastructure of roads, housing, waste removal, and charitable relief.

The Class System[2]

In the 18th century, European society continued to be divided into estates, or legally defined classes, which determined one's status. Though change was evident with the increasing importance placed on wealth, most nations continued to grant privilege for those who claimed hereditary descent from noble blood. Wealthy merchants and cash-strapped nobles often saw the benefit of blending families, fulfilling the twin purpose of raising the status of the merchants while infusing wealth into a threadbare aristocratic line. The chart below provides you with a snapshot of the class system in the 18th century. Keep in mind that this data represents a baseline for comparison's sake to evaluate the social impact of the French Revolution, which began in 1789.

2 SKILL SET

Over the course of the 18th century, economic developments effected changes in the social structure, setting the stage for the French and Industrial Revolutions. As you read through this section, consider the Changes and Continuities Over Time (CCOT) that mark a discrepancy between the traditions of the Old Regime (Three Estates) and those of a more dynamic class structure, linked to the growth of a money economy.

Class	Activities	Status/Standard of Living	Developments/ Assessment
Nobility	*Lived primarily off of their estates, which varied considerably in size. *Often monopolized positions in the military as well as government and judicial offices. *Nobles often had more in common with those of the same class in other nations than they did with peasants in their homelands. *Often received a classical education, spoke French (the language of philosophy and culture in the 18th century), and if male, ventured on a grand tour. *A rite of passage, the grand tour allowed male aristocrats to experience European art, ideas, as well as gambling and **prostitution**.	*Noble status was defined by a set of legal and social privileges—the right to hunt, to be tried in special courts, to hold office, to claim exemptions from taxes. *With advances in commerce, nobles prided themselves on acquiring the newest fashions, carriages, art, and luxury items. *In England, to keep lands intact, families practiced primogeniture and entail, or granting all lands to the eldest son and prohibiting him or his heirs from ever breaking them up. Such laws forced younger sons into business or the clergy and became a hated symbol of privilege. *In imitation of Louis XIV, many nobles built gracious country houses, especially in England. With the grandeur of a palace and the comfort of home, such residences expressed classical style and the increased desire for **privacy**.	*Aristocrats of the 18th century experienced a revival of power following the great age of absolutism. *Remarkably adaptable, nobles used investments and strategic marriages with merchants to meld their noble status with new wealth. *To support a more luxurious lifestyle, nobles tried to wring out of the peasantry whatever taxes, fees, dues, and obligations could be justified from the remnants of the feudal system. *The continued existence of this system of unequal privileges came under increasing attack by Enlightenment philosophes (see next chapter).

Class	Activities	Status/Standard of Living	Developments/ Assessment
Peasants	*The great majority of Europeans (about 80%–85%) continued to work the land as either peasants or **serfs**. ***Free peasants**, who lived primarily in western and some parts of central Europe, often owned their own land or had the right to work the land of a lord. ***Villages** governed the lives of peasants. Decisions regarding agriculture, local disputes, public order, and religion were made by village leaders according to customs and the needs of the community.	*Standards of living for peasants varied significantly, depending on the degree of freedoms, soil/climate conditions, and strength of the nobility. *Those living east of the Elbe River or in southern Italy and the Iberian peninsula often faced more difficult burdens. *Nobles in eastern Europe and Russia were larger in number and exercised greater power over their peasants and serfs. *Despite improvements in diet and transportation, peasants still fell prey to famines and diseases (because of greater susceptibility due to malnutrition).	*In some ways, little changed in peasant life from the 16th to 18th centuries—nobles still held sway, customs dictated everyday life, and fate seemed to rule one's destiny. At the same time, changes were evident. *Peasant life was marginally more secure because of improved diet and better weather. *Discontent over a lingering feudal system often sparked revolts. The most famous of these was the Pugachev Revolt in the 1770s in Russia, the largest peasant uprising in European history. Such revolts underscored the growing dissatisfaction with the unequal class system.
Towns-people/ Bour-geoisie	*Towns attracted both people and capital. *Cities produced wealth through manufacture and trade. *The middle class often owned land in the countryside, living off rents and dues. *Peasants resented the parasitical role of the towns, which seemed to absorb the wealth of the countryside but provide nothing in return.	*Cities technically existed outside the feudal structure and jealously guarded their liberties. *Standards of living varied widely between the **merchant oligarchs** who dominated political and social life, and the petty bourgeoisie of artisans and shopkeepers, down to the menial laborers, beggars, and prostitutes. *Wealthy merchants and entrepreneurs imitated the tastes and styles of the nobility, often intermarrying with them or gaining noble status through purchase of an office.	*Cities in the 18th century paled in comparison with today's teeming industrial metropolises. Europe's largest city was London with around 1 million people. Many towns had only 10,000 to 50,000 inhabitants. *Towns played an important economic and cultural role, attracting migrants from the countryside, capital from investors, and ideas from all over Europe. *Cities suffered under an inadequate infrastructure of streets, houses, and waste removal in the face of growing populations.

Class	Activities	Status/Standard of Living	Developments/Assessment
		*As commerce expanded, cities grew in size and eventually became overwhelmed with the problems of **poverty** and **crime**. Charitable institutions still existed to address needs, but attitudes hardened against professional beggars. Many nations passed laws to house the poor in hospitals or workhouses.	*Belief in a "moral economy" led city-dwellers to demand "fair prices" for grains. *To avoid bread riots, governments also stored grain to provide reasonable prices.

Family Life and Child-Rearing

The 18th-century European family remained predominantly **nuclear**, with the exception of parts of eastern Europe where the tax system promoted extended families living under one roof. Average ages at first marriage in Europe remained high compared with other civilizations in the 18th century—often mid- to late 20s for both men and women–known as the **European marriage pattern**. Couples delayed wedlock until they were able to support themselves economically and provide for children.

Families generally labored together as an economic unit. In agricultural settings, tasks tended to divide based on gender, with men involved in heavier work such as plowing, while women assisted with harvesting, mowing hay, and preparing food. Children were expected to contribute productive labor at an early age. In towns, boys were apprenticed to a local shop or filled any job that augmented the family income. Young women often found themselves in domestic settings as servants and maids, their goal being to earn a sufficient dowry to guarantee a favorable marriage partner. Theoretically, servants were to be treated as members of the family, with the heads of the household responsible for their well-being and moral upbringing. In fact, young women often found themselves subject to verbal abuse and the sexual advances of male family members.

Strong community controls in early modern Europe had ensured that couples avoided having children out of wedlock. As long as the couple was married prior to the birth of the child, social stigma did not attach to premarital sex. However, between 1750 and 1850 a rapid increase of **illegitimacy** occurred. It is unclear what caused this trend. One explanation is that the new opportunities provided by **cottage industry**—earning money at home by finishing products— allowed couples to earn income without access to land or regular employment. Additionally, small children could contribute to the family income quickly as part of this system. Furthermore, migration to cities tended to disrupt traditional patterns of arranged marriages and enforcement of marriage promises by men.

The unfortunate consequences of the out-of-wedlock births led to the related problems of infanticide and child abandonment. Though Europeans used traditional **birth control** methods to limit population, these techniques proved unreliable and dangerous, as in the case of abortion. Unwanted children were often "accidentally" smothered in bed during the night. Some nations even outlawed the common practice of parents and children sharing a bed to discourage these actions. Given the extremes of poverty and inequality that existed in 18th-century cities, it was not surprising that young women felt driven to infanticide. An illustration of this sad practice occurred when the city of Rennes, France opened a storm drain in 1721 only to find the skeletons of 80 infants within[1]. Rather than the extreme measure of infanticide, many couples or mothers abandoned their children on the steps of a church or hospital. Wealthy philanthropists and Catholic religious orders established foundling homes to care for this burgeoning population. However, such homes were often overwhelmed, and the vast majority of the children under their care died before reaching maturity.

Traditionally, children were viewed as sinful "sprigs of Adam," and parents were warned that "to spare the rod was to spoil the child." The modern expression "rule of thumb," in fact, derives from the limitation on the width of a stick a husband was allowed to reprove both children and wife. Children were tightly swaddled to restrict their natural impulsive movements, as parents worked to instill discipline from the earliest ages. Upper-class women relied on wet nurses to provide nutrition for their children, which often meant they went undernourished or neglected.

Such views of children began to change slowly in the 18th century. A result of the ideas of John Locke and the educational writings of Jean-Jacques Rousseau (see next chapter), new attitudes began to stress the view of children as innocent creatures who needed tender love and guidance through progressive stages of development. Rousseau and others denounced the practices of wet-nursing and swaddling. Children, they argued, should be insulated from the adult world of vulgarity and cruelty. Among the upper classes, parents began to provide their children with age-appropriate clothing, reading materials, and games. Books and toys were designed to stimulate children's interest and moral development. Simplified scientific ideas found their way into books like Tom Telescope's *Newtonian System of Philosophy*, probably written by John Newbery (1713–1767). Newbery, also famous for *The Pretty Little Pocket Book*, richly illustrated his books to appeal to children's eyes. Along with the jigsaw puzzle, parents lavished children with dolls, *camera obscuras* (a simple machine for projecting images), and tops. New family practices were also reflected in more government attention being given to primary education (see next chapter)[3].

3 SKILL SET

As practice for Argumentation and Use of Evidence (EVARG), consider the following prompt as you read through this section: How and why did child-rearing attitudes and practices change over the course of the 18th century?

The Dynamic Economy of the Eighteenth Century

At the center of the significant social, cultural, and intellectual developments occurring in 18th-century Europe stood an expanding and changing economy. More than ever, Europe became enmeshed in a global system of trade; at the same time, the continent reaped the fruits of incremental advances in manufacturing and agriculture. Ultimately, the national pursuit of wealth and empire fueled a series of mid-century wars that altered the European balance of power and set the stage for the French Revolution.

Cottage Industry

For centuries, European manufacturing had taken place in towns under the auspices of the guilds. During the 18th century, the system of **cottage industry** expanded, whereby a merchant capitalist paid wages to rural families to finish raw materials. Due to its lack of internal tariffs and weak guild structure, England experienced the most rapid expansion of this **putting-out system**. Though the British Isles later gained the reputation for industrial ingenuity, their manufactures in 1750 were easily surpassed by several other nations. However, England could boast an expanding base of textile production, one of the most basic of consumer goods. The many and varied steps of textile production lent themselves to the decentralized nature of cottage industry. Entrepreneurial expansion of manufacturing in the countryside allowed merchants to reinvest profits from trade and later provided sufficient capital for investment in large-scale industrial enterprises. In addition, cottage industry provided rural families the opportunity to supplement a livelihood often threatened by changes in the nature of agriculture.

---

[1]Isser Woloch, *Eighteenth-Century Europe: Tradition and Progress, 1715–1789* (New York: Norton, 1982), p. 162.

The Agricultural Revolution

An inefficient agricultural system arrested European population growth. The open three-field system wasted a large proportion of useful land, and primitive techniques offered little margin for error, often plunging regions into famine, as had happened in the 1690s. Much of this insecurity was relieved by the Agricultural Revolution of the 18th century. The movement began in the Netherlands and England and featured the introduction of new crops and the application of new techniques. Some have labeled these changes in crop and livestock raising scientific agriculture.

To combat the waste of allowing fields to lie fallow, agricultural reformers like Charles "Turnip" Townsend (1674–1738) supported the use of nitrogen-replenishing crops such as turnips, clover, and alfalfa. Such fodder crops also fed livestock, whose manure was in turn used to further increase the output of fields. One of the crops vital to saving millions from malnutrition proved to be the potato. Easy to grow, rich in vitamins, and versatile, the crop became a staple of the peasant diet in Ireland, Prussia, and Russia. A large family could subsist on as little as an acre of potatoes.

Increasing production also involved solutions as simple as clearing more land. Using new drainage techniques, such as terracing, the Dutch and English were able to reclaim swamps and bogs. Jethro Tull (1674–1741), another reformer concerned about increasing yields, advocated soil aeration through use of the hoe and invention of the seed drill, which pushed the seed safely beneath the soil. Tull thus employed Enlightenment reason and empirical study in service of practical solutions. Improvements in livestock, through selective breeding, served as a natural next step. The English government granted awards to those who could produce the fattest and meatiest cattle, providing additional protein for the average person's diet.

Efficiency often requires doing things in a big way, or what is known as economies of scale. In agriculture, this meant that the traditional open-field system of scattered strips of land had to be abandoned. This process had already been underway in England since the 16th century with enclosure. Advances in agricultural techniques in the 18th century provided an additional spur, as Parliament passed enclosure acts, which allowed wealthy landowners to buy up common land and enclose it within large manors. This destruction of the commons produced an unequal system of landholding in England, with a few large landholders at the top, some independent yeoman and enterprising tenant farmers in the middle, and a mass of landless laborers on the bottom. For this last group, the loss of land rendered them dependent on earning wages, driving them into the newly expanding and industrializing cities as an unskilled labor force[4].

The Commercial Revolution, Phase II

While the Dutch remained important traders, they had been surpassed by the French and the English, both of whose commerce ballooned in the 18th century. East India companies, pooling the resources of numerous investors, were established by numerous nations and exploited the European taste for a whole range of new consumer goods. Triangular trade facilitated the exchange of goods between the continents of Europe, Africa, and the Americas, also promoting the human trafficking in slaves. Europe's sweet tooth caused untold suffering for Africans forced to work in the horrifying conditions of Caribbean sugar plantation "factories."

Europeans continued to demand spices from the East—cinnamon, nutmeg, cloves, pepper, saffron. The new beverages of coffee and tea appeared on the European menu, making the East Indies, India, and Ceylon focal points for colonial interest, and spawning new venues for conversation (tea- and coffee-houses). These colonial areas were also known for the production of fine cloth and rugs. Light, brightly colored silks, calicoes, muslins, and chintzes poured into the homes of Europe's upper classes, as signs of status and refinement. Goods from overseas, as well as porcelain and cloth now produced within Europe, promoted a **consumer revolution** in tastes, as the well-to-do stocked their drawing rooms, boudoirs, and eating areas with genteel decor.

The biggest money-maker of all was sugar. Small sugar islands in the Caribbean easily outpaced the entire North American mainland in value to the British Empire. Throughout the 18th century, sugar production skyrocketed. As sugar increased, so did slavery. Over 600,000 slaves

4 THEME MUSIC

The Agricultural Revolution highlights an overarching question for the PP theme--how technological advances can benefit overall wealth and those who patronize the new processes (e.g., the gentry), yet at the same time create poverty and inequality for others (e.g., smallholders and peasants in traditional settings).

were brought from Africa to the island of Jamaica alone from 1700 to 1786. Originally dominated by the Portuguese then the Dutch, the **slave trade** fell into the orbit of English trading interests after the War of Spanish Succession. Because much of the profit from the slave trade and sugar went directly to England's industrial expansion, it would be fair to conclude that British capitalism resulted in part from the enslavement of Africans. What's more, because profits were so easy to come by on these sugar islands, plantation owners inhumanely treated their slaves, causing one of the highest mortality rates in the world.

Global trade produced a myriad of important results. Let's focus on three for right now:

- The profits from commerce promoted the development of a **market economy** of private property. Governments became much more dependent on entrepreneurs as a source of taxation and to underwrite state borrowing of funds, through banks and other credit institutions.

- As noted above, the accumulation of wealth by the **middle class (bourgeoisie)** tended to facilitate their merging with the aristocracy, as both gained from intermarriage.

- The potential for great riches led to an intensification of **commercial rivalries**, resulting in war. Conflict over territory in Europe merged with overseas competition for colonies and markets, producing the first world wars in history.

Diplomacy and War

Commercial competition invariably led to war in the 18th century. Soon after the Peace of Utrecht (1713–1714), one old rivalry (**Britain vs. France**) reasserted itself while another arose between Prussia and Austria over predominance of German affairs. These two rivalries stood at the center of diplomacy and war in the middle of the century. Spain experienced new life under the Bourbon monarchy of Philip V (1700–1749), and the Netherlands remained important financially, though neither was able to exert influence equivalent to that enjoyed before 1715. In the east, Russia demonstrated that its modernization under Peter the Great made it a reckoning force within the system of European diplomacy.

Before moving on to the wars, we take a quick snapshot of Britain and France after 1715. For purposes of the AP exam, this review is helpful in the case of Britain to note how that nation developed a unique constitutional system following the Glorious Revolution and in the case of France to lay the foundations for the long-term causes of the French Revolution[5].

5 SKILL SET
Since Britain and France battled over power on the European continent and overseas, consider setting up a Venn diagram to illustrate the similarities and differences between their economic, political, and social systems (COMP).

France—Limping Absolutism

The landed and commercial classes in France between 1715 and 1789 increased their power and challenged absolutism under the weak reigns of Louis XV (1714–1774) and Louis XVI (1774–1793). Both proved inadequate to the task of addressing France's pressing problems—Louis XV due to his preoccupation with hunting and controversial mistress and Louis XVI due to his indecision and scandalous wife (Marie Antoinette). The government's need to fund the debt left over from its many wars along with the constant desire of investors to profit from the Commercial Revolution led to an unintended crisis in public finance. Unlike England, France never developed the notion of a public debt funded by banks—the debt was considered the king's *personal* debt—and as a result lagged behind in the development of credit institutions and the ability to borrow money. Not surprisingly, the issues that forced the French monarchy to concede limits on its theoretically absolutist powers in 1789 were government debt and taxation.

Great Britain—the "King in Parliament" and Prime Minister

Following the Glorious Revolution in 1688, Britain developed a unique form of government known as the "king in parliament." In short, English monarchs continued to play an important political role, but worked through Parliament and a Prime Minister to pass legislation and govern. After the last Stuart monarch, Queen Anne (1701–1714), died without an heir, England turned to a related German dynasty—the Hanoverians. Despite the unpopularity of the first Hanoverian, George I (1714–1727), who did not speak English, the dynasty was able to establish a functioning government system by relying on a prime minister and the cabinet system.

A major reason for Britain's commercial success in the 18th century involved the close relationship between government finance and private enterprise. The Bank of England issued stock to finance government debt and also allowed investors to draw on a larger amount of capital than in other nations. As in France, this system almost led to a speculative disaster in 1720. Unlike France, Britain was able to salvage and further develop its system of public finance.

The man largely responsible for the development of Britain's cabinet system of government was Robert Walpole (tenure, 1721–1743), also considered the first prime minister. Walpole appointed ministers to head up government agencies who also served in the Parliament. By carefully managing his parliamentary majority through issuance of government stocks and promises of patronage, Walpole was able to steer legislation through the House of Commons (the more important of the two houses of Parliament). Throughout his tenure, Walpole worked diligently to advance Britain's commercial interests abroad while avoiding war (to keep taxes down), a task he was largely able to accomplish.

Eighteenth-Century Warfare

War in the 18th century was waged between highly trained and professional armies for specific strategic objectives. Soldiers were drawn from the underclass and less productive groups in society, perhaps "recruited" after a drunken night in a tavern. Their aristocratic army officers controlled them through harsh discipline. Because conflict proved less destructive to civilians and land than the religious wars of an earlier age, states entered into it more lightly and also withdrew from it more quickly. Questions of war tended to be calculated and strategic. Armies were expensive to maintain, train, and supply, so generals were reluctant to risk them carelessly in battle, often making warfare a game of movement and of securing supply lines. Infantry played the major role in war, their inaccurate smoothbore muskets and bright uniforms imparting a parade-ground atmosphere to battles. Nonetheless, 18th-century warfare was destructive and disruptive; it only seems less so in comparison with the conflagrations of the 20th century[6].

The War of Austrian Succession, 1740–1748

The War of Austrian Succession began with a cynical attack by Frederick II, the Great (1740–1786), king of Prussia, on Austria in defiance of the Pragmatic Sanction. Like a swarm of vultures, other nations (Bavaria, Saxony, Spain) rushed in to claim territorial prizes from the threatened empire. In continuance of their longtime opposition to the Habsburgs, the French joined the assault in alliance with Prussia. To prevent the dismemberment of Austria and maintain the balance of power on continent, Britain joined the fray on the side of the new Habsburg ruler, Maria Theresa (1740–1780). In this way, the two primary rivalries in European politics merged into a complex conflict, which would be fought in two phases (see Seven Years' War below).

Frederick the Great experienced a difficult youth. More interested in learning French and playing the flute than war, Frederick often feuded with his stern father, Frederick William I (see Chapter 7) who intended to break his son. The young Frederick attempted to escape the kingdom with a friend, whom Frederick William I had executed right before his son's eyes to teach him a lesson. Against odds, Frederick proved to be one the great rulers in German history and a true military genius. The primary target of Frederick's aggression was the resource-rich province of Silesia, which he was able to win and hold until the end of the conflict.

Frederick was almost equally matched by Maria Theresa. In an act of political theater, Maria Theresa held aloft her newborn son (the future Joseph II) before the Hungarian nobles in 1741 to appeal for their support, which they gave in a spasm of chivalric fervor. Though Maria eventually

6 THEME MUSIC
As you read this section, keep in the mind the strong connection between the SP and PP themes. Pursuit of commerce and colonies embroiled nations in conflict, stimulated the growth of military states, and altered the balance of power.

lost Silesia, she did well to hold onto most of her other possessions by treaty (1748), one that reflected an Anglo-French agreement and in which the Habsburg ruler had little say.

Britain and France waged war in several theaters in pursuit of their commercial and colonial objectives. Each side made advances against the other. The antagonists were thus content to return to the situation as it had existed before the war, with Frederick holding on to Silesia. Though the map had changed little beyond Silesia, the War of Austrian Succession had highlighted two issues: (1) France sat in an unfavorable strategic position hamstrung between major continental commitments with its large army and a growing commercial empire in need of naval defense, and (2) Austria and Prussia now uneasily coexisted as two relatively even powers in Germany, with the latter immensely enhanced by its capture of Silesia, which had doubled its population to 6 million and strengthened its economic base. Maria Theresa was just as determined to regain the territory.

The Reforms of Maria Theresa and Diplomatic Revolution of 1756

Maria Theresa embarked on a wide-ranging series of reforms after 1748. To reduce inefficiency, Maria Theresa centralized the collection of taxes and combined the chancelleries (administrative offices) of the various territories of her empire. The army was tripled in size, while a military academy and engineering school were also founded. Later in her reign, Maria Theresa promoted primary education in the interests of economic productivity, promoted smallpox inoculation, outlawed torture and capital punishment, and eased the burdens of serfdom. Though many of these reforms benefited her subjects, her primary goal was to strengthen the state so as to recapture Silesia.

In 1756, the great Austrian diplomat and advisor to Maria Theresa, Count von Kaunitz (1711–1794), engineered one of diplomacy's greatest coups. Von Kaunitz convinced France to give up its traditional opposition to the Habsburgs and enter an alliance against Prussia, a coalition that Russia also joined. This Diplomatic Revolution of 1756 forced Britain onto the side of Prussia to prevent another continental disruption to the balance of power (and a threat to Hanover, ancestral home to Britain's monarchy) and helped reignite the worldwide colonial conflict between France and Great Britain. Once again, despite the switch in alliances, the two key rivalries had merged, this time to produce a true world war with profound consequences for three continents[7].

7 EXAMPLE BASE
Don't be intimidated by the details in this section. If it helps, consider a focus question: How did states manage their economic and political resources in pursuit of power and in addressing both internal problems and external challenges?

The Seven Years' War, 1756–1763

The Seven Years' War stands as Frederick II's darkest and finest hour. Though outnumbered by his enemies almost 10 to 1, Frederick fought brilliantly, even when his capital Berlin was burned to the ground and all seemed lost. Britain provided primarily financial support in order to concentrate its energies on the colonial conflict with France. Frederick was aided by the disorganization of his opponents, who never seemed able to coordinate their attacks, and the French lack of enthusiasm for their new Austrian alliance. Despite his sometimes desperate situation and aging seemingly 20 years in 7 years' time, Frederick once again was able to hold onto Silesia by treaty (1763).

Fighting between France and Great Britain proved more decisive. Under the brilliant leadership of William Pitt the Elder (1708–1778), Britain won victories on land and sea in North America, the Caribbean, and in India. France found itself again depleted by fighting major wars on the continent of Europe and overseas. France and Britain both used their East India companies to exploit the decaying Mogul Empire in India, enlisting local rulers and warlords in pursuit of their interests. However, with its superior naval forces, Britain emerged victorious on balance, a fact that was reflected in the peace treaty.

By the Treaty of Paris (1763), Great Britain secured sole access to North America east of the Mississippi River and gained the dominant position in India, which became the "crown jewel of the British Empire." France was, however, able to win back its profitable sugar islands in the Caribbean. Though Britain clearly came out the dominant maritime power, French commerce continued to grow after 1763 and may have even outpaced Britain. The Treaty of Paris set the stage for major events on three continents. In North America (where the conflict was called the French and Indian War), British colonists were now free of the perennial French threat while the British were determined to make them pay for the costs of empire, a difference in outlook leading directly to the American Revolution. For Europe, the Seven Years' War confirmed the dualism in Germany of Austria and Prussia, but more importantly, set the stage for the French Revolution by increasing the debt of and criticism against the French monarchy. On the Indian subcontinent, Britain oversaw the further dissolution of the Mogul Empire and established a strong colonial presence that would change both civilizations.

Additional Resources

M.S. Anderson, *Europe in the Eighteenth Century, 1715–1783*, 3rd ed. (1987)—Provides a useful overview of political developments in each country.

Jeremy Black, *The Cambridge Illustrated Atlas of Warfare: Renaissance to Revolution, 1492–1792* (1996)—For those students interested in the details of warfare, this book offers excellent maps, concise text, and worldwide coverage.

Olwen Hufton, *The Prospect before Her: A History of Women in Western Europe* (1996)—Strong history of women, especially the chapters on the 18th century.

Steven Mintz, *Sweetness and Power: The Place of Sugar in Modern History* (1985)—For those interested in Europe's sweet tooth.

Isser Woloch, *Eighteenth-Century Europe: Tradition and Progress, 1715–1798* (1982)—A survey in the Norton History of Europe that nicely combines political and social history.

https://en.wikipedia.org/wiki/Tulip_mania–Provides a summary of the psychology and financial practices that can produce speculative bubbles, in this case the tulip.

http://www.pbs.org/wgbh/aia/part1/1narr4.html

http://slaveryimages.org/

http://www.slavevoyages.org/—These three sites offer different types of documents and perspectives on slavery and the slave trade.

http://www.representingchildhood.pitt.edu/eighteencent_child.htm—Brief scholarly essays on the history of childhood.

Practice MC Questions

Questions 1–3 are based on the map below.

ENGLAND
3%
EUROPE
ATLANTIC
OCEAN
NORTH
AMERICA
BRITISH COLONIES
ARAB
ASIA
BERBER
ARAB
SAHARA DESERT
KAARTA
ARAB
WEST INDIES
4%
French 17%
SEGU KANEM-
BORNU
Spanish 13%
British 24%
HAUSA
DAHOMEY
CENTRAL
AMERICA
ASHANTE BENIN
OYO
AFRICA
Dutch 7%
GUIANAS
TEKE
Equator
Portuguese 32%
62%
NSUNDI
KONGO SWAHILI
BRAZIL
MBUNDU CITY-STATES
36%
SOUTH
AMERICA
ANGOLA
MADAGASCAR
2%

Main slave sources
1450 to 1760

SUSU Ethnic groups

James West Davidson, Brian DeLay, Christine Leigh Heyman, Mark H. Lytle, Michael B. Stoff, *Experience History: Interpreting America's Past* (New York: McGraw-Hill Education, 2014), p. 65.

1. All of the following resulted from the trends depicted on the map above during the 17th and 18th centuries EXCEPT:

   A. European states pursued mercantilist economic policies to exploit colonial resources.

   B. European consumers gained wider access to new goods and venues for purchasing them.

   C. Russia rose as a major power in eastern Europe, gaining territory at the expense of its neighbors.

   D. Colonial rivalries increased among Britain, France, the Netherlands, and Spain.

2. The map above could be used most effectively to support which of the following conclusions?

   A. "European colonial powers employed slave labor to enhance their military and naval power."

   B. "European powers effectively controlled the interior of Africa in a race for resources and territory."

   C. "Revolutionary movements in the Americas arose to combat slavery and oppose colonialism."

   D. "European global economic power rested upon a system of transatlantic trade, including slavery."

John Roberts, *Revolution and Improvement: The Western World 1775–1847* (Berkeley and Los Angeles: University of California Press, 1976), p. 35.

3. Which of the following represents the most significant change after about 1750 in the situation depicted in the map?

   A. France replaced Britain as the dominant colonial power in the Americas.

   B. Enlightenment anti-slavery movements attacked the slave trade and slavery.

   C. Africa successfully resisted further European incursions into its territory.

   D. The United States replaced Europe as the major colonial power in the Americas.

Questions 4–6 are based on the text below.

"Across all these assumptions ran an overriding mental conservatism. One of the deepest differences between our own age and the *ancien régime* [old regime] is the pervading conviction of those times that it was innovation which needed to be justified, not the past. A huge inertia generated by usage, tradition, prescription and the brutal fact of simple ignorance, lay heavily upon the institutions of the eighteenth century. As there had been for centuries, there was a self-evident justification for the ways of our fathers, for the forms and laws they had evolved and set down."

John Roberts, historian, *Revolution and Improvement*, 1976

4. The economic feature of the 18th century that best supports Roberts's interpretation was the:

   A. use of cottage industry in rural areas.

   B. reliance on serfdom in eastern Europe.

   C. domination by Europe of global trade.

   D. adoption of scientific agriculture.

5. All of the following contradict Roberts's depiction of the 18th century EXCEPT:

   A. rivalries among the great powers over territory and commerce.

   B. steady population growth due to inoculation and decline of plague.

   C. homes with private space and resources dedicated to child-rearing.

   D. freeing of trade and labor from corporate entities and the state.

6. The strongest continuity in the 19th century with Roberts's portrayal would be the:

   A. mechanization of textiles and other manufactures.

   B. Concert of Europe and influence of Metternich.

   C. positivist approach to social and economic issues.

   D. influence of the middle-class in social and political life.

Questions 7–9 are based on the passage below.

> "It is older than Aristotle, and will be true, when Hobbes is forgot, that man is a sociable creature, and delights in company. Now, [where] shall a person, wearied with hard study, or the laborious turmoils of a tedious day, repair to refresh himself? Or where can young gentlemen, or shop-keepers, more innocently and advantageously spend an hour or two in the evening, than at a coffee-house? . . . Discourse is...the mind's best diet, and the great whetstone and incentive of ingenuity; by that we come to know men better than by their physiognomy [physical appearance] . . . . [S]peak, that I may see [you], was the philosopher's adage . . . . [W]here is there a better library for that study, generally, than here, amongst such a variety of humors, all expressing themselves on divers[e] subjects, according to their respective abilities?
>
> In brief, it is undeniable, that, as you have here the most civil, so it is, generally, the most intelligent society; the frequenting whose converse, and observing their discourses and deportment, cannot but civilize our manners, enlarge our understandings, refine our language, teach us a generous confidence and handsome mode of address . . . "
>
> "Coffeehouses Vindicated," anonymous pamphlet, England, ca. 1675

7. Which of the following contributed most directly to the rise of the phenomenon described in the passage?

   A. Political challenges to absolutism

   B. The expansion of commerce

   C. Increase in population

   D. Scientific explanations of nature

8. Which of the following resulted most directly from the atmosphere described in the passage?

   A. The use of government censorship to control ideas

   B. Widespread discussion of interaction with non-European cultures

   C. The spread of the New Science and Enlightenment ideas

   D. The expansion of new methods of finance and trade

9. The passage supports which of the following conclusions about the period, 1600–1750?

   A. "Colonization and the expansion of overseas commerce created a new consumer culture."

   B. "European governments competed globally for control of resources and influence."

   C. "Civic venues emerged to challenge traditional religious views, resulting in deism and skepticism."

   D. "The arts came to reflect a growing bourgeois and commercial society."

See Chapter 18 for answers and explanations.

Charles W. Colby, ed. *Selections from the Sources of English History, 55 B.C.–A.D. 1832* (London: Longmans, Green, and Co., 1913), p. 211.

Long Essay Question with Sample and Commentary

Analyze how the expansion of global trade in the period 1650–1763 affected European society and diplomacy.
(HTS: Causation)

Europe experienced a major increase in its trade in the 18th century. After the voyages of discovery and colonization, European powers like France, England, Spain, and the Netherlands, continued to seek trade and colonies throughout the world. This led to new methods of trade, like joint-stock companies and triangular trade. One of the more important effects was the increase in new goods, such as sugar, coffee, tea, spices, cloth, and porcelain. As a result, society experienced changes, like increased population and more middle-class influence. Diplomatically, commercial expansion led to one result: war.

All of the new goods that came to Europe changed people's lifestyles. More people desired goods that had been luxury products. These included spices from the East Indies, silks from China, tea from India, and coffee from Java. Wealthy people enjoyed expressing their status by decorating their homes with fancy rugs, fine china, and other trinkets from the "Orient," as Europeans called Asia. Even the lower classes benefited from this trade. New crops like potatoes, corn, and tomatoes helped the European diet. This made the diet better and increased the population, which really increased in the 18th century.

Competition for colonies seemed to lead to conflict among the European powers. At first the Dutch were the "kings of commerce," but they were eventually surpassed by the English, with whom they fought a naval war. Many of the wars revolved around France's goals under Louis XIV, like the War of Utrecht over Spain. Though Spain and France were not united, the Bourbons did come to the throne in Spain, even if Louis got stopped from dominating Europe. Later there were wars between Austria and Prussia over Silesia. This was fought in two phases, the second of which involved France and Britain. This Seven Years' War was also called the French and Indian War in America, because North America was a major area of competition. Each side wanted the goods and commerce from the Americas, as well as India.

Overall, the expansion of goods and commerce in the 18th century had positive and negative effects. On the plus side, it gave European consumers more goods to buy and fill up their homes with luxuries. Without the improved nutrition, there probably would not have been a major increase in the population. On the down side, all of this competition for colonies created huge wars between the commercial powers. These wars tended to make Britain stronger and France weaker. Also, the Seven Years' War led to the French and American Revolutions.

This response begins with an effective introduction and a clear thesis which specifies both social and diplomatic results. The body paragraph on social effects provides stronger focus on the targeted HTS than the one on politics, which tends to fall into a narrative mode and loses its focus on the question. Referring to the War of Utrecht (the name of the treaty that ended the War of Spanish Succession) constitutes a minor error, though it reinforces that the student is not fully in control of his use of examples. Even if the conclusion offers several insights to the essay, the attempt at Synthesis (reference to French and American Revolutions) is undeveloped and does not earn the point. Score: 3 (Thesis, 1 for Targeted HTS, 1 for Use of Evidence)

9 The Enlightenment and Dynamic 18ᵗʰ Century

The great philosopher Immanuel Kant wrote of the 18th-century Enlightenment: "We live in an age of Enlightenment, but not an enlightened age." Kant considered the 18th century a time of significant reform and a questioning of established traditions, optimistically pointing toward progress. At the same time, Kant realized how far Europe still had to go toward the ideals of reason, equality, individualism, and secularism—all principles of the Enlightenment. The Enlightenment, its principles, and its adherents form the central focus on this chapter, but we also examine cultural and political manifestations of Enlightenment thought. As an intellectual movement, the Enlightenment ranks as one of the most important you will study this year and a frequent subject of AP questions.

Key In Chapter 9 addresses the following KCs from the Course Description:

- **KC 2.1** Enlightened absolutism in central and eastern Europe
- **KC 2.3** Enlightenment thought applied to religion, politics, and social reform
- **KC 2.3** Development of civic venues, publications, and literacy
- **KC 2.3** Role of and debate over women in the Enlightenment
- **KC 2.3** Revival of religion and public sentiment

---

1 SKILL SET

Through this section, you are advised to note the similarities and differences (COMP) between elite and popular culture, perhaps by making a Venn Diagram. In addition, you may wish to note the ways and degree to which the Enlightenment shaped the outlook and activities of the two strands of culture.

Elite and Popular Cultures[1]

Despite differences in station and outlook, peasants and nobles partook of similar cultural experiences in early modern Europe. This changed during the 18th-century Enlightenment as elite and popular cultural diverged. Those in the upper classes inhabited a culture of print, reading the latest novels, periodicals, newspapers, and perhaps philosophical treatises. Congregating in salons, coffeehouses, reading clubs, and libraries, members of the aristocracy and bourgeoisie acquired an appreciation for scientific knowledge and secular learning. Peasants and poor townspeople, however, lived within an oral culture, with knowledge and stories transmitted through story-telling, legend, or perhaps the symbolic imagery of a religious service. Once again, we are faced with a paradox of the 18th century—the Enlightenment gaining a strong cultural foothold, while many if not most Europeans remained relatively untouched by and unaware of it.

The Reading Public

If your life had spanned across 18th-century Europe, you would have witnessed a huge increase in the amount of **printed materials** available—newspapers, periodicals, pamphlets, and novels. The phenomenon was both a cause and a result of an increase in the literacy rate, which in turn was supported by improved access to primary education. All classes and groups took part in this increase, though it was strongest among males and the middle classes.

By 1780 most European cities supported publication of at least one daily or weekly newspaper. The phenomenon fed interest and concern regarding public affairs, including government policies, and publishers often catered to specific segments of the population. One of the more notable if short-lived publications was Richard Steele's and Joseph Addison's *Spectator*, which featured articles of public interest and inspired the *Female Spectator*, focusing on domestic topics such as child-rearing and household management. Though books remained expensive, more members of the upper classes willingly invested resources in their purchase. Popularized scientific accounts, history, and philosophical works all competed for shelf space. These works often reflected a secular focus or took a more critical view of religion. For example, Edward Gibbon's (1737–1794) *Decline and Fall of the Roman Empire*, an immense chronicle of its subject, argued that the adoption of Christianity had sapped the Stoic energy of Rome.

Novels proved to be the biggest sellers. England pioneered the development of these works which featured complex plots, character development, and ultimately, a strong moral message. For example, Samuel Richardson's (1689–1761) *Pamela: or, Virtue Rewarded* recounts the tale of a serving girl who resists the sexual advances of her master, who then comes to understand her worth and eventually proposes marriage to her, thus her chastity is rewarded. Reflecting the 18th-century theme of child abandonment, Henry Fielding's *The History of Tom Jones, a Foundling* traces the adventures and ultimate success of the title character, a wily orphan who in traveling around England allows the author to satirize the hypocrisy of the age. Such works illustrated the growth of **public sentiment**, the belief that open emotional displays equated with sincerity, and that humanitarian impulses elevated society by sustaining reform movements.

Governments did attempt to censor works they deemed threatening to public order or blasphemous to organized religion. Efforts at **censorship** rarely succeeded in the long run, due partly to the decentralized nature of intellectual life in Europe and because states lacked the enthusiasm or manpower to enforce them adequately. To illustrate, the French government at one time or another banned publication of the famous *Encyclopédie* as well as works by Voltaire, yet these publications eventually saw the light of day in other nations or the authors went into temporary hiding only to reappear when circumstances had shifted.

Other than the sheer increase in knowledge, why is this increase in reading material important? Two words: **public opinion**. It is hard to imagine the American and French Revolutions occurring without the political energy generated by a reading public which was both informed and concerned about politics[2].

Education

Even in this age of Enlightenment, education (or lack thereof) reflected social inequality. Secondary schools reinforced the hierarchy of European society and focused on a curriculum of classical languages unlikely to provide practical advantages to an aspiring member of the lower classes. Educational reformers also criticized the stale education of the universities, slow to change in their adherence to Greek and Latin and often ignoring the scientific advances of the previous two centuries. Nonetheless, changes were evident. In Germany, *Realschule* were founded, which focused on practical skills to prepare young men for business. Furthermore, if a modern-minded scholar wished to learn the new science, he could attend one of the following universities: Leiden in the Netherlands, Halle in Germany, or Edinburgh in Scotland.

Art and Music

Though the Baroque style in the arts and music continued well into the 18th century, by the 1720s the Rococo style had taken hold, especially in France. Whereas the Baroque expressed power, illusion, and movement—the art of popes and kings—Rococo concentrated on light-hearted and pensive themes of romance and the transitory nature of life. Paintings employed rich creams and golds, subtle curves, and lush settings to portray the graceful material pleasures of the aristocracy.

Nearer the middle of the century, Rococo gave way to another renewal of classical subject matter and motifs. Reflecting the increased attention paid to civic culture in an enlightening age, artists, such as Jacques-Louis David (1748–1825), in their **neo-classical** style drew from stories of ancient Greece and Rome. The David masterpiece *Oath of the Horatii* (1785) recounts the story of three brothers pledging to their father the patriotic sacrifice of their lives. Male figures stand firm and starkly drawn with straight lines and bold colors beneath masculine Doric columns, while emotionally prostrate women await the action in muted colors and passive curves.

2 THEME MUSIC

Here we can see the connection between two course themes (OS and PP), as the increase in wealth during the 18th century allowed for the expansion of a reading public and venues in which to consume these new reading materials.

With the works of Joseph Haydn (1732–1809) and Wolfgang Amadeus Mozart (1756–1791), we move into the great Age of Classical Music (1750–1830). Composers experimented with full orchestration, writing symphonies of several movements that developed simple themes into complex musical patterns. Operas, like Mozart's *Don Giovanni* or *The Magic Flute*, allowed composers to demonstrate mastery of several artistic forms—drama, music, and set design.

Crime and Punishment

Governments of the 18th century lacked modern police forces and prisons. When criminals were captured, they were punished harshly and publicly in order to set an example. An Italian jurist, Cesare Beccaria (1738–1794), condemned the traditional approach in his *On Crimes and Punishments* (1762). According to Beccaria, reason and the certainty of punishment (not its severity) should guide law and the penal system. Torture, breaking on the wheel, and drawing and quartering all served as horrifying spectacles but tended to arouse people's bloodlust and fear of power rather than respect for the law. Beccaria's ideas promoted penal reform and the building of prisons, beginning in the United States, which aimed at rehabilitation of its inmates through discipline and structure. Many enlightened monarchs further reflected humanitarianism by working toward the rational codification of laws to replace the patchwork of local customs and the elimination of torture and even capital punishment (see below).

Medicine

Despite slight improvements, the medical care available to most Europeans remained inadequate and based either on outmoded classical ideas or dubious folk remedies. Life expectancy remained low, even with gradual improvements in urban hygiene and the beginnings of **inoculation**, first developed to address the scourge of smallpox in the 1770s. Most prospective physicians trained at universities that emphasized classical learning and paid little heed to a scientific or clinical approach, an exception being the University of Leiden in the Netherlands, famous as the setting for Rembrandt's paintings of human dissection. To improve standards and training, British physicians formed the first professional group, the Royal College of Physicians, and were followed by surgeons who broke away from barbers to create the Royal College of Surgeons. Professionalization aimed to exclude traditional practitioners, such as midwives and folk healers, as outside the circle of expertise and knowledge of medicine. Though such developments created an improved setting for medical study and practice, the general improvement in Europeans' standard of living in this period owed more to improved diet and nutrition than to medicine.

3 THEME MUSIC AND SKILL SET

A natural human tendency is to prioritize change over stasis. The Enlightenment--also named the Age of Reason--is one such era. No doubt, secular thinking increased during the 18th century, especially among elites. At the same time, religious belief remained strong among the masses; in fact, several revivals of belief occurred in this century, forcing us to balance our understanding of the OS theme and return to sound advice regarding CCOT.

Religious Revival in a Secular Age[3]

Enlightenment philosophes aimed to improve European society through a secular and scientific approach. Many Europeans did not share this goal and clung to a religious worldview. Strong evidence to counter secularism is offered by several movements of religious revival. John Wesley's (1703–1791) Methodism represents the most famous of these movements. Wesley appealed directly to the English lower classes, many of whose lives had been negatively affected by economic changes or alcoholism, with a warm spirituality that emphasized huge open-air meetings highlighted by dramatic stories of conversion. In Germany, Count von Zinzendorf (1700–1760) initiated the Pietist revival within a Lutheran religion that many perceived as stale and institutional. Revivalism crossed the Atlantic as Wesley's conversion tactics were employed liberally on the American frontier, and German Pietists immigrated to the American colonies to practice their religious faith.

Unlike previous centuries, many enlightened monarchs approached religious matters with skepticism and attempted to create a barrier between private religious belief and public expressions of religion, which were of concern to the state. At the insistence of several governments, the papacy in 1773 banned the Jesuit order, which was perceived as beholden to a foreign power, though it was later reinstated in 1814 following the French Revolution. Furthermore, monarchs began to extend **religious toleration** to minorities. Going furthest in this regard was Joseph II of Austria, whose Edict on Toleration (1781) even granted toleration to Jews, allowing them to practice their religion freely, own land, and hold titles of nobility. The process of emancipation for Jews continued into the French Revolution, allowing them to assimilate more fully into economic and intellectual life. However, it should be noted that Jews continued to be subjected to scorn by Enlightenment thinkers and prejudice by popular opinion.

Popular Culture and Leisure

Literacy increased among all classes in 18th-century Europe; however, literate lower class members generally shunned the novels, histories, and treatises of the elites. Many poor towns-people and peasants favored the 24-page cheaply printed chapbooks, as well as almanacs, both of which carried tales of chivalry and religion, folk wisdom, and information about weather. **Oral culture** remained strong among the illiterate, who often told folk and fairy tales to understand their condition and warn the young about the harsh world outside.

Carnival celebrations punctuated the cycle of seasonal work in early modern Europe. Despite government efforts to curtail them during the Protestant Reformation, many clung to the tradition of concentrated indulgence and riotous behavior that the festival offered. The masses could turn to other amusements even if Carnival was restricted. Drink has always played a major social and dietary role in the lives of Europeans. During the 18th century, many of the lower class turned to stronger (and often cheaper) spirits like gin and whiskey for escape. Taverns in Great Britain advertised "drunk for a penny, dead drunk for two." Alcoholism arose as a major social problem for the first time. For further escape, peasants and poor townspeople turned to the bloodsports of bare-knuckle fisticuffs, cockfighting, and bear-baiting (chaining a bear taken from the woods and siccing ferocious dogs upon it). These popular leisure activities serve to remind us of the growing divergence between popular and elite cultures and that the Enlightenment ethos clearly did not reach all members of society.

Enlightenment Thought

Enlightenment philosophy took its cue from the Scientific Revolution of the 16th and 17th centuries. Given this, remember the following brief and useful definition of the Enlightenment:

An application of the methods and principles of the Scientific Revolution to issues of political, economic, and social reform.

In other words, Enlightenment thinkers believed that just as laws guided the movements of the planets or workings of the human body, human reason and observation could discover the same laws of human affairs—for example, in law, politics, or even religion. We have already seen how the skeptical mindset liberated by the Scientific Revolution laid the foundations for the 18th century. Now we look at the social setting in which this philosophy gained currency.

The Setting of the Enlightenment and the Role of Women[4]

To experience the full flavor of the Enlightenment, one needed to live in Paris. Many of the greatest philosophes hailed from France, and French served as the unifying language of intellectual discourse among elites. Scotland, Britain, Germany, and America—all contributed to the Enlightenment, but the movement took its tone and spirit from the salons of Paris. The women who ran the **salons**—known as *salonnières*—attracted philosophers, economists, and writers from all over Europe in an effort to stimulate an ongoing conversation regarding the key issues facing Europe. For 25 years, Madame de Geoffrin (1699–1777) hosted intellectuals, acted as mediator and financial patroness, and invited foreign thinkers and rulers to her famous Parisian salon. Many writers chose the salons of Julie Lespinasse or Suzanne Necker as the settings to introduce newly published works or discuss new theories.

4 THEME MUSIC AND SKILL SET
You may have noted throughout this guide the recurring theme (IS) of women's involvement in various movements of reform, only to be frustrated by lack of change in gender attitudes or practices (CCOT). Though the evidence of women's advance during the Enlightenment is mixed, one proposition seems undeniable: women gained a language of natural rights that would later bear fruit with feminism.

Women clearly participated in the culture of the Enlightenment. Some women and even a few male philosophes like Condorcet advocated the equality of women. A writer and collaborator in radical political movements, Mary Wollstonecraft (1759–1797), penned the first modern statements of the feminist movement. Wollstonecraft's *Thoughts on the Education of Daughters* took issue with Rousseau's gender-based educational philosophy, arguing that only if women were trained for intelligence and self-reliance could they raise children who exhibited these same characteristics necessary for republican government. Later, during the French Revolution, Wollstonecraft defended the movement for equality with *A Vindication of the Rights of Women* (1792), which held that no legitimate basis, other than physical strength, could be devised to discriminate between men and women. Though these works set the feminist agenda for the next century, women gained few tangible benefits from their participation in a movement that targeted religious superstition and intellectual suppression rather than gender inequality.

For those who could not participate in the salons, other venues provided opportunities for the exchange of new ideas. The middle classes congregated in coffeehouses and reading clubs to discuss the New Science or the latest novel. Though most philosophes boasted aristocratic status, the bourgeoisie often imitated noble fashions and intellectual interests, including Enlightenment philosophy. An additional if more secretive setting for the spread of the Enlightenment were the Freemason lodges, founded in the early 1700s. Freemasonry attracted many famous intellectuals, including Mozart and many early U.S. presidents, with its tight-knit camaraderie, select membership, and betterment through education and technology.

The Philosophes and Their Ideals

Who were the philosophes? The majority were not, in fact, professional philosophers, though several, like Hume and Kant, were. Most worked as writers, social critics, and publicists for new ideas. Just as an engineer or political leader uses a plan to guide his actions, the philosophes articulated an intellectual project: to subject all of human custom and tradition to a systematic criticism using reason and the methods of science. Revolution was far from their thinking; progress should occur through gradual acceptance of the Enlightenment message of reform. As you review the important philosophes below, consider how their works reflect the following principles:

- *Reason*—Perhaps the concept most associated with the Enlightenment, belief in reason's ability to discover the relevant laws of nature and humanity expresses the assumption that the world itself is inherently knowable to the human mind and an optimism in the advance of human understanding.

- *Secularism*—Not all philosophes demonstrated hostility to organized religion or advocated **atheism**. Most Enlightenment thinkers attacked the perceived dogmatism of organized religion and sought to quarantine it from public life. Science and rational inquiry should replace theology as the authorities in public affairs. In place of organized religion, many intellectuals adhered to belief in God based on reason, not revelation. This **deism** portrayed God as a kind of Newtonian clockmaker who designed the world with scientific natural laws and then simply allowed it to function. With this natural religion, the prophets, holy books, dogma, clergy, and rituals of organized religion were considered unnecessary.

- *Equality*—Though many philosophes noted the crushing inequality present in European institutions, few trusted the masses to rule. Belief in the betterment of the lower classes did not necessarily translate into support for democracy.

- *Progress*—A natural byproduct of belief in human reason, the notion of progress lay at the heart of the Enlightenment project. According to the foremost American advocate of the Enlightenment, Benjamin Franklin, the pursuit of knowledge should ultimately yield practical benefits for humankind.

Brief biographical and intellectual sketches of the most important figures of the Enlightenment follow:[5]

Denis Diderot (1713–1784)—Diderot, one of the first outspoken atheists, achieved fame for his editing of the *Encyclopédie*, a 17-volume reference work that ambitiously set out to arrange the sum total of human knowledge alphabetically, without deference to ecclesiastical (religious) or political authority. Many of the articles generated controversy by taking a critical perspective on organized religion or by revealing the trade secrets of the guilds. In addition to print articles, the *Encyclopédie* provided illustrations designed to convey practical knowledge of engineering, the military arts, and manufacturing. Diderot possessed an expansive mind, which led him to write in a variety of genres, including drama and education for the deaf, making him a favorite in the salons and at courts like Catherine the Great's of Russia.

David Hume (1711–1776)—A down-to-earth, jovial leader of the Scottish Enlightenment, Hume conveyed a radically empirical approach to human knowledge. According to Hume (see *Enquiry Concerning Human Understanding* [1748]), it was a fallacy of reasoning to say that we *experience* the "laws of nature" or even that personal identity persists through time. Stable knowledge arises from our immediate observations (what Hume called perceptions); the further removed from these we become by forming abstract ideas, the less reliable is our knowledge. Further, in his *Dialogues Concerning Natural Religion* (1779), Hume articulated a **skeptical** and an agnostic attitude toward miracles and the intelligent design argument for God's existence. Finally, Hume argued that the "oughts" of morality cannot arise from the "is'es" of nature; ethics, then, could only be based on our moral sense, or sentiments (feelings), not our reasoning.

Immanuel Kant (1724–1804)—Kant stands as one of the most brilliant and incomprehensible philosophers of the modern age. Rarely traveling outside his home town of Königsberg, Prussia, Kant never married and dedicated his life to developing a complete system of philosophy. Kant's "Copernican revolution" in philosophy combined the empirical and rationalist traditions into one coherent system of knowledge. Our rational intuitions about time, space, and causation (rationalism) do provide us with knowledge about what we experience (empiricism), Kant held, but they can never tell us about the "things in themselves," for these lay beyond our experience. Kant's system is called constructivism, because the perceptual "lenses" of our intuitions construct the world out of our experiences. When it came to ethics, Kant rejected Hume's moral-sense ideas in favor of a purely rationalist approach—the ethical act is objectively determined by testing whether it could be applied universally without contradiction.

Baron de Montesquieu (1689–1755)—Montesquieu's experiences as a French Protestant and member of the Bordeaux *parlement* influenced his writings. Keeping with the new travel literature, Montesquieu in 1721 penned the *Persian Letters*, a satirical account of two foreign visitors' adventures through France as they encounter what seem like strange and often ridiculous beliefs and customs. By far, Montesquieu's most important work was *The Spirit of the Laws* (1748). Based on his investigation of history and contemporary states, Montesquieu concluded that geography, climate, and history determined the forms of government and laws of each nation. Large nations tended toward despotism (like Russia), medium-sized nations toward monarchy (like France), and smaller nations toward republics (like Switzerland). Montesquieu favored a government like Britain's, which incorporated checks and balances to restrain the vices associated with each major political interest: monarchy—tyranny, oligarchy—factionalism, democracy—anarchy.

The Physiocrats and **Adam Smith** (1723–1790)—Scottish thinker Adam Smith built off the ideas of the French Physiocrats, both of whom criticized mercantilism for violating the natural laws regarding economics. Whereas mercantilists believed specie (hard money) to be the true source of wealth, the Physiocrats held it to be land, as that resource provided society with its agricultural sustenance and mineral resources. To produce a higher standard of living, Physiocrats argued, one must free land from the inefficient feudal restrictions placed upon it and promote the development of commercial agriculture. It was the Physiocrats who coined the term "laissez faire"

5 EXAMPLE BASE

As you study the figures in this section, focus on connecting each to the principles articulated above and the project of the Enlightenment--to better human affairs through a scientific approach. Also, these thinkers engaged in a debate regarding a new epistemology (method of knowledge) and cosmology (model of the universe). Make sure that you can explain it.

("let it be") to argue against the kind of continuous government supervision of the economy associated with mercantilism. Adam Smith agreed with Physiocracy's analysis of mercantilism, but provided a somewhat different analysis of the natural laws of economics in his "bible of capitalism," *Inquiry into Nature and Causes of the Wealth of Nations* (1776). Many of his ideas still guide economic thinking today and can be summarized as follows:

1. Labor is the ultimate source of value, as it is labor that mixes with raw materials to make useful products.

2. Economic activity is too complex to be guided by the blunt instrument of government. The "invisible hand of the marketplace" or the laws of supply and demand (i.e., the **free market**) should determine what is produced, how much is produced, and at what price.

3. Nations should allow the free flow of goods across borders and concentrate on producing those goods for which they possess a comparative advantage (e.g., Guatemala produces coffee more efficiently than computers). Mercantilism's assumption of scarcity will be rendered false, as all nations will benefit from this practice of **free trade**, without artificial tariffs that protect inefficient producers and harm consumers.

4. Opposing the traditional guild system, Smith argued for a higher division of labor to produce larger quantities of goods and lower costs. When the production process is broken into its component steps, worker specialization yields greater efficiency.

Voltaire (1694–1778)—The middle-class François-Marie Arouet later took his famous pen name and came to represent the ideals of the Enlightenment. Voltaire's sarcasm, witty style, and commitment to intellectual freedom won him both admiration and resentment. Wide ranging in his interests, Voltaire took aim at religious fanaticism and hypocrisy. During the Calas Affair—when a Protestant father was falsely accused of killing his son to prevent his conversion to Catholicism—Voltaire argued for religious toleration and claimed that revealed religion made people stupid and cruel. His famous battle cry "crush the infamous thing!," indicated his distaste for organized religion. Like many philosophes, Voltaire argued for rational belief in God, or deism. In *Philosophical Letters on the English*, Voltaire expressed his admiration for England's balanced government and relative religious tolerance. Voltaire spent two years at the court of Frederick II of Prussia, with whom he shared a belief in enlightened top-down reform and a distrust of the ignorant masses. In response to the narrow-mindedness and shallow optimism Voltaire believed to be a part of human nature, he wrote the novelette *Candide*, which recounts the misadventures of a young man who ultimately learns the best we can hope for is "to tend our own garden," or develop our intellectual capacities without interference.

The Later Enlightenment

Some historians believe that after 1760, the Enlightenment entered a new phase. According to this interpretation, some philosophes grew more insistent and radical in their criticisms of existing society and called for the adoption of an explicitly mechanistic and materialist view of the world. Though he is difficult to categorize, Jean-Jacques Rousseau is often associated with this more radical view of the Enlightenment.[6]

Jean-Jacques Rousseau (1712–1778)—Unique among the philosophes, Rousseau came from the lower middle class. His life represents a tale of misfortune, as he was a neglected child, lived from job to job, found patronage among older women, and eventually married a local barmaid, with whom he had five children, which he later abandoned. In his many writings, Rousseau developed several themes. Early on, in *Discourses on the Arts and Sciences* and *Discourses on the Origin of Inequality among Men*, Rousseau portrayed civilization as corrupting to humans' natural inclination for mutual association, leading to exploitation and artificial divisions. Rousseau glorified the life of the Noble Savage, exemplified by American Indians, for whom there was no need for reason, as instinct and emotion more reliably produced happiness. Concerned with the

6 THEME MUSIC
Many of the Enlightenment figures, especially Rousseau, later exercised significant influence on the French revolutionaries, as their critique of the Old Regime and prescription for reform provided an ostensible blueprint for a nation based on reason and equality (SP).

moral dimension of human experience, Rousseau wrote in *The Social Contract* (1762) that the fundamental dilemma of any political system was to find a form of political association in which the General Will of the entire society could be realized through pursuit of the common good. Rousseau left the institutional structure of this republican state ambiguous, for the General Will could not be expressed through representative bodies or legal formalities. With *Émile* (1762) and *La Nouvelle Heloise* (1762), Rousseau completed his presentation of a culture of public senti-ment. In the former, Rousseau laid out a new approach to child-rearing and education, with a focus on children's positive experiences rather than rote memorization or a premature focus on reason. Within this system, Rousseau viewed women as naturally fitted for the domestic sphere, where their duties lie with breast-feeding and nurturing their children. For the latter work, a sentimental novel, Rousseau showed how artificial boundaries between two lovers lead to tragedy. In imitation of Rousseau, many began to weep openly, speak emotionally, and glorify nature. Overall, Rousseau stands as one of the most creative and controversial of the philosophes, but also the first figure of the later Romantic movement.

Though many philosophes wished to retain a veneer of spirituality with deism, others were content to push a scientific view of the world to its further limits. Baron d'Holbach (1723–1789) of Germany contributed to the *Encyclopédie* articles attacking Christianity as preventing human-ity from reaching its full moral development. In *The System of Nature* (1770), he boldly asserted that all of existence consisted of no more than particles in motion, guided by built-in natural laws. God, souls, angels, and spirits could not exist since they did not possess a material nature. From this, d'Holbach concluded that human behavior itself was subject to the same material forces and was therefore determined, even if actions *seemed* the result of free choice. Not only churches, but even thinkers such as Voltaire found d'Holbach's ideas repugnant to the spirit of human progress and improvement characteristic of the Enlightenment.

Marquis de Condorcet (1743–1794), an aristocratic mathematician and political scientist, wrote passionately for equality (including women), justice, constitutional government, and individual liberty. His most famous work, *Progress of the Human Mind* (1795), portrays human civilization as an advance toward scientific thinking and freedom and happiness. Condorcet's idealism could not save him from the radicalism of the French Revolution, as he was arrested because of his aristocratic lineage and later died in prison, an example of how the forces unleashed by the Enlightenment could not always be controlled by its creators.

Enlightened Absolutism

Monarchs recognized the potential of Enlightenment methods for the rational ordering of the state. While rulers patronized the Enlightenment and attracted philosophes to their courts, their focus remained on the realities of power. Several rulers in the 18th century fit the label **enlightened absolutism**, but three stand out.[7]

Prussia and Frederick II the Great (1740–1786)

We have already seen how Frederick established the greatness of Prussia through his military exploits and conquest of Silesia (see Chapter 8). A skeptic by nature, Frederick practiced religious toleration, as did his Hohenzollern ancestors, but did not offend the religious sensibili-ties of his people by ridiculing their faith. Whereas Louis XIV proclaimed "I am the state," Frederick believed himself to be "the first servant of the state." In *Forms of Government* (1781), Frederick specified for each social group its necessary function for the smooth operation of the state machinery. His ideal of efficiency and reason did not produce equality, however. Prussian social classes remained legally defined with little or no social mobility between them. Frederick also reversed many of his father's policies related to merit, once again favoring the Junker nobility above others. In addition, outside of Frederick's own crown lands, serfdom grew worse during his reign. Nonetheless, Frederick achieved a higher degree of centralization, codifying the

7 THEME MUSIC

In Chapter 7, we examined the theory and practice of absolutism (e.g., Louis XIV). As you study this section, please note the way in which enlightened thought both changed and left unchanged the practice of absolute monarchy (SP). These monarchs embraced the Enlightenment, but as a means to strengthen the state and often sacrificed ideals when it clashed with the realities of power.

laws of his diverse lands and enforcing them with Prussia's renowned bureaucracy. Frederick invited Voltaire to his court, but their egos were too large for close company. Despite such displays of enlightenment and Frederick's early interest in music and philosophy, the aging monarch often cynically put the interests of state above principles, as with his calculated invasion of Silesia in 1740 and the Polish Partition of 1772.

Austria and Joseph II (1780–1790)

Of all rulers, Joseph II most thoroughly believed in and upheld Enlightenment principles during his brief 10-year reign. Building on the reforms of his mother, Maria Theresa, Joseph pursued reform systematically and often recklessly. Genuinely concerned with the plight of the lower classes, Joseph abolished serfdom, granted religious toleration to minorities (Edict on Toleration, 1781), granted liberty of the press, and introduced legal equality. Though nominally Catholic, Joseph clashed with the pope and insisted on greater control over the church in Austria. His Edict on Idle Institutions disbanded unproductive monasteries and diverted the funds for the establishment of secular hospitals. Joseph also attempted to promote economic development in his empire by advocating Physiocracy. Despite issuing over 10,000 edicts in his life for the betterment of the people, when Joseph died at 49, many of his reforms were reversed. In his effort to centralize his diverse lands and improve the lives of his people, Joseph offended local traditions and alienated important segments of society, such as the clergy and nobility. No one can doubt Joseph's commitment to the Enlightenment principles, but his fast-paced reform and disregard for opposition ultimately proved too much for many in the empire.

Russia and Catherine II the Great (1762–1796)

Catherine may have been the most famous and admired woman of her era. Between Peter the Great's death in 1725 and Catherine's accession in 1762, Russia had been led by a series of weak and unstable rulers, which allowed the nobility to resurrect their power. In addition, Catherine hailed from Germany and gained power via a palace coup against her weak husband. Despite these obstacles, Catherine proved a strong ruler, though one who continuously compromised her adherence to Enlightenment principles in favor of practical political realities. The "philosopher on the throne," Catherine attracted Voltaire and Diderot to her court, wrote a famous Instruction to the Legislative Commission (1767) expressing her belief in reason and equality, established schools for girls, and even abolished torture and capital punishment. On the other hand, she gained a reputation for leaving grandiose projects unfinished and acting ruthlessly when it suited her interests. She allowed serfdom to worsen by selling off crown lands and brutally crushed the subsequent Pugachev Revolt in the 1770s. At the same time, Catherine liberated the nobles from state service with a Charter of the Nobility (1785), while never following up with the proposed constitution for all Russia's people. In her greatest accomplishment, Catherine added more territory to Russia than any ruler in its history, both by defeating the weakening Ottoman Empire and by partitioning neighboring Poland out of existence. Reflecting a double standard toward women, Catherine earned a reputation for sexual promiscuity by taking lovers of her advisers and political allies. One of these, Grigori Potemkin, lends his name to the fake villages set up to impress foreign dignitaries with Russia's greatness. Like the Potemkin Villages, Russia appeared immense and powerful to the outside world, but in Catherine's Russia much suffering and unfinished reform hid behind this façade.

The Realities of Enlightened Despotism and the Partitions of Poland

Enlightened despotism allows us to gauge and assess the ideals and realities of the larger movement. With the problematic exception of Joseph II, enlightened monarchs viewed enlightened ideals primarily as a *tool* to exercise power. When push came to shove, most rulers chose the path of power and compromised on ideals. Even so, enlightened absolutism laid the groundwork for the revolutionary movements of the late 18th and early 19th centuries. By promoting centralization and calling into question traditional authorities, enlightened monarchs provided an agenda and a method for future changes, even if in the future by way of revolution. Since the Middle Ages, monarchy had generally acted as a progressive force for change; by 1780, the enlightened despots had taken their reforms about as far as they could without undermining their hereditary dynasties. Not surprisingly, after the French Revolution, monarchies looked backward instead of forward, attempting to avoid change while supporting tradition.

Poland represented an outlier among European monarchies. Its elective monarchy and powerful nobility never allowed the kingdom to achieve centralized institutions like a tax system, bureaucracy, or standing army. As a result, the three great eastern powers—Austria, Prussia, and Russia—took advantage of Poland's internal instability to eliminate its independent existence. While each of the three partitions (in 1772, 1793, and 1795) was prompted by differing circumstances, each stemmed from the collusion and cynicism of Poland's great power rivals. The **Partitions of Poland** maintained the balance of power in eastern Europe, but at the expense of the old international order, which had often upheld the existence of weaker states like Poland. The enlightened monarchs who helped carve up Poland once again demonstrated how power politics under the guise of enlightened reform held the potential of upsetting the basis for traditional government.

Realizing the Enlightenment in Politics

Reform in Britain

Prior to the great revolution in France (1789), clouds of change wafted across the Atlantic World. We look first at Britain, before traveling to its colonies in America. As part of the humanitarian impulse borne out of the Enlightenment, reformers targeted slavery as one of greatest violations of the principles of equality and freedom. In 1783, the Quakers, who believed all humans possessed an inner light, founded the first abolitionist society in Europe. The **British Abolitionist movement** targeted the slave trade itself for elimination, which achieved success with both Britain's and America's elimination of the practice in 1807.

Within Britain, the system of "rotten boroughs" and patronage came under increasing criticism. Many cities lacked representation, and only the wealthy exercised the vote. Voices for democratic reform rallied around the case of John Wilkes, a radical journalist and member of Parliament who criticized the king's policies. Though the "king's men" excluded Wilkes from Parliament until 1774, his cause animated the crowds of London with cries of "Wilkes and Liberty!" Calls for reform echoed throughout Britain's empire; however, attempts at change in Ireland resulted only in an Act of Union in 1801, which bound it more tightly to Britain. As for India, the rule of the British East India Company grew more centralized under parliamentary supervision. Of these trends toward democratization and centralization, the American colonists took up the first and defied the second.

The Promise of the Enlightenment—The American Revolution[8]

The United States appears on the AP exam only in its relation to European history, which means only sporadically until the First World War. It is not necessary to recount the American Revolution here, but a word is in order to place the Enlightenment in proper context.

First, the American colonists followed events closely in Britain, particularly the Wilkes affair. Such events, as well as the reading of British critics of the king-in-parliament system, inspired America in its own rebellion against British efforts at centralizing the empire. These protests resulted in American independence and later, the first written constitution in the modern age

8 THEME MUSIC

Historians often speak of a transatlantic revolutionary impulse, fed by the winds of the Enlightenment blowing back and forth across the ocean. The American rebellion against Britain inspired the French Revolution, which itself stirred a slave revolt in Saint-Domingue (later Haiti)--all of which drew upon the principles and rhetoric of natural rights and social contract theory from the Enlightenment (INT).

expressing Enlightenment principles. Enlightenment thinking stretched across the Atlantic Ocean, and indeed, several Americans contributed to the movement:

- Benjamin Franklin (1706–1790)—Franklin lived an exceptionally fruitful life, which included the discovery of electricity, several inventions, projects of civic betterment like the postal service, as well as diplomatic contributions as Minister to France. During his term, Franklin wowed Parisians with his humor and intellect, acting as a conduit for the notion that enlightened principles could be realized in a government and an individual.

- Thomas Jefferson (1743–1826)—Jefferson gained fame for crafting the Declaration of Independence, one of the great expressions of Enlightenment thought, justifying natural law, inalienable rights, and the right of revolution. One of the only presidents openly to espouse deism, Jefferson promoted religious toleration and sponsored numerous scientific endeavors. Of course, Jefferson's ownership of slaves demonstrates the limitations to his enlightened philosophy.

- Thomas Paine (1737–1809)—Born in Britain, Paine set sail for America in 1774 just in time for the revolution. Paine's *Common Sense* (1776), which criticized monarchy as unnatural, sparked the movement for independence. Later involved in the French Revolution, Paine defended the radical movement for equality and liberty with *The Rights of Man* (1791) as well as deism with *The Age of Reason* (1794).

As we see in the next chapter, the American Revolution inspired belief that Enlightenment principles could be realized politically, and also, indirectly led to revolution in France by bankrupting that nation's treasury through its support for American independence.

Additional Resources

Robert Darnton, *The Great Cat Massacre: And Other Episodes in French Cultural History* (1985)—Through the author's retelling of fascinating vignettes, we come to understand how historians re-create the mental worlds of the past.

Norman Hampson, *A Cultural History of the Enlightenment* (1969)—A challenging read, but provides strong insight in one focused volume.

Margaret C. Jacob, *The Enlightenment: A Brief History with Documents* (2000)—This slim volume in the Bedford Cultural Series provides primary sources with brief analysis.

Leonard Krieger, *Kings and Philosophers, 1689–1789* (1970)—This volume in the Norton History Series offers effective sections on enlightened absolutism.

Bonnie Smith, *Changing Lives: Women in European History Since 1700* (1988)—Good resource that begins with insightful chapters on the Enlightenment and French Revolution.

http://www.economist.com/node/2281736—Fascinating article from *The Economist* on the role of coffeehouses in the spread of new ideas ("The Internet in a Cup").

Practice MC Questions

Questions 1–5 are based on the text below.

> "Woman and man are made for one another, but their mutual dependence is not equal. Men depend on women because of their desires, women depend on men because of both their desires and their needs....
>
> By the very law of nature women are at the mercy of men's judgments, as much for their sake as for that of their children. It is not enough that they be estimable; they must be esteemed. It is not enough that they be pretty; they must please. It is not enough for them to be temperate; they must be recognized as such. Their honor is not only in their conduct but in their reputation; and it is not possible that a woman who consents to be regarded as disreputable can ever be decent. When a man acts well, he depends only on himself and can brave public judgment; but when a woman acts well, she has accomplished only half of her task, and what is thought of her is no less important to her than what she actually is. From this it follows that the system of woman's education ought to be contrary in this respect to the system of our education. Opinion is the grave of virtue among men and its throne among women."
>
> Jean-Jacques Rousseau, French philosopher and writer, *Emile, or, On Education*, 1761

1. In which of the following ways does Rousseau most contradict the principles of the Enlightenment?

   A. By calling into question the notion that the universe follows natural laws

   B. By reinforcing the belief that legitimate governments are based on a social contract

   C. By denying the emphasis on empiricism and observation for attaining knowledge

   D. By supporting traditional social roles and upholding inequality of the genders

2. Rousseau's writings here and elsewhere reflect which of the following cultural trends?

   A. The expansion of a consumer culture and products for the home

   B. A revival of sentiment and emotion in response to overreliance on reason

   C. The effort by governments to censor materials deemed a threat to the state

   D. Growth of venues for discussion of new ideas, such as salons and coffeehouses

3. Rousseau's analysis of women most closely mirrors Enlightenment depictions of which of the following?

   A. Commercial activities

   B. Scientists and intellectuals

   C. Non-European peoples

   D. Political power and citizenship

4. All of the following are accurate statements regarding the lives of women in the 18th century EXCEPT:

   A. home life was shaped increasingly by concern for privacy, leisure, and consumerism.

   B. the rate of illegitimacy increased, as did use of primitive forms of birth control.

   C. feminists succeeded in establishing property rights and entrance to higher education.

   D. women in cities encountered poverty, prostitution, and increased social controls.

5. Which of the following events caused the greatest change in attitudes toward and the roles of women presented by Rousseau?

   A. Enlightenment

   B. French Revolution

   C. First World War

   D. Cold War

Jean-Jacques Rousseau, *Emile, or, On Education*, trans. Allan Bloom. (New York: Basic Books, 1979), pp. 364–365.

Questions 6–8 are based on the text below.

> "I believe in one God, and no more; and I hope for happiness beyond this life.
>
> I believe in the equality of man, and I believe that religious duties consist in doing justice, loving mercy, and endeavouring to make our fellow-creatures happy....
>
> I do not believe in the creed professed by the Jewish church, by the Roman church, by the Greek church, by the Turkish church, by the Protestant church, nor by any church that I know of. My own mind is my own church.
>
> All national institutions of churches, whether Jewish, Christian or Turkish, appear to me no other than human inventions, set up to terrify and enslave mankind, and monopolize power and profit.
>
> I do not mean by this declaration to condemn those who believe otherwise. They have the same right to their belief as I have to mine. But it is necessary to the happiness of man, that he be mentally faithful to himself. Infidelity does not consist in believing, or in disbelieving; it consists in professing to believe what he does not believe."
>
> Thomas Paine, British political activist and writer, *The Age of Reason*, 1794

6. The beliefs articulated above reflect which of the following religious outlooks?

    A. Toleration

    B. Deism

    C. Atheism

    D. Agnosticism

7. Which of the following contemporary developments most likely influenced Paine's ideas?

    A. The rivalry between Britain and France

    B. Establishment of the first factories in Britain

    C. The rule of the enlightened despots

    D. The policies of French revolutionaries

8. Which of the following is the most accurate comparison between Paine's views and those of Renaissance intellectuals?

    A. Both believed that the state should have no control over religion.

    B. Both emphasized equality, regardless of class, gender, or race.

    C. Unlike Paine, Renaissance intellectuals worked within Christian ideas.

    D. Unlike Paine, Renaissance intellectuals downplayed individualism.

See Chapter 18 for answers and explanations.

Thomas Paine, *The Age of Reason*, Part the First (London: Daniel Isaac Eaton, 1796), pp. A2, 4.

Joseph Wright of Derby, British artist, *An Experiment on a Bird in the Air Pump*, 1768

A. Using the painting by Wright and your knowledge of the 18th century, analyze TWO ways in which the Enlightenment altered conceptions of the natural world and human reason.

B. Briefly explain how the painting reflects changes in culture and/or the visual arts in the 18th century.

(HTS: Contextualization and CCOT)

A. The Enlightenment was also known as the Age of Reason. This is clear in the painting by Wright of Derby. In this work, the figures are viewing an experiment about air pressure, showing the influence of science. Many of the philosophes supported the idea that science was the best way of approaching knowledge, because it involved testing of hypothesis, rather than accepting religious dogma.

 As part of the experiment it appears that a bird will be sacrificed (by suffocation). Enlightenment thinkers wanted to control nature through their use of the scientific method. This attitude of controlling the environment was also applied to human life, as with prison reforms or new educational methods, as presented by Locke and Rousseau.

B. During the 18th century, the Baroque style was prominent. Baroque artists painted canvases with strong colors and shadowing (as shown here) to convey emotion and power. Also, monarchs patronized Baroque art, so this painting was probably sponsored by the British king to show the power and glory of England.

This response starts well enough, with the student using the painting to establish an understanding of the Enlightenment. With the references to experimentation, application of science, and skepticism about religion, the student earns a point in Part A. Additionally, though brief, she connects the attitude toward nature to human concerns, such as education and penal reform, even mentioning two philosophes. However, the response goes off track with the art analysis. Though the Baroque style lingered into the 18th century, this painting is more reflective of neo-classical art that promoted a secular and scientific (or perhaps commercial) perspective. Finally, the supposition that the British monarch patronized the art is off base. Score: 2 points

10 The French Revolution and Napoleonic Era, 1789–1815

When asked in the 1950s about the importance of the French Revolution, Chinese revolutionary Mao Zedong responded, "It's too early to tell." The revolution that gripped France, the European continent, and ultimately the world stands as the crossroads of your course. It is considered the model for all revolutions; it gave us our modern ideologies and our political geography of left and right. Unlike the American Revolution, which today in the United States is considered an accomplished and successful fact, the French public still debates the significance and meaning of this defining event in their nation's existence. This chapter examines the causes and phases of the revolution and also traces its development through the Napoleonic Era. As you study this complex event, you should focus on the following issues: (1) What interaction of factors brought about the French Revolution? (2) What were the accomplishments of the various phases of the revolution? (3) How and why did the revolution become more violent after 1791? and (4) To what extent did Napoleon uphold the ideals of the French Revolution?

Key In Chapter 10 addresses the following KCs from the Course Description:

- **KC 2.1** The causes and course of the French Revolution
- **KC 2.1** Participation of and effects on women and other groups in the revolution
- **KC 2.1** Haitian slave revolt
- **KC 2.1** Rise, policies, and downfall of Napoleon
- **KC 2.3** Application of Enlightenment political, economic, social, and religious principles
- **KC 2.3** Art that emphasized civic themes
- **KC 2.3** Role of nationalism and public sentiment during the revolution

---

Causes of the French Revolution

Observers and historians have debated the causes and meaning of the French Revolution since it began. This debate often revolves around A) which factors keyed the revolution—political, social, intellectual AND B) the legacy of the revolution—positive or negative overall. The revolution seized the attention of Europe and the world because France itself was important. After Russia, France was Europe's most populous nation, the center of Enlightenment culture, and, despite the problems of its monarchy, considered prestigious and stable. For most, the revolution came as a surprise, though it could have been foreseen given the constellation of circumstances facing France in the 1780s.[1]

Social Causes: The Three Estates

France remained separated into three estates, each with its own legal status and privileges. The First Estate, the clergy, amounted to less than 1% of the population, or about 100,000 clerics of different types. Though the position of the church had declined in previous centuries, it remained a social, cultural, and economic force. The church owned about 10% of the land in France and collected the tithe, a tax that amounted to about 3%–5% of individual income. In an age of increasing secularism, many resented the privileges and high social status of the upper clergy—bishops and cardinals—even if many sympathized with their parish priests, known as *curés*.

1 SKILL SET

The historiography on the French Revolution might take a dedicated scholar a lifetime to master (INTR), especially since it grows every year. Though you need not be familiar with particular schools of interpretation for the AP exam, you should appreciate how and why this seminal event provokes such strong historical debate. Further, as you read, consider how you might frame an argument on any of the guiding questions from the introduction above.

Nobles comprised roughly 2% of the population, about 400,000 members, though they often differed widely in income, and owned approximately 25% of France's land. Counter to Marxist interpretations, which emphasize the rigidity of the class structure, bourgeois members of the Third Estate could ascend into the Second Estate, often by purchase of a government office. In fact, about 40% of nobles in 1789 had earned their status in the previous 150 years. Aristocratic status depended on **inherited privilege** (right to hunt on common land, separate courts, right to wear distinctive clothing, etc.) and exemptions from certain taxes. Members of the nobility monopolized positions in government and the military. After the death of Louis XIV in 1715, nobles reasserted their power and as part of a feudal reaction, attempted to support their increasingly extravagant lifestyles by reviving feudal dues and strictly enforcing their collection. Some members of the nobility, particularly the old nobles of the sword, attempted to limit the further entry of the middle classes into their privileged station with the Segur Law (1781), which restricted military positions to those who could trace their noble lineage back four generations.

The vast majority of French people (about 24 million) belonged to the Third Estate, obviously not a monolithic group. Members of the Third Estate varied from the wealthiest merchants down to the few serfs or landless laborers still eking out a living from the soil. The bourgeoisie increased in numbers and economic power significantly in the 17th and 18th centuries with the growth of commerce. In addition to their mercantile and professional interests, the bourgeoisie owned about 25% of the land in France. Many resented the privileges of the aristocracy while at the same time envying their status and imitating their fashions and interests. The petty bourgeoisie of artisans, shopkeepers, and small business owners felt the pinch of, on one hand, rising prices for goods, while on the other, stagnant wages. These *sans-culottes* ("without breeches" worn by the well-to-do) favored equality and played a major role in the radicalization of the revolution. Peasants formed the largest social class. Most were small landowners who wished to be free from the plethora of service obligations, taxes, tithes, and feudal dues that could eat away over 50% of their livelihood. Owning about 40% of the land, peasants tended to be conservative in outlook, wishing simply to be free of the feudal system.

France's social inequality is taken to be the most fundamental cause of the revolution. It would be a mistake, however, to portray the revolution as simply a drama of class struggle, with a discontented lower class overthrowing their oppressors. In fact, aristocrats and bourgeoisie often shared similar lifestyles and outlooks. Further, some members of the nobility influenced by the Enlightenment criticized the inequities of the Old Regime and led the initial phases of the revolution. Also, during the radical phase of the revolution, nobles and peasants shared distaste for the radical policies of Paris. Even with these caveats, the social inequality of the three estates drove the revolution forward and accounts for the depth of its radicalism.[2]

Political Causes

The conflict between the resurgent nobility and a theoretically absolute monarchy constitutes the fundamental political cause of the revolution. French aristocrats accepted and often admired the monarchy but wished it to evolve along English lines. To limit Bourbon pretensions to absolutism, nobles asserted the powers of the *parlements*, the 15 regional law courts, to check the king's ability to tax and legislate arbitrarily. During the weak reign of Louis XV (1715–1774), some progress was made in this regard. However, near the end of his reign in 1771, Louis reasserted royal power and dissolved the Parlement of Paris. As a gesture of goodwill, the young Louis XVI reconvened the body in 1774. This move only emboldened the nobility in their efforts to move France toward a constitutional monarchy.

Many condemned the capricious nature of the monarchy. Hated symbols of arbitrary government were the *lettres de cachet*, which allowed the king to arrest and imprison any individual without judicial procedures. No doubt the stories of an army of political prisoners rotting in the Bastille proved to be exaggerated, but Enlightenment principles of equality and justice spoke against the practice. Additionally, the personalities of **King Louis XVI** (1774–1793) and his Austrian wife, Marie Antoinette (d. 1793) acted as a magnet for discontent with the regime. By all accounts, Louis was a pious, well-meaning family man. However, he also had difficulty

2 THEME MUSIC

The causes and events of the French Revolution reveal the tie between economic and social changes. As mercantile wealth expanded from the Commercial Revolution, there occurred a corresponding increase in the size and importance of the middle class (bourgeoisie). One need not endorse the Marxist view of class struggle (as do some historians) to recognize the ways in which the revolution attacked the privileges and political power of the aristocracy, whose wealth depended on the feudal order.

consummating his marriage, which when combined with Marie's promiscuous reputation, earned the couple ridicule and scandal. As events unfolded, it became clear that Louis lacked the energy and purpose to see his nation through its crisis. The king's behavior during key moments of the revolution often escalated conflict and fueled demands by radicals for a republic.

Intellectual Causes

The Enlightenment did not directly cause the French Revolution; however, it ensured that unfocused discontent and class anger crystallized into a more fundamental criticism of the Old Regime. Ideas from Voltaire, Rousseau, Montesquieu, and other philosophes provided systematic tools for the expression of grievances, though most people gravitated to the salacious underground press with stories of the scandals of the royal couple. Even if readers for high-minded philosophy were lacking, a century of enlightened thought helped create a public concern over political issues, awareness of the larger world, and a strong spirit of criticism.

Economic and Financial Causes

Economic and financial causes for the revolution were distinct but related. France did not fall into revolution because of economic stagnancy; more accurately, the French state and legally defined social system coped poorly with rapid economic change. Between 1714 and 1789, French commerce expanded tenfold, faster than Britain's, and fed the wealth of the nation. However, this wealth was unequally distributed. Though France stood out as one of the wealthiest nations in Europe, it was as if it had one hand tied behind its back.

Due to its semi-feudal nature, the French state never tapped effectively into the nation's wealth. We have already seen how France, unlike Britain, did not develop an extensive credit network. More importantly, France was plagued by an inefficient and regressive tax system. Tax rates varied widely based on geography, the highest class claimed exemptions, and the task of collecting the taxes was franchised out to the Farmers General. This group of wealthy financial families legally skimmed off as much as half of state tax revenue.

Louis XVI realized the dire need for tax reform. The debt of the French monarchy accumulated from numerous wars—most recently the American War for Independence (1778–1783)—threatened to choke the state budget. By 1785, the French treasury was bankrupt, and half of the budget went simply to pay the interest on the debt! Louis attempted several far-reaching efforts at reform but was blocked by restive nobles who insisted on more fundamental changes in the political structure before they would agree to new taxes. If Louis had pursued his plans more consistently or resolutely, he might have staved off disaster. Each time one of his finance ministers encountered opposition, he was dismissed by the king.

Louis began boldly by appointing the noted Physiocrat and economic liberal, Turgot (1774–1776), as Finance Minister. Turgot mercilessly attacked privilege. He proposed converting the *corvée* labor service of the peasantry into a cash payment, eliminated numerous government positions and pensions, attacked government monopolies, slashed spending, advocated free trade, and moved to adopt a single direct tax on land to replace the multitude of confusing indirect taxes. Turgot pursued his plan ambitiously and, as a result, sparked wide opposition. When dismissed by Louis, he was replaced by the talented Swiss Protestant banker, Jacques Necker (1776–1781) (whose wife Suzanne hosted a salon). Necker published a complete accounting of the state budget, the *compte rendu*, which revealed the incredible waste therein. Necker's plans for economy proved too much for entrenched interests, so he was dismissed in 1781. This well-respected symbol of reform was recalled by the king during the early phase of the revolution in 1789.

By 1787, the situation in France turned desperate, for two reasons. First, France stood at the verge of bankruptcy, and the efforts at financial reform were stalled by growing opposition across the nation. Second, during the years 1787–1789, which coincided with the early stages of the revolution, France suffered from the last great subsistence crisis of the century. Poor crops led to high bread prices, sending urban crowds into the streets. Louis sat upon an explosive situation, and little seemed left to do but call the Estates General, which the king did in 1788 after protests spread among the *parlements* to his policies.

The Liberal Phase, 1789–1791

Labeling the first phase of the French Revolution "moderate" or "Liberal" makes sense only if we keep in mind that the violence inherent from the outset paled in comparison to what came later. From the calling of the Estates General in 1788 until the onset of war in the spring of 1792, the revolution accomplished a major reordering of French state and society. Unfortunately, ideological divisions and the revolutionaries' inability to address major economic issues increased violence and strengthened the hand of radicals. For ease of study, the following three sections will provide a timeline with commentary.

Prior to the meeting of the Estates General, Louis XVI asked all French people to set down their grievances in notebooks, called the *cahiers de doléances*, most of which expressed moderate demands for tax equality and the gradual abolition of feudalism. The subsequent national election was France's first since 1614, and both the election and grievances helped politicize the entire country with the expectation of change. As the Estates General convened in 1789, immediate disagreements broke out over two issues: 1) whether to double the number of delegates to the Third Estate, seeing as it represented 98% of the nation, and 2) whether the delegates should vote as individuals ("heads") or by orders, with each of the three estates getting one vote. The first issue was easy enough to resolve, but the Third Estate and many liberal nobles, known as the Committee of Thirty, refused to budge on the second. The pamphlet *What Is the Third Estate?* by clergyman Abbé Sieyès (1748–1836) stoked discontent by arguing that the Third Estate *was* the assembled will of the nation and that the noble caste should simply be abolished.

June 17, 1789—Unable to reach agreement on the issue of voting, the Third Estate declares itself the National Assembly.

June 20, 1789—Finding themselves locked out of their meeting place, the National Assembly adjourns to a nearby tennis court and pledges not to disband until it has written a new constitution for France, an event known as the Tennis Court Oath.

Unsure what to do next, the king begins raising an army possibly to disperse the National Assembly. In addition, he dismisses Finance Minister Jacques Necker in July, signaling his movement away from reform.

July 14, 1789—Fearing the king's military power, the crowds of Paris march to the Bastille, symbol of royal despotism, but also an armory. After accidentally firing on the crowd, the defenders are captured and several executed by beheading. The fall of the Bastille saves the National Assembly and demonstrates the power of mob violence. Soon after, revolutionaries form the National Guard to protect the revolution, appointing Marquis de Lafayette (1757–1834), called the "hero of two worlds" for this support for the American Revolution, as head.

The king is forced to recognize the National Assembly and orders the other two estates to sit with the new legislative body. However, rumors spread in the countryside regarding events in Paris and of plots to undermine the revolution, leading to attacks on nobles.

June–August 1789—In the Great Fear, peasants attack manorial courts and noble manors, directing anger against feudalism. To reestablish order, the National Assembly on the famous night of August 4 dismantles the entire feudal system. In one blow, **feudal privileges**, the tithe, noble hunting rights, labor service, and serfdom are all **destroyed**.

August 26, 1789—The National Assembly completes the Declaration of Rights of Man and Citizen, an expression of Enlightenment principles such as legal equality, freedom of religion, judicial rights, and "liberty, property, security, and resistance to oppression."

October 1789—Angry over high bread prices and fearing the king's opposition to the Declaration of Rights of Man (and August 4 decrees), the women of Paris march on Versailles and break into the queen's chamber, killing several guards and forcibly bringing the royal family back to

Paris, where they would remain as virtually prisoners of the revolution. The actions of women to protect the revolution are termed the October Days.

By the end of 1789, the revolutionaries succeeded in radically restructuring the French state. One of the more important but underestimated actions the assembly took was the abolition of all feudal institutions, *parlements*, estates, provincial law codes, and tariff and tax bodies, to be replaced by 83 equal departments, subdivided into cantons and communes. As a result, France became a centralized national government based in Paris in a way it never had been under royal absolutism.

November 1789–July 1790—In a fateful move that divided the revolution, the National Assembly attacks the privileged position of the Catholic Church. First, the revolution confiscates the lands owned by the Catholic Church and issues paper currency, *assignats*, based on the value of the land, which results in rapid inflation. Later, the church is brought under control of the state—bishops are to be elected and paid by the state, their numbers reduced to 83, and the pope's influence over the clergy eliminated. In addition, after the pope condemns the revolution, the **Civil Constitution of the Clergy** requires all priests to swear an oath of loyalty to the revolution. About half ultimately swear the oath, while the nonjuring clergy (those who would not swear allegiance) later become a rallying point for counterrevolution.

June 1791—The National Assembly completes the Constitution of 1791, a conservative document that creates a single legislative body with a **constitutional monarchy** possessing only the power to delay legislation. Active citizens are those who own substantial property (about half a million men), while those less well-to-do and women are deemed passive citizens. The document indicates that the revolution still rests in the hands of the wealthy bourgeoisie. Nonetheless, the king, under influence from his wife and *émigrés* who had escaped the revolution, decides to flee France. His "flight to Varennes" is stopped just short of safety, and he is brought back to the Tuileries Palace in Paris.

July 17, 1791—A crowd gathers in a public park to demand the overthrow of the king and the declaration of a republic. The National Guard under Lafayette disperses the crowd with gunfire, killing 50. The Champs de Mars Massacre radicalizes public opinion and leads to further distrust of the monarchy.

Political culture in France now openly embraces symbols of the revolution—liberty trees, liberty caps, *citoyen* and *citoyenne* as forms of address, and the replacement of religious with revolutionary icons. Citizens join in clubs to discuss issues and agitate for change. The **Jacobin Club** grows in influence and later produces many of the most important leaders of the radical phase of the revolution.

By the summer of 1791, the revolution has achieved much. However, its laissez-faire policies have not solved the rapid inflation or government debt. Complicating matters are the behavior of the king and growing divisions over how far the revolution should go. The debate extends across Europe as writers, citizens, and governments choose sides. English conservative Edmund Burke (1729–1797) condemns the radical destruction of France's traditions and predicts in *Reflections on the Revolution in France* (1790) that the revolution will end in military dictatorship. Thomas Paine responds (see Chapter 9) with *The Rights of Man* (1791) in defense of the revolution. *Émigrés* from France heighten tensions by working against the revolution from abroad, a situation that seems ripe for war.[3]

The Radical Phase, 1792–1794

Why did the revolution become more radical after 1792? Several factors present themselves:

- *Economic problems*—Rapid inflation continued and the laissez-faire policies of the revolution angered workers stung by high prices and policies directed against union activity.

- *The royal family*—The king clearly harbored reservations regarding key events of the revolution, such as the Civil Constitution of the Clergy. His effort to flee the revolution undermined much of his remaining support.

3 SKILL SET

As subsequent chapters will demonstrate, the French Revolution helped create the political ideologies that dominated debate and fostered action throughout the 19th and 20th centuries. In anticipation of this theme, you may want to compare (COMP) how a supporter (Liberal--Paine, or a nationalist or a socialist) and an opponent (Conservative--Burke) of the French Revolution would interpret the causes, key events, and outcomes of this transformative event.

- *Counterrevolution*—By now, several groups actively opposed the revolution—provinces jealous of the power of Paris, nonjuring clergy, *émigrés*, religious peasants—and worked to thwart it.
- *War*—War radicalizes politics. When France declared war in the spring of 1792, it strengthened the hands of those who called for an even more violent break with the past.

August 1791—The Austrian emperor (brother of Marie Antoinette), along with the Prussian king, issue the Declaration of Pillnitz, promising to restore order in France if other nations provide support.

This declaration, as well as the actions of the king and *émigrés*, convince the Girondins party (a faction of the Jacobins Club from the provinces) that the only way to save the revolution is to spread it across Europe by force of arms. To the strains of *Le Marseillaise*, the revolutionary anthem, the first citizen-soldiers in modern European history depart for the front.

April 20, 1792—France declares war on Austria. The king supports the declaration because he believes France will *lose*, and thus his power would be restored.

July 25, 1792—With the war going badly for France, Austria and Prussia stand on the verge of invading France. Austria and Prussia issue the Brunswick Manifesto, threatening the revolutionaries with violence if any harm comes to the king and queen. The manifesto produces the exact opposite of its intended effect by inflaming violence against the monarchy.

By now, the working people of Paris, known as *sans-culottes*, and other cities oppose the half-measures of the Girondins and are open to the persuasion of radical leaders. The vehement journalist Jean-Paul Marat (1743–1793) with his *L'Ami du peuple* (*The Friend of the People*) newspaper demands the deaths of traitors and for heads to roll. The skilled politician Georges Danton (1759–1794), works to create a revolutionary government in the capital, the Paris Commune, which would play a major role in forcing moderates to adopt more aggressive measures.

August 10, 1792—In an event known as the Second French Revolution, an armed mob storms the Tuileries Palace and forces the arrest of the king. The Constitution of 1791 is abrogated and a more radical National Convention is elected to govern France.

September 1792—Fearing that political prisoners will aid the advancing Austrian-Prussian army, revolutionaries break into prisons across France and massacre thousands, many of them innocent bystanders (September Massacres).

September 20–21, 1792—After victory in the battle of Valmy, which stopped the invading armies, the National Convention abolishes the monarchy and declares France a **republic**, with 1792 as Year I of the new era.

January 21, 1793—The **king** is placed on trial for treason and after being found guilty by the Convention and at the insistence of the Mountain (a faction of the Jacobins), is **executed** by guillotine. With the execution, France enters the **Reign of Terror**.

May–June 1793—Under pressure from the *sans-culottes*, the Paris Commune arrests and executes the leaders of the Girondins. The Mountain, under the leadership of the radical **Maximilien Robespierre** (1758–1794), comes to dominate the Convention. The democratic Constitution of 1793, which calls for universal male suffrage, is passed, though is never put into effect because of the crisis situation.

Over the next year, France is ruled by the Committee of Public Safety, a 12-member executive body elected each month by the Convention, which steers France through the Reign of Terror. It is aided by the Committee of General Security, the police arm of the revolution. An entire province, the Vendée, rises in counterrevolution against the centralizing and anti-Catholic policies of Paris. War continues and justifies further radical measures.

Robespierre emerges as the dominant personality. An ambitious lawyer from northern France, Robespierre served in the National Assembly, gaining notoriety with his calls for universal male suffrage and the abolition (ironically) of capital punishment and slavery in the colonies. Obsessed with creating a new political culture, Robespierre argues that virtue must be combined with terror. Even if they condemn his methods, most historians consider Robespierre sincere in his beliefs; indeed, he earns the nickname The Incorruptible in his lifetime. As a result of the Mountain's policies, revolutionary tribunals arise across France, executing about 50,000 over the course of the terror, and "representatives on mission" ensure that the policies of Paris are followed. Though members of the clergy and aristocracy represent the largest segment of victims as a percentage of their numbers, in absolute terms peasants and the working class make up 70% of the victims.[4]

Many view the Reign of Terror as a period of unnecessary and bloodthirsty excess. Others believe that the radicals enacted many creative reforms that helped see France through its time of crisis.

- *Mass conscription* (*Levée en masse*)—All French citizens are required to contribute to the war effort. Never before in European history has a nation marshaled so many citizens in arms, raising an army of over 1 million men who fought with passion for *liberté, égalité, fratenité*.

- *Law of General Maximum*—Abandoning free-market policies, the Convention establishes maximum prices for key commodities and punishes severely those who break the law. However, this battle against inflation is difficult to enforce.

- *Abolition of slavery*—Ratifying the massive **slave revolt in Saint-Domingue** (**Haiti**) led by **Toussaint L'Ouverture**, the Convention abolishes slavery in all French colonies. Napoleon was later unable to subdue the revolt, and Haiti gained its independence in 1804. Despite L'Ouverture's later capture and imprisonment (where he died), Haitian independence represents the first successful slave revolt in modern history, and it indirectly leads Napoleon to sell Louisiana to the new American republic.

- *Revolutionary calendar*—As part of a **de-Christianization** campaign, the Convention devises a new calendar with months and days renamed after weather conditions and agricultural products. Months are divided into 30 days of three *décade*, allowing for only 1 day of rest in 10, rather than 7. The new republican era begins with 1792 as Year I.

- *Cult of the Supreme Being*—De-Christianization leads to the elimination of saints' names on streets and Notre Dame becoming a Temple of Reason. Robespierre opposes these excesses and attempts to create a new deistic civic religion, which culminates with a Festival of the Supreme Being in June 1794.

- *Standardization of weights and measures*—Following a trend of the moderate phase and reflecting Enlightenment rationalism, the Convention promotes use of the metric system and, as above, restructures time along the same principles.

- *Military victories*—With these policies, France turns around her fortunes on the battlefield, invading the Netherlands in June 1794 and creating a sister Batavian Republic to replace the old Dutch provinces.

March 1794—The Committee of Public Safety acts against extremism on the left. Radicals who advocated complete equality and terror known as Hébertists, or *enragés*, are sent to the guillotine.

May 1794—Danton, the popular leader of the Paris Commune and a growing critic of Robespierre, is executed along with his supporters, known as Indulgents.

By the summer of 1794, France seems to have emerged from its crisis. Counterrevolution has been defeated, French armies are advancing on the battlefield, and the worst of the inflation seems to have passed. Despite these successes, the pace of executions quickens in the summer of 1794. When Robespierre announces in the Convention a new law that allows looser standards for proof of treason and a new list of proposed executions, fearful opponents ally against him.

July 27, 1794—The Convention arrests Robespierre and his supporters. After a failed attempt at suicide, Robespierre, along with his associates, is guillotined. This event ends the Reign of Terror.

4 EXAMPLE BASE

You encounter numerous specific content references in this section. To avoid bogging down in detail, consider the following two interpretive questions: 1) To what extent did the revolution fulfill its stated principles of liberty, equality, and fraternity (nationalism)? AND 2) To what extent was the violence of the radical phase necessary to save the revolution during its crisis from 1791–1794?

Thermidor and the Directory, 1795–1799

The period following Robespierre's fall is known as the Thermidorian reaction (Thermidor, or "heat," was the revolutionary month of Robespierre's execution). Revolutionary violence takes a breather as the Terror subsides and extreme policies are reversed. Jacobin Clubs are closed and a "white terror" instigated against former radicals. To provide order while maintaining republicanism, the Convention once again writes up a plan of government, the Constitution of Year III (1795). Though all males can vote, their votes are filtered through well-to-do electors who in turn choose representatives for the two-chamber assembly. For day-to-day governing, this assembly appoints five directors as an executive body. The regime known as the Directory governs France for four years. During this time, aristocratic fashions return as French politics remain divided over the future course of the revolution. These divisions plague the weak Directory, which faces opposition from both the left and the right.

Spring–Summer 1796—Extremists led by Gracchus Babeuf attempt to establish a socialist government with the Conspiracy of Equals, but they are arrested, tried, and executed.

September 4, 1797—After free elections create a majority for royalists, the Directory, assisted by Napoleon Bonaparte (1769–1821), annuls the results and maintains power in the *coup d'état* of Fructidor.

With little popular support, the Directory remains dependent on battlefield victories to maintain itself in power. The situation seems ripe for an ambitious and successful military leader to overthrow the government and restore order.

The Rise of Napoleon

Some have labeled **Napoleon Bonaparte** the first modern man. His rise to power owed nothing to traditional ecclesiastical, aristocratic, or political institutions. Napoleon was self-made and possessed of immense talent and ambition, qualities that account for both his stunning successes and his crushing defeats. Born into a minor Italian noble family on the island of Corsica, which the French had annexed in 1768 (a year before his birth), Napoleon set out to prove he was the equal of every Frenchmen he encountered in his military academy and the army. Napoleon combined a quick mind that excelled in practical subjects, such as engineering, history, law, and administration, with supreme confidence in his talents and destiny.

Napoleon earned his first fame with the Italian campaign. Defying traditional rules of warfare, the general outmaneuvered and outfought the larger Habsburg army, and then proceeded to negotiate with the Austrian emperor on his own. The subsequent treaty (1797) established several new Italian republics and spread revolutionary ideas throughout the long-divided peninsula. Napoleon followed up his success with a bold move—the invasion of Egypt in 1798–1799. Though his strategic goals were unclear, Napoleon initially defeated the Ottoman army at the Battle of the Pyramids.[5] However, the British fleet cut off Napoleon's supply lines after crushing the French fleet. With bigger stakes in mind, Napoleon abandoned his men in Egypt and found his way back to France, in time to take part in an overthrow of the moribund Directory. Joined by two other conspirators, Napoleon's *coup d'état* of Brumaire succeeded in creating a new government, the Consulate (with three Consuls). Chosen as First Consul, Bonaparte quickly outmaneuvered the other two consuls and in 1801 proclaimed himself First Consul for life. At the age of 32, Bonaparte commanded France and set out to institutionalize the principles of the revolution.

Napoleon's Domestic Policies, 1799–1814

Soon after being named First Consul, Napoleon consolidated his power, culminating with his proclamation of the French Empire in 1804 and his crowning as emperor. It is generally believed that Napoleon promoted equality and nationalism during his rule; however, he implemented his policies from the top down with little democratic input and disregarded individual rights, such as

5 THEME MUSIC

Even when resented by those occupied, Napoleon's invasions exercised a profound impact on conquered nations, often triggering internal reforms or at minimum, debates over revolutionary ideas and modernizing policies. The Egyptian campaign launched Napoleon to power in France, while also stimulating European interest in the Middle East--both strategically and culturally. In addition, the campaign revealed the weakness of the Ottoman Empire (the "sick man of Europe") and stimulated nationalism among the Balkan peoples (INT & SP).

freedom of the press or privacy, whenever it suited his interests. The following provides an idea of the nature of Napoleon's domestic policies in several areas. As you read, consider the extent to which Bonaparte either fulfilled or twisted the ideals of the revolution.

- *Governance and administration*—Keeping with the tradition of the revolution, Napoleon created a constitution for the Consulate and then the Empire. In reality, Napoleon concentrated power in his own hands. Laws were enacted by the Legislative Corps but could not be debated. The body acted in effect as a rubber stamp for the emperor's will. Unlike absolute monarchs, Napoleon succeeded in centralizing administration through the creation of a **centralized professional bureaucracy**. Prefects ran each of the 83 departments but reported directly to Paris. To present himself as a man of the people, Napoleon used plebiscites, or referenda, on specific issues often after the fact, such as whether the people agreed with Napoleon's proclamation of the empire (they did, by a large majority). However, Napoleon would not countenance opposition to his rule. The press was censored, and under the watchful eye of Joseph Fouché (1763–1820), a secret police infiltrated intellectual circles to identify opposition to the regime. Eventually Napoleon became occupied with the trappings of imperial rule, which was reflected in the nation at large with a new Empire Style of architecture and décor.

- *Legal and social policies*—Napoleon announced "careers open to talent" for those like himself who came from middling or lowly station but wished to rise through talent and ambition. Napoleon created a Legion of Honor to recognize the contributions of those who served in the revolutionary wars. It is the **Civil Code** that represented the revolution's ideals of merit and equality and arguably Napoleon's single most significant accomplishment. Guided by the enlightened impulse toward rational systemization, Napoleon created a single legal code for all of France, as well as the many nations he conquered, which stands to this day. However, the Civil Code reinforced patriarchy in the home and limited the rights of women related to divorce, property, and male infidelity.

- *Economic and financial policies*—To enhance industry, Napoleon modernized the infrastructure of France—building/repairing roads and bridges, beautifying the nation with monuments, and establishing the Bank of France. The bank helped in finally eliminating the budget deficit and modernizing the tax system. Napoleon's efforts at industrial simulation—tariffs, loans, public works—proved less successful, as his failed Continental System (see below) against Great Britain hindered French trade.

- *Educational system*—In an effort to modernize France and promote opportunity, Napoleon established a nationwide system of secondary schools, called the *lycée*, open to all social classes. A national system of technical universities was founded, reflecting the emperor's interest and belief in scientific progress.

- *Religious policies*—Napoleon finally ended the war between the revolution and the Catholic Church in his Concordat of 1801 with Pope Pius VII (1800–1823). By the agreement, the pope regained some control of the French clergy, and Catholicism was recognized as the majority religion of France. However, the Church acknowledged the loss of its properties, and the French government retained a veto power over clerical appointments. Of skeptical mindset himself, Napoleon manipulated popular religious belief to his advantage, proclaiming in Egypt, "I am a Muslim," but also extending religious toleration to those in conquered nations.

Napoleonic Warfare, 1796–1814

Regardless of how Napoleon is viewed politically, he revolutionized the practice of warfare. It will not be necessary for you to grasp the complexities of Napoleonic battles and shifting coalitions, except in general outline, but you should understand the role of warfare in Napoleonic diplomacy and the legacy it left in the 19th century.

Though Napoleon met ultimate defeat and blundered strategically, he did not lose a battle on land until 1814. What accounts for his stunning success?

- *Movement*—Conventional military wisdom emphasized maneuver to conserve manpower and guard supply lines and fortresses. Napoleon turned this wisdom on its head and made the enemy army his target by striking quickly.

- *Defying traditional limits*—Napoleon's armies ignored customs regarding when to fight: Sundays, winter, night—all were fair game. The French army learned to live off the countryside, cut off from supply lines.

- *Offensive*—With no patience for drawn-out campaigns, Napoleon aimed to defeat his opponents in a decisive battle, by concentrating force at the enemy's weakest spot.

- *Propaganda*—Napoleon presented himself as a liberator. He proclaimed republics in conquered nations and ended feudalism for peasants.

- **Citizen armies**—The French Revolution helped establish, and Napoleon advanced, the notion that warfare was an affair for free and equal citizens, not paid mercenaries—an idea that remains to this day.

In the period 1792–1815, France fought a number of different coalitions of nations. Despite the general agreement among rulers that the French Revolution should be quarantined, great power politics continued. Nations pursued traditional territorial and political objectives, even if in a more complex revolutionary environment. Britain most consistently opposed French designs, pursuing its traditional objective of preventing the emergence of a dominant power on the continent.

France emerged victorious against the first two coalitions, which failed to stop the advance of the French revolution and its expansion into neighboring nations. In 1802, Napoleon negotiated peace with Britain, the final holdout from the Second Coalition. It would not last, as Napoleon's expansionist designs inevitably clashed with British mercantile interests. During the War of the Third Coalition (1805–1807), Napoleon masterfully defeated each of his continental opponents in turn—Austria, Prussia, and Russia—establishing himself as master of the continent. All major continental nations were either annexed to France, allied with it, or a friendly neutral. Napoleon's plans to defeat Britain outright were thwarted at the Battle of Trafalgar (1805), as a Franco-Spanish invasion fleet was destroyed by the British navy under Horatio Nelson.

To subdue Britain, Napoleon forced continental nations to embargo British goods, known as the Continental System. The plan proved difficult to enforce, harmful to continental trading interests (including France), and highly unpopular. By 1810, Russia had withdrawn from the system, compelling France to launch the fateful Russian campaign. Though many of Napoleon's policies within conquered nations proved popular, his actions also **aroused nationalism**, especially in Germany. These factors, in addition to a decline in Napoleon's tactical skill, led to his final defeat. The Grand Army's retreat from Moscow cost 90% of the men who had set out. Though Napoleon was able to raise another army, he was defeated again in 1814 in Germany (the largest battle prior to the 20th century) and ultimately at Waterloo in 1815.

Napoleon's Foreign Policies, 1799–1814

In foreign policy, Napoleon pursued two goals: 1) institutionalize the ideals of the Enlightenment and French Revolution in conquered lands and 2) gain territory and influence for the French nation. At first, Napoleon captured the imagination of intellectuals across Europe, such as Beethoven and Goethe, as well as the support of the common people for his abolition of the Old Regime. However, his exploitation of subject lands and ruthless imposition of "French values" alienated a critical mass of nations bent on stopping him. In the last analysis, Napoleon was done in by the same superabundant ego that had led to his amazing rise to power. As you review Napoleon's policies below, again consider his adherence to revolutionary principles.

- *Reforms*—Napoleon proclaimed the liberation of conquered nations and implemented many of the revolution's policies. To win over peasants, he announced the abolition of feudalism and the Old Regime, including guilds, old town charters, internal tariffs, and local weights and measures. In their place, Napoleon promoted rational government based on enlightened principles of religious toleration, efficient centralized administration, and equality under the Napoleonic Code. Among progressives, such policies gained support, at least until opinion against Napoleon turned.

- *Creation of new diplomatic system*—Napoleon paid little respect to diplomatic traditions. As he conquered, he created republics in Italy, the Low Countries, and Switzerland, appointing his relatives to ruling positions (a practice of nepotism seemingly at odds with his ideas of merit). After defeating Austria again in 1806, Napoleon simply abolished the long-standing Holy Roman Empire, replacing it with the 35-state Confederation of the Rhine. To gain the support of Polish leaders, Napoleon recreated a smaller version of Poland, the Duchy of Warsaw. Once Napoleon felt secure in his domination of the continent, he attempted to wrap himself with dynastic legitimacy. In 1804, he convinced the pope to attend his coronation as emperor, and when he and Josephine were unable to produce an heir, he married a young Habsburg princess, Marie Louise (which made him by marriage the nephew of the deceased Louis XVI).

- *Continental System*—As noted above, Napoleon attempted to cut the continent off from British trade. This proved difficult because Britain's colonial products could not be easily replaced. Transportation difficulties and differing tariffs among the member states prevented continental trade from taking up the British slack. Not only did the Continental System fail in its objective, it aroused opposition toward a French-dominated Europe.

- *Peninsular war*—In 1808, Napoleon coerced the Bourbon king of Spain to abdicate and replaced him with his own brother Jerome. The Spanish resented Napoleon's high-handed tactics and toleration of religions other than Catholicism. With British support, the Spanish bogged the French down in a guerrilla war, sapping resources and men.

Coda: Women and the Revolution[6]

6 SKILL SET

Though women did not realize the promise of their participation, the French Revolution marks a turning point in the status of women and the feminist movement (PER). To evaluate this claim, you will need to draw upon your understanding of previous movements of change (e.g., Reformation or Scientific Revolution) and anticipate the outcomes for women during the 19th century. You may wish to create a simple timeline or chart that demonstrates these changes and continuities over time (CCOT).

Women played a central role in the French Revolution. But did this participation yield tangible results? It was during the moderate phase that women gained the most—the right to divorce, inherit property, and child custody. Also at this time, Olympe de Gouges (1748–1793) published the Declaration of Rights of Women and the Female Citizen to counter the similarly titled document by the National Assembly, but she was guillotined in 1793 for her revolutionary activities. During the radical phase, some women formed the Society for Revolutionary Republican Women, which agitated for equal rights. The club was banned by the Mountain, because they believed it violated Rousseau's ideals regarding women's domestic role. Finally, the Napoleonic Code, often viewed as a blow for equality, generally excluded women from the principle. The code limited female property rights, restricted divorce, and reinforced the sexual double-standard for adultery. Most women who participated in the revolution probably did so on behalf of their class rather than their gender. Nonetheless, it seemed that once again a movement promising change and equality left women excluded from the revolutionary application of its principles. Taken together, the Enlightenment and the French Revolution, however, established the agenda for the feminist movement over the next century.

Additional Resources

Jack Censer and Lynn Hunt, *Liberty, Equality, and Fraternity* (2001)—A wonderful resource for students, this book is concise, focused, and interpretive. Also see the related website: http://chnm.gmu.edu/revolution/.

William Doyle, *Origins of the French Revolution* (1980)—Provides an account of the events leading up to the revolution, concentrating on the financial crisis and political conflict.

Empires: Napoleon (2000)—A 4-hour PBS documentary that traces the life of Napoleon. Offers a companion website: http://www.pbs.org/empires/napoleon/.

Francois Furet and Mona Ozouf, eds., *A Critical Dictionary of the French Revolution* (1989)—For those who need a comprehensive resource for further study and research.

Georges Lefebvre, *The Coming of the French Revolution* (1967)—This is considered the classic Marxist explanation of the revolution's origins in terms of class struggle.

R.R. Palmer, *Twelve Who Ruled: The Year of the Terror in the French Revolution* (1989)—Engaging study that examines the personalities of the 12 men on the Committee of Public Safety.

Andrew Roberts, *Napoleon: A Life* (2014)—The new standard biography of a major figure of the course.

Simon Schama, *Citizens: A Chronicle of the French Revolution* (1990)—Well-written but challenging work focusing on the new civic culture and the use of violence.

http://alphahistory.com/frenchrevolution/french-revolution-historiography/—

Explains the evolution of scholarship on and interpretations of the French Revolution. Also, see the home page for other resources on the French Revolution.

Practice MC Questions

Questions 1–4 are based on the text below.

> "July 22ⁿᵈ 1789. The Revolution in the French Constitution and Government may now, I think, be looked upon as completed, beyond all fears of any further attempts being made by the Court Party to defeat it. The entrance of the King into Paris was certainly one of the most humiliating steps that he could possibly take...
>
> There certainly never was an instance of so astonishing a Revolution operated almost without bloodshed, and without the people being led on by any leader, or by any party, but merely by the general diffusion of reason and philosophy. We shall soon be able to form a guess what is the nature of the constitution that is intended to be adopted in France.... From what is known of their ideas and principles it is thought the Executive Power will be left solely to the King, who will be deprived of all share in the Legislative Authority, which will be lodged in the National Assembly, formed into one Body, without distinction of Orders."
>
> Report from the British Ambassador on events in France, 1789

1. Which of the following causes of the French Revolution is most directly reflected above?

    A. The financial crisis of the monarchy and inability to resolve its debt

    B. The social divisions among the traditional three estates

    C. The growing criticism of royal absolutism and corruption

    D. The economic crisis caused by rising food prices and famine

2. The development after July 1789 that most contradicted the ambassador's portrayal of the revolution was:

    A. the abolition of serfdom and feudalism.

    B. the confiscation of the lands of the Church.

    C. the Declaration of the Rights of Man and Citizen.

    D. the execution of Louis XVI and Reign of Terror.

3. Which of the following situations most directly parallels that above?

    A. The Protestant attack on the Catholic Church in the 16ᵗʰ century

    B. Opposition to Habsburg centralization during the 17ᵗʰ century

    C. The unification of Italy and Germany during the 19ᵗʰ century

    D. The overthrow of the Russian tsar during the 20ᵗʰ century

4. All of the following represent effects of the French Revolution outside of France EXCEPT:

    A. the use of mass citizen armies to conquer lands and impose revolutionary ideals.

    B. the emergence of a major slave rebellion in the colony of Saint Domingue.

    C. the establishment of a system of stable republics committed to peace.

    D. the creation of an empire under the control of Napoleon Bonaparte.

Despatches from Paris, 1784–1790, selected and ed. from the Foreign office correspondence by Oscar Browning Volume II (1788–1790), Camden Third Series vol. XIX: pp. 229, 230.

French revolutionary calendar, 1794

5. The depiction above was likely influenced most strongly by which of the following?

A. The spread of revolutionary ideals by French armies

B. Romantic themes in and approaches toward in art

C. Enlightenment principles of reason and efficiency

D. Feminist principles of equality and natural rights

6. Which of the following policies of the French revolutionaries most directly coincides with the visual?

A. De-Christianization and nationalization of the Catholic Church

B. Raising of mass citizen armies for total warfare

C. Overthrow of the monarchy and the execution of Louis XVI

D. The creation of a government based on popular sovereignty

Questions 7–9 are based on the map below.

EUROPE, 1810

Legend:
- Confederation of the Rhine Boundary
- French Empire
- Satellite Kingdoms
- Allies of Napoleon
- Hostile to Napoleon
- ☆ Major battle

Dennis Sherman and Joyce Salisbury, *The West in the World: A History of Western Civilization* (New York: McGraw-Hill Education, 2014), p. 510.

7. Which of the following contributed most directly to the situation above?

   A. The mobilization of French women under feminist principles to the revolution

   B. Britain's extensive empire of colonial possessions and dominance of trade

   C. The hostility of foreign governments to the spread of the French Revolution

   D. France's reliance on mass citizen armies motivated by liberty, equality, and fraternity

8. The most significant change on the map above from one depicting Europe in 1648 was:

   A. the dominant position of Russia in eastern Europe.

   B. the elimination of the Holy Roman Empire.

   C. the unification of Italy and Germany.

   D. a state of extended war among the great powers.

9. Which of the following, in the short-term, led to a significant alteration in the situation above?

   A. Nationalist campaigns directed against Napoleon and foreign rule

   B. A revival of the position of the Catholic Church

   C. The expansion of British manufactures and commerce

   D. A civil war in France directed against Napoleon's Empire

See Chapter 18 for answers and explanations.

Long Essay Question with Sample and Commentary

To what extent and in what ways did Napoleon Bonaparte (1799–1814) either advance the ideals of the French Revolution or reaffirm features of the Old Regime? (HTS: CCOT)

Napoleon Bonaparte certainly stands as one of the most influential rulers of all-time, both within and outside of France. Napoleon portrayed himself as a man of the people, and in many ways he was. Born in Corsica, Napoleon had to prove himself through his talent and ambition, one of the major ideals of the French Revolution. When he came to power in 1799, Napoleon set out to bring order back to revolutionary principles. Though sometimes his policies seemed dictatorial or imperial, his ultimate goal was always to preserve the revolution for the people, and in this, he succeeded.

Equality was a major principle of the revolution. Napoleon made sure that opportunity was available for all people in France and in other nations. When he liberated a nation, he proclaimed the abolition of feudal privileges and all the features of the Old Regime. What's more, he did this all with his military and intellectual talent. His actions won him the support of great intellectuals like Beethoven (who dedicated the Third Symphony to Napoleon), as well as citizens who wanted to rise in society. In France, Napoleon created schools, universities, and a Legion of Honor, all for the benefit of those who really contributed to society, unlike the old sponging nobles. The culmination of this was his Napoleonic Code. It threw out all the old feudal and backward legal codes and made one rational equal system for all, including for taxes. If Napoleon overlooked some liberty, it was only because France was in chaos and someone needed to provide reform and order. Even then, Napoleon had a constitution and allowed people to vote in plebiscites.

Napoleon promoted another great ideal of the revolution—nationalism. The reason his soldiers fought so strongly was because they believed they were fighting for their own nation and their equality and liberty. Many foreign nations saw how powerful nationalism could be in their own nations. After Napoleon brought his equal law code and promoted equality, many believed that their nations also could benefit from nationalism. One place where this was especially important was Germany. Many German intellectuals found Napoleon a great figure who showed how a nation could be united, which Germany was not. Philosophers and writers extolled the power of a united state, and how old feudal hierarchies must be eliminated. Just because Napoleon inadvertently promoted the kind of nationalism that led the Germans to get rid of the French does not change the point—Napoleon did promote nationalism!

People who say that Napoleon was a dictator or that he reversed the ideals of the revolution don't understand the situation at the time. France had swung back and forth between royalism and Jacobinism and needed a break. Napoleon was that break—someone who took a mass of rhetoric and grand ideas and made them into something tangible. For centuries, monarchs had failed in creating a rational and centralized state and economy, but Napoleon left a legacy of how to create a truly modern state and win over the people at the same time. Napoleon's approach would influence future leaders like Bismarck and Cavour in unifying their nations, as they governed from the top-down but manipulated nationalism and public opinion to secure their power.

Clearly our student is an admirer of Napoleon, which for the most part, he uses to his advantage. The essay offers a strong thesis, ample factual support, and clearly addresses the targeted HTS. On one hand, the student acknowledges the ways in which Napoleon failed to fulfill revolutionary ideas (liberty), but provides an explanation for this anomaly. The body paragraphs focus on the prompt and provide a fairly wide but relevant range of examples. Finally, the conclusion attempts to earn the synthesis point by connecting Napoleon both to prior monarchs and to subsequent political leaders (Bismarck and Cavour). The essay overlooks obvious counterexamples in its positive portrayal–status of women, conquests, censorship–however, it cannot be denied that the student accomplishes the objective of consistently arguing his point. Score: 6 (Thesis, 2 for HTS, 2 for Use of Evidence, 1 for Synthesis).

The chapters in Period 3 will address the following major developments and events:

- Industrial Revolution in Britain and its spread to the continent
- The social and economic impact of industrialization
- Governmental, reformist, and ideological responses to industrialization
- Congress of Vienna, Concert system, and revolutionary responses
- Romanticism and its influences on the arts
- Unification of Italy and Germany and other nation-building efforts
- 2nd Industrial Revolution and its relation to nationalism and imperialism
- European im perialism into Africa and Asia
- Urban reform and development of a mass society
- Mass politics and pressure groups, including workers, women, and ethnic minorities
- Modernism in the sciences, ideas, and the arts

Each chapter will provide a content review and practice questions to test your understanding of the material. At the conclusion of the content chapters, you will be able both to gauge your grasp of the content and practice historical thinking skills in an online diagnostic test that will include:

- 30 MC questions
- 2 SAQs
- 1 DBQ
- 1 LEQ (choice of 2)

Each chapter will begin with a brief correlation to the Key Concepts from the Course Description. Good luck with your review.

CHAPTER 11 Industrial Society and the Struggle for Reform, 1815–1850

The Industrial Revolution in economic production and the French Revolution in politics combined to transform every facet of European life in the 19th century. Moving on parallel but often intersecting tracks, these two movements are often termed the Dual Revolution. Many historians consider the revolution in production, transportation, and marketing of goods associated with the Industrial Revolution the single most significant event in human history. In this chapter, we address the growth of industry in Great Britain, its spread to the continent, the effort to restore the Old Order at the Congress of Vienna, the development of political ideologies as a response to the Dual Revolution, and the revolutionary echoes rebounding through the first half of the 19th century from the French Revolution, culminating with the revolutions of 1848. This period lays the foundation for modern society, politics, and production, making it a turning point in European history.

Great Britain's Industrial Experience

Definitions and Great Britain's Advantages

Before exploring the reasons for Britain's industrial lead and dominance, let's define what is involved in the term Industrial Revolution. Each of the following three definitions expresses an essential feature of the process:

1. An assault on the scarcity of the Old Regime, leading to a revolution in access to the means supporting human life.

2. The substitution of mineral and mechanical energy (theoretically inexhaustible) for animal and human energy (which tires or wears out).

3. Rising output *per capita* (per person) at declining unit cost; in other words, each worker produces more goods at a cheaper cost, supporting a rising standard of living.

Of course, Europe had enjoyed commercial growth in the past and at times a rising standard of living. Inevitably, these periods of growth ran up against the limits of natural resources or the primitive nature of technology. Britain's accomplishment seemed unique in applying new production techniques and technologies to exploit the full potential of nature's bounty. Owing to the following package of advantages, Great Britain, first among European nations, realized the processes expressed above:[1]

- *Geographic advantages*—Britain's unique island status insulated it from continental strife, freeing it from supporting a standing army while at the same time promoting an overseas empire. No place in Britain was more than 70 miles from the ocean. Profits from trade could be reinvested in manufacturing enterprises. In addition, Britain possessed natural resources, such as coal and iron ore, necessary for industry.

- *Economic advantages*—Promotion of the **Agricultural Revolution** allowed for a larger population and the resulting mobile labor force to staff the new factories. Also, no nation could boast a better financial network of banks and credit institutions able to supply entrepreneurs with the capital necessary for industrial enterprises.

- *Political advantages*—Even if many nations mirrored Britain's industrial potential, chances are those inclined toward industry exercised little influence over government policy. Not so in Britain. Through Parliament, mercantile and industrial interests enacted laws such as the Enclosure Acts to promote commercial agriculture and laissez-faire policies to protect property rights. These groups supported development of the British Navy and the acquisition of colonies, the source of raw materials and markets for British products.

1 SKILL SET

Here we have a major interpretive question of causation (CAUS): Why was Great Britain the first nation to experience industrialization? For practice, consider writing a focused introductory paragraph that not only identifies the relevant causal factors, but also takes a position with which another historian might disagree.

- *Social advantages*—In traditional European societies, elites frowned upon the pursuit of profit (to be distinguished from the accumulation of wealth) as characteristic of the "vulgar bourgeoisie." In Britain, aristocrats and the middle class instead shared an interest in commerce and profit accumulation. Though Protestant dissenters experienced religious toleration, their exclusion from the paid clergy, the university system, and government positions drove them into commercial and industrial pursuits. Their dissenting academies emphasized practical and technical training, and indeed, many of the early inventors derived from this group.

The Classical Economists

Many of the features outlined above correspond with capitalism, but note that industrial development can occur within a command or socialist economic model. The so-called classical economists articulated the nature of a laissez-faire capitalist economic order, though not always with a positive view of its potential. Of the three figures associated with capitalism, one (Adam Smith, "the father of capitalism") was addressed in Chapter 9; now we look at two other important figures:

Thomas Malthus (1766–1834)—Malthus believed that food supplies, which increase only incrementally, could never keep up with natural population growth, which occurs exponentially. Even today, Malthus's *Essay on Human Population* (1798) represents the classic statement of concern for population growth and the need for its limitation. Malthus was pessimistic about the prospects for birth control and technological advance, though he did underestimate the productive capacity unleashed by both the Agricultural and Industrial Revolutions.

David Ricardo (1772–1823)—Taking Malthus's ideas regarding population, Ricardo introduced the concept of the Iron Law of Wages. In the short run, Ricardo argued, if the poor gain higher wages, they will simply produce more children, increasing the labor supply and driving down incomes. Thus, in the long run, humanity could not produce a higher standard of living. Once again, Ricardo miscalculated the potential of new technologies and techniques to generate wealth and the human desire for smaller families within this capitalist, consumerist regime.

Textile Innovations

Textiles led the way during the early Industrial Revolution. The many processes of textile production lent themselves to the development of cottage industry, which took hold in Britain in the 18th century. Several basic technological breakthroughs, beginning in the 1730s, paved the way for the mechanization of spinning under one roof, or the first factories. It is important to keep in mind that production processes like mechanization and the putting-out system often complemented each other in industries with multiple steps, such as textile production. Further, mechanization did not penetrate production in other industries for several generations. As you review the **textile innovations** below, focus more on the incremental nature of technological change rather than the names of the inventors.

- Flying shuttle, 1733: John Kay halved the time of the weaving process and allowed a single loom operator to work with wider cloth by creating a shuttle that could be operated with one hand. The invention increased demand for spun yarn.
- Spinning jenny, 1768: Improving on the traditional spinning wheel, James Hargreaves developed the jenny, which enabled operators to spin eight or more threads with additional spindles.
- Water frame, 1771, and "mule," 1780: Richard Arkwright added water power to the principle of the jenny, allowing for the development of factories near rivers, which could harness this natural resource. Samuel Crompton combined the mechanical principles of the jenny and the water frame to create the spinning mule.

- Power loom, 1785: Edmund Cartwright's power loom took several generations to perfect, and when it finally became cost-effective in the 1830s, it quickly drove the many hand-loom weavers out of business.

By the middle of the 19th century, then, the entire textile industry had become mechanized. Demand for raw cotton jumped exponentially, which, along with the new cotton gin (1793), provided a new lease on life for American slavery. Britain thus established dominance in a key consumer item with its cheap, sturdy cotton cloth.

Steam Power, Coal Mining, Iron, and Railroads

These four industries or technologies were closely related. Developments in one tended to feed demand in the others, like a feedback loop. The first steam engines in the early 18th century pumped water out of coal mines, but did so inefficiently, using more energy than they produced. James Watt (1736–1819), in partnership with the entrepreneur Matthew Boulton, perfected the steam engine by employing a separate condenser to cool the steam and later added rotary motion, essential to the development of locomotion. Watt's invention provided a much-needed source of power for factories, which could now be located anywhere.

Coal mining expanded significantly in Great Britain in the 18th century, driven by the energy needs of the new steam engines and for metallurgical processes. Traditionally, **iron smelting** employed charcoal (fuel produced from burning wood), but this had led to the depletion of English forests. In 1709, Quaker Abraham Darby developed the first blast furnace using coke (a by-product of coal) to heat iron ore, which burned cleaner and allowed for the production of greater amounts of iron. Later in the century, Henry Cort pioneered the puddling and rolling processes that enabled factories to produce higher-quality wrought iron and to shape it more easily for industrial purposes. Soon, all processes were consolidated under one roof, vastly increasing British production of iron in the first half of the 19th century. Metallurgy, in turn, required vast amounts of coal, stimulating both industries.

Eighteenth-century Britain witnessed a great age of canal building. Water transportation proved more reliable and cut the costs of bringing goods to market. Many of the first canals were privately funded, earning huge profits for their investors. With the advent of cheaper iron and the power of the steam engine, **railroads** replaced canals as the most efficient form of transportation. At first, railways consisted of horse-drawn wagons over wooden rails, used to transport coal out of mines to foundries. In 1804, Richard Trevithick designed and built the first steam-powered locomotive. Soon after, engineer George Stephenson created a faster engine, The Rocket, which could travel at the (for-the-time) amazing speed of 24 mph! Railroads soon veined across Britain, providing cheaper goods and a new form of reliable passenger transportation. Railroads decreased isolation and allowed for geographic and social mobility, making them one of the most important inventions of the 19th century.

The great age of railroad building energized the production of iron, steam engines, and the mining of coal. In addition, machine tools, made of more refined and flexible **steel**, enabled engineers to shape, mold, bore, drill, cut, and saw materials with great precision. Together, these industries formed the spine of the British economy and fed other industrial processes.

The Factory System and Other Industries

History's first industrialists combined the roles of inventor, entrepreneur, and manager. Early businesses grew out of limited partnerships and fed off borrowed funds from Britain's extensive credit network. These industrialists eventually realized the benefits of standardization and specialization by combining industrial processes in one locale—a factory. The first **factories** appeared in textile spinning in the 1780s in the new industrial towns of the north, such as Manchester and Liverpool. Josiah Wedgwood (1730–1795) stands as a fine example of the new entrepreneur who extended the factory principle to new industries. Lacking an academic back-ground in chemistry, Wedgwood nonetheless used trial and error to develop new styles of pottery and porcelain. Wedgwood not only centralized and standardized his industrial processes, he also marketed his products with a keen eye to consumer tastes. His Queen's Ware gained fame throughout Europe for its delicate style and refinement.

Like petroleum later, coal processing led to the development of important by-products. Mauvine, the first synthetic dye, was extracted from coal tar in the middle of the century. Synthetic bleaches and dyes replaced laborious traditional processes and opened up new fashion opportunities. Certain colors, such as purple, had been associated with aristocratic status; with cheap textiles and dyes, fashion could now be democratized.

By the mid-19th century, Britain had established its industrial preeminence. To celebrate the nation's accomplishments, British leaders organized the first world's fair in 1851 in London called the Crystal Palace Exhibition. Symbols of technology and progress took center stage and beckoned as examples for the continent to imitate.

2 SKILL SET

Now that you've considered the reasons for Britain's lead, it is time to set out the similarities and differences with the continental experience with industry. As you read this section, you might create a complex Venn diagram to establish how Britain compares with France, Germany, and the lagging nations(COMP).

Industrialization on the Continent[2]

Continental European nations wished to copy Britain's industrial success. Some succeeded; others seemed unable to overcome institutional barriers or limited resources. In some ways, the British lead proved beneficial, as its engineers, technicians, and inventors might be enticed by continental powers to share their industrial secrets. Often, however, governments needed to take a more active role in promoting and overseeing industrial development. This government intervention stands in contrast to Britain's laissez-faire approach. Let's see how this worked with several brief examples.

France: A Gradualist Path

Like Britain, France experienced industrialization, but more gradually and with fewer disturbing side effects. As a legacy of the revolution, France continued a tradition of small, family-based agriculture without the destabilizing impact of enclosure and the Agricultural Revolution. Also, France's large internal market and skilled labor force allowed it to focus on higher-end products, such as silks and intricately patterned textiles. Without extensive reserves of coal and iron ore, France did not develop Britain's level of heavy industry. As a result, French industrial cities were smaller in number and did not grow as rapidly, avoiding some of the worst effects attending those in Britain. It was not until after 1850 that French finance, railroads, and communications were able to bring about a fuller modernization of attitudes and habits related to production and consumption.

Germany: A Shackled Giant

Remember that there was no such nation as Germany in 1815. "Germany" remained divided among several dozen states, each with its own tariffs, tax systems, and state priorities. Though Germany boasted an abundant supply of coal and iron ore, a rich agricultural sector, and a strong craft tradition, its disunity hindered its full economic potential. In the 1830s, Prussian economist Friedrich List (1789–1846) argued for the development of a national economic system, beginning with a customs union that would create a free trade zone among the member German states. This Prussian-led *Zollverein* promoted not only economic integration but laid the basis for Germany's later political unity. In addition, List recognized that Britain's hands-off approach would not work in Germany, so he urged government financing of railroads, subsidies for key industries, and protective tariffs. Germany's economic take-off would await political unity in 1871, but it was already establishing strength in key industrial sectors such as iron, coal mining, and chemicals.

The Lagging Lands

While other regions of Europe, such as Belgium and northern Italy, as well as the United States, had built an industrial base by mid-century, many nations languished in the inertia of resource poverty, backward agriculture based on serfdom, and elitist attitudes that discouraged the profit motive. For example, Spain lacked resources necessary for industry and faced geographic obstacles with a barren plain dominating the center of its nation. However, the most important barriers proved to be the continuing influence of aristocratic privilege and religious other-world-liness. After 1848, Russia remained the only major nation relying on serfdom, an enormous waste of labor and land that effectively hindered its economic development and negated its strong resource base. In some cases, underdeveloped nations adopted outward manifestations of industry, such as a show railroad or a model factory, but the essential economic attitudes and the legal and educational infrastructure needed to secure private property or supply technical skills were sadly lacking.

Social Effects of and Responses to Industrialization[3]

The Industrial Revolution profoundly influenced first British and later European society. Problems such as overcrowding, pollution, worker discontent, and inequality compelled governments, reformers, and radicals to devise a range of contending responses to such issues.

Population Increase

Industrialization supported a marked increase in population. From 1750 to 1850, the population of the British Isles rose 200% from 10 to 30 million. What's more, most of this humanity found itself crowded into the new industrial cities of Lancashire and the Midlands, north of London. Manchester came to symbolize the problems of the new industrial city, growing from 20,000 people in 1750 to almost half a million by 1850, making it the second largest city in Britain. Many migrants to the cities were driven by famine in Ireland or landlessness in the countryside. Though many found work in the new cotton mills, urban problems followed closely behind.

Working and Living Conditions

It is easy to dramatize the conditions in the first factories or urban areas, and even though basis exists for these facts, you should incline toward analysis and specifics for any essay prompts on the Industrial Revolution. Initial factory conditions were deplorable. Workers were expected to labor up to 14 hours per day with inadequate light and ventilation. Strict rules punished tardiness and fraternization among workers. Owners often preferred **children as laborers** for their small hands able to reach into machinery, as well as women, considered more docile and willing to work for lower wages than men. In coal mines and factories, laborers were exposed to toxic substances and particulates, causing lung and other diseases. Finally, because machines often determined the pace of labor, workers found themselves living by a regimented schedule and subject to fatigue that could be deadly if they should fall into the moving parts of machines.

Living conditions mirrored those in the workplace. Because of their rapid growth, cities found that their infrastructure of streets, housing, and sewage disposal could not keep up with the onslaught of new residents. Cramped housing and diseases, such as cholera, dysentery, and typhoid, reduced life expectancies by half compared with rural areas. Air and water pollution rendered even breathing and drinking dangerous activities. In addition to sanitary and environmental problems, crime, prostitution, alcoholism, and family breakdown defined city life.

3 THEME MUSIC

The thematic driver for this section is clearly Poverty and Prosperity (PP), but you will notice how wealth and inequality create issues relevant for other themes: 1) class, gender roles, and family (IS) and 2) government involvement in the economy and reform movements (SP). You should practice establishing connections across themes, as it assists with synthesis and reinforces your grasp of chronology.

As a consequence of the mechanization of labor, the family was transformed from a unit of production to a unit of consumption, i.e., gathering only for activities related to eating and leisure. It is easy to exaggerate how quickly and commonly this occurred; nonetheless, mechanization of labor set the precedent of moving work from the home, where workers exercised control over the pace and conditions, to a process managed by the owners of capital seeking profit by squeezing out costs through lower wages and sacrificing on basic safety conditions. Once the British Parliament passed legislation protecting women and children in the 1830s and 1840s, family life was further altered by separating male "productive" work outside the home from female "reproductive" and domestic labor completed in the home.

New Industrial Classes

Industrialization created new classes. At the top, the **industrial middle class** gained wealth and status from the profits of industry. Though they were still few in number, this growing **bourgeoisie** set a social tone of frugality, respectability, and hard work, exemplifying the ideal of social mobility through self-help. The growth of the unskilled working class, or **proletariat**, paralleled that of the industrial middle class. Owning no capital or personal property of which to speak, unskilled workers were forced to sell their labor at a disadvantage, as the supply of workers continued to grow and employers freely dismissed those deemed unproductive or troublesome. Industrial workers remained a relatively small segment of the population in Europe until after the middle of the 19th century, and therefore could exercise little influence on politics through union activity or political pressure.

Responses: Reform, Rebellion, and Rejection

It is helpful to think of responses to these industrial problems on a continuum from acceptance of the new industrial system on one side to complete rejection on the other. We explore this topic further in the section below on "isms," but for now focus on immediate and practical responses to those issues. You may find the following diagram helpful in imagining how these varying responses relate to one another.

rejection ⟵——————————————————————————————⟶ **acceptance**

Luddism   revolutionary socialism   utopian socialism   Chartism/unions   reform legislation   laissez faire

We have already examined the laissez-faire approach of the classical economists. Many laypeople recognized the obvious problems with industrialization but believed that these side effects naturally attended all economic systems. To tamper with the workings of the free market, in their minds, would only create more suffering in the long run. Eventually the problems became too pronounced for any but the most hardened capitalist to ignore. Reformers feared that if nothing were done to ameliorate horrid working and living conditions, moral breakdown or, worse, revolution, would occur. In 1832, Parliament appointed the Sadler Commission to investigate child labor in mines and factories. The appalling testimony of workers convinced Parliament to pass the Factory Act of 1833, which provided for inspection of factories, a limitation on hours, and at least 2 hours of education per day for children. Sanitary reformer Edwin Chadwick's (1800–1890) writings highlighted the need for improved sewage and sanitary conditions in the crowded and polluted cities. Soon after, the Parliament again responded with the Public Health Act of 1848, providing for the development of sanitary systems and public health boards to inspect conditions. Further acts are discussed below in the section "Reform in Great Britain."

Despite the first tentative steps toward reform, workers voiced a more fundamental need for change, one that involved greater control over the workplace and political power. It became clear that, as individuals, workers could do little to blunt the capitalist system. To exert collective power, laborers formed unions. Skilled engineers formed a trade union, later called the Amalgamated Society of Engineers in 1851, to bargain for better working conditions and higher wages, much like medieval guilds. The more radical Grand National Consolidated Trade Union, encouraged by the industrialist Robert Owen (see below), attempted to organize all industrial workers for strikes and labor agitation. The British government looked with hostility on efforts at worker organization, passing the Combination Acts in the early 19th century to prevent union activity. Many workers favored more direct political activity. The Chartists, named after the founding document of their principles, employed petitions, mass meetings, and agitation to achieve **universal male suffrage** and the payment of salaries to members of Parliament. Chartism became associated with violent disturbances and faded as a movement after 1848, even though many of its goals were later reached.

Since socialism developed into a coherent ideology, it is covered more extensively in the section on "isms." Luddism represented an outright rejection of the principle of mechanization of labor. Named for a mythical figure, Ned Ludd, the supporters of the movement met in secret throughout the early 1810s to plan the destruction of knitting frames and spinning devices they perceived as taking their skilled jobs. Many viewed the perpetuation of an artisanal culture of sturdy skilled craftsmen as preferable to any benefits from industrial efficiency. The British government crushed the movement by exiling or executing those involved. Today, those who oppose technological change are often dubbed by their detractors as Luddites.

The Congress of Vienna and Concert of Europe[4]
The Vienna Settlement, 1814–1815

After the French Revolution and Napoleonic Wars, the great powers of Europe met in Vienna to rebuild a stable diplomatic order. Twenty-five years of violent upheaval and warfare had convinced conservatives of the need to reestablish legitimate governments and create mechanisms to subdue revolutionary movements. Negotiations were interrupted by the escape of Napoleon from Elba and his 100 Days campaign culminating with his defeat at Waterloo. In general, the victorious powers treated France leniently—though somewhat less so after the 100 Days—so as not to saddle the restored Bourbon monarchy with a harsh treaty. The Congress of Vienna, then, was guided by the following three principles:

- *Legitimacy*—Monarchs were restored to those nations that experienced revolutions. This meant the Bourbons back in France (Louis XVIII, brother of the executed king), Spain, and Naples. Though some monarchs conceded constitutions in deference to public opinion, power remained in the hands of conservative interests—"throne, altar, and estate"—that is, monarchy, church, and aristocracy.

- *Compensation*—Nations that lost territory in one area received compensation in another. For example, Austria surrendered possession of the Austrian Netherlands (Belgium) but gained control of several states in northern Italy.

- *Balance of power*—Key to the Congress's deliberations, balance-of-power considerations led to the creation of a series of buffer states to quarantine France should revolution break out there again. The new Kingdom of the Netherlands combined the former Dutch republic and Austrian Netherlands, Prussia gained extensive territory on the Rhine, and Piedmont-Sardinia in Italy was strengthened on France's southern border.

4 THEME MUSIC

The Vienna settlement and Concert of Europe defined diplomacy in the 19th century. To appreciate the diplomatic issues of this period (SP), you may want to create a balance of sheet of the possible positive and negative assessments of this most important of treaties and efforts at collective security.

The chart below provides an overview of the key players and their nations' goals.

Nation	Leader	Goals
Austria	**Klemens von Metternich** (1773–1859)—The dominant personality at the Congress.	As the most multiethnic of the great powers, Austria wished to repress nationalism and build a system of collective security to maintain the status quo. Owing to Metternich's association with the Congress of Vienna, the period 1815–1848 is sometimes termed the Age of Metternich.
France	Talleyrand (1754–1838)—Wily political survivor who represented revolutionary France, Napoleon, and then the restored Bourbons.	France wished to be readmitted into the family of the great powers by demonstrating its return to legitimacy. Talleyrand won over Metternich by exposing the plan of Prussia and Russia to take all of Saxony and Poland without consulting the other powers.
Great Britain	Castlereagh (1769–1822)—Focused on protecting British commercial interests.	Britain saw the Congress primarily as reestablishing the balance of power on the continent, its long-time goal. Britain did not wish to be involved in a kind of international police force to crush revolutions.
Prussia	Prince von Hardenberg (1750–1822)—Older leader often outmaneuvered by Metternich.	Least influential at the Congress, Prussia generally followed the lead of Austria, the other German power. Prussia also desired to incorporate its long-time enemy, Saxony, into its territory.
Russia	Alexander I (r. 1801–1825)—Began as a reformer, but grew conservative and more religious in response to revolution.	The largest of the powers and growing in influence, Russia under the once-Liberal Alexander wanted to control Poland and also gain support for a Holy Alliance of powers committed to stopping "godless" revolution.

The resolutions of the Congress of Vienna reflect the traditional diplomacy of elites redrawing the map of Europe to meet their goals. After almost nine months of deliberations and another war against Napoleon, the great powers finally completed their work in June 1815, with the following decisions:

Territorial adjustments: Some have been addressed above. The Polish-Saxon question almost led to war among the powers, but as a compromise, the Prussians gained 40% of Saxony and the Russian tsar was named King of Poland, though in reality ruled Congress Poland directly. To ensure stability in central Europe, a 39-state German Confederation was created with Austria as the dominant power. France relinquished conquests from the revolutionary wars.

Alliances: To ensure peace and stability, the great powers formed the Quadruple Alliance, which became the Quintuple Alliance with the inclusion of France after 1818. In addition, the three conservative central and eastern European powers—Austria, Prussia, and Russia—created the Holy Alliance, envisioned by Alexander I as a brake on revolutionary movements.

Indemnities: After Napoleon's return and the 100 Days, the victorious powers placed some moderate sanctions on France. The nation was required to return the art Napoleon had stolen from conquered lands and had to support an occupation army, which was removed in 1818.

Collective Security: To ensure peace and stability, the great powers agreed to meet periodically to discuss issues of mutual concern, especially related to war and revolution. This **Concert of Europe** provided a degree of informal security in the first half of the 19th century; however, Britain disagreed with Metternich's vision of collective security as committing the members to the suppression of revolutionary movements.

The Congress System

Several times after the meeting in Vienna, the great powers invoked the Concert of Europe to address revolutionary situations. The details of these meetings follow:

Congress of Aix-la-Chapelle, 1818: Based on French compliance with the treaty, the army of occupation was removed and France admitted to the Concert of Europe and Quintuple Alliance.

Congress of Troppau, 1820: Revolutionaries in Spain and Naples forced the kings of those nations to admit to constitutional limits on royal power. Metternich perceived the situation as the beginning of revolutionary violence and urged the other powers to sign a protocol committed to united action. When France and Britain demurred, Austria (with Prussian and Russian backing) subdued the revolt in Italy.

Congress of Verona, 1822: Two situations preoccupied the great powers—the continuing instability in Spain and Latin American revolts against Spanish control. On the first question, the great powers, excluding Britain, authorized a French army to subdue the threats to the Spanish monarchy and punish the revolutionaries, which was successfully done. Britain strongly objected to armed intervention in Latin America, as it wished to exploit the breakup of the Spanish empire to enhance its own trade. More importantly, the United States issued the Monroe Doctrine in 1823 warning against further European colonial ventures in an American sphere of influence.

No congresses met after Verona, demonstrating the differing visions of the Concert of Europe among the Big Five. Even if the great powers failed to create an institutional structure of collective security, a spirit of cooperation lingered until 1848. In assessing the Vienna settlement, some historians point out how its failure to recognize the forces of Liberalism and nationalism led to over 30 years of continuous revolution. However, the great powers did provide a framework that avoided a general war among all of the great powers for almost a century (until 1914). Regardless of interpretations, clearly the Congress of Vienna fundamentally shaped the political and diplomatic climate for the first half of the 19th century.[5]

Restoration and Reaction

What follows is a review-in-brief of domestic developments relating to the post-1815 theme of states restoring traditional governments and attempting to ensure stability. France and other nations that experienced revolutions are covered in the section "Revolutions and Reform."

Great Britain

Conservative Tories controlled British politics after 1815 and were intent on clearing away latent radicalism in the kingdom, often with censorship. Parliament remained unrepresentative, as none of the new industrial towns in the north elected members. Landed interests passed the Corn Laws protecting British grain from competition, but at the same time the policy harmed consumers by raising prices. Democratic movements agitated for political reform; one such peaceful gathering in 1819 in Manchester was met with armed force, killing 11 and wounding hundreds. Opponents of the government derisively dubbed this event the Peterloo Massacre. A gradual loosening of repression in the 1820s paved the way for Liberal reforms in the 1830s.

5 EXAMPLE BASE
Though the examples in this section go beyond what is specifically required in the Course Description, they will assist you in making an interpretation regarding the success or failure of the Concert system.

Germany

The personality of Metternich dominated politics through the German Confederation. Idealistic young student nationalists formed the *Burschenshaft* to celebrate liberal German culture and discuss political issues. Viewing these fraternities as a threat, Metternich convinced the Confederation to issue the Carlsbad Decrees (1819), forcing the dissolution of the *Burschenshaft*, censoring the press, and appointing government officials to supervise universities.

Russia

With an inconsequential middle-class and autocratic tradition, Russia proved infertile ground for political Liberalism. Nonetheless, army officers influenced by revolutionary ideology had formed the Decembrist Society to push for a constitutional government. When Alexander I died in 1825, the Decembrist Revolt agitated for the accession of Constantine, considered a Liberal, rather than his reactionary brother, Nicholas. Nicholas I (r. 1825–1855) crushed the revolt and ruled Russia in succeeding decades guided by the motto "Autocracy, Orthodoxy, and Nationality," relying on a secret police, religious uniformity, and imposition of Russian language and culture on ethnic minorities.

The "Isms"

The period 1815–1850 was the Age of Ideologies. In response to the issues raised by the Dual Revolution, many Europeans adhered to a set of ideas that provided both a systematic view of human affairs as well as a blueprint for changing the world. Such ideologies or "isms" influenced how people viewed events as well as motivated them to action.[6]

Conservatism

Conservatism should not be equated with complete rejection of change (such adherents are known as reactionaries). Defying the optimistic views of human rationality associated with the Enlightenment and French Revolution, Conservatives believed that human nature was driven primarily by the passions. Edmund Burke (1729–1797) became a leading advocate for change through adaptation, not violent revolution, with his statements against events in France (see Chapter 10). Humans are capable of reason, he argued, but often employ it as an excuse for self-interested actions. Customs and traditions, which have evolved over time to meet the needs of particular human societies, act as checks on the passions and should not be discarded lightly. Along with Burke, French philosopher Joseph de Maistre (1753–1821) demonstrated how once the revolution in France broke from its traditions of church, monarchy, and nobility, it descended into violent chaos. Burke and de Maistre were not opposed to constitutions *per se*—as Burke supported the American Revolution—only those based on abstract and supposedly universal principles not in keeping with a society's experiences. Conservative philosophy supported the restoration governments of the post-1815 order.

Liberalism

Classical Liberalism of the 19th century should be distinguished from the way the term *liberal* is used today. Based on Enlightenment and revolutionary ideals of reason, progress, and individual rights, Liberalism acted as a powerful philosophy of change throughout the 19th century. Economically, Liberals embraced the **laissez-faire** principles of Adam Smith's capitalism and strong protection of private property. Politically, Liberals favored the social contract theory of limited government advocated by John Locke and the French revolutionaries as the surest guarantee of **religious toleration** and **individual rights**. Many if not most Liberals came from the middle class and supported a more representative government and an expansion in suffrage, though only for property holders. British philosopher Jeremy Bentham (1748–1832) articulated the related approach of utilitarianism, wherein "good" was defined as providing pleasure and "evil" as causing pain. Holding that the purpose of government was to promote the "greatest good for the greatest number," Bentham argued for separation of church and state, women's rights, and the end of slavery. Beginning in the utilitarian tradition, John Stuart Mill (1806–1873) later provided in his *On Liberty* (1859) one of the most eloquent defenses of freedom of expression and the dangers of the tyranny of the majority. Mill also collaborated with his wife, Harriet Taylor, and defended the cause of female suffrage in Parliament.

Socialism, Republicanism, and Feminism

Self-proclaimed **radicals** and republicans embraced the "principles of '93" from the French Revolution. Many were drawn from intellectual circles or the working class and favored equality and **universal male suffrage** while opposing the influence of organized religion, as well as monarchy and aristocracy. Republicanism shaded off into socialism. **Socialists** criticized the capitalist system as unequal and unjust, wishing to replace it with social and economic planning. One of the first socialists, ironically, was a textile entrepreneur, Robert Owen (1771–1858). Owen built a model factory in New Lanark, Scotland, to better provide for his workers' needs, with high wages, improved conditions, and provision for schools and other amenities. The industrialist also attempted to export his **utopian socialism** to the United States, constructing an experimental but failed colony in Indiana. Most other early socialists were French, reflecting the legacy of the revolution. Henri de Saint-Simon (1760–1825) and Charles Fourier (1772–1837) embraced an ethos of cooperation and shared property to realize human needs beyond merely the economic. Additionally, the socialist Louis Blanc's idea of "national workshops" for the working class played a key role in the revolution in 1848 in France. Despite the creativity, utopian socialism led to few practical successes and gave way after 1850 to the more militant Marxian version of socialism.

Many advocates of women's rights, such as Mary Wollstonecraft and John Stuart Mill, drew from the Enlightenment tradition of individual rights and social equality. Socialists combined their criticism of the class system with that of gender roles. French female socialist Flora Tristan (1803–1844) argued that the oppression of women, whether as factory workers or in domestic roles, sprang from the unequal ownership of property. Numerous famous female writers of the period, such as Jane Austen, George Sand, and Germaine de Staël, once again demonstrated that women could exercise independent creative voices. By 1850, many **feminists** had established a clear agenda for the movement. obtaining greater access to education along with legal, property, and political rights.

Nationalism

Nationalism proved the most combustible ideology of the 19th century, and it is essential to your understanding of political and diplomatic events after 1800. Spread by the example of the French Revolution, nationalism initially focused on cultural revival and celebration of traditions. Long-divided Germany in particular experienced a wave of cultural nationalism fed by the Napoleonic Wars. Johann Gottfried Herder (1744–1803) replaced the political–judicial conception of state with an organic folk-nation best represented by the term *Volksgeist*, or "spirit of the people." Germans celebrated their music and folklore, as with Beethoven's symphonies or the Grimm Brothers' fairy tales. Such cultural nationalism eventually took on political overtones. The German philosopher Hegel (1770–1831) glorified the national state as the march of destiny through history. History itself consisted of a clash of opposing ideas, called the dialectic, which pointed the way to a new synthesis—the idea of German national unity.

Given the atmosphere of repression and reaction during the post-1815 period, many nationalists formed secret societies to promote their agendas of unity. The Italian Giuseppe Mazzini (1805–1872) first joined the secretive Carbonari, who aimed to expel the Habsburgs from the peninsula, before forming Young Italy in 1831. Mazzini worked to foment national-ist uprisings in his native land, while in his writings argued that the overthrow of the Concert of Europe would lead to free, independent states based on linguistic and ethnic identity. States constituted along national lines would eliminate the need for wars and create true brotherhood and peace. Eastern Europe also experienced a revival of national traditions. Intellectuals representing the diverse group of Slavic speakers—Poles, Serbs, Croats, Czechs, Slovaks—looked to common linguistic and cultural traditions and advocated pan-Slavism, or the unity of all Slavs. Pan-Slavism inspired uprisings in the 1815–1850 period, but given the power of the Habsburg and Ottoman Empires over the Slavs, the subsequent failures of these revolutions demonstrated the need for the patronage of an outside power—namely Russia, the protector of the Slavs.

Romanticism

Romanticism dominated literature, music, and the arts in the first half of the 19th century. Romantics reacted to the Enlightenment's emphasis on reason and science, instead stressing the following:

- *Emotions*—Taking their cue from Rousseau, Romantics emphasized feeling and passion as the wellspring of knowledge and creativity.

- *Intuition*—Science alone cannot decipher the world; imagination and the "mind's eye" can also reveal its truths.

- *Nature*—Whereas the philosophes studied nature analytically, the Romantics drew inspiration and awe from its mysteries and power.

- *Nationalism*—Romanticism found a natural connection with nationalism; both emphasized change, passion, and connection to the past.

- *Religion* (*Supernatural*)—Romanticism coincided with a religious revival, particularly in Catholicism. Spirit, mysticism, and emotions were central to both.

- *The unique individual*—Romantics celebrated the individual of genius and talent, like a Beethoven or a Napoleon, rather than what was universal in all humans.

With these themes in mind, consider the topics and individuals below.**7**

Literature and History

Lord Byron (1788–1824)—As famous for his scandalous lifestyle as for his narrative poems, Lord Byron died from fever on his way to fight for Greek independence, a cause he supported in his writings.

Thomas Carlyle (1795–1881)—Carlyle pioneered history as the story of great men, as with his famous study of the French Revolution.

François-René de Chateaubriand (1768–1848)—In *The Genius of Christianity*, Chateaubriand glorified the mystical pull of religious faith and its connection with the beauties of nature.

Johann Wolfgang von Goethe (1749–1832)—Goethe's *Sorrows of Young Werther* recounted the tale of a passionate young man who commits suicide over an unrequited love. Along with *Faust*, in which the title character sells his soul to the devil, Goethe's works proved enormously influential in combining a neoclassical style with the Romantic themes of intuition and emotion.

Edgar Allan Poe (1809–1849)—With his short stories, Poe demonstrates the Romantic interest in the occult and macabre.

Sir Walter Scott (1771–1832)—Reflecting the Romantic interest in medieval history, Scott's *Ivanhoe* chronicles the conflicts between Norman and Saxon knights in England.

Mary Shelley (1797–1851)—Daughter of Mary Wollstonecraft, Shelley gained fame with *Frankenstein*, a literary warning about the hubris of modern humans and technology gone awry.

Percy Bysshe Shelley (1792–1822)—Shelley gained fame both from his poetry, as with his tale of rebellion against social conventions in *Prometheus Unbound*, and his lifestyle of free love and vegetarianism. Husband of Mary Shelley.

7 THEME MUSIC AND EXAMPLE BASE

Prior to the 19th century, you will have noted the rise of objective thinking toward the natural world (Scientific Revolution, Enlightenment), but with the Romantics, we see one of the first strong reactions to the notion that all knowledge stems from the scientific method (OS). Though not the first to do so, the Romantics embrace the subjectivity of experience in a singular and seductive manner.

William Wordsworth (1770–1850)—Wordsworth's poetry glorified nature and suggested that "one impulse from a vernal wood" would teach humans more "than all the sages can."

Architecture and Painting

Eugene Delacroix (1798–1863)—Delacroix is most famous for his large canvases, bold use of color, and exotic themes. His tribute to the French revolutionary tradition, *Liberty Leading the People*, is his most famous work.

Caspar David Friedrich (1774–1840)—Friedrich's paintings gained notoriety for their portrayals of solitary figures confronting the immensity of nature, as with *Wanderer Above the Sea of Fog*.

Théodore Géricault (1791–1824)—His immense canvas, *The Raft of Medusa*, demonstrated the Romantic fascination with nature as well as a critique of a distant and uncaring monarchy. Gericault's works on the insane illustrate the Romantic interest in the exotic and unique.

Houses of Parliament (1830s)—The most famous architectural example of the neo-Gothic revival in Britain.

J.M.W. Turner (1775–1851)—Turner used vivid colors and atmospheric effects to depict the untamed power of nature in his *Rain, Steam, and Speed* and *Slaveship*.

Music

Ludwig von Beethoven (1770–1827)—Beethoven pushed the classical style to its limits with his sophisticated orchestral arrangements. Despite growing deafness, Beethoven helped establish the Romantic movement in music with his nine symphonies.

Hector Berlioz (1803–1869)—Berlioz developed program music in which a drama parallels the motifs of the music. His famous *Symphonie Fantastique* portrays a drug-induced imagination of a witches' gathering.

Though Romantics occupied themselves primary with cultural expression, many combined their aesthetic vision with political activism. Romantics urged freer lifestyles and political systems, which explains the crossover from Romanticism to nationalism, as well as Liberalism. In fact, many historians term the first half of the 19th century the Age of Romantic Nationalism. As we see below, Romanticism fueled the revolutionary sentiments sweeping across Europe in the period 1815–1850.

Revolutions and Reform

The Restoration political settlement, designed to stop revolution, inadvertently fed the grievances of nationalism and Liberalism in the period 1815–1848. This Age of Revolutions gained fuel from industrial problems and the legacy of unfulfilled promises from the French Revolution. Among the great powers, Great Britain avoided revolutionary outbursts through the enactment of tentative Liberal reforms in this period. Revolutionary turmoil culminated with the revolutions of 1848, one of the more overlooked events in European history.

The Revolutions of 1830–1831

We have already seen how the great powers used the Concert of Europe from 1815 to 1830 to subdue revolutionary movements in Sicily and Spain. However, these successes hid the underlying force of Liberal and national movements. In 1830, the fever of revolution flared again, as usual beginning with France.

The restored Bourbon kings of France reestablished the power of the Catholic clergy and favored the interests of former aristocrats. When elections repudiated the monarchy's policies, it curtailed voting rights and censored the press. Militant republicans and middle-class moderates joined in overthrowing the king, who quickly abdicated. As a compromise, the throne went to a ostensibly reformist relative of the deposed monarch. The new King Louis Philippe (r. 1830–1848), known as the "bourgeois king," promised to abide by the Constitution of 1814.

Events in France inspired revolts in Belgium and Poland in 1830–1831. The Belgians never fully accepted their absorption into a Dutch kingdom and, following the French example, declared their independence. Because the great powers agreed to maintain Belgian neutrality, the new nation was permitted to establish a new Belgian kingdom. However, this was not the case with Poland, which also revolted against Russian authority in 1831. With no outside support, the Polish revolt was brutally crushed by Nicholas I, Congress Poland was eliminated, and the territory directly incorporated into Russia.

When the Christian Greeks revolted against their Islamic Turkish rulers in 1821, the event inspired an outpouring of support by European intellectuals, who praised the ancient Greeks as the founders of western civilization. By the 1820s, the great powers had come over to the cause of Greek nationalism, even Metternich. The Turks were defeated and by treaty (1829), a new independent Greek state was created, a rare example of a successful nationalist revolt in this era.

Reform in Great Britain

Great Britain avoided revolutionary upheaval because of its ability to adapt to the challenge of Liberalism. To incorporate the new industrial bourgeoisie and provide an orderly process of representation for new cities, Parliament passed the Reform Act of 1832, which doubled the number of males who could vote, but retained a property requirement. Further reforms followed with the abolition of slavery in the British Empire in 1833 and the Poor Law of 1834. In reflecting the Liberal notion of self-help, the latter law actually punished the poor by making relief in government workhouses more unpleasant than any job. One of the more important principles favored by Liberals was free trade, thus their opposition to the protective Corn Laws. In the context of the Irish potato famine, Parliament in 1846 finally repealed the Corn Laws, initiating a century of British support for free trade. Conservative Tories supported their own notion of reform—through protective legislation. Following the Factory Act of 1833, Tories in Parliament helped pass the Mines Act, banning children and women from mines, and the Ten Hours Act, limiting hours in textile mills. In giving the middle class a stake in society, British reformers hoped to gain their support for compromise over revolution.

8 SKILL SET

You may note in this section how the unresolved issues of the French Revolution echoed throughout the 19th and into the 20th centuries. Consider the continuities and changes (CCOT) in the issues that prompted revolutions and the rhetoric and strategies employed by revolutionaries to achieve their aims.

The Revolutions of 1848[8]

Revolutions broke out all over Europe in the fateful year 1848. Though few of these revolutions achieved their stated objectives, their consequences proved significant nonetheless. Three major causes account for the stunning outburst of revolutionary activity: (1) Liberals felt profound frustration at the lack of political change toward constitutional and representative government, (2) nationalists chafed under the 1815 Vienna settlement and its blunt rejection of self-determination for ethnic minorities, and (3) the lives of the working class suffered from poor agricultural productivity (the era was known as the "hungry '40s") and jobs lost to new industrial machinery. The combination of these factors made for an explosive compound, and once again the match was lit in France. For an overview of events, review the following chart:

Location	Trigger	Leaders	Events	Results
France	Discontented over the slow pace of reform and corruption in Louis-Philippe's government, Liberals agitate for suffrage expansion. When the government resists, Paris rises in revolt.	*Louis-Philippe—(r. 1830–1848) king who abdicates under pressure of violence in Paris. *Louis Blanc—socialist advocate of national workshops for workers. **Louis Napoleon**—nephew of Napoleon I and opponent of monarchy; elected president of the Second Republic in 1848.	*Following Louis's abdication, a provisional government is formed, composed of moderate and radical republicans. *To appease the working class of Paris, Blanc's national workshops are formed, but end up as a system of poor relief, not of worker control of industry. *In June, radicals attack the democratically elected Constituent Assembly in hopes of creating a socialist republic. *The June Days see class violence between radical republicans and the army, which results in the deaths of 10,000 radicals and the establishment of a moderate republic. *Louis Napoleon is elected president in December by a wide majority and moves to consolidate power.	France establishes the Second Republic, but only after class warfare reveals the divisions in French society between the middle and working classes. Louis Napoleon exploits fears of further social conflict to establish authoritarian control of the nation.
Prussia	Inspired by the French example, Prussian Liberals in March revolt in Berlin against the Prussian monarch, who had resisted sharing power.	*Frederick William IV (r. 1840–1861)—agrees to the election of a Prussian assembly, but refuses the Frankfurt Liberals' offer of a crown of a united Germany; does grant a conservative constitution to his kingdom in 1850.	*Liberals force the election of a Prussian Assembly, which grants autonomy to the Polish minority. *By spring's end, the Prussian army has reestablished control of the nation and reversed the pro-Polish legislation of the Assembly.	Prussian Liberals failed to meet their objectives of political equality and reducing the influence of traditional institutions. However, despite its three-tiered class voting system, the 1850 Constitution provides for representation.

Chapter 11 ◆ Industrial Society and the Struggle for Reform, 1815–1850 **189**

Location	Trigger	Leaders	Events	Results
Frankfurt	After the riots in Berlin, Liberals overthrow the traditional political structures of other German states. After elections, delegates meet in Frankfurt to attempt Germany's unification.		*Deliberations divide over whether the Austrian empire, with its large non-German population, should be included in a unified Germany. This debate causes a fatal delay while conservatives regather their strength. *By December, the Liberals issue a Declaration of Rights for the German people. *In April 1849, the Frankfurt Assembly completes its constitution and offers the crown to Prussian King Frederick William IV.	By the time German Liberals complete a constitution, their moment has passed. Frederick William IV rejects the "crown from the gutter," and the work of German unification would await the wily diplomacy of a conservative (see next chapter).
Austria	Workers and students rebel in March in Vienna, causing Metternich to flee to Britain.	*Klemens von Metternich—conservative Foreign Minister and creator of the Congress System, unable to withstand the revolutions of 1848. *Franz Joseph I (r. 1848–1916)—becomes emperor in December upon his father's abdication.	*Serfdom is abolished throughout the Austrian empire. *Emperor Franz Joseph agrees to a Constitution in 1849.	After the initial nationalist revolts, the new emperor and army reestablish control and crush further opposition. Franz Joseph rejects the Liberal constitution and works toward centralization of power, though the ethnicities issue would fester.
Prague	Seeing the turmoil in the Austrian Empire, Slavic nationalists meet in Prague to discuss the unification of all Slavs.	General Windischgrätz—German army commander who succeeds in dispersing the Prague Assembly.	After initially promising autonomy to Bohemia, whose capital was Prague, the Austrian emperor reverses course and breaks up the Pan-Slav Congress.	Though unsuccessful, Slavic nationalism remains a problem for the Austrian Empire and forms an essential cause of the First World War.

Location	Trigger	Leaders	Events	Results
Budapest	Events in Paris inspire the Hungarian Diet in March to proclaim liberty for Magyars (another name for Hungarians).	Louis Kossuth (1802–1894)— Hungarian Liberal and nationalist who leads the cause of the Magyars.	*In the fall of 1848, Hungarian nationalists proclaim a new constitution that promotes the Magyar language but suppresses the rights of Slavic minorities in Hungary. *After the constitution is rejected by the Austrian emperor, Hungary declares complete independence. *Emperor Franz Joseph in 1849 asks Russian leader, Nicholas I, to crush the nationalist movement in Budapest.	The Austrians exploit Slavic fear of Hungarian power to crush the revolt, with Russian support. However, Magyars remain the most restive of the ethnic minorities in the empire.
Italy	After the March Days in Vienna, several Italian states rise in revolt against Austrian rule.	*Charles Albert (r. 1831–1849)— king of Piedmont-Sardinia who urges the Italian states to resist Austrian rule. *Pope Pius IX (r. 1846–1878)— begins as a reformer, but when expelled from Rome by revolutionary forces, turns against modernism. ***Giuseppe Garibaldi** (1807–1882)— Italian nationalist military leader who helps establish the Roman Republic.	*Charles Albert of Piedmont-Sardinia grants a constitution to his people and declares war on Austria to gain territory in Italy. *Numerous other Italian states rise in revolt against Austrian rule. *When the Pope is expelled from Rome, Mazzini proclaims a Roman Republic. *Austrian authorities agree to abolish serfdom in Italian Habsburg lands, hoping to win over peasants. *The Austrian army defeats Charles Albert and restores authority in the other Italian states. *To win over Catholics, Louis Napoleon in 1849 sends French troops into Rome to restore Pope Pius IX.	Italians experience few specific victories in 1848, other than the abolition of serfdom in some states and a constitution for Piedmont. However, the revolutions set the stage for Italian unification under Piedmont-Sardinia later and its opposition by the papacy.

What began with heady enthusiasm and high hopes ended with bitter disappointment and violent suppression. In general, the Liberal and nationalist revolutions of 1848 failed to achieve their objectives, and for this three key factors are responsible: (1) Though revolutionaries boasted lofty rhetoric and inspiring visions, they lacked the institutional power of conservative forces, such as armies and bureaucracies, (2) conservatives successfully exploited middle-class fears of radical revolution after the June Days in Paris, and (3) rulers pitted ethnic minorities against one another to divide and conquer and reestablish authority. Despite these failures, the revolutions of 1848 may be the most underestimated event in European history. The revolutions set the stage for the rise of socialism and a growing division between the middle and working class. In addition, the Romantic age of revolution seemed dead and, philosophically, many intellectuals turned to a more hard-headed realist and materialist vision of the world. Most importantly, conservatives learned the lesson that they could no longer ignore nationalism, so if they wished to stay in power, they had to appeal to public opinion and sponsor movements of national unity from the top down. It is to this topic that the next chapter is devoted.[9]

Additional Resources

Benedict Anderson, *Imagined Communities: Reflections on the Origin and Spread of Nationalism*, rev. ed. (2006)—Influential perspective on the meaning of nationalism.

T.S. Ashton, *The Industrial Revolution, 1760–1830*, 2nd ed. (1998)—A classic account that briefly traces the process of technological change in a positive light.

Eric J. Hobsbawm, *The Age of Revolution: Europe, 1789–1848* (1996)—Challenging, but packed with insights, this volume is authored by a famous Marxist historian.

Henry Kissinger, *Diplomacy* (1995)—By the former Secretary of State, this book offers chapters on the Vienna settlement and beyond.

Philip A.M. Taylor, *The Industrial Revolution in Britain: Triumph or Disaster?* (1969)—From the Problems in European Civilization Series, this volume provides both primary and secondary readings.

http://spartacus-educational.com/IndustrialRevolution.htm—This site addresses many issues related to the Industrial Revolution with primary and secondary sources.

http://www.victorianweb.org/technology/index.html—Focuses on the technology of industrialization.

9 SKILL SET

One pundit argued that the revolutions of 1848 were "a turning point at which history failed to turn." It will be useful take this notion and turn it into a Periodization (PER) question, identifying the ways in which this statement is true or false by tabulating the evidence, particularly in subsequent decades. The short answer is that they helped establish the modern world. How and why?

Practice MC Questions

Questions 1–3 are based on the text below.

"These, then, are the laws by which wages are regulated, and by which the happiness of far the greatest part of every community is governed. Like all other contracts, wages should be left to the fair and free competition of the market, and should never be controlled by the interference of the legislature.

The clear and direct tendency of the poor laws is in direct opposition to these obvious principles: it is not, as the legislature benevolently intended, to amend the condition of the poor, but to deteriorate the condition of both poor and rich; instead of making the poor rich, they are calculated to make the rich poor; and whilst the present laws are in force, it is quite in the natural order of things that the fund for the maintenance of the poor should progressively increase till it has absorbed all the net revenue of the country, or at least so much of it as the state shall leave to us, after satisfying its own never-failing demands for the public expenditure."

David Ricardo, English political economist, *On the Principles of Political Economy and Taxation*, 1817

1. The argument above reflects the influence of:

    A. the principles of the radical phase of the French Revolution.

    B. Conservative political thought aimed at opposing new economic ideas.

    C. Romantic conceptions of an emotional connection to the nation.

    D. the theories of Adam Smith advocating for capitalism.

2. Which subsequent political philosophy would most have agreed with the ideas conveyed in the passage?

    A. Social Darwinism

    B. anarchism

    C. feminism

    D. Marxism

3. In which of the following ways did continental European policies toward the economy differ most markedly from the ideas in the passage?

    A. Continental states actively sponsored industry and economic growth.

    B. Continental states were slower to develop workers' movements and unions.

    C. Continental states refused to provide reforms to address industrial problems.

    D. Continental states lacked access to natural resources such as coal and iron ore.

J.R. McCulloch, "On Wages." in *The Works of David Ricardo* (London: John Murray, 1888), pp. 57–58.

Questions 4–6 are based on the text below.

"Young Italy is a brotherhood of Italians who believe in a law of progress and duty, and are convinced that Italy is destined to become one nation, convinced also that she possesses sufficient strength within herself to become one, and that the ill success of her former efforts is to be attributed not to the weakness, but to the misdirection of the revolutionary elements within her,–that the secret force lies in constancy and unity of effort. They join this association with the firm intention of consecrating both thought and action to the great aim of reconstituting Italy as one independent sovereign nation of free men and equals..."

Giuseppe Mazzini, Italian politician and activist, Instruction to Members of Young Italy, 1831

4. The ideas above were most likely a response to which of the following events?

A. The abolition of feudalism

B. Napoleon's declaration of the empire

C. The Congress of Vienna

D. The Crimean War

5. Which of the following political ideologies does the passage most reflect?

A. Liberalism

B. Romanticism

C. Socialism

D. Nationalism

6. The fulfillment of the ideas in the passage above occurred:

A. during the revolutions of 1848.

B. with Cavour's policies of *Realpolitik*.

C. with the conquest of Libya.

D. after the Treaty of Versailles ended World War I.

7. Which of the following figures would have disagreed most strongly with the passage?

A. Napoleon

B. Metternich

C. Garibaldi

D. Bismarck

James Harvey Robinson and Charles A. Beard, "The Unification of Italy," in *Readings in Modern European History* (Boston: Ginn & Company, 1909), pp. 115–116.

Questions 8–9 are based on the image below.

Caspar David Friedrich, German painter, *Two Men Contemplating the Moon*, 1819

8. The painting above reflects all of the following principles of Romanticism EXCEPT:

 A. interest in the supernatual.

 B. the preoccupation with nature.

 C. skepticism regarding science.

 D. fascination with individualism.

9. Romanticism, as depicted in the painting, anticipated which of the following general trends in ideas and culture?

 A. The importance of national identities and histories

 B. The subjective nature of experience and knowledge

 C. The questioning of traditional social structure and values

 D. The growth of positivism—the effort to make all knowledge scientific

See Chapter 18 for answers and explanations.

Short-Answer Question with Sample and Commentary

A. Explain ONE similarity between Great Britain and a continental European nation in their approaches to or experiences with industrialization.

B. Explain TWO differences between Great Britain and a continental European nation in their approaches to or experiences with industrialization.

(HTS: Comparison)

A. Great Britain took the lead in industrialization with mechanical developments in textiles, coal mining, and metallurgy. However, industry soon spread to the other nations in Europe. One development that promoted industry in Britain and on the continent was the railroad. The new steam rail system helped bring products to market and lowered costs, making factories viable. Both areas depended on the "iron horse" to make industry go.

B. While Britain raced ahead in the 19th century with technology, Russia languished in backwardness. One reason for this difference was their agricultural systems: whereas Britain adopted scientific approaches and enclosure, Russia relied on the inefficient system of serfdom. Britain could feed an expanding urban population, but Russia couldn't. Also, Britain provided for middle-class representation in Parliament, which meant laws facilitating industry, like free trade. On the other hand, Russia was still dominated by an aristocracy that showed little interest in industry or its benefits, once again holding Russia back.

This student knows her topic. For Part A, the response clearly identifies a similarity between Britain and the continent as a whole—the importance of transportation systems in creating an industrial market, while at the same time showing a recognition of its relationship to other industries. The student chooses a nation (Russia) to emphasize contrasts, pointing out the differences between Britain's Agricultural Revolution and Russia's reliance on serfdom, followed by a brief analysis of how political differences (e.g., middle-class representation in government) can affect policy-making toward industry. An effective and focused response: 3 points.

CHAPTER 12 Realism, Nationalism, and Imperialism, 1850–1914

Failure in the revolutions of 1848 vaulted Europe into a new era. Intellectually, the Romantic temperament faded, as artists, scientists, and politicians adopted a hard-headed mindset of realism and materialism. Military power, industry, organization, electricity, commodities—these products of modern life replaced the imaginary, spiritual, emotional, idealistic, and rhetorical of Romanticism. This chapter reviews the post-1848 realist and materialist ethos in the arts and ideas, its application in national unification projects, in the continuing progress of technological and industrial change, and, ultimately, how all these were deployed in Europe's domination of Asia and Africa through imperialism. The events in this chapter culminate centuries-long developments and represent the zenith of European power in world history.

Key In Chapter 12 covers the following KCs from the Course Description:

- **KC 3.6** Realist and materialist themes in the arts, sciences, and social sciences
- **KC 3.4** Unification of Italy and Germany, as well as other nation-building efforts
- **KCs 3.1 and 3.2** The Second Industrial Revolution and its economic effects
- **KC 3.3** State efforts to address the problems raised by industrialization
- **KC 3.5** European imperialism in Africa and Asia

Realism and Materialism

If the Romantics presented a world of possibilities through the imagination, then the realists refocused their attention on the world as it really was, warts and all. For writers and artists of the second half of the 19th century, industry and technology dominated the lives of Europeans.

Art and Literature

After 1850, writers turned from Romantic themes to the lives of those directly affected by a changing material reality. Characters in realist novels struggled to understand and cope with the impersonal forces of economic and social change. British author Charles Dickens (1812–1870) filled his novels with compelling characters thrown into a world of sooty cities, cruel orphanages, and corrupt business practices. Stories such as *Hard Times* and *Oliver Twist* revealed the underside of Britain's rapid industrialization and the crushing inequality attending material progress. Realist writers abandoned the conventions of Romantic rhetoric in favor of an unsentimental, precise style, as in Gustave Flaubert's (1821–1880) *Madame Bovary*. The title character becomes disillusioned with her mundane middle-class life and marriage, engages in several adulterous affairs, and ultimately commits suicide.

Realist artists turned their canvases into windows on the lives of the downtrodden. French painters led the way in revealing the difficult circumstances of landless peasants and exhausted factory workers. Jean-François Millet (1814–1875) highlighted in paintings such as *The Sower* and *The Gleaners* the backbreaking labor of culling enough from the earth to eke out survival. His paintings were echoed by those of Gustave Courbet (1819–1877), whose *Stonebreakers* eloquently captured the brutal work of two manual laborers crushing stones for gravel. We focus on the physical posture of the workers rather than their faces, which are covered in shadows. As photography developed throughout the century, an additional medium became available to depict difficult social problems.

Positivism marks the culmination of the authority of science and belief in objective knowledge (OS), representing a continuity with the Scientific Revolution and Enlightenment. However, positivism goes beyond a particular epistemology (method of knowledge) to take up a philosophical or cosmological position--that only objects verifiable by the senses can exist.

Positivism[1]

As the influence of organized religion declined in Europe, many substituted it with belief in the potential of science. The power of scientific thought seemed validated by its production of immense material benefits through industry and technology. French philosopher August Comte (1798–1857) captured this faith with the theory of positivism. Comte believed that history had progressed through three stages—the theological, metaphysical (or philosophical), and the scientific. The great revolutions of 1789–1848 faltered, according to Comte, because of their adherence to overly abstract principles. Progress must rely on a hard-nosed and empirical investigation of reality, avoiding wishful thinking and unsupported generalizations. Comte categorized all the sciences and argued for a science of society (sociology), which would become a new secular religion.

Marxism

Karl Marx (1818–1883) claimed the mantle of a "**scientific socialism**" and turned his political philosophy into one of the most influential movements in history. From a middle-class family, Marx studied philosophy and law in college and eventually fell in with German radicals. Working for a series of left-wing publications, Marx hailed the revolutions of 1848 as the beginning of the socialist age. Marx's lifelong collaborator, Friedrich Engels (1820–1895), was the son of a German textile owner who rebelled against his inheritance and had published *The Condition of the Working Class in England* (1844) to highlight the inequalities generated by capitalism. Together the two produced the famous pamphlet, *The Communist Manifesto* (1848), urging the working class to unite and throw off their chains. Though the revolutions of 1848 failed, the manifesto established the outlines of Marxian socialism and a program of nationalization of property, universal suffrage, and the redistribution of property. As the collaborators worked within the newly established First International—founded in 1864 to promote a union of working-class parties—Marx labored at his masterwork of political economy, *Capital*, later finished by Engels in the 1880s. Marx and Engels wove together three diverse strands into their comprehensive critique of capitalism: German philosophy, British industrialism, and French radicalism. Marxian socialism comprises the following pillars:

- Alienation of labor—In his early writings, Marx blamed the increasing division of labor (i.e., specialization) for alienating (or creating a feeling of separation) the worker from his product, his labor, himself, and his fellow man, who exploits him.

- Labor theory of value—Borrowing from the British classical economists, Marx held that the value of a product equaled the amount of labor that went into producing it. Therefore, the difference between the worker's wages and the ultimate price of the products—what the factory owner calls profit—robs the worker of his uncompensated "surplus labor."

- Dialectical materialism—Marx took Hegel's historical notion of the clash of opposing forces as producing change (thesis → antithesis → synthesis) and applied it to clashing systems of production. Whereas Hegel emphasized a dialectic of *ideas*, Marx held that antagonistic *material forces* produced change, called economic determinism. Marxism, thus, offered a complete view of history, in keeping with German philosophy.

- Class struggle—Each economic system is associated with a dominant class that owns the means of production. In feudalism, for example, the aristocracy owns the essential resource (land) and exercises power based on this ownership. The **bourgeoisie** who own capital (factories, banks, etc.) represent the most productive class in history, but their exploitation of the propertyless unskilled workers who are forced to sell their labor, the **proletariat**, inevitably produces the system opposing capitalism—socialism. As workers increase in number, they will develop **class identity** (consciousness) and eventually unite to overthrow those who oppress them.

- Revolution—Marx condemned early utopian socialists and the anarchists of eastern and southern Europe for what he considered unrealistic schemes. Rule by the oppressed proletariat would only result from organization, agitation, and planning, not by separate communes and assassinations. Though Marx hoped for a worldwide movement of the working class, he believed it possible, if unlikely, that the revolution might succeed through democratic means in some nations.

Marxism exercised wide influence among all working-class movements, both revolutionary and democratic. Even those who rejected Marx's critique of capitalism had to confront his powerful ideology of change. Many have claimed that the appeal of Marxism lies in its similarity to an organized religion, though Marx rejected religion as the "opiate of the masses." Marxism offers its adherents religious-like symbols: prophets (Marx and Engels), holy books (Marx's writings), a chosen race (proletariat), and an end of the world (history's culmination with **communism**, where the state "withers away"). Marxism would finally gain power in the 20th century, though some claim that these national experiments represent a distortion of Marx's doctrine, suggesting that there may be "as many Marxisms as there are Marxists."[2]

National Unification

It seems each century produces an event that completely transforms the diplomatic landscape. In the 19th century, the unifications of Italy and Germany altered the entire framework of European diplomacy. European political structures proved unable to incorporate successfully the emergence of these two new powers, leading to the most destructive wars in history in the 20th century. Italy and Germany had been divided for centuries. What allowed for their unifications in the middle of the 19th century? Once again, we must look to the failed outcomes of the revolutions of 1848.

The Crimean War, 1853–1856

Revolutions in 1848 undermined the Concert of Europe—the agreement of the great powers to resolve issues collectively—and paved the way for the mid-century **Crimean War**. The Crimean War seemed avoidable and was poorly fought, but ultimately proved of great importance for subsequent diplomacy.

For centuries after its last foray into central Europe in 1683, the Ottoman Empire slowly receded in power. The empire found itself prey to continual attacks by a Russian nation intent on gaining a warm-weather seaport. Only the intervention of Britain, which opposed Russian expansionism into the Mediterranean, kept the "Sick Man of Europe" on life support. When Napoleon III of France in 1853 wrung concessions from the Ottoman sultan to protect Christian minorities within the empire, the Russians demanded the same treatment. Fearing the further growth of Russian power, the French and British stiffened the sultan's resistance to Russian intrusion. When war ensued, the Russian navy shattered the archaic Ottoman fleet in the Black Sea and moved into two Turkish-held provinces (current-day Romania). France and Britain demanded that the Russians evacuate the provinces or face war. Even though Russia complied, the two western powers declared war anyway because of anti-Russian public opinion in their nations. Austria now used the situation to its own benefit. Russia had aided Austria in 1849 by crushing the Hungarian revolt. Instead of repaying the favor, Austria exploited Russia's predicament by moving into the recently evacuated provinces. Isolated, Russia attempted to defend itself against the combined weight of France, Russia, and the Italian kingdom of Piedmont-Sardinia.

The Crimean War represents the inaugural industrialized conflict, with the first use of trenches, telegraphs, and railways. Nonetheless, poor communication, strategic errors, and disease cost an inordinate number of lives. The only hero of the struggle was Florence Nightingale (1820–1910), who helped found the nursing profession and demonstrated the ability of women to take on productive public roles. By 1855, the new Russian tsar, Alexander II, realized that the war had underscored Russia's technological and economic backwardness. With the Treaty of Paris (1856), Russia agreed to demilitarize the Black Sea and halt its expansion into the Balkans.

2 SKILL SET

This section distills orthodox Marxism; however, the theory has been altered and fitted to many contexts, including the most backward of the industrial powers (during the Russian Revolution) and used by anticolonial powers to establish economic independence and promote global equality (CCOT).

Though the war was over, the issues raised by it were not. By forever destroying the Concert of Europe, the Crimean War encouraged states to pursue national interests with little regard for the effects on the international order. Napoleon III considered the war a great victory and was falsely convinced of France's strength and prominence. British leaders felt disappointed at the cost and outcome of the war and fell into "splendid isolation" for half a century, standing aside while Italy and Germany unified. With its overly subtle diplomacy, Austria had isolated itself, a fatal error as it would face two wars in the next 10 years. Before the ink was dry on the treaty, Russia was determined to reform internally and continue its expansion at the first opportunity. Finally, by its involvement, little Piedmont-Sardinia won itself a great power patron in its drive for unification.

The Unification of Italy[3]

Background and Romantic Nationalism

The Italian peninsula was divided since the time of the Roman Empire. Though Italy pioneered the Renaissance, its diverse city-states lost their independence as a result of foreign invasion. Since the 16th century, foreign powers dominated politics in Italy. The nationalism of the French Revolution and the policies of Napoleon revived dreams of a united Italy. The Congress of Vienna's restoration of traditional rule frustrated these aspirations. Despite failure to expel foreign rule in the revolutionary period 1815–1848, Italian nationalists could now look to leadership from Piedmont-Sardinia and exploit the increasingly tenuous position of Austria, the foreign power blocking unification.

Many Italian nationalists preferred the creation of a united republic, which would require a takeover of the Papal States. Following the Congress of Vienna, the resurgence of Italian nationalism was fueled by two republican advocates: Giuseppe Mazzini (see Chapter 11) and **Giuseppe Garibaldi**, the charismatic leader of the Red Shirts. Both represented the spirit of romantic nationalism. Much of the practical work for Italian unity, however, was accomplished by a bookish and wily moderate, **Camillo Benso di Cavour** (1810–1861).

The Role of Piedmont-Sardinia and Cavour

Because of Piedmont-Sardinia's anti-Austrian role in the revolutions of 1848, many Italian nationalists looked to it for leadership. In 1848–1849, the king granted a constitution and attempted to unite the other Italian states in a war of liberation against Austria. Owing to his failure, the king abdicated in 1849, turning power to his son Victor Emmanuel II (r. 1849–1878). In 1852, the new king appointed Cavour as prime minister. Cavour supported Liberal ideas and had urged the unification of Italy in his newspaper, *Il Risorgimento*. Cavour understood practical affairs, having made a fortune in agriculture and business. As prime minister, Cavour looked to modernize the Piedmontese state—updating the tax and budget system, building railroads, pursuing free trade, limiting the power of the Catholic Church, and building a small but strong army. Though Cavour was willing to use Romantic ideals to his advantage, he favored a realistic (*Realpolitik*) approach to Italian unity. And this required a foreign ally.

With the Treaty of Plombières (1858), Cavour persuaded Napoleon III of France to join Piedmont-Sardinia in a joint attack on Austria. By the treaty, Piedmont would gain the Italian states of Lombardy and Venetia, while Napoleon would reconfirm French leadership of nationalism and exercise influence in Italy. In the ensuing war, Piedmont and France defeated the Austrian army, setting off revolutions in the northern Italian states. Fearing that the situation was spinning out of control, Napoleon III signed a separate agreement with Austria, leaving Cavour high and dry. However, the northern Italian states in 1860 voted via plebiscites (elections related to issues not candidates) to join the Piedmontese state, which Napoleon acknowledged in exchange for Nice and Savoy from Piedmont.

Cavour now urged Garibaldi to take advantage of the revolutionary situation brewing in the Kingdom of the Two Sicilies, the backward Bourbon monarchy controlling the southern half of the peninsula. With just over a thousand of his Red Shirts, Garibaldi rallied the countryside to his

3 SKILL SET

To ensure your understanding of the new politics of realism (*Realpolitik*), compare and contrast (COMP) the tactics used by Cavour and Bismarck, respectively, to unify Italy and Germany.

cause and moved up the peninsula. Once again, concerns over the position of the papacy complicated matters. Cavour did not wish to involve French troops guarding Rome in the situation, so he and Victor Emmanuel met Garibaldi south of Rome and asked him to relinquish his conquest to Piedmont-Sardinia. Though a republican, Garibaldi consented, and plebiscites confirmed the unification of the northern and southern halves of the peninsula. In March 1861, the new Italian kingdom was proclaimed, with Victor Emmanuel as its first monarch. Two months later, Cavour died, one might say from complications of nation-birth. Thus, it has been said that the new Italian kingdom represented the "passion of Mazzini, the audacity of Garibaldi, and the cunning of Cavour."

Italy completed its unification by gaining Venetia in 1866 and Rome (excluding the Vatican) in 1870 when Prussia, with whom Italy was allied, defeated Austria and then France in war. Though united, Italy experienced significant problems—opposition by the papacy to the new Italian state, economic underdevelopment, a corrupt political system known as *trasformismo* (the bribing of political opponents), and the wide cultural and economic differences between northern and southern Italy. Because it came so late to national unity, Italy often compensated by aggressively seeking colonies and attempting to regain "unredeemed" Italian-speaking territories.

The Unification of Germany

Background: German Dualism

Like Italy, Germany's limbs had lain severed in central Europe for centuries. Conflicts between the Holy Roman Emperor and papacy in the Middle Ages stymied either from unifying Germany. Due to its elective nature, the emperor never became a strong absolutist ruler like the kings of France. Religious conflict in the 16th and 17th centuries splintered German politics, formalized with the Westphalia settlement in 1648. In the 19th century, the dualism of two German powers— Austria and Prussia—effectively checked either from consolidating the smaller German states into one nation unified around German language and ethnicity. When Liberals failed in 1848 at Frankfurt to unify Germany, it opened the door for a different path to the same objective.

Prussia's great military tradition had decayed since the time of Frederick the Great (d. 1786). The kingdom entered the French revolutionary wars late (1807) and then was defeated decisively by Napoleon. Moreover, Austria under Metternich dominated German politics after the Congress of Vienna, leaving Prussia to play second fiddle. When William I (r. 1861–1888) inherited the Prussian throne from his faltering brother, he set out to reestablish Prussia's power.

With his first act, William introduced long-overdue reforms in the army. At the advice of his generals, William called for the expansion of the army, regular conscription (the draft), the creation of a General Staff (to devise war plans), and the introduction of modern rifled weapons, such as the breech-loading needle gun. According to the Prussian Constitution of 1850, representatives to the Reichstag (lower house of the parliament) were apportioned by a unique three-tiered voting system, designed to favor the wealthy Junker elite. However, as Germany industrialized, the power of the middle-class Liberal Party grew in Prussia. Liberals in the Reichstag resented the conservative influence of the army as well as the Junker class who dominated it and opposed the king's reforms. Neither king nor Reichstag would budge, plunging Prussia into a constitutional crisis.

The Work of Bismarck

To solve the crisis, William turned in 1862 to **Otto von Bismarck** (1815–1898), appointing him Chancellor. Bismarck hailed from the Junker class, but surpassed that often provincial and mediocre group with his intelligence and ambitions. A romantic turned conservative, Bismarck gained wide diplomatic experience representing Prussia to France, Russia, and the German Confederation. In his political approach, Bismarck played the consummate game of *Realpolitik*. Bismarck possessed no predetermined plan for the unification of Germany; rather, he took advantage of opportunities presented to him. To deal with the political crisis in Prussia, Bismarck turned the tables on the Liberals in the Reichstag, claiming that they held no constitutional power to block needed reforms. He appealed to Prussian patriotism, arguing that the other German states did not look to Prussia's liberalism—that was the mistake of 1848—but to its "iron and blood." When the Reichstag continued to refuse taxes to implement the army reforms, Bismarck simply instructed the bureaucracy to collect the taxes anyway.[4]

To unify Germany, Bismarck waged three separate wars. His opponent in each war found itself diplomatically isolated and maneuvered into appearing as the aggressor. When the Poles revolted against Russian authority in 1863, almost every great power expressed support for their national aspirations, but without tangible assistance. Bismarck calculated that he needed the future friendship of great power Russia, so he supported their crushing of the Polish revolt. In 1864, Denmark formally incorporated the mainly German-speaking provinces of Schleswig and Holstein (which it had occupied since 1848) into the Danish kingdom, violating an international treaty. Nationalism flared in Germany. Rather than working through the German Confederation as Austria preferred, Bismarck suggested a joint approach by the two leading powers. Austria relented, and the two powers easily defeated their enemy in the Danish War, occupying the two provinces of Schleswig and Holstein.

The joint occupation of the two provinces offered ample opportunity for conflict between the two German powers. The dispute festered, as Bismarck intended, and eventually Austria turned to the German Confederation for relief. Citing a violation of the occupation agreement, Prussia went to war against Austria. Before entering the conflict, Bismarck ensured Austria's isolation—Russia was favorable after Bismarck's support for the Polish revolt; Napoleon was bought off with vague promises of French expansion; Italy hoped to gain Venetia from Austria; and Britain maintained its splendid isolation. In the ensuing Austro-Prussian War (or Seven Weeks' War) of 1866, Prussia's superior railroads, staff organization, and needle gun overwhelmed the Austrians. Despite the designs of William, Bismarck treated Austria leniently; they lost only Venetia and, more importantly, were forced to bow out of German affairs. Prussia annexed the states of north Germany, and in 1867 Bismarck created the North German Confederation, insisting that its Reichstag be elected by universal male suffrage. What's more, the Reichstag hailed Bismarck's achievement by retroactively approving the illegally collected taxes with the Indemnity Bill of 1866.

The mostly Catholic German states stood outside this union. Anticipating future conflict with France, Bismarck convinced these states to join in an alliance with the North German Confederation should war break out with France. When the Spanish throne became vacant in 1870, Bismarck had his pretext. The Spanish nobles offered the throne to a Hohenzollern relative of William's, an offer that Bismarck pressed the candidate to accept. Not wishing to be surrounded by Hohenzollerns, the French vehemently objected. William relented and encouraged his cousin to drop the offer. Now Napoleon III of France overplayed his hand and demanded an apology from William via the French ambassador. Bismarck edited an account of the meeting, known as the Ems Dispatch, to make it seem as if the king had insulted the French ambassador. Napoleon took the bait and declared war. Once again, Bismarck's opponent was isolated; the French were easily defeated in the Franco-Prussian War and embarrassingly, Napoleon himself was captured at Sedan. The resulting treaty imposed a 5-billion franc indemnity on the French, and, more importantly, they lost Alsace-Lorraine, which became a source of enmity between the two nations throughout the 20th century. In January 1871, Bismarck's work was complete with the proclamation of the German Empire with William I as Kaiser (emperor).

Though Bismarck helped engineer a federal constitution that respected the traditions of the other German states and allowed elements of democracy, power was still exercised in an authoritarian fashion. Government ministers reported to the Kaiser, not the Reichstag, and Bismarck effectively concentrated key positions in his own hands (Chancellor, Prussian Minister of State), which allowed him to exploit democratic mechanisms to ensure his domination of policy. This new German empire immediately upset the balance of power in Europe. Its economic and military potential threatened to dwarf its neighbors. Even though Bismarck worked to maintain peace in Europe after 1871, some historians believe that he laid the foundation for the militarism and state glorification that gave rise to the Nazis in the 20th century.

4 THEME MUSIC
Certainly the unification of Germany represents one of the turning points of the course (PER), and it may be useful for you to identify its effects. As the Prime Minister of Britain noted at the time: "There is not a diplomatic tradition which has not been swept away. You have a new world, new influences at work, new and unknown objects and dangers with which to cope....The balance of power has been entirely destroyed." Consider how subsequent political and diplomatic events were shaped by the creation of this new restless empire (SP).

Other Nation-Building Efforts

Italy and Germany represent the most salient examples of nationalism's power to unify states. However, already territorially unified states, such as France and Russia, worked toward greater internal cohesion through reform. The following states demonstrate three different models of reform.

France: Napoleon III and the Second Empire

After being elected president of the Second Republic, Louis Napoleon quickly consolidated his power. Presenting himself as a man of the people, he dissolved the legislature over the issue of universal male suffrage. In a *coup d'etat* in 1851, Napoleon rescinded the 1848 republican constitution. With popular approval through a plebiscite, Napoleon announced in 1852 the Second Empire with himself as Emperor Napoleon III. Though Napoleon's foreign adventures proved disastrous—loss of control over Italian and German unification, a failed effort to create an empire in Mexico—he did modernize France internally.

Working through a professional and centrally controlled bureaucracy, Napoleon focused on France's economic development. He founded a national bank, built railways, promoted French industry, and in his most celebrated reform, rebuilt the city of Paris. Napoleon hired the talents of the architect and engineer Baron von Haussmann (1809–1891), who tore down old city walls and housing, constructed a modern sanitary system, built grand boulevards, and adorned it all with a feast of opera houses, theaters, and shopping centers. As Napoleon said, "I found Paris stinking, and left it smelling sweet." Due to increasing criticism, Napoleon after 1860 allowed more legislative input, relaxed press censorship, and pursued a policy of free trade with Great Britain. But such reforms could not rescue Napoleon from his foreign policy failures, and in 1870, the emperor himself was captured by the Prussian army (see above) and the empire ended. Workers of the shiny new Paris refused to surrender, however, and established a revolutionary Paris Commune, which harkened back to the principles of 1793 with its socialist program. Eventually, a popularly elected Constituent Assembly crushed the Paris Commune and established the Third Republic. Another French republic started off with the taint of class violence and military failure.

Russia: Alexander II's Modernization

The Crimean War demonstrated Russia's weakness *vis-à-vis* the other great powers. Recognizing the backwardness of his nation, Alexander II (r. 1855–1881) embarked on a series of top-down reforms that proved ultimately too little too late to save the Romanov dynasty. Fearing violent peasant upheaval, Alexander abolished serfdom in 1861. By terms of the liberation, peasants continued to live on the village *mirs* until they paid for the land they received. Russian agriculture continued to suffer from land shortages and rural overpopulation into the 20th century. In addition, Alexander introduced equality into the legal system, abolished corporal and capital punishment, created local assemblies known as *zemstvos*, and reformed the army. These wide-ranging reforms did not heal the growing rift in Russian society between those who emphasized Russia's unique traditions (called Slavophiles) and those who believed Russia must become more modern (Westernizers). Led by discontented intellectuals, such as Alexander Herzen and Mikhail Bakunin (1814–1876), **anarchism** gained support in the context of an autocratic and archaic Russia. Eventually, an anarchist-inspired movement known as the People's Will succeeded in 1881 in assassinating Alexander after numerous failed attempts.

Austria-Hungary: The Dual Monarchy

The tattered Austrian empire was until the First World War ruled by Franz Joseph I (r. 1848–1916), a leader not known for his decisive action or ambitious projects. Franz Joseph attempted to hold together his diverse realm through the bureaucracy, the army, and loyalty to the Habsburg dynasty. Following the revolutions of 1848, Austria focused on internal development, building railroads and promoting industry, as well as centralization around the German language. These policies further alienated the Slavic and Magyar ethnic minorities. Following losses in the Italian and German wars of unification, Franz Joseph allowed the creation of the **Dual Monarchy** in 1867. This new **Austro-Hungarian** monarchy allowed autonomy for the Magyars but maintained unity through common ministries of finance, foreign affairs, and war. However, neither of these kingdoms was democratic. In fact, the Hungarians pursued Magyarization in their part of the empire, suppressing Slavic languages and culture. Not until 1907 did Austria grant universal male suffrage and even then, the imperial Reichsrat so often descended into ethnic conflict that Franz Joseph was forced to rule by decree. Austria-Hungary's ethnic problems laid the powder trail that ignited into the First World War.[5]

The Second Industrial Revolution

Historians point to the year 1850 as roughly dividing the initial phase of industrialization from a new one characterized by a larger scale of industrial enterprises, a further geographic expansion of industry, and a much closer relationship between theoretical science and its application in technology. This new phase we call the Second Industrial Revolution.

New Technologies and Methods

The period 1875–1910 represents arguably the greatest concentration of technological advance—including our own age—in the history of the human race. Steam engines now powered larger factories, as mechanized production became the predominant form of manufacture. American Henry Ford pioneered a new form of **mass production**, the assembly line, which allowed for increased economies of scale (i.e., reduced costs at high levels of production) and cheaper products. With the Bessemer process, steel replaced iron as the essential metal in construction, railways, and for military use. Reinforced concrete and steel girders allowed for the development of skyscrapers, adding a new element to modern cities.

Theoretical advances in chemistry boosted the chemical industry. Germany quickly became the dominant producer of chemicals, which had numerous industrial, pharmaceutical, and military uses. Europeans harnessed the power of **electricity** to light cities, power streetcars, and provide for a seemingly inexhaustible source of energy. After its discovery in 1859, petroleum grew into a mineral resource vital to the needs of the new **internal combustion engines** and to nation-states dependent on its potential power. This catalog above only scratches the surface; refrigeration, photography, elevators, kitchen appliances, motion pictures, synthetic fabrics, TNT, X-rays, and many others could also be included.

Transportation and Communication

Technological advances revolutionized transportation and communications. Steamships allowed for faster ocean journeys and greater geographic mobility, establishing an essential means for European control of distant empires. The completion of the Suez (1869) and Panama Canals (1914) reduced transoceanic travel times even further. Invented in 1903, airplanes would not alter passenger travel for several generations, but did yield immediate military applications. New power sources also allowed for the development of city streetcars and subways and, by extension, the creation of suburbs and the further separation of home and work.

The technology of human communication had not changed much since the invention of the printing press in the 1450s. The late 19th century witnessed a series of inventions that made the world smaller and allowed European power a truly global reach. A transatlantic telegraph cable was laid in the 1870s to create the first instantaneous communication over continents; the invention of the telephone was not far behind. To facilitate railway schedules, standardized time zones were introduced in the 1880s. Marconi's discovery of radio waves translated in the early 20th century into a means for states to coordinate military power and control public opinion.

Business Cycles and Managing Markets

Despite the great wealth generated by this technological dynamo, the European economy suffered from **boom–bust cycles** in the period 1873–1896. Overproduction and unpredictable commodity prices routinely plunged Europe into recession, creating fear for governments of worker unrest and corporate bankruptcies. To manage the market, businesses became more organized. The **modern corporation**, with its complex administrative structures, accounting procedures, and stocks, dates from the late 19th century. Some industries informally collaborated in cartels to control the production and thus the prices of their manufactures. Banks pooled investment resources in consortia to control interest rates. These **monopolies** represented an attempt by companies to control an unpredictable market. Though governments continued to rely on market mechanisms and the gold standard to ensure stable currencies, many states began to move away from free trade toward **protective tariffs** to shield domestic industries.

Technological advances translated into new goods. Former luxuries became necessities. To reach consumers, corporations began to exploit communication advances for marketing purposes. Advertising in billboards, newspapers, and catalogs opened a new world of **consumerism** to European citizens. With its modernization, Paris sponsored the first **department store**, Bon Marché, in the 1870s. An increasingly sophisticated economy opened new employment opportunities in so-called white collar areas, such as retail, marketing, communications, and services.[6]

The Balance of Power and Global Integration

New developments in industry shifted the balance of economic power worldwide. Within Europe, Germany by 1900 surpassed Britain in steel, iron, coal mining, and chemical production. The United States arose as a competitor outside Europe, besting Britain and Germany both in steel and coal production also by 1900. European capital, however, commanded the world. With huge profits and sophisticated banking and investment methods, European corporations and governments came to dominate the functioning of the world economy. Imperial powers like Britain, France, and Germany invested in Asian, African, and Latin American ventures, influencing those regions' economic decisions, if not controlling them outright. By 1914, economic activity had become truly global, with developments in one area of the world rippling throughout.

Imperialism

European control of global markets was nothing new in the 19th century. However, the period 1763–1871 saw a net decline in European colonial control, with American independence and Europe's preoccupation with revolutionary movements and internal development. Following the unification campaigns of Italy and Germany, as well as other internal nation-building programs, Europe's aspirations for national greatness turned outside the continent. With the advance of technology and organization stemming from the Second Industrial Revolution, European powers as of 1870 possessed both the means and motives for further penetration of the global market. Compared with earlier colonization, what distinguished European imperialism in the period 1871–1914 was more direct control of foreign territory and greater emphasis placed on colonies' internal infrastructure development.

Motives and Means

Motives for European imperialism can be divided into three basic categories—economic, political, and cultural. As you might expect, Marxist historians stress economic motives stemming from the expansion of capitalism. However, other historians contend that the pursuit of even financially valueless colonies demonstrates the power of national prestige as a driving force,

6 THEME MUSIC
The Second Industrial Revolution reveals the tension inherent in the Poverty and Prosperity theme (PP), as it provided immense wealth to industrialists and European powers, at the same time left other groups (unskilled laborers, poor peasants, colonial areas) with inequality and dependence.

or that the cultural impulse to "civilize inferior peoples" acted as more than a cynical pretext, but as a genuine idealistic mission.

- *Economic motives*—As nations industrialized, they needed access to **raw materials**, particularly with the sophisticated industries of the Second Industrial Revolution. Rubber, oil, bauxite, copper, diamonds—all could be found in great supply in Asia, Africa, and Latin America. With European rivalries heating up, great powers feared dependence on potential enemies for strategic resources; colonies opened the door for self-sufficiency. With the problem of overproduction, nations also desired colonies as **markets** for finished products and outlets for investment of profits. However, most of the imperialist powers' capital went into more established industrialized areas, such as the United States or other European nations.

- *Political motives*—Imperialist powers coveted strategic locations. Great Britain bought up shares in the Suez Canal Company and eventually formed a protectorate (a nominally independent state indirectly controlled by another state) over Egypt in 1882 because of the geopolitical value of the Suez as a "lifeline to the British Empire." When the United States became an imperial power in 1898 after the Spanish-American War, it looked at the Philippines and Pacific islands as important coaling stations or military bases. Nations like Italy pursued colonies at great cost primarily as a claim to status as one of the great powers. After 1871, the European powers carved up Africa with a **nationalistic fervor** driven by public opinion. In Germany, Bismarck disdained colonies in Africa but pursued them anyway to appease public opinion; colonies are "for elections," he said. Finally, many feared that the mushrooming European population (from 260 million in 1850 to 450 million in 1914) would lead to political discontent. Colonies might act as an outlet for surplus population; indeed, 30–50 million immigrants left Europe in this period, but most went to the United States, the Americas, or Australia.

- *Cultural motives*—Missionaries arrived first in Africa. The famous David Livingstone traveled to the Dark Continent as a medical missionary and was followed by British middle-class Victorians who believed it their duty to civilize the supposedly inferior races. This paternalistic European attitude found expression in Rudyard Kipling's (1865–1936) famous poem "The White Man's Burden," which some view as an endorsement of the civilizing mission, whereas others view it as a satire. By the 1870s, the influence of Charles Darwin's ideas (see next chapter) had seeped into the consciousness of writers, businessmen, and political leaders. Many viewed history as an ongoing struggle among races for resources and territory. According to **Social Darwinism**, war elevated the nation by calling for self-sacrifice and establishing the proper hierarchy among the victors and the defeated. Europeans often took their easy subjugation of technologically less-advanced tribal peoples as a moral endorsement of their imperial ambitions.

How was it possible for the small continent of Europe to control, directly or indirectly, almost two-thirds of the world's population by 1914? First, European control arose directly from the technological advances of the Second Industrial Revolution. Steam power, telegraphs, **medical advances** (e.g., the discovery of quinine to treat malaria), and railroads allowed for global trade and communication as well as penetration of the interior of Africa and Asia. Second, with the industrialization of war, Europeans gained an overwhelming military superiority. The Asian civilizations of India and China, not to mention the tribal societies of Africa, proved no match for high-powered artillery, armored battleships, and machine guns. Finally, the complex and highly organized nature of modern corporate capitalism sustained a long-term presence in colonies and provided for the systematic exploitation of resources.

The Partition of Africa

AFRICA, 1914

Dennis Sherman and Joyce Salisbury, *The West in the World: A History of Western Civilization* (New York: McGraw-Hill Education, 2014), p. 615.

As of 1870, Europe had colonized little of Africa; most areas inland from its coasts were unknown. The pursuit of African colonies got under way with the founding of the International Congo Association in 1878 by King Leopold II (r. 1865–1909) of Belgium. Private bankers financed Leopold's venture, which was an entirely personal rather than a national concern. To manage the possible opening of Africa, Bismarck in 1884–1885 called the Berlin Conference among the great powers. The imperial powers agreed to create the Congo Free State as Leopold's personal fiefdom and devised procedures for the orderly establishment of colonies. Leopold's rule proved to be one of the harshest in Africa, as he ignored the prohibition on slavery, plundered the nation of rubber and ivory, all while the Congolese population was decimated by disease and overwork.

The Berlin Conference produced the opposite of the intended effect. By simply establishing coastal control, European nations could claim huge swaths of Africa's interior by drawing lines on a map, usually with no regard for linguistic or tribal divisions. Imperialists exploited Africans' lack of experience with European legal and economic concepts, as tribal leaders often unknowingly signed away trade and resource concessions. By 1900, all except Liberia and Ethiopia had fallen under direct European rule.[7]

To understand the nature of African imperialism, we briefly examine the British example. Early on, colonial secretary Joseph Chamberlain (1836–1914), fearing the spread of independence movements, proposed a tariff union between Britain and its colonies, thereby binding the

7 THEME MUSIC

From the beginning of the course (1450), Europe had expanded its influence across the globe. The drive for resources and power stimulated exploration in the 15th and 16th centuries, created the Columbian Exchange and Commercial Revolution, and here culminates with the establishment of a European-dominated global economy via imperialism (INT).

colonies together in a system of imperial preferences. Gradually these dominions (self-governing areas such as Canada) would achieve complete self-rule but maintain strong economic ties with the mother country. Chamberlain's idea would later bear fruit with the commonwealth system following World War I. African imperialism seemed to belong to adventurers like Cecil Rhodes (1853–1902) rather than statesmen like Chamberlain. Britain had already established in 1815 control of the Cape of Good Hope on the southern end of Africa, dispossessing the Dutch settlers who trekked overland to create the Orange Free State and Transvaal. When Rhodes was made prime minister of this Cape Colony, he dreamt of establishing a Cape-to-Cairo connection to cement Britain's dominance of Africa and the exploitation of his diamond interests. Rhodes went too far by trying to provoke war with the two Dutch republics and was forced to resign.

Imperial pursuits in Africa demonstrated the potential for conflict involving the great powers. To secure control of the Egypt, Britain extended its power into Sudan. This intrusion brought resistance by Muslim troops, and the retaliatory expedition in 1898 at Omdurman demonstrated the lethal advantage of machine guns and artillery over musket and spears, as the British lost only 48 men to 10,000 for the Sudanese. After their victory, British troops almost fell into conflict with the French, who controlled much of north and west Africa, at Fashoda. Cooler heads prevailed, and war was avoided. Such was not the case with the Dutch Boers. Rhodes's policies eventually embroiled Britain in the costly Boer War (1899–1902), in which Britain's use of concentration camps and scorched-earth policies led to international condemnation. The potential for further conflict in Africa shook Britain out of its isolation as it went shopping for allies.

Imperialism in Asia—Three Examples

ASIA, CA. 1900

The British in India Compared to Africa, European powers employed indirect control of Asia. Because civilizations like India and China already possessed complex political and social hierarchies, European imperialists preferred to "plug in" to the existing power structure to establish control. In India, Britain had exploited that country's political divisions to gain local allies and establish indirect control through the British East India Company. In 1857,

Paul Edward Dutton, Suzanne Marchand, Deborah Harkness, *Many Europes: Choice and Chance in Western Civilization* (New York: McGraw-Hill Education, 2014), p. 641.

soldiers (called sepoys) in the Indian army revolted against Britain's insensitivity toward Hindus and Muslims. Britain subdued the Sepoy Mutiny with great brutality, dissolved the East India Company, and established direct rule, with Queen Victoria (1837–1901) as Empress of India.

Though India boasted its own manufacturing base, Britain turned the country into a raw materials producer. At the same time, Britain attempted to modernize India's infrastructure by building railroads, instructing the population in English, and educating elites at British universities so they might become effective civil servants. Ironically, many such students imbibed western ideas of nationalism and equality, tools that would be used by the likes of Mohandas Gandhi (1869–1948) and Jawaharlal Nehru (1889–1964) to establish Indian independence later.

The Carving of China[8] China disdained contact with foreigners and generally dismissed them as uncivilized. However, the weakness of the Qing Dynasty (1644–1911) allowed westerners to exploit China's growing disintegration to their advantage. Though Europeans coveted Chinese goods, the only commodity Europeans seemed able to sell in China was opium. When the Chinese government attempted to stop the import of the noxious substance, the British responded with overwhelming military force. After several such Opium Wars at mid-century, Britain and France had imposed upon China trading and other concessions. By the Treaty of Nanking (1842), China surrendered Hong Kong and was forced to create free-trade treaty ports.

Soon Russia and Germany had joined in carving out spheres of influence in China. Even worse for the Chinese, Europeans were subject only to the laws of their home nation, not to those of China, an indignity known as extraterritoriality. In an attempt to keep open the Chinese market, the newly imperial United States secured agreement to the Open Door Policy, an effort to maintain China's territorial integrity and the free access of each power to the others' treaty ports. Anger against foreign control resulted in the Boxer Rebellion in 1900, led by a secret Chinese society. The imperial nations crushed the revolt and imposed even more indemnities and controls on the faltering Chinese government.

Japan's Modernization Only Japan seemed able to resist the onslaught of European imperialism. When Commodore Perry of the United States arrived in 1853, he encountered a united and prosperous civilization that had been virtually isolated for 300 years. Foreign contact brought down the Tokugawa Shogunate and almost led to a Chinese-style treatment of Japan. However, under reforming samurai, the authority of the emperor was restored and the most rapid modernization in history followed. During the so-called Meiji Restoration, Japan borrowed from the West liberally—its industrial techniques, educational practices, and military arts.

By 1890, Japan had established itself as an industrial, military, and imperial power in its own right. Japan surprised the world in 1894 by defeating the much larger China and establishing dominance over the Korean peninsula. In a sign of Japan's newfound prestige, Britain allied with the new Asian power in 1902. Conflict with Russia over resources in Manchuria soon led to the Russo-Japanese War of 1904–1905. Japan shocked the world by defeating the Russians on land and sea, destroying the Russian fleet at Tsushima Strait. The outcome represented the first time in modern history that an Asian power had defeated a European power in war. Profound consequences issued from the Russo-Japanese War: first, Russia turned back toward expansion in the Balkans, setting the stage for the First World War; second, Russia's weak showing led to the **Revolution of 1905**, a warm-up for the great Russian Revolution of 1917; and finally, Japan had demonstrated to the rest of the world that Europeans could be defeated by turning their own weapons against them.

Critics and Consequences

Though many Europeans saw great glory in imperialism, some condemned it. Two of the most famous critiques came from J.A. Hobson (1858–1940), a British economist, and the great Russian revolutionary, V.I. Lenin (1870–1924). Hobson argued that European imperialism was

8 EXAMPLE BASE
Though you have choices, the Course Description requires that you understand how colonial areas responded to and resisted European imperialism. As you read through this section, consider the range of responses, perhaps making a visual organizer to show similarities and differences, or provide a brief assessment of effectiveness.

driven by the accumulation of capital, which in turn required overseas investment and markets. If corporations would simply invest in workers' wages and if governments taxed excess wealth and redistributed it to the poor, the impulse to export European capital would diminish. In his *Imperialism, the Highest Stage of World Capitalism* (1916), Lenin contributed to Marxist theory by claiming that the phenomenon of imperialism indicated the crisis inherent in capitalism. By concentrating power in fewer and fewer hands, capitalism inevitably expanded its geographic boundaries in pursuit of further areas of exploitation, leading directly to the First World War. Some historians dispute these assertions; the case of Italy is instructive. Italy desperately pursued colonies in Africa. In fact, at the hands of Ethiopia in 1898, Italy experienced the first major defeat by a European power in Africa. Nonetheless, Italy persisted in its ventures, risking war and diplomatic isolation, to gain in 1911 Libya, a vast expanse of desert hardly worth the cost in men, money, and resources.

How did European imperialism change Europe and the world? There are several arguments:

- *Rise of new powers*—As a result of colonial opportunities, the United States and Japan both rose as imperial powers. After the Spanish-American War (1898), the United States acquired its first overseas possessions—Hawaii, the Philippines, and control of Cuba and the Panama Canal. The rise of these two Pacific powers would lead to conflict in World War II.

- *Intensification of European rivalries*—The First World War did not begin in Africa or Asia, but the seeds of war were planted in colonies. To illustrate, conflicts between Russia and Britain over Persia and between Germany and France in the Moroccan Crises (1905, 1911) helped cement the mutually antagonistic alliance systems that escalated that conflict.

- *Decolonization and dependency*—Europe's hold on its colonies weakened after World War I and was severed after World War II. Today, no European nation possesses a colonial empire, yet issues of colonial dependence and resentment toward former European (and American) dominance show up in the issues of terrorism, tribal conflicts, and persistent economic underdevelopment.

Imperialism reveals a domestic connection as well. Colonial ventures acted as a laboratory for some to test the ideas of Darwinism and eugenics (the pseudoscience of studying racial characteristics), as well as new industrial and military technologies. The overseas drive for colonies reveals the intense domestic pressures operating at home—social, intellectual, and political. In the next chapter, we turn to these issues.

Additional Resources

Gordon Craig, *Germany, 1866–1945* (1980)—The interested student will find a strong narrative of German unification.

T.S. Hamerow, *Otto von Bismarck: A Historical Assessment* (rev. 1993)—This volume provides various interpretations on a key figure of the period.

Eric Hobsbawn, *The Age of Empire, 1875–1914* (1989)—An insightful account of the period from a famous Marxist historian.

Adam Hochschild, *King Leopold's Ghost: A Story of Greed, Terror, and Heroism in Colonial Africa* (1998)—A gripping account of one of the worst experiences under imperial rule.

Thomas Pakenham, *The Scramble for Africa* (1992)—Strong narrative account of the partitioning of Africa.

Norman Rich, *Great Power Diplomacy, 1814–1914* (1991)—A survey of European diplomacy in an important era.

www.postcolonialweb.org/—This site provides literature from the perspective of former British colonies.

Practice MC Questions

Questions 1–4 are based on the map below.

EUROPEAN RAILROADS, 1870 AND 1914

1. **The map best supports which of the following conclusions about the European economy?**

   A. Governments played a more important role on the continent than in Britain in promoting industry.

   B. Mechanization and the factory system became the predominant modes of production by 1914.

   C. German industrialization experienced a significant stimulus with its unification in 1871.

   D. Transportation developments like railroads helped create more fully integrated national and international economies.

2. **The most direct result of the trends shown in the map was:**

   A. the growth of a new consumer economy.

   B. the development of rival alliance blocs.

   C. the creation of the feminist movement.

   D. the expansion of leisure time and activities.

Paul Edward Dutton, Suzanne Marchand, Deborah Harkness, *Many Europes: Choice and Chance in Western Civilization* (New York: McGraw-Hill Education, 2014), p. 671.

3. The differences shown on the map between western and eastern Europe can be explained by:

   A. the prevalence of volatile business cycles in western Europe.

   B. better access to natural resources in western European states.

   C. the dominance of agricultural elites in eastern Europe.

   D. the control over eastern European states by Russia.

4. Which of the following technologies or processes would be most comparable in its effects to those depicted on the map?

   A. The printing press during the Renaissance

   B. Advances in navigation during exploration

   C. Military weapons and tactics in the 17th century

   D. Astronomical discoveries of the Scientific Revolution

Questions 5–8 are based on the text below.

"But the crux of the global economic situation was that a number of developed economies simultaneously felt the same need for new markets. If they were sufficiently strong their ideal was 'the open door' on the markets of the underdeveloped world; but if not strong enough, they hoped to carve out for themselves territories which, by virtue of ownership, would give national business a monopoly position or at least a substantial advantage. Partition of the unoccupied parts of the Third World was the logical consequence."

Eric Hobsbawm, historian, *The Age of Empire*, 1987

5. Which of the following developments in the period 1850–1914 relates most directly to the interpretation above?

   A. The development of Racial Darwinism

   B. Nationalist competition among states

   C. Unification of Italy and Germany

   D. The Second Industrial Revolution

6. How did Europe's interaction with the world described above differ most significantly from Europe's interaction with the world during the period 1450–1600?

   A. The reliance on notions of European cultural superiority

   B. Imbalances of technology between Europeans and non-Europeans

   C. The economic demands produced by an industrializing economy

   D. Widespread conversion of non-Europeans to Christianity

7. Which of the following ideologies most likely influenced the historian's interpretation?

   A. Positivism

   B. Marxism

   C. Nationalism

   D. Darwinism

8. The historian could use all of the following as evidence to support his interpretation EXCEPT:

   A. the persistence of backward agricultural practices in areas of Europe.

   B. transportation advances such as railroads and steamships.

   C. reliance on monopolies by governments and corporations.

   D. volatile business cycles of boom and bust in Europe.

See Chapter 18 for answers and explanations.

E. J. Hobsbawm, *The Age of Empire: 1875–1914* (New York: Pantheon Books, 1987), pp. 66–67.

Long Essay Question with Sample and Commentary

Compare and contrast the nation-building efforts of any TWO nations in the period 1850–1914.
  (HTS: Comparison)

The revolutions of 1848 ambitiously attempted to undo the hated Congress of Vienna and fulfill national goals. Both Italy and Germany waged futile campaigns to unite their nations. They failed because they lacked real power. Cavour of Italy and Bismarck of Germany later united their nations using top-down methods–diplomacy, war, and industry. Since both leaders practiced *Realpolitik*, they were similar in their wily tactics; one major difference was that Italy needed outside help whereas Germany used diplomacy to keep other powers at bay while they fought their wars of unification.

Many Italian nationalists, like Mazzini, were passionate republicans. They created revolutionary groups and met in secret around campfires. However, it was a shrewd businessman like Cavour who actually accomplished Italian unification. After he became Prime Minister of Piedmont, Cavour built up industry, reformed the state, and created a good army. Even though it had no real interests in the Crimean War, Piedmont joined in the fighting, just so it could gain an ally. Which they did when Piedmont allied with Napoleon III of France against Austria, the nation that controlled most of Italy. After this war, Piedmont gained territory but also many states flocked to join them. Cavour did not stop there; he told the famous revolutionary Garibaldi to attack the king of southern Italy. Then when he did this, Cavour actually convinced Garibaldi to turn it over to Piedmont. The new kingdom of Italy was born, all because one man practiced Machiavellian politics like a maestro conducting a symphony. Though Italy was united, it still faced problems of regionalism and a somewhat backward economy, which would make it one of the weaker great powers before WWI.

Bismarck also practiced *Realpolitik*, but he used diplomacy to keep other powers neutral while he fought three wars. When Bismarck became Chancellor of Prussia in the 1860s, the nation was in a crisis between the king (Wilhelm) and the Reichstag, which would not approve taxes for the army. Bismarck simply collected the taxes without the approval of the legislature, and later when his policies proved successful, they voted the taxes legal. In other words, Bismarck was so good at *Realpolitik*, he got the legislature to ratify his illegal acts! After this, Bismarck put that army to use in three separate wars—against Denmark, Austria, and France. In each of these conflicts, Bismarck made sure his opponents were isolated and made them appear in the wrong, like when Napoleon declared war on Prussia because of a fake insult that Bismarck had manufactured. In some cases, Bismarck even treated the defeated nation with lenience, as with Austria in 1866. He was counting on being allies with them later and did not want to anger them too much. Bismarck was able to do what many German leaders had failed to do for centuries—unite his nation. Though Bismarck said Germany was a "satisfied giant," this advice was not followed by Wilhelm II, whose aggressive policies led the new empire into WWI and caused its downfall.

Both of these leaders practiced realistic politics to a tee. They focused on real means of power; they used armies and diplomacy alike to unite their nations. However, the unification of Germany proved the more important outcome, as its economic and military potential upset the balance of power, which happened under the young kaiser. After two world wars and massive destruction, Europe was still trying to figure out how to fit Germany into its diplomacy. With its division during the Cold War and then reunification after, Germany now seems a strong part of Europe.

This is a strong essay. First, the student provides some useful historical context on the revolutions of 1848 that helps set up the thesis. Though straightforward, the thesis identifies a similarity (use of *Realpolitik*) and a difference (diplomacy toward the other great powers). The student's analysis of comparison and contrast can be implicit, but he clearly develops an understanding of similar tactics and explains two important differences, the last of which is developed further in the conclusion (impact of German unification). Moreover, the response offers ample and varied evidence, which is applied to the thesis. Finally, the concluding paragraph not only reinforces the thesis, it also earns the Synthesis point in looking forward to the role of Germany within European diplomacy in the 20th century and beyond. Score: 6 (Thesis, 2 points for Targeted HTS, 2 points for Evidence, Synthesis).

13 The Challenges of Modern Europe, 1850–1914

By 1914, Europe had reached the zenith of its power and influence in the world. Many observers hailed this era of technological advance, scientific discovery, democratic reform, and creativity in the arts as *la belle époque*, the golden age. Optimists proclaimed a coming utopia in which problems would be solved by application of the scientific method and tapping the energies of Europe's industrial and political structures. Concurrent with Europe's greatest accomplishments, modern trends toward mass politics, mass society, and mass production threatened to overwhelm classical Liberal ideas of individualism and rationality. Outsiders demanded inclusion in the political process and often used violence to liberate themselves from traditional restrictions. Ideas emphasized themes of struggle, the irrational, and glorified violence and war. Art moved from the objective portrayal of reality to subjective emotional states and abstraction. Amid the power and prosperity, many sensed an impending explosion of either revolutionary violence or war. This fear provides a contrasting pessimistic perspective on this era of plenty—the *fin de siècle*, or the end of an era.

Key In Chapter 13 covers the following KCs from the Course Description:

- **KC 3.2** The social impact of industrialization, including on class, gender, family, and consumption
- **KC 3.3** State, reform, and ideological responses to the problems of industrialization and urbanization
- **KC 3.3** Growth of mass politics and movements for political equality
- **KC 3.5** Impact of encounters with non-Europeans on culture and ideas
- **KC 3.6** Modern trends in the sciences, social sciences, ideas, and arts

---

Mass Society

Demographic Trends

From 1850 to 1914 industrialization and improved public health and medicine supported a rapidly expanding European population. During the period, Europe's population soared by 75% from 260 to 450 million. Much of the increase was fueled by a drop in the death rate, not a rise in the birth rate. Europe began to adopt the modern population trend of smaller family sizes with an increasing life expectancy. In addition to the rising population, more people congregated in industrial cities. By 1914, Great Britain housed more than half its population in urban areas. Cities ballooned in size, taxing infrastructure and causing a myriad of problems for governments to address. This new urban context formed the breeding ground for a culture of mass leisure and mass politics.

Medicine

The late 19th and early 20th centuries stand as the heroic age of medicine. Central to this breakthrough was the discovery of bacteria and the germ theory of disease. Louis Pasteur (1822–1895) demonstrated how microorganisms caused disease and devised a method for killing them in liquids, called pasteurization. To combat infectious diseases, Pasteur advanced the field of vaccination, developing a rabies vaccine, and helped to create the modern field of immunology. Using Pasteur's ideas, Joseph Lister (1827–1912) developed the first antiseptic treatment for wounds and for use by physicians before surgery. Surgery itself became safer with the development of anesthetics by American William T.G. Morton, who pioneered the use of ether. Improved clinical training allowed for the continuation of such discoveries. In the United States, Johns Hopkins University was incorporated in Baltimore along the German university model, with a focus on research; its medical program and associated hospital set the standard for a new scientific and clinical approach to medicine. Governments recognized the importance of **public health** in an urban setting, wishing to avoid infectious disease outbreaks and potential unrest among the working classes. The British government, for example, tracked the spread of disease, established public health boards, sponsored vaccinations, and introduced modern sewage and sanitation.[1]

Urban Reform and Mass Leisure

By 1870, most governments recognized the need for urban reform. In the late 19th and early 20th centuries, states began to address pollution, working and living conditions, and transportation needs. Moreover, urban planners advocated for development of public parks, architectural attractions, and cultural amenities. We have already addressed how Baron von Haussmann (1809–1891) helped rebuild Paris to include grand boulevards, opera houses, theaters, shopping areas, and modern sewage and sanitation to make it the cultural center of France and a venue for **consumerism**. In the process, many workers and poorer residents lost their housing to the new grandiose buildings. This Haussmannization was completed in other European major cities, notably in Vienna with its Ringstrasse, a famous boulevard circling the city and an attraction with its architecture, history, and shopping. New technological developments, such as electricity, provided cleaner power sources and allowed for the construction of subways and streetcars. Social reformers addressed the need for public housing for the poorer classes, and though states responded slowly, they did provide increased regulation and higher minimum standards. They also encouraged municipal and private charitable efforts. In Britain, Octavia Hill symbolized a new public spirit by championing local associations in providing social housing for the poor.

An increase in **leisure time** coincided with urban reform. With the recognition of unions and protective legislation by governments, workers began to see improved wages and shorter working hours. Many reformers were concerned about the lower classes using this time for excessive drinking, crime, or revolutionary agitation. Cities created organized leisure pursuits to meet this need, such as dance halls, amusement parks, and sporting contests. With their competitive ethos, team spirit, and regimentation, sports teams paralleled military discipline. Rules for soccer, tennis, cricket, and others were formalized in this period to allow for orderly play and avoid violence. Nationalists created gymnastics associations to promote discipline and physical fitness. The ideas of Racial Darwinism influenced notions of national health and spurred the physical fitness ethos. Not surprisingly, the competitive nations of Europe established the modern Olympiad, first held in 1896 in Athens.

Education and Literacy

Literacy rates increased markedly in the period 1850–1914, with some states in western Europe achieving nearly universal literacy. Governments came to view state-supported compulsory education as essential to their national interests. Educated citizens could handle the more complex demands of an industrial and increasingly service-oriented economy. Under the Liberal administration of William Gladstone, the Parliament passed the Education Act of 1870, establishing the basis for elementary education in Britain. For nations like Germany, the traditional *Gymnasia* and *Realschule* systems were expanded and extended to all classes. Literate citizens held political opinions and could read dissenting opinions; however, governments increasingly exploited nationalism and xenophobia for purposes of national unity.

1 THEME MUSIC

Modern societies produce a particular demographic profile. As efficiency and wealth increase, and state power penetrates more areas of life, populations tend to evolve toward smaller family size with increased life expectancy. These trends over time (CCOT) can alter the relationship between the individual and society (IS)—for example, with family life geared toward consumption (rather than production) and high expectations for state involvement in social life (e.g., universal schooling and regulation of business).

Family and Childhood

In Britain, Queen Victoria (1837–1901) became the model of domestic propriety; this Victorian ideal reflected distinct gender roles for men and women. Males were to dominate the rough-and-tumble public sphere of business, politics, and war while women managed the domestic sphere. In this model, the home was viewed as a refuge from the harsh world outside and women its moral guardians. Isabella Beeton published her *Book of Household Management* (1859) to introduce women to domestic engineering, reflecting this **cult of domesticity**.

With the decline in birth rates, European families invested increasing resources in the upbringing of their children. Enlightenment attitudes of childhood as a distinct phase of development seeped slowly down to all classes. New attitudes were reflected in governmental legislation restricting child labor and providing for **compulsory schooling**. Reformers and educators created special games, toys, books, clothing, and activities for children. Reflecting the trend toward **mass leisure** and physical fitness, the Boy Scouts and Girl Scouts were both founded in the first decade of the 20th century.

Mass Politics

Historians speak of the rise of mass politics in the second half of the 19th century. Mass politics arose from the Dual Revolution—the ideal of representative government and public opinion as reflected in the French Revolution AND the development of transportation and communication technologies as a product of industrialization. Three basic features characterize mass politics in the period 1850–1914:

- *Mass communication*—With telegraphs, telephones, radios, and cheap newspapers, governments both responded to and manipulated public opinion. Literate and educated citizens demonstrated awareness of political issues and expected governments to reflect national interests.

- *Democracy AND Authoritarianism*—Despite democratic forms such as elections, representation, and constitutions, authoritarian structures (ruling dynasties, bureaucracies, the military) continued to play the decisive policy-making role in most states.

- Increase in conflict—Public opinion also sharpened ethnic and class conflict. Outsiders, such as women, workers, and ethnic/religious minorities demanded inclusion in the political process while demagogues (those who appeal to prejudice and fear) fanned popular hatreds like **anti-Semitism** and extreme nationalism.

Liberal Accomplishments and Challenges[2]

The 19th century marked the high tide of classical Liberalism. By 1880, Liberals had accomplished many of the items on their economic, social, political, and religious agenda. Symbols of the Liberal achievement include:

- Constitutional government
- Representative assemblies
- Free trade
- Expansion of suffrage (the vote)
- Guarantees of rights (though not always observed)
- Middle-class influence in government
- Spread of education and literacy
- Weakening of established churches
- Self-determination for nations (though not for all)

2 THEME MUSIC

You may be familiar with political labels like "liberal" and "conservative," but note that the usage of these labels has mutated over time. Classical liberals (of the 19th century) were closer to present-day libertarians. With the expansion of industry and cities, most liberal parties adopted a social welfare approach around the turn of the 20th century to promote equality through state action. This shift reflects a new conception of the state's power (SP) and of how progress can be accomplished through science and technology (OS), rather than the "hands-off" view prior to 1870.

Most of the above reflects the Liberal concern for individual rights, representative government, economic freedom, and the expansion of opportunity. Despite these significant outward achievements, classical Liberalism was already weakening by 1880. Mass politics mobilized citizens in large groups and allowed authoritarian leaders to manipulate public sentiment; individual and minority rights were often threatened by this trend. With an increasingly complex industrial economy, it became difficult to sustain a laissez-faire approach to the side effects of industrialization—urban blight, crime, poor working conditions, and boom-and-bust cycles. Already by 1880, many governments had abandoned free trade in favor of protecting domestic markets. Many Liberal parties had by 1900 abandoned the notion of pure capitalism in favor of extending social welfare benefits to those in need. Finally, rising nationalism, imperial conflicts, and the militarization of society strengthened the hand of authoritarian interests, who seemed ready to subvert Liberal ideas and institutions in times of crisis or emergency. Next, we'll look at how mass politics played out in several nations.

France and the Tensions of the Third Republic

Ideological conflicts have marked French politics since 1789, and the Third Republic (1870–1940) proved no exception. You may recall the poor start to the Third Republic—class conflict followed the end of the Second Empire and loss in the Franco-Prussian War. Moderate republicans crushed the revolutionary government of the Paris Commune and either shot or exiled 30,000 of its participants. By 1878 and after exploiting divisions within the royalist camp, moderates had succeeded in establishing the basis for a parliamentary democracy. Nonetheless, important groups, like the Catholic Church and monarchists, never reconciled themselves to the existence of republican government, which they associated with the worst excesses of the French Revolution.

The Dreyfus Affair, a highly publicized scandal, highlighted the divisions within the Third Republic. In 1894, a French military court found Captain Alfred Dreyfus, a Jewish officer, guilty of treason on thin evidence. Despite indications Dreyfus was innocent and was the victim of anti-Semitism, he was sent to Devil's Island, and the army refused to reopen the case. Republicans and even foreign governments rallied to Dreyfus's cause, which became the legal case of its day. French author Emile Zola (1840–1902) condemned authoritarian institutions in his pamphlet *J'Accuse* (*I Accuse*) and made the issue a test of republican strength in France. Eventually the government pardoned Dreyfus, but the fallout grew. Republicans conducted an anticlerical campaign culminating in the complete separation of church and state in 1905 and the secularization of education by the state.

Parliamentary Democracy in Britain

Britain's Victorian Age represented prosperity, imperial greatness, and evolution toward genuine parliamentary democracy. Unlike the continent, reform in Britain was driven by the competing visions of two mass political parties—the Conservatives and the Liberals—and was implemented locally rather than by a centralized bureaucracy. Parliament passed two further reform bills in 1867 and 1884, expanding the vote to almost all adult males. The brilliant though occasionally arrogant William Gladstone (1809–1898) led the Liberal reform effort, geared toward expanding opportunity and lifting religious and political restrictions on citizens. Under Gladstone's first prime ministry, the Parliament enacted universal schooling, the secret ballot, and legalized unions; introduced civil service exams; and lifted religious requirements for universities. Conservatives under Benjamin Disraeli (1804–1881) pursued a philosophy of protecting workers from the worst effects of industrialization, passing acts regulating public housing and sanitation.

By 1900, the Liberal party had abandoned its laissez-faire economic approach, and in an effort to combat support for the new Labour Party (see below) moved toward the development of a **social welfare state**. Between 1906 and 1916, the Liberal Party initiated a wide-ranging system of sickness, accident, old-age, and unemployment insurance (National Insurance Act—1911). To conciliate labor, restrictions on strikes and unions were lifted. To pay for these programs, the Parliament passed progressive income and inheritance taxes. When the House of Lords attempted to block the legislation, its veto power was removed with the Parliament Act of 1911. Despite these efforts, workers continued to agitate for improved working conditions, initiating a wave of strikes in 1911 and 1912. Moreover, women's groups, called suffragettes (see below), pushed for the vote, using militant tactics to gain publicity for their cause and provoking embarrassing conflicts with police and government. Britain's most difficult issue, however, continued to be the situation in Ireland. Though Gladstone had disestablished the Anglican Church in Ireland and assisted tenant farmers there, the Catholic Irish demanded home rule. Home Rule split the Liberal Party and was not granted until 1914, but implementation was delayed until 1922 because of the outbreak of the First World War. Though an age of greatness, the Victorian Age also saw Germany and the United States surpass Britain in industrial production and the increased tensions of mass parliamentary democracy.

Germany's Growing Pains

After its unification, German industrial, political, and military power soared. However, this rapid development placed great strains on an authoritarian political system struggling to incorporate democratic principles. One figure dominated German imperial politics until 1890—Chancellor **Otto von Bismarck** (1815–1890). Bismarck successfully manipulated democratic politics and the party system in the Reichstag to enact his policies. First, Bismarck allied himself with the Liberal Party, who supported his attack on the Catholic Church in Germany. The *Kulturkampf* (struggle for culture) arose from the complex situation surrounding Italian unification. Pope Pius IX (r. 1846–1878), who lost the Papal States in 1870, condemned modern ideas such as religious toleration, nationalism, and Liberalism, in his *Syllabus of Errors* (1864), and in 1870 called the First Vatican Council to enunciate the doctrine of papal infallibility (the acceptance of papal decrees on doctrine without question). In response, Bismarck pushed laws through the Reichstag restricting the powers of the clergy, expelled the Jesuits, and jailed a number of bishops. When the campaign proved unsuccessful, and after Pius died in 1878, Bismarck abandoned it and formed an alliance with the Catholic Center Party.[3]

Bismarck then moved to restrict the power of the Social Democratic Party (SPD). Though Marxist in theory, the SPD, in fact, operated as a moderate socialist party interested in obtaining benefits for the working class through the exercise of political power. Using several assassination attempts against Kaiser William I (r. 1861–1888) as pretext, Bismarck won approval for several Anti-Socialist Laws, which restricted the ability of the SPD to meet and publish its newspaper. To win over workers, Bismarck initiated a welfare program (what he termed "state socialism"), the first in Europe, of old age, accident, unemployment, and health benefits. Despite these efforts, support for the SPD continued to grow. To appease extreme nationalists like the Pan-German League and industrialists, Bismarck moved further away from Liberalism in the 1880s with protective tariffs and the pursuit of colonies in Africa. When the young, erratic, and ambitious Kaiser William II (r. 1888–1918) ascended to the throne after his father's sudden death, he dismissed Bismarck and embarked on a more conciliatory policy toward the SPD at home and a more aggressive foreign policy abroad. With immense potential power, emerging conflicts at home, and an insecure ruler, Germany was poised for entrance into the First World War.

Austria-Hungary: Ethnic Tensions

Austria-Hungary continued to experience ethnic tensions after the creation of the Dual Monarchy in 1867. Within Hungary, large landholders continued to dominate, and the Magyars imposed their language and culture on the many Slavic minorities in their half of the empire. To manage the political situation in Austria, the government expanded voting rights and tried to win over the Czechs, Slovaks, and Poles by including them in the Imperial Parliament (Reichsrat) and appealing to their loyalty toward the Habsburg emperor. German nationalists resented these

3 EXAMPLE BASE

This section on mass politics offers numerous specific examples. As you read over each nation, focus on how it illustrates the features and tensions that define mass politics. Consider similarities between states and unique features within each nation. Also, these conflicts will influence decision-making and strategic concerns as each nation enters the First World War (1914).

policies, and the resulting tensions often led to the breakdown of parliamentary function. Anti-Semitism emerged as a political force in Austrian politics with the rise of the Christian Social Party. From 1897 to 1910 (when Hitler lived in the city), Karl Lueger (1844–1910) served as mayor of Vienna and pursued policies of restriction and exclusion against Jews. It seemed that on the eve of the First World War, the Habsburg Empire was fracturing along nationalist and ethnic lines.

Other Areas and Developments

As noted in the previous chapter, Italy faced a rocky road after unification. Liberal parties in the parliament engaged in the suspect practice of *trasformismo*, whereby political leaders attempted to keep out extremist nationalists on the right and socialists on the left by use of bribery and personal alliances. As a result, Italy did not develop political parties around consistent ideas or programs but along shifting personal relationships. To illustrate, the leader most associated with the practice of *trasformismo*, Giovanni Giolitti, served as prime minister five different times between 1892 and 1922. Economically, northern Italy industrialized while the south remained mired in poverty and illiteracy. Irrational anti-parliamentary ideologies and an active anarchist movement also plagued Italian political life.

Spain lingered on the periphery of European events in 19th century. Despite its constitutional monarchy and parliamentary democracy, Spain continued to be dominated by conservative interests, such as large landowners and the Catholic Church. Spain's defeat in the Spanish-American War (1898) led to a loss of its empire and calls for social reform, urged by a group of intellectuals known as the Generation of 1898. Like other less-developed nations, Spain encountered anti-state violence. In 1909, anarchists in Barcelona resisted government efforts to call up army reserves, leading to an armed clash. Because of its preoccupation with internal divisions, Spain did not enter either of the world wars in the 20th century.

Parliamentary democracy had taken root in most European nations by 1914. All but Romania and Hungary allowed universal male suffrage prior to the First World War. Political parties developed modern techniques of electioneering, communication, and institutional organization. In short, political life in many ways was more institutionalized and democratic than it had ever been. However, many still felt excluded from the political process and agitated for change, often straining the new foundations of democratic government.

Outsiders in Mass Politics

Workers and Socialist Variants

By the late 19th century, workers leveraged their growing numbers into political influence. Early unions faced the difficulties of government opposition and small numbers. By the 1870s and 1880s, most states had recognized the rights of unions to bargain collectively for better wages and working conditions. Many **trade unions** supported such a "bread-and-butter" approach. Workers suffered from the boom-and-bust cycles of the period 1873–1896 and used strikes to achieve their demands. Strikes became more violent and persistent in many nations on the eve of the First World War.

With the expansion of suffrage, the working classes also created political movements to agitate for change. One of the more successful efforts occurred in Germany with the Social Democratic Party (SPD), founded in the 1870s by moderate socialists. Though officially adhering to the Marxist doctrine of class warfare, the SPD in reality functioned as a mass-based political party dedicated to winning seats in the German Reichstag. Despite Bismarck's efforts to eliminate the party, the SPD grew into the largest party in the Reichstag by 1912. Other socialist parties were founded in France, Italy, and Russia in the late 19th century. To organize for the coming socialist revolution, the leaders of these parties formed the Second International in 1889, which eventually broke up amidst the nationalism unleashed by the First World War. British labor leaders and intellectuals, such as H.G. Wells (1866–1946) and George Bernard Shaw (1856–1950), advanced a more moderate, or Fabian, socialist movement. In 1900, Scottish worker James Kier Hardie (1856–1915) helped organize the movement into the Labour Party, which won 29 seats in 1906 and eventually became Britain's second political party.

By 1900, it was clear to many socialists that the Marxist prediction of impending revolution was a way off. In addition, many believed that participation in democratic processes might better secure workers' rights than violent means. These insights led to the development of Revisionist socialism, or the brand of socialism represented by most of the western and central European socialist parties. In Germany, the primary voice of this evolutionary path was Eduard Bernstein (1850–1932), and in France, Jean Jaurès (1859–1914). Militant socialists condemned this "sell-out" to capitalism and worked to expel them from the International.

In less-developed nations where workers were smaller in numbers, revolutionary movements focused more on violent tactics or mass political agitation. French workers boasted a strong tradition of militant action stemming from the French revolution. Influenced by the ideas of French philosopher Georges Sorel (1847–1922), anarcho-syndicalists worked to create a single industrial union aimed at shutting down the nation through the General Strike, an act that gained the force of mythological proportions. Pure **anarchism** arose out of the Russian experience—no democratic tradition or social institutions. Mikhail Bakunin (1814–1876) opposed all governmental systems as a corruption of human freedom and a tool of the privileged classes. Anarchists believed that assassination (the Act) would sever the head (the leader) from the body (the state), thus opening the way for voluntary and mutual associations of free individuals. Despite thousands of assassinations across Russia and of other European leaders, anarchism seemed only to deepen government repression in the face of such terrorism.

The New Woman and Feminism

During this period, feminists articulated a clear agenda for change and achieved some significant economic and political gains. Economic developments during the Second Industrial Revolution allowed women to establish a measure of autonomy. White-collar jobs in new economic sectors—telephone operators, clerks, nurses, teachers—provided many women with income and better working conditions. However, many working-class women found themselves strapped with the dual responsibility of raising children at home while aiding the family income through the assembly of simple items, known as "sweating." The measure of autonomy from these jobs led many women, particularly those in the middle class, to demand economic and legal reforms.

The first area women targeted for reform was the legal system. In some western nations between 1850 and 1914, women won the right to control property, divorce, and gain custody of their children. Most states prohibited the publication and distribution of information regarding birth control. Annie Besant of Britain (1847–1933) and Margaret Sanger of the United States (1879–1966) both championed the cause of birth control in the face of obscenity laws, believing female control of reproduction a vital element of the feminist program. Reflecting the double standard regarding sex, the British Parliament in the 1860s passed the Contagious Diseases Acts, which required prostitutes to submit to tests for venereal disease and be confined to prison hospitals if found to be infected. Due to the unyielding efforts of reformer Josephine Butler (1828–1906), Parliament repealed the laws in 1886.

Some women viewed the vote as the logical culmination of the advance towards women's equality. Suffragettes, as they were called, established a transatlantic movement to push for the right to vote. These suffragettes were led in Britain by the Pankhurst family—Emmeline (1858–1928) and her daughters Christabel and Sylvia (1882–1960). The Pankhursts' organization, the Women's Social and Political Union (WSPU), participated in militant actions to gain the vote—throwing eggs at public officials, arson, chaining themselves to public buildings, engaging in hunger strikes, and in the case of Emily Davison, throwing herself in front of the king's horse at a racing event. Government officials even attempted to force-feed the jailed protestors. Eventually, many nations in western and northern Europe granted women the vote immediately after the First World War, a recognition of their contributions to that conflict.

The independent figures highlighted above earned the designation of New Women. Though many if not most women accepted as natural the dependent and domestic role prescribed by tradition, the New Women articulated and lived an autonomous existence. They were not confined to an explicitly feminist agenda. Italian education reformer Maria Montessori (1870–1952) pioneered a child-centered elementary curriculum. Florence Nightingale (1820–1910) and others founded the modern nursing profession. British-born Elizabeth Blackwell (1821–1910) became the first woman in the United States to earn an M.D. degree and established a hospital for the poor in 1857. Literature also reflected themes of independent women. In Henrik Ibsen's play *A Doll's House*, his character Nora Helmer eventually leaves her traditional marriage and children to establish her own personhood; the play provoked controversy for its scathing critique of the sexual double standard inherit in the Victorian ideal.

Jews, Anti-Semitism, and Zionism[4]

With the Enlightenment and French Revolution, many governments liberated Jews from their segregated existence in ghettoes and from legal restrictions. Throughout the 19th century, this emancipation led to the assimilation of Jews into business, medicine, law, and academia. Prominent Jewish intellectuals, such as Marx, Freud, and Einstein, not only contributed significantly to developments in the period but also seemed to provoke a backlash of **anti-Semitism**. Anti-Semitism was nothing new to Europe and traditionally was based on religious discrimination. In the late 19th century, anti-Semitism took on a new racial tone, indirectly influenced by Charles Darwin's ideas of struggle among species. Mass politics fed the creation of popular anti-Semitic political movements, especially strong in central Europe. In response to anti-Semitism, some prominent Jews called for the creation of a Jewish homeland. Appalled by the Dreyfus Affair in France, Austrian journalist Theodor Herzl (1860–1904) founded **Zionism** in the 1890s, which resulted in the immigration of thousands of Jews to Palestine, then controlled by the Ottoman Empire. Some nations, such as Russian, organized persecutions against Jews, called pogroms, to divert popular energies away from potential antistate activities. Despite the assimilation of millions of Jews into European cultural and economic life, they remained a vulnerable religious and ethnic minority. It is not difficult to see the outlines of the future Holocaust already taking shape in the 19th century.

Modern Ideas

As an intellectual framework, modernism was born in the period 1850–1914. In philosophy, the sciences, and the social sciences, thinkers fulfilled the Enlightenment project of using reason to discover the laws of nature in various fields. However, many cherished Enlightenment notions were called into question by the emerging trends of **irrationality**, subjectivity, randomness, and **struggle**.

New Ideas in Science

Darwinian Evolution

Theories of evolution predated the 19th century. Previous versions explained evolution by the inheritance of acquired characteristics. After studying the diversity of finches on the Galapagos Islands (off the coast of Ecuador), Charles Darwin (1809–1882) concluded that the species he observed descended from a common ancestor. Knowing his theory would be controversial, Darwin waited 25 years to work out the details before publishing *On the Origin of Species* (1859), one of the most influential scientific works ever written. Darwin borrowed from Malthus's population theories to argue that species are locked in a constant struggle for resources and survival. Through random variations (what we would call mutations, but Darwin did not understand the mechanism that produced them), some organisms gained a survival advantage in a local environment. If an evolutionary change was adaptive, the mutation would spread within a species population through reproduction, eventually producing new species. What Darwin called natural selection, and others later termed "survival of the fittest," suggested that biological development occurred *randomly*, not through design or purpose. All of nature seemed in chaotic flux, with no role for the permanent and the good, as defined in theological terms.

Darwin's theory caused an immediate uproar and was condemned by religious figures, particularly those committed to biblical literalism. Not only did Darwin reject the hand of God in creation, his theory suggested that the earth was millions, not thousands, of years in age. Geological developments in the 19th century lent credence to Darwin's rejection of a young earth. Many scientists and intellectuals, such as T.H. Huxley (1825–9184), known as Darwin's Bulldog, rushed to Darwin's defense. Austrian monk Gregor Mendel (1822–1884) later provided additional support for natural selection by articulating the gene theory of reproduction. With *The Descent of Man* (1871), Darwin applied his theory to the evolution of the human race from earlier primate species, once again undermining humanity's special place in the universe. Though some counseled dialogue between religion and science, partisans on both sides drew the cultural lines sharply between "atheistic science" and "superstitious religion."

The New Physics

Newtonian physics ruled science for two centuries. In addition to providing accurate explanations of natural phenomena, Newtonian mechanics offered an appealing vision of the cosmos as orderly and predictable. Quantum mechanics and relativity theory undermined this confidence. Accepted theory held that the atom was the simplest particle and indestructible, the fundamental building block of reality. Accumulating scientific evidence proved this atomic theory incorrect. Marie Curie (1867–1934) demonstrated how atoms emitted radioactive energy as they disintegrated. British scientists J.J. Thomson and Ernest Rutherford elaborated a more complex view of the atom as made up mostly of empty space and comprising subatomic particles. Such discoveries provided practical applications, as with William Röntgen's (1845–1923) discovery of the X-ray and its ability to see within the human body.

German physicist Max Planck (1858–1947) in 1900 articulated the **quantum theory**. According to Planck, particles did not emit or absorb energy in constant streams but in packets of energy. Further, experiments demonstrated how light acted sometimes as a particle and sometimes as a wave, depending on the circumstances of observation. More jarring to the Newtonian view, it was demonstrated that the behavior of many particles could only be expressed by probability, not with objective certainty.

It took the great physicist **Albert Einstein** (1879–1955) to transform our commonsense assumptions regarding time and space. Through a series of scholarly articles, Einstein argued that absolute time and space do not exist, but rather are relative to the observer and their status of motion. For example, Einstein showed how for objects that traveled at or near the speed of light, time slows down relative to a stationary observer. To our three-dimensional universe, Einstein's **relativity theory** thus added another dimension—space-time. In the presence of a massive object, such as the sun, space and time *both* curve, as was confirmed from observations of a solar eclipse in 1919. In addition, Einstein expressed how matter and energy were interconvertible in the famous formula, $e = mc^2$. This discovery suggested how the destruction of an atom might potentially liberate massive amounts of energy and/or destruction.

Advance of the Social Sciences

As European civilization became more complex, the social sciences offered further explanation for human behavior. Many of the social sciences were born during the Enlightenment but reached their modern expression during this period. Psychology, political science, anthropology, criminology, and sociology each demonstrated how human behavior resulted from impersonal economic, political, and social forces. And many of these theories radically altered Europeans' conception of human nature.

Freudian Psychology and the Irrational

Enlightenment philosophes glorified human reason. **Sigmund Freud** (1856–1939), in contrast, revealed the instinctual and unconscious nature of human behavior. Based on his systematic clinical studies, Freud developed his theory and practice of psychoanalysis, wherein the therapist attempted to unlock the hidden desires, fears, and memories of the patient that had caused his mental illness. Freud divided the psyche into the id (the pleasure principle), the ego (reason), and superego (conscience), and claimed that unresolved conflicts among these parts created neuroses. Unpleasant or painful memories might be buried in the **subconscious**, though such memories could be explored through hypnosis and analysis of the patient's dreams, a conclusion articulated in *The Interpretation of Dreams* (1900). Perhaps most controversially, Freud claimed that sexual feelings occurred early in life, with children developing through a series of stages, each marked by a conflict, such as the hidden desire to replace the parent of the same sex in the eyes of the parent of opposite sex (the Oedipal or Electra complex). Freud's ideas gained increasing currency during the 20th century and added a new psychological vocabulary to everyday experiences.[5]

Sociology

Freud's work showed that human action often resulted from factors other than human choice. His work found support with further discoveries. Russian psychologist Ivan Pavlov (1849–1936) famously demonstrated how he could condition dogs to salivate automatically at a particular signal, and suggested that human behavior could also be controlled through appropriate stimuli. Criminologists gathered statistics and performed studies to show that criminal behavior might result from genetic inheritance rather than deliberate choice, a conclusion subversive to the cherished notion of free will. Sociologists such as Max Weber (1864–1920) and Emile Durkheim explored the influences of impersonal bureaucratic structures and crowd mentalities on the individual. In Weber's study, he determined that only a charismatic individual could overcome the inertia of large institutions.

Social scientists borrowed the methods and ideas of science. Many recognized the power of Darwinian theory to explain cultural and historical evolution. British sociologist Herbert Spencer (1820–1903) applied Darwin's ideas to society with **Social Darwinism**. Spencer argued that inequalities and divisions with classes or races resulted from the same process of natural selection when applied to human affairs. Public aid and charity for the destitute would only weaken the genetic pool and cause more suffering in the long run; it was Spencer who coined the phrase "survival of the fittest." Nationalists distorted Darwinian science to advance their ideas of racial inferiority, producing support for European imperialism of Africa and Asia. Francis Galton, a half-cousin of Darwin's, developed the pseudoscience of race, known as eugenics, in an attempt to better the human race through selective breeding. In the context of competitive nation-states, Darwin's ideas eventually found their way into justifications for war as a natural mechanism to separate the fit from the unfit.

Philosophy: A Flight to the Irrational

Philosophy had long upheld reason, but in the late 19th century, the most influential philosophers showed the power of irrationality. French thinker Henri Bergson (1859–1941) introduced his theory of vitalism, which held that nature could not be divided into analyzable units or discrete parts, as premised in the scientific method. According to Bergson, irreducible vital forces pervaded the natural world, suggesting that human behavior was driven by the same forces and therefore not capable of being reduced to any set of explanatory factors.

Beginning with the provocative assertion "God is dead," German philosopher Friedrich Nietzsche (1844–1900) embraced the chaos and flux inherent in nature. Ideas did not actually represent reality, which was inaccessible to human reason. Human systems of thought and morality represented a "will to power" and constituted tools for the individual to overcome himself. Nietzsche also recognized that human nature comprised both the rational and the instinctual. Christianity twisted human nature by teaching people to suppress their natural tendencies toward domination and self-assertion. Morality, for Nietzsche, was personal and beyond common conceptions of good and evil. Ultimately, Nietzsche called on the best Europeans—not the "herdlike masses"—to create a new, more honest system of values and to make of their lives a "work of art."

5 SKILL SET

The period 1850–1914 represents one of most significant in the course, as you can confirm by noting KC 3.6. As you consider the methods and ideas of modernism, you may want to formulate an argument for how and why this era represents a turning point (PER) in the history of Europe and intellectual life.

Religion: The Challenge of Modernism

Modern ideas produced a crisis for Protestant and Catholic Christianity. As is clear from the above descriptions, scientific and philosophical works stressed secular if not openly anti-Christian approaches to knowledge. Even within religious communities, some scholars attempted to update religious beliefs to reflect modern techniques of understanding. French historian Ernst Renan (1823–1892) in his *Life of Jesus* explained the origins of Christianity as if Jesus were merely human and a result of historical, not providential, forces. Being more committed than Catholics to the Bible as the source of authority, Protestants found it difficult to shield members from such ideas. As a result, Protestant denominations began to split between modernists and fundamentalists, as church attendance declined or merely expressed adherence to customs.

The long and conservative pontificate of Pope Pius IX (r. 1846–1878) represented the high tide of the Catholic Church's negative reaction against modernism and the perceived new **relativism in values**. His successor, Leo XIII (r. 1878–1903), attempted to tone down antimodern attacks and advance the cause of social justice. Leo ended the prohibition of Catholics' participation in Italian politics and formulated a social doctrine that combined a belief in private property with a concern for poverty and inequality. In the encyclical *Rerum Novarum* ("of modern things"), Leo suggested that much in socialism reflected Christian teachings, but he firmly rejected Marxist ideology as materialist and antireligious. Perhaps with the Galileo incident firmly in mind, the church refrained from issuing any condemnations of Darwinian theory, adopting a wait-and-see attitude. Catholic Church attendance remained fairly stable through the period, but the Church's full reconciliation with modern trends would not occur until the second half of the 20th century.

The Avant-Garde in the Arts

A diversity of cutting-edge artistic movements marked the period 1850–1914. Artists placed a premium on experimentation and self-expression within the media of paint, architecture, print, and music. As you review below, keep in mind the dominant themes of industrialization, nationalism, mass politics, and imperialism.[6]

6 EXAMPLE BASE
For Contextualization (CTX) practice, find some of the works of art mentioned here and analyze them in more detail, attempting to connect the subject matter and style to other developments in the 1850–1914 era.

Painting: Beyond Representation

Photography altered the purpose of the artist. By 1860, the technology of picture-taking was perfected, and photography emerged as both an artistic medium and a means of photojournalism. Danish-American Jacob Riis (1849–1914) used his camera to document the underworld of New York City's slums and back alleys in his book *How the Other Half Lives*. While photography provided new tools to journalists, it seemed to undermine a traditional purpose of painting—to represent life and nature—as the camera could accomplish this more directly.

Impressionism

The first major artistic trend following the invention of photography was **Impressionism**. A self-named movement, Impressionism attempted to capture how the eye really sees, with off-center positioning, visible brushstrokes, fleeting glimpses of street scenes, and exploration of light and shadow. Claude Monet (1840–1926) named the French-centered movement and became famous for his depictions of water lilies, haystacks, and the Notre Dame Cathedral at different times of day or year. For depictions of the Impressionist interest in middle-class scenes of urban life and its interest in glimpses of reality, see Renoir's (1841–1919) *Dance at Le Moulin de la Galette* or *Luncheon of the Boating Party*. In Edgar Degas's (1834–1917) paintings of ballet studios, we appreciate the Impressionist experimentation with perspective and off-centered framing. Demonstrating the international flavor of the movement, American Mary Cassatt (1844–1926) exhibited her works of domestic scenes, such as a mother bathing her child, with her European compatriots in Impressionism.

Postimpressionism

Postimpressionists moved away from the Impressionist fascination with light and shadow. More interested in form and structure, major postimpressionist painters included Vincent Van Gogh (1853–1890), Paul Cézanne (1839–1906), Paul Gauguin (1848–1903), and Georges Seurat (1859–1891). Though Van Gogh sold only one painting in his lifetime, his paintings today garner tens of millions of dollars at auction. Expressing his inner psychological torment, Van Gogh painted with swirling brushstrokes and, showing the influence of Japanese woodblock prints, distorted perspective and a strong palette of yellows. Van Gogh's unique style is best seen in *Starry Night* and the *Night Café*. Van Gogh's suicide in 1890 seemed to capture the archetype of the tortured artist. Cézanne incorporated a geometric approach in his paintings and with his still lifes, how depth and the passage of time might be captured if we look at an object with a binocular vision, first with one eye and then the other. Frustrated by what he considered the overly artificial nature of European painting, Paul Gauguin traveled to Tahiti and developed a primitive style of bulky figures and simple lines reminiscent of the artistic styles of of the Pacific. Georges Seurat created a related movement named pointillism, after the small dots of color, which when combined, formed a clear picture of shadow and light. Seurat's *Sunday Afternoon on the Island of La Grande Jatte* provides a view of the individualistic leisure of the modern city.

Expressionism

Near the turn of the century, artistic experimentation accelerated. A group of French painters known as the Fauves, or "wild beasts," emphasized strong fields of color and simple lines to convey expression over detail. When Henri Matisse (1869–1954) received criticism for his work *Green Stripe*, a portrait of his wife with a green stripe down the middle of her face, he replied, "I have not made a woman, I have painted a painting." Like the later **Expressionists**, Matisse demonstrated that the key task of the artist was not to represent nature but to convey an emotional stance. To appreciate the intensity of expressionist distortion and use of color to capture the angst and alienation of modern Europe, one must view Norwegian Edvard Munch's (1863–1944) *The Scream*, in which a ghostly figure's silent scream wafts into an ominous red sky. Painting gradually moved toward abstraction, as with the Russian Wassily Kandinsky's (1866–1944) canvases exploding with color, designed to convey musical compositions in visual form—a genre known as abstract expressionism.

Cubism and Futurism

Prior to the First World War, the movements of **Cubism** and futurism most directly show the influence of technology on artistic representation. Founded by Georges Braque and Pablo Picasso (1881–1973), Cubism broke apart scenes into analyzable parts and reassembled them in unique ways to provide the viewer with simultaneous multiple perspectives. In this way, Cubists employed the revolutionary insights of Einstein's theory of relativity to art. One of the first paintings in the Cubist style was Picasso's *Les Demoiselles d'Avignon* (1907), which stirred controversy for its unconventional depiction of female beauty by portraying a group of prostitutes with African and Oceanic masks for faces. Picasso painted in many styles, creating one of the most prolific and influential collection of works by any artist. The Italian futurists F.T. Marinetti and Umberto Boccioni (1882–1916) glorified speed and technology in art as a means to achieve political change. Not content simply with artistic creation, the futurists published manifestoes calling for the abolition of traditional aesthetics (such as nudes, religion, and historical paintings) in favor of automobiles, airplanes, and industrial plants, though many of Boccioni's works, like *Dynamism of a Cyclist,* portray *motion* as their subject. Futurism fizzled out in the technological nightmare that was World War I.

Modern Architecture

Modern buildings express the ideal that "form follows function." Instead of employing ornamentation or classical motifs, modern architects allow the functional requirements of a building to determine its shape and logic. The first modern architects were American and used the new building materials of concrete, reinforced steel, and glass. Louis Sullivan (1856–1924) created the first skyscrapers and designed buildings with simple, clean lines and few decorative elements. Frank Lloyd Wright (1867–1959) strove to create a new aesthetic for single-family homes, replacing "Victorian monstrosities" with horizontal lines and earth tones, in his Prairie Style homes. After the First World War, modernism emerged as the dominant architectural style.

Literary Trends

Like art, literature reflected the larger social and intellectual context of the time. Darwin's ideas influenced the literary movement of Naturalism. French author Émile Zola (1840–1902) wrote a series of novels portraying the destructive influence of heredity on the lives of his characters, as they seemed unable to choose their actions freely. Zola's frank depiction of sex, alcoholism, and violence brought him condemnation from traditionalists. This period also represents the great age of Russian literary genius, best shown in the works of Leo Tolstoy (1828–1910) and Fyodor Dostoevsky (1821–1881), both of whom explored the themes of suffering and spirituality. Tolstoy's *War and Peace* presents the reader with a tapestry of events and characters designed to show how social and economic forces override the designs of great men. In *Crime and Punishment*, Dostoevsky raised the moral dilemma of whether good ends justify evil acts. Dostoevsky's lifelong theme of the individual struggling to find meaning in a world of suffering and alienation helped lay the foundations for existential philosophy in the 20th century.

Music: Romanticism and Nationalism

Romanticism did not die in music after 1848. Many composers worked to establish national styles and continued to explore national traditions. The most influential of these figures was the German Richard Wagner (1813–1883), who used his music to express a vision of a revolutionary and nationalist Germany. Wagner envisioned music as a *Gesamtkunstwerk*, or total work of art, combining all artistic genres and capable of transforming national culture. Wagner synthesized music and drama through the use of leitmotifs—musical themes that coincided with particular characters or plot lines. The *Ring Cycle*, a series of four operas spanning 16 hours, represents the culmination of Wagner's grandiose vision and is one of the most ambitious pieces of music ever written. Russian Igor Stravinsky (1882–1971) also explored national themes in his *Rite of Spring*. When the ballet was first performed in 1913 in Paris, its theme of pagan fertility rituals, dissonant primitive music, and unorthodox dance maneuvers caused a riot in the theater.

Postscript—The Road to World War I

The riot following the performance of *Rites of Spring* demonstrates the divided legacy of modernism. On one hand, advances in industry, technology, ideas, and the arts demonstrate the intense dynamism of modern European civilization. On the other hand, the themes of revolutionary liberation, racial and national struggle, and the glorification of the irrational reveal the destructive potential of Europe's modern achievements. These two themes would merge tragically in the First World War.

Additional Resources

Jacques Barzun, *Darwin, Marx, Wagner: Critique of a Heritage* (rev. 1981)—The author explores how each of the figures undermined classical Liberalism.

Stephen Kern, *The Culture of Time and Space* (1983)—This challenging but worthwhile book examines how technology altered conceptions of time and space.

Stephen J. Lee, *Imperial Germany, 1871–1918* (1999)—A slim interpretive volume with documents, from Routledge's Questions and Analysis in History series.

Barbara Tuchman, *The Proud Tower: A Portrait of Europe Before the War, 1890–1914* (1996)—A popular historian explains the unsettled nature of European culture and politics amidst prosperity through a series of vignettes.

Robert Wohl, *The Generation of 1914* (1981)—This book examines the experiences of the generation that came of age right before the First World War.

www.artchive.com/—A helpful supplement to this guide, you can search by artist or movement.

www.clas.ufl.edu/users/rhatch/pages/02-TeachingResources/readingwriting/darwin/05-DARWIN-PAGE.html—This site provides links to resources on Charles Darwin and related topics.

http://legacy.fordham.edu/halsall/science/sciencesbook.asp#New Science: Darwin, Freud, Einstein—From the Internet History of Science Sourcebook, this page is an excellent clearinghouse for documents on the intellectual life of this important period.

http://spartacus-educational.com/—Comprehensive site that provides biographies of key figures in women's suffrage, women's organizations, and feminist tactics and campaigns.

Practice MC Questions

Questions 1–3 are based on the passage below.

> "In the advanced countries of western Europe during the 1870s, when liberalism was at its zenith...liberal governments, abandoning the liberal opposition to the power of the state and seeing the state as the most effective means of securing the liberal conception of freedom in changed circumstances, accepted the early steps toward the inevitable extension of the functions of government and the use of unprecedented state compulsion on individuals for social ends..."
>
> F.H. Hinsley, historian, "Introduction," *The New Cambridge Modern History*, Vol. XI, 1962

1. All of the following developments in the 19th century help explain the phenomenon described by the historian above EXCEPT:

   A. volatile business cycles associated with the Second Industrial Revolution.

   B. communication and transportation technologies that led to a more complex economy.

   C. the emergence of new consumer goods and an increase in leisure time.

   D. growth of urban areas and issues of economic and social equality.

2. The reference to "the liberal conception of freedom" involved which of the following principles?

   A. A government based on popular sovereignty

   B. The sharing of property for the common good

   C. Glorification of the state based on common ethnicity

   D. Distrust of reforms based on the perfectibility of humans

3. Which of the following events resulted in the most serious challenge to liberalism as outlined by Hinsley?

   A. The pursuit of colonies in Africa and Asia

   B. The experience of total war during World War I

   C. The granting of women equal political rights

   D. Scientific theories such as relativity and natural selection

Charles Darwin, *The Origin of Species,* The Harvard Classics, Vol. 11, Charles W. Eliot, ed. (New York: The Collier Press, 1909), pp. 528–529.

PERIOD 3

"It is interesting to contemplate an entangled bank, clothed with many plants of many kinds, with birds singing on the bushes, with various insects flitting about, and with worms crawling through the damp earth, and to reflect that these elaborately constructed forms . . . have all been produced by laws acting around us. These laws . . . being Growth with Reproduction . . . Variability from the indirect and direct action of the external conditions of life, and from use and disuse; a Ratio of Increase so high as to lead to a Struggle for Life, and as a consequence to Natural Selection, entailing Divergence of Character and the Extinction of less-improved forms. Thus, from the war of nature, from famine and death, the most exalted object which we are capable of conceiving, namely, the production of the higher animals, directly follows. There is grandeur in this view of life, with its several powers, having been originally breathed into a few forms or into one; and that, whilst this planet has gone cycling on according to the fixed law of gravity, from so simple a beginning endless forms most beautiful and most wonderful have been, and are being, evolved."

Charles Darwin, English biologist and naturalist, *The Origin of Species,* 1859

4. Which of the following Enlightenment attitudes does Darwin draw on in the passage above?

   A. The equivalence of humans with other forms of animal life

   B. The emphasis on struggle for life and change through random forces

   C. The glorification of nature and as a source of emotional inspiration

   D. The idea that physical phenomena proceed according to natural laws

5. All of the following resulted, either directly or indirectly, from the ideas above EXCEPT:

   A. Europeans justified imperial conquests through theories of racial superiority.

   B. Art moved away from representation toward abstraction and subjectivity.

   C. Political theorists glorified warfare as a means of improving humanity.

   D. Traditional religious and ethical views were called into question.

6. In what way does the passage reflect a broader intellectual trend in the period after the revolutions of 1848?

   A. A focus on themes of realism and materialism in science and the arts

   B. Relativism in values and loss of confidence in the idea of objective knowledge

   C. Romantic emphasis on intuition and the subjectivity of experience

   D. Revival of classical forms and themes of ancient history and culture

LA GALERIE DE LA RUE DE BABYLONE

Bon Marché Department Store, Paris, late 1800s

7. The illustration provides support for all of the following 19th-century developments EXCEPT:

   A. the realization of feminist goals of economic rights and acceptance of public roles.

   B. the growth of consumerism as a result of the Second Industrial Revolution.

   C. urban reforms that provided amenities such as electricity and leisure pursuits.

   D. an increase in wealth due to efficiencies of production and transportation systems.

8. In what way does the image demonstrate a contrast of 19th-century economic activities with those of the early modern period (1500–1700)?

   A. An interest in luxury items, such as imported cloth and spices

   B. Urban markets as a venue for the display and purchase of goods

   C. Mass production of goods and mass marketing techniques

   D. The role played by the bourgeoisie in trade and industry

See Chapter 18 for answers and explanations.

9. Which of the following period characterizations is best supported by the image?

   A. Age of Nationalism

   B. Age of Industry

   C. Age of Mass Politics

   D. Age of Empire

PERIOD 3

Louis Marcoussis, Polish-French painter, *The Musician*, 1914

A. Explain how the painting above reflects a modern approach toward art.

B. Identify and explain ONE difference between the painting above and another specific work of art from a <u>previous</u> artistic style.

C. Explain how the painting reflects the general intellectual and cultural climate in Europe, 1850–1914.

(HTS: Comparison, Contextualization, CCOT)

> Modern art was all about challenging the viewer, and that is certainly what Marcoussis does in this painting. We see a of jumble of jagged lines and shapes, what is supposed to be a musician, which would not be obvious to the first-time viewer. The subject is given a Cubist look, where perspective has been destroyed and then put back together. This work reflects the intellectual and cultural mood of the period 1850–1914. Intellectuals and artists began to question objective knowledge and the idea of progress through technology. For example, in his theories of psychoanalysis, Sigmund Freud emphasized the ways in which humans were motivated by instincts and irrational impulses–for sex, power, aggression, and even death. His ideas influenced politics and even art, as with surrealist paintings that showed dream-like states and strange placement of objects.

It is clear that this student knows the period and the specific content of the question; however, he did not earn all the possible points. First, the response adequately explains the features of modern art ("challenging the viewer," "Cubist," "perspective destroyed," surrealism), which earns the point for Part A. Although the student notes a contrast with earlier works of art, he does not cite or fully develop a contrast with a specific work of art, costing his response the point for Part B. However, he recovers strongly to explain the general intellectual climate of the period 1850–1914 with an application of Freud's ideas to the period. This analysis earns the point for Part C. Once again, you are encouraged to label each part of your SAQ response, both to remind yourself to answer all parts of the prompt and to show the reader that you have done so. Score: 2 points

PERIOD 4

The chapters in Period 4 will address the following major developments and events:

- The causes, nature, and course of World War I

- The debate over the Treaty of Versailles settlement and its immediate aftermath

- Causes and course of the Russian and Bolshevik Revolutions, including establishment of the Soviet Union

- Causes, effects, and responses to the Great Depression, including extremist movements

- Rise of totalitarian governments in fascist Italy, Nazi Germany, and the Soviet Union under Stalin

- Trends in elite and high culture in the interwar period

- Failed attempts to appease fascist powers and the causes of World War II

- The experience of total war from 1939–1945, including mobilization of home fronts and genocide

- Causes, course, and effects of the Cold War, 1943–1991

- Development and fall of the Soviet Union after 1945 and its relationship to Eastern Europe

- Decolonization and international conflicts since the collapse of communism

- Western European recovery and policies of economic and political unity

- Social and economic developments in post-1945 Europe, including growth of the welfare state, demographics, and feminism

- Advance of medical and industrial technologies and their environmental impact

- Developments in ideas, culture, and religion within the framework of modernism and postmodernism

Each chapter will provide a content review and practice questions to test your understanding of the material. At the conclusions of the content chapters, you will be able both to gauge your grasp of the content and practice historical thinking skills in an online diagnostic test that will include:

- 30 MC questions

- 2 SAQs

- 1 DBQ

- 1 LEQ (choice of 2)

Each chapter will begin with a brief correlation to the Key Concepts from the Course Description. Good luck with your review.

14 The First World War and Russian Revolution

The First World War and Russian Revolution represent the defining events of the 20th century. For decades, intellectuals and political leaders had predicted the coming of a great war, but few expected the devastation and disillusionment that broke upon Europe in 1914. This chapter examines the complex causes of World War I—one of the most analyzed events in European history—the course and nature of the war, how various nations organized for the first total war, and how the war ended in revolution and a controversial treaty settlement at Versailles. It also explores the fall of the Romanov Dynasty in Russia—a consequence of the country's poorly organized involvement in World War I and a growing discontent with the tsarist rule. By 1921, the Bolsheviks (later Communist Party) defeated their foes in a civil war, purging enemies of the state in the Red Terror and securing control of the new Soviet Union (USSR), Europe's first socialist government. The existence of the Soviet Union coincides directly with the 20th century that helped create it, a century that began in violence and revolution.

Key In Chapter 14 covers the following KCs from the Course Description:

- **KCs 3.4 and 4.1** The causes and course of World War I
- **KCs 4.1 and 4.4** The experience of total war on the battlefields and home fronts
- **KC 4.3** How World War I affected attitudes toward technology and progress
- **KC 4.2** The causes and course of the Russian Revolution
- **KC 4.2** Bolshevik victory in the Russian civil war and consolidation of power
- **KC 4.1** The Versailles Peace Settlement, rise of the U.S. as a global power, and anti-colonial movements

---

The Causes of the First World War

Who or *what* caused the First World War is a hotly debated historical issue. Long-term diplomatic and political clashes building up for over a century were ignited by the assassination of the heir to the Austro-Hungarian throne, Archduke Franz Ferdinand. As you review below, consider how long-term and short-term factors interacted to produce the conflict.[1]

MAIMIN'

Students often find mnemonic devices helpful in recalling content. The standard for World War I's causes is MAIN. However, this formula tends to overlook the importance of internal and intellectual causes, which are harder to identify precisely but important nonetheless. Therefore, we use **MAIMIN'**. The following provides a bird's-eye view of these causes.

Militarism and **Military Plans**—After the wars of unification in the mid-19th century, armies exploded in size and firepower, driven by mass production and the dynamic Second Industrial Revolution. These technological and industrial advances rendered warfare even more efficient and deadly. Never before or since have greater percentages of populations served in their nations' military. Conscription (the draft) and regular military training militarized society by creating **mass citizen armies**. Government leaders associated national greatness with a strong military, and many adopted military dress in public ceremonies. In preparation for the upcoming conflict, nations expanded their armaments and navies.

Germany's desire to build a world-class fleet of battleships antagonized Great Britain and made an enemy out of a potential ally. Kaiser William II's (r. 1888–1918) reading of American Admiral A.T. Mahan's *The Influence of Sea Power on History* (1890) convinced him that if Germany wanted a "place in the sun," it must develop a commercial empire akin to Britain's. Given the Kaiser's erratic and bombastic personality, this threat to British naval dominance represented the first of many actions by Germany upsetting the balance of power after 1890. As often occurs in history, the Great War was preceded by arms and naval races.

Upon the completion of the Franco-Russian alliance in 1894, Germany began work on the Schlieffen Plan, designed to fight a two-front war against Russia (to the east) and France (to the west). Germany's was only the most famous of such plans; each nation developed complex blueprints involving railroad timetables, troop movements, and battle strategies that often significantly affected *political* decisions. These plans often limited, or were perceived to limit, the options open to policy makers and, in most cases, escalated regional clashes into a world war.

1 SKILL SET
Historians have debated the question of causation (CAUS) for the First World War since it began, a common reaction to a devastating event brought about by a seemingly minor loss (the assassination of Franz Ferdinand). The issue makes for an ideal historiographical question (INTR) and one that requires you to make an argument (ARG) by considering the range of evidence (EVARG) from both long- and short-term factors. As you read this section, consider these interpretive questions: 1) Which causal factor played the most essential role?, 2) Could the conflict have been avoided? If so, how?, and 3) How would one apportion national responsibility for actions bringing about the conflict?

For example, when Germany began mobilizing troops in 1914 in accordance with the Schlieffen Plan, all hopes of political negotiations to prevent war were lost.

Alliance System—After Germany's unification in 1871, Chancellor Otto von Bismarck worked to maintain the balance of power and prevent war through a complex system of interlocking alliances. As Bismarck put it, Germany was a "satisfied giant" that desired no additional territory. He believed a war among the great powers would be a disaster for Germany. Bismarck aimed to isolate a French nation bent on avenging the loss of Alsace-Loraine and to stay allied with three of the five great powers. To achieve this purpose, Bismarck attempted to mediate the potential for dispute in the Balkans by forming the Three Emperors' League in 1873 between Germany, Austria, and Russia. This agreement proved difficult to maintain, so Bismarck formed a strong mutual defense treaty with Austria (Austro-German Alliance) in 1879 and the Triple Alliance with Italy and Austria in 1882. When Russia refused to revive the alliance with both Germany and Austria, Bismarck convinced the Russians to sign the Reinsurance Treaty in 1887 simply with Germany. Moreover, Bismarck maintained friendly relations with Great Britain and even avoided antagonizing France. Within the Bismarckian alliance structure, no great power could count on the support of any other should it initiate aggressive war, and might in fact trigger a hostile alliance against it.

Kaiser William dismissed Bismarck in 1890 and quickly undid his alliance system. William allowed the Reinsurance Treaty with Russia to lapse, counting on his personal relation with the Russian tsar (they were cousins), which freed Russia to complete the Franco-Russian alliance in 1894. As it industrialized and pursued colonies more vigorously, Germany's potential military and economic might created concern among the other great powers. William's efforts to match Britain's navy, and his militant personal style, drove France and Britain together with the Entente Cordiale (friendly understanding) in 1904. Soon after, in 1907, Russia, smarting from its military defeat to Japan, agreed with Britain to the Anglo-Russian Entente to compromise their contending interests in central Asia. These series of loose agreements among Britain, France, and Russia came to be known as the Triple Entente, which now opposed the Triple Alliance. Within a generation, William had destroyed Bismarck's alliance system and caused Germany's encirclement. As of 1907, two mutually antagonistic alliances faced off, with the potential of a minor conflict between Austria and Russia dragging the whole of Europe into war. The alliance system thus acted as a chain of causation leading to an all-out war once the first trap was sprung.

Imperialism—World War I did not begin over colonial issues; however, conflicts among imperial powers increased tension and hardened the emerging alliance structure. Italy's pursuit of colonies in North Africa brought it into conflict with France and led in 1882 to its joining the Triple Alliance. To test the new alliance between France and Britain (Triple Entente), William provoked the Moroccan Crises of 1905 and 1911, disputes over French control of the North African region. His aggressive actions produced the opposite of the intended effect, as the two Atlantic nations drew closer in their joint military plans. In addition, Britain's isolation during the Boer War (1899–1902) led it to approach Japan, France, and Russia in the next decade to ensure its security vis-à-vis an expansive Germany. Finally, Italy's attack on the crumbling Ottoman Empire in pursuit of the North African colony of Libya (1911) triggered a series of crises in the Balkans culminating in the First World War.

Mass Politics—By 1914, many European states faced significant internal problems—strikes, ethnic violence, extremist groups, and outsiders demanding rights. To promote unity, governments promoted imperialism and fanned nationalist sentiments. As leaders contemplated the momentous decision for war in July 1914, they may have viewed the crisis as an opportunity to solve domestic issues. When war broke out, citizens celebrated in European capitals, and political dissenters called for an end to internal disputes. Kaiser William announced a *Burgfrieden*, or civil peace, for the duration of the war, while in Britain, female suffrage and Irish home rule were tabled. Socialist parties, which wished to unite workers of all nations, generally supported the call to arms, in spite of their Marxist ideology. Mass politics had worked only too well in promoting popular nationalist sentiment in favor of war.

Intellectual Context—Many observers of the European scene sensed that a major war loomed on the horizon. It had been 40 years since the Franco-Prussian War, and with the advent of Darwinism and irrationality in philosophy, some glorified war as a natural product of human advance—how it called upon patriotism and sacrifice and separated the weak from the strong nations. For example, German writer Friedrich von Bernhardi, in *The Next War* (1912), welcomed the prospect of demonstrating Germany's national greatness and predicted that technological advances would render warfare brief and decisive. Europeans' faith in technological and scientific solutions to problems and belief in the productivity of warfare seem naïve today only because of the results of the war they produced.

Nationalism—**Nationalism** caused the First World War in two ways: (1) by making it difficult for nations to compromise what they perceived as their national honor and (2) by feeding the ethnic tensions in the Balkans that drew Austria and Russia into conflict there.

European Diplomacy, 1871–1914[2]

By destroying the Concert of Europe, the Crimean War not only opened the way for the unification of Italy and Germany, it effectively destroyed an international mechanism for containing conflict. Germany's defeat of France in the last of its unification wars established the perennial rivalry at the base of the First World War. With this unstable diplomatic situation and intense national rivalries, all that was needed was a *casus belli* (cause of war). This proved to be the volatile situation in the Balkan peninsula, involving Austria, Russia, and the Ottoman Empire.

Like Russia, the Ottoman Empire realized its backwardness during the Crimean War. However, efforts by reformers, known as Young Turks, to introduce national citizenship, abolish religious hierarchies, and establish legal equality only provoked a conservative backlash. The Sick Man of Europe seemed unable to stem the disintegration of its multiethnic realm, which drew in Russia as the protector of its brother Slavs and in its perennial drive to gain territory at the Ottomans' expense. The ensuing Russo-Turkish War (1877–1878) resulted in Russia's clear victory but one that seemed to threaten the balance of power in the region and Britain's control of the Suez Canal. To prevent further conflict, Bismarck acted as an "honest broker" and called the Congress of Berlin (1878) to resolve the issue. The Congress reduced the territory Russia gained and allowed Austria to occupy (but not annex) Bosnia-Herzegovina, coveted by nationalistic Serbs. Most viewed the Congress of Berlin as a defeat for Russia. The subsequent anti-German feeling in Russia led Bismarck to conclude an Austro-German alliance in 1879; however, Germany and Russia eventually reestablished friendly diplomatic relations with the Reinsurance Treaty. Nonetheless, the conflict revealed the explosive potential of the Balkans.

During the first decade of the 20th century, the Balkans experienced a series of crises. In a rare sign of cooperation, Austria and Russia in 1908 concluded a secret agreement at the expense of an Ottoman Empire once again undergoing internal instability. In exchange for allowing Russia to take the strategic Dardanelles (straits from the Black to Mediterranean Seas), Austria was to annex Bosnia-Herzegovina, which it already occupied. Fearing the dismemberment of the Ottoman Empire, the other great powers blocked Russia's advance into the Mediterranean. Meanwhile, Austria took Bosnia anyway, demonstrating the power of coercion over diplomacy. Russia was humiliated, while its smaller neighbor Serbia was incensed, viewing Bosnia's Slavic population as rightfully belonging to a future greater Serbia. Soon after, Serbian pan-Slavists formed the terrorist Black Hand, bent on expelling Austrian influence from the Balkans.

Like a flock of vultures, the smaller Balkan nations circled the carcass of the dying Ottoman Empire. After Italy's defeat of the Turks in 1911, the smaller nations formed the Balkan League (Serbia, Bulgaria, Greece, and Montenegro) and attacked the Ottomans in the First Balkan War (1912–1913). Following the Balkan League's victory, Serbia stood poised to gain access to the Adriatic Sea. At the London Conference, Austria, Italy, and Germany forced upon Serbia and its protector Russia the creation of an independent Albania, designed specifically to block Serbian access to the sea. Once again, Russia had been forced to back down in its own backyard. When the victors could not agree on how to divide the conquered territory of Macedonia, Bulgaria

2 THEME MUSIC
Much of this chapter addresses the SP theme, particularly the structure of diplomatic rivalries, balance of power, and the state's power over the economy and society. In many ways, World War I formed a turning point. It laid the groundwork for totalitarian movements of subsequent decades, planted the seeds of the Second World War, and set the stage for the superpower rivalry between the U.S. and USSR.

(created in 1878 at the Congress of Berlin) faced off against the other Balkan nations and the Ottomans in the Second Balkan War (1913). Bulgaria was easily defeated. The two conflicts heightened the animosity between Serbia and Austria, convinced Russia of the need to save face in the next crisis, and set the stage for the ultimate conflict.

The July Crisis of 1914

Archduke Franz Ferdinand (1863–1914), the heir to the Austrian throne, visited the capital of Bosnia (Sarajevo) with the intention of building support for his solution to the ethnic problems in the Balkans—a Triple Monarchy. Franz Ferdinand hoped to appease the Slavic minorities in the region by granting them autonomy *within* the Habsburg empire (like the Magyars); however, the Black Hand feared the plan would undermine its goal of establishing a unified independent Serbian kingdom. To stop Ferdinand's plan and punish Austria, the Black Hand trained a group of young assassins to kill the Archduke and his wife, Sophie. On June 28, 1914, the 23-year-old Gavrilo Princip fulfilled his mission, plunging Europe into crisis.

Austria believed the Serbian government was behind the assassination and a month later issued it an ultimatum. Kaiser William of Germany gave his only reliable ally a "blank check" to settle its ethnic issue permanently, emboldening Austria to take a hard line and risk war with Serbia's ally, Russia. Fearing Germany's military plans, France in turn stood firm behind its ally Russia. Meanwhile, Britain refused to signal its intentions clearly, trying in vain to mediate the dispute. When Serbia rejected one point of Austria's ultimatum, Austria declared war against it, an action that prompted Russia's declaration of war against Austria. Russia's war plan presumed a war against *both* Germany and Austria, forcing Tsar Nicholas to mobilize his army on both nations' borders. Despite a last-minute flurry of telegrams between cousins Willy and Nicky, Germany declared war on Russia, triggering the trap of the alliance system. France quickly joined the conflict, and because Germany's Schlieffen Plan had violated Belgian neutrality, Britain too declared war on Germany. Europe was now engulfed in the war for which many had planned but of a nature that few expected.

Fighting on the Fronts

Europe did not get the war it expected. What was supposed to be over by Christmas turned to stalemate by the end of 1914. Though the war eventually involved the nations of six continents, the hinge turned on the Western Front. It is most important for you to understand the nature of the war and its phases; do not be overly concerned with battles.

The Nature of the War

Military tactics often lag a generation behind technologies. The First World War illustrates this adage in bold type. Generals of the day learned the Napoleonic tactics of rapid movement and the massed infantry assault. Military theorists assumed that the new technologies of airplanes, high-powered artillery, and machine guns would favor the offensive by overwhelming a static opponent with massive firepower. The reverse turned out to be the case, as these weapons and technologies proved advantageous to entrenched defensive positions. In all, almost 10 million Europeans (almost all soldiers) were killed during the First World War, largely the result of an inability to conceive of new tactics in dealing with defensive weapons.

Once the Western Front settled down to a stalemate, each side entrenched positions and fortified them with barbed wire. In between stood "no-man's land," an expanse denuded of trees, houses, and crops. Generals attempted to soften up enemy positions with artillery bombardments, often lasting days, as a prelude to "over the top," where infantry ran exposed through no-man's land in a vain effort to overwhelm the enemy trench. Though trenches had been used during the Crimean War and the U.S Civil War, the combatants in this war relied on them extensively. Trench warfare emerged as a dehumanizing and absurd symbol of the futility of the First World

War. Many other important technological breakthroughs occurred or were first used in World War I, but none exercised the decisive impact as hoped and only increased the body count: tanks, airplanes, flamethrowers, submarines (U-boats), high-powered artillery, grenades, poison gas, barbed wire, zeppelins, and aerial bombardment.

The War of Illusions: 1914

Germany gambled that its Schlieffen Plan would defeat France before Russia could mobilize. The plan called for a huge right-flanking maneuver in August 1914 through Belgium to hit Paris from the rear and trap the French army at Alsace-Lorraine. Violation of Belgium neutrality brought Britain in the war on the side of the Entente (Allied Powers), and moreover, Belgium put up unexpected resistance to German forces. This resistance led to the first atrocities of the war against Belgian civilians, providing the Allies with an important propaganda weapon against Germany.

As the German advance toward Paris stalled, the French regrouped and hit the German flank at the Marne River. The Miracle of the Marne halted the German offensive. After each side unsuccessfully tried to outflank the other by racing to the English Channel, the Western Front had settled down by Christmas to a stalemate, with a string of trenches from the English Channel to the Swiss frontier—300 miles in length. On the more open and less populated Eastern Front, the Germans met with more success by capturing an entire Russian army at Tannenberg. This battle was the prelude to the generally poor performance of the Russian army, whose men were captured in much larger numbers than any combatant nation.

Stalemate: 1915

To break out of the stalemate, the Central Powers (Austria-Hungary, Germany) and the Allied forces (Russia, France, Britain, Belgium) expanded the war by bidding for new allies. To recapture its lost territories, Turkey joined the Central Powers in November of 1914. The Allies, meanwhile, bribed Italy, via the Treaty of London, with the promise of Austrian territory to join the war against the Central Powers. From 1915 to 1917, Bulgaria, Romania, and Greece all entered the conflict to achieve territorial objectives left over from the pre-1914 Balkan conflicts.

Each side engaged in probing offensives aimed at finding the enemy weak spot. To knock out the Turks and secure Europe's "soft underbelly," the British in April 1915 launched the poorly planned Gallipoli campaign, an amphibious assault designed to capture Constantinople and the Dardanelles. British forces found themselves pinned down on a narrow ridge and after months of futile assaults withdrew in early 1916.

Germany and Great Britain both attempted to blockade the other and starve it into submission. The German navy's reliance on the submarine made blockades dangerous—the U-boat had to either surface to inspect enemy ships, making it vulnerable to enemy fire, or gamble and destroy the potential enemy craft. This problem almost brought the United States into the conflict when a German U-boat sank the British liner *Lusitania* off the coast of Ireland, killing 1,200, including 128 Americans. President Wilson was able to maintain U.S. neutrality while extracting a promise from the German government to avoid unrestricted submarine warfare. However, U.S. exports and loans to Britain and France skyrocketed as aid and trade to Germany fizzled.

Slaughter: 1916–1917

By 1916, the effects of total war were exhausting all nations involved in the conflict. To break the deadlock, Germany rolled the dice on another bold plan. In February 1916, Commander Erich von Falkenhayn launched a massive surprise attack at the key position of Verdun in the French line. Though the attack met with initial success, the Germans were unable to maintain their momentum. They did not call off the battle, however, until January 1917, making Verdun the longest battle of the war and one of the deadliest in history. In all, the French and German armies combined experienced 1.1 million casualties.[3]

3 EXAMPLE BASE

Few of the specifics in this section constitute required knowledge per se; however, you can employ examples from the fighting to examine how military stalemate and technology affected mobilization, home front issues, and the relationship between governments and science.

To take the pressure off the French, the British launched the Somme offensive in July. The battle proved a disaster for the British army, which lost 30,000 dead in the first 3 hours of the attack, known as the bloodiest day in British military history. In addition, the Russian command surprised the Austrian army with the Brusilov Offensive, driving their enemy back hundreds of miles before the Germans stabilized their collapsing ally. One success for the Central Powers was their victory over Serbia; this country was knocked completely out of the war, losing a greater percentage of its population than any other warring nation.

In one of the ironies of the war, the large battleships that had provoked such animosity between Britain and Germany generally stayed in port, with leaders fearful of destroying such large investments. The only major naval engagement of the war occurred in 1916 off the coast of Denmark at Jutland. Both sides were bloodied but survived, and the German battleships returned to port. After the armistice, the Germans scuttled (sank) their expensive fleet rather than allow it to fall into enemy hands.

Exhaustion and Revolution: 1917–1918

In 1917, the Allied forces lost a key nation: Russia. At the same time, they gained perhaps an even greater force: the United States. Russia's deteriorating economic and political situation resulted in the fall of the Romanov Dynasty, and in late 1917 the newly empowered Bolsheviks pulled Russia out of the war. Germany once again rolled the dice to end the war, betting that unrestricted submarine warfare around the British Isles, in violation of an earlier pledge, could knock Britain and France out of the conflict before the United States could effectively mobilize. They were wrong. The announcement of Germany's U-boat campaign, combined with the Zimmerman Telegram—in which the German ambassador promised Mexico the recovery of lands lost to the United States if it entered the war—drew the United States into the war in April 1917. Contrary to German plans, American involvement proved decisive.

By mid-1917, it looked as if the Central Powers might prevail. Austrian and German forces routed the Italian army at Caporetto, forcing the diversion of French and British forces into the difficult Alpine fighting to prop up their ally. In Belgium, British, ANZAC (Australian and New Zealand Army Corps), and Canadian forces worked to retake the town of Passchendaele. In the subsequent battle, thousands drowned in muddy shell holes, a morbid symbol of the futility of warfare. By March 1918, the Germans imposed on the Bolsheviks the draconian Treaty of Brest-Litovsk, costing Russia significant territory and resources.

In Germany's final gamble of the war, its High Command launched one last major offensive in Spring 1918 on the Western Front. Despite initial gains, which brought the Germans to within 30 miles of Paris, American troops began to inject fresh manpower and morale into the Allied cause. American and French counteroffensives pushed the German lines back by early Fall 1918. By this time, ethnic minorities were establishing independence from the Austrian Empire, and Germany faced a revolutionary situation at home from an exhausted populace. Though few troops stood on German soil, the German High Command asked for an armistice on November 11, 1918. The Armistice ended fighting, yet Europe faced a revolutionary situation in which a return to the prewar world proved impossible.

Organizing for Total War

The Great War involved full mobilization of each nation's resources and populations. Despite modern industrial, military, and bureaucratic techniques, most nations found the burdens of fighting the war an enormous strain, fueling a revolutionary situation.

Government and Economy

Pressures of total war forced the abandonment of laissez-faire practices. Governments moved quickly to oversee wartime production to ensure an adequate supply of matériel. To appreciate the demands of the Great War, you may consider that at the battle of Verdun more projectiles were dropped than in all previous warfare in human history combined! Many combatant nations managed production via bureaucratic centralization—that is, running the war effort as one large industry. In Germany, industrialist Walter Rathenau (1867–1922) helped Germany deal with severe shortages and maintain adequate supplies by overseeing production in the War Ministry. When Britain experienced a shortage of shells in 1915, future Prime Minister David Lloyd George (1863–1945) was made Minister of Munitions to avoid shortfalls. Because of such policies, large businesses and labor unions benefited, as governments found it more efficient to award government contracts to and oversee large enterprises.

To pay for the war, governments exercised three options: raise taxes, depreciate currencies, and borrow money. Raising taxes could only go so far; as the war dragged on, governments grew fearful of placing any additional demands on an already strained populace. By the end of the conflict, France and Britain had borrowed significant amounts from the United States, making it a creditor for the first time in its history. All nations appealed to their citizens' patriotic duty to purchase war bonds. In all, the war cost the nations involved over $350 billion. Inflation acted as a hidden tax and resulted in currency depreciation, a situation that rendered a return to prewar economic stability impossible when the war finally ended.

Nationalist Unrest and Agitation

Almost every nation experienced internal ethnic conflicts, and their enemies attempted to exploit them. For example, the German government gave aid to Irish rebels wishing for independence from the British in the Easter Rising of 1916. Though British men and resources were diverted, the attempt failed. Not to be outdone, the Allies promoted the creation of independence committees for various minorities within the Austro-Hungarian Empire, especially for the Poles and Czechs, an effort that yielded the dissolution of the empire by 1918. Most famously, the British sent Colonel T.E. Lawrence ("of Arabia," 1888–1935) to promote the cause of Arab nationalism within the Ottoman Empire. Though these efforts did not play a decisive role in the outcome of the war, they did set up future conflicts in the **Middle East**, often over the new strategic resource of oil.

The Home Fronts

The First World War represents the culmination of the trend toward mass politics in the previous half-century. Governments called on citizens to sacrifice for the war effort by enlisting, buying war bonds, and rationing. Rationing went furthest in Germany. By 1916, the Kaiser had turned the government over to the famous generals Erich Ludendorff (1865–1937) and Paul von Hindenburg (1847–1934), who quietly established a military dictatorship, part of which involved allotting families ration books for a particular number of calories per day. By the end of the war, many Germans agonized over eating sawdust bread and shortages of essential fats and oils.

Because of the manpower shortage, many women entered the workforce outside the home for the first time. In Britain, industrialists employed women in the production of TNT and shells. Neglect of safety conditions led tragically to the poisoning and infertility of thousands of female laborers. These "women with yellow hands" demonstrated the potential public role of women and helped to earn them the vote in many nations after the war ended. The Provisional Government of Russia even formed a military unit, the Women's Battalion of Death, which saw action at the front and in defense of the state. Among other groups, skilled workers gained the most, as they won wage increases and recognition of union collaboration in production. Nonetheless, strikes did occur. Governments often responded with the promise of improved conditions and the threat of violence if the strike continued. By the end of the war, union discontent broke out into open rebellion, helping to bring down teetering governments in the Fall of 1918. On the other hand, small business owners, those in traditional crafts, and the lower middle-class often found themselves struggling with competition from large businesses favored by government officials.

Freedom is often the first casualty of war. Though states worked to build positive support for their war efforts, they were also quick to crush dissent. Early in the war, the British Parliament passed the Defense of the Realm Act (DORA), which in addition to regimenting the lives of British citizens, censored the press and allowed the government to requisition war supplies from private citizens. All states, including the United States, established stricter laws against treasonous activities and dissent against the government. Germany used spies to infiltrate radical unions, while many governments simply jailed the most outspoken opponents of the war effort.

4 SKILL SET

World War I elevated mass politics to a new level with its need for mobilization. Governments employed propaganda to motivate citizens both to sacrifice and to view enemies as less than human. Using the firstworld-war.com site below, peruse some of the propaganda posters from various nations and place them in historical context, considering how and why they might have motivated combatants and citizens (CTX).

Propaganda and Genocide[4]

Propaganda came of age during the First World War. To motivate citizens, governments employed both positive patriotic appeals with national symbols and negative attacks on the enemy, portraying the war as a battle over civilization against a brutal and inhuman foe. Demonizing the enemy seemed a logical culmination of mass political pressures in the previous half-century—anti-Semitism, xenophobia, extreme nationalism, and glorification of struggle. A tragic culmination of this logic was the first genocide of the 20th century. In 1915, the Ottoman government feared that its Armenian Christian minority might aid the Russian war effort. Several hundred leaders of the Armenian community were executed, while thousands of Armenians were deported to camps with inadequate facilities, where between 500,000 and 1.5 million died from neglect, disease, and starvation. Even today, the Turkish government rejects the notion of an Armenian Genocide, though most independent scholars classify the event as such.

The Treaty of Versailles and Revolution

The Treaty of Versailles ending the First World War represents one of the most significant diplomatic events you will study this year and is essential to your understanding of the 20th century. The Versailles settlement is often compared with the Congress of Vienna in 1814–1815 regarding their respective schemes for collective security and the success of their decisions. Though the Allies negotiated treaties with each of the Central Powers, the settlement with Germany proved most important for future events.

Revolutionary Fallout

When the Allied victors met starting in January 1919 in the Palace of Versailles, they found it nearly impossible to put Humpty Dumpty back together again. Revolutionary violence led to the toppling of four empires—Austro-Hungarian, German, Ottoman, and Russian. What would replace these traditional diplomatic entities remained an open question. Allied leaders were prepared to confirm the **creation of new states** out of the former Habsburg Empire (Austria, Hungary, Czechoslovakia, Poland, Yugoslavia, and the Baltic states of Lithuania, Latvia, and Estonia) and promote democratic governments there and in Germany. Even after the completion of treaties, revolutionary unrest continued, often fed by the existence of a new socialist government in the east, the Soviet Union.

Differing Goals for and Visions of the Peace

President Woodrow Wilson (1856–1923), the first American president to travel abroad, set foot on European soil a hero. He authored the renowned Fourteen Points, his idealistic vision for reconstructing Europe and "making the world safe for democracy." He also declared that WWI should be the "war to end all wars." Wilson dreamed of a new diplomatic order guided by open diplomacy, freedom of the seas, arms reduction, **national self-determination**, and collective security. Representatives from African and Asian colonies attended negotiations in hopes of gaining autonomy only to be thwarted as former German and Ottoman colonies were granted to Britain and France under **mandates**, granting them control until the colonies were ready for self-governance. Collective security was to be achieved by the creation of an international governing body to mediate disputes—the **League of Nations**. Wilson knew that Germany must be punished but hoped that drastic action might be avoided to build a more secure foundation for democratic government after the war.

French Premier George Clemenceau (1841–1929), nicknamed the Tiger, considered Wilson's vision utopian, and concentrated on security for France by emasculating Germany's military and economic potential. British Prime Minister David Lloyd George stood somewhere in between Wilson and Clemenceau (famously remarking, "I had God on one side and the devil on the other") in wanting to punish Germany but not utterly destroy it. And though Prime Minister Vittorio Orlando (1860–1952) represented Italy in negotiations, he eventually walked out in protest over Italy's lack of territorial spoils. Importantly, Russia sat out the negotiations, as the new Bolshevik leader Lenin denounced the gathering as a capitalist plot. The Allies rejected German participation and continued the naval blockade until June 1919 when Germany signed the treaty; in all, approximately 750,000 Germans died of starvation during and after World War I. Given these circumstances, it is not surprising that the treaty pleased no nation.

The Final Product

After months of negotiations, the reluctant German delegates signed the Versailles settlement in the the palace's famous Hall of Mirrors on June 28, 1919 (5 years to the day from the start of the war). By all accounts, the treaty represented a harsh peace:[5]

- *Territorial Losses*—Germany lost 13% of its territory and 12% of its population. The important Saar industrial region was placed under League of Nations control until 1935. East Prussia was cut off from the rest of Germany to provide the new Polish state with access to the sea. Finally, German surrendered its overseas colonies.

- *Demilitarization*—The German army was reduced to 100,000 men, the nation's naval fleet was severely curtailed (including the banning of U-boats), and its air force was eliminated. Fearing further German aggression, the French insisted on the demilitarization of the Rhineland, adjacent to France.

- *War Guilt*—In the most controversial provision of the treaty, Germany was forced to accept full responsibility for the war via Article 231.

- *Reparations*—Based on the War Guilt clause, the Allies in 1921 set a reparations amount for the German government of 132 billion marks (some $33 billion), a figure most German observers considered exorbitant.

- *League of Nations*—To promote collective security, the Allies agreed to Wilson's idea of a League of Nations. However, because the U.S. Senate refused to ratify the treaty, the United States never joined, and the new Soviet Union and Germany were initially excluded.

Consequences and Conflicts

Few were fully satisfied with the Treaty of Versailles, but none less so than Germany. Germany's new postwar government, the **Weimar Republic**, started off with two strikes against it, being saddled with what most Germans perceived as a dictated peace. Discontent over the treaty was fed by extremists groups like the Nazis and played a major role in bringing down Germany's short-lived experiment with democracy. Almost immediately, observers condemned the economic arrangements of the treaty. Economist John Maynard Keynes (1883–1946) attended the negotiations on behalf of Britain and afterward predicted in his *Economic Consequences of the Peace* (1919) the ruination of the world economy, which was not long in coming. Overall, the inability of the victors to establish a consistent diplomatic approach torpedoed their efforts at establishing a stable balance of power, but perhaps the complexity of the issues and intensity of the conflicts might have doomed any settlement. Certainly a major reason for the treaty's failure proved to be the subsequent isolation of both the United States and the Soviet Union. America's

5 SKILL SET

The Treaty of Versailles's Article 231, which assessed full responsibility for the war to Germany, represents the first official interpretation of the war's origins (INTR) and of great political consequence, since it was used to justify the victors' actions against the defeated. To sharpen your skill of Comparison (COMP), make a balance sheet or Venn Diagram of the Congress of Vienna and the Treaty of Versailles. Which was more successful in addressing its respective situation and promoting collective security?

unwillingness to guarantee French security after 1920 and the fear of Soviet communism opened the way for a revival of German power. Without a full commitment to collective security and the League of Nations, Europe in the next two decades drifted toward an even more destructive war.

The Russian Revolution: Importance and Causes

Like the First World War that sparked it, the Russian Revolution helped define the political and ideological issues of the 20th century. Historians often compare it with the earlier French Revolution. Both revolutions proceeded through several phases, appealed to those outside their borders, and forced philosophical divisions throughout the world. One difference, however, was that France stood as Europe's leading nation in 1789 when their revolution began, whereas Russia lagged behind in 1914. Russia's revolution did prove more immediately successful, though, as the Bolsheviks secured power and held it for three-quarters of a century. In France, the Old Regime returned to control in 1814, just 25 years after the struggle began. Without the Russian Revolution, the history of the 20th century—including the Second World War, the Cold War, decolonization, and the nuclear arms race—would be a different story.

Long-Term Causes, 1861–1905

Throughout its history, Russia faced two perennial and irresolvable problems: (1) its technological and economic backwardness vis-à-vis the other European powers and (2) its inability to develop a form of government that successfully harnessed the will of its people. The Russian Revolution can be viewed as a drastic solution to these problems.

Following Alexander II's (r. 1855–1881) reforms, Russia seemed to be moving in the right direction. However, each top-down move by the government engendered a new set of problems. Following the abolition of serfdom, former serfs were forced to continue living on the *mirs* (rural communities practicing subsistence agriculture) until they had paid for their lands. Moreover, large landholders (the gentry) garnered most of the best lands for themselves, sticking former serfs with the rest. Rural overcrowding and a shortage of land led to continual unrest in the countryside, which served as a magnet for revolutionary groups.

Russian intellectuals were divided between those who lauded the unique features of Russia's Slavic culture (called Slavophiles) and those who believed the nation needed to become more like the West to survive (Westernizers). As Russia industrialized after 1880 under the leadership of Finance Minister Sergei Witte (1849–1915), these divisions deepened. Many of the worst problems of industrialization previously experienced by western European nations seemed accentuated within Russia's undemocratic political system. Moreover, the rapid pace of advance proved problematic. Industry and the resulting urban problems of overcrowding, pollution, and poor working/living conditions were concentrated in two cities—Moscow and St. Petersburg. Russian manufacturing enterprises tended to be large, making it easy for workers to organize politically. As such, large cities and factories emerged as centers of proletarian unrest and revolution in subsequent decades.

Reform only seemed to fuel the growth of movements that wished to take things further. Among the Slavophiles, an anarchist movement known as the People's Will succeeded in assassinating Alexander II in 1881, causing a brutal suppression of revolutionary groups by his successor, the reactionary Alexander III (r. 1881–1894). Anarchists succeeded, in fact, in assassinating thousands of Russian officials between 1870 and 1914. Less violent but also radical were the Social Revolutionaries, who favored a socialism led by the peasants that stressed Russia's rural tradition. Westernizers divided strongly between the Constitutional Democrats (Cadets), who favored the development of a capitalist economy and a parliamentary democracy like Britain's, and the Social Democrats, a Marxist party founded in 1898 in exile. Even within the Social Democrats, divisions existed; the Mensheviks wished to establish a mass-based political party like the SPD in Germany, and the **Bolsheviks** claimed that only a conspiratorial group of professional agitators could survive in Russia's autocratic political climate.

Revolution of 1905

The divisions in Russian society burst to the fore under the ongoing pressure of the country's repeated military defeats. Russia's poor showing in the Russo-Japanese War (1904–1905) produced an economic crisis and a breakdown of the nation's infrastructure. Revolutionary groups looked to exploit the situation to foment change. Strikes broke out in the major cities, the small number of university students rallied, and a group of peaceful protestors marched on the tsar's Winter Palace to request reform. Though unprovoked, the Tsar's troops fired on the crowd, killing hundreds, in an event known as Bloody Sunday. To calm the furor that followed, Tsar Nicholas II (r. 1894–1917) issued the October Manifesto promising the creation of a legislative assembly, known as the Duma, and further reforms. For the moment, these actions appeased the moderate reform parties.

Any moderate efforts toward the evolution of a constitutional monarchy were undermined by the actions of Nicholas II. Much like Louis XVI, Nicholas appeared a well-meaning and religious family man who, while espousing divine right rule, proved incapable of upholding what this ideal entailed. Nicholas's prime minister, Peter Stolypin (1862–1911), offered the last chance to pull Russia through its difficult transition. Stolypin introduced a series of far-reaching reforms in the decade before WWI designed to move Russia toward a functioning parliamentary democracy and a modern economic system. Peasants were finally allowed to sell their land shares to the *mir* and move to cities; property rights were advanced; and the provincial zemstvos (government councils) were strengthened. Unfortunately, Nicholas thwarted Stolypin's attempts to work with the Duma in creating parliamentary coalitions, exercising his royal prerogative to suspend the legislative whenever its policies annoyed him. When Stolypin was assassinated in 1911, it marked the end of Russia's chance for a peaceful transition to modernity.

The March Revolution and Provisional Government

World War I served as the proverbial straw that broke the camel's back of the Romanov Dynasty. Russia did not fare well in the conflict, experiencing a lack of supplies, poor morale among troops, and numerous casualties. Once again, war had exposed Russia's economic and technological weakness in comparison with the western European powers. As political divisions deepened, Tsar Nicholas II in 1915 dissolved the Duma. Following failures at the front, Nicholas then took personal control of the troops, a task for which he was woefully unprepared. Many soldiers were sent into battle with inadequate clothing and weapons. Meanwhile, public opinion turned against the monarchy, as it became increasingly viewed as distant and corrupt. Discontent toward the royal family centered on the mysterious figure of Rasputin (1869–1916), a dissolute monk who exercised sway over the tsarina (tsar's wife) because of his supposed ability to cure her son, Alexis, of hemophilia. Nobles at the court decided to end Rasputin's corrupting influence by assassinating him in December 1916.

Only a crisis was needed to topple the tsarist regime. On March 8, 1917, International Women's Day, a food riot broke out over the high cost of bread in an event eerily similar to the women's march on Versailles during the French Revolution. Revolutionary agitators pushed the crowd toward a political insurrection. When nearby troops refused to fire on the crowd, the Romanov Dynasty collapsed like a house of cards. Two new governments came to the fore as a result of the March Revolution. First, the **Provisional Government** replaced the deposed tsar and was led by constitutional democrats and moderate socialists. Second, more radical groups founded councils of workers, sailors, and soldiers known as **soviets**, the most important of which was the Petrograd Soviet (the city of St. Petersburg had been changed to Petrograd because it sounded less German). The Petrograd Soviet played much the same role as the Paris Commune during the French Revolution, pushing the government further to the left.

The Provisional Government opted to continue the war effort and honor its treaty commitments. Meanwhile, peasants seized land from the gentry, and discipline among troops dissolved. The Petrograd Soviet aided the latter development by passing Army Order No. 1, which provided for democratically elected committees to run the army, causing the breakdown of all discipline. In April 1917, the German army sent Lenin through their lines in a sealed train to Petrograd in the hope that he would further undermine the Provisional Government.

The Bolshevik Revolution

The Role of Lenin

V.I. Lenin (1870–1924) provided the intellectual and organizational energy behind the Russian Revolution. From an upper middle-class family, Lenin became radicalized when his brother was executed for indirect involvement in an assassination attempt against Tsar Alexander III. Unable to find work and arrested for his revolutionary affiliations, Lenin went into exile in Switzerland, where he joined the Social Democratic Party and urged a hard line against capitalism. Lenin's writings, such as the *April Theses* issued upon his arrival in 1917 in Russia, adapted Marxism to the experience of Russia. His contributions to socialist ideology include:

- *Imperialism*—As noted in Chapter 12, Lenin incorporated the phenomenon of imperialism into Marx's critique of capitalism. Lenin claimed that imperialism represented the highest stage of capitalism's concentration of power into fewer and fewer hands and signaled an imminent crisis.

- *Vanguard Party*—Lenin insisted, in contrast to the Mensheviks, that only a small group of professional revolutionary conspirators could operate successfully in Russia's undemocratic political climate.

- *"Weakest link in the chain"*—Orthodox Marxism held that the revolution would occur first in the most developed capitalist nation, such as Britain or Germany. Lenin countered that because capitalism operated as a worldwide system, revolutionaries should concentrate on the weakest link—Russia—enabling the spread of revolution to the other links.

- *Telescoping*—Many Russian socialists cooperated with the Provisional Government, believing Russia unready to enter into a socialist phase of development before its complete industrialization. Lenin rejected this notion and claimed that the time was ripe for revolution. He further claimed that Russia's rapid industrialization could occur under the dictatorship of the proletariat.

- *Revolutionary tactics*—To stir the masses, Lenin and the Bolsheviks focused on simple slogans and uncompromising opposition to the Provisional Government. "Peace, bread, and land" and "All power to the soviets!" indicated clearly the thrust of the Bolshevik message.

Bolshevik Consolidation of Power

By November 1917, Lenin judged that the hour for action had arrived. Troops in Petrograd voted to support the Bolshevik-controlled soviets. The Bolsheviks easily seized key communication, transportation, and utilities, while the Provisional Government fled for lack of support. Lenin and the Bolsheviks timed their takeover to coincide with the Congress of Soviets, which elected Lenin the head of the Council of People's Commissars, an executive body. Bolshevik leaders quickly moved to consolidate their power by confirming peasant seizures of land and worker control of factories. More importantly, the Bolsheviks in January 1918 disbanded the recently elected Constituent Assembly, which had produced majorities for the Social Revolutionaries and Mensheviks. This action plunged Russia into civil war. Claiming to speak on behalf of the proletariat, the Bolsheviks (now the Communist Party) proclaimed a dictatorship in their name.

The Treaty of Brest-Litovsk

Now preoccupied with a civil war, Lenin desperately needed to end Russia's involvement in the First World War. In March 1918, the Bolsheviks signed the harsh Treaty of Brest-Litovsk with

Germany. By the agreement, Russia recognized the independence of the Baltic provinces, Poland, and Ukraine. In the process, the Bolsheviks lost the most densely populated regions of their nation, important mineral resources, and some of Russia's best farmland. Bolshevik leaders gambled that Russia would regain these lands amid the inevitable socialist revolution accompanying the collapse of the war effort all around.

Russian Civil War, 1918–1922

To fight the civil war, the Bolsheviks formed the Red Army. Led by the brilliant organizer and former head of the Petrograd Soviet, Leon Trotsky (1879–1940), the army faced a motley collection of former tsarists, Cadets, Mensheviks, and Social Revolutionaries known as the White Army. Organizing the war effort was accomplished through war communism. The Bolsheviks nationalized key industries, allowing workers to run factories but dealing harshly with peasants who hoarded grain and refused to surrender their crops and livestock for the Reds' worthless paper money. Bolshevik policies, exacerbated by economic problems, produced class warfare, especially between wealthy peasants on one side and landless laborers and urban dwellers on the other. Complicating the situation, Allied governments landed armies under American, Japanese, and Czech control to aid the Whites and bring Russia back into World War I.

Despite being outnumbered, the Bolsheviks were able to survive. Several factors account for this. First, the Bolsheviks were united in a common vision, in contrast with their enemies who could only agree that they hated the Bolsheviks. Second, intervention by foreign powers allowed the Bolsheviks to paint their opponents as traitors. Third, efforts by the White Army were hindered by exterior lines of communication, making it difficult for them to coordinate their attacks and allowing the Bolsheviks to travel on the inside of the circle they controlled to meet any incursion. Finally, the Bolsheviks simply exhibited a more ruthless willingness than their opponents to maintain their newly won power. Soon after their revolution, the Bolsheviks formed a secret police to infiltrate and eliminate centers of opposition.

Though the situation remained fluid, by 1922 the Bolsheviks had secured control of the nation. In fact, the Red Army recaptured some of the lands lost in the Treaty of Brest-Litovsk and from ethnic minorities that had declared independence since 1918. Once the Bolsheviks had secured power, they engaged in a Red Terror designed to eliminate class enemies. Under the influence of the Cheka (security police), thousands of former bourgeoisie, gentry, and White Army collaborators were shot summarily without trial. The Bolsheviks determined not to repeat the mistakes of French revolutionaries who allowed supporters of the Old Regime to survive or escape. Estimates run to over 2 million for those killed by the Bolsheviks; no Russian after 1922 would openly call for a return to traditional or even antisocialist government.

The Union of Soviet Socialist Republics (USSR)

By 1922, the Bolsheviks felt secure enough in their power to create the **Union of Soviet Socialist Republics (USSR)**, also known as the **Soviet Union**. Eventually the new nation consisted of 15 such republics. It is important to remember that only about 50% of the citizens in this new USSR claimed Russian ethnicity and language. In that sense, the USSR acquired an international character. During the 1920s, many communists continued to hold out hope for the imminent overthrow of capitalism. To this purpose, the Bolsheviks in 1919 created the Third International of communist parties, or Comintern, to replace the Second International, which had divided over entry into the First World War. Supposedly an alliance of socialist parties, in actuality, the Comintern represented a Soviet effort to control the international communist movement.

Party-State Structure

The political structure of the Soviet Union reflected a unique party-state dualism. For each function of government, there existed both a party and a state organ. Because the party acted as the driving force of the revolution and direct representative of the proletariat, it played the primary policy-making role. State organs essentially worked to carry out policies. Constitutions were created in 1924 and 1936 to outline the complex workings of a strongly centralized government. Elections featured only one party, the CPSU (Communist Party of the Soviet Union), and authority worked according to the principle of democratic centralism, a feature of Lenin's political philosophy. Elections and discussion flowed upward to the top, where decisions were made and adhered to by all party members. At the top of this centralized structure stood the Politburo (policy bureau) of a dozen individuals who dominated the decision-making process. Once Stalin came to power, the position of General Secretary (of the CPSU) took on an important role in maintaining strict discipline, selecting members to key positions, and enacting policy.

The Nationalities Issue

For centuries, the Russian tsars had unsuccessfully attempted to Russify the 50 different ethnic groups of their empire, in which over a hundred languages were spoken. To address the nationalities issues, the Bolsheviks adopted a federal structure of government whereby the various republics, and less important autonomous regions, could theoretically secede. In fact, the dominance of the Communist Party, many of whose officials were appointed by Russian leaders of the CPSU, prevented any movement away from the Soviet Union's centralized structure. However, the minority issue never died, and under Mikhail Gorbachev's rule (1985–1991) once again came to the fore in the form of national independence movements, leading to the disintegration of the Soviet empire.

The New Economic Policy (NEP)

As a result of the ravages of the First World War, civil war, and resulting famine, the Soviet economy stood at only a small fraction of its prewar productivity. To jump-start production, Lenin introduced the **New Economic Policy (NEP)** in 1921, a strategic retreat from communism and compromise with capitalism. Under the NEP, peasants were allowed to sell their grain themselves, and middlemen in towns and cities began exchanging goods for profit. A new class of wealthy peasants, called **kulaks**, arose in the countryside, often resented by landless laborers. Though the NEP did help to revive production, the Soviet economy by 1928 had just returned to its prewar level. Moreover, the policy provoked a split in the Politburo between those who favored continuing the NEP and those who wished to move further toward communism.

Social and Cultural Changes

The 1920s were a decade of experimentation in the Soviet Union. Legal changes provided women with a measure of equality—the vote in 1918, the right to divorce, and access to birth control and abortion. Such reforms did not always translate into immediate changes in the daily lives of women, especially as families struggled to rebuild after a disastrous decade of violence. One of the more prominent women involved in the building of a socialist society was Alexandra Kollontai (1872–1952), appointed People's Commissar for Social Welfare. Kollontai helped found Zhenotdel, a women's bureau designed to fight illiteracy and educate women about the new marriage laws. Sparking controversy, Kollontai argued that as a natural instinct, sexuality should be freed from oppressive traditions, which mainly harm women. As for children, the Soviet Union created the Communist Youth League, or Komsomol, to promote socialist values and promote membership in the CPSU.

Artists and intellectuals eagerly assisted in the government's efforts to promote literacy. The great filmmaker Sergei Eisenstein pioneered new techniques of portraying action and political themes. Soviet leaders sponsored Eisenstein's famous film about the revolution, *Potemkin* (1925), critically acclaimed by film critics for its innovations. Radical artists incorporated the style of futurist art with a socialist message. Eventually, Stalin ended this period of experimentation, enforcing a cultural orthodoxy of socialist realism in the arts, celebrating factories and tractors, and reversing many of the provisions regarding women's equality.[6]

6 THEME MUSIC

The Russian Revolution initially promoted women's rights (e.g., granting suffrage); however, the end of social experimentation after 1928 coincided with a harsher time for women. Take note of how revolution and total war in the first half of the 20th century altered attitudes and practices toward women and other social groups (IS), such as workers, peasants, and ethnic minorities (e.g., Jews).

Stalin versus Trotsky

Soon after the Russian Civil War, Lenin fell ill from a series of strokes. Behind the scenes, General Secretary Josef Stalin (1879–1953) and Leon Trotsky—a true intellectual force in socialism and the organizer of the Red Army—battled for control of the party. Trotsky condemned the NEP as a sell-out to capitalism, calling for "permanent revolution" and protesting the bureaucratization of the communist party. Stalin proved the more organized and ruthless. With his control of patronage in the CPSU and by wrapping himself in the mantle of Lenin, Stalin engineered Trotsky's dismissal from the party and then his exile. By 1928, Stalin had secured his absolute hold on power and moved to implement his plans to modernize the Soviet Union.

Results of WWI and the Russian Revolution

It would be difficult to overestimate the combined impact of the First World War and Russian Revolution on European and world history. In 1914, Europe stood at its zenith of power. Less than a decade later, total war and revolution had altered that situation. First, violent and extreme forces liberated by the war and revolution would bear full fruit with the totalitarian movements of the 1920s and 1930s. Second, laissez-faire ideas regarding the economy were abandoned under pressure of the war effort, and the Versailles settlement laid the seeds for the Great Depression. Third, World War I and the Russian Revolution both radically altered diplomatic structures and destroyed the balance of power. Fourth, prewar cultural trends toward irrationality and alienation gained currency from a decade of upheaval and dominated ideas during the interwar period. Though the Treaty of Versailles attempted to remake a stable world order, the task proved too much given the extreme circumstances facing Europe in 1919. The 20th century achieved its violent birth amid the chaos of the First World War and Russian Revolution.

Additional Resources

Christopher Clark, *The Sleepwalkers: How Europe Went to War in 1914* (2014)—One of the more provocative books to emerge in the centennial year of WWI's beginning.

Sheila Fitzpatrick, *The Russian Revolution, 1917–1932*, 3rd ed. (2003)—Concise and somewhat sympathetic analysis of the founding of the Soviet Union.

Paul Fussell, *The Great War and Modern Memory* (2013)—One of the great nonfiction books, this volume explores how British writers interpreted their war experiences.

G.J. Meyer, *A World Undone: The Story of the Great War, 1914 to 1918* (2007)—Lengthy, but a pleasure to read, with character profiles and vivid writing.

John Mosier, *The Myth of the Great War: A New Military History of World War I* (2002)—The author argues that Germany fought the most effectively, with only the United States saving the Allies. For military history aficionados.

Theodore H. von Laue, *Why Lenin? Why Stalin? Why Gorbachev?: The Rise and Fall of the Soviet System*, 3rd ed. (1998)—The author analyzes the continuities and difficulties of Russian history.

Erich Maria Remarque, *All Quiet on the Western Front* (1929)—The classic antiwar novel.

Jay Winter, *The Experience of World War I* (1989)—Combining a wealth of text, special features, and maps, this coffee-table book presents the war from the perspectives of politicians, generals, soldiers, and civilians.

The Great War and the Shaping of the Twentieth Century, 8 VHS tapes (1998)—An outstanding BBC/PBS documentary focusing on the psychological impact of the Great War.

http://www.firstworldwar.com/—This excellent site offers interpretive essays, primary sources, and thousands of visuals.

Practice MC Questions

Questions 1–4 are based on the map below.

SOUTHEASTERN EUROPE, 1914

Serbia, Greece, Romania, and Ottomans Fight Bulgaria, 1913

Dennis Sherman and Joyce Salisbury, *The West in the World: A History of Western Civilization* (New York: McGraw-Hill Education, 2014), p. 658.

1. The map above depicts which of the following causes of the First World War?

    A. The increase in armaments and influence of military plans

    B. The growth of mass politics and power of nationalism

    C. Tensions in the Balkans that drew in the great powers

    D. Policies of *Realpolitik* that led to the emergence of new powers

2. The map reflects which of the following diplomatic issues of the period, 1850–1914?

    A. The unifications of Italy and Germany

    B. The competition for colonies

    C. Nationalist tensions within the Austrian Empire

    D. The decline of the Ottoman Empire

3. Comparing the situation above with the diplomacy of Europe in 1815, all of the following express major differences between the two situations EXCEPT:

    A. the Concert of Europe provided a mechanism for the great powers to avoid war.

    B. nationalist impulses created tensions and caused revolutionary upheaval.

    C. the alliance system made it difficult for European powers to compromise in 1914.

    D. the industrialization of warfare created potential for more destructive conflicts.

4. Which of the following events represents the most significant change in the alliance system before 1914?

    A. The dismissal of Bismarck as German Chancellor in 1890

    B. The Berlin Conference over African imperialism, 1884–1885

    C. The British effort to subdue the Boer revolt, 1899–1902

    D. The defeat of Russia in the Russo-Japanese War, 1904–1905

"Does it matter?—losing your legs? ...

For people will always be kind,

And you need not show that you mind

When the others come in after hunting

To gobble their muffins and eggs.

Does it matter?—losing your sight? ...

There's such splendid work for the blind;

And people will always be kind,

As you sit on the terrace remembering

And turning your face to the light.

Do they matter?—those dreams from the pit? ...

You can drink and forget and be glad,

And people won't say that you're mad;

For they'll know you've fought for your country

And no one will worry a bit."

Siegfried Sassoon, British WWI soldier and poet,
"Does it Matter?," 1918

5. The poem above reflects which of the following outcomes of the First World War?

A. The creation of a disillusioned and cynical lost generation

B. The fall of traditional empires and creation of new republics

C. The movement toward subjectivity and experimentation in the arts

D. The economic problems of hyperinflation and high unemployment

6. The style of the poem was most likely influenced by:

A. the Renaissance emphasis on classics.

B. the Reformation concern with morality.

C. the Romantic preference for subjectivity.

D. the realist preoccupation with vivid descriptions.

Siegfried Sassoon, "Does it Matter?" in *Counter-Attack and Other Poems*, (New York: E.P. Dutton & Company, 1918), pp. 131–132.

Questions 7–9 are based on the poster below.

Bolshevik propaganda poster, 1920

Caption: "On the ruins of capitalism, let us walk towards fraternity: farmers and workers are walking towards the peoples from all over the world"

7. The poster reveals which of the following causes of the Russian Revolution?

   A. The incompetence of the tsarist government

   B. Discontent created by social inequality

   C. Incomplete industrialization and economic development

   D. Conflict among various revolutionary groups

8. The poster above was likely intended to:

   A. drive foreign powers from Russian soil.

   B. overthrow the Provisional Government.

   C. collectivize Russian agriculture.

   D. help the Bolsheviks win the Russian civil war.

9. In contradiction to the message of the poster, the Soviet Union after 1921:

   A. requisitioned grain and supplies from the peasants.

   B. adopted centralized planning to promote industrialization.

   C. adopted limited free-market ideas in the New Economic Policy.

   D. liquidated the wealthy kulak peasant class in Ukraine.

See Chapter 18 for answers and explanations.

Long Essay Question with Sample and Commentary

Analyze how and why the assassination of Archduke Franz Ferdinand, heir to the Austro-Hungarian throne, sparked the First World War (1914–1918).

(HTS: Causation)

World War I was one of the most significant events in history. Ironically, it began with the assassination of a man nobody really liked very much—Franz Ferdinand. When the heir to the Austrian throne was killed, it set in motion of chain of events that led to one of the worst conflicts in European history. Without the issues of nationalism in the Balkans, domestic pressures at home, and the alliance system, World War I might have remained another regional war among the great powers.

The Balkans is the most complex region in Europe, consisting of many different ethnic groups and languages. Slavic languages and peoples dominate the region and had been ruled for centuries by the crumbling Ottoman Empire. As the Sick Man of Europe faded like an old photograph, the Slavic Russians moved in to lead the Slavic peoples there and seek their warm-weather port. However, the Austro-Hungarians controlled many of the Slavs and did not want them to establish strong independent nations, because then their Slavic groups, especially the Serbs, would want to join with them. This was shown clearly in 1878, when a war in the region led to the creation of a few states but also Austria's control of Bosnia, which the Serbs thought should be theirs. Later on, these new Balkan states attempted to gain more territory in the two Balkan Wars, which almost led to war when Austria and Germany stood firm in blocking Serbia's access to the sea. Russia was humiliated, as it had been in 1878, and was determined not to lose its great-power position in the Balkans.

Mass politics made governments respond more to pressures. With nationalism, leaders had to appeal to all the people and act like they represented them. This meant that many new groups wanted to get more rights, such as workers, women, and ethnic groups. Workers formed socialist parties, went on strike, and even used assassinations if they were anarchists. Suffragettes demanded the vote. With all of this chaos, governments tried to manipulate nationalism to "rally round the flag." Before 1914, this meant that states pursued colonies, like Italy and Germany, mostly to appeal to their public's demand for national glory. Urban areas grew larger and industrialization created many new problems. All of these issues placed great strain on governments. Why is this relevant? When the decision for war came, many leaders considered that a war might rally the public around the government. In fact, many citizens celebrated the declaration of war and groups, like the SPD in Germany, decided to support the war effort, even though they were supposed to be socialist.

All of these factors would not have mattered without the alliance system. Without the two opposed alliances, the crises in the Balkans probably would have stayed between Austria and Russia. When Bismarck ran Germany, he focused on keeping the balance of power and isolating France. His alliance system was really complex and few understood it. However, when Kaiser William got rid of Bismarck in 1890, he decided to get Germany's "place in the sun" by building up the navy and getting colonies. His actions alienated Russia and Britain, who joined with France in an alliance. Though Germany was allied with Italy, their only really ally was Austria. This meant that Germany depended on a weak nation with lots of nationalism problems. Germany was encircled and feared losing its only ally, so when Austria took a hard line against Serbia in 1914, the Kaiser issued the "blank check." When Russia defended Serbia, this drew in Germany, France, and eventually Britain.

Political science uses a "rational actor" model to study decision-making, as when John F. Kennedy created an advisory group to settle the Cuban Missile Crisis. This model, however, fails when we look at WWI. It is better to consider a "bureaucratic" perspective, in which the momentum of military plans and alliances dictated to leaders what they should do. In fact, leaders often put aside logic and reason and put faith in their institutions, leading to the tragedy that was the First World War.

This is an excellent student response, a paragon of the student being in control of the question. From the outset, he demonstrates a grasp of the historical context and clearly identifies relevant causes to earn the Thesis point. Body paragraphs begin with a strong topic sentence and then proceed to explain *how* and *why* the particular causal factor is relevant. The student chooses the examples judiciously and applies them explicitly to demonstrate *how* and *why* each factor acted as a cause, earning both points for the targeted HTS and for Use of Evidence. Though brief, the conclusion effectively extends the discussion by drawing on a different discipline (political science) to provide a further perspective. Score: 6 (Thesis, 2 points for targeted HTS, 2 points for Use of Evidence, Synthesis)

15 Democracy, Totalitarianism, and the Second World War, 1919–1945

Europe struggled to return to peace after the First World War. Though the continent had never before boasted so many democratic governments, in the next two decades, most of these new democracies crumbled under the onslaught of the Great Depression and the rise of totalitarian ideologies, such as fascism and communism. Nineteenth-century intellectual trends combined with the extreme circumstances of the First World War to produce the totalitarian movements. Dictators exploited new technologies of mass communication to mobilize their populations. At the same time, themes of alienation and disillusionment permeated high culture. Ultimately, Europe's inability to deal with the dual crises of economic depression and extreme political movements culminated in the most destructive conflict in history—the Second World War.

> **Key In** Chapter 15 covers the following KCs from the Course Description:
>
> - **KC 4.1** Effects of the Versailles settlement on diplomacy and the balance of power
> - **KC 4.3** Intellectual and cultural impact of the First World War
> - **KCs 4.1 and 4.2** Rise of totalitarian movements and the conflict among fascism, Soviet communism, and liberal democracy leading to World War II
> - **KC 4.2** Economic problems caused by World War I and the struggle of democracies to address the Great Depression
> - **KCs 4.1 and 4.4** Total war on the battlefield, home front, and resulting genocide

An Uncertain Peace: Enforcing the Treaty of Versailles

After the First World War, France attempted to enforce the Versailles settlement vigorously. This proved difficult without the active support of Great Britain and the United States, both isolationist in sentiment, and due to the Bolshevik Revolution, which eliminated Russia as a counterweight to a revived Germany. Many in Europe preferred to rely on the new **League of Nations** to ensure collective security. The League unfortunately lacked enforcement mechanisms as well as the membership of Germany, the Soviet Union, and the United States. For security, France turned to the less satisfactory alternative of allying with those new eastern European democracies sandwiched between Bolshevik Russia and a vengeful Germany. France's Little Entente with Poland, Czechoslovakia, and Romania proved no substitute for France's recent WWI allies in balancing Germany. When Germany agreed in 1922 with the Rapallo Pact to supply manufactures to the Soviet Union and engage in joint military maneuvers, it signaled the potential danger to France's security system and to the position of the new eastern European democracies.

1 SKILL SET

It is easy to overlook the nations of eastern Europe. This section provides an important reminder to evaluate the political, diplomatic, and economic trends of the era against the experience of the new states created after the Versailles settlement. As you read, it is recommended that you think in terms of the changes and continuities (CCOT) in the situation of these states from 1815 to 1945.

The Advance of Democracy in Eastern Europe

Europe enjoyed a general but short-lived trend toward democracy after the First World War. Women earned the right to vote in many nations, labor unions gained power, and governments enacted social legislation to benefit their citizens. An entire new region experienced democracy for the first time. In eastern Europe, the new states of Czechoslovakia, Yugoslavia, Austria, Hungary, Poland, and the Baltic nations emerged out of the former empires. Other than Czechoslovakia, none of these new nations drew from a democratic tradition. Though these new states were formed around the notion of national self-determination, each confronted an ethnic minority problem (e.g., the presence of millions of ethnic Hungarians in Romanian Transylvania). More ominously, millions of ethnic Germans lived in Czechoslovakia and Poland.[1]

In addition, conservative interests opposed the new democracies on one hand, while extreme socialists worked to overthrow them on the other. The specter of Bolshevism hung over eastern Europe, as in 1919 when radical leader Béla Kun attempted to establish a Soviet regime in Hungary, before his ouster in 1920. Even the great social change in the region—land reform—failed to solve the problem of underdevelopment. The new democracies lacked the integrated economies they had experienced as part of former empires. Though peasants were confirmed in ownership of their small farms, the development of a middle class—the traditional basis for parliamentary democracy—lagged far behind western Europe. Other than Czechoslovakia, the new eastern European democracies proved thin reeds and fell over easily with the crisis of depression and the threat of dictatorship.

Germany's Failed Experiment with Democracy: The Weimar Republic

Germany's Weimar Republic began with two strikes against it. Born amidst the turmoil accompanying the end of the First World War, the republic faced a myriad of economic and political problems. Many influential Germans, particularly military officials, judges, and civil servants, opposed the new government as a weak substitute for imperial Germany. Extremists on both the left and the right attempted to overthrow the government in its first years of existence.

Two parties helped found the republic and draw up its constitution—the Social Democratic Party (left-center) and the Catholic Center Party (right-center). The former had all but abandoned its Marxist rhetoric and seemed more concerned with advancing Germany's welfare system; both wished to avoid communist and rightist takeovers. In 1919, a Soviet-inspired communist movement, known as the Spartacists and led by Rosa Luxembourg and Karl Liebknecht, attempted an overthrow of the Berlin city government but were captured and executed by the *Freikorps*, a right-wing paramilitary group. Then in 1920, the *Freikorps* itself attempted a takeover known as the Kapp putsch. Only the intervention of the working class saved the republic from an early death. Political violence seemed to mark the short history of Weimar, as when Foreign Minister Walter Rathenau was assassinated in 1922 by two conservative army officers.

According to the Weimar constitution, delegates to the Reichstag (the popular branch of the parliament) were chosen by proportional representation, meaning that if a party received 10% of the vote, it would earn approximately 10% of the seats in the Reichstag. Though this allowed for a diversity of views, the system also made it difficult to establish stable majority government and easier for extreme views to gain a political voice. Also, in times of "imminent danger," the president of the republic could suspend parliament and rule by decree. This so-called suicide clause (Article 48) provided a pretext for those who wished to undermine democratic rule.

Perhaps most damaging to Weimar was its association with the Versailles settlement. Even left-of-center Germans viewed the treaty as a *Diktat*, or dictated peace. Demagogues like Hitler perpetuated the myth that the German army in 1918 stood on the verge of victory when it was "stabbed in the back" by the "Jews, socialists, communists, and democrats" bent on establishing republican government at any price. No matter how untrue and unfair this charge, it allowed right-wing groups to scapegoat the Weimar Republic for Germany's problems. When this catalogue is added to the economic problems of reparations, hyperinflation, and the Great Depression, Weimar's failure is not difficult to understand.[2]

Reparations, the Ruhr, and Hyperinflation

In 1923 the Weimar Republic fell behind on its reparations payments. In response, the French and Belgians invaded the industrial Ruhr Valley to extract the payments in the form of coal and steel. The result benefited neither France nor Germany. Weimar leaders encouraged workers to engage in a campaign of passive resistance and refuse to operate the factories and mines. This action required the Weimar Republic to pay the workers' benefits and wages in ever-increasing amounts of paper money. By November 1923, the German mark had plummeted to catastrophic levels. At the worst of this hyperinflation, $1 equaled 4 trillion marks. Overnight, middle-class

2 THEME MUSIC AND SKILL SET

In this section, we address the factors explaining the failure of democratic governments, especially the Weimar Republic, whose failure held profound consequences for Europe's future. Americans may take for granted how natural democracy seems, but if you consult the SP theme, you'll realize the struggles many states have experienced along the road to or even away from democracy. When finished with the chapter, consider writing a focused paragraph explaining how and why democracy faltered during the interwar period (ARG and EVARG) savings, pensions, insurance policies, and interest income all become worthless. Confidence in the Weimar Republic plunged, emboldening **Adolf Hitler** (1889–1945) and his Nazi party to attempt to overthrow the Bavarian government in the Beer Hall putsch (1923). Though the coup failed, Hitler received only a 5-year sentence from a justice system always more lenient on right-wing than left-wing violence. While in prison, Hitler wrote his political testament, *Mein Kampf* (1924), which outlined his racial ideas and goals for Germany.

Great Britain and the United States criticized France for its provocative gesture. To defuse the situation, the U.S. intervened economically. Because America's former allies claimed that they could not pay back loans to the United States without German reparations, the U.S. extended loans to Germany and rescheduled the reparations payments in exchange for a French withdrawal of the Ruhr. Funds from the Dawes Plan aided a short-lived economic revival in Germany, while a new spirit of cooperation emerged from the French and Germans. However, the French learned an important lesson; its vigorous action brought down the government and earned it the criticism of allies fearful of another war.

The Spirit of Locarno

The period 1924–1929 produced optimistic hopes of peace and prosperity. Moderate leaders emerged in the principal nations who were dedicated to resolving disputes through negotiation and diplomacy, most importantly, Gustav Streseman (1878–1929) of Germany and Aristide Briand (1862–1932) of France. In 1925, these two leaders engineered the Locarno Pact, which contemporaries considered the true end to the First World War. Germany recognized its western borders as permanent (meaning the loss of Alsace-Lorraine) and agreed to revise its eastern borders with Poland and Czechoslovakia only by common agreement. As a result, Germany was allowed to enter the League of Nations in 1926. The "spirit of Locarno" culminated with the Kellogg-Briand Pact of 1928, by which the 65 signatory nations condemned war as an instrument of international politics.

Like the Kellogg-Briand Pact, the League of Nations lacked the means to enforce its decisions. When Japan invaded Manchuria in 1931 and Italy invaded Ethiopia in 1935, the League made rhetorical protests and contemplated sanctions, but took few concrete actions to punish the aggressors. Such diplomacy left underlying issues unresolved and lulled some nations into adopting isolationist policies in deference to the league. In 1930, France began work on a set of defensive fortifications along the German border known as the Maginot Line, a term that symbolizes a false notion of security behind an imaginary strong frontier.

The Great Depression
Causes

The First World War and Treaty of Versailles sowed the seeds for the Great Depression. Before 1914, economic activity had become increasingly global, meaning that disturbance in one area was transmitted quickly to other areas. During the period of international stability, 1924–1929, the world economy was marked by prosperity, especially in new sectors such as automobiles, household appliances, and communications. This prosperity proved shallow, however, and was hindered by the following factors:

- *Strong inflationary pressures*—During the First World War, governments engaged in rationing, borrowed money at record rates, and depreciated their currencies in an effort to reduce their debt. Inflation complicated the return to a peacetime economy and wreaked havoc on the world system of stable currencies that had existed before 1914.

- *Disrupted markets*—While Europe fought World War I, competitors moved into its worldwide markets. For example, India developed its own textile industry and was less interested in British imports following the war. North America and Australia established themselves as major exporters of grain. When the war ended, European nations found it difficult to reestablish former trade patterns.

- *Agricultural depression*—A glut of grain worldwide drove down prices and left many farmers bankrupt or destitute.

- *Economic nationalism*—To protect fragile domestic markets and head off unrest, most states enacted high tariff barriers. The United States, in particular, refused to replace Great Britain as financial world leader; rather than lower tariffs to allow Germany to accumulate capital from trade and thus pay off reparations, the United States enacted some of its highest barriers ever.

- *Reparations*—The cycle of world capital flowed from the United States to Germany, then from Germany to France and Britain, and finally back to the United States. This unnatural arrangement disrupted investment, while making world economic activity unusually reliant on American financial conditions.

- *Credit financing*—The advent of the installment plan allowed consumers to defer payment on purchases. In addition, expanding American stock market activity occurred on margin, by borrowing up to 90% of the stock's value. Any small economic downturn threatened to burst this speculative bubble.

When the U.S. **stock market crashed** in October 1929, it triggered the components of the above trap into place, causing a downward economic spiral.

Effects

Europe had experienced economic cycles throughout its history, but nothing compared with the Great Depression in the 1930s for length and depth of contraction. Stock values plunged from 1929 to 1932 as businesses cut back production and laid off workers. Investment and world trade plummeted. Unemployment reached shocking proportions, strengthening those parties who promised extreme solutions to problems. Germany and the United States were hardest hit; as many as 35% of workers were idled in both nations. Due to the unstable credit situation, the stock market crash rippled throughout the financial world, causing global bank failures. In 1931 the failure of the leading Vienna bank, the *Creditanstalt*, sparked additional financial collapses.

Most nations experienced a drain on their treasuries to pay off debts. Currency values depreciated even further, wrecking the stable gold-backed system dating from the mid-19th century. Investors lost confidence in the British pound, causing a massive sell-off. Long the world financial leader, Great Britain was forced off the gold standard in 1931, followed soon after by the United States and the rest of the industrialized world. In many cases, trade reverted to **bilateral agreements** and even barter, wherein one nation would exchange goods directly with another. Such arrangements hindered world trade and made it difficult for nations to obtain necessary products and to earn income from exports.[3]

Democratic Responses

The Great Depression created a crisis for democratic governments. Economy orthodoxy seemed impotent in addressing the downward spiral. According to Liberal economic theory, in times of depression, states should pursue austerity much like individual families: cut the budget and raise taxes. However, these policies failed to stimulate production and increased the misery of the unemployed. British economist John Maynard Keynes (1883–1946) introduced an alternate approach to economic stimulation in his *General Theory of Employment, Interest, and Money* (1936). Contrary to accepted wisdom, Keynes argued that governments needed to "prime the pump" through deficit financing, by cutting taxes and spending on government programs to aid the needy. Though few nations consistently followed such policies before the Second World War, Keynesian economics emerged as the new orthodoxy after 1945. On the AP exam, questions tend to focus on the general structure of the economy during this period; however, the following brief review of democratic responses illustrates the depth of the crisis.

3 THEME MUSIC
The Great Depression reveals the fragility of the post-WWI settlement. Also, the Depression represents a critical moment in the PP theme, in that it changed the relationship between the government and economy and laid the foundations for the modern welfare state.

Great Britain: Of all the industrial nations, Great Britain depended most on trade. The First World War and Great Depression both struck a blow against Britain's dominant position. Welfare legislation enacted before the war eased some of the burden on the unemployed. Despite the negative economic conditions, workers were reluctant to surrender gains made in wartime. Conflicts with industry led in 1926 to a General Strike, which was eventually squashed by government intervention. Politically, the Labour Party replaced the Liberal Party and, after gaining power in 1924 and again in 1929, aimed to extend the rights of workers. In 1931, former Labour Prime Minister Ramsay MacDonald (1866–1937) joined with Conservatives in a National Government that attempted to reduce the budget deficit through traditional retrenchment. To address imperial issues, Britain provided autonomy for Egypt and the Irish Free State in 1922, and in 1931 formalized relations with former colonies such as Canada, Australia, New Zealand, and South Africa by granting dominion status. The combined problems of economic stagnation, diminished world status, and political tension placed Britain in a weakened position to confront Nazi aggression.

France: France escaped some of the worst effects of the Great Depression. Less dependent on trade than Britain, France was not as hard hit by the world downturn. In addition, the nation succeeded in stabilizing the *franc* at a fraction of its prewar level, making French exports cheaper on the world market. Amid the growth of right-wing and fascist groups, a coalition of left-wing parties, called the Popular Front, held power briefly from 1936 to 1938 and promoted a series of significant reforms—the 40-hour workweek, paid vacations, and stronger collective bargaining rights for unions. Socialist Prime Minister Léon Blum's (1872–1950) government eventually fell victim to heightening ideological tensions, particularly after the outbreak of the Spanish Civil War. However, France preserved its republican government for the time being and enacted legislation that still benefits French workers today.

Scandinavia: The Scandinavian nations of Norway, Sweden, and Denmark demonstrated that governments could effectively combine elements of socialism and democracy. These states enacted the most social welfare programs to curb the worst effects of the Great Depression. Additionally, Scandinavian nations most eagerly embraced creative and Keynesian approaches, such as producers' cooperatives to regulate the price of agricultural products and state ownership of key industries.

Totalitarianism

Totalitarianism arose during the interwar period, yet it also claims roots in the pre-1914 period. Mass politics and intellectual trends after 1870 fueled the development of irrational ideologies. You may recall the growth of political anti-Semitism, anarchism's glorification of violence, and the rabid nationalism associated with imperialism. In addition, Darwinian evolution emphasized the importance of struggle, a notion taken up by racists and extremists to justify domination of the "weaker." During the First World War, states grew significantly in their powers of regimentation and mobilization, employing propaganda to control public opinion. Communication advances in the interwar period, such as radio and motion pictures, provided additional means for controlling the populace.

Dictatorship was not new to Europe, so how can we distinguish totalitarianism from the absolutism of the 17th and 18th centuries? Absolute monarchs like Louis XIV derived their power from traditional dynastic and aristocratic institutions, and it extended to those areas deemed essential to the state's interest, such as trade, taxes, and religion. Even then, geographic and customary obstacles hindered centralization. Totalitarian dictators exploited mass media to mobilize the public to fanatical support of the movement, not simply passive obedience, as with absolute monarchs. Twentieth-century dictators aimed at total control of society; any independent civic or social life must be subordinated to the party, movement, and leader. Modern communications allowed for such control but also increased the potential for catastrophic violence, as would be clear during the Second World War.

Fascism and Mussolini's Italy

The traumas of the interwar proved fertile ground for the European and even world phenomenon of fascism. For many, fascism provided a third way between faltering Liberal democracies and revolutionary, class-based Marxism. With its origins in 19th-century irrational ideologies but feeding on the unstable conditions of the 1920s and 1930s, fascism posed a genuine threat to supplant democracy as the wave of the future. Before turning to the Italian variant of fascism, the following list may prove helpful in understanding the nature of fascist ideology:

- *Militarism*—Fascists extolled war as the proving ground of national identity and for sorting out the hierarchy of nations.

- *Glorification of the state*—Not only was the state seen as all-powerful, it also represented the culminating force in historical evolution.

- *Führer principle*—German for "leader," the Führer principle stated that the voice of the people reached its highest expression not in assemblies or representation but in a single person, for example, Mussolini or Hitler.

- *Anti-democracy*—Fascists scorned the weakness of democratic mechanisms of government and argued that the national spirit cannot be captured by specific institutions.

- *Anti-communism*—Though communists and fascists shared many tactics, fascists condemned class warfare and upheld the importance of racial and national identity, in contrast to communists who condemned racism and nationalism.

- *One-party rule*—In fascist states, democratic mechanisms such as elections, multiparty systems, and the free press were suppressed.[4]

The Rise of Fascism in Italy Italy came out of the First World War as a victor, but in name only. Right-wing nationalists condemned the Versailles settlement for not allowing Italians to recapture unredeemed lands from Austria and the new nation of Yugoslavia. To make matters worse, the Italian economy suffered from unemployment, inflation, and high budget deficits. Workers engaged in numerous strikes, often fanned by extremist groups hoping to institute a socialist state. Already low before the war, respect for Italy's parliamentary democracy sank further.

Into this atmosphere strode **Benito Mussolini** (1883–1945) and his fascists (after the Latin *fasces*, or bundle of sticks carried by ancient Roman officials to symbolize state power). Named for a Mexican revolutionary, Mussolini began as a revolutionary left-wing journalist but moved rightward with the outbreak of World War I. Influenced by the writings of Sorel and Nietzsche regarding the irrational, Mussolini glorified the state and violence as a means of combating Italy's perceived enemies. To gain power, Mussolini used the paramilitary *squadristi* (or Blackshirts) to intimidate political opponents and promote the breakdown of parliamentary order. Though the Fascist movement won only a small percentage of parliamentary seats in the 1921 election, Mussolini continued to gain adherents, who ironically saw him as a champion of law and order against the threat from the left. By 1922, Mussolini decided the moment had arrived for his movement to seize power. In October of that year, thousands of fascists converged on the capital to intimidate the king into appointing Mussolini as head of government. The so-called March on Rome convinced Victor Emmanuel III to name Mussolini as premier.

The Italian Fascist State Under Mussolini Mussolini moved quickly to exploit the emergency powers he was granted to cement his hold on the government. To ensure a functioning majority, the parliament passed an amendment that granted two-thirds of the seats to the party gaining the most votes in elections. With help from this law and the tactics of the *squadristi*, the fascists in 1924 gained control of the parliament. Soon after the election, a respected Socialist deputy, Giacomo Matteotti, was assassinated by fascist thugs for exposing corruption and violence within the government. Public outrage demanded the resignation of Mussolini, who, nonetheless, used the incident to secure his hold on power.

4 THEME MUSIC AND SKILL SET

Totalitarian governments represent, on one hand, the culmination of the trend toward mass politics since the French Revolution, and on the other, a unique manifestation of the extreme conditions existing during the interwar period (SP). The entire 20th century might be viewed as a three-sided struggle among Liberal democracy, communism, and fascism—each representing a specific conception of legitimate government and manner of expressing popular will. If you consider the historical context (CTX), perhaps you can explain how and why totalitarian governments differed from absolute monarchies of the 17th and 18th centuries (COMP).

By 1926, fascism had censored the press, eliminated all opposition parties, and employed a secret police, the OVRA, to ferret out dissent. In keeping with fascist ideology, Mussolini condemned laissez-faire capitalism, democracy, and Marxist appeals to class. National solidarity and glory, symbolized by Mussolini himself (called *Il Duce*—the Leader), replaced a pluralistic society. In economic affairs, Mussolini introduced corporatism, in which the economy was run as 22 separate corporations, with representatives from business, fascist-organized labor unions, and the state. State interest dictated actual policy and production priorities, though private property and profit were allowed.

In social and cultural life, the fascists worked to orient the lives of Italians around the state. To end the conflict with the Catholic Church dating from 1870, Mussolini signed the Lateran Accord in 1929, which recognized the sovereignty of the church over the Vatican in exchange for the papacy's promise not to interfere with the functions of the state. To address Italy's declining birthrate, Mussolini provided incentives for larger families, gave awards for fertile mothers, and created holidays to honor motherhood. In a fascist state, women were clearly to play the domestic role of rearing strong children for the state. A healthy race demanded a regimen of physical fitness. Schools required calisthenics, and the government sponsored recreational and outdoor activities through the state-sponsored *Dopolavoro*.

The fascist corporate state failed to address effectively the problems of the Great Depression. Mussolini turned to a program of public works to provide jobs—swamps were cleared, roads built, and self-sufficiency in wheat and power was attempted. Though it was said that Mussolini "made the trains run on time," he was forced increasingly after 1935 to engage in imperialist adventures to revive support for his flagging movement. Despite fascist efforts, Italy was never able to realize the totalitarian state to the degree of Nazi Germany or Stalinist Soviet Union.

Nazi Germany

Hitler and the Rise to Power No political movement in history is associated more with a single person than Nazism under Adolf Hitler. Hitler came from a lower-middle-class Austrian family of unremarkable circumstances. The young Hitler moved to Vienna to pursue his artistic aspirations. After failing entrance to the Viennese art academy, Hitler survived by selling watercolors and postcards. While in Vienna, Hitler absorbed the anti-Semitism of its mayor, Karl Lueger, and grew to hate the "mongrel" Habsburg Empire with its ethnic diversity and aristocratic airs. To avoid being drafted into the Austrian army at the outset of World War I, Hitler crossed the border into Bavaria and enlisted in the German army. The young corporal served with distinction at the front as a message runner, and ended the war in a hospital the victim of a poison gas attack, where he heard the news of the armistice. Hitler believed his war experience the most significant of his life and joined a military-style political group in 1920 known as the National Socialist German Workers' Party (NSDAP), later known as National Socialists, or simply **Nazis**. The ragtag group of political misfits soon recognized the spellbinding quality of Hitler's oratory and made him their leader.

After the failed Beer Hall putsch of 1923, Hitler and the Nazis focused on a legality strategy of exploiting parliamentary politics to create a mass movement capable of taking power when democracy broke down. The Nazi message was simple: Weimar represented rule by the worst— democrats, socialists, Jews—and Germany needed a strong national state based on race. As Hitler laid out in *Mein Kampf*, Germany required *Lebensraum* (living space) in the east, as part of a new European order organized around a hierarchy of race. At every opportunity, Hitler blamed Germany's problems on the Treaty of Versailles and pledged to restore German honor. Members of the S.A. (Brownshirts or Stormtroopers) provoked street fights with rival political groups and received lenient treatment from sympathetic officials and judges. Initially, the Nazis pitched their message to workers but gained little support, earning less than 3% of the vote in 1928. Two developments caused a turnaround in Nazi fortunes: (1) the Great Depression and (2) a switch in Nazi tactics to appeal to the middle class.

The Nazis used modern electoral tactics to gain support. Nazi leaders gave speeches tailored to specific audiences and portrayed themselves as the party of the young and dynamic. Hitler made effective use of modern technologies, as with his Hitler over Germany campaign, in which he visited 50 cities in 15 days via airplane. By 1932, the Nazi vote total had increased to 37%, winning 230 seats in the Reichstag and making it the largest party. As early as 1930, the Weimar Republic already subsisted on life support, with the chancellor ruling by decree. Some old-line conservatives believed Hitler represented the best hope to defeat communism and restore order in Germany. Intriguers behind President Hindenburg convinced the aged and perhaps senile leader to appoint Hitler chancellor in January 1933. It was believed that Hitler could be controlled by other members of the cabinet, certainly one of the most egregious miscalculations in political history.[5]

The Nazi Total State It did not take long for Hitler to consolidate his power. Soon after his appointment, the parliament building caught fire. The Nazis blamed the Reichstag fire on the Communist Party, which they banned as illegal, arresting its leaders. In response, the Nazis rammed through the Reichstag an amendment allowing Hitler to rule by decree for 5 years. This Enabling Act essentially made Hitler a dictator, and it was followed by the 1933 Civil Service Act, requiring all government employees to swear a personal oath of loyalty to the Fuhrer.

In 1934, Hitler removed the last obstacles to his power. First, all parties but National Socialism were declared illegal. All federal governments, such as Bavaria or Saxony, were eliminated in favor of a unitary state. To win over the army leadership, Hitler agreed in June 1934 to purge the leadership of the S.A., grown to 500,000 men and perceived as a threat to the army's monopoly of military force. With Hitler in power, the S.A. no longer seemed necessary, and its leader, Ernst Röhm (1887–1934), represented one of the last potential challenges to Hitler's unquestioned leadership of the party. On the night of June 30, 1934, top leaders of the Brownshirts, in addition to numerous other political opponents, were summarily executed in what became known as the Blood Purge. When President Hindenburg died 2 months later, Hitler assumed the position of president.

Terror comprised an elemental weapon of Nazi rule. Internally, a secret police, the Gestapo, arrested real and imagined opponents, committing thousands to a constellation of concentration camps. Following the S.A. purge, the S.S. (*Schutzstaffel*) emerged as the primary perpetrators of terror, eventually absorbing control of the Gestapo, running the death camps, and forming the leading edge of a new Aryan racial elite. Another ingredient of the total state involved coordinating independent social and civic organizations—charities, youth groups, unions—into Nazi organizations. Though only one-tenth of Germans belonged to the Nazi Party, all social activity was to be geared around the state and its goals. The Nazi Party also positively promoted loyalty through propaganda, such as the annual Nuremberg rallies, a spectacle of pageantry and regimentation captured effectively in the film *Triumph of the Will*.

To solve Germany's economic problems, the Nazis attempted to spend Germany out of the Depression with public works projects and rearmament. By 1936, the Nazis had developed a Four-Year Plan to promote the goal of self-sufficiency (autarky) in strategic commodities such as fuels and rubber. Hitler won over industrialists with the promise of government contracts for rearmament and eliminating the perceived socialist threat. In addition, the independent labor unions of the Social Democratic Party were replaced by the National Labor Front, a state-run union requiring each worker in good standing to carry a booklet in order to procure a job. With projects like the Autobahn, many Germans credited Hitler with getting Germany back to work, even if his pump-priming did not represent a long-term solution to Germany's problems.

Nazi racial policy touched all areas of life. Boys were enrolled in the Hitler Youth and girls in the League of German Maidens to reinforce traditional gender roles and build a strong racial stock. Women were expected to fulfill the domestic duties of "church, kitchen, and children," while their public and economic roles were limited by the state. Anti-Semitic policies reflected the Nazi racial vision. At first, Jews were excluded from the civil service and army. To clarify the position of Jews in Germany, the Nazis passed the Nuremberg Laws of 1935, which defined who was a Jew, stripped Jews of citizenship, and prohibited sexual relations with Aryans. Many Jews

5 EXAMPLE BASE
Example Base: Among the specific examples in this section, try to employ them to explain the nature and manner of totalitarianism and to test whether these regimes actually realized the degree of control claimed by the theory.

preferred to remain in Germany, hoping to ride out the Nazi tide. However, Nazi policies turned violent with the *Kristallnacht* (Night of Broken Glass) of November 1938, in which synagogues were burned, businesses destroyed, and hundreds of Jews killed or arrested. To further the goal of racial purity, the Nazis also engaged in campaigns of sterilization for the mentally unfit and euthanasia for the terminally ill, insane, and physically deformed. This so-called T-4 program killed approximately 200,000 between 1939 and 1941 before protests by religious groups slowed and eventually halted it. For the attentive, the genocidal program laid out in *Mein Kampf* was apparent before the onset of World War II.

The Soviet Union Under Stalin, 1928–1939

In the 10-year period 1928–1938, the Soviet Union under Stalin experienced one of the most rapid modernizations in history. After expelling Trotsky, Stalin ended the **New Economic Policy** (NEP; see Chapter 14) and began building "socialism in one country." It was clear by 1928 that world revolution was not imminent, and Stalin wished to push forward the Soviet Union's industrialization as rapidly as possible, appropriating Trotsky's ideas regarding strong central planning to accomplish it. As Stalin saw it, "We are fifty or a hundred years behind the advanced countries. We must make good this distance in ten years. Either we do it, or we shall be crushed."

To move forward, Stalin instituted the first of several Five-Year Plans in 1928. Its goals were to build a strong base of heavy industry, aim for self-sufficiency, and create a modern infrastructure of electricity, roads, and factories. Overseeing every intricate detail of production and resource allocation was Gosplan, a central government agency staffed by thousands of party bureaucrats. Because the Bolsheviks had repudiated the tsarist debt and could not draw on foreign capital, funds for industrialization had to come from the agricultural sector. During the NEP, a class of wealthy peasants developed who accumulated land and often hired labor among the landless. These **kulaks** were resented by many. To absorb the excess capital of the kulaks, Stalin forced them and all peasants onto collective farms. The kulaks resisted the forced collectivization of agriculture, often by destroying crops and slaughtering livestock. Though by 1932 almost all peasants lived on collective farms, the cost proved high—millions of kulaks were killed for resisting collectivization, and millions more died in the **famine** that ensued in Russia and Ukraine from the disruption in agriculture.

By some measures, the Five-Year Plans proved remarkably successful. The Soviet Union avoided the economic contraction of the Great Depression and soon became the world's largest producer of tractors and railway locomotives. Overall, only the United States and Germany surpassed the Soviet Union in productive capacity. Soviet authorities extolled socialist heroes like the miner Stakhanov, who exceeded his quota for coal by 1300%. However, many Soviet manufactures were of poor quality, and consumer goods lagged far behind. The exponential growth in the Soviet economy is explained partly by its start from such a low level.

Stalin imposed a rigid totalitarian system on the Soviet Union. Independent political parties, labor unions, and free expression were eliminated. Government controlled cultural life—art, literature, film—for propaganda purposes. The cultural experimentation of the 1920s was ended; socialist realism, glorifying factories and workers, became the accepted standard. Huge posters of Stalin adorned factories and street corners as part of a cult of personality. To rid himself of any real or potential enemies, Stalin initiated the Great Purges. Aimed at the Old Bolsheviks, the purges ultimately eliminated leftists who supported Trotsky, now in exile in Mexico, and rightists charged with supporting capitalism. During the Great Terror, from 1934 to 1938, it is estimated that almost 4 million were charged with crimes against the state, and close to 800,000 were executed. Though Soviet citizens experienced an improved basic standard of living, it came at a high cost. Ethnic minorities and perceived opponents, for example, filled Siberian gulags, or hard-labor camps. Women, also, found that many of the reproductive rights gained in the 1920s were reversed as part of a campaign to increase the birth rate, forcing them to balance work and family obligations. Regimentation of Soviet social life came as the by-product of its astounding economic successes.

The Culture of the Interwar Period

Cultural developments from 1918 to 1939 reflected two distinct trends: (1) the disillusioning effects of the First World War in high culture and (2) the further development of a truly mass culture based on new communications technologies. We address both of these areas in turn.

Experimentation and Alienation in High Culture

The writers, artists, and intellectuals who came of age during the First World War became known as the **Lost Generation**. Prewar trends of **irrationality**, **subjectivity**, and alienation were confirmed by the experience of war. German historian Oswald Spengler (1880–1936) reflected this sense of pessimism in his book *The Decline of the West*, which argued that Europe's golden age was coming to end due to its tendency toward self-destructive acts, and was fated for eclipse by other civilizations. Writers of fiction worked in similar themes. Franz Kafka (1883–1924) described characters caught up in an incomprehensible world with no capacity to alter their fates. In one of the great antiwar novels, Erich Maria Remarque's (1898–1970) *All Quiet on the Western Front* showed matter-of-factly how war destroys innocence and meaning. T.S. Eliot's epic poem "The Waste Land" (1922) captured a similar sense of decline and the absurdity of human existence.

Many writers experimented with stream-of-consciousness styles and unstructured works to convey the subjective nature of experience. Marcel Proust's *Remembrance of Things Past* explores the narrator's memories of childhood experiences amid a half-waking state. James Joyce's *Ulysses* stands as the masterwork of modernist literature, examining one day in the life of Dublin resident Stephen Dedalus through mental associations and word play. Virginia Woolf experimented with similar techniques but combined them with feminist themes. Expatriates (those who live outside their culture or nation) from the United States—Ernest Hemingway, F. Scott Fitzgerald, and Gertrude Stein—worked in similar styles and themes and demonstrated the growing influence of American culture as well as the profound sense of alienation in the western world as a whole.[6]

Modern art grew incredibly diverse in the 20th century. Weimar Germany, and Berlin in particular, became a center of experimentation in the arts; in painting, German artists such as George Grosz and Hannah Hoch employed expressionist and Dadaist techniques to critique the perceived weakness and corruption of Weimar. Dadaism represented an anti-art movement, using artistic media to show the absurdity of life. Examples include collages of disconnected images or distorted caricatures. Abstraction reduces reality down to its essentials—line, shape, and color. In the massive mural *Guernica* (1937), Pablo Picasso conveys the horror of a fascist atrocity during the Spanish Civil War through the spare use of symbols and Cubist multiple perspective. Furthermore, Freud's ideas regarding the unconscious began to influence painting with the artistic movement of surrealism. Spanish surrealist Salvador Dali (1904–1989) gained fame for his bizarre juxtaposition of objects and dreamy landscapes, as in his ubiquitous *The Persistence of Memory* (1931). In architecture, modernists from the Bauhaus school worked with concrete, steel, and glass to design straightforward "boxes with windows." When the Nazis took power in 1933, they condemned the works of such architects and other artists as degenerate and drove them out of the country.

The sciences and the social sciences confirmed prewar trends toward the irrational and the uncertain. In *Civilization and Its Discontents* (1931), **Sigmund Freud** argued that aggressive human drives inevitably lead to violence and war, an observation given credence by the First World War. Building on Freud's ideas, Swiss psychiatrist Carl Jung (1875–1961) developed the notion of the collective unconscious, the part of a person's psyche common to all human beings and made up of archetypes, basic character types grounding all experiences. Physicists continued to explore the structure of the subatomic world and time. Werner Heisenberg (1901–1976) demonstrated with his **uncertainty principle** how one could not observe *both* the position and momentum of a particle, as the act of observation itself alters the behavior of what is observed. Heisenberg's theory supported the quantum notion of probabilities over objectively determined realities.

6 SKILL SET

As during the Enlightenment, elite and popular culture diverged strongly in the interwar period. Identify the themes and focus for both high and popular culture (COMP) and be prepared to explain how each reveals the mood and developments of the 1920s and 1930s (CTX).

Mass Culture and Leisure

The experience of shared suffering during World War I provoked a shift in public morals. During the Roaring Twenties, displays of sexuality grew more open, women smoked in public, and dance halls gained popularity. Fashion challenged traditional gender roles, as women wore less defining and more revealing clothing. In many European states, laws against the distribution of birth control were abandoned. Germany's Cabaret culture featured sultry jazz music along with frank themes of sexuality. African-American Josephine Baker took Europe by storm with exotic and erotic dance routines. These developments divided Europeans between those who celebrated the new openness as part of a general democratization and those who condemned it as a decadent feature of post-WWI society.

During the prosperous 1920s, many businesses developed installment plans and allowed buying on credit. Advertising, often using celebrities and sports figures, fed a new **consumerism** in household appliances, beauty aids, and automobiles. Governments openly encouraged the purchase of radios and attendance at motion pictures. New communication technologies offered opportunities to shape public opinion and promote propaganda. Nazi Germany ensured that all citizens owned a radio so as to hear Hitler's speeches. Minister of Propaganda Joseph Goebbels (1897–1945) elevated visual spectacle to new heights in Nazi films and festivals. Democratic states also recognized the potential of mass communication; in 1927, the British Broadcasting Corporation (BBC) was chartered. Ironically, filmmakers like Charlie Chaplin with *Modern Times* (1936) and Fritz Lang with *Metropolis* (1927) used the medium to critique the modern obsession with technology.

With increased leisure time, Europeans engaged in more air travel and tourism. Totalitarian states encouraged such activities around state-run agencies, such as *Kraft durch Freude* (Strength Through Joy) in Nazi Germany, which sponsored camping, hiking, and boating trips. In tune with racial ideologies and eugenics, governments promoted a "cult of the body" through organized sports, such as gymnastics, soccer, and track and field. Nazi Germany held the 1936 Berlin Olympics as a showplace for the superiority of the Aryan race. Though Germany did win the most medals, African American track star Jesse Owens stole the show with five gold medals.

The Road to World War II, 1933–1939: Appeasement

Though historians still debate the causes of the First World War, those of World War II lack controversy—the ambitions of Nazi Germany to overturn the Versailles settlement. Seemingly every year after taking power until the commencement of hostilities in 1939, Adolf Hitler provoked an international crisis related to his goals of creating a New European Order around race. Hitler sought first to regain those lands lost at Versailles; second, to subdue France and bring Britain to friendly terms; third, to turn east and conquer Slavic Europe as a vast granary and slave labor force; and finally, in the process, to eliminate "culture destroyers" such as Jews and Gypsies. That Hitler almost accomplished these goals demonstrates the fragility of the post-WWI diplomatic order.

To avoid another war, the western democracies engaged in **appeasement**, or an attempt to meet Hitler's demands through diplomacy. Today, the term suggests cowardice and folly, but at the time was driven by several concerns: (1) lack military preparedness due to budget constraints created by the Great Depression, (2) a greater fear of Soviet communism, and (3) the genuine feeling that the horrors of Verdun and the Somme must not be repeated. The following chronology serves to demonstrate the evolution of Hitler's goals and tactics, as well as the application and eventual abandonment of appeasement. Without the active diplomatic support of the Soviet Union (due to its exclusion) and the United States (due to its **isolation**), it seemed an almost impossible task to deter Hitler or Mussolini, not to mention the Japanese.

1931: In pursuit of natural resources, Japan invades the Chinese province of Manchuria. Rhetorical denunciations by the League of Nations provoke Japan's withdrawal from that body.

1933: Hitler withdraws Germany from the League of Nations and Geneva disarmament conference, primarily to consolidate domestic support for his regime.

1935: Hitler openly repudiates the Versailles provisions related to demilitarization. Great Britain rewards Germany's rearmament with a naval agreement, allowing Hitler to build up his fleet.

To avenge Italy's defeat in 1896, Mussolini invades Ethiopia without provocation. In a failure of collective security, Britain and France's half-hearted economic sanctions and military actions fail to prevent Italy's conquest of Ethiopia.

1936: Rejecting Versailles and the Locarno Pact, Hitler boldly remilitarizes the Rhineland. France and Britain do nothing, convincing Hitler of their weakness.

Since 1931, Spain had been ruled by a republic. The republican government moved against the entrenched power of the Catholic Church and large landowners. Elections in 1936 lead to the creation of a Popular Front of leftist parties aimed against monarchists, clerical supporters, and army officers. Military officers, led by **General Francisco Franco** (1892–1975) and aided by the fascist Falange movement, attempt to overthrow the republic, plunging the nation into a vicious civil war between Nationalists and Loyalists. The **Spanish Civil War** (1936–1939) becomes a test of rival ideological forces—fascism vs. communism—and a warm-up for World War II. Other than a few idealists from the democracies, the only nation willing to commit significant resources to the anti-fascist battle is the Soviet Union. Fascist forces launch aerial bombardments aimed at civilians in Madrid, Barcelona, and Guernica, a preview of the horrors to come. By 1939, Franco gains control of the nation, but only at the cost of 600,000 lives—Spain's deadliest conflict.

In the wake of the Spanish Civil War, Hitler signs the Rome-Berlin Axis with Mussolini and the Anti-Comintern Pact with Japan.

1937: Japan launches an all-out invasion of China proper, leading to its control of China's coastal cities. Though China moves inland to continue the fight, Japanese forces capture Nanking, in the process indiscriminately killing 250,000 civilians and raping thousands of women in an atrocity known as the Rape of Nanking.

1938: With Mussolini's approval, Hitler marches into his native Austria, directly incorporating it into the German Reich. In a subsequent plebiscite, the Austrian people overwhelmingly approve the annexation (*Anschluss*).

Hitler demands incorporation of 3 million Germans of the Czech Sudetenland. Czechoslovakia represents the most democratic, industrial, and strategically vital nation of Eastern Europe. Tied to France through the Little Entente and with strong defenses, Czechoslovakia seems an ideal place to stop Hitler's aggression. Nonetheless, British Prime Minister Neville Chamberlain (1869–1940) urges compromise at a four-power meeting (Britain, France, Germany, Italy). The western democracies exclude the Soviet Union and Czechoslovakia itself at the Munich Conference, which signs over the Sudetenland to Germany. Upon arriving back in Britain, Chamberlain proclaims he has achieved "peace in our time."

1939: Violating the Munich Agreement, Hitler in the spring marches into Moravia and Bohemia, creating a Czech protectorate, while making Slovakia a puppet government. In addition, Mussolini moves into Albania to establish a foothold for his *mare nostrum* ("our sea") project of controlling the Mediterranean. These actions cause a decisive shift in public opinion within the west against appeasement; however, France and Britain prove unable to win over a suspicious Soviet Union into a joint alliance against Nazi Germany.

Shocking the world, Hitler and Stalin in late August conclude the Nazi-Soviet Non-Aggression Pact, giving Hitler a free hand for his next project—an invasion of Poland to regain the Danzig corridor, which cuts off East Prussia from Germany proper. A secret protocol provides for the division of Poland, the Baltic States, and Finland between the supposedly bitter ideological enemies. A week later, Hitler invades Poland to begin World War II.

World War II, 1939–1945

The Second World War stands as the most destructive conflict in history, killing an estimated 60 million people. It involved the nations of six continents and decisively altered Europe's position in the world. As with any war, new technologies—radar, rockets, jet airplanes, atomic weapons—played a major role. Never before had the line between soldier and civilian been so blurred, with civilians and entire ethnic groups targeted for extermination. The chart below provides a general understanding of the nature and course of the conflict.[7]

7 SKILL SET
Total war's effects extend beyond the death toll and material destruction. As you read this section, apply selected examples to this prompt: "To what extent was the Second World War a turning point in the government's relation to the economy, society, and science?" In addressing this question, you will draw on the ARG, EVARG, and PER skills.

Phases of the Conflict

Phase	Goals and Strategy	Actions and Results	Assessment
Blitzkrieg, 1939–1941	*In the early phase of the war, Hitler takes the initiative and attacks Poland. The following spring, the Nazis move against Norway, the Low Countries, and France. *In its first defeat, Germany is unable to bring Britain to its knees. Without directly entering the conflict, President Franklin Roosevelt of the United States provides aid to Great Britain with the Lend-Lease Act and signs the Atlantic Charter with Winston Churchill (British PM), outlining Anglo-American war aims. *By the end of 1941, Japan's attack on the United States and Hitler's invasion of its former ally, the USSR, cements the Grand Alliance against the Rome-Tokyo-Berlin Axis powers.	*With armored divisions and aerial bombers, Hitler's *blitzkrieg* ("lightning war") defeats Poland in a matter of weeks. *Soviet troops move into the Baltic states, eastern Poland, and attack Finland. *In the Spring of 1940, Hitler secures his northern flank vis-à-vis Britain and supplies of iron ore by taking Norway. The Nazis next defeat the Low Countries and France. German forces occupy the northern two-thirds of France, allowing the creation of the collaborationist Vichy government in the south. Free French forces under Charles de Gaulle (1890–1970) continue resistance. *Under the strong leadership of Prime Minister Winston Churchill (1874–1965), Britain defeats Germany in the Battle of Britain. The German Luftwaffe loses twice the planes of the Royal Air Force (RAF). Bombing of cities by the Nazis only hardens British resistance. *Mussolini's attempted invasion in 1941 of Greece falters, drawing German forces into the Balkans. *In the largest land battle in history, Hitler invades the Soviet Union in June 1941, capturing huge swaths of territory before stalling in front of Moscow in December. *The Japanese capture French colonies in Indochina, leading the United States to cut off oil and scrap metal shipments. In retaliation, the Japanese launch the surprise attack on Pearl Harbor, drawing America into the war.	*By the end of 1941, Hitler still holds the initiative. Nazi Germany continues to dominate Europe and works toward a joint strategy with Japan to link forces in Central Asia. Churchill and Roosevelt agree to concentrate on the war in Europe, with the Pacific theater taking a back seat. *Hitler's invasion of the USSR takes Stalin by surprise and also allows for the beginning of the systematic **genocide** of Slavs, Roma, and Jews.

Phase	Goals and Strategy	Actions and Results	Assessment
Turning of the Tide, 1942–1944	*Hitler divides his armies into three groups in the Soviet Union—aimed at Leningrad (formerly St. Petersburg), Moscow, and the Caucasus oil fields. *The Japanese attack on Pearl Harbor is followed by the expansion of its empire through-out the Pacific, which reaches its height in Spring 1942. *German and Italian forces attack British forces in North Africa, threatening the Suez Canal. *In a series of counterattacks, the Allies defeat the Axis in North Africa, the Soviet Union, and in the Pacific.	*Soviet forces regroup and capture an entire German army in February 1943 at Stalingrad. At the tank Battle of Kursk, the Soviet Union decisively turns the tide and begins an inexorable advance toward Germany. *The German-Italian advance toward the Suez Canal in North Africa is stopped in July 1942 at El Alamein. An Anglo-American invasion pushes German forces under Erwin Rommel out of North Africa. *Anglo-American forces launch an invasion of Sicily and move slowly up the peninsula of Italy. Mussolini is captured by Allied forces in 1943 but rescued by German paratroopers. The Allied drive up the peninsula stalls outside Rome as German forces take up the fight. *The American naval victory at Midway deals a decisive blow to Japan's surface fleet. At Guadalcanal, the U.S. amphibious invasion blunts Japan's threat to Australia.	*By 1943, the tide turns against the Axis powers. In late 1943, the Big Three (Churchill, Roosevelt, and Stalin) meet at the Teheran Conference and agree on the unconditional surrender of the Axis powers, and the Anglo-Americans plan to open a second front in France. Before launching an amphibious assault, the United States must secure control of the seas from German submarines, accomplished by early 1944. *In the Pacific, American forces begin the strategy of "island hopping" to gain a base of operations directly against the Japanese home islands.

Phase	Goals and Strategy	Actions and Results	Assessment
End-game, 1944–1945	*Anglo-American forces establish a second front in France and along with the advance of Soviet forces, move toward the German homeland. Soviet forces divert into the Balkans to ensure Soviet control of Eastern Europe following the war. *U.S. forces close in on the Japanese home islands. Following fierce fighting, the Pacific war ends with the dropping of two atomic bombs on Hiroshima and Nagasaki.	*At the D-Day invasion of Normandy (June 1944), the United States and Britain establish a beachhead in France, which leads to the liberation of Paris by August. *Soviet forces advance toward but pause outside Warsaw in September 1944 to allow the Nazis to destroy the western-backed Polish Home Army during its effort to liberate the city, a bloody precursor to Cold War conflicts over Eastern Europe. *In the Pacific, U.S. forces retake the Philippines, capture Iwo Jima and Okinawa after fierce fighting, and begin aerial bombing of Tokyo. *Widespread targeting of German cities begins, exemplified by the fire-bombing of Dresden in February 1945. *A last-ditch German advance in Belgium (Battle of the Bulge) is turned back, and Anglo-American and Soviet forces end the war in the Germany in May 1945. *After the dropping of the atomic bombs, Japan sues for peace in September 1945.	*The combined manpower and economic potential of the Allied powers exercises a decisive influence on the course of the war. In addition, strategic errors by the Axis powers as well as the unification of numerous groups opposed to the brutal rule of the Nazis eventually works in the Allies' favor. *America's use of the first atomic weapons ends the Second World War but also marks the beginning of the **Nuclear Age** and the Cold War.

Mobilization of the Home Fronts

The Second World War required an even higher level of mobilization and sacrifice among civilians than did the First World War. Many governments centralized production, instituted rationing programs, and called on all citizens to contribute to the war effort in some way. The following are several examples of such mobilization:

   Germany: Despite the perception of Nazi efficiency and invincibility, Germany did not mobilize effectively for wartime production. Hitler was reluctant to employ women in the workforce or call on German citizens to sacrifice consumer goods, recognizing the collapse of the war effort in 1917–1918. Nazi Germany relied extensively on slave labor from conquered and occupied territories for armaments production. It was not until 1942 that Hitler appointed a young architect, Albert Speer (1905–1981), to centralize production as Minister of Armaments. Only in 1944, when the war was nearing its end, did Germany move toward full mobilization, closing down popular amusements and rationing goods. German women never did enter the work force in large numbers.

   Soviet Union: For the Soviet Union, the conflict was known as the Great Patriotic War, a fight for its very survival. Over 20 million Soviet citizens perished in the war, by far the most of any combatant. Once the Nazis had captured some of the best agricultural lands and threatened key industrial cities, the Soviets moved entire factories inland, which commenced production before the walls went up. Stalin promoted supercentralization of the economy around the war effort and reduced the already paltry production of consumer goods, allowing the USSR to win the "battle of the machines." The city of Leningrad endured a 900-day siege, its residents often surviving on mice; spring thaws revealed thousands of corpses in the streets. Women also served in the armed forces, unique among the combatants, as with the famous Night Witches fighter pilots protecting Stalingrad.

Great Britain: Great Britain effectively centralized its economy for wartime production. Almost every able-bodied adult assisted the war effort—women went into armament production and older citizens joined the Home Guard. The government created ministries to oversee and distribute fuel, food, and war supplies. In addition, citizens were encouraged to develop self-sufficiency in food production, as with Dig for Victory gardens. Citizens received ration books with coupons and received only those goods assigned to them. The shared sacrifice of rationing continued until after the war, ending only in 1951.

United States: President Roosevelt urged the United States to become the "arsenal of democracy" for the Allied powers. Though no nation was producing more tanks, planes, and ships by the end of the conflict, the United States never entered a complete wartime production footing. Though rationing was practiced, it did not reach the levels of European control, particularly with fuel consumption. After Pearl Harbor, thousands of Japanese citizens of the U.S. on the west coast were forced into internment camps for fear of their conspiring with the Japanese Empire.

Collaboration and Resistance

Europeans of occupied nations faced stark choices—to collaborate or resist. A major reason for Nazi success militarily and with genocide involved the active cooperation or apathetic acceptance of many in occupied lands. Conservatives in many nations welcomed the Nazi takeover as a solution to indigenous political problems. To assist in ruling occupied lands, Nazi Germany created puppet governments. In Norway, Vadkun Quisling lent his name, as a synonym, to those who betray their nation by assisting a foreign power's conquest. Though nominally independent, the Vichy regime in France cooperated with Nazi authorities, assisting in the Nazi Final Solution (see below). Reprisals against thousands of collaborators followed right after the armies of liberation. In the complex Balkans, the Ustashe, a nationalist and Catholic government of Croatia, assisted the Nazis in taking reprisals against Orthodox Serbs.

Anti-Nazi movements gained momentum as the tide of war turned. Resistance groups engaged in acts of sabotage and assassination, hindered production, rescued ethnic minorities, and spread anti-Nazi or nationalist propaganda. Strongly organized movements arose in France under Charles DeGaulle and in Yugoslavia under Joseph Broz Tito (1892–1980). Due to the latter's efforts, Yugoslavia became the only nation in eastern Europe that did not require the aid of the Soviet army to liberate itself from Nazi rule. The Polish council, Żegota, saved hundreds of Jews in Poland, while Denmark was able to engineer the rescue of almost all 8,000 of its Jewish population. Within Germany, a group of idealistic university students, named the White Rose, distributed pamphlets against the Nazis before being caught and executed. Conservative army officers attempted but failed to assassinate Hitler in July 1944, leading to the execution of thousands.

The Holocaust[8]

Soon after taking power, the Nazis established a network of concentration camps to punish political prisoners and other undesirables. From that point, Nazi policy moved step by step, from exclusion to concentration to extermination, or the Final Solution—the elimination of all of Europe's Jews, as well as **Roma**, Slavic intellectuals, Russian prisoners of war, Jehovah's Witnesses, and **homosexuals**. Mass killing began with the Nazi invasion of the Soviet Union in 1941; mobile killings squads, known as *Einsatzgruppen*, machine-gunned thousands and buried them in mass graves.

In 1942, top Nazi officials met at the Wannsee Conference. Led by Reinhard Heydrich (1904–1942), the head of the S.S. security office, the meeting decided on the implementation of the Final Solution to the "Jewish problem." The Nazis erected a system of death camps in

8 | THEME MUSIC
Total war requires regimentation of societies, and in the process, the individual is subsumed. This is no more true than with genocide. During the First World War, Armenians were targeted; during the Second, the Nazis took these efforts to an even higher level of industrialized murder in their policies toward Jews and other ethnic minorities. The Holocaust reveals a frightening level of political control (SP) but also the power of propaganda and racialism to create a sense of "otherness" (IS) toward a vulnerable and outsider group.

Poland—<u>Auschwitz</u>, Treblinka, and others—designed to kill thousands per day in gas chambers, their bodies destroyed in crematoria. Even as the war turned against the Nazis on the battlefield, Hitler continued to pour resources into this race war, stepping up the extermination as Allied armies approached. Only the participation of thousands of people, including those in the occupied nations, made such a massive and systematic process possible. By the end of the war, 6 million Jews had been killed (the **Holocaust**), along with another 5 million from the above categories, in the Nazi genocide.

Results of the Second World War

By 1945, much of Europe lay in ruins; some cities, like Warsaw, experienced complete devastation. The Second World War represents the lowest point for European civilization. Some of the results can be measured in numbers; others would become clear only in subsequent years.

- 60 million dead, mostly civilians
- Widespread destruction of infrastructure
- 30–50 million displaced persons (DPs) wandering the continent
- Europe's hold on its colonies nearly broken
- Traditional values questioned in postwar Europe
- Economic activity brought to a standstill
- Conditions laid for the Cold War

All analyses aside, the Second World War stands as the single largest event in the history of the human race.

Additional Resources

William S. Allen, *The Nazi Seizure of Power: The Experience of a Single German Town, 1922–1945* (rev. 1989)—A local study offering strong insights into how the Nazi party operated.

Judith Tydor Baumel and Walter Laqueur, *The Holocaust Encyclopedia* (2001)—A comprehensive and well-written resource.

Hannah Arendt, *The Origins of Totalitarianism* (rev. 1966)—Explores the meaning and development of a major political development in the 20th century; by a well-known political philosopher.

Peter Gay, *Weimar Culture: The Outsider as Insider* (rev. 2001)—A noted historian examines cultural experimentation amid a fractured political climate.

Mark Mazower, *Dark Continent: Europe's Twentieth Century* (1999)—Portrays the era as a violent clash between democracy, fascism, and communism.

Ron Rosenbaum, *Explaining Hitler: The Search for the Origins of His Evil* (1999)—A psychologist pursues various theories to explain the nature of human evil.

Gerhard Weinberg, *A World at Arms: A Global History of World War II* (rev. 2005)—Strictly for military history buffs, the most comprehensive and riveting account of the war.

www.loc.gov/exhibits/archives/—This Library of Congress site features formerly secret documents from the Soviet archives.

http://spartacus-educational.com/GERnazigermany.htm-—Spartacus site on Nazi Germany.

www.ushmm.org/—The official site of the United States Holocaust Museum in Washington, D.C.; features a searchable encyclopedia.

http://www.fallen.io/ww2/-—Fascinating video providing a statistical sense of WWII within the context of world history.

Practice MC Questions

Sigmund Freud, *Civilization and its Discontents*, James Strachey, trans. and ed. (New York: W.W. Norton & Company, 1961), p. 70.

Questions 1–4 are based on the text below.

> "Men are proud of those achievements, and have a right to be. But they seem to have observed that this newly-won power over space and time, this subjugation of the forces of nature, which is the fulfillment of a longing that goes back thousands of years, has not increased the amount of pleasurable satisfaction which they may expect from life and has not made them feel happier. From the recognition of this fact we ought to be content to conclude that power over nature is not the only precondition of human happiness, just as it is not the only goal of cultural endeavor..."
>
> Sigmund Freud, Austrian psychologist and neurologist, *Civilization and its Discontents*, 1930

1. Freud's analysis most directly reflects which of the following trends of the period?

    A. High unemployment brought about by the Great Depression

    B. Failure of the League of Nations to provide collective security

    C. Loss of confidence in human reason and the role of science

    D. The threat of violent revolution from the communist Soviet Union

2. Freud's perspective was a reaction to:

    A. Darwin's theory of natural selection.

    B. devastation and death caused by World War I.

    C. the rise of the Nazi party in Germany.

    D. women's entrance into the work force.

3. All of the following cultural developments would support Freud's perspective EXCEPT:

    A. the challenge to Newtonian physics from quantum and relativity theories.

    B. literature that emphasized the subconscious and addressed controversy.

    C. art that satirized western values and emphasized subjective experience.

    D. mass production that created a consumer culture in domestic comforts.

4. The most accurate characterization of an historical period supported by the passage is the:

    A. Clash of Ideologies.

    B. Age of Anxiety.

    C. Great Depression.

    D. Age of Totalitarianism.

Questions 5–7 are based on the photograph below.

German woman burning money for fuel, 1920s

5. Which of the following most directly caused the situation above?

   A. The rise of fascist political movements

   B. Reparations assigned to Germany at Versailles

   C. Tariff and trade policies of the United States

   D. Loss of German territory and colonies

6. The situation depicted in the photograph led to:

   A. the rise of extremist movements and ultimate failure of the Weimar Republic.

   B. a treaty between Germany and the Soviet Union to oppose western democracies.

   C. new artistic movements that satirized western values and standards of beauty.

   D. entrance of large numbers of women in the work-force to supplement family income.

7. This situation would likely have been avoided after the Second World War through all of the following EXCEPT:

   A. American financial aid and leadership.

   B. continental economic and political integration.

   C. extension of widespread social welfare benefits.

   D. adoption of centralized command economy.

> "THE HIGH CONTRACTING PARTIES,
> In order to promote international co-operation and to achieve international peace and security
> by the acceptance of obligations not to resort to war,
> by the prescription of open, just and honorable relations between nations,
> by the firm establishment of the understandings of international law as the actual rule of conduct among Governments, and
> by the maintenance of justice and a scrupulous respect for all treaty obligations in the dealings of organized peoples with one another,
> Agree to this Covenant of the League of Nations.
>
> ARTICLE 10.
> The Members of the League undertake to respect and preserve as against external aggression the territorial integrity and existing political independence of all Members of the League. In case of any such aggression or in case of any threat or danger of such aggression the Council shall advise upon the means by which this obligation shall be fulfilled."
>
> Charter of the League of Nations, 1919

8. The charter most directly reflects the influence of:

   A. the conflicting goals of the victors at Versailles.

   B. the idealistic vision of American President Wilson.

   C. French aims to punish and disarm Germany.

   D. fear of Soviet communism spreading across Europe.

9. Which the following most affected the success of the goals indicated by the charter?

   A. The onset of the Great Depression and widespread unemployment

   B. A loss of confidence in western values and aesthetic standards

   C. Weakness of the new democracies in central and eastern Europe

   D. Lack of participation of major powers such as the United States

10. Which of the following actions in the 1930s most directly undermined the provision of Article 10 of the charter?

   A. Agreeing to the rearmament of Nazi Germany and fascist Italy

   B. Allowing fascist powers to absorb territory from League members

   C. Excluding the Soviet Union from membership in the League until 1934

   D. Depending on American capital for the functioning of the European economy

See Chapter 18 for answers and explanations.

Short-Answer Question with Sample and Commentary

A. Explain ONE difference between absolute monarchies of the 17th and 18th centuries and totalitarian regimes of the 20th century.

B. Choose TWO of the regimes below and explain ONE way in which each did OR did <u>not</u> fulfill the theory of totalitarianism.

- Fascist Italy (1922–1943)
- Nazi Germany (1933–1945)
- Soviet Union under Stalin (1928–1945)
  (Skills: Comparison, Argumentation, and Use of Evidence)

There were many differences between the absolute monarchies of the 17th and 18th centuries and the totalitarian dictators of the 20th century. Louis XIV was an absolute monarch, and he tried to control religion in France by taking away the right of Huguenots to worship in their Protestant ways. However, totalitarian dictators didn't really care about religion and made no policies related to it. Mussolini of Italy wasn't really a strong dictator, certainly not as much as Hitler and Stalin. Though he tried to increase his population through incentives and to enforce a reproductive role for women, the population didn't actually increase and it also created opposition to Mussolini. The story in the Soviet Union was much different. Stalin focused all of his attention on building up the military and invading countries around him, like when he took over Eastern Europe during the Cold War. This shows how his totalitarian control went beyond his own country and into others.

Unfortunately, this response offers underdeveloped analysis along with some errors. The student did not earn the point for Part A, as the statement regarding religious policies is incorrect. Both Hitler and Mussolini attempted to replace loyalty to religion with loyalty to the state or party. Also, each fascist regime signed agreements with the Catholic Church. Further, the ideology of the Soviet Union was officially atheistic and openly hostile to organized religion, viewed as a prop of the tsarist system. In Part B, the student earns a point for the correct explanation of the failure of Mussolini's population policy; however, her analysis of Stalin is outside the specified time period and does not relate directly to the principles of totalitarian rule, as many previous (Russian) regimes have pursued territorial expansion. Short-answer responses may be brief, as is this one, but this one would benefit from further explanation, as well as indicating which parts of the prompt are being addressed. Score: 1

16 The Cold War and European Recovery

Looking across Europe in 1945, one saw a civilization in ruins. Europeans suffered through one of the coldest winters on record in 1945–1946; Germans called this time their *Stunde Null* or zero hour. Destruction and devastation created a power vacuum in Europe, into which rushed the new contending superpowers of the United States and the Soviet Union. Due to fundamental economic and political differences and a cycle of action/reaction by each side, by 1947 the two superpowers were locked in a Cold War that divided Western from Eastern Europe. Competition between the superpowers decisively shaped the contrasting development of the two regions: the West toward economic recovery and integration and the East under Soviet domination and ultimately rebellion. In the final analysis, Europe rose like a phoenix from the ashes after 1945, but its recovery has been marked by fits and starts, successes and failures. By 1991, a new era opened with the collapse of communism and the Soviet Union itself, an opportunity for the continent to work toward a European identity that combined East and West.

Key In Chapter 16 covers the following KCs from the Course Description:

- **KC 4.1** Origins and nature of the Cold War, including impact on Western and Eastern Europe

- **KC 4.1** The movement toward economic and political integration, with continuing issues of nationalism

- **KC 4.1** Causes, course, and consequences of decolonization

- **KC 4.2** Postwar economic recovery in Western Europe

- **KC 4.2** Soviet control of Eastern Europe and the collapse of communism

---

The Cold War, 1943–1991

Origins of the Conflict

The Grand Alliance between the Anglo-American powers and the Soviet Union had always been a marriage of convenience; it was a relationship based on a battle against a common enemy—the Nazis. Since the Bolshevik Revolution, relations between the new Soviet Union and the west had been strained: (1) the Allies sent assistance to the White Army during the Russian Civil War; (2) the United States did not recognize the Soviet Union until 1933; (3) the western democracies excluded the Soviet Union from interwar diplomacy while appeasing Hitler; and (4) Stalin and Hitler joined in dividing Poland to initiate the Second World War.

During World War II, the so-called Big Three (Stalin, Churchill, Roosevelt) met several times to forge common policies; these meetings also revealed strains in the alliance. In February 1945 at Yalta, just months from victory, the Big Three met to discuss the layout of postwar Europe. Soviet armies stood within 40 miles of Berlin and dominated most of Eastern Europe. This reality determined much of the Anglo-American posture toward Stalin, though Roosevelt tended to see himself as the mediator between the more *Realpolitik*-oriented Churchill and Stalin. The parties agreed to the Declaration on Liberated Europe, which promised national self-determination and free elections in Eastern Europe. Stalin was especially concerned with controlling postwar Poland, which territorially was moved 300 miles west at the expense of Germany and to the benefit of the Soviet Union. As for Germany, the three leaders agreed it must be disarmed and denazified, though they differed over Stalin's proposal for its complete dismemberment and the extraction of $20 billion in reparations. Finally, the Big Three agreed to create the **United Nations** in hopes of resolving future security issues. Despite the agreements, it soon became clear that the Anglo-Americans and Soviets interpreted their decisions differently, particularly free elections. Later critics viewed Roosevelt's position as a sell-out of Eastern Europe in order to gain Soviet support for the continuing war against Japan.

When the Allies next met at Potsdam in July 1945, the war in Europe had ended. In the interim, Roosevelt had died and his successor, Harry Truman (1884–1972), harbored suspicion of Stalin's intentions. Also, during the conference, Labour leader Clement Attlee was voted into office as prime minister, replacing Churchill. The Allies agreed to hold war crimes trials of the top Nazi leaders at Nuremberg, divide Germany into four occupation zones, and provide reparations for the rebuilding of the Soviet Union. However, disagreements between the United States and Soviet Union deepened over Poland and other Eastern European states. When the United States abruptly ended aid to the Soviet Union (but not Great Britain) in Spring 1945 and developed its monopoly on atomic weapons, Soviet suspicions of American intentions mounted. By 1947, a series of disagreements led to a fracturing of the wartime alliance and open if often restrained conflict between the former allies.

Nature of the Conflict[1]

The Cold War played out as a complex, multipronged worldwide competition between the superpowers of the United States and Soviet Union.

Political: The United States and Soviet Union vied to spread their respective political influence throughout the world. Beginning in Europe, the Cold War soon spread to Asia, and eventually to the Middle East, Latin America, and Africa. In some cases, direct control was exercised, as with the Soviet sphere of influence in Eastern Europe; in others, indirect economic control, as with U.S. policy in Latin America, proved sufficient to maintain bloc solidarity. The system of Liberal democracy and free markets became known as the First World, the Soviet system of planned economies and one-party rule as the Second World, and those nonaligned nations refusing to choose sides as the Third World, a term often used to signify less-developed nations. Both sides developed alliances to maintain collective security in their blocs. In response to the Berlin Crisis of 1948–1949, the United States entered into its first peacetime alliance, the **North Atlantic Treaty Organization (NATO)**, later followed by CENTO in the Middle East and SEATO in Southeast Asia. When the West rearmed Germany in 1955, the Soviets responded with the **Warsaw Pact** to defend the Eastern bloc.

With its expressed goal of spreading world revolution, the Soviet Union created fear among the western capitalist and democratic nations. During the late 1940s and early 1950s, President Truman relied on the expertise of former diplomat and historian George Kennan (1904-2005) to develop the strategy of containment. Containment employed a variety of techniques—war, diplomacy, economic aid, intelligence, funding rebel groups—to halt the spread of communism around the world. To support its new international presence, the U.S. Congress passed the National Security Act (1947), which created the National Security Council (NSC, also with a National Security Advisor), the Central Intelligence Agency (CIA), and reorganized the Department of Defense. Numerous novels and films have since reflected the cloak-and-dagger spy battles between the CIA and Soviet KGB to gain the upper hand.

Military: Nuclear weapons technology led to an **arms race** between the two superpowers. The Soviet Union exploded its first atomic weapon in 1949, and both nations developed the hydrogen bomb after 1952. Under the leadership of Nikita Khrushchev, the Soviet Union in 1957 launched its first satellite—*Sputnik*—bringing the arms race to outer space. Fearing a so-called missile gap, the United States hurriedly worked to develop rocket technology, culminating with Intercontinental Ballistic Missiles (ICBMs) capable of reaching the Soviet Union from silos in America or Europe. By the 1970s, both sides combined boasted about 25,000 long-range nuclear weapons. Moreover, each side developed nuclear submarines with the capacity to fire missiles from the depths of the ocean, forming a nuclear triad—on land, in the air, and under the sea.

An ironic consequence of the Nuclear Age was the doctrine of Mutual Assured Destruction (MAD): neither side had an incentive to launch a first strike because it was sure to incur unacceptable casualties from the opponent's missiles. Therefore, "missiles that kill people" kept the peace by precluding a nuclear strike, but "missiles that kill other missiles" (Anti-Ballistic Missiles—ABMs) threatened to upset the nuclear balance by providing an incentive to launch a first strike and were thus banned by the superpowers in a 1972 agreement. During the height of the Cold War, the Soviet Union may have spent as much as 25–30% of its gross domestic product on military expenditures, a massive commitment of resources for a modern society and a tremendous drain on its economy.

Economic: Perhaps never in history had one nation so dominated the world economy as did the United States at the end of the Second World War. Fully 80% of the world's trade passed through American hands, and 50% of the world's productive capacity was American. The United States thus stood in the unique position of helping to rebuild the world economy, which it wished to do by promoting free markets and access to American goods. To pursue this goal, the United States extended aid to Europe in the form of the **Marshall Plan** (1947), aid that the Soviet Union prohibited its Eastern European satellites from accepting, viewing the plan as a capitalist plot aimed at the Soviet sphere. In response, the Soviet Union organized the Eastern bloc around the rival **Council for Mutual Economic Assistance (COMECON)**, an effort to create a specialization of production among its satellites.

As the Cold War expanded, the United States often exploited the power of its multinational corporations to control the economies of underdeveloped nations, particularly in Latin America. For example, when a socialist government was elected to power in 1954 in Guatemala with the intention of nationalizing U.S. fruit companies that dominated that nation's banana industry, the U.S. government engineered a CIA-backed coup deposing the government. Many such underdeveloped nations and former colonies sympathized with the Soviet critique of capitalism and adopted state planning to promote internal development and gain control of resources vis-à-vis the former colonial powers of the West. Both superpowers often extended aid in strategic regions with the goal of gaining allies.

Ideological: At its heart, the Cold War represented a battle over rival views of the world, a combat of antagonistic ideologies. Each side hoped to win hearts and minds with propaganda. In 1946, Winston Churchill fired the first salvo in the war with a speech in Fulton, Missouri, when he announced that an **Iron Curtain** had descended across the continent of Europe, dividing the free peoples of the West from the oppressed peoples of the East. The United States established the Voice of America and Radio Free Europe to broadcast messages from "free and prosperous citizens" across the Iron Curtain. Internally, the United States in the 1950s plunged into a Red Scare, or McCarthyism (named after Wisconsin Senator Joseph McCarthy), aimed at real and imaginary communist enemies in the upper reaches of government and in Hollywood.

Though Soviet propaganda tended to be more heavy-handed, it also aimed to control public opinion within its bloc. In 1948 the Communist Information Bureau (Cominform) was created to replace the old Comintern suspended during World War II. The notion that each side struggled for a cherished way of life—the future of civilization itself—added intensity to the Cold War not fully captured by traditional conceptions of geopolitical maneuvering.

Chronological Development of the Cold War

This section is designed to suggest the scope and duration of the Cold War. It is divided chronologically into phases, with brief explanations of the main areas of conflict. Consider it a supplement to the conceptual overview above.[2]

Beginnings, 1945–1953 *The Cold War began with mutual suspicions related to the status of Germany, control of Eastern Europe, nuclear weapons, and eventually the spread of rivalry into Asia.*

1945: Germany is divided into four zones of occupation—British, American, Soviet, and French. Additionally, the city of Berlin (entirely within the Soviet zone) is divided into four occupation zones. Germany and, more specifically, Berlin become the epicenter of the emerging Cold War.

2 THEME MUSIC
The Cold War played out on a global scale, facilitated decolonization, and forced world conflicts into an artificial bipolar divide between capitalism vs. command economy, liberal democracy vs. communism. Europe's relationship to the rest of the world was redefined as it sat uneasily between the two superpowers (INT).

The United States explodes atomic bombs over Hiroshima and Nagasaki in Japan, ending the Pacific War but also initiating the **Nuclear Age**.

Soviet troops occupy all of the nations of Eastern Europe except Albania and Yugoslavia. At first, coalition governments of socialist/communist parties rule along with democratic and/or free market parties.

1946: Winston Churchill delivers his **Iron Curtain** speech.

1947: The United States extends Marshall Plan aid to the nations of Europe to be funneled through the Office of European Economic Cooperation (OEEC) rather than to each nation individually.

Fearing the spread of communism in Greece and Turkey, President Truman offers financial assistance to any nation facing "insurgencies by armed minorities." Along with the Marshall Plan, this Truman Doctrine establishes the early outlines of a new interventionist approach by the United States in European affairs.

In most Eastern European nations, Western-backed parties are pushed out of power, while in Italy, elections vault the pro-U.S. Christian Democrats to leadership while limiting the influence of the usually strong Socialist and Communist parties.

1948: Concerned over economic conditions in Germany and Soviet reparations policies, the United States, Britain, and France merge their three occupied German zones and introduce a new *Deutschmark* currency. In response, the Soviet Union imposes the Berlin Blockade, cutting the western part of the city off from rail and auto traffic, threatening to starve it out. Rather than confront the Soviets directly, President Truman begins the Berlin Airlift, an almost year-long enterprise designed to supply the basic needs of West Berliners.

Noncommunists are kicked out of the Czechoslovakian government in a coup. The leader of the noncommunists, Jan Masyrk, is later found dead outside his window, either a suicide or murder.

1949: Stalin ends the Berlin Blockade, and the division of Germany becomes formal with the creation of West Germany and East Germany. Under American leadership, Western Europe forms a mutual defense system known as NATO to defend against future Soviet provocations.

Communists under Mao Zedong (1890–1976) gain control of the Chinese mainland, driving the Nationalists onto the island of Taiwan. In addition, the Soviet Union explodes its first atomic bomb. These two events spur the Red Scare in the United States.

1950: Communist North Korea invades the Western-backed government of South Korea. Taking advantage of the Soviet boycott of the Security Council, President Truman builds a UN coalition to combat the invasion and signify the American commitment to the policy of containment. The Korean War drags on for 3 years and involves fighting between the United States and China.

1953: Joseph Stalin's death opens a new era in Cold War diplomacy. The Korean War ends with the division into North Korea and South Korea at the 38th parallel.

Coexistence and Confrontation, 1953–1970 *This period begins with an effort at peaceful coexistence, but rivalries reheat over Berlin, control of the vital Middle East, and Soviet intrusion into America's perceived sphere of influence in Latin America, which almost bring the superpowers to nuclear war in 1962.*

1954: Vietnamese resistance fighters under Communist leader Ho Chi Minh (1890–1969) defeat French colonial forces at Dien Bien Phu, leading to Vietnam's division along the 17th parallel between communist North Vietnam and Western-backed South Vietnam.

The United States supports a coup against socialist Guatemalan leader Jacobo Arbenz Guzman to prevent the nationalization of land owned by U.S. fruit companies.

1955: NATO agrees to rearm West Germany, leading to the Soviet creation of the **Warsaw Pact** alliance in Eastern Europe.

Secretary of State John Foster Dulles announces the American policy of massive retaliation, threatening an all-out nuclear attack in response to Communist aggression anywhere in the world.

A summit in Geneva, Switzerland, between President Dwight Eisenhower (1890–1969) and Khrushchev leads to the evacuation of forces from Austria and its neutralization.

1956: Soviet leader **Nikita Khrushchev** (1894–1971) gives a secret speech to the 20th Party Congress of the Communist Party of the Soviet Union condemning the excesses of the Stalin period and signals his goal of **de-Stalinization**. Khrushchev also suggests the possibility of peaceful coexistence between the capitalist West and communism.

Taking their cue from Khrushchev, the leadership of the Polish and Hungarian Communist Parties begins a liberalization of economic and intellectual life. The Hungarian revolt goes too far for Khrushchev and is crushed by Soviet forces.

1957: Soviet leaders announce the launching of the first satellite into outer space—*Sputnik*. The United States follows with the creation of the National Aeronautics and Space Agency (NASA), indicating the beginning of the space race.

1959: Leftist forces under Fidel Castro (1926–) overthrow the U.S.-backed government of Cuba. Castro nationalizes the sugar industry, seizes American assets, and establishes strong ties with the Soviet Union.

1960: Soviet forces shoot down a U-2 spy plane over Russian territory, forcing the United States to recant previous statements denying such flights. The incident forces the cancellation of a planned superpower summit.

1961: A U.S.-backed invasion of Cuba by exiled Cubans ends disastrously with the capture of such forces at the Bay of Pigs.

Another crisis over control of the city of Berlin leads to the erection of the Berlin Wall by East Berlin to prevent its citizens from escaping to the West.

1962: Soviet plans to install nuclear missiles in Cuba lead to a 2-week crisis, pushing the world to the brink of nuclear war. The Cuban Missile Crisis ends when President John F. Kennedy (1917–1963) assures Khrushchev that the United States will not invade Cuba in exchange for the removal of the missiles.

1963: The superpowers agree to the creation of a Hot Line establishing direct contact in times of crisis. In addition, the two sides, along with Great Britain, agree to the Limited Nuclear Test Ban Treaty, prohibiting the testing of nuclear weapons except underground.

1964: America's commitment to fighting in Vietnam, between the communist north and U.S.-backed south, deepens with the Gulf of Tonkin Resolution, allowing President Lyndon Johnson (1908–1973) greater latitude to involve American forces.

1967: Israel attacks its Arab neighbors and seizes the West Bank, Sinai Peninsula, and Golan Heights. In this Six-Day War, the United States backs Israel while the Soviets support Arab forces.

1968: Soviet forces crush the Czechoslovakian reform movement, known as the Prague Spring, and announce the Brezhnev Doctrine, whereby a perceived threat to socialism in one nation is taken as a threat to socialism everywhere.

Détente, 1970–1978 *A French term, détente means an easing of tensions. During the decade, the superpowers work to normalize relations between their two rival blocs and to accept the permanent existence of the rival side.*

1970: The Treaty of Moscow between West Germany and the Soviet Union establishes diplomatic relations between the two nations and formalizes the split between East and West Germany. Soon after, both nations are admitted to the United Nations.[3]

1972: Soviet and American negotiators agree to the first limitations on nuclear weapons, the Strategic Arms Limitation Talks (SALT I), which also recognizes the nuclear parity that exists between the superpowers. In addition, both sides agree to an Anti-Ballistic Missile (ABM) Treaty to reduce the potential for a first-strike launch.

President Richard Nixon (1913–1994) becomes the first U.S. president to visit the People's Republic (Communist) of China, which leads to formal diplomatic relations later in the decade.

1973: The United States removes its last major military units from fighting in Vietnam. In 1975, North Vietnam captures Saigon, the South Vietnamese capital, ending the war with Vietnam's unification under communism.

The Yom Kippur War between Israel and its Arab neighbors once again almost brings the two superpowers to blows.

3 EXAMPLE BASE

Use the examples in this section as evidence in pursuit of the interpretative questions posed above. Only those in bold are required knowledge; however, the illustrative examples may serve as a fodder for your conclusions.

1975: Signed by all nations of Europe, including the United States, Canada, and USSR, the Helsinki Accords bring a formal end to the Second World War by acknowledging existing national boundaries. In addition, human rights provisions open the door for dissent within the Soviet Union and in the Eastern European satellites. This represents the height of détente.

Revival and End, 1979–1991 *The period of détente ends with a series of actions by both the United States and Soviet Union that increase Cold War tensions. However, Mikhail Gorbachev's accession to leadership of the Soviet Union helps bring an end to the Cold War by the late 1980s.*

1979: To prop up a communist regime on its border, the Soviet Union invades Afghanistan, bogging it down in a Vietnam-style quagmire until 1988. In response, the U.S. Senate refuses to ratify the SALT II agreement to limit nuclear weapons, and President Jimmy Carter (1924–) limits grain shipments to the Soviet Union and boycotts the 1980 Olympics in Moscow. Further, the United States provides aid to Afghan freedom fighters known as the *mujahadeen*.

1983: President Ronald Reagan (1911–2004) denounces the Soviet Union as the "evil empire" and pledges to install intermediate range nuclear weapons in Europe. World concerns grow over the proliferation of nuclear weapons and the dangers of nuclear power.

A Korean commercial jet strays into Soviet airspace and is shot down by Soviet forces, killing all 269 people aboard.

1985: Mikhail Gorbachev (1931–) becomes the new Soviet leader and works toward an internal reform of the Soviet system that requires a reduction in Cold War tensions.

1987: After several inconclusive superpower summits, Reagan and Gorbachev agree to the Intermediate-Range Nuclear Force (INF) Treaty, which eliminates an entire class of weapons on European soil.

1988: Gorbachev withdraws the final Soviet troops from Afghanistan.

Reagan and Gorbachev sign the Strategic Arms Reduction Treaty (START), which reduces the number of long-range missiles on both sides.

1989: Communist governments in Eastern Europe collapse as Gorbachev refuses to employ Soviet troops to defeat the peoples' revolutions. The **Fall of Communism** results in the end of Germany's division (by 1990) and the movement toward democracy and free markets in the former Soviet satellites.

1991: After a failed coup by communist hardliners fails, the **Soviet Union collapses** into its member national republics. Soviet President Mikhail Gorbachev resigns with the official end of the USSR.

International Conflicts Since 1990

With the end of the Cold War, the existential threat of widespread nuclear war seemed to abate; however, because the bipolar nature of Cold War diplomacy tended to repress nationalist and religious conflicts in both Europe and globally, these have come back to the fore since the collapse of communism.

The first opportunity to test the post-Cold War diplomatic order was the Gulf War. In 1990, Iraqi forces under command of leader Saddam Hussein (1937–2006) invaded Kuwait, claiming it as a historic province of Iraq. Ironically, the United States lent support to Hussein during the brutal Iran-Iraq War (1980–1988), which followed Iran's Islamist revolution (against the U.S.-backed government of the Shah) and subsequent hostage crisis of U.S. embassy personnel. President George H.W. Bush (1924–) pledged that the aggressive action would not stand and secured agreement from both the Soviet Union and China on the UN Security Council for a multinational force to liberate Kuwait. With minimal casualties, the U.S. Desert Storm Operation of 1991 defeated Iraqi forces in Kuwait but left Saddam Hussein in power.

Following the Second World War, the United States became more deeply involved in the Middle East, driven by securing strategic oil supplies and supporting its Israeli ally. The presence of American military bases and troops in many undemocratic Middle Eastern nations, as well as U.S. support for Israel, inspired terrorist incidents beginning in the 1970s, such as the Palestine

Liberation Organization's (PLO) killing of the Israeli Olympic team in 1972 in Munich and the hijacking of western airliners. Such terrorist incidents caused concern for the U.S. government but posed no direct threat to United States itself.

The situation changed when al-Qaeda—a terrorist group supported by the radical Islamist Taliban regime in Afghanistan—crashed hijacked commercial jets into the World Trade Center in New York City and the Pentagon in Washington, D.C., on September 11, 2001, causing the deaths of 3,000 people. In response, President George W. Bush (1946–) pledged a war on terror. With broad international support, American forces successfully deposed the Taliban regime in Afghanistan, and eventually captured or killed many top leaders of al-Qaeda, including eventually Osama bin Laden. However, the Bush administration's subsequent War in Iraq (2003), based on the presumption of Saddam Hussein's possession of weapons of mass destruction, won only limited support among its European allies and caused a rift in the alliance. Though President Obama (1961–) moved to bring both wars to a close, the Middle East has continued to draw the attention of the Western alliance, whether through encouragement of the Arab Spring (2011) or combatting the efforts of the Islamic State of Syria (ISIS) to establish an Islamist state in the region as well as launch terrorist attacks on European and American soil.

The Soviet Union: From Superpower to Collapse

Cold War Repression Under Stalin

Stalin continued his dictatorship in the Soviet Union during and especially after World War II. Rigid controls over economic, intellectual, and cultural life resulted in millions of persons being sent to forced labor camps (gulags) for deviations from the official line. During Stalin's final years, the KGB (secret police) increased in power; right before Stalin's death, official anti-Semitism led to fabricated charges against a group of Jewish doctors accused of poisoning Kremlin officials. Fortunately for the accused, Stalin died before a new round of executions and imprisonment could commence in the so-called doctor's plot.

Khrushchev's Abortive Reforms

After a short period of collective leadership in the USSR, **Nikita Khrushchev** emerged as the Secretary General of the Communist Party of the Soviet Union (CPSU). Khrushchev secured his leadership by distancing himself from his predecessor, initiating a campaign of **de-Stalinization** with a 1956 speech. Soviet intellectual life thawed, as writers were encouraged to publish the excesses of the Stalinist period. One example is Alexander Solzhenitsyn's grim depiction of the gulag system, *One Day in the Life of Ivan Denisovich* (1962). Khrushchev dramatically stated his goal of surpassing the U.S. economy by 1980 with the phrase "We will bury you." Despite Soviet space successes like *Sputnik*, Khrushchev's decentralization of the economy and focus on consumer goods failed to come close to overtaking American productivity. More importantly, Khrushchev failed to fix the woeful productivity of Soviet collective farms; his so-called virgin lands project of opening Soviet Central Asian lands to cultivation did little to address the bureaucratic structure of Soviet agriculture. Khrushchev found his way blocked by party bureaucrats, known as *apparatchiki*, who feared the effect of his reforms on their power. Along with his provocative foreign policy failures over Cuba, Berlin, and the break with Communist China, Khrushchev's incomplete reforms led to his downfall in 1964.

Nuclear Parity and Domestic Drift: Brezhnev

Soviet life in the era of Leonid Brezhnev (1907–1982) reminds one of the Potemkin villages in the era of Catherine the Great (see Chapter 9)—a glittering façade of power to the outside world that hides the rot within. Party leaders specifically selected Brezhnev for his status quo credentials; his goal was "no experimentation," that is, to maintain the influence of the army, *apparatchiki*, and state-owned industrial enterprises. Brezhnev did preside over an important diplomatic achievement—nuclear parity with the United States by the 1972 SALT agreement. In addition, Soviet leaders could boast of a formidable space program, scientific community, and Olympic athletic success. With the Brezhnev Doctrine (see below), the Soviet Union stood poised to maintain a sphere of influence on its borders without American interference. However, these successes could not compensate for the staggering Soviet economy. Successive Five-Year Plans barely met established quotas and hid the fact that in an emerging computer age, the nation continued to focus on production of heavy industry—tractors, steel, construction equipment. Economic life drifted amid a lack of consumer goods and poor productivity. Many workers failed to show up for work (absenteeism), and alcoholism became rife. Important indicators of social health, such as infant mortality, suicide, and life expectancy, experienced troubling reversals.

Gorbachev: *Perestroika* and *Glasnost*

Soviet leadership in the late 1970s and early 1980s resembled a geriatric ward. Following Brezhnev, two aged leaders maintained the status quo. When Mikhail Gorbachev was chosen General Secretary of the CPSU in 1985, he came as breath of fresh air to the Soviet Union. At 54, he was the youngest member of the Politburo. Gorbachev recognized the problems within both the Soviet economy and social life; he hoped to save the Soviet system by creating "socialism with a human face." The centerpiece of the Gorbachev's reform movement was *perestroika*, or restructuring, of the centrally planned Soviet economy. Gorbachev wanted to produce more consumer goods and to decentralize control of the inefficient state-owned enterprises. The new Soviet leader underestimated the entrenched power of Soviet bureaucrats and soon added another fundamental principle to his reform—*glasnost*, or openness. Soviet citizens were encouraged to discuss openly the failures of the past; an underground press, *samizdat*, came out into the open, as Gorbachev allowed Soviet Jews to emigrate and promoted religious freedom. Nuclear disaster at Chernobyl in 1986 actually strengthened Gorbachev's hand by demonstrating the vital need for Soviet modernization and reform.[4]

By 1988, Gorbachev found himself in an increasingly difficult position, pinched between hard-line defenders of the old system and advocates of free-market capitalism. Agriculture presents a good example of the Soviet leader's dilemma. Gorbachev allowed small farmers to lease plots from the government collectives, but the state remained the sole owner of the land. As a result, commercial agriculture never developed, and productivity remained low. Politically, Gorbachev moved power from the party over to state institutions, as with the creation of a Congress of People's Deputies, which then elected him president. Dramatic by any standard, these reforms nonetheless proved inadequate either to save the old system or create a new one. Ironically, as approval for these measures plummeted in the Soviet Union, Gorbachev's reputation and celebrity in the West skyrocketed as the liberator of Eastern Europe and an ender of the Cold War.

Reformers and defenders of the old system both began to lose faith in Gorbachev. Many reformers turned to the newly elected maverick president of the Russian republic—Boris Yeltsin (1931–2007)—who had been expelled from the CPSU by Gorbachev in 1987. More importantly, *perestroika* and *glasnost* had inadvertently sparked independence movements by the many ethnic minorities within the Soviet empire, particularly among the Baltic republics. Gorbachev veered between threats of force and conciliation to prevent the break-up of the USSR. However, the Soviet leader worked out a union treaty with the 15 republics (except for the Baltic States and Georgia) for greater autonomy within the USSR to take effect in August 1991. Before the treaty could be implemented, communist hard-liners attempted to overthrow Gorbachev. The August 1991 coup failed miserably due to lack of planning, popular resistance, and the opposition of Yeltsin. Gorbachev returned to power, but not for long; Yeltsin outlawed the Communist Party in Russia, and the Soviet Union was voted out of existence by the federation council of the various republics. The entity that had coincided with and helped define the turbulent 20th century no longer existed.

4 SKILL SET

Mikhail Gorbachev represents one of the most significant figures of the latter part of your course. By the end of his political career, Gorbachev drew more respect from outside than inside the (former) Soviet Union. As a way to consider the long- and short-term problems of the USSR, take a position on this question (ARG and EVARG): To what extent was Mikhail Gorbachev responsible for the collapse of the Soviet Union?

Russia Since 1991

Russia's history since 1991 has been a troubled one. Following the collapse of the USSR in 1991, 12 republics agreed to form the loose Commonwealth of Independent States (CIS). Like Gorbachev, Yeltsin veered back and forth with reforms. Pushing for a strong presidential republic, Yeltsin in the spring of 1993 dissolved the legislature and called for new elections. Hard-liners in the legislature refused to leave the building, leading to a violent clash that left 100 dead. Though Yeltsin won the battle and his new constitution took effect, public support for reform flagged, as shown by the return of Communists and Soviet nationalists to the new Duma. In addition, Yeltsin from 1994 to 1996 bogged the now-decrepit Russian army down in an ethnic conflict with separatist Chechnya, a small Islamic enclave. The conflict involved atrocities on both sides, but Russia was able to restore nominal control of the breakaway republic.

Before his resignation in 1999, Yeltsin sponsored the rise of his handpicked successor as president, Vladimir Putin (1952–). Putin has worked to advance Russia's independent position in world affairs, promote economic development, and centralize state authority. Putin's presidency has been marked by an increase in state control of the media and repression of internal opponents of his regime. However, Putin retains high approval ratings internally for restoring Russian power, as with his annexation of Crimea (from Ukraine) in 2014, hosting the Sochi Olympics (also in 2014), and defying U.S. diplomacy in the Middle East and elsewhere. These tensions have led some to characterize Putin's presidency as fomenting a new cold war between Russia and the western alliance.

Eastern Europe: In the Soviet Shadow

Stalinization

After suffering two invasions by Germany in 30 years and in keeping with its perennial expansion, Russia under Stalin was determined to create a buffer zone to its west. Disagreements over the fate of Eastern Europe helped precipitate the Cold War between the superpowers. By 1948, all but Albania and Yugoslavia lay firmly within the Soviet sphere of influence. To combat the Marshall Plan, the Soviet Union developed its own framework for integration in the East known as COMECON. Communism and socialism in Eastern Europe found wide appeal after the war anyway, but Stalin wanted to assure himself of pro-Soviet communist regimes on his western border and so forced purge trials of any independent-minded homegrown leftists. Therefore, the Soviet Union imposed Stalinist regimes on the Eastern European satellites, a trend that involved the following to greater or lesser degrees:

- *One-party police states*—Once the Cold War broke open, all political parties but the Communist Party and its direct allies were banned. Eastern European states closely controlled speech, culture, and religious expression.

- *Planned economies*—The Soviet model of centralized control via party bureaucrats was exported to Eastern Europe. Moreover, the USSR assigned specific economic roles to the various nations, with, for example, East Germany focusing on heavy industry, Romania on oil production, and Bulgaria on agricultural products.

- *Collectivization of agriculture*—During the interwar period, most Eastern European states redistributed land to peasants in smaller plots. The Soviet Union now reversed this trend by requiring its satellites to collectivize agriculture and establish communal farms; in the more western-oriented nations such as Poland and Hungary, this process did not include all farmland.

These policies fomented discontent among key segments of the populations of Eastern Europe—small farmers, the middle class, nationalists, and intellectuals. However, the ever-present fear of Stalinist repression kept a tight seal on such discontent.

De-Stalinization, Revolt, and the Brezhnev Doctrine

Stalin's death in 1953 prompted revolts and hopes for change. East Berliners toppled statues of Stalin, but their revolt was quickly suppressed. A more momentous push for change came with Khrushchev's official policy of **de-Stalinization** in 1956. Several Eastern European states took the Soviet policy as their cue to liberalize their own economic and political systems.

Communist leaders in Poland and Hungary wished to establish a system more in keeping with national traditions. Polish party officials turned to reformer Wladyslaw Gomulka (1905–1982), who halted collectivization of agriculture, relaxed control over the economy, and improved relations with Poland's strong Catholic Church. Soviet leaders warned the Polish leaders that their reform had gone too far, but Gomulka stayed in power by promising allegiance to the Warsaw Pact and because the Soviets faced a bigger issue in Hungary.

Events in Poland sparked protests in Hungary. The Communist Party replaced hard-line leaders with the former Prime Minister Imre Nagy (1896–1958), who had previously been expelled from the party for "deviation." Nagy freed political prisoners and worked toward liberalizing Hungary's political and economic system. When Nagy announced Hungary's withdrawal from the Warsaw Pact and called on the world to recognize his nation's neutrality, the Soviets forced the Hungarian Communist Party to depose Nagy and appoint János Kádar (1912–1989) as the new leader. Soviet tanks now rolled in and crushed the uprising, at the cost of about 100,000 lives. Over 200,000 Hungarians fled the country, and Nagy himself was captured and hanged. The message was clear: reform must not threaten the Soviet sphere of influence.

Despite the failed promise of de-Stalinization and the imposition of even harsher Soviet controls after 1956, many Eastern European satellites continued to desire greater autonomy. As part of a worldwide youth protest movement, Czechoslovakia attempted to liberalize its communist system during the Prague Spring of 1968. Reformers within the Communist Party replaced its Stalinist leaders with the Slovak reformer Alexander Dubček (1921–1992). Dubček encouraged a new spirit of openness and promised the relaxing of political controls, all in an effort to create a humane socialism. Though Dubček reassured Soviet leaders of his nation's commitment to the Warsaw Pact, he ultimately could not control the euphoria of the movement in Czechoslovakia and the concern of the surrounding Warsaw Pact leaders, who feared the spread of reform to their own nations. In August 1968, Soviet troops ended the reform and declared in the Brezhnev Doctrine that deviations from the socialist line would not be tolerated. As with Hungary, the United States tacitly accepted the Soviet action.

The Fall of Communism, 1989–1990

The collapse of communism during 1989–1990 represents one of the most momentous and surprising events of the 20th century. Reasons for the collapse divide into 1) propellant forces *toward* change and 2) the *lack* of restraining forces *against* it. By the 1980s, the economies of the Eastern European states were losing ground to the more technological Western Europe. Also, high oil prices and inefficient state-owned enterprises had created huge government debts. Politically, the desire for national autonomy, religious freedom, and political rights lingered under the surface of passive obedience. Given these conditions, the presence of the Soviet army *and* the satellites' agreement to maintain their borders (to prevent refugees from escaping) acted as the only checks on a revolutionary situation. When these props were removed by Gorbachev and some members of the Warsaw Pact, the Berlin Wall came tumbling down.

With this general context in mind, we survey developments in the major Eastern European nations leading to the collapse of communism:

Poland: Gomulka began as a reformer, but price increases by the government in 1970 caused his ouster. The replacement, Edward Gierek, embarked on economic reforms, but borrowing from the West forced upon the nation an austerity program. Once again, price increases in 1980 led to discontent and strikes by workers. Uniquely in a Communist nation, workers founded an *independent* labor union called <u>Solidarity</u>, led by the militant shipyard worker Lech Walesa

(1943–), which soon claimed a membership of 10 million workers. Emboldened by the Catholic Church and a newly elected Polish pope, John Paul II (r. 1978–2005), workers demonstrated for free elections and a share in government. Fearing Soviet intervention, the new Communist leader General Wojciech Jaruzelski (1923–2014) declared martial law in 1981. Walesa was arrested and Solidarity driven underground. When Gorbachev embarked on his *perestroika* reforms, pressure grew on the satellites to liberalize. By 1989, Solidarity had convinced the government to allow free elections, which resulted in a universal repudiation of Communist rule, as Solidarity won all but one seat in the legislature. The following year, Nobel Peace Prize winner Walesa was elected president in a stunning reversal of fortunes.

Hungary: Following the Soviet crushing of the Hungarian revolt, Jánós Kádar maintained strong political control while allowing a more decentralized economy. By the 1980s, like the other satellites, Hungary experienced economic stagnation and rising debt. Communist party leaders quietly pushed Kádar out of power in 1988 and soon opened the door to a more social democratic economy and multiparty elections. In an act of reconciliation with its past, Hungary rehabilitated Nagy and the other leaders of the revolt and provided a burial with honors for those who had been killed. More important for future events, Hungary removed the barbed wire "iron curtain" around its borders, triggering a flood of refugees from nearby East Germany.**5**

East Germany: Since 1961, the aged and increasingly out-of-touch Erich Honecker (1912– 1994) strictly ruled East Germany with the aid of the state police, the Stasi. East Germany possessed the strongest economy in Eastern Europe; however, East Germany's leaders always felt insecure in the presence of their larger and more dynamic sister (West Germany), an insecurity that accounts for the Berlin Wall. When Hungary opened its borders, the action prompted a flood of East German refugees fleeing west. When Gorbachev visited East Germany in 1989 to celebrate its 40th anniversary, he inadvertently sparked mass demonstrations calling for reform and open travel. Though Honecker contemplated military repression using the Stasi, the Communist Politburo removed him and opened travel through the Berlin Wall. Soon after, a euphoric populace destroyed the hated symbol, and the Communists were kicked out of power. Momentum became unstoppable toward the **unification of Germany**. With the approval of the four WWII Allied powers, including the Soviet Union, Germany was reunified in October 1990.

Czechoslovakia: Events in Eastern Europe began to resemble the proverbial snowball rolling downhill. Inspired by the revolts in Poland, Hungary, and East Germany, mass demonstrations broke out in the fall of 1989 in the capital city of Prague. A group of intellectuals, Charter '77, led by the jailed playwright Vaclav Havel (1936–2011), became a rallying point against the Stalinist regime. By this point, Communist leaders had lost both their nerve and remaining moral authority; within weeks, the Communist monopoly on power evaporated to be replaced by free elections, a free press, and emergence of Havel as the president of Czechoslovakia. Observers dubbed the nonviolent change the Velvet Revolution. Because of its democratic past, the nation moved quickly toward a multiparty political system and a free-market economy. In the aftermath, Slovakia pressed for independence, accomplished through the so-called Velvet Divorce that created the Czech Republic and Slovakia in 1993.

Romania: Since 1965, the iron-fisted Nicolae Ceausescu (1918–1989) had ruled Romania. Ceausescu justified his regime by striking an independent pose in foreign policy—opposing the Soviet invasion of Czechoslovakia in 1968 and building friendly ties with Western nations. Through rigid one-person rule, Ceausescu wished to force Romania into the modern industrial age; however, Ceausescu compromised the nation's standard of living to pay off foreign debt and support his family's extravagant lifestyle. Ceausescu brutally crushed any opposition with his Securitate police. Encouraged by the revolts across Eastern Europe, protests erupted in the city of Timisoara, which the Securitate smashed, at the cost of hundreds of lives. Violent street battles broke out among the regular army, which now supported the revolutionaries, and the Securitate. Ceausescu's forces collapsed and the dictator, along with his wife, were captured and executed on Christmas Day 1989. The National Salvation Front reform movement emerged to oversee the nation's difficult transition to democracy and capitalism.

5 SKILL SET

Since Europe was officially divided into East and West during the Cold War, the question of comparisons naturally arise. As you read through the material on each bloc, make a diagram in which you note differences AND similarities (for LEQs, you'll usually need to address both) in areas like economic, political, social, and intellectual life. Can you devise a focused thesis for this question?

Following the Velvet Revolution, new president Havel proclaimed, "Czechoslovakia is reentering Europe." In that spirit, many of the former Soviet satellites have rejoined the West by entering NATO and the European Union (EU); for some nations, such as Romania, Bulgaria, and Albania, the evolution toward parliamentary democracy and free markets has proven more painful but continues today.

Yugoslavia: The Balkans Again

The most violent break from communism occurred in multiethnic Yugoslavia. A diverse collection of Slavic ethnic groups, Yugoslavia was always an artificial state. Though Croats and Serbs speak the same language, the former historically were tied more to the West religiously (Catholicism) and politically, whereas the latter were oriented more toward Russia and Orthodox Christianity. The Nazi invasion of 1941 led to the creation of a Croat fascist movement, the Ustashe, which committed atrocities against Serbs. Communist resistance leader Marshal Tito liberated his nation from the Nazis while also resisting Soviet domination. To maintain control of Yugoslavia, Tito experimented with a decentralized though socialist economic system and a federation of ethnic states, kept tightly together by the authority of the Communist Party.

Following Tito's death in 1980, ethnic tensions reemerged and burst into the open with the events of 1989–1991. The Western-oriented republics—Croatia, Slovenia, and Bosnia—voted in 1991 for independence. However, significant minorities of Serbs lived in each of these regions, prompting a series of violent wars between 1991 and 1999. Led by the nationalist Slobodan Milosevic (1941–2006), Yugoslavia (now simply Serbia and Montenegro) attacked Bosnia to recapture Serb territory; in the process, Serbian troops used **ethnic cleansing** campaigns against Bosnian Muslims involving mass killing, rape, and the destruction of homes. Croatian armies responded with their own atrocities against Serb civilians. Europe stood appalled and impotent at the sight of ethnic conflict thought to be a relic of the WWII era. Finally in 1995, NATO and the United States engineered a cease-fire and with the Dayton Peace Accord, the parties agreed to the partition of Bosnia, enforced by UN peacekeepers. Now Milosevic turned to the historically important province of Kosovo, populated primarily by ethnic Albanians known as Kosovars. To halt another ethnic cleansing campaign, President Bill Clinton (1946–) led a NATO bombing operation that once again ended the killing and the placement of peacekeepers. By 2001, Milosevic had been voted out of office and placed on trial at The Hague, Netherlands, for crimes against humanity; however, he died in 2006 before his trial was completed.

Western Europe: Pulling Back and Together

In 1945 Western Europe lay in ruins. By the mid-1950s, however, it had experienced a remarkable recovery. How? First, the nations of Western Europe pulled back from their imperial commitments, either surrendering or losing their colonies, thus freeing themselves from the expense of defending empires. Second, the two world wars threw an icy bucket of water in the face of extreme nationalism. After 1945, the peoples of Western Europe, prompted by the United States, worked toward economic and political unity. The Atlantic alliance (NATO) provided collective security while economic unity produced a stunning turnaround.

Recovery and Reconstruction

Following the Second World War, Western Europe faced immense devastation. Important industrial areas had been bombed to oblivion, infrastructure lay in ruins, and regular economic structures such as currencies and trade had collapsed. Complicating recovery was the issue of displaced persons (DPs)—the 30–50 million refugees seeking relatives and shelter, and the ethnic minorities (mostly Germans) forcibly removed in the redrawing of postwar boundaries. What's more, harsh winters and poor harvests from 1945 to 1947 increased fears of the spread of communism.

With its dominant economy and readiness to enter decisively into European affairs, the United States offered **Marshall Plan** aid (totaling $12 billion) to the nations of Europe. American leaders insisted that such aid be funneled through the Organization for European Economic Cooperation (OEEC) to promote unity—both for efficiency's sake and to create bloc solidarity as the Cold War heated up.[6]

Learning lessons from the post-WWI settlement, industrial nations began creating international economic institutions even before the Second World War ended. The Allied nations in 1944 adopted the Bretton Woods system, which included an International Monetary Fund (IMF) for currency stabilization. Currencies were to be backed by gold and exchange rates fixed to ensure stability. Based on the strength of the U.S. economy, the dollar evolved into an unofficial reserve currency, at least until 1971, when President Nixon was forced to abandon the gold standard due to inflation, returning the industrial world to a system of floating currencies. In addition, the International Bank of Reconstruction and Development (World Bank) provided loans for the modernization of infrastructure (e.g., dams, roads, and sewers). To avoid the economic nationalism of the interwar period, Western nations embraced free trade. The informal General Agreement on Trade and Tariffs (GATT) worked toward the reduction and elimination of trade barriers and eventually gave way to the more formal World Trade Organization (WTO) in 1997. In all, these institutions performed admirably in regulating the world economy and promoting growth, though they came under increasing criticism from opponents of economic globalization in the 1990s.

Western European governments accepted the need for state management of a capitalist economy. Keynesian economics emerged as the reigning theory; states employed tax and budget policies to promote growth and cushion recessions. In Britain, the new Labour government signaled its commitment to full employment and the **social welfare state** by following the recommendations of the wartime Beveridge Report (1942). Some European states nationalized key industries, such as utilities and transport, to ensure the public welfare, but these new mixed economies (free markets *and* government regulation) did not approach the rigid controls of Soviet-style planned economies. European growth continued throughout the 1960s but stalled with the oil shock of the 1970s and 1980s. Staglation (inflation *and* unemployment) forced a reappraisal of Keynesian theory and a move to reduce the welfare state and government regulation in favor of supply-side economics.

6 THEME MUSIC
Western Europe's unexpectedly rapid recovery from the destruction of World War II was termed an "economic miracle." Though this economic engine provided new forms of prosperity, it also raised continuing issues of inequality and, for the first time, the potential for environmental devastation (PP).

Decolonization

World War I shook Europe's control of its colonies, and World War II severed it. By 1945, most European nations no longer possessed the means or the inclination to continue as colonial powers. Also, the senior member of the Western alliance, the United States, generally opposed Europe's continued domination of colonial empires. Nonetheless, the road to independence proved rough in many cases both for the mother country and the colony. On the AP exam, if you encounter this topic, it is likely to be couched in a comparative framework. What follows are three approaches to decolonization.

Great Britain: The new Labour government lacked enthusiasm for the British Empire. After the First World War, Britain ruled several areas of the world under **mandates**, a system of tutelage (protection and guidance) leading to independence. After World War II, Britain adopted a strategy of "partition and depart" for its colonies and mandates, encouraging the contending groups to sort out the political settlement. In the case of Palestine, a proposed partition in 1947 led to the founding of the state of Israel in 1948 and the first of several wars between Palestinians and Israelis. Both Hindus and Muslims had for decades urged Britain to leave India, led by Gandhi's campaign of nonviolent resistance (Indian National Congress). Britain's partition of the subcontinent in 1947 left Muslim East and West Pakistan divided between India; this geographic anomaly, along with dispute over the border region of Kashmir, has fed a succession of conflicts between Muslim Pakistan and mainly Hindu India, both now nuclear powers.

In Africa, the push for independence accelerated after 1960 and is demonstrated by the increase in UN membership from the 51 original members to around 195 today. Britain faced its most difficult situation on the continent in Egypt. After overthrowing the British-backed government in 1952, Egyptian leader Gamal Abdul-Nasser (1918–1970) announced the nationalization of the Suez Canal, sparking an invasion by British, French, and Israeli forces. The Suez Crisis of 1956 ended when the United States and Soviet Union denounced the invasion and forced its withdrawal. This defeat is usually taken to signify the end of Britain's status as a world power. Britain's retreat from direct colonial control continued throughout the 1950s and 1960s in Asia as well, though many former colonies retained political and economic contacts with Britain through the commonwealth system.

Low Countries: During the Second World War, Japan "liberated" many Asian colonies of the European powers, including the Dutch East Indies. Even before the war, an Indonesian Nationalist Party under Sukarno (1901–1970) agitated for autonomy. After the expulsion of Japan in 1945, the movement actively sought independence. Attempts to subdue the revolt failed, and the Netherlands withdrew from the archipelago and refocused on European issues. After 1949, Indonesia faced a number of difficult transitional issues, such as a communist threat, government corruption, and political violence over East Timor (a Christian enclave among a Muslim majority). However, Indonesia has haltingly moved toward democracy and become a major economic and political power in Asia.

Belgium planned to grant independence to its African colony, Congo, over a 30-year period following World War II. Faced with increasing pressures, Belgium changed its position and pulled out in 1960. Chaos ensued, due to separatist movements, rival political factions, and army mutinies. With UN support, Belgian forces returned in 1961 to restore order, but a leftist rebellion continued. Eventually, the Congo was ruled as a brutal and corrupt dictatorship by Mobuto Sese Seko. Because of Congo's vast but untapped resources, its political problems spilled over into neighboring Burundi and Rwanda. The latter nation descended into ethnic violence in 1994 between rival tribes (Hutus and Tutsis); after several of its peacekeepers were killed, Belgium pulled out of the country as a genocide took almost 1 million lives.

France: To reestablish prestige after its poor showing in the Second World War, France was determined to hold onto its colonial empire. It soon faced a nationalist and communist insurgency in Indochina with the Viet Minh, led by Ho Chi Minh. The conflict represents an appropriate example of how communism and anticolonialism often became fused in the context of the Cold War. As noted above, the French were forced to withdraw in 1954, only to have the United States take up the battle in its own war in Vietnam. France's more agonizing war occurred in Algeria. Unlike Indochina, much of the Algerian population were French settlers (*colons*), and the postwar French government resolved to defend their interests. A militant and nationalist group, the National Liberation Front (FLN), waged an almost 8-year war against the French, with atrocities on both sides. The war produced a crisis for the French government, eventually bringing down the Fourth French Republic and leading to the reemergence of Charles de Gaulle. President De Gaulle ended the war in 1962, despite opposition from the army, and granted Algerian independence.

As these examples demonstrate, European nations came to realize the inevitability of independence at different times and with varying approaches, some of which proved violent. Before refocusing on Europe, you should keep in mind that Europe's involvement with its former colonies did not end with independence—issues of terrorism, peacekeeping, **guest workers**, and colonial dependence continued.**7**

7 THEME MUSIC AND SKILL SET

Decolonization fittingly culminates the theme of Europe's interaction with the world (INT), including the indirect effects of immigration and terrorism. Consider what impact decolonization has had both upon Europe and the world (CAUS).

Western European Unity and Economic Integration

Putting aside the narrow nationalism that had brought them low, Western and Central Europeans moved incrementally in the postwar period toward economic and political integration. Key to this unity was the partnership between France and West Germany. In 1952, two practical men of business and politics, both from Alsace-Lorraine—Jean Monnet (1888–1979) and Robert Schuman (1886–1963)—proposed the **European Coal and Steel Community (ECSC)**, involving Belgium, the Netherlands, and Luxembourg (Benelux nations), France, Italy, and Germany. These nations (Inner Six) eliminated tariff barriers and placed coal and steel production under a High Authority. Within 5 years, production had doubled. Flush with success, the Inner Six in 1957 agreed to the Treaty of Rome, creating the **European Economic Community (EEC)** or **Common Market**, which worked toward the abolition of trade barriers, the free flow of capital, and common economic policies. In addition, the six agreed to coordinate their nonmilitary atomic research and development under the European Atomic Community (Euratom).

At first, Great Britain stood aside from the Common Market, owing to its special relationship with the United States and its commonwealth. Later in the 1960s when the British changed their minds, De Gaulle of France vetoed their entry for fear Britain's overseas commitments would dilute European unity. Eventually, the British joined the EEC in 1973, along with Denmark and Ireland. During the 1980s and 1990s, more nations on the Mediterranean and in Eastern Europe—with the fall of communism—joined the growing community. After the passing of the oil shock of the 1970s, the European Community moved toward a stronger integration. In 1991, the member states signed the Maastricht Treaty aimed at creating a single Europe. This new **European Union (EU)** was governed by an elected European Parliament and a centralized decision-making European Commission of civil servants and administrators. Recent expansion has increased the number of EU members to 28. More importantly, 12 EU members in 2000 (now 19) adopted the new **euro** currency to replace their national currencies. Some have criticized the distant and bureaucratic nature of the EU—and indeed the movement toward a truly United States of Europe has moved in fits and starts and still lies a way off—but progress since the late 1940s has resulted in an economic bloc of over 500 million people and which accounts for about 40% of the world's trade. During the global financial crisis of 2007–2009, many of the weaker EU nations (such as Portugal, Spain, Greece, Ireland, and Cyprus) experienced severe budget shortfalls that required bailout packages from the stronger states (e.g., Germany), as well as unpopular austerity measures. Though the situation has been stabilized for now, the crisis has once again demonstrated the difficulties of coordinating such a diverse economic entity and continued popular discontent with the distant power of EU bureaucrats and bankers.

Western European National Politics[8]

Though the themes of Western Europe as a region take precedence, you will find it useful to draw from specific nations in applying your understanding of broader themes. To keep this material to manageable size, consult the chart of Western European nations after 1945 on the following page:

8 EXAMPLE BASE

Many observers prematurely predicted the end of nationalism or other ideological conflicts with the fall of communism. You are encouraged to identify and explain several instances of how nationalist and separatist movements have continued to trouble policymakers and citizens on the European continent.

Nation	Issues	Leaders/Groups	Events	Analysis
Great Britain	Since 1945, Britain has faced an older and less advanced economic infrastructure than the other Western European nations. In addition, it has battled high unemployment and its adjustment to a second-tier power.	*The Labour and Conservative Parties have alternated control of the government, with Labour working toward the expansion of the welfare state. *Margaret Thatcher (1925–2013)— ideological ally of President Reagan, Thatcher curbed the size of the welfare system, denationalized industries, attacked the power of labor unions, and reasserted British power abroad. *Tony Blair (1953–)—Labour Prime Minister from 1997 to 2007, Blair appealed more to the middle class, promoted economic growth, and supported U.S. efforts against terrorism.	*The "Troubles" in Northern Ireland between the Catholic Irish Republic Army (IRA) and Protestants led to continued violence, though a peace agreement has largely held since 1998. *In 1982 Thatcher aroused British nationalism with the Falklands War against Argentina over control of an island chain off of South America *In 1973, Britain joined the Common Market but not the euro, and recently (2016) voted to leave the EU ("Brexit") in protest against the effects of globalization. *Britain has "devolved" political decision-making to its various nations, such as Scotland and Wales.	Britain continues to face decaying industrial cities and lower economic productivity, while trying to retain a British identity that unites its several nations.
France	The postwar Fourth Republic (1945–1958) struggled with the legacy of collaboration during the Vichy regime and political instability yet enacted important reform legislation. With the Fifth Republic's (1958–) strong presidency under De Gaulle, France left the NATO military alliance and pursued a more independent line in foreign affairs, known as Gaullism.	*Charles de Gaulle (1890–1970)— De Gaulle supported European integration but an independent foreign policy vis-à-vis the United States. *Francois Mitterand (1916–1996)—Socialist president from 1981 to 1995, Mitterand at first expanded the welfare state but was forced to retrench and cohabit with conservative prime ministers. *Jean Monnet (1888–1979)— architect of European unity.	*In 1961, France pulled out of the NATO military alliance (remaining in the political alliance). *France developed independent nuclear weapons. *Student revolts in 1968 led to violence in Paris and almost brought down the De Gaulle government. *Colonial conflicts in Indochina and Algeria caused internal political conflict and changes.	France benefited from its involvement in the EU and partnership with Germany. French assertions of political and diplomatic power have not always coincided with its economic power, which is second in Europe to Germany's.

Nation	Issues	Leaders/Groups	Events	Analysis
(West) Germany	West Germany —Germany after its reunification in 1990—has worked to demonstrate its allegiance to democracy and the Western alliance by distancing itself from the Nazi past. It has played a crucial role as the banker of the EU.	*Konrad Adenauer (1876–1967)— known as the founding Chancellor, he led the Christian Dem-ocratic Party (CDs), a right-center party favoring laissez-faire economics and close ties to the U.S. *Ludwig Erhard (1897–1977)— economic minister and brains behind Germany's economic miracle. *Willy Brandt (1913–1992)— Socialist chancellor whose Ostpolik ("opening to the East") normalized relations between East Germany and the Soviet Union.	*In 1955, Germany rearmed and joined NATO. *Germany joined the UN in the 1970s as part of détente. **German reunification** came soon after the collapse of the Berlin Wall in 1989.	Germany seems firmly established as a democracy and committed member of the Atlantic Alliance. Reunification has cost trillions of marks and the eastern part still suffers from higher un-employment and environmental problems. Germany's economic power makes it the strongest member of the EU.
Italy	Following World War II, Italy abolished the monarchy and worked toward economic modernization. Leftist parties proved resilient, and Italy's parliamentary system has produced more than 60 different governments since 1945.	*Alcide de Gaspari (1881–1954)— Christian Democratic prime minister who helped establish Italy's new parliamentary system and membership in the Atlantic alliance. *Socialists finally gained power in 1983 but their policies differed little in practice from the CDs.	*In 1946, Italians by a small majority voted to abolish the monarchy for its involvement with fascism. *Eurocommunism, centered in Italy, rejected ties to the Soviet Union and the radical features of Marxism-Leninism. *In 1993, Italy restructured its system of proportional representation, which has allowed for longer-lived governments and more stability.	Italy recovered economically after the war, but was hard hit by the oil shock. It continues to deal with the lack of development in the south and corruption in government.

Additional Resources

Timothy Garton Ash, *In Europe's Name: Germany and the Divided Continent* (1993)—The author examines the roots of German reunification.

Timothy Garton Ash, *The Magic Lantern: The Revolution of '89 Witnessed in Warsaw, Budapest, Berlin, and Prague* (1993)—A gripping journalistic account of the fall of communism.

John Lewis Gaddis, *The Cold War: A New History* (2005)—A noted diplomatic historian incorporates the latest interpretations of the conflict.

Samuel Huntington, *The Clash of Civilizations and the Remaking of the World Order* (1996)—The author argues controversially that the post-Cold War world has been defined by rising conflicts over culture and religion.

Tony Judt, *Postwar: A History of Europe Since 1945* (2006)—Strong resource and the best single-volume history of the period.

Paul Kennedy, *The Rise and Fall of the Great Powers: Economic Change and Military Conflict, 1500–2000* (1989)—With broad historical perspective, the author examines the importance of economic productivity and imperial overreach in the rise and decline of great powers.

David Remnick, *Lenin's Tomb: The Last Days of the Soviet Empire* (1994)—A journalist's account of the fall of the Soviet empire.

Laura Silber and Alan Little, *Yugoslavia: Death of a Nation* (1997)—Clearly written story of a nation's collapse into ethnic conflict.

John O'Sullivan, *The President, the Pope, and the Prime Minister: Three Who Changed the World* (2008)—Argues for the primacy of its three figures in the collapse of communism.

www.almaz.com/nobel/peace/1990a.html—Biographical information related to Mikhail Gorbachev, including primary sources.

http://www.johndclare.net/cold_warA1.htm—Resources and perspectives on the Cold War

http://chnm.gmu.edu/1989/—Materials and lessons on the collapse of communism

https://www.washingtonpost.com/national/10-seismic-changes-since-911/2013/09/10/4499cf18–19b4-11e3-82ef-a059e54c49d0_gallery.html—From the Washington Post, the ways the world has changed since 9/11.

Practice MC Questions

Questions 1–5 are based on the text below.

> "In an ironic sense Karl Marx was right. We are witnessing today a great revolutionary crisis, a crisis where the demands of the economic order are conflicting directly with those of the political order. But the crisis is happening not in the free, non-Marxist West, but in the home of Marxist-Leninism, the Soviet Union. It is the Soviet Union that runs against the tide of history by denying human freedom and human dignity to its citizens. It also is in deep economic difficulty....Over-centralized, with little or no incentives, year after year the Soviet system pours its best resource into the making of instruments of destruction. The constant shrinkage of economic growth combined with the growth of military production is putting a heavy strain on the Soviet people. What we see here is a political structure that no longer corresponds to its economic base, a society where productive forces are hampered by political ones."
>
> U.S. President Ronald Reagan, Address to the British Parliament, June 8, 1982

1. The speech suggests all of the following features of the Cold War EXCEPT:

   A. American economic and military influence over Western Europe.

   B. an arms race between the superpowers with the threat of nuclear war.

   C. covert actions and limited "hot wars" globally to secure power and influence.

   D. the division of Europe into rival blocs, known as the Iron Curtain.

2. Which of the following Soviet leaders would have most likely agreed with Reagan's analysis of the Soviet Union's situation?

   A. Lenin

   B. Stalin

   C. Khrushchev

   D. Gorbachev

3. Which of the following was the direct result of the situation Reagan outlines?

   A. A new period of cooperation between the U.S. and Soviet Union

   B. The fall of the Berlin Wall and reunification of Germany

   C. The collapse of the communist system and break-up of the Soviet Union

   D. A renewal of nationalism in the Balkans and wars of ethnic cleansing

4. How does U.S. policy toward Europe, as suggested by Reagan's speech, differ most significantly from U.S. policy following the First World War?

   A. The U.S. guaranteed Western European security with the NATO alliance.

   B. The U.S. joined the United Nations and other international organizations.

   C. The U.S. promoted its economic interests through trade and financial policies.

   D. The U.S. President visited Europe and engaged in direct diplomacy.

5. A 19th-century supporter of which ideology would have agreed most with the content and tone of Reagan's speech?

   A. Conservatism

   B. Liberalism

   C. Socialism

   D. Nationalism

Questions 6–9 are based on the text below.

"At that time I acted for Germany as the German Chancellor, but also a firm believer in Europe. Because I believe in Europe, I proposed that my parliament, the German Bundestag, take unusual and previously unimagined routes in order to help Greece and thus to ensure the stability of the eurozone as a whole. I was motivated to do so by the European project. This is the only reason why I decided to implement a short-term solution for the rescue package as well as ambitious reforms and strict austerity programmes for Greece and other countries. I faced severe criticism for this: For some it was too slow, for others too fast. But I believe it was the right thing, on the one hand, to insist that countries which caused such a crisis will have to take action themselves in the future and, on the other hand, to make clear that we bear a shared European responsibility. I think that today everyone in Europe agrees that on the whole this was the right way to bring Europe back from the brink of disaster."

Angela Merkel, German Chancellor, speech to students at the College of Europe in Bruges, Belgium, November 2, 2010

6. The post-World War II trend in European politics most strongly reflected above is:

A. the end of the Cold War between the superpowers.

B. the commitment of the United States to European security.

C. the recovery of Germany from the devastation of the war.

D. the movement toward continental cooperation and unity.

7. All of the following institutions would be consistent with Merkel's perspective EXCEPT:

A. the European Coal and Steel Community (ECSC).

B. the North Atlantic Treaty Organization (NATO).

C. the Council for Mutual Economic Assistance (COMECON).

D. the European Union (EU).

See Chapter 18 for answers and explanations.

8. Which of the following represents the most significant turning point in German politics after 1950?

A. Its admission into NATO in 1955

B. The building of the Berlin Wall in 1961

C. The election of SPD Chancellor Willy Brandt in 1969

D. The reunification of West and East Germany in 1990

9. Which of the following post-World War II trends has worked most strongly against Merkel's vision?

A. The independence of African and Asian colonies

B. The revival of nationalist and separatist movements

C. The collapse of communism in Eastern Europe

D. Establishment of the UN and other international organizations

Angela Merkel, German Chancellor, speech to students at the College of Europe in Bruges, Belgium, November 2, 2010, https://www.coleurope.eu/content/news/Speeches/Europakolleg%20Brugge%20Mitschrift%20englisch.pdf, page 3.

Long Essay Question with Sample and Commentary

Compare and contrast the economic and political impact of the Cold War on Western Europe and Eastern Europe.
(HTS: Comparison)

The Cold War had a big impact on Europe after WWII. However, different parts of Europe were affected differently. Western Europe really gained a lot from being allied with the United States, but the East was dominated by the Soviet Union. In this essay, I will discuss the different policies of the superpowers and how the Cold War created blocs of countries that opposed each other over the Iron Curtain.

Western Europe was ruined in 1945. At first, the United States did not know what to do about the situation. Soon conflict with the Soviet Union broke out over Berlin and free elections in Eastern Europe. To oppose communism, the United States tried to help rebuild Europe; American leaders knew that communism could spread if conditions continued to be bad. So the United States provided Marshall Plan aid and promoted the unity of the West. NATO was created and West Germany was admitted into it. This alliance tried to defend against the spread of communism. Also, Western Europe began to pool their resources together. They created the Coal and Steel Society and eventually the Treaty of Rome to knock down tariff barriers. These two organizations promoted an "economic miracle" and helped Europe get back on its feet. Some leaders, like De Gaulle of France, did not like U.S. domination of Europe but most in the West realized that they needed an American ally to fight the Soviet threat.

The Soviet Union wanted to dominate Eastern Europe, because the Soviets were all about world domination. It was part of their Marxist-Leninist philosophy. Communist governments were imposed on the satellite nations, called this because they revolved around the Soviet Union. Oppression reigned in the East and all the bad features of communism were imposed on these nations—gulags, no free press, and rigid bureaucratic economies. Some states rebelled against the Soviet Union like Hungary, because of their domination. This did not help the unity of the East because it was unity imposed by the Soviet Union. This is shown later when the nations of Eastern Europe revolted against the USSR with the fall of the Berlin Wall in the late 1980s.

Western European nations like France and Germany experienced growth in their economies from 1945–1960 and banded together to oppose communism. NATO protected them against the Soviet Union. On the other hand, the East was dominated by the Soviet menace. Nations had to toe the Soviet line or face invasion. So in the long run, the West was positively unified but East was negatively unified. This division was similar to what happened in Europe during the religious wars, especially after the Peace of Westphalia, when countries supported either the Protestant or Catholic Church. Eventually the religions decided to "coexist peacefully" however, with the superpowers, one of them no longer exists.

The student addresses the question, but might do so more explicitly. Several similarities are offered (e.g., both superpowers unifying their blocs), but he concentrates primarily on contrasts, often with a negative portrayal of the Soviet Union. Certainly there is evidence to support this view, but the response grows repetitious in its assertions by the end of the essay. Despite a relatively weak introduction–inadequate thesis and minimal historical context–the student does provide two cogent body paragraphs. Much of the analysis of similarities and differences remains implicit, yet the response does provide a range of examples as evidence, as well as earn the synthesis point with appropriate extension of the argument to the religious wars. Score: 5 (Thesis, 1 point for Targeted HTS, 2 points for Use of Evidence, Synthesis).

CHAPTER 17 Contemporary European Society and Culture

Wars not only reorder the balance of power and diplomatic structures, they also work major changes in society and culture. This truism applies to the period following World War II. Pent-up demand for products and the need for reconstruction fed an **economic miracle**, especially in Western Europe. Prosperity, in turn, promoted a population increase, consumerism, and technological advance. Most governments committed themselves to a more active role in economic regulation and ensuring a social welfare system. Renewed prosperity and the specter of the Cold War also worked a downside. Numerous outsiders—students, feminists, environmentalists, terrorists—offered various critiques of European society in the years after 1945. Culturally, experimentation flourished in the postwar intellectual climate but also revealed divisions between traditionalists and modernists, and even postmodernists. Following World War II, Europe's problems are increasingly seen in a global context.

Key In Chapter 17 covers the following KCs from the Course Description:

- **KC 4.2** The nature and impact of Europe's economic miracle
- **KCs 4.3 and 4.4** Advances in science/technology and economic production, with both positive and negative effects
- **KC 4.4** Demographic trends and their impact on women, family, and sexuality
- **KC 4.4** Reform movements and critics of western society
- **KC 4.1** Nationalist, separatist, and domestic terrorist movements
- **KC 4.3** Diverse intellectual and cultural trends in postwar Europe
- **KC 4.3** Changing role of religion, growth of secularism, and shifting religious identities

---

The Economic Miracle and Its Consequences

Europe's amazing recovery from the destruction of the Second World War produced a higher standard of living and increased life expectancy but also negative side effects. In this section, we examine the social changes provoked by the changing European economy and the advance of technology.

The Baby Boom and After

The Great Depression and World War II dampened European birth rates. After 1945, the western world underwent a steady increase in the birth rate, known as the **Baby Boom**. Governments encouraged the trend in an effort to replace lost population from the war and also to allay a labor shortage in the period. State policies of <u>neonatalism</u> subsidized additional births, infant nutrition, and day care. Also aided by an influx of immigrants, Europe's population increased by 25% between 1945 and 1970. With the onset of artificial means of contraception, particularly the <u>birth control pill</u>, the birth rate trended downward after the mid-1960s. The Baby Boomers born in this interval and who grew up amidst prosperity and **consumerism** benefited from the increased standard of living but also came to criticize it, along with their parents' values.

Since the 1970s, and especially since 1990, the population of many European nations has stagnated. In some states, like Germany and much of Eastern Europe, populations have already begun to decline. This trend affects politics for two reasons. Government provision for generous retirement benefits must be funded by taxes from the young. When these programs were first implemented, 20 workers funded the benefits of one retiree. That ratio has decreased to between

3–5 workers per retiree, creating a potential entitlements time bomb in the next few decades. Europe's prosperity also attracts immigrants from Asia, the Middle East, and elsewhere. Greater ethnic diversity has increased social tension and led to the growth of nationalist and **anti-immigrant political parties**. With the decline in religious observance among European Christians, some estimate that Muslims will outnumber Christians during the 21st century. It is likely that this demographic shift will be attended by increased conflict, as witnessed by recent violence over publication of cartoons satirizing Muhammad (Denmark, 2006; France, 2011 and 2015) and the assassination of Theo Van Gogh in 2004 in response to his (Dutch) film critical of Islam. Such tensions have arisen not only due to conflicting religious loyalties but more fundamentally over the status of religion in state and society and the growing divide between secularism and religiosity.[1]

Growth of and Challenge to the Welfare State

Western and Eastern governments both significantly expanded **welfare benefits** (known as **cradle-to-grave**) following World War II. In Eastern Europe, this trend coincided with the establishment of Marxist governments dedicated to social equality and providing the basics for all of their citizens. In the West, the trend was driven by the dominance of Keynesian economic theory and fears about socialist exploitation of class conflict. Western nations provided old-age pensions, unemployment, and disability insurance; subsidized or socialized medical care; and redistributed income through progressive taxation. For the most part, this social safety net proved popular, though it came under increasing criticism during the stagnant 1970s and 1980s.

The late 1970s and early 1980s witnessed a resurgence of conservative political parties in several nations, such as Great Britain and the United States. Leaders like British Prime Minister Margaret Thatcher and President Ronald Reagan criticized the overregulated economy and bloated government bureaucracy as causing the high inflation and unemployment of the period. Even Socialist Francois Mitterand of France was forced to abandon the more ambitious elements of his social reform program by the mid-1980s due to budget deficits and stagnating productivity. Supply-side economists argued that economic productivity would result from a reduction of taxes, regulation, and government spending on the welfare state. Supply-side policies did produce growth in the 1980s and early 1990s, but leftist groups believed the costs too high in poverty, inequality, and decline of organized labor.

Consumerism and Its Critics

Postwar prosperity brought a flood of new consumer goods. Pent-up demand from two decades of retrenchment during the Depression and WWII burst open with a spree of kitchen appliances, television sets, automobiles, and clothing fashions. **Mass marketing** techniques grew in sophistication, employing TV spots and computer technology to sell the good life. Images and sounds of blue jeans and Coca-Cola were beamed across the Iron Curtain to demonstrate the superior abundance of Western society. Marketers often employed sexuality to sell products, a fact condemned both by religious conservatives and some feminists who decried the objectification of women. The Western economies (including the United States) began a shift away from traditional heavy industry toward services and information processing. While this postindustrial economy created new opportunities and wealth, it also gutted jobs from older industrial areas, such as the Midland cities of Britain—Leeds, Liverpool, Manchester, and Sheffield.

Many across the political spectrum—from traditionalists to socialists—found the new consumerism shallow and extravagant. Environmentalists objected to the waste of nonrenewable resources and levels of pollution. Socialists found confirmation of theories for Marxist alienation in Western society's high levels of crime, suicide, and social dislocation. British economist E.F. Schumacher (1911–1977) argued for balancing society's need for efficiency and productive centralization with humanistic values of community and the dignity of labor. In his famous work *Small Is Beautiful* (1973), Schumacher argued for sustainable development that would take into account the needs of future generations and the impact of production on the health of the planet.

1 THEME MUSIC

We are said to live in an age of globalization, with the easy transmission of goods, information, and people. As such, events in the non-European world have exercised growing influence on the Continent. A recent global trend affecting Europe has been the refugee crisis, with victims of war and state collapse from the Middle East (and other regions) seeking refuge in Europe. Such large population movements rarely occur without conflict or contest, as is apparent in Europe today.

Technological Advances

Continued scientific progress marked the postwar era. Major advances in medical care almost doubled life expectancy during the 20th century. Antibiotics cured formerly deadly infectious diseases. Medical personnel first used penicillin widely during the Second World War to fight infections following surgeries and amputations. In addition, vaccines also helped curtail a number of other dreaded diseases; Jonas Salk in 1955 pioneered an easily administered vaccine against polio. Safe and effective surgery, including organ transplantation, became common after the 1970s. Due to worldwide public health efforts, often sponsored by the United Nations, smallpox was eradicated by the 1970s. However, the threat of global pandemics, such as AIDS (acquired immunodeficiency syndrome) and avian flu, have intensified with the further development of global trade and travel.

Much scientific research in the postwar period has been funded by governments. With the onset of the Cold War, both superpowers invested huge resources in obtaining a technological edge over the other—in rocket technology, nuclear power, and the space race. The space race produced the first moon landing by America's Apollo program in 1969. Not all applauded these advances. In his farewell address, President Eisenhower warned of the political dominance of a military-industrial complex, comprising large, bureaucratic armed forces, arms manufacturers, and corporations, all of whom held an interest in the continuation of the arms race or even war. A new class of technocrats—engineers, managers, scientists—seemed to wield authority out of proportion to their numbers and outside democratic political processes. Moreover, many European nations adopted **nuclear power** as a beneficial side effect of the Cold War nuclear arms race. Currently, France supplies more than 75% of its energy needs via nuclear power. Opponents feared that reliance on nuclear power would lead to environmental problems, such as waste disposal and nuclear meltdowns, as occurred at Chernobyl in 1986 and almost occurred at Three Mile Island, Pennsylvania, in 1979.

Critics and Outsiders in European Society

Despite renewed economic prosperity, many Europeans felt either left out or alienated by postwar society. These groups offered critiques of consumerism, conformity, and inequality that often crossed the political spectrum.

Youth Revolts and the Generation Gap

The postwar Baby Boom generation was the first to attend college in large numbers. However, universities became a victim of their success in attracting students. Classes tended to be large and impersonal, and the professors distant. Students criticized living conditions in the dorms and demanded the addition of more up-to-date and relevant courses and programs in psychology, sociology, and women's studies. Youth criticisms were not unique to Europe; the years 1967–1968 saw worldwide protests against repression and bureaucratization. European protests began in Italy and Germany before spreading to France; these **revolts of '68** evolved into the most fundamental critique of postwar society and nearly brought down President De Gaulle's government.

French students considered De Gaulle an elderly and distant figure, more interested in foreign affairs than domestic reform. In addition, many students and those sympathetic to leftist ideologies, such as Maoism and Trotskyism, opposed America's involvement in Vietnam and other Cold War colonial conflicts. Many students were attracted to the New Left critiques of neo-Marxist thinkers like Herbert Marcuse (1898–1979), whose *One-Dimensional Man* (1964) condemned both the bureaucratic centralism of Soviet ideology and the rampant consumerism of Western society in favor of a culture of protest and rebellion.

In May 1968, the University of Paris exploded with student unrest. Students seized control of campus buildings and battled police, demanding better conditions and a more open and less bureaucratic society. Workers initially supported the students with a nationwide general strike.

When it looked as if De Gaulle's government would collapse, he defused the situation by co-opting the workers with wage increases and by ensuring the support of the army for his government. Now isolated, the students eventually settled for concessions such as input into university governance and relief of overcrowding. Though the students' more ideological demands were not met, their actions highlighted growing divisions within European society.

Young people often conflict with parents as they establish autonomy. However, some have referred to a "generation gap" to describe the widely divergent experiences of parents who grew up in the Great Depression and World War II with their children who experienced Cold War pessimism and economic prosperity. Youth culture embraced themes of rebellion, symbolized by the slogan "sex, drugs, and rock 'n roll." Postwar European governments **decriminalized gay and lesbian relationships** and abortion, and made birth control widely available. The resulting sexual revolution sought to separate sexual expression from family and commitment. Many young people embraced premarital sex and open sexuality as acts of rebellion against a society they perceived as rigid and conventional. During the 1960s, the recreational use of drugs such as marijuana and LSD grew as a way to experiment with new states of consciousness. Postwar music also expressed themes of rebellion. The Beatles' long hair, irreverent attitudes, and drug references introduced a generation to rock 'n roll music. American protest music from Bob Dylan and Janis Joplin linked social consciousness with popular culture. Fittingly, the children of the Boomers launched their own musical rebellion in the 1980s with punk and alternative.

Feminism

Militant feminism began as a transatlantic movement and coincided with the push for civil rights in the United States during the 1960s. Now that women had gained the vote in almost all European nations after World War II, this Second Wave Feminism turned toward economic and cultural criticism. Women's liberation was inspired by several key works. First, French philosopher Simone de Beauvoir (1908–1986), in *The Second Sex* (1949), demonstrated how gender represented a social construction of expectations and attitudes rather than a biological category. Throughout history, de Beauvior argued, women have been treated as **the Other**, that is, a deviance from the "default" male gender, rather than beings in their own right. American Betty Friedan's *The Feminine Mystique* (1963) encouraged women to battle subtle oppression that limited women's entrance into leadership positions in academia, business, and government.

Indeed, women in Eastern and Western Europe entered the workforce in larger percentages than ever before. Moreover, many women attained **high political office** during the postwar era. Scandinavian legislatures claim close to 50% of seats held by women. Several famous women were elected for the first time in modern history as heads of government or state, such as Margaret Thatcher in Britain, Angela Merkel in Germany, Golda Meir in Israel, and Indira Gandhi in India. Feminists advocated for reproductive rights, such as access to birth control and legalized abortion, as essential to this progress. Worldwide, Europe led the way for the liberation of women, and European feminists have proven instrumental in pushing the United Nations to develop programs for female literacy, contraception, and universal rights in those developing regions where women often suffer the brunt of oppression and poverty.

Environmentalism[2]

Postwar economic growth created a host of environmental problems, such as pollution, acid rain, and global climate change. American zoologist Rachel Carson (1907–1964) spawned the global environmental movement with her investigation of the effects of pesticides on the food chain in *Silent Spring* (1962). Environmental groups sprung up in response and agitated for ecological protections, the more radical of which demanded a complete reassessment of the nature of global, consumerist capitalism. The fall of communist states in Eastern Europe revealed that socialist economies could despoil the environment as much as capitalist ones; in fact, much of the cost of German reunification has involved bringing the former East Germany up to similar ecological

2 THEME MUSIC AND EXAMPLE BASE

For the examples in this section, consider how they help flesh out your understanding of the Individual and Society (IS) theme. More than ever, the lives or individuals were shaped by forces—economic, environmental, technological—beyond their control. You will notice that people will often form groups, such as reform movements or political parties, to address issues of concern.

standards as the rest of Germany. In the 1980s **Green parties** sprung up in Central Europe, advocating for sustainable development and supporting other leftist causes, such as social justice and pacifism. Germany's Green Party has proved most successful, having served in coalition with the Social Democratic Party from 1998 to 2005. Environmentalists often combined forces tactically and philosophically with feminists and the antinuclear movement in the 1980s and 1990s.

Most industrialized nations now support at least some of the environmental agenda. In 1992, 178 nations sent representatives to the first Earth Summit, held in Rio de Janeiro, to address concerns over global warming. Science has confirmed that human burning of fossil fuels (anthropogenic climate change) has increased global temperatures and reduced the ozone layer. To address the issue further, 150 nations signed the Kyoto Protocol to halve so-called greenhouse gases by 2010; however, the largest producer of such gases, the United States, has of this date declined to ratify the agreement. Another issue of concern for the environmental movement has been world population growth. At the beginning of the 20th century, the Earth's population stood at 1.7 billion; as of today, it stands at over 7 billion. Much of this growth has occurred in the developing world, often complicating global problems of poverty, illiteracy, and lack of infrastructure. Controversy over measures to address this issue, such as promotion of birth control, often provokes controversy among differing cultural and religious traditions.

Guest Workers and Immigration

During the economic boom times of the 1950s and 1960s, Europe allayed its labor shortage by enticing immigrants from southern Europe, Africa, and the Middle East. As with the United States today, these Gastarbeiter (as they are called in Germany) often performed jobs that local populations were reluctant or unwilling to assume. Moreover, governments often refused to extend citizenship or state benefits to these workers. When the European economy slowed in the 1970s and 1980s, local populations urged the **guest workers** to leave. When the fall of the Berlin Wall led to increased unemployment in the former East Germany, anti-immigrant parties and neo-Nazi groups urged their expulsion, or worse, attacked ethnic enclaves. In France, Jean-Marie Le Pen's National Front Party called for an end to immigration and supported economic nationalism; Le Pen polled enough votes in the 2002 presidential election to force a run-off before losing. An heir to the pan-German nationalist parties of the 19th century, the anti-immigrant Austria Freedom Party won almost 27% of the 1999 legislative vote, before falling back in subsequent elections. Issues of immigration and refugees (from the Middle East) highlight the growing diversity of European culture in an age of global capitalism and the challenges of successfully integrating new groups and redefining what it means to be European.

Domestic Terrorism

Indigenous European terrorist movements took root in the 1970s and divided basically into two groups: leftists and nationalists. Leftist groups arose out of the violent youth movement of the late 1960s, especially among those influenced by Maoist and Trotskyite ideologies. The Red Brigade used armed violence to force (unsuccessfully) Italy's withdrawal from the Western alliance. Most famously, it kidnapped and assassinated Prime Minister Aldo Moro in 1978; its influence has declined since the late 1980s. Germany's Baader-Meinhof Gang also employed assassinations and kidnappings of public and business officials, most famously in the so-called German Autumn of 1977. Since the collapse of communism, the influence of the group has decreased.

Ethnic **separatist movements** in Northern Ireland and Spain have used tactics similar to leftist groups. The Troubles in British-ruled Northern Ireland began in 1968–1969 with communal clashes between Protestants wishing to remain in the United Kingdom and Catholics wishing to unite with the Republic of Ireland. The Irish Republican Army (IRA) campaigned against the British presence with car bombs, assassinations, and hunger strikes. Not until 1998 had the two sides worked out a power-sharing agreement; in late 2005, the IRA announced that it had abandoned all of its weapons. Similarly in Spain, the ETA has agitated with assassinations and bombings for a separate socialist government representing the Basque people, the oldest ethnic group in Europe and one of the few not speaking an Indo-European language.

Intellectual and Cultural Trends

The experience of two world wars has fomented experimentation in the arts and reevaluation in the realms of philosophy and religion.[3]

3 SKILL SET

From the rubble of 1945, many Europeans reevaluated their civilization. As a focal point, consider the following interpretation (INTR): To what extent and in what ways was the Second World War a turning point in European intellectual and cultural life? To practice the skill of Periodization (PER), try writing a focused thesis paragraph in response.

Modernism and Postmodernism

We often use the term "modern" simply to mean contemporary. Modernism, however, is associated with the Enlightenment project—that is, the effort to discover the laws of nature and of human society, and thereby reach objective knowledge of the world. Once humans possess objective knowledge, they can harness nature for their flourishing and achieve progress. These notions define developments in ideas, economics, politics, and culture from the 18th into the 20th centuries. The wrenching experiences of the two world wars and disgust over the crimes of absolutist ideologies like Nazism and communism have produced a movement in opposition to modern assumptions of objective knowledge, a movement known as **postmodernism**.

Postmodernism's roots lay in the 19th-century ideas of Friedrich Nietzsche and Danish philosopher Søren Kierkegaard (1813–1855), both of whom emphasized the lack of objective values in the world and the importance of **subjective experience**. In the postwar intellectual world, postmodernism has exercised a significant influence on literary criticism, philosophy, the writing of history, architecture, and film. Postmodernists aim to deconstruct texts—fiction and nonfiction—to find the underlying sociopolitical structure of gender, class, and race embedded in the authors' works. All ideas carry the baggage of their creator's biases and drive for power. As Thomas Kuhn (1922–1996) argued in his *The Structure of Scientific Revolutions* (1962), not even science possesses objective authority, instead representing a series of paradigm shifts that deal only with fact and theory, not truth. Postmodernists express interest in how knowledge is constructed rather than its correspondence with truth, since the latter does not exist. In art, postmodernists employ irony and satire and promiscuously blend traditional and modern styles.

Existentialism

Existentialism dominated the postwar intellectual world. The philosophy arises out of humanity's modern predicament—our feeling of angst amid a world of dizzying economic and technological change, the decline of traditional religious values, and the horrors revealed of humanity during the 20th century. Most but not all existentialists began with Nietzsche's premise "God is dead." If this is so, then man must "create himself." As a movement, existentialism took hold among French intellectuals wrestling with the agonizing issues of resistance or collaboration during the Nazi occupation of France. Jean-Paul Sartre (1905–1980) was captured by the German army during World War II and later founded a resistance movement. Sartre argued that for humans, "existence precedes essence," meaning that we "turn up on the scene" without choosing to exist; because we have no creator, our essence must be defined by our own choices and values. As is demonstrated in Albert Camus's (1913–1960) novels *The Stranger* (1942) and *The Plague* (1947), humans must face the absurdity of existence by making life-defining choices alone and with incomplete knowledge of their surroundings. Human experience is thus subjective, and because no objective values exist for us to draw on, we must accept our radical human freedom and act with authenticity—without self-deception and by accepting responsibility for our choices. Existentialism significantly influenced the arts (see below), and with its emphasis on subjectivity and criticism of modern society, it helped lay the foundations for postmodernist thought.

Art, Theater, and Music

Signifying the increasingly important role of the United States in European affairs, the center of the Western art world shifted to New York City following World War II. Two styles dominated art in the contemporary era: <u>abstract expressionism</u> and <u>pop art</u>. In abstract expressionism, the artist does not portray anything, but instead uses the canvas and paint to express an emotional attitude or mood. American painter Jackson Pollock (1912–1956) popularized the style with his drip technique of pouring and splashing paint on immense canvases lying on the floor. Pop art is associated with both the rise of consumerism in the postwar Western world and also the irony and satire of postmodernism. Artists such as American Andy Warhol (1928–1987) and Roy Lichtenstein (1923–1997) employed advertising, celebrities, and comic books in their art to comment ironically on the artificiality of consumer capitalism. When contemplating Warhol's Campbell's soup cans or Lichtenstein's comic strips, the line between advertising and artistic creativity becomes blurred.

The ideas of existentialist Albert Camus directly influenced the so-called Theater of the Absurd. Whereas traditional drama concentrates on the development of plot and character, absurdist drama provokes the question, "What is happening now?" Along with the characters, the audience attempts to ascertain the significance of what is occurring on stage. Perhaps the most famous absurdist drama is Irish playwright Samuel Beckett's *Waiting for Godot* (1954), in which two tramps arrive on stage and discuss waiting for a figure named Godot; Godot never shows, but the audience is never told why this person is important. In Tom Stoppard's *Rosencrantz and Guildenstern Are Dead* (1967), two characters from Shakespeare's *Hamlet* discuss their upcoming fate but seem unable to prevent their untimely deaths—a play within a play.

While popular music incorporated rebellion and consumerism, composers of avant-garde (cutting edge) music experimented with serialism. Serialist composer Arnold Schoenberg (1874–1951) employed a 12-note scale and used mathematical series of tone rows to create a more abstract sound than standard tonal and melodic music. Pioneering American composer John Cage (1912–1992) experimented with chance music, where elements of a composition occur randomly. Most famously, Cage "played" his composition "4'33'" in concert, a piece consisting of not a single note; Cage simply timed the composition and then closed the piano cover. In conclusion, perhaps many of these works strike the reader as far-fetched, ridiculous, or nonsensical; with postwar culture, it may very well be that the point is that there is no point.

4 THEME MUSIC

How relevant is organized religion in an age of technological and intellectual pluralism? There are no easy answers to this question. Before responding, draw on what you've learned from the role of religion throughout the relevant themes of the course—in shaping views of the world (OS), influencing political life (SP), and affecting society (IS).

Religion in the Modern World[4]

As noted, religious belief in Europe declined markedly in the postwar period. Nonetheless, religious developments continued to play a role in European culture after 1945. For the Catholic Church, the most important development has been the ecumenical movement, or the effort to reach out and establish common ground with other, particularly Christian, religions. Since the Council of Trent (1545–1563), the Church had generally been on the defensive against modern ideas and culture. When Pope John XXIII (r. 1958–1963) called the **Second Vatican Council** (1962–1965), it signaled the willingness of the Catholic Church to update doctrine and practice more in keeping with modern developments. John opened dialogues with different faiths and called on wealthy nations to support social justice and work toward human rights. His successor, Paul VI (1963–1978), continued the work of Vatican II but sparked controversy with his encyclical *Humanae Vitae* (1968), which condemned artificial means of birth control.

Paul's death in 1978 opened the door for a historic change in the Church, the election of the first non-Italian pope since 1522 and the first Slavic pope ever. <u>John Paul II</u> (1978–2005), often considered the first postmodern pope, lived under both Nazi and Soviet oppression in his native Poland. This experience shaped John Paul's concern with what he later called the 20th century's "culture of death." As pope, John Paul supported the <u>Solidarity</u> movement in Poland and worked toward the end of communist oppression in Eastern Europe but also condemned the nuclear arms race and the excesses of consumer capitalism. John Paul's long reign also witnessed his many efforts to reconcile the Catholic Church with its past, apologizing for the Crusades, Galileo's persecution, and the failures of the Catholic Church during the Holocaust. Though progressive on economic issues, John Paul adhered to a conservative line on Church dogma, upholding bans on contraception, female and married priests, and abortion. Though it will likely take decades, if at all, for radical changes to occur in Catholic doctrine, Pope Francis (2013–) has worked to humanize the Church further, with a humble style and a more accepting rhetorical stance toward the above-mentioned divisive issues.

Most European Protestant denominations have reconciled themselves to modern biblical scholarship and have adapted their faiths in keeping with modern science. Nonetheless, Protestant theologians like the Swiss Karl Barth (1886–1986) took reformed Christianity back to its roots in biblical revelation. Barth held that divine revelation stood on its own feet, without the possibility of being judged by human reason. The European Protestant experience has differed markedly from that of the United States since 1945. Evangelical Christianity along with a renewed fundamentalism has experienced widespread growth in America, trends that have not generally touched Europe. Formerly communist Eastern Europe suffered under religious persecution, which effectively killed religious belief in several nations. This unchurched Europe often conflicts with United States when it comes to issues like Darwinian evolution and foreign policy.

Globalization

Since the beginning of this course, Europe's place in the world has been a recurring theme. More than ever, the issues confronting the world today reflect those facing Europe. With global communication developments, such as cell phones, the Internet, and social media, it is no longer possible for one region of the world to wall itself off from the rest. Recognition of past mistakes in this regard is already apparent with postwar efforts to build a common European identity through economic and political integration. In some ways, Europe has renewed its power and prestige after the horrors of the 20th century, yet it continues to struggle with its role and place in the world, as seen in the belated response to the Balkan conflicts of the 1990s, recent struggles over the euro currency and EU, and conflicts with shifting religious diversity. As confirmed by history since 1945, many Europeans seem to recognize that their continent functions increasingly within a global context.

Additional Resources

Karen Armstrong, *The Battle for God* (2001)—A comparative and critical analysis of the growth of fundamentalism among the monotheistic faiths.

Sarah Bakewell, *At the Existentialist Café: Freedom, Being, and Apricot Cocktails with Jean-Paul Sartre, Simone de Beauvoir, Albert Camus, Martin Heidegger, Maurice Merleau-Ponty and Others* (2016)—Explores the meaning and context of those who made a new philosophy.

Albert Camus, *The Stranger* (1942) and *The Plague* (1947)—Two well-known novels that convey the existentialist ethos well and raise profound questions about the human condition.

Thomas Friedman, *The World Is Flat: A Brief History of the Twenty-First Century* (2007)—The author examines the process of global economic and technological change.

Steven R.C. Hicks, *Explaining Postmodernism: Skepticism and Socialism from Rousseau to Foucault* (2011)—Introduces a recent and complex movement by examining it historical roots.

Tony Judt, *Postwar: A History of Europe since 1945* (2005)—A well-received history that offers powerful insights and the author's unique voice.

Mark Kurlansky, *1968: The Year That Rocked the World* (2005)—Interesting analysis of the personalities involved in a year of upheaval.

www.art-for-a-change.com/Paris/paris.html—This site provides text and posters of the student revolts in 1968 Paris.

Practice MC Questions

Questions 1–4 are based on the chart below.

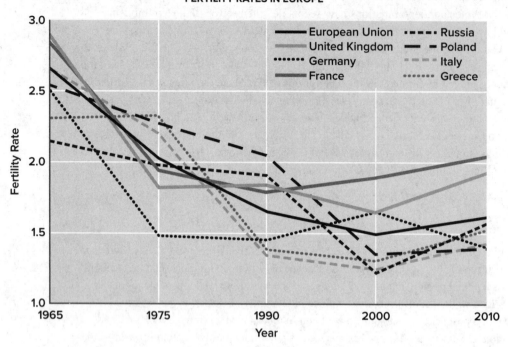

FERTILITY RATES IN EUROPE

1. The levels at the beginning of the chart are explained by all of the following EXCEPT:

   A. government policies to increase birthrates.

   B. economic recovery and a rising standard of living.

   C. improved political stability after the world wars.

   D. the threat of Soviet communism and nuclear war.

2. Fertility levels after 1965 reflect which of the following?

   A. The growth of gay and lesbian rights

   B. A youth culture emphasizing rebellion

   C. Advances in artificial birth control

   D. Immigration of workers from outside Europe

3. The later fertility trends have prompted debates over:

   A. whether women should have the right to vote.

   B. the benefits of European economic unity.

   C. the role of technology in European society.

   D. the economic feasibility of the welfare state.

4. A feminist would most likely use the data to support which of the following conclusions?

   A. "New conceptions of marriage and motherhood have freed women from a solely domestic role."

   B. "High fertility rates cause significant problems of environmental degradation and resource overuse."

   C. "Emigration from overseas should be curtailed to provide European women with greater job opportunities."

   D. "Western European nations have provided higher status and greater rights to women than those in Eastern Europe."

Paul Edward Dutton, Suzanne Marchand, Deborah Harkness, *Many Europes: Choice and Chance in Western Civilization* (New York: McGraw-Hill Education, 2014), p. 860.

Questions 5–8 are based on the image below.

Advertisement for Belling electric cooker, Britain, 1954

5. The image above most strongly reflects the postwar economic trend of:

   A. continental integration.

   B. central planning.

   C. consumerism.

   D. American aid.

6. The image coincides with which of the following postwar trends?

   A. Competition from the Soviet economic bloc

   B. Economic recovery and rising standard of living

   C. Existential concern for freedom and individualism

   D. Concern with technology's destructive potential

7. A European historian would mostly likely use this art as evidence of:

   A. the growing cultural influence of the United States.

   B. a general decline in the belief in progress.

   C. attitudes toward gender and family.

   D. the effectiveness of the social welfare policies.

8. The postwar development represented by the image would have received the strongest criticism after 1970 from

   A. the Green Party.

   B. guest workers.

   C. national separatists.

   D. postmodernists.

See Chapter 18 for answers and explanations.

Short-Answer Question with Sample and Commentary

A. Choose TWO post-1945 technological changes and explain their respective impacts on European society, using ONE piece of evidence for each.

B. Explain ONE critical reaction against the developments above with ONE piece of evidence.

(HTS: Causation and Use of Evidence)

A. After World War II ended, many Europeans were concerned about the destructive nature of technology. However, these concerns did not stop the progress of science and technology. One can argue that the most important technology was nuclear power. Some nations, especially France, used it to reduce their reliance on Middle Eastern oil, and it made relatively cheap power available to millions. However, this also presented the problem of nuclear waste, as with the meltdown at Chernobyl in the 1980s, not to mention the constant threat of nuclear war, which almost happened over missiles in Cuba.

    Another socially impactful invention was the birth control pill. When it became widely available in the 1960s, it reduced the Baby Boom birthrates and more to the point, gave women a new reproductive freedom and helped create the sexual revolution. This new freedom was expressed in the youth revolts of 1968.

B. Ironically it was these very same youth that criticized these technologies. They viewed society—like their professors and parents—as being materialistic and too focused on consumer pleasures. To show their displeasure, young people in Paris and many other cities rose in rebellion, using leftist ideologies to show displeasure with capitalism.

Here we have a model response. The student provides sufficient analysis and detail while respecting the SAQ format, i.e., to be concise. In Part A, he briefly sets the context of WWII before explaining an example (nuclear power) that bridges to the Cold War, offering two ways that technology affected society. Switching gears, the response notes the impact of the birth control pill on women's lives and in sexuality more generally. The reference to 1968 once again allows the student to bridge to Part B, where the analysis is extended to the student revolts and their critique of consumer capitalism. Score: 3 points.

Chapter 4

1. **Answer: C. HTS—CTX & INTR; Theme—OS; KC—1.1.** All of the terms listed apply to the Renaissance. This reminds you that stimulus-based questions will often present several appealing choices. In the last paragraph, Burckhardt explicitly calls out individualism (C) and presents this value as characterizing the break between the attitude of the Renaissance and the Middle Ages, which according to Burckhardt, promoted identity based almost exclusively within groups, such as classes or church. Choices A, B, and D can only be inferred from the passage.

2. **Answer: A. HTS—CAUS; Theme—OS; KC—1.1.** These choices reflect accurate features of art prior to the French Revolution. Only A expresses an attitude of the Renaissance (both northern and Italian) toward art. In addition, A connects most explicitly to the theme of individualism tested in Question 1. Choice B reflects features of the Baroque, while D captures Dutch art. Choice C represents an overstatement of art during this period.

3. **Answer: B. HTS—CCOT; Theme—OS; KC—3.6.** As you try these questions, you will encounter several like this—requiring knowledge of topics you may not have covered. I've included them here-and-there to give you practice with cross-chronological thinking and to sharpen your powers of inference. Again, all the choices express intellectual movements during Burckhardt's life, yet B connects most strongly to the origins of modernism that the author seeks to find in the Renaissance (note the word "objective"). A is incorrect since there are no references to class conflict. C and D would seem to be excluded by the references to individualism and challenging the status quo in the Renaissance.

4. **Answer: D. HTS—PER & INTR; Theme—OS; KC—1.1.** B is not addressed within the content of the passage, and though Burckhardt presents the Renaissance favorably, his purpose goes beyond merely applauding it (A). Certainly C is true, but historical figures will always reflect their historical context, a trivial point. Burckhardt seeks primarily to find within the Renaissance those features that came to dominate the modern ethos—individualism, secularism, and rationalism (D).

5. **Answer: C. HTS—CAUS; Themes—IS & OS; KCs 1.1 & 1.2.** Since this is an EXCEPT question, we are seeking the one cause that does not apply. The printing press (A) facilitated the spread of literacy and promoted the Protestant focus on reading the Bible (B). The tone clearly indicates the importance placed upon the role of forming morality through education; not to mention that the source comes from a municipal government (D). C is the correct answer, both because of its inapplicability to the stem and also since the emperor failed to centralize power during this period.

6. **Answer: B. HTS—COMP & EVARG; Themes—IS & OS; KC 1.3.** Each of the figures relates to issues of religious reform during the 16th century; however, it was Calvin who most strongly promoted education. Not only did Geneva found its own academy for training of pastors, but like most mainstream reformers, Calvin placed strong emphasis on Bible reading and seeking knowledge as a way of glorifying God. As rulers, Charles (A) and Henry (C) focused on other issues, and Anabaptists (D) concentrated more on living simply in small Christian communities.

7. **Answer: A. HTS—COMP; Themes—IS & OS; KCs 1.1 & 1.3.** One of the key differences between the Italian and northern Renaissances (and Reformation) was the former's emphasis on secular values. Both pursued education and revived classical texts, but as can be seen from the ordinance, northern religious reformers saw education primarily in religious terms. The other choices (B-D) express attitudes of both movements.

8. **Answer: B. HTS—CCOT; Themes—IS & SP; KC 3.3.** Here again you are asked to apply your understanding of a topic (education) across a time period. After around 1850, most governments legislated universal education for all citizens, in part to support the skills necessary to sustain a more complex economy but also to inculcate national loyalties (B). D is the opposite of this idea, and governments would certainly not wish to promote violence against the state (C). In both periods, education addressed moral concerns, such as formation of character and promoting group affiliation—to regions, religion, or the state (A).

Chapter 5

1. **Answer: C. HTS—CAUS; Theme—INT; KC 1.4.** The scene depicted is the largest mining operation in the Americas, established by the Spanish with the enslaved labor of indigenous peoples. The question aims at explaining how it is that Spain (and other European states) were able to establish such colonies. Since this is an EXCEPT question, you should look for the one factor that does not apply. Though C may have happened, the depiction of mythological civilizations did not motivate states directly to seek colonies, nor did it provide the means to do so. Choices A, B, and D played key roles in sustaining European exploration and colonization.

2. **Answer: B. HTS—CCOT & CAUS; Theme—PP; KC 1.5.** The mining operation extracted precious metals and injected these into the European economy, This fact, in addition, to the trade in goods from colonies, stimulated the development of new financial and banking practices (B). The influence of precious metals indirectly influenced the growth of landed elites (A), and affected serfdom even less so (C). Though hierarchy continued to guide social relations, the new money economy tended to undermine this notion (D).

3. **Answer: D. HTS—COMP; Themes—INT & PP; KCs 1.4 & 2.2.** In this question, you compare the effects of exploration on the Americas and Africa. The main impact on Africa, which also affected the Americas, was the trade in slaves, most of whom ended up working on plantations in the Americas producing sugar, cotton, indigo, tobacco, etc. Large

territorial empires did not occur in Africa until the 19th century (A). States did compete over the slave trade in Africa, among other resources, so B is incorrect. As with all regions, the further integration of the global economy (C) affected Africa, as we see with the slave trade.

4. **Answer: C. HTS—EVARG; Theme—INT; KC 1.4.** Here you are asked to think like an historian. Each of the choices reflect possible uses of the document, but to settle on the key, make sure you look again at the depiction. It shows brutal labor and reveals conditions of the indigenous peoples (C). We can infer European motivations from the activities and manner of the work, but other sources would work better to reveal these facts (A). Since this does not seem like a work of fine art, we can exclude B. Of course, exploration affected European rivalries, but these issues are not raised by the image (D).

5. **Answer: B. HTS—CAUS; Theme—SP; KC 1.3.** You are asked here about the causes of the Thirty Years' War, the settlement of which is shown on the map. A, C, and D all express major causes and motivations of the powers involved. Though England and Britain had by this time established colonies outside Europe, their long competition for overseas dominance did not begin until later and did not affect the Thirty Years' War.

6. **Answer: B. HTS—CAUS & CCOT; Theme—SP; KCs 1.2 & 1.3.** By 1648, Spain had begun its decline, so we can exclude A. Westphalia confirmed the decline of the Holy Roman Empire, the opposite of C. With the military revolution that helped define the conflict, the state gained greater control over warfare, eliminating D. We are left with the major impact of the peace–the establishment of state sovereignty over religious matters and the end of religion as a key motive for warfare (B).

7. **Answer: D. HTS—PER; Theme—SP; KCs 1.2 & 1.3.** The Peace of Westphalia confirmed state control of religion, removing it as a source of conflict between states (D). Since the aristocracy continued to dominate political offices, we exclude A. Choice B did occur, but the Thirty Years' War did not involve the issue of colonies. The papacy, in fact, declined in political influence, excluding C.

8. **Answer: C. HTS—CAUS; Theme—SP; KCs 1.2 & 1.3.** Choices A, B, and D either gained from the treaty (e.g., Sweden, with lands in the Baltic) or experienced no reduction in their diplomatic situation. Spain, however, failed to maintain itself as the political leader of Catholicism and, in attempting to do so, futilely expended much of its wealth. Along with population decline and cultural stagnation, the Thirty Years' War pushed Spain outside the ranks of the great powers of Europe (C).

Chapter 6

1. **Answer: D. HTS—CTX & EVARG; Theme—OS; KC 1.1.** Galileo engaged in all the activities expressed by these choices, as evidenced by appealing to his patron's wife in this letter (B). And though he stirred controversy with his written works (A) and helped create an international dialogue with other scientists such as Kepler (C), it was his questioning of biblical and church authority in the context of the Counter-Reformation and later Thirty Years' War that brought him before the Roman Inquisition (D).

2. **Answer: C. HTS—CCOT; Theme—OS; KCs and 2.3.** A is clearly not the answer, since Galileo's trial reflects conflicts, not to mention later issues during the French Revolution and scientific theories like Darwin's. Galileo, in fact, took scientific ideas beyond ancient thinkers, eliminating B. Though states patronized science, scientists did not generally appeal to their authority to bolster their ideas. We are left with C: the Scientific Revolution led directly to a mechanistic worldview based on the invocation of natural laws and application of mathematics. This approach would sustain the 18th-century Enlightenment.

3. **Answer: C. HTS—CTX; Theme—OS; KC 1.1.** As an EXCEPT question, you are seeking the one choice that does not apply. The visual demonstrates a use of empiricism to make conclusions about blood flow. A, B, and D all represent important features of the new science and which are explicitly or implicitly demonstrated in the visual. Though C is true, folk traditions are not portrayed in the visual and were not considered a defining feature of the new science.

4. **Answer: D. HTS—CTX & CAUS; Theme—OS; KC 1.1.** This is a straightforward factual question, inferred from the visual. William Harvey discovered the modern theory of blood flow, through a system of arteries and veins (and later capillaries). Paracelsus (A) formed a bridge between Galenic and modern anatomy but worked more by trial and error. Vesalius (B) also contributed to anatomical discoveries but not specifically with blood flow. Bacon (C) helped establish the scientific method but was not known for specific discoveries related to anatomy.

5. **Answer: B. HTS—COMP & CCOT; Theme—OS; KCs 1.1 & 3.6.** Here you are asked to project the methods and ideas of the Scientific Revolution forward. Between 19th-century positivism and the new science of the 16th and 17th centuries, there are many similarities. These include A, C, and D. However, by the completion of the Newtonian cosmology (around 1690), most scientists had moved beyond their fascination with alchemy and astrology as part of project of explaining nature.

6. **Answer: A. HTS—CTX; Theme—OS; KC 1.1.** In the painting, we see a physician demonstrating the features of human anatomy through direct observation. An interested group of spectators stand around, rapt by the exhibition. This scene reveals the importance of empiricism (A) to the new science. Of course, math was also a key feature (B), but not shown in the painting. One might make deductions from these observations, but this process is not revealed directly in the visual (C). Finally, no particular model of the universe is depicted, eliminating D.

7. **Answer: C. HTS—CAUS; Themes—OS, PP & SP; KCs 1.1 & 2.2.** This question asks you to connect intellectual/cultural developments with the features of Dutch society and politics. The Netherlands was generally considered the most tolerant area of Europe (A) and oriented toward trade and commerce (B and D). However, the Netherlands was a decentralized oligarchic republic dominated by the wealthy merchants. It was not controlled by a strong, central monarchy (C).

8. **Answer: B. HTS—CTX & EVARG; Theme—OS; KCs 1.1 & 2.3.** All of the statements accurately express purposes of art; however, the Enlightenment did not occur during the 17th

century, eliminating it. Though the painting arguably employs Baroque style, it certainly does not advance a religious or political outlook (A). C can be excluded, since the painting does employ perspective and, because of its scientific subject matter, embraces a natural style. That leaves us with B, which does accurately express an artistic trend that is shown in the painting–the idea of advancing our understanding of the human body to address illness and promote medicine.

Chapter 7

1. **Answer: A. HTS—CTX; Theme—SP; KCs 1.2 & 2.1.** Each statement is accurate in itself; however the two passages illustrate the conflict between the English Parliament and the Stuart monarchs (James I) over political sovereignty. Neither employs scientific language to justify its position (eliminating B); instead the Parliament calls on tradition and James invokes God. Neither passage bears on question of beliefs about the cosmos (C) or the issue of commerce (D). A is the only choice that captures the notion of conflict and conveys the debate over absolutism.

2. **Answer: C. HTS—COMP; Theme—SP; KC 2.1.** In Source 2 James argues for an absolutist divine-right monarchy, most akin to what Louis XIV aimed for in France (B). However, this question asks for the *exception* to the ideal. Since Russia was an autocracy, it is also eliminated (A). Though Spain declined in this period, its monarchs maintained strong political and religious power (D). Poland, however, struggled during this period with an elective monarchy and was ultimately partitioned out of existence by 1795, demonstrating its weakness (C).

3. **Answer: B. HTS—CCOT; Theme—SP; KCs 1.2 & 2.1.** The Parliament achieved its recognition of sovereignty by English monarchs with the Glorious Revolution in 1689 (B). Of course, England participated in the Commercial and Scientific Revolutions (A and C), as well as the Protestant Reformation (D); however, Parliament's goals were primarily political (with religious issues as a complicating factor), making B the best choice.

4. **Answer: C. HTS—EVARG; Themes—SP & OS; KCs 2.1 & 2.3.** John Locke supported the Glorious Revolution with his *Two Treatises on Government* and provided a theoretical foundation for limited government and the social contract, ideals that later influenced revolutions (C). Since Calvinism tended to be a minority religion, it did express some anti-monarchical strains, but without the theoretical foundations of Locke and not in the appropriate historical context (A). B can be eliminated, since Hobbes provided a secular defense of absolutism in opposition to Locke's later ideas. D can be safely eliminated, as Louis represents the strongest strain of absolutist thinking, more in line with Source 2.

5. **Answer: B. HTS—INTR & CAUS; Theme—SP; KCs 1.2, 1.3 & 2.1.** Blanning's interpretation focuses on the results of the Peace of Westphalia, which provided for religious diversity within the Holy Roman Empire. Now that states came to control religion, warfare shifted toward secular concerns, as noted in B. A, B, and D are accurate statements; however, A and D have little to do with religion directly, while C violated the principle of pluralism.

6. **Answer: A. HTS—INTR & PER; Theme—SP; KCs 1.2, 1.3 & 2.1.** Blanning argues for the significance of 1648 as a turning point in politics and diplomacy. One such justification for this claim is given in A, since states turned to issues of rivalry over commerce and territory on the heels of the Commercial Revolution. The year 1648 does not weigh substantially on the arts (since the Baroque style bridges the date–B), nor does it for commerce and finance (since these trends evolved over time–C) or for the Scientific Revolution (which began with Copernicus in 1543 and ended with Newton in 1687–D).

7. **Answer: D; HTS—CAUS & CCOT; Theme—SP; KC 2.1.** This is a difficult question, as it asks you to project forward from 1648 and anticipate the structure of diplomacy in central Europe. From the Thirty Years' War there emerged two strong German powers–the Austrian Empire and Brandenburg-Prussia—each of which prevented the other from unifying the German-speaking peoples (until diplomacy changed in the 19th century), giving D as the key. A is true but did not directly affect the settlement and pattern of diplomacy. B and C are also true in their periods; however, they represented developments complicating the essential division of Germany and did not change that division directly.

8. **Answer: D; HTS—CAUS, CCOT & INTR; Theme—SP; KC 2.1.** B was already in process and did not directly affect German politics. The United States did not substantially affect European diplomacy until World War I (eliminating C). Industrialization eventually altered the balance of power in central Europe, but only after Germany had been unified (in 1871, A). It was the spread of revolutionary ideas and upheaval to the traditional state system (D) that opened the door to new patterns of diplomacy and allowed Prussia to defeat Austria and unify the other German-speaking states.

Chapter 8

1. **Answer: C. HTS—CAUS; Themes—PP & SP; KCs 2.2 & 2.1.** The map displays the economic effects of the slave trade, connecting this practice to the development of a European-dominated global economy. Except for C (the key), all of the choices did result directly or indirectly from the slave trade. To manage their trade and exploit colonies, most states practiced mercantilist policies, such as France under Colbert (A). This competition led to rivalries and commercial wars (D), as well as put new goods (such as sugar) in the homes of Europeans, stimulating a consumer culture. However, Russia did not participate in the Atlantic trade and was primarily a commercial power (C).

2. **Answer: D. HTS—EVARG; Themes—PP & SP; KCs 2.2 & 2.1.** Slave labor was not widely employed in military and naval operations, excluding A. European powers did not come to control the interior of Africa until after 1871 (B). Though C is true, the map does not support that conclusion directly and such a development would follow in subsequent decades. This leaves D as the key, which ties the question back to a major theme of the course and close to the wording of KC 2.2 itself.

3. **Answer: B. HTS—CCOT; Themes—PP & OS; KCs 2.2 & 2.3.** This CCOT question asks you to project beyond the map data and consider how the issue of slavery and the slave trade changed after the middle of the 18th century. You may recall that the 18th century was, in part, defined by the

Enlightenment, which critiqued inequality in institutions, including slavery (B). A is incorrect, as the reverse is true (due to the Seven Years' War). European powers continued to intrude into Africa, at least along the coasts and in North Africa (C). Though the U.S. did emerge as a major power and considered the Americas as its sphere of influence, it did not generally become a formal colonial power (D).

4. **Answer: B. HTS—CTX & INTR; Theme—PP; KCs 1.5 & 2.2.** Roberts portrays the 18th-century old regime as lacking in innovation and oriented toward the preservation of traditional norms. This coincides with the prevalence of serfdom in eastern Europe (B). The areas suggested by A, B, and D represent innovations in the economy, all of which increased productivity and challenged the control of traditional groups (e.g., guilds, nobles) over production.

5. **Answer: A. HTS—INTR & EVARG; Themes—SP, PP & IS; KCs 2.1, 2.2, & 2.4.** Here you are asked to consider evidence that runs counter to the historical interpretation. Since Roberts argues for the static nature of the old regime, your job is to find the one that supports it (since this is an EXCEPT question). Rivalries among the great powers of Europe were nothing new to the 18th century, making A the answer. Each of the choices represented by B, C, and D express major new developments in the areas of demographics, social life, and economic organization.

6. **Answer: B. HTS—CCOT; Theme—SP; KC 3.4.** Since Roberts argues for the inherent conservatism of the 18th century, we need to find the expression of conservatism in the 19th century. The answer is B: through the Concert of Europe, Metternich (of Austria) attempted to suppress the revolutionary fallout from the French Revolution. Mechanization of textiles replaced the old system of guild production, making it an innovation (A). Positivism developed after 1840 along with the success of science and technology in seeming to provide new means to address human problems (C). Along with the growth of commerce, and especially industry in the 19th century, the middle class grew in influence, which fed the revolutionary ideologies of the period (D). Thus, B-D represent key changes defining the 19th century, counter to the view of Roberts in the 18th century.

7. **Answer: B. HTS—CAUS; Themes—PP & IS. KCs 2.2 & 2.4.** Each of the choices represents an accurate statement of 18th-century trends. The passage connects a cultural venue (coffeehouses) with a new product from overseas expansion, reflecting the development of a new consumer culture (B). Though A may have occurred as a result of the phenomenon, it is not directly addressed in the passage. Population did increase (C) in the 18th century; this, however, was more the result not the cause of the introduction of new goods into Europe. Patrons of coffeehouses certainly discussed new ideas (D), as the passage implies, but a better explanation relates to how coffeehouses helped spread such ideas rather than the reverse.

8. **Answer: C. HTS—CAUS; Themes—PP & OS; KCs 2.2, 2.3 & 2.4.** This question effectively reverses the Causation issue of the previous one. Governments practiced censorship, but the practice predated the development of coffeehouses (and in most states proved ineffective–A). B also occurred, but this result did not prove as consequential as the application of scientific ideas

to society–i.e., the Enlightenment (C). As for D, this was more the cause than the result of the coffeehouse (and related development of civil society) captured by the passage.

9. **Answer: A. HTS—EVARG; Themes—PP; KC 2.2.** Let's remember to focus on connecting your content knowledge to what is indicated by the passage. European governments did compete for global control of resources, but the passage does not address that point (B). Controversial new religious views did emerge from new civic venues (such as coffeehouses and salons), but the text does not address that point (C). The same can be said for D–true as well, but not addressed by the passage. A is the correct answer, as the pamphlet addresses a new venue and atmosphere created by a new product (A).

Chapter 9

1. **Answer: D. HTS—CTX & EVARG; Themes—OS & IS; KC 2.3.** In this passage, Rousseau reinforces his gendered perspective on social roles and intellectual capacities. Though few Enlightenment philosophes endorsed feminism, most did embrace the notion of inherent sexual differences as strongly as Rousseau (D). A and B both state important principles of the Enlightenment and ones that Rousseau would have endorsed in his other writings. C would contradict enlightened thought, but Rousseau does not explicitly reject empiricism in the passage.

2. **Answer: B. HTS—CTX; Theme—OS; KC 2.3.** Rousseau introduced new concepts to the Enlightenment, but also stands apart from the other philosophes in questioning the exclusive focus on reason and in upholding the importance of sentiment. We can see the latter in his sentimental view of the female role in marriage and the household (B). Consumer goods did expand during the 18th century (A); however, this phenomenon does not relate to the passage, nor does the passage address censorship (C) or the growth of civic venues (D).

3. **Answer: C. HTS—COMP; Themes—OS, INT, & IS; KCs 2.2 & 2.3.** In erecting an insurmountable gender barrier, Rousseau's establishes an "otherness" to women akin to how Enlightenment figures drew on travel narratives to portray non-European peoples (Africans, Native Americans, Oceanians) as either uncivilized brutes or, positively, as "noble savages." Enlightenment writers addressed commerce (A), science (B), and themes of citizenship (D), but they did so positively, not negatively, as Rousseau does with women.

4. **Answer: C. HTS—CTX & CCOT; Themes—IS & PP; KCs 2.3 & 2.4.** Statements A, B, and D express important features of social life affecting women. Feminists drew on the language of natural rights to argue for female equality (e.g., Mary Wollstonecraft), but the statement is overstated and premature. Women did not gain the rights listed until the middle of the 19th century at the earliest (C).

5. **Answer: C. HTS—CCOT & PER; Themes—IS & SP; KCs 2.3 & 4.4.** This is a challenging question that requires a sensitivity to how important movements of change actually played out for women and gender attitudes. Both the Enlightenment (A) and French Revolution (B) saw the involvement of women and arguments for female equality; however, women often found efforts at equality stymied by intellectual limitations and male leadership focused on other concerns. The Cold War (D) certainly affected women, as with any other

group, yet it did not directly contribute to major changes in women's lives, though such changes did occur *during* the Cold War. This leaves us with C, as it was during the First World War that women entered the workforce (outside the home) in large numbers and gained the right to vote in many nations.

6. **Answer: B. HTS—CTX; Theme—OS; KC 2.3.** In the text, Paine endorses a view of the Supreme Being commensurate with scientific and secular attitudes toward nature, a position known as deism (B). Though Paine would also have embraced toleration (A), this principle is not the focus of the text. Paine clearly expresses a belief in a Supreme Being, eliminating C and D.

7. **Answer: D. HTS—CAUS & CTX; Themes—OS & SP; KCs 2.1 & 2.3.** Here is where a sensitivity to historical context can assist your ability to infer correct answers. This passage was published during the de-Christianization campaign of the French Revolution, possible in support of the secular policies of that regime (D). Paine explicitly rejected monarchy in other writings, eliminating C. Though Paine hailed from Britain, the text does not treat directly with A, and choice B seems early for writings on conditions of textile factories.

8. **Answer: C. HTS—COMP & CCOT; Theme—OS; KCs 2.3 & 1.1.** A is false, as Renaissance intellectuals did not argue for separation between church and state, merely a more secular outlook on life. Paine endorsed equality, but B overstates the Renaissance attitude, which tended to accept some hierarchies as natural. Both Paine (as shown in the passage) and Renaissance humanists strongly endorsed individualism (D). Despite their purported secularism, Renaissance humanists accepted the authority of the church and did not reject Christianity as a belief system.

Chapter 10

1. **Answer: C. HTS—CAUS & CTX; Theme—SP; KC 2.1.** All of the choices represent causes of the French Revolution; however, the passage makes no reference to economic or financial issues, excluding A and D. In addition, although the last line refers to the elimination of "Orders" in the new National Assembly (B), the primary thrust of the passage centers around discontent with the monarchy and the desire by revolutionaries to strip the king of his powers and force upon him a constitutional form of government. Making C the correct choice.

2. **Answer: D. HTS—CCOT & EVARG; Themes—SP & IS; KC 2.1.** The British ambassador presents the revolution in its early stages as a bloodless constitutional change. Even so, many of the early events of the revolution involved outright violence or conflict, including A and B. The Declaration of the Rights of Man would fit directly in with the passage, as it marks another legal change from above (C). However, the execution of Louis and subsequent Reign of Terror clearly do not fit the portrayal of a relatively smooth transition to a new regime (D).

3. **Answer: D. HTS—COMP; Theme—SP; KCs 2.1 & 4.2.** You are asked here to make an historical comparison across time periods. The French Revolution most closely parallels the Russian Revolution (D), in that both involved a fundamental political reordering against a perceived inept and corrupt

monarchy, fueled by a combination of economic grievances and new political ideologies (Enlightenment and socialism). The Protestant Reformation caused political changes but was primarily religious in character (A), and opposition to the Habsburgs occurred within the basic structure of early modern dynastic politics (B). Finally, choice C expresses an almost-opposite outcome–a political revolution that created unity under a stronger monarchy.

4. **Answer: C. HTS—CAUS & CCOT; Themes—SP & INT; KC 2.1.** The stimulus reminds you that all areas of Europe took note of the French Revolution; thus, the stem asks in turn to gauge the effects of the revolution outside Europe. The French employed mass citizen armies effectively to spread the ideals of the revolution (A), through which Napoleon also created an empire that dominated Europe for a decade (D). In addition, the revolution led to the abolition of slavery in French colonies and a revolt in Saint Domingue (Haiti)–A. This leaves C as the only false outcome (remember, this is an EXCEPT question). Though Napoleon did impose such republics, they did not prove long-lived and certainly not committed to peace, since warfare defined the continent from 1792–1815.

5. **Answer: C. HTS—CTX & CAUS; Themes—OS & SP; KCs 2.3 & 2.1.** This image was used by radical revolutionaries to promote the new calendar, which replaced the "religious" Gregorian calendar, as part of a de-Christianization campaign, based on the Enlightenment trend toward rationalizing law and weights and measures (C). If anything, the style of art is neoclassical, not Romantic (B). Though the figure is a woman, it is not aimed at women's rights–which were not advanced during the radical phase–instead, the figure is more akin to a goddess of liberty/reason (D). Of course, French armies spread the ideals of the revolution, but this image does not touch on that issue (A).

6. **Answer: A; HTS—CTX & EVARG; Themes—SP & OS; KCs 2.1.** As noted above, the calendar (among other reforms during the radical phase) coincided with the general effort to expunge the features of the Old Regime believed to be "superstitious and fanatical," particularly religion (A). Each of the other developments occurred during the French Revolution; however, they are not addressed by the image. Once again, the visual does not touch on military affairs (B), nor does it deal with the execution of the king (C). A government based on popular sovereignty preceded the calendar and occurred with the early actions by the National Assembly (D).

7. **Answer: D; HTS—CTX & CAUS; Theme—SP; KC 2.1.** The map portrays the height of Napoleon's empire, a feat that was accomplished primarily by force of French arms, relying on mass citizen armies (D). With the levy in mass, women were asked to contribute to the war effort, but not to promote feminist ideals (A). Britain, of course, possessed an extensive empire, but because of this fact, it tended to act as the most consistent opponent of Napoleon, which would not have aided his conquests (B). Finally, the hostility of foreign governments resulted from but did not cause the situation on the map (C).

8. **Answer: B; HTS—COMP & CCOT; Theme—SP: KCs 1.3 & 2.1.** Russia's dominance in the east predates the map (A), and even though Russia had grown since 1648, it had been the largest power in the east since the 16th century. C did not occur

until later in the 19th century, and both periods witnessed extended war among the great powers (e.g., Thirty Years' War), eliminating D. That leaves B, and indeed, the Holy Roman Empire had dominated central Europe since the Middle Ages until Napoleon abolished it in 1806.

9. **Answer: A. HTS—CAUS & CCOT; Theme—SP; KC 2.1.** C occurred but not specifically in relation to the diplomatic situation depicted, rather due to internal British policies and circumstances. The Catholic Church never did regain the power it had lost during the early modern movements of reform, including the French Revolution (B). Despite serious blunders, Napoleon did not provoke a civil war in France related to his rule. However, the great powers of Europe eventually felt emboldened by Napoleon's errors to wage campaigns of nationalist liberation, defeating him for good at Waterloo (A).

Chapter 11

1. **Answer: D; HTS—CTX; Themes—PP & OS; KCs: 2.3 & 3.1.** In the passage, Ricardo–one of the classical economists–argues for the unfettered operation of a free-market economy, echoing the principles first articulated by Adam Smith (D). During the radical phase of the French Revolution, its leaders attempted to regulate prices–not what Ricardo advocates (A). The laissez-faire approach presented in the passage was associated with Liberalism, not Conservatism during the 19th century (B). Finally, Ricardo does not address the typical concerns of the Romantics, many of whom were skeptical of industrialization (C).

2. **Answer: A. HTS—EVARG & CCOT; Theme—OS; KCs 3.1 & 3.6.** It is clear that Ricardo does not endorse Marxism (D), since this passage argues for a free-market economy. Also, there is no mention or implication of feminism (C). Though Ricardo calls for a limited government, it is a government nonetheless, excluding anarchism (B). This leaves us with Social Darwinism, and indeed, supporters of this application of Darwin's ideas argued for a "survival-of-the-fittest" philosophy toward the economy.

3. **Answer: A. HTS—COMP; Themes—PP & SP; KC 3.1.** Ricardo's passage tends to parallel the British government's approach toward industrialization–providing a framework of property rights and the economic infrastructure and then allowing market forces to work. However, continental nations, playing catch-up with Britain, relied much more on government subsidies and protective tariffs to support industry (A). Unions tended to be a function of the pace of industrialization, and thus, continental nations paralleled Britain; in fact, the German SPD became Europe's strongest socialist movement (B). All states were eventually forced to address the problems of industry, eliminating C. Some nations did lack natural resources (e.g., Spain); however, many like Germany and Belgium drew effectively on their resource base (D).

4. **Answer: C. HTS—CTX & EVARG; Themes—SP & OS; KCs 3.3 & 3.4.** Mazzini writes from a strong nationalist perspective, within a nation lacking unity (Italy). The reason for Italy's lack of unity relates to decisions made at Vienna (C). Napoleon's invasion of Italy and proclamation of a republic (1796–1797) stimulated nationalist sentiment, but Mazzini's writing is too removed in time for this to be the key (B). Napoleon also abolished feudalism in most parts of Italy,

but again, the passage does not address this issue (A). Finally, the Crimean War (1853–1856) had not yet occurred (D).

5. **Answer: D. HTS—CTX; Themes—OS & SP; KC 3.3.** Though Mazzini had Liberal (A) and Romantic (B) tendencies, his writing here focuses on the bonds of nationhood and the need to create a unified state (D). Mazzini believed in political equality, but the text does not support any notions of collective ownership of property or redistribution of income (C).

6. **Answer: B. HTS—CCOT & PER; Theme—SP; KC 3.4.** Attempts at Italian unity (A) failed during the revolutions of 1848; however, it was the work of Cavour (Prime Minister of Piedmont-Sardinia) that established the new Italian kingdom in 1861 (B). Both C and D occurred after Italy became unified, though they do relate to Italian nationalism.

7. **Answer: B. HTS—EVARG & COMP; Themes—SP & OS; KCs 3.3 & 3.4.** Napoleon, Garibaldi, and Bismarck were all nationalists of one variety or another (A, C, and D), even if Bismarck achieved nationalism from the top-down rather than the bottom-up. However, Metternich attempted through the Concert of Europe to blunt nationalism, an obvious tactic for a minister of a multi-ethnic empire (B).

8. **Answer: C. HTS—CTX; Theme—OS; KC 3.6.** In this painting, two figures contemplate a moonrise amidst a ancient trees and rock-strewn hills. Romantics embraced the supernatural (A), and this scene suggests the spiritual dimension of human experience. The painting also reveals Romantic preoccupation with nature (B) and fascination with individuals (D). Though Romantics critiqued the Enlightenment overemphasis on reason, this work does not comment on that feature of the movement (C), making it the outlier for this EXCEPT question.

9. **Answer: B. HTS—CCOT; Theme—OS; KCs 3.6 & 4.3.** Both A and C express characteristics of Romantic thought, but it is arguable that these tendencies originally stemmed from it. D is incorrect, as Romanticism often criticized the very attitude that only science yields knowledge. Choice B is a rephrasing of KC 3.6, which reminds you that a familiarity with the KCs and Concept Outline will serve you well on the MC questions.

Chapter 12

1. **Answer: D. HTS—CTX & EVARG; Theme—PP; KC 3.1.** The map shows the expansion of European railways over a span of about 40 years. Of course, several economic processes during this period (Second Industrial Revolution) relate to transportation developments. A is true, but the map does not provide any inferences about government involvement in the economy. Mechanization did become the predominant form of manufacturing; however, that process was separate from transportation developments (B). Germany's unification did stimulate its industrialization, yet the map does not address that issue (C). The option most directly related to the map remains the integration of the European and world economies, since these would depend on the cost-effective ability to reach (far-flung) markets (D).

2. **Answer: A. HTS—CAUS; Theme—PP; KCs 3.1 & 3.2.** Choices B, C, and D all occurred during this period; however, they were only affected indirectly if at all by the growth of railroads. However, railroads reduced the cost of products and

enabled a wider geographic scope to purchase goods, including those that had once been expensive luxuries but now became accessible to the middle- and even working-class (A).

3. **Answer: C. HTS—CAUS; Themes—PP & SP; KC 3.1.** It is true that Europe experienced volatile business cycles during this era, but these were not unique to western Europe and did not overall impede industrialization (A). Resource access relates to industrial development; however, even states in eastern Europe with the means to industrialize often failed to do so because of poor government policy (B), which suggests the answer of C: most polities in eastern Europe were dominated by aristocrats tied up in traditional landholding and thus averse to promoting industry. Though Russia often influenced eastern European diplomacy, it too suffered from many of the same drawbacks as those smaller nations, many of which were controlled by the technologically backward Ottoman Empire (D).

4. **Answer: B. HTS—COMP; Theme—PP; KCs 1.5, 3.1 & 3.5.** The map depicts an economic and transportation development and suggests its effects on the development of a larger and more integrated market. The choice most related to this trend in a different period is B, as navigational advances helped created a global economy. The printing press spread ideas, but relates less to economic integration (A). Choices C and D occurred and significantly affected warfare and diplomacy, on one hand, and ideas on the other–not connected to the economy.

5. **Answer: D. HTS—CTX & INTR; Themes—PP & INT; KCs 3.1 & 3.5.** The passage focuses on the economic imperatives driving imperialism, suggesting the answer is D. Choice A does not relate to the passage, even if it did facilitate imperialism. Though the passage touches on the behavior of nations, Hobsbawm's interpretive focus is on economic motivations, excluding B and C.

6. **Answer: C. HTS—COMP & CCOT; Themes—PP & INT; KCs 1.5, 3.1 & 3.5.** This question asks you to consider the similarities and differences between the era of exploration (15th and 16th centuries) and imperialism (19th and 20th centuries). In both instances, Europe's relation to the non-European world was affected by notions of superiority (A), technological imbalances (B), and conversions to Christianity (D). The main difference between the two periods relates to the development of an industrial economy in the latter period, which both drove and allowed for widespread European control of overseas territory.

7. **Answer: B. HTS—INTR & EVCS; Themes—INT & OS; KCs 3.5 & 3.6.** Any of the options relates to the time period described in the passage, but the question directs your attention to the historian's (implicit) philosophical commitments. Given the focus on the driving force of capitalism and industry in promote imperialism, Choice B emerges as the most appealing choice. Hobsbawm does not glorify science per se (A), nor does he endorse nationalism (C) or Darwinism (D).

8. **Answer: A. HTS—EVARG & INTR; Themes—PP & INT; KCs 3.1 & 3.5.** Choices B, C, and D all describe features of the Second Industrial Revolution and thus relate to the economic analysis provided by Hobsbawm. However, backward agricultural practices were both diminishing around the turn of the 20th century and certainly did not promote imperialism, since those areas relying on traditional agriculture tended to be isolated from the world economy (A).

Chapter 13

1. **Answer: C. HTS—INTR, CCOT & CAUS; Themes—PP & SP; KCs 3.1, 3.2 & 3.3.** The passage explains the shift in classical liberalism from laissez-faire individualism to government intervention to promote equality. For choices, you are presented with four economic developments, all of which represent accurate statements about the late 19th century. A, B, and D posed new social and political problems for governments that required some degree of regulation or policy initiative. However, the growth of consumer goods and leisure time (C) did not in themselves require government action, as they tended to be ancillary to the more fundamental changes in the structure of the economy.

2. **Answer: A. HTS—CTX; Themes—SP & OS; KC: 3.3.** Liberal political theory emphasized that legitimate governments are based on the will of the people, as with the American and French Revolutions (A). The sharing of property (B) characterizes socialism and would undermine the Liberal notion of the free market. C better expresses a principle of nationalism, and the skepticism regarding the perfectibility of human nature relates more closely to conservatism (D).

3. **Answer: B. HTS—CAUS & CCOT; Theme—SP; KCs 4.1 & 4.2.** Given that the passage focuses on the shift toward intervention, you should look for the choice that most strongly promoted it. The demands of total war (B) forced governments to expand their powers significantly and establish new precedents for state power in many areas. A is more the result than the cause of government expansion, as imperialism required a high degree of state power. Women did gain new rights during this era (C); however, these would represent more of a fulfillment of classical Liberalism's notion of natural rights. Though new scientific theories posed cultural challenges, they did not directly affect the issue of state intervention (D).

4. **Answer: D. HTS—CTX & CAUS; Theme—OS; KCs 2.3 & 3.6.** Enlightenment philosophes interpreted nature primarily through the operation of natural laws, as does Darwin in this passage (D). Darwin does endorse A and B, yet these do not express principles of the Enlightenment, which promoted the uniqueness of human reason and the assumption of rationality in human relations. The glorification of nature as a source of emotion represents more of a Romantic attitude and less an enlightened one (C).

5. **Answer: B. HTS—CAUS; Themes—SP & OS; KCs 3.3, 3.5 & 3.6.** This EXCEPT question asks you to identify the least connected outcome of Darwinism. The theory of natural selection certainly raised religious and ethical controversies (D). Also, many theorists applied the theory to political, social, and military affairs, as is indicated accurately in Choices A and C. One area that saw limited direct impact of Darwinism was in the arts, or at least it was not directly responsible for the shift away from representation and toward abstraction (B).

6. **Answer: A. HTS—CTX & CCOT; Theme—OS; KCs 3.3 & 3.6.** The failure of Romantic revolution in 1848 caused political and intellectual figures to adopt a more hard-headed

and realistic attitude toward an industrializing Europe, making A the key. B is true, but this trend stems more from other ideas in the sciences and social sciences (such as Freud), not to mention that Darwin endorses objective knowledge based on the scientific method in the passage. Though there is a poetry in the excerpt, Darwin does not endorse a primarily emotional attitude toward nature, as would the Romantics (C). Finally, there is no reference here to classical or ancient themes, excluding D.

7. **Answer: A. HTS—CTX; Theme—PP; KCs 3.1 & 3.2.** The image depicts one of the new urban amenities of reformed cities–a department store (C). Further, the scene provides the viewer with a testament to the new consumerism with its conspicuous displays of goods for purchase (B). This abundance of goods at relatively low prices can be attributed to advances in production and transportation (D). Though women are portrayed in the image, they are presented in the traditional role as purchasers of household goods and not holders of new rights or independent actors, making A a false choice to the EXCEPT question.

8. **Answer: C. HTS—COMP & CCOT; Theme—PP; KCs 1.5, 2.2 & 3.1.** This question wants you to compare two eras in their economic patterns, aiming for the area of difference. Both the early modern and industrial eras emphasized luxury goods (A), urban markets (B), and the key role played by the middle-class in commerce (D). However, the early modern period relied for production on guilds and crafts, as opposed to the ability of an industrial economy to mass-produce goods at lower prices, making them available to a wider public (as shown in the department store), giving C as the key.

9. **Answer: B. HTS—PER; Theme—PP; KCs 3.1 & 3.2.** All of the labels given might accurately characterize the period 1850-1914. However, the image relates primarily to the advances produced by industrial production (B) and only indirectly, if at all, to nationalism (A), mass politics (C), or the pursuit of colonies (D)–all of which would be related on indirectly to the scene depicted.

Chapter 14

1. **Answer: C. HTS—CAUS; Theme—SP; KCs 3.4 & 4.1.** The map shows the Balkan peninsula right before WWI. Even if you didn't recall the two Balkan Wars that occurred there (1912–1913), you should be prompted by the map to note the smaller Balkan nations, especially Serbia, adjacent to Austria-Hungary and Russia. It was tensions here that drew in Austria and Russia and then sprung the trap of the alliance system (C). Choices A, B, and D all express causes of WWI, but these are not portrayed on the map.

2. **Answer: D. HTS—CTX; Theme—SP; KCs 3.4 & 4.1.** As the Ottoman Empire declined, the Slavic minorities worked toward independence, often aided by the Slavic power of Russia. This deterioration of a major empire created instability in the region (D). The map does not portray Germany (A) nor colonies (B). Though Austria-Hungary appears, the map does not break down the ethnic composition of that empire, eliminating C.

3. **Answer: B. HTS—COMP & CCOT; Theme—SP; KCs 3.4 & 4.1.** This is a challenging question, as it asks you to make a comparison across eras and select the one false difference. It

is true that Concert of Europe in 1815 provided a means for the great powers to address security issues, while no such mechanism existed in 1914 (A). Whereas in 1815 there existed a consensus among the great powers, pre-1914 diplomacy struggled to reconcile the interests of two rival alliance blocs (Triple Alliance vs. Triple Entente)–C. Finally, warfare had been altered in the century between 1815 and 1914 due to industrialization of weapons as would be revealed in WWI (D). This leaves B as the correct answer, and indeed, both eras involved nationalist conflicts that threatened revolution and forced the great powers to act.

4. **Answer: A. HTS—CCOT & PER; Theme—SP; KCs 3.4 & 4.1.** Through Bismarck's alliance system (1871–1890), Europe avoided major wars among the great powers. However, with Bismarck's dismissal by William II, Germany moved toward a more assertive international posture, which led to a more rigid system of alliances and a series of conflicts (A). The Berlin Conference did stimulate African imperialism, but the resulting conflicts among the great powers did not cause actual warfare (B). Britain was criticized for its actions in the Boer War, and as a result, shopped for allies, but again, this action was not as critical as A (C). Finally, Russia's defeat by Japan shocked it into reconciling with Britain, yet this was still not as critical as Germany's actions leading up to 1914 (D).

5. **Answer: A. HTS—CTX & CAUS; Themes—OS & IS; KCs 4.3 & 4.4.** Hopefully you noted the tone of sarcasm in the poem, representing the disillusionment many experienced with the First World War, creating a cynical "lost generation" (A). The poem does not address politics per se, eliminating B. Though there are references to the economic struggles of the soldier, the poem conveys more about the psychology of the veteran rather than an analysis of economic matters (D). C does express a trend in the arts (making it an appealing choice); however, this poem does not reveal this trend as directly as Choice A.

6. **Answer: D. HTS—CAUS & CTX; Theme—OS; KCs 3.6 & 4.3.** The writer tackles a difficult topic through vivid description and irony (the supposedly wonderful opportunities that exist for wounded soldiers returning home), which is expressive of a realist approach to literature, as in the writings of Dickens and Zola (D). There are no classical references here (A), nor does the text promote Christian morality (B). One might argue that the passage conveys subjectivity, but it certainly does not employ the typical Romantic subjects, such as nature (C).

7. **Answer: B; HTS—CTX & CAUS; Themes—PP & SP; KCs 3.4 & 4.2.** The poster requires you to make inferences. Given the depictions of peasants and working classes, you would correctly conclude that the message relates to how the revolution would overthrow the inequality of the tsarist government (B); however, there are no specific critiques given of government itself, eliminating A. Choice C does express a cause of the Russian Revolution, but this issue does not appear as directly as does the key. By 1920, the Bolsheviks were eliminating other revolutionary parties in the Russian Civil War and certainly wouldn't be keen to remind Russians of that in their propaganda (D).

8. **Answer: D. HTS—CTX & CCOT; Themes—SP & PP; KC 4.2.** In 1920 Russia was entrenched in a deadly civil war. Though A relates to this objective, the poster does not address

this issue directly. B had already been accomplished by 1920, and C would occur only later under Stalin (C). This leaves us with Choice D, and we may surmise that the poster was designed to motivate the Russian people to support its agenda of "peace, bread, and land" during the Civil War.

9. **Answer: C. HTS—CTX & CCOT; Theme—PP & OS; KC 4.2.** To stimulate the dead-in-the-water Russian economy, Lenin compromised with capitalism with the New Economic Policy (NEP), which allowed for limited free market activity (C). These policies caused a rift in the Politburo between "leftists" (led by Trotsky) and "rightists" (led by Bukharin), though later Stalin eliminated both groups and adopted B and D as policies in his drive for modernization, both of which could be interpreted as attacks on capitalism. Choice A occurred during the Russian Civil War, but one might argue that such shared sacrifice is in keeping with the spirit of the poster.

Chapter 15

1. **Answer: C. HTS—CTX; Theme—OS; KC 4.3.** Freud calls into question the power of science and its technological fruits to resolve the fundamental condition of humanity. His writings reflect the disillusionment of the interwar era with notions of progress (C). A, B, and D express problems of the interwar period of a political or economic nature, but they do not relate to the crux of Freud's argument.

2. **Answer: B. HTS—CAUS; Theme—OS; KC 4.3.** World War I caused profound disillusionment in western civilization, reversing the course of technological and material progress prior to 1914 (B). Darwin's theory certainly raised questions about the human condition; however, it was more remote in time (1859) from Freud's concerns. The Nazi party had not yet risen to power when Freud wrote this passage, eliminating C. Women did enter the work during the war, but this does not seem to touch on Freud's points (D).

3. **Answer: D. HTS—EVARG; Themes—OS & PP; KCs 4.3 & 4.4.** Since Freud critiques the notion of progress (and this is an EXCEPT question), we are looking for an example that represents progress. A, B, and C express themes of disillusionment in high culture, or that questioned objective knowledge. D represents a significant improvement in the ability of economies to raise the standard of living through mass production, not fitting with Freud's point.

4. **Answer: B. HTS—PER; Theme—OS; KC 4.3.** Some historians refer to the interwar period as the Age of Anxiety (B), which also fits well given Freud's field of psychiatry. Each of the other labels (A, C, and D) also fits the interwar period; however, they do not touch on the main point of Freud's writing (and its title): the doubt seeping into the project of western civilization.

5. **Answer: B. HTS—CAUS; Themes—PP & SP; KCs 4.1 & 4.2.** The picture shows the absurd effects of the hyperinflation that broke upon Germany in the early 1920s. Along with poor policies, this situation was caused most directly by the imposition of reparations from the Versailles settlement (B). Fascism had not yet gained a foothold in Germany, and in any case, fascism *resulted* from such economic problems. The trade policies of the U.S. did not help the situation (C), but such policies played a more central role in bringing on the

Depression. Germany did lose territory and colonies under Versailles (D), which created resentment, but these decisions bear only indirectly on the economic situation portrayed here.

6. **Answer: A. HTS—CAUS; Themes—SP & PP; KCs 4.1 & 4.2.** The inability of democracies like the Weimar Republic to address economic crises led directly to support for fascist and communist parties (A). Germany and the Soviet Union did sign the Rapallo Pact in 1922, but this preceded the hyperinflation (B). There was no relation between the hyperinflation and C and D.

7. **Answer: D. HTS—CCOT & COMP; Themes—PP & SP; KC 4.2.** Learning the lessons of the past, governments in both Western and Eastern Europe after 1945 instituted strong welfare programs (C). In addition, the United States (in a policy reversal from after WWI) extended significant aid to Western Europe (A) and encouraged successful policies of integration (B). This leaves us with the outlier (D) and in fact, this statement applies only to Eastern Europe, whose policies of central control provided for less prosperity than obtained in Western Europe.

8. **Answer: B. HTS—CTX & CAUS; Theme—SP; KC 4.1.** President Wilson championed the League of Nations as a means to prevent further security breakdowns and wars, one of his justifications for U.S. entrance into the conflict (B). Versailles was beset by conflicting goals among the victors (A), French desires for vengeance (C), and fear of Soviet Communism (D)–a reason this nation was excluded–but these issues are not reflected in the League charter itself.

9. **Answer: D. HTS—CAUS; Theme—SP; KC 4.1.** Each of the choices represents problems of the interwar period. This section of the League charter deals primarily with collective security, a goal that was seriously compromised by the non-adherence or exclusion of the United States, Germany, and the Soviet Union (D). The Great Depression fomented the rise of extremist groups (A), but this did not bear directly on the weakened structure of the League. The loss of confidence in western values may have contributed to lack of confidence in the League (B), but this did relate as directly to its failure as D. Certainly the weak new democracies in central and eastern Europe created challenges for a reconstruction of the balance of power (C), but this issue only accentuated but did not cause the failure of the charter (with WWII).

10. **Answer: B. HTS—EVARG & CCOT: Theme—SP; KC 4.1.** In some ways, the League seemed to participate in its own death, primarily by undermining the security mechanism of Article 10 with the appeasement of the fascist powers (B). Though the decision to allow Germany and Italy to rearm contributed to the failure of security, it was not in itself the failure described in Article 10 (A). Choice C does not apply, since the appeasement of fascism occurred *after* the admission of the USSR. Dependence on U.S. capital relates more directly to economic issues and the onset of the Depression and less to collective security (D).

Chapter 16

1. **Answer: C. HTS—CTX; Themes—SP & PP; KC 4.1.** Reagan explicitly addresses the Cold War division of Europe into blocs, excluding D. Also, he implies the drain of the arms race on the Soviet Union (B). Further, the very fact that

Reagan appears before the British Parliament suggests the influence exercised by the U.S. during the Cold War (A). This leave C, and covert actions and "hot wars" (e.g., Korea) did feature as part of the Cold War, but these are not covered by the speech.

2. **Answer: D. HTS—EVARG; Themes—SP & PP; KCs 4.1 & 4.2.** Reagan notes the difficulties present in a Soviet economy geared toward production of heavy industry and weapons, sacrificing consumer goods. Khrushchev (C) attempted some reforms, but these did not extend as far as Gorbachev's policies of perestroika and glasnost (D). Lenin (A) and Stalin (B) established the command economy of the Soviet Union that Reagan critiques.

3. **Answer: C. HTS—CAUS; Theme—SP; KC 4.1.** The passage suggests the problems associated with the communist system, particularly with production of goods. In fact, Reagan presented his speech as Cold War tensions revived, eliminating A. Choice B relates to the prompt, but more indirectly, since it addresses Germany and not the Soviet Union. The better choice is C, which did occur from 1989–1991, for many of the reasons that Reagan identifies in the speech. Balkan nationalism revived after communism's collapse, but this phenomenon is not the purpose of the address to Parliament (D).

4. **Answer: A. HTS—COMP & CCOT; Theme—SP; KC 4.1.** This question asks you to consider the shift in U.S. foreign policy following each world war. Both Wilson and here Reagan visited Europe to engage in diplomacy, even if Wilson's vision for the League of Nations fell short (D). In both cases, the U.S. pursued its economic interests in relation to Europe, even if in a more enlightened way after WWII with the Marshall Plan (C). Both A and B state differences between each era; however, Choice A relates directly to American involvement with Europe, such as NATO, whereas the U.S. might have joined the UN without becoming a guarantor of European security.

5. **Answer: B. HTS—COMP & CCOT; Themes—SP & OS; KCs 3.3 & 4.1.** Reagan employs themes of freedom–both economic and political–throughout the speech. The ideology most associated with freedom in the 19th century was Liberalism (B). Keep in mind that the meaning of "liberal" and "conservative" shifted around the turn of the 20th century, so even though Reagan may have presented himself as a "conservative," his rhetoric draws from laissez-faire Liberalism of the 19th century (A). Clearly Reagan espoused free markets, eliminating C, and while he may have promoted American exceptionalism (D), that theme is not addressed in this passage.

6. **Answer: D. HTS—CTX; Themes—SP & PP; KCs 4.1 & 4.2.** Merkel recommits Germany to the notion of a single Europe economically and politically in this address (D). By 2010, the Cold War was well over, but the passage does not relate to this development, nor does it consider the U.S. role in Europe (B). Of course, Merkel's position is predicated on C, but Germany's recovery was well established by 2010; in fact, it forms the bases of Merkel's leadership on the euro crisis, as referenced in the passage. However, her focus remains on the "Europe project," not the particular situation of Germany.

7. **Answer: C. HTS—EVARG & COMP; Themes—SP & PP; KCs 4.1 & 4.2.** Choices A, B, and D all represents transnational economic, political, or military organizations aimed at Western European security and cooperation during the Cold War. COMECON united the Eastern bloc under Soviet influence, making it the outlier here (C).

8. **Answer: D; HTS—PER; Theme—SP; KC 4.1.** This question does not require the stimulus directly. Each of these choices expresses a key date in German politics; however, the defining fact of German politics after WWII was its division into East and West, which was overcome with its reunification in 1990 (D), following the fall of the Berlin Wall. A and B reflect this division, and though Brandt's Chancellorship did help ease tensions between the two Germanies, it did not change the official divide between them (C).

9. **Answer: B; HTS—EVARG & COMP; Theme—SP; KC 4.1.** Merkel focuses on the common heritage of Europe and the importance of unity. A prerequisite for this unity may have been decolonization (A), eliminating this choice. Choice C facilitated Merkel's vision, as it opened the door for former Eastern bloc nations to join the EU and euro. Choice D also fits in with Merkel's ideas, though on a broader and more global scale. This leaves B, and indeed, such conflicts as the Balkan Wars, the Basque separatist campaign, or the Troubles in Northern Ireland reveal the continuing power of nationalism in the postwar period (B).

Chapter 17

1. **Answer: D. HTS—CAUS; Themes—IS, PP & SP; KC 4.4.** The beginning of the chart depicts the end of the Baby Boom, marked by increased birth rates from 1945–1965, often promoted by government pronatalist policies (A). Pent-up demands for products after two world wars and the Great Depression led to increased prosperity and confidence in the future (B), boosting births. Despite the Cold War, Europe generally enjoyed political stability and the absence of military destruction (C), which also promoted fertility. This leaves D, and although such threats (communism and nuclear war) existed, they exercised little if any causal influence on birth rates.

2. **Answer: C. HTS—CAUS; Theme—IS; KC 4.4.** Here we are looking for which choice best explains the decline in the birth rates. Advances in artificial birth control (e.g., the pill) largely explain this decline (C). Though A, B, and D occurred (in fact, immigration fertility rates were higher than established residents), they do not explain how and why birth rates continued to decline during this period.

3. **Answer: D. HTS—CCOT; Themes—IS, PP, & SP; KC 4.2 & 4.4.** Women already exercised the vote in most European states before the dates in the chart (A), eliminating that option. European unity has been debated, but not in the context of fertility rates, but rather due to lingering nationalism (B). Many technological developments, including birth control, have prompted debates in European cultural life; at this point, however, artificial birth control has won general acceptance, except from the hierarchy of the Catholic Church (C). With an expanding welfare state, many of the benefits go to the elderly (pensions, sickness, disability); in an age of declining population growth, fewer young tax-paying workers will support a larger, aging population–meaning either benefit cuts or higher taxes (D).

4. **Answer: A. HTS—EVARG; Theme—IS; KC 4.4.** In this question, you are asked to take the perspective of a feminist, who in the postwar era worked to provide women with improved opportunities for education and public life. Access to such opportunities required greater control of fertility, to free women from an exclusively reproductive and domestic role (A). B may be true, but the data show a decline in birth rates after 1965 (B). Overseas emigration occurred, but it played a minimal role in affecting the opportunities of existing populations in Europe (C). It is also true that Western European nations provided a higher standard of living than their Eastern European counterparts, but this fact is not derivable from the chart itself (D).

5. **Answer: C. HTS—CTX; Theme—PP; KC 4.2 & 4.4.** Pent-up demand from the sacrifices of two world wars and the Great Depression led to an expansion in production and consumption of new products, such as the appliance depicted here (C) along with cars, new foods, and leisure pursuits. Though continental integration indirectly aided this process, it cannot be inferred from the ad (A). The same is true for D. Given that the ad portrays women in a domestic role, D seems out of place.

6. **Answer: B. HTS—CTX; Theme—PP; KC 4.2.** Each of the choices provides an accurate development of the era, but B links most closely with the image, since it showcases a new consumer item. Though competition with the Soviet Union may have aided the West's economic miracle, it did so only indirectly (A). Existentialists generally derided consumerism as conformist and inauthentic, running counter to the portrayal of it here as liberating (C). Finally, D seems out of place, as the ad presents appliances in a positive light, with no suggestion of consumerism's destructive potential.

7. **Answer: C. HTS—EVARG; Theme—IS; KC 4.4.** Several of the choices pose an attractive possibility, so we must consider which is most directly illustrated. The answer is C, since the ad portrays a traditional domestic role for women during the Baby Boom (when many governments promoted the birth rate) increase in population. Though the cultural influence of U.S. culture expanded post-1945, this ad seems to be for a British product and British consumers, eliminating A. It certainly does not suggest a general decline in the belief in progress; instead it portrays progress as arising from improved use of technology, dropping out B. Welfare systems did expand after World War II, but the ad provides the historian with a glimpse into the operation of a free-market system (D).

8. **Answer: A. HTS—CCOT & COMP; Themes—PP & SP.** The Green Party reacted strongly to the type of consumerism promoted in the ad, believing that it produced waste and environmental destruction (A). Having arrived primarily for economic reasons, guest workers focused their attention on building a new life and gaining citizenship rights (B). National separatists focused on issues of identity and political influence, far removed from the domestic concerns of the ad (C). Postmodernists, such as Pop artists, often employed advertising to comment ironically on culture, providing a more ambivalent attitude toward such advertising (D).

Section III
Practice Exams

Practice Exam 1 | Section 1, Part A

⏱ **55 minutes | 55 questions**

Directions Each of the questions or incomplete statements below is followed by four suggested answers or completions. Select the one that is best in each case.

Source materials have been edited for the purpose of this exercise.

Questions 1–3 are based on the text below.

> "And first, where I affirm the empire of a woman to be a thing repugnant to nature, I mean not only that God, by the order of his creation, has spoiled [deprived] woman of authority and dominion, but also that man has seen, proved, and pronounced just causes why it should be. Man, I say, in many other cases, does in this behalf see very clearly. For the causes are so manifest, that they cannot be hid. For who can deny but it is repugnant to nature, that the blind shall be appointed to lead and conduct such as do see? That the weak, the sick, and impotent persons shall nourish and keep the whole and strong? And finally, that the foolish, mad, and frenetic shall govern the discreet, and give counsel to such as be sober of mind? And such be all women, compared unto man in bearing of authority. For their sight in civil regiment is but blindness; their strength, weakness; their counsel, foolishness; and judgment, frenzy, if it be rightly considered."
>
> John Knox, Scottish reformer, *The First Blast of the Trumpet Against the Monstrous Regiment of Women*, 1558

1. Knox's views on women were most likely prompted by which of the following?

   A. The prevalence of women involved in spreading Renaissance humanism

   B. Reformation reforms that initiated debates over women's nature and roles

   C. Weakness among the new monarchies in addressing religious dissent

   D. Economic changes that enhanced the status of women within households

2. Which of the following was most important in allowing views such as Knox's to gain an audience?

   A. Stability provided by increased state control over religion and administration

   B. An expanding consumer economy fed by exploration and colonization

   C. The invention and expansion of the printing press and printed materials

   D. Scientific discoveries that allowed for increased control of nature

3. For an historian researching the lives of ordinary women in the 16th century, which of the following sources would be most useful?

   A. Statistics on rates of marriage and childbirth

   B. Laws enacted by female monarchs

   C. Paintings of well-known female intellectuals

   D. Diagrams of female anatomy by scientists

John Knox, *The First Blast of the Trumpet Against the Monstrous Regiment of Women*, Edward Arber, ed. (London: University College, 1878), pp. 11–12.

Questions 4–6 are based on the graph below.

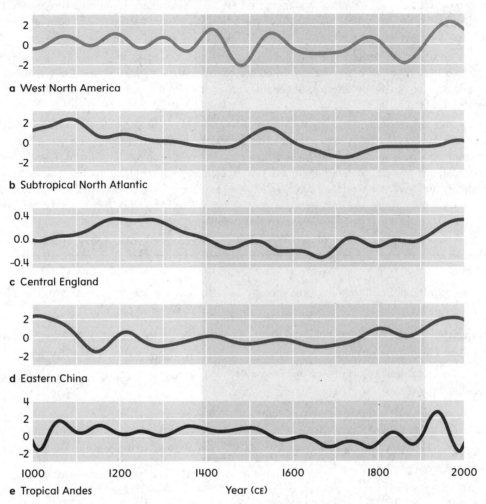

ESTIMATED RELATIVE TEMPERATURE VARIATIONS, 1000–2000

a West North America

b Subtropical North Atlantic

c Central England

d Eastern China

e Tropical Andes

Year (CE)

Paul Edward Dutton, Suzanne Marchand, Deborah Harkness, *Many Europes: Choice and Chance in Western Civilization* (New York: McGraw-Hill Education, 2014), p. 425.

4. Which of the following phenomena is depicted in the graph?

   A. The Price Revolution

   B. The Age of Crisis

   C. The Little Ice Age

   D. The Black Death

5. Which of the following resulted from the trends depicted in the graph?

   A. Europeans delayed marriage and childbirth, restraining population growth.

   B. Landowners enclosed common lands and increased agricultural productivity.

   C. Cities and states began to regulate morality and restrict traditional freedoms.

   D. Serfdom was codified into law in much of eastern and central Europe.

6. In the period after 1945, a similar issue to that depicted above was:

   A. the development of ideas that challenged objective knowledge and reason.

   B. the increase in immigrants from the Middle East and Asia.

   C. the Cold War division between Eastern and Western Europe.

   D. the impact of consumerism and burning of fossil fuels.

"There are two means by which states are maintained in their weal and greatness—reward and penalty: the one for the good, the other for the bad. And, if the distribution of these two be faulty, nothing else is to be expected than the inevitable ruin of the state....

Now, if there is any means to appease the wrath of God, to gain his blessing, to strike awe into some by the punishment of others, to preserve some from being infected by others, to diminish the number of evil-doers, to make secure the life of the well-disposed, and to punish the most detestable crimes of which the human mind can conceive, it is to punish with the utmost rigor the witches....

Now, it is not within the power of princes to pardon a crime which the law of God punishes with the penalty of death—such as are the crimes of witches. Moreover, princes do gravely insult God in pardoning such horrible crimes committed directly against his majesty, seeing that the pettiest prince avenges with death insults against himself. Those too who let the witches escape, or who do not punish them with the utmost rigor, may rest assured that they will be abandoned by God to the mercy of the witches. And the country which shall tolerate this will be scourged with pestilences, famines, and wars; and those which shall take vengeance on the witches will be blessed by him and will make his anger to cease."

Jean Bodin, French jurist and political theorist, *On the Demon-Mania of Witches*, 1580

7. Which of the following political trends is most strongly reflected in the passage?

   A. The expansion in power of commercial and professional groups in government

   B. Noble challenges to royal power based on defense of traditional privileges

   C. Development of a new competitive state system based on sovereign nations

   D. Growth of monarchical power and theories justifying centralization

8. All of the following contributed to the trend discussed in the final paragraph EXCEPT:

   A. persistence of folk ideas regarding natural events.

   B. negative gender stereotypes regarding women.

   C. humanist literature emphasizing individualism.

   D. poor economic conditions and social breakdown.

9. The attitudes expressed in the final paragraph had changed among elites:

   A. as they adopted the New Science.

   B. with the onset of the French Revolution.

   C. as they sponsored industrialization.

   D. with the growth of positivism.

10. How does the passage differ most strongly from political writings in the 18th century?

    A. The latter did not concern themselves with strong state power.

    B. The latter relied on natural law principles to justify authority.

    C. The latter did not seek to identify or punish perceived outsiders.

    D. The latter emphasized the importance of central legal codes.

George L. Burr, ed., "The Witch Persecutions" in *Translations and Reprints from the Original Sources of European History*, 6 vols. (Philadelphia: University of Pennsylvania History Department, 1898-1912) vol. 3, no. 4, pp. 5–6, Hanover Historical Texts Project, https://history.hanover.edu/texts/bodin.html.

Questions 11–14 are based on the poem below.

> "I own I am shock'd at the purchase of slaves,
> And fear those, who buy them and sell them, are knaves;
> What I hear of their hardships, their tortures, and groans
> Is almost enough to draw pity from stones.
>
> I pity them greatly, but I must be mum,
> For how could we do without sugar and rum?
> Especially sugar, so needful we see?
> What, give up our desserts, our coffee, and tea!
>
> Besides, if we do, the French, Dutch, and Danes,
> Will heartily thank us, no doubt, for our pains:
> If we do not buy the poor creatures, they will,
> And tortures and groans will be multiplied still."
>
> William Cowper, English poet and evangelical Christian,
> *Pity for Poor Africans*, 1788

11. Which of the following nations initiated the practice referenced by the poet?

    A. Spain
    B. Portugal
    C. England
    D. Netherlands

12. Which of the following developments in the Americas coincided most closely with the practice referenced by the poet?

    A. The destruction of indigenous cultures
    B. The conversion of indigenous peoples to Christianity
    C. The development of plantation economies
    D. The rivalry among colonial powers

13. The practice referenced in the poem led to:

    A. the widespread colonization of Africa.
    B. the growth of a consumer culture in Europe.
    C. the development of new political theories.
    D. the decline in political power of the nobility.

14. Which of the following movements stimulated opposition to the practice referenced by the poet?

    A. Exploration
    B. Protestant Reformation
    C. Enlightenment
    D. Industrial Revolution

Questions 15–18 are based on the text below.

> "That the only purpose for which power can be rightfully exercised over any member of a civilized community, against his will, is to prevent harm to others. His own good, either physical or moral, is not a sufficient warrant. He cannot rightfully be compelled to do or forbear because it will be better for him to do so, because it will make him happier, because, in the opinions of others, to do so would be wise, or even right. These are good reasons for remonstrating with him, or reasoning with him, or persuading him, or entreating him, but not for compelling him, or visiting him with any evil, in case he do otherwise. To justify that, the conduct from which it is desired to deter him, must be calculated to produce evil to some one else. The only part of the conduct of any one, for which he is amenable to society, is that which concerns others. In the part which merely concerns himself, his independence is, of right, absolute. Over himself, over his own body and mind, the individual is sovereign."
>
> John Stuart Mill, English philosopher, *On Liberty*, 1859

15. All of the following developments most likely influenced the ideas above EXCEPT:

    A. the Enlightenment.

    B. the French Revolution.

    C. the Concert of Europe.

    D. the rise of mass political parties.

16. Which of the following 19th-century political ideologies does the passage reflect?

    A. Romanticism

    B. Liberalism

    C. Republicanism

    D. Nationalism

17. What most directly caused the ideology above to change by the end of the 19th century?

    A. The need for government intervention due to problems of industrialization

    B. The pursuit of colonies and resources in Africa and Asia

    C. The shifting balance of power due to the unifications of Italy and Germany

    D. The rise of a feminist movement demanding equal economic and political rights

18. Which of the following figures would have agreed most strongly with the ideas above?

    A. René Descartes

    B. John Locke

    C. Jean-Jacques Rousseau

    D. Maximilien Robespierre

John Stuart Mill, *On Liberty* (London: Longmans, Green, and CO., 1867), p.6.

Questions 19–22 are based on the two passages below.

President Harry S. Truman, Address Before a Joint Session of Congress, March 12, 1947. The Avalon Project, Yale Law School, http://avalon.lawyale.edu/20th_century/trudoc.asp; Andrew Rothstein, ed., *History of the Communist Party of the Soviet Union* (Moscow: Foreign Languages Publishing House, 1960), p. 609.

<u>Source 1</u>

"One way of life is based upon the will of the majority, and is distinguished by free institutions, representative government, free elections, guarantees of individual liberty, freedom of speech and religion, and freedom from political oppression.

The second way of life is based upon the will of a minority forcibly imposed upon the majority. It relies upon terror and oppression, a controlled press and radio; fixed elections, and the suppression of personal freedoms.

I believe that it must be the policy of the United States to support free peoples who are resisting attempted subjugation by armed minorities or by outside pressures."

President Harry Truman, speech to U.S. Congress, 1947

<u>Source 2</u>

"The U.S.A. decided to take advantage of the economic and political difficulties in the other leading capitalist countries and bring them under its sway. Under the pretext of economic aid the U.S.A. began to infiltrate into their economy and interfere in their internal affairs. Such big capitalist countries as Japan, West Germany, Italy, France and Britain all became dependent on the U.S.A. to a greater or lesser degree."

B.N. Ponomaryov, *History of the Communist Party of the Soviet Union*, official publication of the Soviet government, 1960

19. The two sources above reveal which of the following causes of the Cold War?

A. Military confrontation and the race to develop nuclear weaponry

B. Competition over strategically and economically valuable areas of the world

C. Fundamental differences over economics, ideology, and politics

D. Failure of the United Nations to moderate conflict in the postwar period

20. All of the following resulted from the U.S. policies referenced in both sources EXCEPT:

A. a higher degree of economic, political, and military coordination in Western Europe.

B. an economic recovery that increased the standard of living and consumerism.

C. an increase in the birth rate (Baby Boom), often promoted by government policy.

D. expansion of cradle-to-grave welfare programs and accompanying higher taxes.

21. The Soviet Union responded to the American policies addressed in the sources by:

A. imposing central planning and specialized production in Eastern Europe.

B. reforming the communist system through *perestroika* and *glasnost*.

C. promoting de-Stalinization and peaceful coexistence with the West.

D. crushing revolts in Eastern Europe through the Brezhnev Doctrine.

22. Which of the following is the <u>strongest</u> limitation for an historian using either of the sources as a basis for attributing responsibility for the Cold War?

A. Source 1 is drawn from a speech, attempting to persuade for political purposes.

B. Source 1 does not refer to specific geographic areas or indicate monetary amounts.

C. Source 2 is from an official government publication under a regime lacking a free press.

D. Source 2 does not explain the background or motivations of its author.

Questions 23–27 are based on the text below.

"In the year 5280* (1519/20), our lord, the Emperor Charles, was crowned king. I came to him and to his servants to plead for our people and our inheritance. We...obtained comprehensive privileges for all of Germany. Notwithstanding this, in the same year, charters were issued authorizing the expulsion of [the Jews] from Rosheim and from the *Vogtei* of Kaysersberg. With the help of God, blessed be He, I interceded with the King, and succeeded in having the expulsion from the *Vogtei* of Kaysersberg cancelled altogether, with the annulment of that particular charter of expulsion. However, the charter to Rosheim was not rescinded, [nor was that city's decision to expel the Jews]. By dint of supreme efforts we succeeded time after time, with great difficulty, in obtaining yet another postponement. To this day we still do not know [how matters will turn out], and we can but place our trust in our Father in Heaven. He will redeem us and save us from [our] assailants. May it be His will. Amen."

*according to the Jewish calendar

Josel von Rosheim, Jewish rabbi and merchant, memoirs, 1540s

23. How does the text above reflect the political nature of the Holy Roman Empire?

A. It shows the ability of Charles V to draw on the wealth of his Spanish Empire.

B. It demonstrates the spread of the ideals of Christian humanism to Germany.

C. It shows the inability of the Holy Roman Empire to centralize like other new monarchies.

D. It reflects the rise of new commercial and professional elites to challenge the nobility.

24. In which of the following ways did religious reform in the 16th century likely affect the status of Jews in Germany?

A. It provided wealth from the confiscation of church lands.

B. It allowed them the option to convert to Protestantism.

C. It prevented them from emigrating to areas of religious diversity.

D. It posed a threat due to heightened concern for religious orthodoxy.

25. The key turning point for the issues Jews faced in the text came with the:

A. Commercial Revolution.

B. Enlightenment.

C. Industrial Revolution.

D. world wars of the 20th century.

26. Which of the following subsequent developments worsened the situation faced by Jews in the text?

A. Darwin's theory of natural selection

B. Voltaire's criticism of organized religion

C. Rousseau's notion of the noble savage

D. Marx's emphasis on class struggle

27. All of the following groups faced similar situations EXCEPT:

A. women accused of witchcraft.

B. nobles exiled for opposing absolutism.

C. Africans taken for the slave trade.

D. peasants executed for revolting.

Chava Fraenkel-Goldschmidt, ed., trans. Naomi Schendowich, trans. Adam Shear, ed., (English Edition), *The Historical Writings of Joseph of Rosheim: Leader of Jewry in Early Modern Germany* (Leiden, The Netherlands: Brill, 2006), pp. 315–316.

Questions 28–31 are based on the interpretation below.

"[Napoleon] Bonaparte belongs to the Revolution, surely, in matters that seemed irreversible at the time—civil equality, the destruction of feudalism, the ruin of the privileged position of the Catholic Church. As for the rest, the enjoyment of liberties, the form of political institutions, there had been since 1789 so much instability, so many contradictions between grand principles and the practice of governments, so much persistent uncertainty on the outcome of the war and the unity of the nation, that the field lay open for a strong man who, on condition of preserving the essential conquests of the Revolution, would do something new in the matter of government and refuse to be embarrassed by scruples. By anchoring France securely to the shores that the Constituent Assembly had been unveiling to leave, Bonaparte accomplished somewhat late in the day that 'revolution from above' of which the old monarchy had been incapable."

Louis Bergeron, historian, *France Under Napoleon*, 1981

28. Which of the following labels would the historian most likely apply to Napoleon?

   A. New monarch
   B. Divine-right ruler
   C. Enlightened absolutist
   D. Totalitarian dictator

29. Which of the following best accounts for the situation in France prior to Napoleon, as outlined by the historian?

   A. The meeting of the Estates-General
   B. The abolition of serfdom and feudalism
   C. The Declaration of Rights of Man and Citizen
   D. The threat of invasion and counterrevolution

30. Napoleon responded to the historical situation he inherited, as described by the historian, by:

   A. curtailing rights behind a façade of democracy.
   B. extending citizenship to women.
   C. provoking nationalist responses in other nations.
   D. reaffirming popular revolutionary violence.

31. All of the following leaders imitated many of Napoleon's political strategies EXCEPT:

   A. Cavour
   B. Metternich
   C. Napoleon III
   D. Bismarck

Louis Bergeron, *France Under Napoleon*, R.R. Palmer, trans. (Princeton, New Jersey: Princeton University Press, 1981), p. 4.

Jean-Honoré Fragonard, French artist, *The Visit to the Nursery*, 1775

32. The scene reflects all of the following economic and social features of the 18th century EXCEPT:

   A. the nuclear family as the predominant social and economic unit.

   B. the development of privacy within the family home.

   C. a rise in the rate of illegitimate births.

   D. a consumer revolution with more resources dedicated to child-rearing.

33. The thinkers most responsible for the attitude toward children shown above were:

   A. Voltaire and Diderot.

   B. Locke and Rousseau.

   C. Smith and Quesnay.

   D. Montesquieu and Beccaria.

34. Which of the following developments of the 19th century would confirm the attitudes expressed in the painting?

   A. The development of political ideologies that challenged the status quo

   B. The mechanization of production that increased the standard of living

   C. Growth of private reform movements to aid the poor and disadvantaged

   D. Restrictions on factory labor and provision for universal compulsory education

35. An historian might use the painting as evidence for which feature of the Enlightenment?

   A. Social reforms based on empirical and rational principles

   B. Expansion of printed materials and increase in literacy

   C. Development of public venues, like salons, to spread ideas

   D. Skeptical approaches toward traditional religious beliefs

Questions 36–37 are based on the chart below.

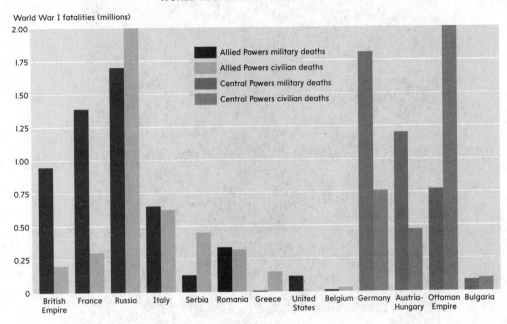

WORLD WAR I FATALITIES (IN MILLIONS)

World War I fatalities (millions)

Legend:
- Allied Powers military deaths
- Allied Powers civilian deaths
- Central Powers military deaths
- Central Powers civilian deaths

Countries: British Empire, France, Russia, Italy, Serbia, Romania, Greece, United States, Belgium, Germany, Austria-Hungary, Ottoman Empire, Bulgaria

36. Which of the following best explains the overall pattern for the data above?

A. New technologies overwhelmed traditional military strategies.

B. Widespread fighting disrupted trade and led to famine.

C. The strain of total war led to insurrection and revolution.

D. Military stalemate led to widening of the war to a global conflict.

37. All of the following resulted from the data depicted above EXCEPT:

A. women entered the industrial workforce in large numbers.

B. a disillusioned and cynical "lost generation" was created.

C. peace movements were successful in reestablishing stability.

D. the hold on power of traditional elites was destroyed.

Questions 38–40 are based on the poster below.

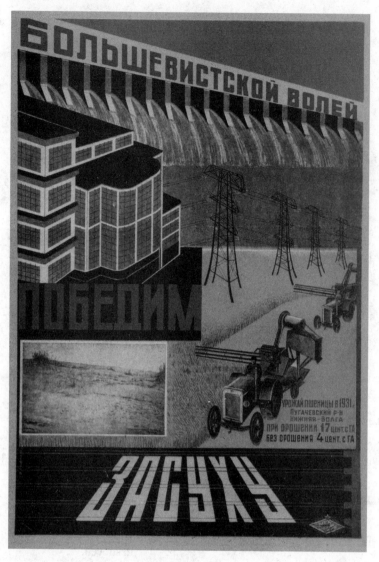

Soviet propaganda poster, 1933

38. The poster reflects Stalin's goal of:

   A. establishing his control of the Bolsheviks.

   B. rapidly modernizing the Soviet economy.

   C. promoting revolution through the Comintern.

   D. embracing Lenin's New Economic Policy.

39. A major result of pursuing the initiatives depicted above was:

   A. the liquidation of the kulak class.

   B. closer relations with western Europe.

   C. Soviet admission to the League of Nations.

   D. new rights and status for Soviet women.

40. The most significant change after 1945 in the initiatives depicted in the poster came through the policies of:

   A. Lenin.

   B. Khrushchev.

   C. Brezhnev.

   D. Gorbachev.

Questions 41–44 are based on the text below.

> "Up to the year 1856, the year before the outbreak, there had been for a whole century a continuous, aggressive advance of the British power, till it completed the ring fence of the empire...some provinces being brought under its direct administration and others being left as feudatory or vassal states under their native rulers. At the start the old Mogul dominion had been in a hopeless state of decay...and some of the native principalities had gladly turned for safety to the shelter of English protection and supremacy.
>
> ....The benefits of civilized rule, of the *Pax Britannica*, were felt only skin-deep, and the old fierce instincts, the outcome of centuries of strife and oppression, were still in the ascendant. The memory of injuries was still keen and vivid, the newer cases helping to recall the old ones, and to reopen sores that might otherwise have been getting healed; so that, briefly, the mood and temper which prevailed were those of a conquered people who had wrongs and humiliations to remember, and were chafing at having to endure the sway of aliens in race and creed."
>
> P.R. Innes, British colonial officer, "Review of the English progress in India from 1757 to 1857," 1885.

41. The beginning of the process that Innes describes stemmed from Britain's rivalry with:

   A. the Netherlands.

   B. France.

   C. Germany.

   D. Russia.

42. What does Innes likely mean by the "benefits of civilized rule"?

   A. Communication and transportation technologies, like railroads

   B. Medical technologies that allowed European states to conquer empires

   C. Advanced weaponry that overpowered colonized nations

   D. New artistic styles that provided realistic depictions of nature

43. Which of the following provided the most decisive turning point in the relationship explained by Innes?

   A. Boer War

   B. Russo-Japanese War

   C. Founding of the League of Nations

   D. Second World War

44. Colonial peoples responded to the situation outlined above in all of the following ways EXCEPT by:

   A. modernizing their economies and societies.

   B. refusing to join the United Nations after 1945.

   C. establishing national resistance movements.

   D. emigrating to Europe in search of new opportunities.

Questions 45–47 are based on the texts below.

Source 1

"The map of Europe will be redrawn. The countries of the Peoples, defined by the vote of free men, will arise upon the ruins of the Countries of Kings and privileged Castes, and between these Countries harmony and fraternity will exist. And the common work of Humanity, of general amelioration, and the gradual discovery and application of its Law of Life, being distributed according to local and general capacities, will be wrought out in peaceful and progressive development and advance."

Giuseppe Mazzini, Italian politician and journalist, *The Duties of Man*, ca. 1820s–1830s

Source 2

"But Prussia must keep her strength intact for the favorable moment, which is too often missed. Prussia's borders are not favorable for a healthy, vital state; it is not by speeches and majority resolutions that the great questions of the time are decided—that was the big mistake of 1848 and 1849—but by iron and blood."

Otto von Bismarck, Prussian Chancellor, Speech to the Prussian Reichstag, 1862

45. Both of the sources note a situation that was NOT conducive to the goals of the author and speaker. Which of the following most likely produced this situation?

   A. The revolutions of 1848

   B. The growth of industry

   C. The Congress of Vienna

   D. The pursuit of colonies

46. Which of the following historical developments best explains the differences in the tone and goals of the sources?

   A. The adoption of nationalism by conservative politicians

   B. The spread of the Romantic movement in the arts

   C. The growth of the labor movement and socialism

   D. The situation created by the Crimean War

47. Which of the following developments most directly contributed to the achievement of the goals of both sources?

   A. Growth of factories and transportation systems

   B. Breakdown of the Concert of Europe

   C. Creation of the Dual Monarchy in Austria

   D. Nationalist tensions in the Balkans

Joseph Mazzini, *The Duties of Man* (London: Chapman & Hall, 1862), p. 88.; James Harvey Robinson and Charles A. Beard, *Readings in Modern European History, Volume II: Europe Since the Congress of Vienna* (Boston: Ginn & Company, 1909), pp. 142–143.

Bauhaus building, Walter Gropius, German architect, 1919

48. The building above reflects which of the following cultural trends?

   A. Irrationality and the notion that struggle leads to progress

   B. New theories in the sciences that undermined Newtonian physics

   C. Growth of spaces dedicated to consumerism and mass leisure

   D. A modernist focus on the abstract and efficient use of space

49. Which of the following economic trends most directly-produced such buildings?

   A. Production of materials like steel during the Second Industrial Revolution

   B. The expansion of European states into African and Asian markets

   C. A move toward protective tariffs to shield domestic production from competition

   D. Improvement in working conditions and wages for unskilled laborers

50. The building contrasts most strongly with one built during the 16th through early 19th centuries in its:

   A. emphasis on natural light.

   B. explicitly economic focus.

   C. lack of ornamentation.

   D. solitary geographic location.

51. Which of the following events created the most decisive shift in cultural attitudes in the half century around when this building was created?

   A. Scramble for Africa

   B. First World War

   C. Great Depression

   D. Second World War

Questions 52–53 are based on the passage below.

"The strongest nation has always been conquering the weaker; sometimes even subduing it, but always prevailing over it. Every intellectual gain, so to speak, that a nation possessed was in the earliest times made use of—was invested and taken out—in war; all else perished. Each nation tried constantly to be the stronger, and so made or copied the best weapons, by conscious and unconscious imitation each nation formed a type of character suitable to war and conquest. Conquest improved mankind by the intermixture of strengths; the armed truce, which was then called peace, improved them by the competition of training and the consequent creation of new power."

Walter Bagehot, British journalist and businessman, *Physics and Politics*, 1872

52. Bagehot's ideas were most directly influenced by the:

A. development of workers' movements and socialism.

B. ideas of natural selection developed by Charles Darwin.

C. pursuit of colonies and resources in Africa and Asia.

D. growth of populations and influence of mass politics.

53. Which of the following led to the strongest criticism of ideas like Bagehot's?

A. Growth of the feminist movement

B. Freud's theories of the unconscious

C. Effects of World War I and World War II

D. Abandonment of laissez-faire economics

Walter Bagehot, *Physics and Politics: Or, Thoughts on the Application of the Principles of "Natural Selection" and "Inheritance" to Political Society* (New York: The Colonial Press, 1899), p. 31.

French Women's World Cup Soccer Team, 2014

54. The photograph above reflects which of the following post–1945 trends most directly?

  A. The spread of new technologies that promoted globalization

  B. Immigration into Europe from the Middle East, Africa, and Asia

  C. The rise of nationalism following the collapse of communism

  D. An economic miracle that increased the standard of living

55. Independence in the post–1945 period for many of the nations represented above was delayed for which of the following reasons?

  A. Cold War geopolitical competition between the superpowers

  B. Use of nationalist and separatist violence alienated potential supporters

  C. A loss of faith in progress and the ability of science to solve problems

  D. Military technologies that allowed for genocide and the threat of nuclear war

Practice Exam 1 | Section 1, Part B

⏱ 50 minutes | 4 questions

Directions Read each question carefully and answer all parts of the question. Use complete sentences; an outline or bulleted list is not acceptable. Your response should be contained within one side of a sheet of paper. Sources have been edited for the purposes of this exercise.

Louis XIV and Minister Jean-Baptiste Colbert at the Royal Academy of Sciences, 1671
Etching by Sebastian Léclerc, French artist

1A. Identify and explain TWO ways in which the image above conveys the principles of the Scientific Revolution.

1B. Identify and explain ONE way in which the image above conveys the relationship between science and politics during the 17th century.
   (HTS: Contextualization and Use of Evidence)

2A. Explain TWO ways in which the Catholic Church pursued reform and/or responded to the Protestant Reformation.

2B. Briefly assess the success of the Catholic Church's response to the Protestant Reformation in the 16th century.
   (HTS: CCOT)

3A. Pick ONE of the following dates and provide TWO reasons why it represents the most significant turning point in the politics and/or diplomacy of Europe.

3B. Pick ANOTHER date and explain why it is not as important as the one you selected.

- French Revolution (1789)
- Napoleon takes power (1799)
- Congress of Vienna (1815)
- Revolutions of 1848
   (HTS: Periodization and CCOT)

> "What no one understood, at the beginning of 1989, was that the Soviet Union, its empire, its ideology—and therefore the Cold War itself—was a sand pile ready to slide. All it took to make that happen were a few more grains of sand. The people who dropped them were not in charge of superpowers or movements or religions: they were ordinary people with simple priorities who saw, seized, and sometimes stumbled into opportunities. In doing so, they caused a collapse no one could stop. Their 'leaders' had little choice but to follow.
>
> One particular leader, however, did so in a distinctive way. He ensured that the great 1989 revolution was the first one ever in which almost no blood was shed...People did die, but in remarkably small numbers for the size and significance of what was happening. In both its ends and its means, then, this revolution became a triumph of hope. It did so chiefly because Mikhail Gorbachev chose not to act, but rather to be acted upon."
>
> John Lewis Gaddis, historian, *The Cold War: A New History*, 2005

4A. Explain ONE specific example that helped bring about the situation described in the first paragraph.

4B. Explain ONE policy that supports the historian's interpretation in the second paragraph.

4C. Considering a revolution from a *different* time period, explain ONE reason for its outcome that differed from the one described by the historian.

  (HTS: Causation, Use of Evidence, Interpretation, Comparison)

Question 1 (Document-Based Question)

Suggested reading and writing time: 55 minutes

It is suggested that you spend 15 minutes reading the documents and 40 minutes writing your response.

Note: You may begin writing your response before the reading period is over.

Directions Question 1 is based on the accompanying documents. The documents have been edited for the purpose of this exercise.

In your response you should do the following.

- **Thesis**: Present a thesis that makes a historically defensible claim and responds to all parts of the question. The thesis must consist of one or more sentences located in one place, either in the introduction or the conclusion.

- **Argument Development**: Develop and support a cohesive argument that recognizes and accounts for historical complexity by explicitly illustrating relationships among historical evidence such as contradiction, corroboration, and/or qualification.

- **Use of the Documents**: Utilize the content of at least six of the documents to support the stated thesis or a relevant argument.

- **Sourcing the Documents**: Explain the significance of the author's point of view, author's purpose, historical context, and/or audience for at least four documents.

- **Contextualization**: Situate the argument by explaining the broader historical events, developments, or processes immediately relevant to the question.

- **Outside Evidence**: Provide an example or additional piece of specific evidence beyond those found in the documents to support or qualify the argument.

- **Synthesis**: Extend the argument by explaining the connections between the argument and one of the following.

    o A development in a different historical period, situation, era, or geographical area.

    o A course theme and/or approach to history that is not the focus of the essay (such as political, economic, social, cultural, or intellectual history).

    o A different discipline or field of inquiry (such as economics, government and politics, art history, or anthropology)

1. To what extent and in what ways did the Italian Renaissance fulfill humanist ideals in culture and society?
   (HTS: Periodization)

Document 1

Source: Peter Paul Vergerius, Italian educator, *On Noble Manners and Liberal Studies*, letter to Ubertinus Carrara, ca. 1404

We call those studies liberal which are worthy of a free man; those studies by which we attain and practice virtue and wisdom; that education which calls forth, trains and develops those highest gifts of body and of mind which ennoble men, and which are rightly judged to rank next in dignity to virtue only. For to a vulgar temper, gain and pleasure are the one aim of existence, to a lofty nature, moral worth and fame. It is, then, of the highest importance that even from infancy this aim, this effort, should constantly be kept alive in growing minds. For I may affirm with fullest conviction that we shall not have attained wisdom in our later years unless in our earliest we have sincerely entered on its search.

Document 2

Source: Alessandra Strozzi, wife of Florentine merchant, letter to her son, Filippo, April 20, 1464

Concerning the matter of a wife [for you], it appears to me that if Francesco di Messer Guglielmino Tanagli wishes to give his daughter, that it would be a fine marriage....Now I will speak with Marco [Parenti, Alessandra's son-in-law], to see if there are other prospects that would be better, and if there are none, then we will learn if he wishes to give her [in marriage].... Francesco Tanagli has a good reputation, and he has held office, not the highest, but still he has been in office. You may ask: 'Why should he give her to someone in exile?'* There are three reasons. First, there aren't many young men of good family who have both virtue and property. Secondly, she has only a small dowry, 1,000 florins, which is the dowry of an artisan....Third, I believe that he will give her away, because he has a large family and he will need help to settle them....

*Filippo and his family had been banned for opposing the Medici

Document 3

Source: Unknown Artist, *Portrait of Federico da Montefeltro and his Son Guidobaldo*, mercenary soldier and later Duke of Urbino [Federico], ca. 1476

PHOTO: Florilegius/Alamy; TEXT: Petrus Paulus Vergerius, *The New Education*, ca. 1404, The Internet Medieval Source Book, http://sourcebooks.fordham.edu/source/vergerius.html; Gene Brucker, ed., *The Society of Renaissance Florence: A Documentary Study* (Toronto: University of Toronto Press in association with the Renaissance Society of America, 1998), pp. 37–38.

Document 4

Luca Landucci, *A Florentine Diary from 1450 to 1516*, Alice de Rosen Jervis, trans. (London: J. M. Dent & Sons Ltd., 1927), pp. 130–131.; Julia Cartwright, *Isabella D'Este, Marchioness of Mantua 1474-1539: A Study of the Renaissance* (London: John Murray, 1903), pp. 324–325.; *The Historical, Political and Diplomatic Writings of Niccolò Machiavelli*, trans. C. E. Detmold (Boston: J. R. Osgood, 1882), p. 58; revised.; Count Baldesar Castiglione, *The Book of the Courtier*, 1528, Leonard Eckstein Opdycke, trans. (New York: Charles Scribner's Sons, 1903), pp. 175–176.

Source: Luca Landucci, Florentine shopkeeper, diary entry, February 27 (Carnival), 1497

There was made on the Piazza de' Signori a pile of vain things, nude statues and playing-boards, heretic books, Morganti [poems], mirrors, and many other vain things, of great value, estimated at thousands of florins. Although some lukewarm people gave trouble, throwing dead cats and other dirt upon it, the boys nevertheless set it on fire and burnt everything, for there was plenty of small brushwood....[A]lthough it was Carnival, Fra Girolamo* said mass in San Marco, and gave the Sacrament with his hands to all his friars, and afterwards to several thousand men and women; and then he came on to a pulpit outside the door of the church with the Host, and showing it to the people, blessed them, with many prayers...There was a great crowd, who had come in the expectation of seeing signs; the lukewarm laughed and mocked, saying: 'He is excommunicated, and he gives the Communion to others.' And certainly it seemed a mistake to me, although I had faith in him; but I never wished to endanger myself by going to hear him, since he was excommunicated.

*Girolamo Savonarola was a Dominican monk who took over the city government of Florence and was later executed for heresy

Document 5

Source: Isabella d'Este, regent of Mantua and humanist, letter to Leonardo da Vinci, May 1504

To Master Leonardo da Vinci, the painter. M. Leonardo,—Hearing that you are settled at Florence, we have begun to hope that our cherished desire to obtain a work by your hand may be at length realized. When you were in this city, and drew our portrait in carbon, you promised us that you would some day paint it in colors. But because this would be almost impossible, since you are unable to come here, we beg you to keep your promise by converting our portrait into another figure, which would be still more acceptable to us; that is to say, a youthful Christ of about twelve years, which would be the age He had attained when He disputed with the doctors in the temple, executed with all that sweetness and charm of atmosphere which is the peculiar excellence of your art. If you will consent to gratify this our great desire, remember that apart from the payment, which you shall fix yourself, we shall remain so deeply obliged to you that our sole desire will be to do what you wish, and from this time forth we are ready to do your service and pleasure, hoping to receive an answer in the affirmative.

Document 6

Source: Niccolò Machiavelli, Italian diplomat, philosopher, and writer, *The Prince*, 1516

A prince should be a fox so as to spot the traps set out for him and a lion to frighten the wolves. Those princes who only employ the lion's nature mistake their business. A prudent ruler, therefore, cannot and should not keep his promises when it is to his disadvantage or when the reasons that inclined him to make the promise have ceased to exist. If men were entirely good, this advice would be wrong, but since men are at their core rotten and will not stand by their promises to you, you similarly need not keep your promises to them. A prince never lacks legitimate reasons for breaking his promises. I could cite innumerable modern examples to show this....Rulers who know how to act as foxes have always been the most successful. But the prince should also know how to disguise his character and to be a consummate hypocrite and a brazen liar, for men are so naïve and so governed by their immediate desires that the deceiver will always find a fool willing to allow himself to be duped...

Document 7

Source: Baldassare Castiglione, Italian diplomat and writer, *The Book of the Courtier*, 1528

For I believe that many faculties of the mind are as necessary to woman as to man; likewise gentle birth, to avoid affectation, to be naturally graceful in all her doings, to be mannerly, clever, prudent, not arrogant, not envious, not slanderous, not vain, not quarrelsome, not silly, to know how to win and keep the favor of her mistress and of all others, to practice well and gracefully the exercises that befit women. I am quite of the opinion, too, that beauty is more necessary to her than to the Courtier, for in truth that woman lacks much who lacks beauty.

...I say that in a lady who lives at court methinks above all else a certain pleasant affability is befitting, whereby she may be able to entertain politely every sort of man with agreeable and seemly converse, suited to the time and place, and to the rank of the person with whom she may speak, uniting with calm and modest manners...

Directions Choose EITHER Question 2 or Question 3.

In your response, you should do the following.

- **Thesis**: Present a thesis that makes a historically defensible claim and responds to all parts of the question. The thesis must consist of one or more sentences located in one place, either in the introduction or the conclusion.

- **Application of Historical Thinking Skills**: Develop and support an argument that applies historical thinking skills as directed by the question.

- **Supporting the Argument with Evidence**: Utilize specific examples of evidence to fully and effectively substantiate the stated thesis or a relevant argument.

- **Synthesis**: Extend the argument by explain the connections between the argument and ONE of the following.

    o A development in a different historical period, situation, era, or geographical area.

    o A course theme and/or approach to history that is not the focus of the essay (such as political, economic, social, cultural, or intellectual history).

    o A different discipline or field of inquiry (such as economics, government and politics, art history, or anthropology).

2. Compare and contrast the periods 1650–1815 and 1914–1991 in terms of Europe's economic and political interactions with the non-European world.
    (HTS: Comparison)

3. Compare and contrast the periods 1500–1700 and 1815–1914 in terms of European family life and leisure activities.
    (HTS: Comparison)

Answers and Sample Responses: Multiple Choice

1. **Answer: B. HTS—CAUS; Themes—IS & OS; KCs 1.5 & 1.3.** Though some women, such as Isabella d'Este, did patronize the Renaissance, Knox writes well after that event and clearly seems more concerned with moral issues (A). Knox himself expressed Calvinist dissent within Mary, Queen of Scots Catholic state, thus eliminating C. The early modern period did witness major economic changes, like rising prices and enclosure, but women generally did not benefit from these (D). This leaves us with B as the answer: women played a key role in spreading ideals of religious reform and this involvement sparked concern among males regarding their proper role in society.

2. **Answer: C. HTS—CAUS; Theme—OS; KCs 1.1 & 1.3.** A major factor in spreading ideas of religious reform was the printing press, providing an audience for views like Knox's (C). States did exercise increased state control over religion during this period, but only after significant upheaval and even civil war (A). Though B and D originated in the 16th century, these developments were not germane to Knox's concerns in the passage.

3. **Answer: A. HTS—EVCS; Theme—IS; KC 1.5.** Here we have a skills-only question that asks you to consider the approaches that historians employ in reconstructing the past. The key in the stem is "ordinary women," whose lives were often dominated by cycles of marriage and reproduction, giving us A as the key. B and C indicate other forms of useful evidence, but these artifacts would be of service primarily to reconstruct the lives of elite women. Many male scientists who made diagrams of female anatomy did so under the assumption and with the purpose of reinforcing female inferiority, making these unreliable as evidence for women's actual lives (D).

4. **Answer: C. HTS—CTX; Themes—PP & IS; KC 1.5.** The chart depicts the lower temperatures between 1400 and 1700, termed the Little Ice Age (C). No economic data are shown, eliminating A. Though a portion of this period was known as the Age of Crisis, that term refers to phenomena beyond weather, such as religious upheaval and high crime rates (B). There was no correlation between weather and the Black Death, which preceded the drop in average temperature anyway (D).

5. **Answer: A. HTS—CAUS; Themes—PP & IS; KC 1.5.** All of the choices express important features of early modern social and economic life; however, only A resulted directly from the changing weather patterns, as families under economic stress—due to poor crop yields and repeated famine—responded by delaying standard family events such as marriage and children, until conditions improved. Enclosure occurred in response to the growing money economy (B), and serfdom was codified (D) due to the strength of the nobles and weakness of peasant bargaining position in central and eastern Europe. C is true, but regulation of morality evolved from the goals of religious reformers to apply new dogma to practices.

6. **Answer: D. HTS—CCOT & COMP; Theme—PP; KC 4.4.** The chart invites us to compare an issue—weather—over two time periods. In the contemporary era, weather concerns revolve around global climate change and the human contribution to it, making the key D. Choices A, B, and C all describe developments after 1945 but are not relatable to the chart in a direct way.

7. **Answer: D. HTS—CTX; Theme—SP; KC 1.2.** In this passage, Bodin argues for a vigorous use of state power to address a moral issue—witchcraft. During the period of his writings, many theorists, including Bodin, argued for stronger monarchical power—over religion and to maintain stability and security (D). Though choices A, B, and C all portray accurate developments during the early modern period, they do not relate directly or are not referenced in Bodin's writings.

8. **Answer: C. HTS—CAUS; Themes—OS & IS; KC 1.5.** The focus of the excerpt is the fear of witches, which led to a widespread persecution of the accused between 1550–1680. Prior to the spread of the new scientific methods, most thinkers attributed causation to supernatural forces (A). Of those accused of witchcraft, women comprised about 85% of the total, primarily because of stereotypes that portrayed women as credulous and carnal, thus open to the seduction of the devil (B). Fears during this era were heightened by community breakdown with the shift from communal to commercial agriculture, rise of a money economy, and unstable prices and food supply (D). This leaves us with C, and indeed, humanist literature did not generally emphasize the danger of witches.

9. **Answer: A. HTS—CCOT; Themes—OS; KCs 1.1 & 1.5.** As the new scientific thinking based on empiricism and natural laws took hold, elites gradually abandoned folk explanations and the culture of the masses (A). Witchcraft accusations subsided well before the French Revolution (B) and industrialization (C) and positivism (D) in the 19th century.

10. **Answer: B. HTS—COMP & CCOT; Theme—SP; KCs 1.2 & 2.1.** Political theorists of the 18th century operated in the environment of the Enlightenment, which applied the methods of the new science to politics, particularly the notion that it operates according to natural laws (B), as in the writings of Montesquieu and Rousseau. Both periods emphasized the importance of strong state power (A) and the centralization of legal codes (D), though the 18th century took the latter further. Even if the 18th century saw few witchcraft persecutions, outsiders who were perceived as a threat to the state, such as radicals or ethnic minorities, continued to bear the brunt of discriminatory policies, just as perceived witches in the 16th century (C).

11. **Answer: B. HTS—CAUS; Themes—INT & PP; KCs 1.4 & 2.2.** This is a straightforward factual question asking about the origins of the slave trade. You may recall that Portugal initiated European contact with the west coast of Africa, which included trade in slaves (B). The other nations mentioned (A, C, D) eventually participated in the slave trade, even surpassing Portugal.

12. **Answer: C. HTS—CTX & COMP; Themes—INT & PP; KCs 1.4 & 2.2.** It is true that destruction of indigenous cultures in the Americas (A) stimulated the slave trade; however, the slave trade's massive expansion in the 17th and 18th centuries occurred with the exploitation of unfree labor on American plantations, growing products such as sugar, cotton, and tobacco (C). European powers often converted indigenous peoples to Christianity, yet this practice was not correlated directly with the slave trade. Finally, colonial powers competed for resources (D), but this competition did not center on the slave trade.

13. **Answer: C. HTS—CAUS; Themes—INT & PP; KC 2.2.** The spread of new goods into Europe on the backs of slave labor transformed both the economy and the culture. Sugar, tea, coffee, rum, tobacco, molasses—these goods shifted from luxuries to common commodities consumed by the growing middle class (B). African colonization did not occur until after 1850, eliminating A. New political theories also developed during this era but generally not in direct response to slavery (C). Though the trade associated with slavery increased the wealth and power of the bourgeoisie, the nobility continued to dominate positions in government and political power (D).

14. **Answer: C. HTS—CCOT; Themes—INT, OS, & PP; KCs 2.3 & 2.2.** Exploration promoted the slave trade, so A is out. The Protestant Reformation related minimally if not at all to the slave trade, causing B to drop out. Instead of stimulating opposition to slavery, the Industrial Revolution in fact benefited indirectly from

slavery—by producing capital for investment in manufacturing—eliminating D. This leaves C, and indeed, Enlightenment philosophes in their advancement of natural rights came to oppose a practice in such blatant violation of personal liberty (C).

15. **Answer: C. HTS—CAUS; Themes—OS & SP; KCs 2.1, 2.3, 3.3, & 3.4.** Mill presents a classic case for personal autonomy from a Liberal perspective—the right for each individual to be sovereign over his or her own affairs. His ideas were inspired by Enlightenment beliefs in natural rights and individualism (as in the writings of Locke, Voltaire, and Montesquieu), as well as many actions of the French revolutionaries, such as the Declaration of Rights of Man (A and B). In addition, Mill shows concern about the "tyranny of the majority," a concern that arose with the development of mass politics (D). However, the Concert of Europe acted primarily as a diplomatic mechanism, and though it might have limited political change, Mills does not condemn conservatism *per se* (C).

16. **Answer: B. HTS—CTX; Themes—OS & SP; KC 3.3.** As noted above, Mill's ideas represent one of the classic expositions of 19th-century Liberalism, with an emphasis on individual freedom (B). His argument is based on reason rather than emotion, eliminating A. Mill does not necessarily endorse the elimination of monarchy, one of the central tenets of republicanism (C). Though Mill's ideas may be commensurable with nationalism, he expresses skepticism regarding ideologies that can overwhelm the individual—a danger with nationalism (D).

17. **Answer: A. HTS—CCOT; Themes—SP & PP; KC 3.3.** Each of these developments occurred during the 19th century, but it was the recognition by Liberals of the need to address the intractable problems of industrialization, such as poverty and social breakdown, with the powers of the state that transformed its laissez-faire attitude (as expressed by Mill) into a more interventionist approach (A). Choices B, C, and D only indirectly influenced the development of Liberalism, at least in comparison to the pressing problems of industrial development.

18. **Answer: B. HTS—COMP & EVARG; Themes—OS & SP; KCs 2.1 & 3.3.** Though Locke lived prior to the age of ideologies, his ideas of contract theory and empiricism are considered the foundations for Liberalism (B). Descartes did not speak directly to political issues (like Mill), dropping out A. Rousseau promoted social contract theories; however, his unique ideas of the General Will would run counter to Mill's fears about the oppressive nature of majority opinion (C). Finally, Mill would likely cite a figure like Robespierre

as exactly the type of leader who must be avoided in a state organized around individual rights, since the latter used the power of the state during the French Revolution to curtail liberty (D).

19. **Answer: C. HTS—CTX & CAUS; Themes—SP, INT, & PP; KCs 4.1 & 4.2.** All of the choices express the causes and nature of the Cold War. However, the two sources focus on the strong distrust between the superpowers fed by their fundamentally different visions of the world, making C the key. There are no specific references to nuclear weaponry (A). Certainly the US and USSR competed for strategic areas, especially Europe, but these concerns are secondary to the differing ideologies highlighted by the two sources (B). Though the United Nations was created to resolve security issues, the two superpowers never engaged in direct warfare and the failure of the UN was secondary to the differences between the rival Cold War blocs (D).

20. **Answer: D. HTS—CAUS; Themes—INT, PP, SP, & IS; KCs 4.1, 4.2, & 4.4.** American aid was channeled through institutions that promoted European unity, which stimulated efforts toward greater coordination of European economies (A). The flood of aid promoted an economic recovery that lifted the standard of living and provided funds for pent-up demand in consumer goods (B). Economic recovery promoted a higher birth rate (Baby Boom), as families had the means to support more children (C). This leaves D, and although European states promoted welfare programs, these policies did not directly relate to American aid, particularly since the US did not promote nor adopt them (D).

21. **Answer: A. HTS—CAUS & CCOT; Themes—INT, SP, & PP; KCs 4.1 & 4.2.** In response to US aid to Western Europe, the Soviet Union worked to organize economic activity in the Eastern bloc, primarily through imposing a central, collective economic on its satellites (A). The reforms mentioned in B came much later with Mikhail Gorbachev (1980s). Both de-Stalinization and the rhetoric of "peaceful coexistence" were attempted under Khrushchev, but those Soviet responses were only after those mentioned in A. The Brezhnev Doctrine (D) was articulated in 1968 as justification for crushing the Prague Spring reform movement, once again removed in time from the sources.

22. **Answer: C. HTS—EVCS; Theme—SP; KC 4.1.** This question considers the question of reliability in use of sources. Though all the choices address potential drawbacks of the source, C represents the most problematic situation. It is unlikely that an official government publication would promote any position other than the party line. All speeches attempt to persuade (A), but

they can still provide useful insights into the attitudes of decision-makers. The lack of specific data in the speech (B) does not present a specific limitation on *that type of source*, though it would if the source were a statistical report. As for D, most sources require inference and context for interpretation, so this fact would not constitute a problem for the source *per se*.

23. **Answer: C. HTS—CTX & CAUS; Theme—SP; KC 1.2.** Unlike the other new monarchies, the Holy Roman Empire suffered from an unusually high degree of localism, being divided into over 300 different principalities, cities, and states. Even with a prestigious title, the emperor struggled to counter these centrifugal forces, as Rosheim relates with the laws regarding Jews (C). Charles did draw from the wealth of Spain, but the passage does not address that particular issue (A). Further, there is no mention or suggestion of Christian humanism (B), nor does the text deal with class conflict (D). Rather, the text shows religious persecution and localism.

24. **Answer: D. HTS—CAUS & EVARG; Themes—SP, OS, & IS; KCs 1.2 & 1.3.** Religious reformers confiscated church lands in Germany; however, Jews did not generally benefit from this practice, eliminating A. Though Luther hoped Jews would convert to Christianity with his reform, he grew disenchanted with Jews when these conversions did not materialize, dropping out B. The status of Jews in most states proved precarious; however, mass emigration occurred primarily in areas like the Iberian Peninsula where the state sponsored campaigns to achieve religious uniformity (C). This leave us with D, and indeed, the higher degree of concern over religious doctrine during the Reformation tended to increase persecution until the end of the religious wars after 1648.

25. **Answer: B. HTS—CCOT & PER; Themes—SP, OS, & IS; KCs 1.3 & 2.3.** Many of the first treatises arguing for toleration of Jews and granting citizenship emerged during the Enlightenment, with its emphasis on natural rights and secularism (B). The Commercial Revolution increased cultural contact but did not address the status of Jews directly (A). By the Industrial Revolution, Jews in many states had been granted (at least in theory) full civic rights (C). If anything, the two world wars rendered the status of Jews even more precarious, as the unstable conditions fueled anti-Semitism (D).

26. **Answer: A. HTS—CAUS & CCOT; Themes—OS & IS; KCs 3.3 & 3.6.** Anti-Semitism shifted in nature with the popularization of Darwin's theories, as it took on a racial and political focus (A). The undermining of organized religion, particularly Catholicism, would have tended to improve the status of Jews by making

religious homogeneity more suspect, eliminating B. Rousseau's glorification of precivilization man caused a general questioning of all religions, not supporting or condemning Judaism specifically (C). Marx himself came from a Jewish background (though became an atheist) and many Jews took up socialism/Marxism, but the theory shifted the focus from religion and race toward class as a category of analysis (D).

27. **Answer: B. HTS—COMP; Theme—IS; KCs 1.5 & 2.2.** This question relates to the IS Learning Objective of "the Other," or the tendency for majority groups to alienate minorities through language, symbols, and depictions. Such groups tended to live in precarious situations and fell prey periodically to persecutions, sometimes popular, sometimes state organized (as with Jews in Russia). Choices A, C, and D capture such marginalized and often powerless groups. This leaves B as the key—though some nobles did experience exile for opposing absolutism, they were not targeted as a group and did not suffer from a general lack of social and political power.

28. **Answer: C. HTS—EVARG & CTX; Themes—SP; KC 2.1.** The passage conveys two key notions regarding Napoleon: 1) that he accepted the reformulation of the French state by the revolutionaries and 2) that he brought order to the faltering ideals by exercising strong power from above. These principles are most in keeping with enlightened absolutism (C), the embrace of rational reform from the top-down in order to strengthen the state. New monarchs of the 16th century preceded such enlightened reforms, canceling out A. Napoleon manipulated religion to gain support but did not claim to derive his power from God (B). Though Napoleon employed popular appeals, he did not have access to the communication and transportation technologies of the 20th century to exercise total rule, causing D to fall out for chronological reasons.

29. **Answer: D. HTS—CAUS & CCOT; Theme—SP; KC 2.1.** The historian portrays France as amidst chaos prior to Napoleon, thus explaining the appeal of his movement toward central power and order. The situation most responsible for this development is expressed by D, which seemed to require the extreme measures of the Reign of Terror. The other choices (A, B, C) represent more lasting achievements or events of the early (Liberal) phase of the revolution.

30. **Answer: A. HTS—CAUS & CCOT; Theme—SP; KC 2.1.** As the reading suggests, Napoleon's success lay in his ability to portray himself as a child of the revolution and to use popular impulses to justify his accumulation of power (A). Though the Napoleonic Code granted some

rights to women, they were rendered second-class citizens and stripped of some rights (such as divorce under most circumstances), excluding B. Napoleon did provoke nationalist responses in conquered nations, but this outcome was not intended as a policy (C). Once again, the passage reminds us that Napoleon eschewed popular violence in favor of a top-down regime, leaving off D.

31. **Answer: B. HTS—CCOT & COMP; Theme—SP; KCs 2.1 & 3.4.** Napoleon initiated a new type of rule that led to the *Realpolitik* practitioners of the later 19th century. This characterization includes Cavour (A), Napoleon III (C), and Bismarck (D), all of whom used nationalism and popular appeals to build support for what were essentially authoritarian regimes. However, Metternich, as an old-style conservative who helped overthrow Napoleon, rejected the popular passions of the revolutionary era in favor of unabashed elite rule, hearkening back to the Old Regime (B).

32. **Answer: C. HTS—CTX & CAUS; Themes—PP & IS; KCs 2.2 & 2.4.** The Fragonard painting portrays the growing "cult of sentiment" surrounding family life and greater resources dedicated to child-rearing with the consumer revolution, as seen by the wealth of the family (D). We see depicted two parents, their two young children, a newborn infant, and likely a wet nurse, indicating a nuclear family, the predominant social unit of this era (A). The title and scene suggest that this space is dedicated to one or more of the children, with parents sleeping separately, a relatively new development in the 18th century (B). This leaves the EXCEPT answer C. Note that though illegitimacy increased during this period, it is not portrayed in the painting.

33. **Answer: B. HTS—CAUS; Themes—OS & IS; KCs 2.3 & 2.4.** This is a straightforward content question, asking for the intellectual causes of new attitudes toward children. Locke wrote a famous treatise, *Some Thoughts Concerning Education* (1693), arguing for a new approach toward children, which emphasized psychological over physical persuasion. In *Émile, or Treatise on Education* (1762), Rousseau critiqued the overemphasis on rote learning and urged society to adopt an experiential method of education (B). Though the other sets of thinkers (A, C, and D) listed here also partook of the Enlightenment focus on empiricism and reason, none were noted for writing tracts about childhood or education.

34. **Answer: D. HTS—CCOT; Themes—PP, IS, & SP; KC 3.3.** The painting depicts a protective and humanitarian attitude toward children. Political ideologies did not generally address the issue of children and their welfare directly, excluding A. Mechanization of production, in fact, often benefited from child labor, the

opposite of the stem in this question (B). C represents the best distractor, but movements to aid the poor focused more on issues of class inequality rather than the notion of childhood as a particular phase of human development. This leaves us with D, and indeed, governments eventually passed legislation aimed at protecting children from the rigors of factory labor and to require basic education, at least around the turn of the 20th century.

35. **Answer: A. HTS: EVARG & CTX; Theme—OS; KC 2.3.** As noted in Question 32, the new attitude toward children arose in part from the application of scientific principles to issues of social and political reform, known as the Enlightenment (A). Printed materials increased significantly during the 18th century, but this fact is not central to the image (B). In addition, the period did see the growth of public venues; however, the painting shows *private* space, eliminating C. No reference or implication regarding religion is portrayed, though skepticism does constitute a feature of Enlightenment thought (D).

36. **Answer: A. HTS—CAUS & CTX; Theme—SP; KC 4.1.** All of the choices relate to features of the First World War. The casualties listed are military, excluding B, which refers principally to civilian casualties. The same is true for C. Though military stalemate led to the spread of the war globally (D), this outcome was itself the result of the discrepancy between traditional military strategies (mimicking Napoleon) and new technologies that favored the defensive. Thus, the key is A.

37. **Answer: C. HTS—CAUS; Themes—SP, IS, & OS; KCs 4.3 & 4.4.** With men at the front and with loss of life, women entered the industrial work force to maintain munitions production (A). Due to its tragic nature, World War I spawned a cynical and disillusioned lost generation (B). Instead of the French Revolution, it was in fact World War I that severed the hold of traditional elites (monarchies and nobility) on political power (D). This leaves C as the false choice: the Versailles settlement did establish peace but it was directed by the great powers and did not result in a stable Europe, hence the Depression and rise of totalitarian regimes.

38. **Answer: B. HTS—CTX; Themes—SP & PP; KC 4.2.** The poster depicts various features of Stalin's Five-Year Plans to collectivize agriculture and accelerate industrial production (B). By the time of this project, Stalin had already purged any threats to his power (A). It is true the Soviet Union controlled the Communist International (Comintern), ostensibly to promote world revolution; however, Stalin preferred to focus on building "socialism in one country" before

turning to the spread of Bolshevism (C). Finally, the goals depicted reversed Lenin's New Economic Policy (NEP), which had temporarily compromised with capitalism (D).

39. **Answer: A. HTS—CAUS; Themes—SP & IS; KC 4.2.** The movement toward collective agriculture led Stalin to steamroll those wealthy peasants (kulaks) who stood in his way, leading to their slaughter (A). The other choices either did not occur or were unrelated to Stalin's forced industrialization. As the lone communist nation, the Soviet Union was isolated diplomatically (B), and even if it was later admitted to the League of Nations, this occurred despite, not because of, Stalin's centralization of power (C). Theoretically women achieved equality of status with men in the USSR; in reality, women did double duty as homemakers and factory workers, while reproductive rights were curtailed in favor of increasing population (D).

40. **Answer: D. HTS—CCOT; Themes—SP & PP; KC 4.2.** Lenin died prior to the policies depicted, eliminating A. Khrushchev supported de-Stalinization and a movement toward consumer goods; nonetheless, his policies did not dismantle the collective planning of the Soviet system, nor did they meet their goals (B). Brezhnev, who followed the controversial Khrushchev, preached "no experiments" and reinforced the command economy and continued to focus on military and industrial production (C). It was Gorbachev who fundamentally attempted to reconstruct (perestroika) the Soviet economy, an undertaking so ambitious that it led to the collapse of the entire Soviet system.

41. **Answer: B. HTS—CAUS & CCOT; Themes—INT & SP; KCs 2.1, 2.2, & 3.5.** The author addresses the century previous to 1856, which refers to the beginning of the Seven Years' War, a major continental and colonial struggle between Britain and France (B). One of the battlegrounds in this conflict was India, with the British emerging victorious and extending their control through the process presented by Innes. The other nations (A, C, and D) had been rivals at one point or another in British history (including Russia in Central Asia during the 19th century), but Britain's most consistent rival was France.

42. **Answer: A. HTS—CTX; Themes—INT, PP, & SP; KC 3.5.** Choices B, C, and D all enabled European colonial powers to establish dominance in Africa and Asia, so they could not be presented to colonial peoples as "benefits." However, one claim made by European colonizers was that they modernized the infrastructure of colonial nations, by building road, railroads, and introducing modern sanitation and hygiene (A).

43. **Answer: D. HTS—PER; Theme—INT; KCs 3.5 & 4.1.** Each of the conflicts affected the relationship between European powers and their colonies. The Boer War shook Britain out of its half-century of isolation and caused it to seek new allies (A), but it did not radically alter the state of colonial empires. Though the Russo-Japanese War proved that an Asian power could defeat a European power, its effects were not felt across the colonies until decades later, not to mention that Japan used its new modern power to engage in imperialism itself (B). The League of Nations held the promise of self-determination, but it also confirmed mandates strengthening (temporarily) British and French control over territories in the Middle East, Africa, and the Pacific (C). It was, in fact, the vast devastation and moral failings of the Second World War that severed Europe's hold over its colonies and a reappraisal of their value to European security (D).

44. **Answer: B. HTS—CCOT & CAUS; Theme—INT; KCs 3.5 & 4.1.** With an EXCEPT question, we are looking for the outlier, and it is B. Former colonial nations did not refuse to participate in the United Nations; in fact, it was one of the few forums where former colonies and developing nations had a voice that could influence the great powers, who dominated the Security Council (B). The other choices represent actions taken by colonial peoples: modernizing economies, such as the Indian textile industry or Egypt building the Aswan Dam (A); establishing national resistance movements, like the Viet Minh in Indochina (B); and emigrating to Europe, seeking jobs with the European economic miracle (D).

45. **Answer: C. HTS—CTX & CAUS; Theme—SP; KCs 3.3 & 3.4.** Though the revolutions of 1848 both dealt with Italian and German unification, they were more an attempt to overthrow the established order in an effort to establish territorial states. Even though they failed in this goal, this failure set the stage for unification, eliminating A. Industry played less of a role than diplomacy, but if anything, the growth of industry would have facilitated unification by creating a more unified market (B). The dates of the quotes are too early for the pursuit of colonies (D). This gives us the Congress of Vienna, and if you recall, it was this diplomatic settlement (led by Metternich) that stifled the idea of nationalism and retained the division and/or foreign occupation of each nation (C).

46. **Answer: A. HTS—CCOT & CAUS; Themes—SP & OS; KCs 3.3 & 3.4.** With the failure of Romantic revolution in 1848, conservatives took up the cause of nationalism, but from the top down. We can see this in the quote by Bismarck (A). The year 1848 represents the end of the Romantic spirit (except for music),

canceling out B. Socialism gained influence during the 19th century, but that fact does not bear directly upon the changes in nationalism (C). The Crimean War certainly set the stage for unification, but it bears less directly on the *tone* of the sources (D).

47. **Answer: B. HTS—CAUS; Theme—SP; KC 3.4.** Diplomacy and warfare produced the modern Italian and German states. This possibility opened with the fall of Metternich's Concert of Europe, aimed at repressing revolutionary nationalism and maintaining the status quo. When the Concert collapsed after 1848, the path opened toward unification (B). Industrialization (A) aided the achievement, but it was secondary to diplomacy. The creation of the Dual Monarchy occurred later (1867) and relates to Austria rather than to Italy or Germany (C). Nationalist tensions in the Balkans played a more central role after Germany's rise as a great power and on the eve of World War I (D).

48. **Answer: D. HTS—CTX; Theme—OS; KCs 3.6 & 4.3.** All of the choices reflect cultural trends of the era, but upon considering the building, you will likely note its unornamented appearance and use of modern materials, such as glass and steel. This relates most closely to D. The other developments (A, B, and C) do not pertain to this particular building, or do so only incidentally.

49. **Answer: A. HTS—CAUS; Themes—PP & OS; KC 3.1.** As noted above, new building materials allowed for new approaches to architecture, such as skyscrapers (A). Expansion into African and Asian markets coincided with modern architecture, but the latter was not dependent on the former (B). European states did move toward protectionism after 1875; however, this trend did not affect architecture *per se* (C). Same for D—working conditions improved but this was not causally related to new building styles.

50. **Answer: C. HTS—COMP & CCOT; Themes—SP & PP; KCs 1.1, 2.3, & 3.1.** Modern buildings like the Bauhaus building generally lacked ornamentation in favor of an appearance of economic efficiency (C). Choices A, B, and D do not express significant differences between classical and modern architectural styles.

51. **Answer: B. HTS—PER; Theme—SP; KC 4.3.** Prior to the onset of World War I, European culture embraced a technological utopianism and the notion of progress. These attitudes were largely undermined by the tragic consequences of the Great War (B). The scramble for colonies in Africa did not appreciably alter the trend of European culture in these directions (A). Though the Great Depression and World War II represented fundamental challenges to Europe (C and D), the tone

of disillusionment and wariness of technology had already been established by World War I.

52. **Answer: B. HTS—CTX & CAUS; Themes—OS & SP; KC 3.6.** Bagehot glorifies the importance of competition and struggle in interstate relations, an idea central (at least in biology) to Darwin's *On the Origin of Species* (B). Though workers struggled for equality and in Marxism embraced violent revolution, socialism condemned war among states as serving the interests of capital, excluding A. It would be more accurate to argue that Bagehot's attitudes (or at least those like his) *caused* the pursuit of colonies rather than vice versa (C). Though his ideas reflected the growth of mass politics, this development ran parallel to, rather than caused, the embrace of struggle (D).

53. **Answer: C. HTS—CCOT; Theme—OS; KCs 3.6 & 4.3.** Feminists could also be pacifists, but many suffragettes (e.g., Pankhursts) supported the very ideas of struggle and violence Bagehot addresses, excluding A. Both Freud and Darwin tended to undermine the Enlightenment notions of rationality and progress; thus Freud may have endorsed the competitive urge outlined by Darwin as the analog to the *id*, or drive for power (B). It was not the abandonment of laissez-faire that countered Bagehot's Social Darwinist view; rather, D emerged as a response to such criticisms. We are left with C, and indeed, the immense and pointless destruction of the two world wars led to a more critical outlook toward war and even moved European nations to move toward unity.

54. **Answer: B. HTS—CTX; Themes—INT, IS, & PP; KC 4.4.** One is struck by the multiethnic composition of this national soccer team, reflecting the immigration trend following World War II, stimulated by European prosperity (C). New technologies contributed to globalization, but many nations of immigrant origin lacked them, excluding A. The immigrant trend preceded the collapse of communism in 1989 (C). D represents an appealing choice, but its causal relationship (noted above) was more indirect than direct.

55. **Answer: A. HTS—CAUS; Themes—INT & SP; KC 4.1.** Many former colonies won independence following the Second World War, though the real wave occurred after about 1960, delayed by concern that former colonies might become communist outposts (A). Separatist violence provoked backlashes, but often, as in Algeria, it was the means to gain independence (B). Choice C expresses an accurate trend but one that was generally unrelated to colonial autonomy. The same is true for D.

SAQ 1 Response and Commentary

1A. The painting shows many of the features of the Scientific Revolution. On the floor of the Academy, we see a model of the universe according to the new heliocentric theory by Copernicus, a major change in the way people looked at the world. In addition, the scene is filled with many measuring devices, presumably to chart the planets and gain knowledge from new astronomical discoveries. The etching also reflects empirical knowledge gained from dissections and plants and animals, as seen behind the assembled figures.

1B. Many political figures endorsed scientific discovery as it promoted the idea that their state was the best. In this painting, Louis visits the science academy he founded to learn about its research. Political rulers like him encouraged these discoveries first-hand as it also created an aura for the public that they were well-rounded in all subjects. Also, since Louis was the Sun King, he wanted to extend his power over Europe through trade and military technology.

This concise response earns all 3 points. First, in Part A the student notes the astronomical model as representing the heliocentric theory of Copernicus. Further, she uses specific objects in the image to highlight the importance of empirical observation and measurement. Next in Part B, the student explains the state's interest in science, such as prestige and commercial and military advances, though "well rounded" sounds generic. 3 points

SAQ 2 Response and Commentary

2A. The Catholic Church first attempted reform with the Council of Trent. This was a meeting of the highest officials in order to address the problems the church was facing. This meeting came about soon after Luther posted his Ninety-Five Theses and was the first step to solve the problems of division he created. The Church also attempted reform in creating religious orders. They created groups like the Jesuits order for people to join to reform their faith. This also promoted the idea of perfect followers of God as models. They also spread the faith to the New World.

2B. The Counter Reformation took a long time to respond to the Protestants. Religious wars occurred throughout the 16th century, as in France and Holy Roman Empire, and after these wars, religion was divided. So in that sense, the Catholic Reformation did not succeed.

For Part A, the response provides 2 appropriate pieces of evidence (Council of Trent and Jesuits), and explains them accurately, earning 2 points. However, the explanation in Part B incorrectly focuses on the religious wars, a topic that is causally connected but not synonymous with the Catholic Reformation. No point earned for this section of the SAQ. 2 points

SAQ 3 Response and Commentary

3A. The Revolutions of 1848 were the most significant turning points because they introduced the political system of mass politics. Because leaders feared another violent attempt at revolution, they began to appeal to the public. In addition, the revolutions changed the Romantic ideals of leaders and shifted it to a more realistic view of the world. The violence of the revolution ended the obsession with nature and beauty. Now leaders focused on the technological advancements of their state.

3B. The Revolutions of 1848 were more of a turning point than the Congress of Vienna because the Congress of Vienna obviously failed to accomplish its goals. If it didn't, then the Revolutions of 1848 would never have happened. Therefore, the Revolutions of 1848 were more significant as they actually accomplished a true change.

Again, this response models a concise approach to the SAQs, providing 2 accurate arguments for the revolutions of 1848 as a turning point-introduction of mass politics and shift from Romanticism to realism. Next, the student not only argues against the Congress of Vienna but also connects it to the turning point (1848) she selected in Part A. 3 points

SAQ 4 Response and Commentary

4A. The Soviet Union was on the brink of collapse in 1989. One example is the Cold War. With all of the money spent on missiles and arms, the Soviet Union could not keep up with the United States and Reagan's infamous Star Wars defense shield.

4B. Gorbachev wanted to reform the Soviet Union through structural change. This was known as perestroika. He took actions like increasing consumer products, decentralizing control, and other examples of openness, or glasnost, to fix problems. He did not try to resist the change that was inevitable, and this shows how he was acted upon for the better of the people.

4C. This outcome is not always the same, and this can be shown with the French Revolution. The French Revolution failed to solve its problems and clearly did not end with the same positive outcomes as the historian described. Napoleon can be compared to Gorbachev, but it is clear that their actions and outcomes differed.

Though the student provides an accurate cause of the collapse of the Soviet Union, it is not drawn from the quote, which in the first paragraph, focuses on popular discontent, not issues of national security. No point earned. In Part B, the response briefly but accurately outlines Gorbachev's perestroika program and the goals behind it, earning a point. The reference in Part C to the French Revolution is apropos, but the explanation provided is too general and undeveloped to earn the point. 1 point

DBQ Response and Commentary

The Italian Renaissance, occurring from 1350 to 1550, gave rise to a new set of views on life and humanity that stimulated cultural and social growth and improvement in Italy. As a result, humanism swept across Italy during the Renaissance, planting seeds that would reverse the nature of Europe completely prior to the Renaissance. Humanism is described as an ideology in which human potential and nature are glorified through means of art and literature to convey deeper meanings. Thus, the Renaissance greatly fulfilled humanist ideas in culture and society by revamping the traditional practices of religion, family life, politics, and introducing new secular ideas that greatly influenced new views on humanity and nature.

Humanism during the Renaissance promoted equality in society which in return, caused an increase in activities that promoted human potential and glorified the human body and mind. According to Peter Paul Vergerius, classical studies provide free men the virtues and wisdom to train the noble gift of the body and soul (Doc. 1). In his interpretation, we notice that the social impacts of humanism led to a rise in equality and human talent, enabling free men access to literature and education which was not common during the Medieval age. Thus, we can conclude that Vergerius suggests that the Renaissance fulfilled humanist goals by promoting education and equality in society that caused the rise of ideas associated with human ability. Vergerius' role as an educator shows that education has became more prevalent in the process of advancing humanity through education. Furthermore, humanist impacts on society is exemplified by the Portrait of Federico da Montefeltro and his son Guidobaldo, depicting a mercenary reading a book (Doc. 3). This painting aligns my argument above stating social changes during the Renaissance on human potential. The emphasis fulfills humanism because it allows humans the right to education, which glorifies the human race. This unknown painter's artwork is an accurate representation of daily society as it conveys the activities of a commoner during the Renaissance, showing how effective and impactful the Renaissance truly was. In addition, social activities and practices during the Renaissance fully satisfied the humanist ideology as shown through politics and new practices. Machiavelli states that a ruler should be just

and capable of reacting to his subjects by being both a lion and a fox (Doc. 6). Not only is he describing humanist ideas of how a ruler should be just and equal to his subjects, but Machiavelli is also promoting human intelligence by advocating that a ruler should be sly in certain situations and stern in other situations. Prior to the Renaissance, politics in Italy remained corrupt and decentralized with great feudalism and corruption during the Medieval age. With the introduction of Greek and Latin classics, politics and humanity were significantly improved and altered to become more civilized and efficient. Thus, politics in Florence are shown to fulfill humanist beliefs of human glorification and equality. Machiavelli's background as a diplomat suggest that he has had full experience and is aware of the newly evolved Renaissance politics. Overall, the Italian Renaissance did fulfill the expectations of humanism fully in the social aspect of human equality, human potential, and city-state politics.

Not only did the Renaissance influence Humanism in society, but culturally, Italy experienced some of the greatest changes in history in fields such as religion and the rise of secularism, gender roles and marriages, and uses for art to portray and glorify human nature. With the rise of humanism, wealth and status became more emphasized in marriages and between families. As shown by the letter written by Alessandra Strozzi to her son, Filippo, Strozzi is concerned with the status and dowry of the bride's family (Doc. 2). This shows that humanist ideas on glory, which is related to wealth, is considered when arranging marriages. Although equality was promoted, emphasis of marrying with a family of same or similar status remained popular. Nonetheless, roles of women remained similar throughout marriages and relationships. Humanist ideas were incorporated in the expectations of a wife as shown by Baldassare Castiglione's book, *The Book of the Courtier*. In this writing, Castiglione advocates that the minds of women are very similar to men, but the female brain is employed to act naturally graceful and delicate (Doc.7). Humanism is shown by the cultural practices of women during the Renaissance by using human qualities to promote gender roles and gender expectations. Castiglione's role as a diplomat shows that he often visits noble families, thus his vision of women during the Renaissance would only be geared towards wealthy families and not the common people. In addition, humanist ideas are reflected during the Renaissance in religion as the rise of secularism affected the popularity of religion. In a diary entry by Luca Landucci, he describes Girolamo Savonarola, who was excommunicated, yet people had faith in him (Doc. 4). The entry shows how the rise of secularism and skepticism towards the church allowed for people to begin defining the church's orders, such as associating with the excommunicated. The effects of humanism played a major role in religion as it caused a rise in secular ideals and undermined the credibility of the church. Therefore, Landucci's entry was written in the aspect of a commoner, showing the true humanist changes that sunk into cultures. Last, humanist ideals were demonstrated effectively during the Renaissance through artwork and paintings. Isabella d'Este patronized Leonardo da Vinci for his realistic and natural portraits of the human body. In her letter to da Vinci, Isabella shows the desire to be similar to the divine, requesting for her portrait to be converted (Doc. 5). Her request shows how the humanist idea of glorification of the human body has became significant in artworks. Thus, from her request we learn that the Renaissance did indeed impact cultural traditions by incorporating the glory of the human body in the arts. Isabella is a renowned humanist during her times, and her background clearly supports her cause and demonstrates the full effect of humanism during the Renaissance. Overall, humanism is evidently crucial and prevalent during the Renaissance in cultural activities such as arts, family arrangements, and religion.

In conclusion, the Renaissance did significantly fulfill the humanist ideas by subjecting major changes towards society and culture. Social changes in law and human rights abide the humanist cause whereas the cultural changes in arts and family demonstrate the effects of humanism during this time period. This topic relates to the later Scientific Revolution, when further secularism took place and attacked the power of the Catholic Church.

Despite providing solid background on Italy and humanism, these references are within the parameters of the prompt itself and do not earn the Contextualization point; however, the student does earn the Thesis point for the reference to secularism in humanism. Further, even though the student consistently pursues her thesis, there needs to be further recognition of historical complexity and document interaction to earn the Argumentation point. The response employs all 7 documents, but misinterprets Document 4, which focuses on a religious reaction to the materialism of the Renaissance. However, the student does earn the Content Use point by employing 6 documents to make arguments related to the Renaissance and humanism. There are several Source Analysis attempts here, but some fall short, costing the student the point. For Document 1, the reference to Vergerius's role as an educator is not explained as it relates to the content of the document. For the painting (Document 3), the reference to da Montefeltro being a commoner is inaccurate (the attribute notes that he became a duke), and no further explanation is given. However, the point of view

analysis for Machiavelli as a diplomat provides adequate support for reliability. Also, the similar strategy works for the Castiglione document (Doc. 7), providing a second successful effort. However, the reference to the authors of Document 4 (commoner) and Document 6 (humanist) fall short in linking the source's identity to its content. Though brief, the content reference to politics during the "Medieval age" is adequate for the Evidence Beyond Document point, though this is not the case with the Synthesis attempt in the conclusion, as the connection with the Scientific Revolution is in need of further analysis. Score: 3 (Thesis, Document Content, Evidence Beyond Documents).

LEQ 2 Response and Commentary

In both these periods, European nations tried to dominate other areas of the world. During the 1650–1815 period, Europe tried to set up colonies in the Americas and in Asia, seeking silks, silver, and other goods. The situation was defined by Europe's superior technology, like cannons and joint-stock companies. In the later period, Europe still tried to gain advantage from colonies; however, because of Europe's declining power from the world wars, it was forced to give up its colonies. This decolonization was a major difference between the two periods.

Europe sought many goods and helped expand trade from 1650–1815. This was the age of the Commercial Revolution. One of the greatest powers was the Dutch Republic. With its center based in Amsterdam, the Dutch traded with all areas of the world, even the colonies of other powers. Into Europe flowed new consumer goods, such as coffee, tea, sugar, potatoes, calicoes, and cotton. Many of these products were made on the backs of slaves, imported from Africa and sent to plantations in the New World. This competition for goods created rivalries among European nations, especially between France and Great Britain. These two nations warred over North America, the Caribbean, and India. After the 7 Years War, Britain became the dominant power, but not for long. The French helped the British colonies gain their independence with the American Revolution, and this would set the stage for other revolts based on Enlightenment principles and nationalism.

In 1914, Europe stood at the top of its power, with colonies all over the world. But this would all come toppling down with the two world wars and the Cold War. Even though Britain and France gained mandates after 1918, places like India and Indochina were claiming they should have the same "self-determination" granted to nations that came out of the empires that collapsed at the end of the war. The breaking point came with Europe's utter devastation after 1945. Britain decided on a "partition and run" strategy in places like

India, while France tried to hold onto to colonies like Algeria. Now weaker, European nations no longer could hold on to their colonies and instead focused much more on internal problems like recovering from the war. Recovery came with Marshall Plan funds and new institutions like the ECSC and EU.

Though Europe had fewer colonies in 1991 than 1815, it had certainly learned some lessons. By realizing that it's not worth it to waste so much power controlling other nations, Europe focused more on its own problems. This new attitude helped it recover and make a better argument that it was a "civilizing" power.

Here we have a student who conveys a good range of content knowledge and generally uses it in service to analysis. Though the thesis does not consist of a single statement, the introduction clearly outlines both similarities and differences of the two periods, earning the Thesis point. The student provides ample evidence for both periods, capturing 2 points for Use of Evidence. Though much of the analysis is implicit, the student adequately accounted for (rather than merely describing) the reasons for the similarities and differences in each period, thus gaining both points for the Targeted HTS. However, the conclusion's brevity does not allow a sufficient development of the Synthesis point. Score: 5 (Thesis, 2 points for Targeted HTS, 2 points for Use of Evidence).

LEQ 3 Response and Commentary

We are all born into families, and they define how we live. This was true in both of these periods, 1500–1700 and 1815–1914. In both periods, families were important and had a great influence over social life. However, in the earlier period, families had an even more important role, since people worked together to produce goods, either on farms or in shops. During the later period, families mostly got together to consume things, like meals or to go shopping and have leisure.

During the period before industry, most people lived on farms and worked together to form a living. As seen in many Bruegel paintings, both men and women brought in the hay and crops. Children were valued for their labor and were often portrayed as little adults in images. Fathers had almost absolute powers over the family and looked to have children who could inherit their wealth. For fun, communities did things together, like Carnival, a time when there was much drinking and frivolity. Since there were no shopping malls, people had to find their amusements with each other. This helped build bonds within the community.

In the later period, the Industrial Revolution was changing all of economic and social life. With the advent of factories, families now separated and worked outside the home. Later on, women would control the domestic sphere while men labored in factories or offices. This was a big change and in some ways, loosened the importance of families. At first, children worked in factories too, but many states—like England with the Factory Act of 1833—put limits on children working and required them to get schooling. When cities began to reform after about 1850, they built places for families to enjoy leisure, such as department stores, museums, and parks, like the one depicted in Seurat's "Sunday on Le Grande Jatte." This painting is unique because it uses dots of color that, when combined, form a complete image of Paris during a beautiful summer day. Most of the painting seems very still—with people fishing, boating, and having a picnic—yet there is some movement, like a girl chasing a butterfly or dogs chasing one another. Impressionist painters focused more on scenes of everyday life like this, which shows how the new leisure activities worked more on a weekday basis instead of by the seasons, as before.

The economic issues during each period basically defined what family life was like and what types of leisure pursuits were available. While the later period may have had more choices, it is possible that families were actually closer when they had to depend on each other for survival.

Though uneven, this essay earned all of the rubric points. Despite a brief introduction, the essay does identify both similarities (families "define how we live") and differences ("working together" to "consuming together"), which earns the Thesis point. Clearly, the second body paragraph provides a higher level of detail and analysis; however, the brief paragraph on the earlier period is on point and does provide a linkage to the agricultural setting of early modern Europe with some specific examples (Bruegel paintings, "little adults," paternal power, Carnival). The discussion in each paragraph goes beyond description and links effectively, albeit basically, to the historical context, earning 2 points for the Targeted HTS and 2 points for Use of Evidence. This student earned the Synthesis point for the extended analysis using Art History with the Seurat painting, and to a lesser extent, with the Bruegel painting. Score: 6 (Thesis, 2 points for Targeted HTS, 2 points for Use of Evidence, Synthesis).

Section III
Practice Exams

Practice Exam 2 | Section 1, Part A

⏱ **55 minutes | 55 questions**

Directions Each of the questions or incomplete statements below is followed by four suggested answers or completions. Select the one that is best in each case.

Source materials have been edited for the purpose of this exercise.

Questions 1–4 refer to the passage below.

> "For some women are concerned with parting their hair correctly, adorning themselves with lovely dresses, or decorating their fingers with pearls and other gems...[O]thers wish to gaze at lavish banquet tables, to rest in sleep, or, standing at mirrors, to smear their lovely faces. But those in whom a deeper integrity yearns for virtue, restrain from the start their youthful souls, reflect on higher things, harden the body with sobriety and trials, and curb their tongues, open their ears, compose their thoughts in wakeful hours, their minds in contemplation, to letters bonded with righteousness. For knowledge is not given as a gift, but [is gained] with diligence.
>
> Laura Cereta, Italian humanist and feminist, *Letter to Bibulus Sempronius: A Defense of the Liberal Education of Women*, 1488

1. Cereta's criticism of the behavior of some women in the passage was most likely caused by which of the following developments in the late 15th century?

   A. The persistence of folk beliefs in witchcraft and the supernatural

   B. The increase in luxury items brought about by exploration

   C. The spread of reading materials due to the printing press

   D. The denunciation of the abuses of the Catholic Church

2. Cereta's attitude toward education was most likely influenced by:

   A. The growth of civic humanism.

   B. Patronage of the arts by elites.

   C. Scientific observations of the human body.

   D. Revival of classical texts and languages.

3. As reflected in the passage, Renaissance Italy would have been most similar to the rest of Europe in which of the following ways?

   A. High level of urbanization and economic development

   B. The growth of a new merchant and banking elite

   C. The movement toward centralized monarchy

   D. Continuing importance of hierarchy and social status

4. Cereta's concerns about women were most strongly addressed and changed in the period:

   A. 1517–1648.

   B. 1789–1850.

   C. 1850–1920.

   D. 1920–1945.

Margaret L. King and Albert Rabil, Jr., eds., trans., *Her Immaculate Hand: Selected Works By and About The Women Humanists of Quattrocento Italy* (New York: Center for Medieval and Early Renaissance Studies, State University of New York at Binghamton, 1992), p. 83.

"There remains simple experience; which, if taken as it comes, is called accident, if sought for, experiment. The true method of experience first lights the candle, and then by means of the candle shows the way; commencing as it does with experience duly ordered and digested, not bungling or erratic, and from it deducing axioms, and from established axioms again new experiments."

Francis Bacon, English natural philosopher, *Novum Organum*, 1620

5. In the passage, Francis Bacon argues for which of the following approaches toward knowledge?

A. Revival of classical learning

B. Reliance on mathematics

C. Inductive method

D. Astrology and alchemy

6. The method above changed ideas in the 16th and 17th centuries most significantly in:

A. astronomy.

B. medicine.

C. biology.

D. chemistry.

Questions 7–8 are based on the text below.

"5. The Committee of Public Safety is charged to take all necessary measures to set up without delay an extraordinary manufacture of arms of every sort which corresponds with the ardor and energy of the French people. It is, accordingly, authorized to form all the establishments, factories, workshops, and mills which shall be deemed necessary for the carrying on of these works, as well as to put in requisition, within the entire extent of the Republic, the artists and workingmen who can contribute to their success.

6. The representatives of the people sent out for the execution of the present law shall have the same authority in their respective districts, acting in concert with the Committee of Public Safety; they are invested with the unlimited powers assigned to the representatives of the people to the armies."

Levée en masse ("mass levy"), Decree of the French National Convention, August 23, 1793

7. An historian might use this source as evidence for all of the following EXCEPT:

A. the growth of citizen armies during the French Revolution.

B. divisions across Europe caused by revolutionary ideologies.

C. the exclusion of women from citizenship and legal and economic rights.

D. an increase in the power of the state during the Reign of Terror.

8. In what ways did the ideas expressed in the decree remain most consistent under Napoleon?

A. Napoleon's reliance on warfare and mass armies to spread the revolution

B. Napoleon's conquest of foreign nations and creation of an empire

C. Napoleon's policies of religious toleration and compromise with the Catholic Church

D. Napoleon's restriction of women from full citizenship and economic and legal rights

Frank Maloy Anderson, ed., *The Constitutions and other Select Documents Illustrative of the History of France, 1789–1901* (Minneapolis: The H.W. Wilson Company, 1904), p. 184.   Will Durant, *The Story of Philosophy: The Lives and Opinions of the Great Philosophers of the Western World* (New York: Simon & Schuster, 2006), p. 102.

Questions 9–12 are based on the two texts below.

J.F.C. Harrison, ed., *Society and Politics in England, 1780–1960: A Selection of Readings and Comments* (New York: Harper & Row, 1965), p. 70;   W.B. Crump, ed., *The Leeds Woolen Industry 1780–1820* (Leeds: The Thoresby Society, 1931), p. 318.

<u>Source 1</u>

"The Humble ADDRESS and PETITION of Thousands, who labour in the Cloth Manufactory.

SHEWETH, That the Scribbling-Machines* have thrown thousands of your petitioners out of employ, whereby they are brought into great distress, and are not able to procure a maintenance for their families, and deprived them of the opportunity of bringing up their children to labour: We have therefore to request, that prejudice and self-interest may be laid aside, and that you may pay that attention to the following facts, which the nature of the case requires.

The number of Scribbling-Machines extending about seventeen miles south-west of LEEDS, exceed all belief, being no less than *one hundred and seventy!* and as each machine will do as much work in twelve hours, as ten men can in that time do by hand, (speaking within bounds) and they working night-and day, one machine will do as much work in one day as would otherwise employ twenty men."

*carding machines in textile manufacture

Petition of Leeds Woollen Workers to Cloth Merchants, Great Britain, 1786

<u>Source 2</u>

"At a time when the People, engaged in every other Manufacture in the Kingdom, are exerting themselves to bring their Work to Market at reduced Prices, which can alone be effected by the Aid of Machinery, it certainly is not necessary that the Cloth Merchants of Leeds, who depend chiefly on a Foreign Demand, where they have for Competitors the Manufacturers of other Nations, whose Taxes are few, and whose manual Labour is only Half the Price it bears here, should have Occasion to defend a Conduct, which has for its Aim the Advantage of the Kingdom in general, and of the Cloth Trade in particular; yet anxious to prevent Misrepresentations, which have usually attended the Introduction of the most useful Machines, they wish to remind the Inhabitants of this Town, of the Advantages derived to every flourishing Manufacture from the Application of Machinery; they instance that of Cotton in particular, which in its internal and foreign Demand is nearly alike to our own, and has in a few Years by the Means of Machinery advanced to its present Importance, and is still increasing."

Letter from Leeds Cloth Merchants, 1791

9. All of the following explain the phenomenon referenced in the sources above EXCEPT:

   A. Britain's ready supply of raw materials such as coal and iron ore.

   B. government intervention in the form of subsidies and regulations.

   C. effective entrepreneurial human capital and credit institutions like banks.

   D. representation of commercial and industrial interests in Parliament.

10. The difference between the two sources reflects which of the following trends of industrialization?

   A. The persistence of agricultural elites in many areas of Europe

   B. A heightened consumerism as a result of newly available products

   C. Growth of class distinctions between the bourgeoisie and proletariat

   D. Social problems created by rapid migration from rural to urban areas

11. Which of the following sources would an historian most likely research to reach a conclusion regarding the differing interpretations presented in the sources?

   A. Blueprints of new industrial machines

   B. Data on wages and standards of living

   C. Population statistics for industrial cities

   D. Journals and letters of industrial entrepreneurs

12. By 1870, most European governments would respond to these issues by:

   A. providing an extensive system of social welfare.

   B. granting suffrage to all citizens, regardless of wealth or gender.

   C. pursuing colonies in Africa and Asia to access key resources.

   D. expanding regulation and reforming cities to improve health.

EUROPEAN STEEL PRODUCTION

13. Which of the following developments best explain the overall trends in the chart?

   A. Adoption of the mechanization of production and new technologies

   B. Steady population growth and resulting emigration to the Americas

   C. Ability of working class movements to pressure for higher wages

   D. Increases in agricultural productivity due to introduction of new crops

14. Which is the best explanation for the changes over time in Germany's economic position as shown on the chart?

   A. The borrowing of British technology and methods

   B. Rivalry with the competing power of France

   C. The benefits provided by a unified economy and polity

   D. Development of a major colonial empire in Africa

15. All of the following coincided with the developments shown on the chart EXCEPT:

   A. the growth of consumerism and advertising.

   B. volatile business cycles and periodic unemployment.

   C. the spread of Liberal notions of laissez-faire.

   D. pursuit of colonies in Africa and Asia.

Dennis Sherman and Joyce Salisbury, *The West in the World: A History of Western Civilization* (New York: McGraw-Hill Education, 2014), p. 627.

Questions 16–18 are based on the text below.

United States of America Congressional Record: Proceedings and Debates of the 84th Congress Second Session, Volume 102 - Part 7, May 22, 1956, to June 11, 1956 (Washington, D.C.: United States Government Printing Office, 1956), p. 9402.

> "Comrades, in order not to repeat errors of the past, the central committee has declared itself resolutely against the cult of the individual. We consider that Stalin was excessively extolled. However, in the past Stalin doubtless performed great services to the party, to the working class, and to the international workers' movement.
>
> We should in all seriousness consider the question of the cult of the individual. We cannot let this matter get out of the party, especially not to the press. It is for this reason that we are considering it here at a closed congress session. We should know the limits; we should not give ammunition to the enemy; we should not wash our dirty linen before their eyes.
>
> Comrades, we must abolish the cult of the individual decisively, once and for all; we must draw the proper conclusions concerning both ideological-theoretical and practical work."
>
> Nikita Khrushchev, Soviet leader, secret speech delivered at the Twentieth Party Congress of the Communist Party of the Soviet Union, February 25, 1956

16. To support his portrayal of Stalin, Khrushchev might have noted all of the following policies EXCEPT:

    A. liquidation of the kulaks.

    B. purge of Old Bolsheviks.

    C. Nazi-Soviet Non-Aggression Pact.

    D. forced labor camps (gulags).

17. A major result of Khrushchev's speech and subsequent policies was:

    A. reforms and revolts within Eastern European nations.

    B. an increase in the arms race between the superpowers.

    C. defeat of the United States in the Korean War.

    D. further efforts toward Western European unity.

18. Which of the following facts (all of which are accurate) would act as the most serious limitation on the speech as a source for Stalin's policies?

    A. Khrushchev was later dismissed (in 1964) by the Soviet leadership for economic and diplomatic failures.

    B. Khrushchev supported Stalin's purges and carried many of them out as governor of Ukraine.

    C. Under Khrushchev, the Soviet Union surpassed the United States in the space race, launching a satellite and the first persons to orbit the Earth.

    D. The Soviet Union controlled the press, establishing a state-run news service and official government newspaper.

Questions 19–22 are based on the map below.

EXPLORATION AND CONQUEST, 15TH AND 16TH CENTURIES

19. All of the following facilitated the process depicted above EXCEPT:

    A. advances in navigation and map-making.

    B. superior military technology, such as cannons.

    C. the desire for luxury items, such as silks and spices.

    D. a shift in power from the Mediterranean to the Atlantic.

20. The economic theory that came to be associated with the process depicted was:

    A. feudalism.

    B. mercantilism.

    C. capitalism.

    D. monetarism.

21. A major political effect of the process depicted was:

    A. the centralization of the new monarchies.

    B. a decrease in the power of the Catholic Church.

    C. rivalries among European powers over trade.

    D. the outbreak of revolts in the Americas.

22. Which of the following represents the most significant turning point in the process depicted?

    A. Protestant Reformation

    B. Scientific Revolution

    C. French Revolution

    D. Unification of Germany

Dennis Sherman and Joyce Salisbury, *The West in the World: A History of Western Civilization* (New York: McGraw-Hill Education, 2014), p. 364.

Questions 23–24 are based on the image below.

Maria Sibylla Merian, German naturalist and illustrator, illustration from *The Metamorphosis of the Insects of Suriname*, 1705

23. The illustration above reflects all of the following trends in early modern Europe EXCEPT:

   A. an increasing focus on investigation of the physical world.

   B. the ability of Europeans to interact with overseas environments.

   C. an improvement in women's economic rights and opportunities.

   D. the expansion of printed materials, such as books and periodicals.

24. Which of the following figures would have agreed most strongly with the illustrator's method of inquiry and approach toward nature?

   A. Denis Diderot

   B. René Descartes

   C. Aristotle

   D. Karl Marx

"Let the business [of marriage] be carried as Prudently as it can be on the Woman's side, a reasonable Man can't deny that she has by much the harder bargain. Because she puts herself entirely into her Husband's Power, and if the Matrimonial Yoke be grievous, neither Law nor Custom afford her that redress which a Man obtains. He who has Sovereign Power does not value the Provocations of a Rebellious Subject, but knows how to subdue him with ease, and will make himself obey'd; but Patience and Submission are the only Comforts that are left to a poor People, who groan under Tyranny, unless they are Strong enough to break the Yoke, to Depose and Abdicate, which I doubt wou'd not be allow'd of here."

Mary Astell, English writer and feminist, *Some Reflections Upon Marriage, Occasion'd by the Duke and Dutchess of Mazarine's Case; Which is Also Consider'd*, 1700

25. Which of the following movements would Astell most likely have drawn from to address marriage practices as described above?

A. Scientific Revolution

B. Commercial Revolution

C. Glorious Revolution

D. Enlightenment

26. Which of the following developments of the 18th century would most directly have contradicted Astell's portrayal of family life?

A. The ideas of Jean-Jacques Rousseau

B. Growth of companionate marriage

C. Continued importance of the family economy

D. Rise of the number of out-of-wedlock births

27. Astell's ideas would be most applicable to the 18th-century reform movement of:

A. advocating for more appropriate treatment and education of children.

B. promoting the use of inoculation and vaccination to prevent disease.

C. applying new techniques and technologies to improve crop yields.

D. urging the abolition of the slave trade and slavery in the colonies.

Mary Astell, *Some Reflections Upon Marriage, Occasion'd by the Duke and Dutchess of Mazarine's Case; Which is Also Consider'd* (London: Printed for John Nutt, near Stationer-Hall, 1700), pp. 28–29.

Questions 28–30 are based on the map below.

THE REVOLUTIONS OF 1848

28. All of the following caused the events depicted above EXCEPT:

   A. frustration over the Vienna settlement of 1814–1815.

   B. grievances caused by poor economic conditions.

   C. the effort by France to expand its political influence.

   D. resentment against the persistence of the old regime.

29. Which of the following resulted from the events depicted above?

   A. The reestablishment of the Concert of Europe

   B. A turn toward realism in politics and culture

   C. An alliance of the middle and working classes

   D. The rapid industrialization of eastern Europe

30. Which of the following historical situations had similar causes but had a differing outcome than the one depicted on the map?

   A. The Thirty Years' War and Peace of Westphalia

   B. The unification of Italy and Germany

   C. The Nazi-Soviet Non-Aggression Pact and World War II

   D. The collapse of communism in central and eastern Europe

"The fact that with the consolidation of the capitalist system of production, the marital/family union develops from a production unit into a legal arrangement concerned only with consumption, leads inevitably to the weakening of marital/family ties. In the era of private property and the bourgeois-capitalist economic system, marriage and the family are grounded in (a) material and financial considerations, (b) economic dependence of the female sex on the family breadwinner—the husband—rather than the social collective, and (c) the need to care for the rising generation. Capitalism maintains a system of individual economies: the family has a role to play in performing economic tasks and functions within the national capitalist economy. Thus under capitalism the family does not merge with or dissolve into the national economy but continues to exist as an independent economic unit."

Alexandra Kollontai, Russian revolutionary, "Theses on Communist Morality in the Sphere of Marital Relations," 1921

31. Which of the following economic and/or social developments of the period 1850–1920 would Kollontai most likely cite in support of her analysis?

   A. The pursuit of colonies in Africa and Asia by the Great Powers

   B. The development of the cult of domesticity within families

   C. The movement among reformers to aid the poor

   D. Feminist pursuit of legal, economic, and political rights

32. Which of the causes of the Russian Revolution does the passage most strongly reflect?

   A. The failure of Russia's infrastructure during World War I

   B. The limitations of the abolition of serfdom and land reform

   C. Inability of the tsarist regime to incorporate disaffected elements

   D. Russia's haphazard industrialization and resulting social inequality

33. Of all the following accurate facts about Kollontai, which would be most useful in providing context for the passage?

   A. In 1908, Kollontai went into exile in Germany after publishing pamphlets that urged Finns to resist the oppression of Russian rule.

   B. Kollontai was originally a member of the Menshevik Party, but switched to the Bolsheviks in 1915, after the onset of World War I.

   C. Kollontai headed Zhenotdel, the women's department under the Bolsheviks, aimed at advancing the opportunities and status of women.

   D. After 1923, Kollontai's political influence waned, and she served as a diplomat in several ambassadorial posts, most notably to Norway.

Alix Holt, trans., *Selected Writings of Alexandra Kollontai* (Westport, Conn.: Lawrence Hill and Company, 1977), pp. 225–226.

Questions 34–35 are based on text below.

> "A spirit of collective pacifism possessed them, and made the people content with the lazy approval of high ideals, the verbal condemnation of injustice, chicanery and oppression. Holding all the power, the Western democracies disdained to use it, so long as the status quo was in any way tolerable. The attitude of America was not dissimilar, except that here the League idea was rejected and the Monroe doctrine was still regarded as America's contribution to world peace."
>
> R.H.S. Crossman, historian, *Government and the Governed*, 1940

34. In which of the following ways did European culture in the interwar period (1918–1939) most directly reflect the attitude explained in the passage?

   A. The movement toward subjectivity and irony in the arts

   B. The spread of mass communications such as radio and film

   C. The growing influence of the United States in consumer culture

   D. The development of new theories and technologies in science and medicine

35. All of the following examples support the historian's interpretation above EXCEPT:

   A. the structure and actions of the League of Nations.

   B. Western democracies' actions in the Spanish Civil War.

   C. creation of mandates and involvement in the Middle East.

   D. the economic and financial policies of the United States.

Questions 36–38 are based on the map below.

RELIGIONS IN EUROPE, CA. 1600

Legend:
- Anglican Areas
- Calvinist Areas
- Calvinist-Influenced Areas
- Roman Catholic Areas
- Lutheran Areas
- Boundary of the Holy Roman Empire
- Major Protestant Universities
- Major Roman Catholic Universities

0 250 mi
0 500 km

Dennis Sherman and Joyce Salisbury, The West in the World: A History of Western Civilization (New York: McGraw-Hill Education, 2014), p. 341.

36. Which of the following conclusions can be drawn from the map above and your knowledge of European history?

   A. Catholicism was no longer the dominant religion within any major state.

   B. Denmark had become the leading Protestant state.

   C. Calvinism presented a challenge to many Catholic states.

   D. Germany had created a stable state around religious toleration.

37. Which of the following most directly resulted from the situation depicted above?

   A. States no longer concerned themselves with religious uniformity.

   B. The Council of Trent reformed clerical abuses and reaffirmed Church doctrine.

   C. Europe's center of power shifted to the Atlantic seaboard.

   D. Religious division led to internal conflict and interstate warfare.

38. The most conclusive resolution to the situation depicted was the:

    A. Peace of Augsburg (1555).

    B. Edict of Nantes (1598).

    C. Peace of Westphalia (1648).

    D. French Revolution (1789).

Questions 39–41 are based on the text below.

> "All the parts of this realm of England and Wales be presently with rogues, vagabonds, and sturdy beggars exceedingly pestered, by means whereof daily happen in the same realm horrible murders, theft, and other great outrage, to the high displeasure of Almighty God, and the annoyance of the commonweal. If a person be duly convicted of his or her roguish or vagabond trade of life...then immediately he or she shall be adjudged to be grievously whipped and burnt through the right ear with a hot iron of an inch around."
>
> Act for Punishment of Vagabonds and Relief of the Poor, parliamentary statute law, approved by
> Queen Elizabeth I and her parliament, 1572

39. The problems referenced in the passage were most likely the result of which of the following economic developments in early modern Europe, 1500–1650?

    A. Innovations in banking and finance that promoted a money economy

    B. The gradual replacement of subsistence with commercial agricultural practices

    C. Discovery of the Americas and the importation of New World crops

    D. Growth of literate and professional elites in service of the state

40. Which of the following changes in the treatment of poverty during the early modern period, 1500–1650, is demonstrated by the passage?

    A. The adoption of widespread social welfare benefits to promote equality

    B. Creation of professional police forces and penitentiaries (prisons)

    C. Reassertion by landlords of the right to tax and control peasants

    D. Governments assuming control of moral regulation from religious institutions

41. Which of following developments in Eastern Europe during this period parallels the situation raised in the passage?

    A. The growth of population to its pre-plague levels

    B. The codification of serfdom into law

    C. The growth of new economic elites

    D. The focus on the nuclear family

The Statutes of the Realm. Printed by Command of His Majesty King George the Third. In Pursuance of an Address of The House of Commons of Great Britain, Volume the Fourth (reprinted London: Dawsons of Pall Mall, 1965), p. 590.

"If, contrary to the principles of liberty and the Constitution, some citizens associated in the same professions, arts, and crafts hold deliberations or make agreements among themselves tending to refuse by mutual consent or to grant only at a determined price the assistance of their industry or their labor, such deliberations and agreements, whether accompanied by oath or not, are declared unconstitutional, in contempt of liberty and the Declaration of the Rights of Man, and noneffective; administrative and municipal bodies shall be required so to declare them. The authors, leaders, and instigators who have provoked, drafted, or presided over them shall be cited before the police court, at the request of the communal attorney, each condemned to a fine of 500 livres*, and suspended for a year from the employment of all rights of active citizenship and from admittance to the primary assemblies."

*the currency of France

The Le Chapelier Law, passed by French National Assembly, June 14, 1791

42. The act above was aimed primarily against:

   A. the economic features of the old regime.

   B. the arbitrary nature of absolute monarchy.

   C. the powerful position of the Catholic Church.

   D. the control of the nobility over offices.

43. Which action of the radical phase of the French Revolution contradicted the law above?

   A. Requirement of a national military conscription

   B. Execution of the king and Reign of Terror

   C. Imposition of controls on prices and wages

   D. Limitation of women's right to assembly

44. The legislation above would have coincided with the 19th-century ideology of:

   A. Conservatism.

   B. Liberalism.

   C. socialism.

   D. nationalism.

John Hall Stewart, A Documentary Survey of the French Revolution (New York: The Macmillan Company, 1951), pp. 165–166.

Questions 45–47 are based on the chart below.

ETHNIC COMPOSITION OF THE AUSTRIAN EMPIRE, 1910

Language	Number	%
German	11,853,000	22.85
Hungarian	9,944,000	19.2
Czech	6,436,000	12.4
Polish	4,968,000	9.6
Serbo-Croatian	5,495,000	10.6
Ukrainian	3,983,000	7.7
Romanian	3,223,000	6.2
Slovak	1,946,000	3.75
Slovene	1,253,000	2.4
Italian	768,000	1.5
Other	ca. 2,000,000	3.8
Total	**51,869,000**	**100.00**

A.J.P. Taylor, *The Habsburg Monarchy, 1809–1918: A History of the Austrian Empire and Austria-Hungary* (London: Hamish Hamilton, 1951), Appendix, pp. 262–269.

45. In which of the following ways during the 19ᵗʰ century did the Austrian rulers attempt to address the situation reflected in the chart shown above?

    A. Expand territory in the Balkans

    B. Create a Dual Monarchy with Hungary

    C. Ally with Germany and Russia

    D. Abolish serfdom and feudalism

46. In which of the following ways did the Versailles settlement (1919) attempt to resolve the situation shown above?

    A. The dissolution of empires into ethnically based nation-states

    B. Attribution of responsibility for World War I to the Central Powers

    C. Creation of a League of Nations to address issues of collective security

    D. The involvement of the United States in European diplomacy

47. The chart above could best be used to support which of the following interpretations on the causes of the First World War?

    A. "If not for the system of mutually antagonistic alliances, a regional conflict in the Balkans might have remained limited to the powers with a direct interest in the region."

    B. "The massive increase in armaments and reliance of military leaders and military plans limited the decision-making of political leaders and virtually forced them into war."

    C. "Leaders contemplated global war in 1914 because the principles of Darwin, Freud, and Nietzsche told them that war and struggle were not an evil to be avoided but a force for the good of the race."

    D. "Multi-ethnic empires had survived the twists and turns of history, but they could not escape the crucible of nationalism, stoked by agitation throughout the nineteenth century."

"My fellow citizens! Napoleon spoke of the press as 'the seventh great power'....The radio will be for the twentieth century what the press was for the nineteenth century. With the appropriate change, one can apply Napoleon's phrase to our age ["the press is the seventh great power"], speaking of the radio as the eighth great power. Its discovery and application are of truly revolutionary significance for contemporary community life. Future generations may conclude that the radio had as great an intellectual and spiritual impact on the masses as the printing press had before the beginning of the Reformation."

Joseph Goebbels, Nazi Minister of Propaganda, speech, August 1933

48. Which of the following trends in European history are most directly related to Goebbels's analysis?

A. The expansion of leisure time

B. Domination of the world economy

C. The growth of mass politics

D. Conflict among the great powers

49. Goebbels invokes Napoleon as support for his position. In which of the following ways were the policies of Napoleon and the Nazis under Hitler most DIFFERENT?

A. Reliance on mass political propaganda

B. Use of warfare to promote nationalism

C. Appeal to a charismatic leader

D. Empire based on racial ideology

50. Which of the following contemporary nations or regimes would most likely have agreed with the methods, if not the goals, identified by Goebbels?

A. Poland

B. Spain

C. Soviet Union

D. France

51. Hitler and the Nazis exploited all of the following developments in gaining and consolidating power in Germany EXCEPT:

A. the policy of appeasement by the Western democracies.

B. fear of a communist takeover and threat from the Soviet Union.

C. lack of support for and weakness of the Weimar Republic.

D. frustration over economic problems such as inflation and unemployment.

Anson Rabinbach and Sander L. Gilman, eds., *The Third Reich Sourcebook* (Berkeley: University of California Press, 2013), p. 420.

Questions 52–55 are based on the text below.

> - "We want structures that serve people, not people serving structures."
> - "Barricades close the streets but open the way."
> - "Professors, you are as senile as your culture, your modernism is nothing but the modernization of the police."
> - "The more I make love, the more I want to make revolution. The more I make revolution, the more I want to make love."
> - "How can you think freely in the shadow of a chapel?"
> - "You will end up dying of comfort."
>
> Graffiti slogans from 1968 revolts in Paris

52. The slogans above reveal all of the following post–1945 issues EXCEPT the:

    A. stresses caused by the Baby Boom and expansion of college attendance.

    B. influx of guest workers and the changing identity of Europe's population.

    C. environmental and ethical concerns over prosperity and consumerism.

    D. growth of dissident voices demanding liberation and political rights.

53. Which of these historical developments most likely influenced those revolting?

    A. The revival of classical texts during the Renaissance

    B. The reform of the Catholic Church in the 16th century

    C. The development of the New Science in the 17th century

    D. The attack on the Old Regime during the French Revolution

54. Which of the following 20th-century developments regarding women most directly parallels the slogans?

    A. Women became increasingly involved in work and mobilization during the world wars.

    B. Women gained leisure time due to advances in mass production and household technologies.

    C. Women were granted the vote and gained positions of leadership in government.

    D. Women experienced increased birth rates after 1945 due to government pro-natalist policies.

55. The movement most similar to the one expressed in the slogans was the:

    A. Algerian War for independence.

    B. Prague Spring in Czechoslovakia.

    C. fall of the Berlin Wall.

    D. defeat of the Nazis in World War II.

Ken Knabb, ed. trans., *Situationist International Anthology* (Berkeley, California: Bureau of Public Secrets, 2006), pp. 447, 450, 453, 454.

Directions Read each question carefully and answer all parts of the question. Use complete sentences; an outline or bulleted list is not acceptable. Your response should be contained within one side of a sheet of paper. Sources have been edited for the purposes of this exercise.

Source 1

"The second reason [for exploration] was...many kinds of merchandise might be brought to this realm, which would find a ready market . . . because no other people of these parts traded with them, nor yet people of any other that were known; and also the products of this realm might be taken there, which traffic would bring great profit to our countrymen.

The fifth reason was his [Prince Henry, the Navigator] great desire to make increase in the faith of our Lord Jesus Christ and to bring to him all the souls that should be saved . . . . [F]or so many souls as were saved by the efforts of this Lord, he will have so many hundreds of guerdons [rewards] in the kingdom of God, by which his spirit may be glorified after this life in the celestial realm."

Gomes Eannes de Azurara, Portuguese chronicler, account of voyages of 1452–1453

Source 2

"In the new Reich we have of late got into an economic situation which is oppressive, which is truly alarming . . . . Great though the growth of our prosperity may have been in the last few decades compared with earlier times, yet we are still on the whole poor, and the strength and resilience of our national prosperity are not at all proportionate to the plenitude of political power which we have acquired . . . . The most important factor in the so unfavorable development of the German situation, however, is the rapid rise in the rate of population growth, a circumstance which is of the most far-reaching economic significance, but one which is still quite insufficiently recognized as such, with the result that so far almost nothing has been done to deal with it."

Friedrich Fabri, German theologian and writer, *Does Germany Need Colonies?*, 1879

1A. Using the sources and your knowledge of European history, explain ONE similarity in the reasons for pursuit of colonies during each period.

1B. Using the sources and your knowledge of European history, explain ONE difference in the reasons for pursuit of colonies during each period.

1C. Explain ONE historical development that accounts for the difference addressed in Part B.
(HTS: Comparison and CCOT)

2A. Using ONE example for each, explain TWO ways in which the printing press represented a turning point in European intellectual and cultural history, 1450–1650.

2B. Choose an invention from another period and using ONE specific example, explain how it also represented a turning point in European history.
(HTS: Periodization and Comparison)

Gomes Eannes de Azurara, *The Chronicle of the Discovery and Conquest of Guinea*, Charles Raymond Beazley and Edgar Prestage, trans. (London: The Hakluyt Society, 1896), pp. 28–29.;   Friedrich Fabri, *Does Germany Need Colonies?*, orig. pub. 1879, in Volume 4: Forging an Empire: Bismarckian Germany, 1866–1890, http://germanhistorydocs.ghi-dc.org/pdf/eng/618_Fabri_Germany%20Colonies_198.pdf, pp. 1–2.

A FAUT ESPERER Q'EU JEU LA FINIRA BEN TOT.

French Political Cartoon, 1788

3A. Based on the cartoon above and your historical knowledge, explain ONE specific cause of the French Revolution.

3B. Explain TWO policies of the French revolutionaries that addressed the concerns depicted in the cartoon.
(HTS: Causation and CCOT)

EUROPE, 1919–1939

ICELAND

ATLANTIC
OCEAN

NORTH
SEA

BALTIC SEA

NORWAY

SWEDEN

FINLAND

UNITED
KINGDOM

IRELAND

DENMARK

ESTONIA
1934–1937

LATVIA
1934

LITHUANIA
1926

DANZIG

EAST
PRUSSIA

UNION
OF
SOVIET
SOCIALIST
REPUBLICS

NETHERLANDS

BELGIUM

LUXEMBOURG

FRANCE

SWITZERLAND

GERMANY
1933

POLAND
1926

CZECHOSLOVAKIA

AUSTRIA
1934

HUNGARY
1920

ROMANIA
1938

PORTUGAL
1926

SPAIN
1923–1930, 1939

ITALY
1922

YUGOSLAVIA
1929–1931

BULGARIA
1934

BLACK
SEA

ALBANIA
1925–1928

GREECE
1936

TURKEY

MEDITERRANEAN
SEA

Parliamentary Democracies

Communist Governments, 1917

Parliamentary Governments that became, at least temporarily, totalitarian or right-wing authoritarian regimes (with dates of change).

Dennis Sherman and Joyce Salisbury, *The West in the World: A History of Western Civilization* (New York: McGraw-Hill Education, 2014), p. 713.

4A. Explain TWO reasons for the trends depicted on the map.

4B. Explain ONE effect of the trend depicted for European diplomacy.
(HTS: Causation)

Question 1 (Document-Based Question)

Suggested reading and writing time: 55 m inutes

It is suggested that you spend 15 minutes reading the documents and 40 minutes writing your response.

Note: You may begin writing your response before the reading period is over.

Directions Question 1 is based on the accompanying documents. The documents have been edited for the purpose of this exercise.

In your response you should do the following.

- **Thesis**: Present a thesis that makes a historically defensible claim and responds to all parts of the question. The thesis must consist of one or more sentences located in one place, either in the introduction or the conclusion.

- **Argument Development**: Develop and support a cohesive argument that recognizes and accounts for historical complexity by explicitly illustrating relationships among historical evidence such as contradiction, corroboration, and/ or qualification.

- **Use of the Documents**: Utilize the content of at least six of the documents to support the stated thesis or a relevant argument.

- **Sourcing the Documents**: Explain the significance of the author's point of view, author's purpose, historical context, and/or audience for at least four documents.

- **Contextualization**: Situate the argument by explaining the broader historical events, developments, or processes immediately relevant to the question.

- **Outside Evidence**: Provide an example or additional piece of specific evidence beyond those found in the documents to support or qualify the argument.

- **Synthesis**: Extend the argument by explaining the connections between the argument and one of the following.

  o A development in a different historical period, situation, era, or geographical area.

  o A course theme and/or approach to history that is not the focus of the essay (such as political, economic, social, cultural, or intellectual history).

  o A different discipline or field of inquiry (such as economics, government and politics, art history, or anthropology)

1. Compare and contrast the Enlightenment and Romanticism in their attitudes toward the natural world and religion.

   (HTS: Comparison)

<u>Document 1</u>

Source: David Hume, Scottish philosopher, "Of Miracles," from *An Enquiry Concerning Human Understanding*, 1748

"A miracle is a violation of the laws of nature; and as a firm and unalterable experience has established these laws, the proof against a miracle, from the very nature of the fact, is as entire as any argument from experience can possibly be imagined . . . . Nothing is esteemed a miracle, if it ever happen in the common course of nature. It is no miracle that a man, seemingly in good health, should die on a sudden: because such a kind of death, though more unusual than any other, has yet been frequently observed to happen . . . And as a uniform experience amounts to a proof, there is here a direct and full *proof*, from the nature of the fact, against the existence of any miracle; nor can such a proof be destroyed, or the miracle rendered credible, but by an opposite proof, which is superior."

Source: Jean-Jacques Rousseau, Swiss/French philosopher, *A Discourse on the Moral Effects of the Arts and Sciences*, 1750

"We cannot reflect on the morality of mankind without contemplating with pleasure the picture of the simplicity which prevailed in the earliest times. This image may be justly compared to a beautiful coast, adorned only by the hands of nature; towards which our eyes are constantly turned, and which we see receding with regret. While men were innocent and virtuous and loved to have the gods for witnesses of their actions, they dwelt together in the same huts; but when they became vicious, they grew tired of such inconvenient onlookers, and banished them to magnificent temples. Finally, they expelled their deities even from these, in order to dwell there themselves; or at least the temples of the gods were no longer more magnificent than the palaces of the citizens.

. . . . As the conveniences of life increase, as the arts are brought to perfection, and luxury spreads, true courage flags, the virtues disappear; and all this is the effect of the sciences and of those arts which are exercised in the privacy of men's dwellings."

Document 3

Source: Frederick II, the Great, king of Prussia, *Political Testament*, 1752

"Catholics, Lutherans, Reformed, Jews and other Christian sects live in this state, and live together in peace. If the sovereign, actuated by a mistaken zeal, declares himself for one religion or another, parties spring up, heated disputes ensue, little by little persecutions will commence and, in the end, the religion persecuted will leave the fatherland, and millions of subjects will enrich our neighbors by their skill and industry.

It is of no concern in politics whether the ruler has a religion or whether he has none. All religions, if one examines them, are founded on superstitious systems, more or less absurd. It is impossible for a man of good sense, who dissects their contents, not to see their error; but these prejudices, these errors and mysteries, were made for men, and one must know enough to respect the public and not to outrage its faith, whatever religion be involved."

Document 4

Source: Joseph Wright of Derby, British artist, *A Philosopher Giving A Lecture at the Orrery* [mechanical model of the universe], c. 1765

PHOTO: Digital Image: Yale Center for British Art; TEXT: Jean-Jacques Rousseau, G.D.H. Cole, trans., *The Social Contract & Discourses* (London: J.M. Dent & Sons, LTD., 1920), p. 145.; George L. Mosse, Rondo E. Cameron, Henry Bertram Hill, and Michael B. Petrovich, eds., *Europe in Review* (Chicago: Rand McNally & Company, 1964), pp. 111–112.

Document 5

Source: François-René de Chateaubriand, French politician and writer, *The Genius of Christianity*, 1802

"The forests of Gaul [ancient France] were, in their turn, introduced into the temples of our ancestors, and those celebrated woods of oaks of thus maintained their sacred character. Those ceilings sculptured into foliage of different kinds, those buttresses which prop the walls and terminate abruptly like the broken trunks of trees, the coolness of the vaults, the darkness of the sanctuary, the dim twilight of the aisles, the secret passages, the low doorways,—in a word, every thing in a Gothic church reminds you of the labyrinths of a wood; every thing excites a feeling of religious awe, of mystery, and of the Divinity."

Document 6

Source: Lord Byron, English Romantic poet, *Manfred, A Dramatic Poem*, 1817

"I do remember me, that in my youth,
When I was wandering, – upon such a night
I stood within the Colosseum's wall,
'Midst the chief relics of almighty Rome;
The trees which grew along the broken arches
Waved dark in the blue midnight, and the stars
Shone through the rents of ruin....

While Caesar's chambers, and the Augustan halls,
Grovel on earth in indistinct decay
And thou didst shine, thou rolling moon, upon
All this, and cast a wide and tender light,...

As 'twere, anew, the gaps of centuries;
Leaving that beautiful which still was so,
And making that which was not, till the place
Became religion, and the heart ran o'er
With silent worship of the great of old!"

Source: Caspar David Friedrich, German painter, *The Dreamer*, ca. 1820s–1840s

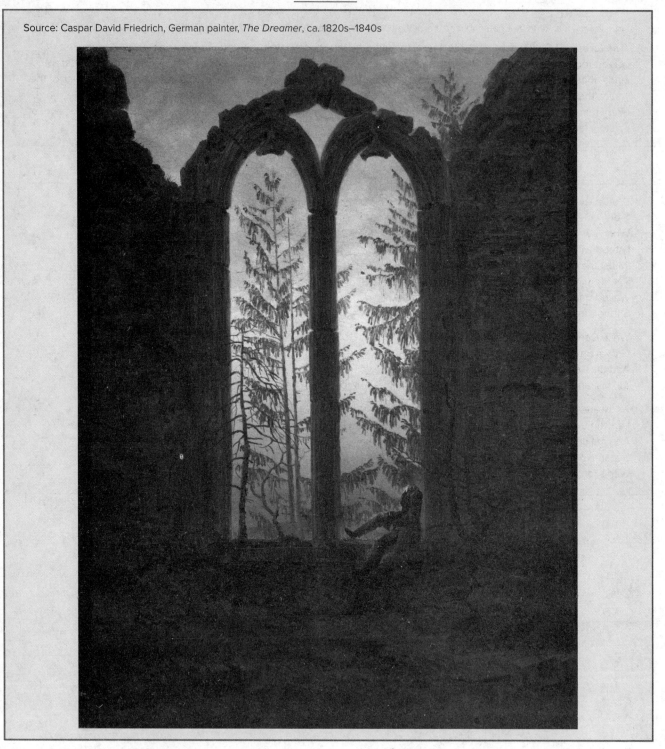

Directions Choose EITHER Question 2 or Question 3.

In your response, you should do the following.

- **Thesis**: Present a thesis that makes a historically defensible claim and responds to all parts of the question. The thesis must consist of one or more sentences located in one place, either in the introduction or the conclusion.

- **Application of Historical Thinking Skills**: Develop and support an argument that applies historical thinking skills as directed by the question.

- **Supporting the Argument with Evidence**: Utilize specific examples of evidence to fully and effectively substantiate the stated thesis or a relevant argument.

- **Synthesis**: Extend the argument by explaining the connections between the argument and ONE of the following.

    o A development in a different historical period, situation, era, or geographical area.

    o A course theme and/or approach to history that is not the focus of the essay (such as political, economic, social, cultural, or intellectual history).

    o A different discipline or field of inquiry (such as economics, government and politics, art history, or anthropology).

2. Analyze the causes and results of the unifications of Italy and Germany, 1848–1914.
   (HTS: Causation)

3. Analyze the causes and results of Europe's economic recovery after the Second World War, 1945–1991.
   (HTS: Causation)

Answers and Sample Responses: Multiple Choice

1. **Answer: B. HTS—CTX & CAUS; Themes—INT, IS & PP; KCs 1.4 & 1.5.** In the passage, Cereta makes a contrast between women of appearance and women of substance. The former seem to her preoccupied with displaying luxuries, many garnered from the trade with overseas ports (B). No mention is made of folk beliefs (A), nor does Cereta relate her discussion of gender to organized religion, other than references to piety and ethics (D). Rather than criticize women for engaging in intellectual pursuits (promoted by print media), Cereta encourages them in this endeavor, dropping out C.

2. **Answer: D. HTS—CTX; Theme—OS; KC 1.1.** Cereta advocates an approach toward education that would develop within women their virtues and abilities, influenced by and consistent with the revival of humanist texts from ancient Greece and Rome (D). This was an age of civic humanism, but Cereta draws her attention more to the private behavior of women, excluding A. No mention is made of art patronage (B) or anatomical discoveries (C).

3. **Answer: D. HTS—COMP; Theme—IS; KC 1.5.** Because of its urban setting, Italy provided an environment conducive for the spread of Renaissance ideas, but in this respect it was unique (excluding A). The growth of a new economic elite eventually spread to the rest of Europe, but in the 15th century was focused on Italy (B). Italy did not develop a centralized monarchy (due to its thriving city-states), making it different than other states with new monarchies (C). However, social life in all of Europe concerned itself with status and hierarchy, as shown in the passage with women distinguishing themselves by appearance or by the implicit condemnation of women being viewed from the lens of patriarchy (D).

4. **Answer: C. HTS—CCOT; Theme—IS; KCs 1.5 & 3.3.** Consider when feminism began to emerge as a consistent ideology and make progress in obtaining rights for women. Of these periods, the strongest case can be made for C (1850–1920), when feminism evolved in response to the 19th-century revolutions and when women gained economic rights and the vote (after 1918). The period 1517–1648 saw little progress for women, and though the 1789–1850 held promise, women's participation in revolutions met with few tangible results (B). Due to the instability of the

interwar period and growth of totalitarian governments, the 1920-1945 era marks a holding pattern for feminism, to be revived in the post-1945 era (D).

5. **Answer: C. HTS—CTX; Theme—OS; KC 1.1.** Bacon advocates for observation and experimentation, his contribution to the scientific method, also known as inductive reasoning (C). This passage makes no mention of classical learning, which Bacon hoped to surpass by moving toward direct examination of nature, excluding A. Though Bacon's counterpart Descartes articulated a geometric approach to learning, Bacon's focus here is on empiricism, not math (B). No reference is made to folk beliefs like astrology and alchemy (D).

6. **Answer: A. HTS—CCOT; Theme—OS; KC 1.1.** Using the new scientific method of direct observation, astronomers like Galileo and Brahe articulated new theories of the cosmos (A). Though new anatomical discoveries paralleled those in astronomy, these did not yield advances in medicine until much later (B). Though Leeuwenhoek used the microscope to introduce microbiology, these changes were not as profound in altering European worldviews as those in astronomy (C). Robert Boyle also changed the approach in chemistry by using the notion of elements, yet again, these advances did not pose the same challenge as the upheaval in the geocentric model (D).

7. **Answer: C. HTS—EVARG & CTX; Themes—SP, OS, & IS; KC 2.1.** Radical revolutionaries adopted the mass levy defend the revolution through total war against internal and external enemies. The armies are briefly referenced in Section 6; however the entire law relates to their employment (A). War occurred because of the upheaval caused by dissent over the revolution's course (B). Clearly this law grants the state significant powers to organize the nation for war (D). This leaves C as the EXCEPT outlier, and even though the statement is correct, it does not relate to the passage itself.

8. **Answer: A. HTS—CCOT; Themes—SP & IS; KC 2.1.** Napoleon succeeded in manipulating nationalism to promote his military and political objectives, reaping the benefits of new citizen armies (A). Eventually the armies of revolutionary France turned the tide and invaded neighboring states, spreading revolutionary ideals. Napoleon did the same; however, this law relates to defense of the revolution, not conquest, excluding B. Choices C and D indicate goals and policies of Napoleon, but neither is indicated or referenced in the decree.

9. **Answer: C. HTS—CAUS; Theme—PP; KC 3.1.** Both of these sources address, albeit with differing

perspectives, the mechanization of textile production, the first phase of the Industrial Revolution. Thus, you are asked what caused industrialization. Britain's advantages included: access to raw materials (A), an entrepreneurial spirit and advanced credit institutions (C), and representation of industrial interests in Parliament (D). In contrast to continental nations, Britain did not rely upon the active intervention of the government in promoting industry, instead employing a more laissez-faire approach (B).

10. **Answer: C. HTS—CAUS & CCOT; Themes—PP & IS; KCs 3.1 & 3.2.** The sources show differing takes on the mechanization of traditional craft production, or the growth of self-conscious classes, the bourgeoisie (owners of capital) and proletariat (newly unskilled workers), indicating C as the key. No mention is made here of agricultural elites, crossing off B. Though textile manufacture did produce new consumer goods, that is not the focus of the sources. Social discontent is offered, but it does not arise from migration or urbanization, but instead from the fear workers directed against machines perceived as taking away their traditional employment (D).

11. **Answer: B. HTS—EVCS; Themes—PP & IS; KCs 3.1 & 3.2.** The two passages provide varying perspectives on the standard of living (both material and psychological) produced by the new textile machines. To judge the issue, historians might draw on statistical measures (B). The designs of the machines themselves are not central to the disagreement (A). Since the passages deal only implicitly with urbanization, population measures would not resolve the issue (C). Though the writings on entrepreneurs would provide further data for that group, these would not assist the historian in gaining a more objective sense of the disagreement (D).

12. **Answer: D. HTS—CCOT; Themes—PP, SP & IS; KC 3.3.** The year 1870 preceded the development of social welfare systems (A). Further, it was not until just before World War I that most states adopted universal male suffrage, and not until after the war (even WWII in some nations) for women (B). European states did pursue colonies for a variety of reasons but not primarily to address social discontent (C). This leaves D, and indeed, most states realized by mid-century that some public health and regulatory measures were necessary to blunt the worst problems created by industrialization.

13. **Answer: A. HTS—CAUS & CTX; Theme—PP; KC 3.1.** The chart shows the significant increase in steel production, owing to new methods (Bessemer Process)

and the mechanization of production (A). Demographic growth was more likely the result rather than the cause of industrialization, as mechanization supported a higher population, excluding B. Workers did seek higher wages during this period through union activity, but that fact is separate from the increase in productivity (C). Industrialization depended in broad terms on the increase in the food supply, allowing for the transition in labor to cities, but this trend does not explain steel production directly (D).

14. **Answer: C. HTS—CAUS & CCOT; Themes—PP & SP; KCs 3.1 & 3.4.** Germany's level of industrialization in 1882 compared unfavorably to Britain's; however, over several decades Germany reaped the benefits of a uniform economy with standardized weights and measures and central policy direction (C). Certainly Germany borrowed some techniques from Britain, but so did other nations that did not fare as well as Germany (A). France and Germany bore enmity in the fallout of the Franco-Prussian War, but this rivalry focused more around diplomatic and territorial concerns, and further, it does not explain German industrialization generally (B). Bismarck pursued colonies tardily and reluctantly, and Germany's new colonial empire contributed to its economic expansion minimally (D).

15. **Answer: C. HTS—CAUS; Themes—INT, PP & SP; KCs 3.1 & 3.5.** Industrialization promoted the growth of a consumer culture in new goods (A); however, it also spawned boom/bust cycles, especially between 1873 and 1896, leading many governments to abandon free trade and corporations to manage the market through informal arrangements (B). To secure the raw materials needed for industrialization and gain markets for manufactured goods, European powers pursued colonies in Africa and Asia (D). However, as noted above, economic volatility led to the eventual abandonment of a hands-off (laissez-faire) approach, the opposite of C.

16. **Answer: C. HTS—EVARG; Themes—SP & PP; KC 4.1 & 4.2.** Khrushchev's speech criticizes the excesses of Stalin's policies within the Soviet Union, not foreign policy. This excludes C, as it deals with the agreement Stalin made with Hitler in 1939, primarily due to the western allies' neglect of the Soviet Union (key: C). Choices A, B, and D all represent ways in which Stalin repressed various groups in the single-minded pursuit of his goals.

17. **Answer: A. HTS—CAUS; Theme—SP; KC 4.2.** Though Khrushchev attempted to keep his critique of Stalin secret, his speech inadvertently inspired resistance to Soviet authority in Eastern Europe, leading to revolts in Poland and Hungary, the latter being crushed (A). The Cold War was defined by an arms race between the superpowers, but this was incidental to Khrushchev's speech (B). The Korean War resulted in stalemate and ended three years before this speech, eliminating C. The progress toward Western European unity was well under way and generally separate from the policies within the Soviet bloc (D).

18. **Answer: B. HTS—EVCS; Theme—SP KC 4.2.** Since Khrushchev condemns Stalin in his speech, any fact that casts doubt on that central point would be of interest to the historian. Khrushchev did support Stalin's purges, undermining his supposed outrage at Stalin's excesses, making B the key. The others (A, C, and D) would be of interest to an historian, but more likely for other interpretive issues related to Khrushchev or the Soviet Union.

19. **Answer: D. HTS—CAUS; Themes—INT, PP & SP; KC 1.4.** The map depicts the European outreach toward new goods and colonies. The process was facilitated by the ability to sustain overseas voyages (A), asymmetries in military technology between Europeans and non-Europeans (B), and the pursuit of profit (C). The shift in power to the Atlantic was the *result* not the cause of this process (D).

20. **Answer: B. HTS—CTX & CAUS; Themes—INT, PP & SP; KCs 1.4 & 1.2.** New colonial empires required management of their resources from European states, which were guided by the assumption that real wealth required the accumulation of specie, or hard money, known as mercantilism (B). Exploration undermined feudalism (A) by promoting a money economy around trade. Since we are not dealing with free markets or free trade, C is excluded, though the shift to a money economy laid the foundations for capitalism. Monetarism, or the belief that controlling the money supply is the key to economic growth, developed in the 20th century to address inflation after World War II (D). If anything, the colonial powers' importation of gold and silver created unpredictable fluctuations in the money supply.

21. **Answer: C. HTS—CAUS & CCOT; Themes—INT, SP & PP; KCs 1.4.** Centralization of monarchies was more the *cause* than the result of exploration, excluding A. The encounter with colonies allowed the Catholic Church (often through the Jesuits) new venues for religious conversion, countering B. The demographic catastrophe in the Americas precluded organized revolts, so these movements did not gain traction until the 18th century with the growth of Enlightenment ideals (D). This leaves C, and as the map indicates,

several powers sought wealth and colonies, creating conflict and later commercial wars.

22. **Answer: C. HTS—CCOT & PER; Themes—INT, PP, SP & OS; KC 2.1.** The French Revolution spread ideologies of natural rights and self-rule worldwide, best exemplified by the Haitian slave revolt (1790s) and the Latin American move for independence (1810s)—C. The Reformation may have even stimulated further control of colonies through religious conversion (A). Also, the Scientific Revolution provided further technologies, navigational and military, for suppression and control of colonies (B). Finally, the unification of Germany did not reverse this process and even stimulated German pursuit of colonies in the late 19th century (D).

23. **Answer: C. HTS—CTX; Themes—OS, INT & PP; KCs 2.2, 2.3 & 2.4.** Here we see precise and detailed illustrations of insects, with the emerging field of entomology. This level of detail comes from a focused investigation of nature (A) and the ability to interact with areas of the world where "exotic" insects inhabit (B). In addition, the 18th century witnessed a huge increase in the number and range of printed materials (D), which helped popularize the new science. Despite the drawings being created by a female scientist, women in general did not experience an increase in rights during this era, making C the key.

24. **Answer: A. HTS—EVARG & COMP; Theme—OS; KC 2.3.** As a popularizer of the Enlightenment, Diderot urged an empirical and scientific approach to natural and human questions, as laid out in his famous *Encyclopédie* (A). Though Descartes helped establish the scientific method, his contribution lay more in a geometric or a deductive (vs. inductive) method of reasoning (B). The new science suggested by the illustrations generally undermined the Aristotelian world view, eliminating C. Marx argued for a scientific socialism in the 19th century, but he relied more on grand theories than on experimentation, canceling out D.

25. **Answer: C. HTS—CAUS & CTX; Themes—OS & SP; KCs 2.1 & 2.4.** Several of these make appealing choices; however, the language Astell adopts involves rebellion against tyranny, pointing to the Glorious Revolution (Astell is British), which had occurred just over a decade before she wrote (C). The scientific revolution did stimulate new theories of politics, but it would have had only an indirect effect on Astell's writings (A). Also, the year 1700 would be early for the Enlightenment (D). Astell, moreover, does not draw from commerce in her analysis of marriage, excluding B.

26. **Answer: B. HTS—CCOT & EVARG; Themes—IS & OS; KCs 2.3 & 2.4.** Each choice expresses an actual development in the 18th century. Rousseau's ideas provided further support for the unequal gender balance in marriage that Astell condemns (A). Family production as a unit (C) tended to support male control of the family, since men usually directed its labor. The rise of illegitimacy in the 18th century does not support Astell's depiction, but it did not contradict either, since it didn't involve marriage itself (D). This leaves us with B, and indeed, the notion that men and women should marry for companionship, rather than for economic pragmatism, tended to elevate the role of women within marriage, counter to Astell's portrayal of it (B).

27. **Answer: D. HTS—COMP; Themes—INT, OS & PP; KC 2.2.** At the end of the passage, Astell employs language to express women's oppression reminiscent of slavery ("groan under Tyranny" and "break the Yoke"); in fact, the antislavery movement gained steam throughout the 18th century due to evangelical Christianity and the Enlightenment (D). The closest distracter would be A, but even here, it was not so much that children were oppressed in the household, more that philosophes came to a more nuanced understanding of childhood. Both B and C did occur, but do not relate to the theme of liberation from oppression.

28. **Answer: C. HTS—CAUS; Themes—SP & PP; KCs 3.4.** The map depicts the spread of revolutionary agitation during the fateful year of 1848. These revolutions stemmed from the political and economic causes expressed by A, B, and D. As usual, the revolutions began in France, reminiscent of the quote, "When France sneezes, Europe catches a cold"; however, revolution in France did not constitute an agenda to spread its political influence, though the new president, Louis Napoleon, would eventually attempt to do so as emperor. Thus, C is the outlier here.

29. **Answer: B. HTS—CAUS; Themes—SP & OS; KCs 3.4 & 3.6.** Rather than reestablish the Concert of Europe, the revolutions of 1848 undermined it, dropping out A. The class conflict that emerged in places like newly republican France revealed the gap between the aspirations of the middle and working classes, which would grow with the rise of socialism (C). Eastern Europe's industrialization was delayed until the 20th century due to a range of economic and political obstacles (D). With the failures of 1848, the era of Romantic revolution ended, and a new realism and materialism took its place, as reflected in *Realpolitik*, Darwinism, and Marxism (B).

30. **Answer: D. HTS—CCOT & COMP; Theme—SP; KCs 3.4 & 4.2.** The Thirty Years' War was prompted by religion, evolved into a struggle among the great powers and was resolved with the advent of religious toleration, showing few parallels with 1848 (A). Even with external diplomacy, the unifications of Italy and Germany resulted primarily from internal policies, rather than the spread of ideological discontent, as with 1848 (B). On the eve of World War II, Nazi Germany and the Soviet Union (under Stalin) cynically signed an agreement that gave each a free hand to divide Poland; again, this shows only minor similarities to 1848 (C). However, it was the combination of nationalist resentment against Soviet control of Eastern Europe and poor economic prospects that pushed over the Berlin Wall in 1989, a much more successful outcome than in 1848, but one driven by similar grievances (D).

31. **Answer: B. HTS—CAUS & EVARG; Themes—PP & IS; KCs 3.2 & 3.3.** Kollontai notes how the rise of capitalism shifts families from a unit of production to one of consumption, with women more dependent upon men for material sustenance. To sustain this development, bourgeois thinkers supported the cult of domesticity, extolling women as guardians of the home (B). The passage does not address imperialism, and it is only tangentially related to Kollontai's analysis (A). Though reformers did seek to aid the poor, the text addresses family life in particular, excluding C. Feminists did pursue rights during 1850–1920, but that fact would not support Kollontai's analysis, since her treatise addresses female inequality (D).

32. **Answer: D. HTS—CAUS; Theme—SP & PP; KC 4.2.** All of the choices express causes of the Russian Revolution; however, Kollontai's analysis primarily addresses the effects of industrialization and issues of inequality arising from them, which could be extended to other groups (D). The passage does not address Russia's failures during World War I (A), nor issues related to agriculture or serfdom (B). As a revolutionary, Kollontai would have opposed the out-of-touch Romanov dynasty, but the focus of her analysis is not political incompetence but more fundamental economic and social processes (C).

33. **Answer: C. HTS—EVCS; Theme—IS & SP; KCs 4.2 & 4.4.** Since the excerpt addresses the issue of female equality, any factor that would help understand Kollontai's role would be of strongest interest to an historian—giving us C as the key. The other portions of her life (A, B, and D) certainly round out her biography but would not be as central as C.

34. **Answer: A. HTS—INTR & CTX; Themes—INT, SP & OS; KCs 4.1 & 4.3.** Crossman's interpretation emphasizes the lack of confidence and initiative by the western democracies after World War I. The prewar confidence in technology and progress had been undermined by slaughter on the Western Front, leading to an embrace of subjectivity and irony in the arts (A). The spread of mass communications did not directly undermine democratic government, though dictators later employed it to establish totalitarian control, excluding B. Though the passage mentions the role of the U.S., its influence in consumerism was not matched by a diplomatic commitment to European security, as noted in the passage (exclude C). Since the passage deals with lack of confidence, we can eliminate the advance of science (D), which would confirm notions of progress.

35. **Answer: C. HTS—EVARG & CTX; Themes—INT, SP & PP; KCs 4.1 & 4.2.** Here we are looking for the outlier—an example that runs counter to the portrayal of the western democracies as on the defensive. Since the League of Nations failed to maintain collective security without the assistance of the United States, we can eliminate A. The western democracies stood aside while fascist Italy and Nazi Germany helped Franco win the Spanish Civil War, arguing against B. Though the U.S. provided loans to Germany, its trade and financial policies helped lead to the Great Depression, excluding D. With the Versailles settlement, Britain and France actually advanced their colonial empires in the Middle East, Africa, and the Pacific, a move that advanced its power, at least temporarily. C is the key.

36. **Answer: C. HTS—CTX & EVARG; Themes—SP & OS; KCs 1.2 & 1.3.** The map shows the religious division of Europe, with many states facing significant religious minority populations. In states like France, the Holy Roman Empire, and Poland, the dominance of Catholicism was challenged by the spread of Calvinism, later leading to religious warfare (C). Clearly, states like Spain upheld a dominant Catholic position, excluding A. By 1600, England had emerged as the dominant Protestant state, due to its defeat of the Spanish Armada in 1588, which excludes B. Germany's religious division led not to toleration but to the Thirty Years' War in subsequent decades, eliminating D.

37. **Answer: D. HTS—CAUS; Theme—SP; KCs 1.2 & 1.3.** The concern with religious uniformity led in part to the subsequent Thirty Years' War, dropping out A. The Council of Trent ended in 1563, so could not be a result

of the situation shown (B). The power center of Europe did shift toward the Atlantic states, but this development owed more to the Commercial Revolution than to religious division. Since the religious divisions depicted were not yet accepted by Protestants and Catholics, warfare dominated the political landscape from 1517 to 1648, making D the answer.

38. **Answer: C. HTS—PER; Theme—SP; KCs 1.2 & 1.3.** The Peace of Westphalia provided for the permanent religious division of the Holy Roman Empire and the independence of Protestant states (Dutch Republic and Switzerland), making it the last of the religious wars (C). Though the Peace of Augsburg divided Germany by religion, it proved a temporary solution, since the Thirty Years' War took place a century later (A). The Edict of Nantes provided toleration for the Huguenots, but it was revoked by Louis XIV in 1685 (B). Finally, the French Revolution promoted a secular state, but the policies of the radicals repressed religious belief during the de-Christianization campaign, not exactly a solution to religious pluralism (D).

39. **Answer: B. HTS—CAUS; Theme—PP & IS; KC 1.5.** Several early modern developments contributed to the problems of poverty and begging. The expanding money economy produced new forms of wealth, but also caused inflation and stagnated manufacturing wages (A), but the more significant factor was the movement toward commercial agriculture. The break-up of agricultural communities displaced small shareholders, many of whom sought their livelihoods in nearby cities, where they often resorted to begging (B). New World crops would have provided a food outlet to address subsistence problems, excluding C. Choice D represents an accurate development but one largely unrelated to the issue of poverty (D).

40. **Answer: D. HTS—CTX; Themes—SP, PP & IS; KC 1.5.** Social welfare provisions were not enacted until the late 19th century, so we can cancel out A. The same is true for the developments in B. Landlords did often attempt to revive elements of feudalism, but this phenomenon would have promoted poverty not resolve it (C). Since Protestants rejected the Catholic notion of good works as a means to salvation, they turned moral regulation and poor relief over to municipal or state entities, as shown in this text from England, a Protestant state (D).

41. **Answer: B. HTS—COMP; Themes—PP & SP; KC 1.5.** The text shows the tightening of regulations to achieve a higher degree of social and economic control. In eastern Europe, the correlate development was the codification of serfdom, as in Russia (B). Though

European population reached a post-plague peak in 1600, the law does not deal with this issue directly, excluding A. With its dominance by nobles, eastern Europe lagged in the development of new economic elites, such as merchants or the gentry (C). Not only does the law omit mention of families, eastern Europe was, with its taxation system based on household, more likely to support extended families (D).

42. **Answer: A. HTS—CCOT & EVARG; Themes—PP, SP & IS; KCs 2.1 & 2.2.** The Le Chapelier Law here abolished the guilds in favor of a free-market system and as such represented an attack on the vestiges of the old regime (A). The role of the monarchy (B) and Church (C) appear nowhere in the law, though they would be attacked with other legislation. The Declaration of Rights of Man, cited in the passage, also attempted to remove exclusive noble control over offices, but this law does not address that issue, making D false.

43. **Answer: C. HTS—CCOT & EVARG; Themes—PP & SP; KC 2.1.** During the radical phase, the Mountain enacted laws to control wages and prices, in response to agitation from the artisans and shopkeepers of Paris (sans-culottes). This ran counter to the free-market system of the Le Chapelier Law here (C). Choices A, B, and D all express actions of the radical phase of the revolution, but they do not bear directly on the economic issues discussed in the law.

44. **Answer: B. HTS—CCOT & EVARG; Themes—PP & SP; KCs 2.1 & 3.3.** Of the choices, the ideological framework most likely to endorse the free movement of labor and goods would be Liberalism (B). The other groups' attitudes toward this issue would have ranged from ambivalence (A and D) to hostility (C), leaving us with B.

45. **Answer: B. HTS—CAUS; Theme—SP; KC 3.4.** The chart shows Hungarians as the largest ethnic minority, and indeed, Hungarians briefly established independence during the revolutions of 1848. To appease this largest minority group, the Austrian (German) rulers of the empire allowed for the creation of the Dual Monarchy, providing a high degree of autonomy to Hungarians (B). Any expansion of territory in the Balkans—as with the annexation of Bosnia in 1908—would only further complicate the ethnic situation given in the chart (A). At points after 1871, Austria formed an alliance with Germany and Russia, but this did not directly address its festering ethnic situation (C). Serfdom and feudalism had been abolished in 1848, and though it pleased peasants, it did not address ethnic issues (D).

46. **Answer: A. HTS—CCOT; Theme—SP; KC 4.1.** The Allies fought World War I (especially after U.S. involvement in 1917) with the idea of allowing self-determination, which spelled doom for multiethnic empires like Austria, which were broken up (A). Though the Allies blamed the Central Powers and created the League of Nations, these actions did not directly address ethnic issues within states, such as those shown on the chart (B and C). The level of U.S. involvement diplomatically declined with the Senate's refusal to approve the Versailles Treaty and join the League of Nations, and these actions, once again, did not bear directly on ethnicity (D).

47. **Answer: D. HTS—EVARG; Theme—SP; KC 4.1.** Each of these choices, emphasizing a particular cause of the war, could be supported with examples from the period prior to 1914. But our question deals specifically with the ethnic issues represented in the chart, so the interpretation most closely aligned is D, and not A, B, or C.

48. **Answer: C. HTS—CTX & CAUS; Theme—SP; KCs 3.4 & 4.2.** Goebbels focuses on the potential of new communication devices (such as the radio) to alter the relationship between the state and the individual, a major feature of mass politics after 1850 (C). Dictatorships also promoted state-run leisure, but the expansion of leisure in the 19th century is only indirectly related to Goebbels's analysis (A). The passage does not address or bear directly upon imperialism (B) or interstate conflict, though Goebbels (as a Nazi) would certainly have an eye toward this possibility in the future…with the radio as a means to mobilize the German population (D). C is the best choice.

49. **Answer: D. HTS—COMP & CCOT; Theme—SP; KCs 2.1 & 4.1.** Napoleon and Hitler both appealed to the masses (A), employed warfare to promote internal unity (B), and manipulated their images to gain support for their regimes (C). However, Napoleon, unlike Hitler, did not seek to create a racial empire; his motives were more personal and political. Thus, D is the outlier.

50. **Answer: C. HTS—COMP; Theme—SP; KC 4.2.** Both Hitler and Stalin created totalitarian regimes and employed media to establish a cult of personality, giving us C. The other states ranged from republics to authoritarian regimes, and either did not embrace Hitler's goals (D) or could not mobilize such a high degree of popular support (A and B).

51. **Answer: A. HTS—CAUS; Theme—SP & PP; KC 4.2.** This question does not require the stimulus, so you can draw directly from your historical knowledge. You may recall that the policy of appeasement *followed* the establishment of Nazi rule, thus rendering it moot as a cause (A). A main pillar of Nazi ideology was anti-Communism, which Hitler used to gain absolute control after accusing communists of starting the Reichstag fire, shortly after he was appointed Chancellor (B). Since the Weimar Republic lacked support from key elites (C) and failed to address (or worsened) Germany's economic problems (D), Hitler was able to promise a strong hand in reestablishing stability, prosperity, and power.

52. **Answer: B. HTS—CTX; Themes—PP & IS; KCs 4.3 & 4.4.** These slogans express discontent as part of the 1968 student revolts. As population and college opportunities expanded, universities experienced the stress of overcrowding and rebellion against the bureaucratization of college life—the fundamental causes of the revolts (A). Despite the post–1945 economic recovery, the students condemn the consumerist values of their elders in the slogans (C). Clearly the theme of liberation runs through all of the slogans (D). However, we see no reference to the post–1945 trend of increased immigration from outside Europe, giving B as the key.

53. **Answer: D. HTS—CAUS & CCOT; Themes—SP, OS & IS; KCs 2.1, 4.3 & 4.4.** The key requires drawing a connection across a significant time period. In the slogans one is struck by the theme of liberation, and the movement among those given most closely associated with this theme is D (French Revolution). Though the other movements altered features of European life, they did embrace the rhetoric of violence against the old regime as presented by the student revolutionaries, thus eliminating A, B, and C.

54. **Answer: C. HTS—COMP; Themes—IS & SP; KC 4.4.** Choices A, B, and D all occurred within the context of traditional values and did not necessitate an alteration of values regarding women or give rise to their liberation. Many women returned home after involvement in wartime manufacturing (A). Increased leisure time without access to autonomy would not coincide for women with the desire for liberation in the slogans. Pro-natalist policies reinforced the notion of women as mothers and homemakers (D). We are left with C, and yes, many women gained increased access to positions of power (e.g., Margaret Thatcher) and served increasingly in legislatures (especially in Scandinavian nations). Thus, the students and women both sought access to power.

55. Answer: B. HTS—COMP; Themes—SP, PP & IS; KCs 4.2 & 4.4. Each of these choices coincides with movements against repression. However, the student revolts in Paris were echoed in that same year (1968) by the Prague Spring, another youth movement aimed against bureaucracy and an out-of-touch government (B). The Algerian War employed a much higher degree of violence and lasted much longer (A). Unlike the fall of the Berlin Wall, the 1968 revolts did not meet with ultimate success (C). The defeat of the Nazis was caused primarily by powerful states marshaling all of their resources, rather than a discontented segment within a state (D).

SAQ 1 Response and Commentary

1A. It is clear from both sources that Europeans desired goods and profit from foreign lands. In Source 1, during the period of exploration, de Azurara notes the exotic goods that are unavailable from European markets and that will bring great profit to his nation. Fabri also cites economic reasons for pursuing colonies, and he seems to think the newly united Germany must secure access to important materials with great urgency, since it faces difficult economic problems.

1B. There are significant differences in the passages as well. On one hand, de Azurara notes that Prince Henry the Navigator wanted to convert souls for the glory of God and also to achieve rewards in heaven, expressing the great age of faith during the fifteenth century. Fabri, on the other hand, is much more practical and sees colonies as an outpost for a growing German population. Addressing this potential internal problem seems important because of the competition among states during this period.

1C. In the later period, Europe had moved toward industry, nationalism, and a more secular outlook. For the early period of exploration, nations wanted to save souls and gain knowledge of the world, all while making some money. Competition among states and the demands of a more complex economy raised the ante, and we can see the urgency in Fabri's writing to gain a colonial empire for Germany.

In this focused response, the student earns all 3 points. First, she identifies and explains a similarity—pursuit of goods and profit—with attention to historical context (e.g., unified Germany). Second, she provides an appropriate difference—spreading Christianity vs. an outlet for population growth—again, with historical context ("age of faith," "competition among states"). Finally, our student evinces a solid knowledge of context by identifying the features of the latter period ("more complex economy," "colonial empire") that explain the change over time. Score: 3 points

SAQ 2 Response and Commentary

2A. The printing press revolutionized intellectual life by making ideas more easily accessible. During the Renaissance, the printing press allowed for more standard editions of works, like Machiavelli's writings and other Latin and Greek classics. Also, it helped spread the Renaissance to northern areas, such as the Netherlands and Germany. Another effect of the printing press was the spread of Darwin's ideas of natural selection. His portrayal of humans as animal-like provoked religious controversy and caused the rise of racial ideologies of superiority among Europeans.

2B. A different invention that changed life was television. With this vivid new media technique, dictators like Hitler and Stalin were able to send images of massive rallies and propaganda that made them look like gods. People tended to believe what was presented to them, making the TV a great way to sway the masses.

In this response, we see the dangers of chronological errors. In Part A, the student earns a point for accurately explaining the spread of the Renaissance to the north, as well as the standardization of texts. However, the reference to Darwin is well outside the time period (by 200 years) and thus not responsive to the prompt. Although the discussion of dictators' use of propaganda in the 20th century is on target, the student incorrectly attributes the phenomenon to television, which did not play a major cultural role until well after World War II. Perhaps the student meant to discuss motion pictures or the radio. Score: 1 point

SAQ 3 Response and Commentary

3A. The unfair treatment of the Third Estate was a main cause of the French Revolution. The Third Estate made up ninety-eight percent of the population but was lower than the other two Estates due to the social hierarchy of France. Also, the third Estate was the poorest of the three Estates but was the only one that had to pay taxes, which led to a wider wealth gap between the upper and lower classes. As depicted in the cartoon, the lower class literally carried the French economy, since they were the only ones required to pay the state.

3B. The Declaration of the Rights of Man and Citizen by the National Assembly was created to abolish the social inequality in France and bring more rights to the Third Estate in comparison with the other two Estates, as it created legal equality and freedom of religion. The creation of 83 equal departments throughout France shows the Third Estate's restructuring of the French state. This got rid of the parliaments and estates, leading to a new centralized government in France without royal absolutism and an unjust social hierarchy.

This student responds directly to each part of the question. In Part A, she effectively explains the inequality of the three estates of France, including how the issue of taxation is represented in the cartoon. For Part B, the response identifies and explains two specific policies created to address this inequality—the Declaration of Rights and Man and the establishment of 83 equal and centralized departments to replace the old feudal provinces. The latter example is an oft-forgotten yet important reform of the revolutionaries. Score: 3 points

SAQ 4 Response and Commentary

4A. One of the reasons for the populist authoritarian governments gaining popularity over democracies is the rising distaste for democracy that grew out of the Great Depression. This is no better shown than in Germany under the Weimar Republic. The failures of the Weimar Republic would provide a platform by which the Nazis gained popularity. Secondly, one reason for the rise in authoritarian forms of governments is the creation of weak democracies during the interwar period as part of the Treaty of Versailles. This would allow for that situation because, in these democracies there was no tradition of democracy and thus they would be susceptible to authoritarian forms of government that were more in line with their traditions.

4B. One effect that the rise of the Soviet Union had on the diplomacy of Europeans is that it would promote movements toward unity by creating a common enemy. One such example of the unity movements created to combat the USSR is NATO, created explicitly by the US as a part of their containment policy. Although the Soviet Union would actually split Europe in two, the movements toward unity would rise out of the western blocs created to protect against communism and other forms of totalitarianism.

On one hand, the response deals effectively with Part A by explaining two reasons for the spread of authoritarian and totalitarian regimes in the interwar period. First, he explains how the Great Depression undermined faith in the new Weimar Republic and led to the rise of the Nazis. Next, the student briefly notes how the Treaty of Versailles created fragile states with a limited tradition of democracy. However, the discussion in Part B errs in invoking the Cold War and NATO, as these examples lie outside of the 1919–1939 era indicated by the map. Score: 2 points

DBQ Response and Commentary

The Enlightenment and Romanticism were two events that occurred back-to-back, with the Enlightenment expressing control over nature and disproving religion, while Romanticism emphasized a revival of religion and the power of nature. The Enlightenment, which occurred just after the Scientific Revolution, was an attempt by Europeans to apply the methods of the new science, such as empiricism and natural laws, to all areas of human life. This movement encouraged humans to see their power over nature and often disproved religion, because it is not tangible. Romantics, who emerged about a century later, responded to the Enlightenment by reviving religion and discovering the awe that nature possessed.

Europeans' view of nature had traditionally been subjective, as they often followed what they had been told by their religions and other traditional authorities. Some even resorted to folktales and mysticism to dictate the happenings of the universe. However, this changed with the Scientific Revolution and its application to everyday life, which was known as the Enlightenment. With the Enlightenment, the application of fixed laws of nature became prominent within European societies. Artists, such as Joseph Wright (Doc. 4), often reflected this in their works, especially through the impressionism art movement, which experimented with light, shadow and scientific discoveries. This source is an accurate representation of the Enlightenment laws and how they are applied, because of its depiction and detail. The children and adult onlookers seem intrigued by the orrery demonstration, which was a typical response to all information that was being discovered about gaining control of nature. Similar to the painting, many philosophers used the fixed laws of nature to disprove mysteries of the universe, such as miracles. David Hume (Doc. 1) discusses how "a uniform experience amounts to a proof," which cannot be destroyed. His interpretation was a typical one of the time period. He also discovers how miracles "are violations of the laws of nature," which were shown to be true during the Scientific Revolution. However, it is not surprising that he would take this standpoint, given that he is a philosopher and intends to spread his new discoveries to everyone. Unlike the two documents and the Enlightenment approach of nature, Romantics did not see nature to be controlled, but they were in awe of its prestige and power. For example, Document 7 is a painting by German painter Friedrich, which shows a man sitting at an old ruin admiring the tall trees and nature around him. Friedrich's painting reflects the classic view of Romantics, who respected nature and wished to become one with it. The views of nature drastically changed from the Enlightenment period to next century of Romanticism, which was almost a direct response to science.

In addition to fixed laws of nature, the Enlightenment also contained intellectuals who encouraged the idea of the "General Will" of the people and that humans should have choices when it came to religion. Also from the Enlightenment grew enlightened despots, such as Frederick II the Great of Prussia, who used Enlightenment ideals in their ruling. Doc 3 addresses the fact that politics and religion should not be concerned with each other, and that rulers should not be able to choose their subjects religion. He also expresses how Lutherans, Catholics, Jews and other religions lived in peace. It is not surprising that Frederick II would express this sentiment, seeing that he is a ruler and wants to spread his popularity among citizens in Prussia. Another enlightened despot, who expressed similar beliefs except with women was, Catherine the Great of Russia, who encouraged women's rights and education. Although Romantics never really expressed an opinion on religious pluralism and toleration, they encouraged it in an attempt to express religiosity and its greatness. For example, in Doc. 5, Chateaubriand of France discusses the awe that nature brings and expresses through religion that old Gothic style buildings and broken tree trunks excite a feeling of "religious awe, mystery and divinity." His works are significant because they expressed the feeling of awe that nature brought to religion, in contrast to the scientific view of the control of nature. Similar to Chateaubriand, Doc 6 is a poem by an English romantic poet, Lord Byron, who was famous for his poetry and controversial lifestyle. His poem, "Manfred" expresses the revival of religion by saying that "silent worship of the Great of Old" would bring wonder and success to the people of Europe. His works expressed the revival of a powerful religion, that was thought to be disproved by scientists, by showing that science and fixed laws were not always the end-all-be-all.

The Enlightenment and Romanticism and their different views on nature and religion show how movements can respond to one another. Romantics revived religion and a sense of awe of the wonders of nature, proving that knowledge doesn't always have to derive from direct science and reason. Romanticism was significant because it gave way to later developments such as Freud's theories and glorified irrationality.

This is a solid response that, with some further development, might have earned a top score. Though the introductory paragraph sets up the question well—earning the Contextualization point for its brief connection of the Scientific Revolution with the Enlightenment—it never identifies a similarity between the Enlightenment and Romanticism. This omission here and in the conclusion costs the Thesis point. However, the student does go on to earn the Argumentation point by effective juxtaposition of the documents to show corroboration (Documents 4 and 1) and contradiction (Documents 4 and 1 vs. Document 7). All 7 documents are used to make an argument on the two movements, earning Document Use. Though the student provides acceptable Source Analysis for three documents— Document 1 (point of view), Document 7 (historical context), and Document 3 (purpose)—the attempt with Document 4 falls short, due to lack of explanation and the inaccurate connection to Impressionism. However, Evidence Beyond Documents is earned (minimally) through the reference to Catherine the Great. Finally, the Synthesis attempt related to Freud falls short, as it requires further elaboration of its connection to the question. Score: 4 (Argumentation, Document Use, Contextualization, Evidence Beyond Documents).

LEQ 2 Response and Commentary

After the French Revolution, nationalistic ideologies were beginning to peak in the 19th century. However, while the Congress of Vienna may have tried to contain riots and revolts within nations that were spurred by Napoleon's policies and ideas, the subsequent Crimean War and the Revolutions of 1848 escalated the urge for unification and decimated the Concert of Europe. Thus, nationalism and the development of *Realpolitik*, a diplomatic method of using mass politics and strategies to increase the power of a nation, caused the unification of Italy and Germany. Nonetheless, since many smaller states were becoming unified, there was a great deal of change in the balance of power as both nations industrialized more efficiently and expanded their armies.

Cavour and Otto von Bismarck both instituted *Realpolitik* approaches to their diplomacy, and therefore, used nationalistic woes to heighten the unification of Italy and Germany respectively. To begin, Cavour strategically made decisions that benefited the joining of the Italian states. He persuaded France to help Piedmont-Sardinia fight against Austria and won in doing so. As revolutions were taking place in the north, he urged Garibaldi, the leader of the Red Shirts, to use his army and move up the peninsula. Since many people welcomed the unification of Italy, little violence was necessary and it was deemed a nation in 1861. Bismarck also made tactical decisions when the opportunity presented itself. For instance, he partook in three wars against isolated countries and made Germany easily defeat them. During the Austro-Prussian war, he made sure the surrounding countries did not help Austria, as Bismarck supported the Russian conquest of the Polish revolt, presented France with thoughts of expansion, and gave Italy hope of land. He also provoked France to call war upon Germany with the Ems Dispatch, making it seem as if the king insulted the French ambassador, and easily triumphed in the war. Thus, he used prudent judgments to assist the nation. However, both nations witnessed nationalistic ideologies reach a new height because of its presence in the French Revolution and in the policies of Napoleon, which only promoted the fusion of states.

Nonetheless, since Italy and Germany were unified, their ability to develop a stronger economy and an increase in political standing were promoted, and thus shifted the delicate balance of power. Italy industrialized more efficiently as it was open to new resources that facilitated economic growth, and sustained imperialistic lands abroad. For Germany, Bismarck wanted to get as much power as possible, and made sure he continued to be Chancellor and Prime Minister of State, which gave him control in diplomatic relations. He also tried restricting the growth of the Social Democratic Party by executing welfare programs, which in turn supported the economy. Yet, when the hot-headed Kaiser William II dismissed Bismarck, his inability to negotiate and keep peace, and his focus in matching Germany's naval power to Britain's, helped lead into WWI. However, since Italy and Germany unified, their economic and military potential did thwart the balance of power within Europe that was previously set by the Congress of Vienna.

Italy and Germany's unifications were spurred by nationalistic beliefs taking hold and also new methods of political negotiations. As they both took a larger economic foothold within Europe, their political influence increased. This nationalistic outlook also influenced art and culture of the period. In Delacroix's *Liberty Leading the People*, the artist shows the symbol of the French nation (a vulnerable woman) rallying the people against the oppression of the corrupt monarchy. This is similar to the famous painting of Bismarck at the center of the scene in the Hall of Mirrors as the German Empire is proclaimed. It is clear that nationalism unified states and shaped cultural outlooks.

The response begins with a strong introduction, as the student provides effective background on the Congress of Vienna, revolutions of 1848, and Crimean War, linking these to the growth of nationalism and impulse toward national unity. Though not as effective, the references to a shifted balance of power and industry address the results of unification. For the Targeted HTS, the student both describes and explains the reasons for and effects of the unifications, though with stronger detail on Germany with effects, earning both points. Also, abundant examples are given and, while there is some narration, the student brings the analysis back to applying the examples to the argument, earning both points. To conclude the essay, he provides a creative extension of the argument regarding nationalism to the arts. Score: 6 (Thesis, 2 points for Targeted HTS, 2 points for Use of Evidence, Synthesis).

LEQ 3 Response and Commentary

Immediately after World War II, many European countries, especially Britain and Germany, were crippled economically because of the astronomical sums of money they used for the war. This is not even factoring in the amount of money that Germany had to make for reparations. Both countries borrowed large amounts of money from the US, and this plunged them into even greater debt later on. Luckily, both countries regained their former standing and economical power thanks to the US Marshall Plan.

After WWII, many European countries, especially the largest such as Russia, Britain, and Germany suffered from both bombed out cities and destroyed factories, as well as horrible economic deficits. Both Britain and Germany started borrowing large sums from the US, which were funneled back to the US from Germany's reparations. Many countries started printing tons of money, spurring inflation, to avoid going bankrupt. Though this worked in the short term, it eventually devalued currencies, decreasing the ability of the workers to buy food and clothing even more.

Even after all of these horrible things, Europe's market was able to go back to the way it was, and even surpass its old power. This is largely due to three different reasons: first, Europe wasn't at war anymore, allowing it to sell its goods, which during the war could not really be exported, as well as leaving it open to foreign investment, and, without the Allies (or Axis) destroying factories and fields, the economy could grow back to its pre-war might. Second, the Marshall Plan, named after Secretary of State George Marshall, which pooled money from countries not so badly impacted by the war, and spread that money throughout the other European states, with the exception of Russia and the Eastern Bloc countries, so that they could again rebuild to their former glory. Last, but certainly not least, the Axis stifled the ability of many countries to buy or sell goods, and all of this need for goods built up until the end of the war. Also, as a side note, the pressures and needs of total war prepared the European countries for rebuilding of both their economy and the internal systems, such as apartments and farms, because the machines and techniques used to create bunkers could easily be turned for use by the government to create infrastructure.

The change from poverty-stricken Europe to economic giant Europe was created by the lessons that Europe learned from all of the nationalist destruction, working toward some unity.

This is because all of the governments tried to think of ways in which to solve the many problems arrayed before them and caused by the war. The states learned how to work together and spread the wealth from the problems caused by total war, and used this new knowledge quite a bit in the future.

This essay suffers from two problems—it conflates the post-World War II situation with that of post-World War I and it does not address the effects of Europe's economic recovery in any systematic way. An adequate Thesis that addresses both parts of the question cannot be found in either the introduction or the conclusion. Since the essay does not address effects in its analysis and provides a confused discussion of causes, it does not earn either of the points for the Targeted HTS. However, the student does provide some relevant examples, despite vagueness and simplifying, to address the question—Marshall Plan, pent-up demand, nationalism to unity. Because of the confusion, the examples are not applied consistently to the thesis, limiting the Use of Evidence point to 1. Finally, without further specifics or explicit connections, the brief conclusion falls far short of the Synthesis point. Score: 1 (Use of Evidence).

INDEX

A

abortion, 299

absolute monarchies, 114, 120

absolutism, 94, 97, 107, 114–116, 151

advertising, 264

Afghanistan, 280

African imperialism, 207–208

African slavery, 87

Age of Ideologies, 184–186; conservatism, 184; feminism, 185; liberalism, 184; republicanism, 185; romanticism, 186; socialism, 185

agriculture, 90; forced collectivization of, 262

Agricultural Revolution, 135, 175, 178

airplanes, 204, 239

alchemy, 102, 104, 106

Alexander II, 199, 203, 244

Algeria, 288

alienation, 263

Allies, 239–243

American Revolution, 153

Anabaptists, 78

anarchism, 203, 220

anatomy, 104

anesthetics, 215

anti-immigrant political parties, 296

anti-Semitism, 215–216, 221, 242, 260

antiseptic, 214

applied science, 108

appeasement, 264

Arab nationalism, 241

architecture, modernism in, 226

Aristotle, 102

Armenian genocide, 242

arms race, 276

army, 117

art, 65–66, 68–69, 81, 117, 120, 145, 197; abstract expressionism, 302; avant-Garde in, 224–226; cubism, 225; expressionism, 225; impressionism, 224; painting, 224; pop art, 302; postimpressionism, 225

astrolabe, 85

atheism, 148

Auschwitz, 273

Austria, 121–123

Austria-Hungary, 203, 218

Austro-Hungarian monarchy, 204

B

baby boom, 296, 298

Bach, J.S., 120

Bacon, Francis, 104

Bakunin, Mikhail, 203, 220

balance of power, 88 70, 114, 202

balance of trace, 89 117, 121, 205

Bank of Amsterdam, 118

Bank of England, 137

barbed wire, 239

Baroque Art, 81, 117, 120, 145

Basque people, 301

Battle of Vienna, 122

Bauhaus school, 263

Bayle, Pierre, 106, 108

Beccaria, Cesare, 146

Beethoven, Ludwig von, 187

Bergson, Henri, 223

Berlin Conference, 207

Bernini, Giovanni Lorenzo, 81, 120

bilateral agreements, 257

Bill of Rights, 120

birth control, 133, 296

Bismarck, Otto von, 201–202, 206–207, 218, 236

black death, 65, 66

blitzkrieg, 266

bloodsports, 147

Bolshevik Revolution, 254, 275

Bolsheviks, 240, 244, 246–247

Book of Common Prayer, 79, 119

boom-bust cycles, 205

Bosnia–Herzegovina, 237

Bosnian Muslims, 286

bourgeoisie, 88–89, 132, 136, 148, 162, 176, 180, 188, 198

Boxer Rebellion, 209

Brezhnev, Leonid, 281, 284

Britain vs. France, 136 159

British abolitionist movement, 153

British East India Company, 89

Bruegel, Pieter, the Elder, 74

Brunelleschi, Filippo, 69

Bruni, Leonardo, 67

Burgundy, 94

Burke, Edmund, 162

Butler, Josephine, 220

Byron, Lord, 186

Byzantine Empire, 65, 67, 71, 73

C

calendar, 103

Calvin, John, 77

Calvinism, 77–78, 81, 93–95, 117. *See also* Huguenots

capitalism, 88–89

Carlyle, Thomas, 186

Carnival, 80, 92, 147

Cartesian coordinate system, 105

Castiglione, Baldassare, 67–68

Catherine II, 152

Catholic, 87, 92–96

Catholic Center Party, 255

Catholic Church, 65, 71–72, 76, 81, 162, 302

Catholic Reformation, 64, 79–81

Catholic Revival, 80–81

causes of WW I, 235–238; alliance system, 236; imperialism, 236; intellectual context, 237; mass politics, 236; nationalism, 237; military plans, 235

Cavour, Camillo Benso di, 200–201

celestial navigation, 103

censorship, 145, 166

centralized professional bureaucracy, 166

Central Powers, 239–240, 242

Cereta, Laura, 70

Cézanne, Paul, 225

Charles I, 119

Charles V, 76–77

Chartists, 181

Chechnya, 283

child labor, 179

Christian humanism, 73–74

Christianity, 65, 74, 75, 77, 102, 108

Christian Social Party, 219

church calendar, 92

cities, growth of, 91

citizen armies, 167

civic humanism, 67

Civil Code, 166

Civil Constitution of the Clergy, 162

classics, 67

class systems, 131–132; Bourgeoisie, 132; nobility, 131; Peasants, 132

coffee, 89

coffeehouses, 89, 144, 148

Colbert, Jean-Baptiste, 117

Cold War, 275–281; nature of, 276–281; origiins, 275

colonial empires, 86–87

colonization, 85, 88–89

Columbian Exchange, 87; new crops, 87; new diseases, 87

commerce, 114, 117, 119

Appendices: Chronological Supplement—Timelines

To assist in your chronological mastery of the course, you will find three different timelines in this section. With the first timeline, you can identify the major eras and developments by centuries. Next is a list of important dates to provide you with a strong base of chronology that supports your application of HTS. It is strongly recommended that you commit these dates to memory as guideposts. Finally, you can consult the more developed timeline categorized by the themes to make connections across the themes and the time periods.

Timeline 1: Important Eras and Developments (by century)

Renaissance—1350–1550
Exploration—1450–1600
Protestant and Catholic Reformations—16th century
Religious Wars—1520s–1650
Early Modern Society—1500–1700
Price Revolution—16th century
Dutch Commercial Dominance—1550–1650
Age of Crisis—1550–1650
Witchcraft Scare—1580–1680
Scientific Revolution—1543–1687
Baroque Art—1600–1750
Conflict between Parliament and King in England—1603–1689
Age of Louis XIV—1643–1715
Absolutism—1650–1750
Commercial Wars—1650–1763
Rise of Prussia—1650–1763
Rise of Russia—1689–1815
Commercial Revolution—17th and 18th centuries
Rococo Art—1720–1760
Rise of the Middle Class—18th century
Enlightenment—18th century
Agricultural Revolution—18th century
Age of Revolutions—1789–1848
Feminism—1790s–1980s
Romanticism—First half of 19th century
Rise of Nationalism—1790s–1914
Unification and Nation–Building—1850–1875
Rise of Liberalism—1830s–1870s
Industrial Revolution—1750–1850
Realism and Materialism—1850–1870s
Second Industrial Revolution—1850–1914
Imperialism—1850–1914
Modern Ideas and Science—1850–1920s
Modern Art—1870–1920
Rise of Modern Society—Second half of 19th century
Totalitarianism—1920s–1945
World Wars—1914–1945
Cold War—1945–1991

European Unity—1945–present
War on Terror—2001–present

Note: A century refers to the hundred years numerically prior to the number of the century (e.g., the 16th century covers the 1500s).

Timeline 2: Important Dates to Commit to Memory

1348–1351—Black Death
1415–1417—Council of Constance burns Hus and ends Great Schism
1453—Fall of Constantinople; end of Hundred Years' War
1455—Invention of printing press
1492—Columbus encounters America; completion of *reconquista* in Spain
1517—Luther posts 95 Theses
1519—Cortez conquers Aztecs
1534—Act of Supremacy in England creates Anglican Church
1536—Calvin establishes reformed faith in Geneva
1543—Copernicus publishes heliocentric theory
1545—Council of Trent opens
1555—Peace of Augsburg ends religious war in Germany; Charles V abdicates
1588—Defeat of Spanish Armada
1598—Edict of Nantes ends French religious wars
1600—Dutch East India Company founded
1603—Stuart monarchy begins in England
1648—Peace of Westphalia ends Thirty Years' War
1649—Charles I executed in England
1687—Newton publishes *Principia Mathematica*
1688–1689—Glorious Revolution; Peter the Great's reign begins in Russia
1694—Bank of England founded
1713–1715—Peace of Utrecht; death of Louis XIV
1740—War of Austrian Succession begins
1763—Treaty of Paris ends Seven Years' War
1776—American Revolution; Smith publishes *Wealth of Nations*
1789—French Revolution begins
1792—Wollstonecraft begins feminist movement with *Vindication of Rights of Women*
1799—Napoleon comes to power in France
1815—Abdication of Napoleon; Congress of Vienna
1830–1831—Revolution in France; Belgian and Greek independence
1848—Revolutions of 1848; Marx and Engels publish *Communist Manifesto*
1851—Crystal Palace Exhibition in Britain
1857—Britain establishes direct rule of India
1859—Darwin publishes *On the Origin of Species*
1861—Italy unified; Russian serfs emancipated
1871—Unification of Germany; Paris Commune and Third Republic in France
1884–1885—Berlin Conference over imperialism in Africa
1900—Freud publishes *Interpretation of Dreams*
1905—Einstein publishes relativity theory; Revolution of 1905 in Russia
1914—World War I begins
1917—Bolshevik Revolution in Russia
1919—Treaty of Versailles ends World War I
1922—Fascists and Mussolini come to power in Italy

1929—Great Depression begins

1933—Hitler comes to power in Germany

1938—Munich Conference—height of appeasement

1939—World War II begins

1945—World War II ends; United Nations founded

1949—NATO formed

1951—European Coal and Steel Community (ECSC) formed

1953—Stalin dies

1956—Khrushchev's de-Stalinization speech; Hungary revolt

1957—Treaty of Rome creates European Economic Community (EEC); Sputnik launched

1958—Fifth Republic in France under De Gaulle

1961—Berlin Wall erected

1962—Cuban Missile Crisis

1962—Second Vatican Council begins

1968—Student revolts; Czech Prague Spring revolt

1975—Helsinki Accords—height of détente

1978—John Paul II elected pope

1979—Soviet Union invades Afghanistan; Thatcher elected prime minister in Britain

1980—Solidarity founded in Poland

1985—Gorbachev comes to power in Soviet Union

1989—Berlin Wall falls and collapse of communism

1991—Break-up of Soviet Union; Balkan conflicts begin in former Yugoslavia

1992—Maastricht Treaty creates European Union (EU)

2001—Terrorist attacks on United States

2002—Euro currency released into circulation

2005—Angela Merkel elected Chancellor of Germany

2009—European debt (euro) crisis begins

2014—Russia annexes Crimea and occupies parts of Ukraine

2015–2016—Terrorist attacks in Paris and Brussels

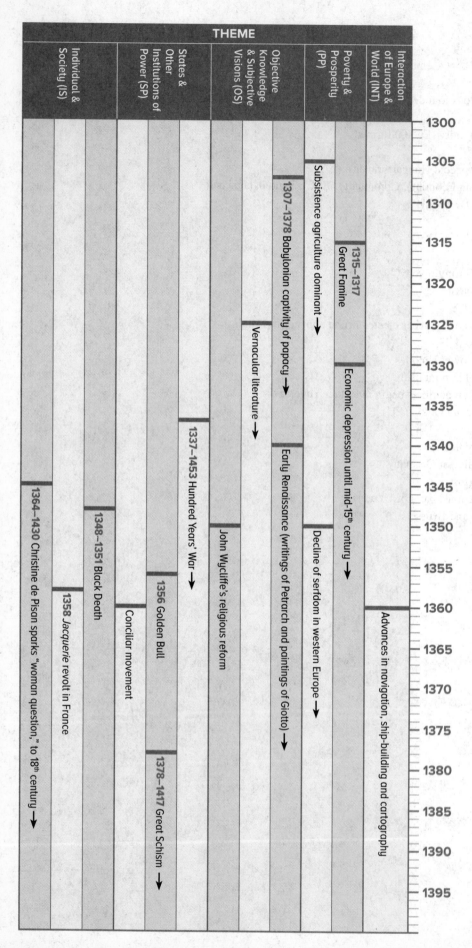

THEME

Interaction of Europe & World (INT)	Advances in navigation, ship-building and cartography →
Poverty & Prosperity (PP)	**1315–1317** Great Famine Economic depression until mid-15th century → Decline of serfdom in western Europe →
Objective Knowledge & Subjective Visions (OS)	Subsistence agriculture dominant → **1307–1378** Babylonian captivity of papacy → Vernacular literature → Early Renaissance (writings of Petrarch and paintings of Giotto) → John Wycliffe's religious reform
States & Other Institutions of Power (SP)	**1337–1453** Hundred Years' War → **1356** Golden Bull Conciliar movement **1378–1417** Great Schism →
Individual & Society (IS)	**1348–1351** Black Death **1358** *Jacquerie* revolt in France **1364–1430** Christine de Pisan sparks "woman question," to 18th century →

Timeline years: 1300, 1305, 1310, 1315, 1320, 1325, 1330, 1335, 1340, 1345, 1350, 1355, 1360, 1365, 1370, 1375, 1380, 1385, 1390, 1395

THEME

Interaction of Europe & World (INT)
- Slave labor imported from Africa into Europe (until ca. 1500) →
- 1415 Prince Henry founds navigation school
- Rise of Portuguese trading empire →
- 1492 Columbus's voyage to Americas

Poverty & Prosperity (PP)
- Economic recovery, until mid-16th century →

Objective Knowledge & Subjective Visions (OS)
- Florence emerges as center of Italian Renaissance →
- 1455 Gutenberg invents printing press
- High Renaissance in Rome, after 1490

States & Other Institutions of Power (SP)
- 1417 Council of Constance ends Great Schism
- 1415 Jan Hus burned for heresy
- 1430 Medicis come to power in Florence
- Rise of New Monarchs, to mid-16th century →
- 1454 Peace of Lodi
- 1453 Constantinople captured by Turks
- 1455–1485 War of the Roses in England
- 1469 Isabella and Ferdinand unify Spain
- 1492 Spain completes Reconquista and expels Jews
- 1494 French invade Italy

Individual & Society (IS)
- Arranged marriages in Italy, age gap between husbands and wives →

Timeline scale: 1400, 1405, 1410, 1415, 1420, 1425, 1430, 1435, 1440, 1445, 1450, 1455, 1460, 1465, 1470, 1475, 1480, 1485, 1490, 1495, 1500, 1505, 1510, 1515, 1520, 1525

THEME

Chronological timeline (1500–1655), organized by theme.

Interaction of Europe & World (INT)
- 1519 Cortez conquers Aztecs
- 1519–1521 Magellan's circumnavigation
- Spanish and Portuguese colonization
- Columbian Exchange
- Shift in power from Mediterranean to Atlantic

Poverty & Prosperity (PP)
- Enclosure movement begins
- Innovations in banking & finance
- Price Revolution, 16th century
- Rise of Netherlands as commercial power

Objective Knowledge & Subjective Visions (OS)
- Writings of Erasmus
- Christian humanism
- 1513 Machiavelli's *The Prince*
- 1517 Luther posts 95-Thesis
- 1527 Castiglione, *The Courtier*
- 1536 Calvinism in Geneva
- Protestant Reformation
- 1543 Copernicus publishes heliocentric theory
- 1543–1687 Scientific Revolution
- Catholic (Counter-) Reformation
- re-Catholicization of central & eastern Europe
- 1560s–1600 Mannerist art
- 1564 Michelangelo dies
- 1564–1616 Shakespeare in England
- Baroque art, late 16th century–1720s

States & Other Institutions of Power (SP)
- 1494–1559 Habsburg Valois Wars
- 1500–1650 Military revolution
- 1516–1556 Charles V, ruler of Spain/HRE
- 1527 Rome sacked (ends Renaissance in Italy)
- 1534 Henry VIII creates Anglican Church
- 1540 Jesuits founded
- 1545–1563 Council of Trent
- 1555 Peace of Augsburg
- 1558–1603 Elizabeth I of England
- 1562–1598 French Religious Wars
- 1566–1648 Dutch Revolt vs. Spain
- 1572 St. Bartholomew's Day Massacre
- 1588 Defeat of Spanish Armada
- 1598 Edict of Nantes

Individual & Society (IS)
- 1500–1700 Early modern society
- Population recovers to pre-plague levels
- 1524–1525 German Peasants' Revolt
- Anabaptism spreads among commoners
- 1550–1650 Age of Crisis
- 1560–1680 Witchcraft persecutions
- Stricter regulation of public morals

Year scale: 1500, 1505, 1510, 1515, 1520, 1525, 1530, 1535, 1540, 1545, 1550, 1555, 1560, 1565, 1570, 1575, 1580, 1585, 1590, 1595, 1600, 1605, 1610, 1615, 1620, 1625, 1630, 1635, 1640, 1645, 1650, 1655

THEME

Timeline (1600–1725)

Interaction of Europe & World (INT)
- 1600 Dutch East India Company
- Commercial Revolution 17th–18th centuries →
- Development of triangular trade
- Transatlantic slave trade →
- 1650–1763 Commercial Wars →

Poverty & Prosperity (PP)
- ca. 1600–1750 Mercantilism →

Objective Knowledge & Subjective Visions (OS)
- Bacon advocates empirical science
- 1610 Galileo's *Starry Messenger*
- Dutch Golden Age
- 1627 Harvey publishes circulatory theory
- 1637 Descartes's *Discourse on Method*
- 1600–1750 Great Age of Opera and Baroque music →
- 1633 Galileo before Inquisition
- 1651 Hobbes's *Leviathan*
- Development of deism
- 1687 Newton's *Principia Mathematica*
- 1690 Locke's *Second Treatise on Government* & *Essay Concerning Human Understanding*

States & Other Institutions of Power (SP)
- 1590s–1613 Time of Troubles in Russia
- 1603–1714 Stuart monarchy in England →
- 1618–1648 Thirty Years' War
- 1642–1649 English Civil War
- Numerous local and regional revolts vs. centralization & high taxes
- 1648 Peace of Westphalia / Rise of absolute monarchies
- 1650s Cromwell & Protectorate
- Rise of Prussia →
- 1643–1715 Age of Louis XIV
- 1683 Ottomans besiege Vienna
- 1685 Revocation of Edict of Nantes
- 1688–1689 Glorious Revolution
- 1689–1725 Peter the Great's reforms →

Individual & Society (IS)
- Population peaks and valleys throughout 17th century
- Widespread famine during "Little Ice Age"
- High crime rates, 17th century
- European marriage family and nuclear family →
- Codification of serfdom in eastern Europe
- Malthusian Trap (until ca. 1850) →

Time scale: 1600, 1605, 1610, 1615, 1620, 1625, 1630, 1635, 1640, 1645, 1650, 1655, 1660, 1665, 1670, 1675, 1680, 1685, 1690, 1695, 1700, 1705, 1710, 1715, 1720, 1725

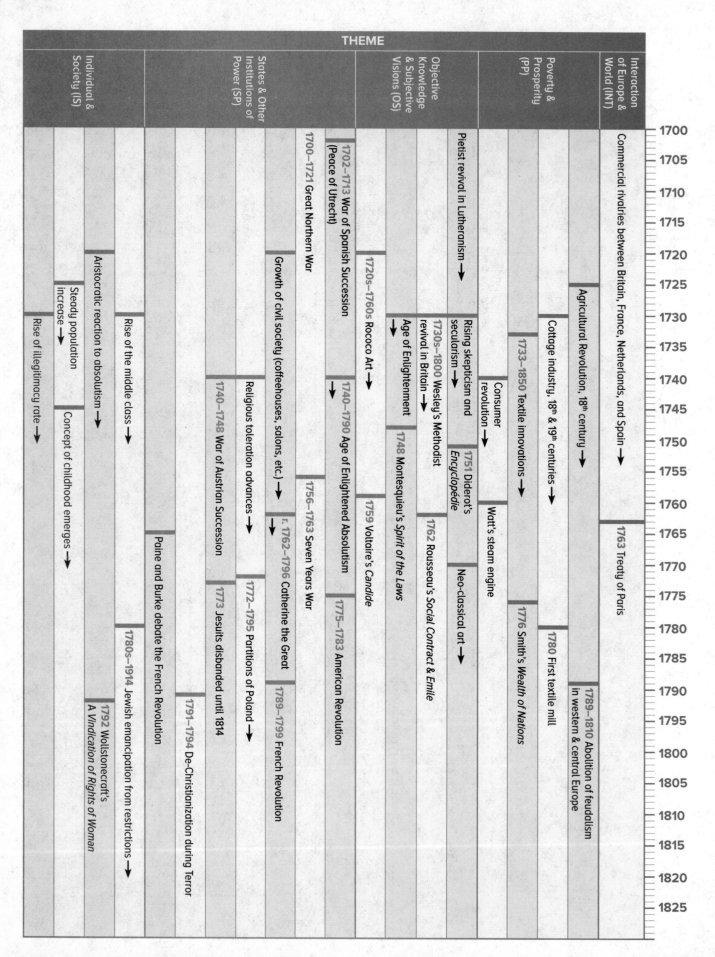

THEME

Interaction of Europe & World (INT)	Commercial rivalries between Britain, France, Netherlands, and Spain →		1763 Treaty of Paris	1789–1810 Abolition of feudalism in western & central Europe

Interaction of Europe & World (INT)
- Commercial rivalries between Britain, France, Netherlands, and Spain →
- 1763 Treaty of Paris
- 1789–1810 Abolition of feudalism in western & central Europe

Poverty & Prosperity (PP)
- Agricultural Revolution, 18th century →
- Cottage industry, 18th & 19th centuries →
- 1733–1850 Textile innovations →
- Consumer revolution
- Watt's steam engine
- 1776 Smith's *Wealth of Nations*
- 1780 First textile mill

Objective Knowledge & Subjective Visions (OS)
- Pietist revival in Lutheranism →
- 1720s–1760s Rococo Art →
- Rising skepticism and secularism →
- 1730s–1800 Wesley's Methodist revival in Britain →
- Age of Enlightenment
- 1751 Diderot's *Encyclopédie*
- 1748 Montesquieu's *Spirit of the Laws*
- 1762 Rousseau's *Social Contract & Emile*
- Neo-classical art →
- 1759 Voltaire's *Candide*

States & Other Institutions of Power (SP)
- 1700–1721 Great Northern War
- 1702–1713 War of Spanish Succession (Peace of Utrecht)
- Growth of civil society (coffeehouses, salons, etc.) →
- 1740–1790 Age of Enlightened Absolutism
- Religious toleration advances →
- 1740–1748 War of Austrian Succession
- 1756–1763 Seven Years War
- r. 1762–1796 Catherine the Great
- 1775–1783 American Revolution
- 1772–1795 Partitions of Poland
- 1773 Jesuits disbanded until 1814
- 1789–1799 French Revolution
- 1791–1794 De-Christianization during Terror

Individual & Society (IS)
- Aristocratic reaction to absolutism →
- Rise of the middle class →
- Steady population increase →
- Concept of childhood emerges →
- Rise of illegitimacy rate →
- Paine and Burke debate the French Revolution
- 1780s–1914 Jewish emancipation from restrictions →
- 1792 Wollstonecraft's *A Vindication of Rights of Woman*

Timeline years: 1700, 1705, 1710, 1715, 1720, 1725, 1730, 1735, 1740, 1745, 1750, 1755, 1760, 1765, 1770, 1775, 1780, 1785, 1790, 1795, 1800, 1805, 1810, 1815, 1820, 1825

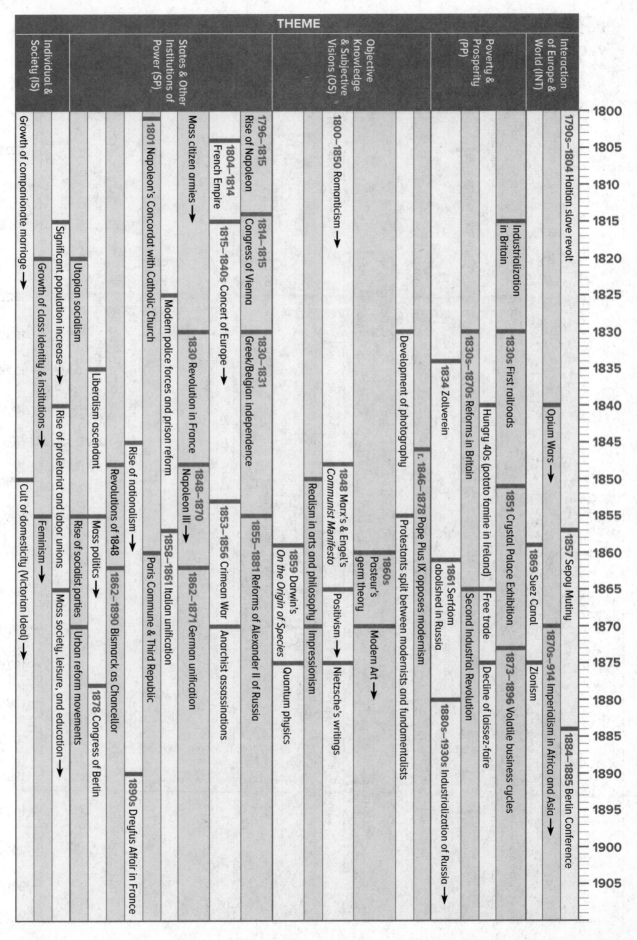

THEME

Interaction of Europe & World (INT)

Poverty & Prosperity (PP)

Objective Knowledge & Subjective Visions (OS)

States & Other Institutions of Power (SP)

Individual & Society (IS)

1790s–1804 Haitian slave revolt

Industrialization in Britain

1800–1850 Romanticism →

1796–1815 Rise of Napoleon

1801 Napoleon's Concordat with Catholic Church

Growth of companionate marriage →

1804–1814 French Empire

Mass citizen armies →

Significant population increase

1814–1815 Congress of Vienna

1815–1840s Concert of Europe →

Growth of class identity & institutions →

1830s First railroads

1830s–1870s Reforms in Britain

1834 Zollverein

Development of photography

1830–1831 Greek/Belgian independence

1830 Revolution in France

Modern police forces and prison reform

Utopian socialism

Rise of proletariat and labor unions

Opium Wars →

Hungry 40s (potato famine in Ireland)

r. 1846–1878 Pope Pius IX opposes modernism

Realism in arts and philosophy

1848 Marx's & Engel's *Communist Manifesto*

Liberalism ascendant

Revolutions of 1848

Rise of nationalism →

1848–1870 Napoleon III →

Feminism →

1857 Sepoy Mutiny

1851 Crystal Palace Exhibition

1869 Suez Canal

1859 Darwin's *On the Origin of Species*

Protestants split between modernists and fundamentalists

1855–1881 Reforms of Alexander II of Russia

1853–1856 Crimean War

Paris Commune & Third Republic

1858–1861 Italian unification

Mass politics →

Rise of socialist parties

Cult of domesticity (Victorian Ideal) →

1870s–1914 Imperialism in Africa and Asia →

Zionism

Free trade

Decline of laissez-faire

Second Industrial Revolution

1861 Serfdom abolished in Russia

1860s Pasteur's germ theory

Positivism →

Impressionism

Quantum physics

Modern Art →

Nietzsche's writings

1862–1871 German unification

Anarchist assassinations

1862–1890 Bismarck as Chancellor

1878 Congress of Berlin

Urban reform movements

Mass society, leisure, and education →

1884–1885 Berlin Conference

1873–1896 Volatile business cycles

1880s–1930s Industrialization of Russia →

1890s Dreyfus Affair in France

1800
1805
1810
1815
1820
1825
1830
1835
1840
1845
1850
1855
1860
1865
1870
1875
1880
1885
1890
1895
1900
1905

THEME

Timeline 1900–2005

Interaction of Europe & World (INT)
- 1900 Boxer Rebellion
- 1904–1905 Russo-Japanese War
- 1905 & 1911 Moroccan Crises
- 1919–1940s Mandate system →
- Decolonization →
- Postwar international economic institutions

Poverty & Prosperity (PP)
- Modern medicine, life expectancy rises →
- 1920s Hyperinflation in Germany
- 1919–1945 League of Nations →
- 1921–1924 New Economic Policy in Russia
- 1928 Soviet 5-Year Plans
- 1930s Soviet collectivization
- Great Depression
- Keynesian economics →
- Economic recovery in Western Europe
- 1945 United Nations
- Rise of U.S. as world power →
- Marshall Plan and COMECON
- Growth of welfare state →
- 1951 ECSC
- 1957 EEC
- 1960s Birth control pill
- 1970s Oil shock and stagflation
- 1992 Maastricht Treaty & EU

Objective Knowledge & Subjective Visions (OS)
- 1900 Freud's *Interpretation of Dreams*
- Modern medicine →
- 1903 Airplane
- 1905 Einstein's relativity theory
- "Lost Generation" culture
- Interwar mass culture and leisure →
- Radio & Motion Pictures
- 1927 Heisenberg Uncertainty Principle
- Existentialism
- Abstract expressionism
- Rock music →
- 1957 Sputnik
- Pop Art
- Space race & ICBMs
- Postmodernism
- 1980s Personal computers

States & Other Institutions of Power (SP)
- Balkan tensions
- Revolution of 1905 in Russia
- 1914–1918 World War I
- 1917–1921 Russian Revolution and Civil War
- 1918–1933 Weimar Republic
- 1919 Treaty of Versailles
- 1922–1943 Fascist Italy →
- 1930s Appeasement
- 1933–1945 Third Reich
- 1936–1939 Spanish Civil War
- Popular Front governments
- 1939–1945 World War II
- 1945–1991 Cold War →
- 1949 NATO
- 1950s Khrushchev de-Stalinizes
- 1955 Warsaw Pact
- 1962 Cuban Missile Crisis
- 1968 Prague Spring
- 1970s Détente
- 1980 Solidarity in Poland
- 1985–1991 Gorbachev in power
- 1989–1991 Fall of communism
- 1991–1999 Yugoslavia and Balkan Wars

Individual & Society (IS)
- Women's suffrage →
- 1935 Nuremberg Laws
- 1939–1945 Holocaust
- Postwar Baby Boom
- 1956 Hungarian revolt
- 1960s feminism
- Guest workers
- Gay and lesbian rights →
- r. 1978–2005 John Paul II →
- 1960s–1980s 2nd Wave feminism
- Rise of Green Party
- 1962–1965 2nd Vatican Council
- Generation Gap
- 1968 Student revolts
- 1990 German reunification

Year scale: 1900, 1905, 1910, 1915, 1920, 1925, 1930, 1935, 1940, 1945, 1950, 1955, 1960, 1965, 1970, 1975, 1980, 1985, 1990, 1995, 2000, 2005

THEME						
Individual & Society (IS)	States & Other Institutions of Power (SP)	Objective Knowledge & Subjective Visions (OS)	Poverty & Prosperity (PP)		Interaction of Europe & World (INT)	

2000

2001 Terrorist attacks on U.S.

2001 War on Terror →

2002 Euro released

2005

2009 European debt crisis →

2010

Internet, cellphones, and social media

2015

Terror attacks in Madrid, Paris, Brussels

2020

Migration & refugee conflicts

2025

2030

2035

2040

2045

2050

2055

2060

2065

2070

2075

2080

2085